POLITICAL CRIMINAL TRIALS

How to Defend Them

CRIMINAL LAW SERIES

Searches & Seizures, Arrests and Confessions
by William E. Ringel

Eye-Witness Identification: Legal and
Practical Problems
by Nathan R. Sobel

New York Criminal Practice Under the CPL
by Robert M. Pitler

Prisoners' Rights Sourcebook
Edited by Michele G. Hermann
and Marilyn G. Haft

POLITICAL CRIMINAL TRIALS

How to Defend Them

by

JOHN M. SINK

Clark Boardman Company, Ltd.
New York, New York
1974

Library of Congress Catalog Card Number: 73–89533

ISBN 0–87632–103–1

Portions of the following works are reproduced in this book by permission of the copyright owners:

"Epitaph On An Army Of Mercenaries" from *The Collected Poems of A. E. Housman*, copyright 1922 by Holt, Rinehart and Winston, Inc., copyright 1950 by Barclays Bank Ltd.; also by permission of The Society of Authors (as the literary representative of the Estate of A. E. Housman) and Jonathan Cape, Ltd., publishers;

California Jury Instructions—Criminal (CALJIC) (P. Richard ed. 3d rev. ed. 1970) copyright © 1970 by West Publishing Company;

The Institutio Oratoria of Quintilian (H. Butler transl. 1921) (The Loeb Classical Library) by permission of Harvard University Press;

D. Hammett, *The Maltese Falcon* from *The Novels of Dashiell Hammett*, copyright © 1965 by Alfred A. Knopf, Inc.

To Jinny

FOREWORD

Political trials have been rather frequent in this country, although some readers might suppose them limited to ten or twelve conspiracy trials they read about in the national press. Hundreds of lesser-known cases have occurred in state courts in just the last four years; and it may be that political trials are an historical constant of Anglo-American law. They are not uniquely the aftermath of political demonstrations. A person on his way to something about to happen at an Indian reservation may find himself facing a roadblock a thousand miles from his destination—with political consequences; someone whose telephone has been tapped by a law enforcement agency for ideological reasons may find himself facing unusual criminal charges that would have come to him in no other way. Electronic communications and data retrieval are often referred to as opening technological doors, but they are also capable of slamming prison doors behind people.

The political cases I have had the privilege of defending have been the best and most personally satisfying part of my practice; I would not willingly have missed them. Apparently this evaluation is far from representative of a majority of the American bar.

This book is intended for lawyers about to defend a political criminal case for the first or second time. Large parts are addressed to young lawyers, because in my recent memory young lawyers have often been the only ones who would defend relatively unknown (and unremunerative) political cases. There have been satisfying exceptions, and indeed if this observation were measured solely by the better-known political trials, it would be indefensible, since experienced men were found to defend those cases.

Anyone reading this book for an indictment of the jury system is going to be disappointed; on the other hand, an otherwise unstated proposition of these pages is that law schools, the organized bar and their adjuncts, the legislatures, have failed to deter political prosecutions or to provide remedies to persons caught up in them. As anyone knows who has been through a few, getting acquitted is a world in itself; but acquittal is not redress for the shock, the risk or any part of the experience. Nobody has ever heard of a prosecutor being called before a bar committee for conducting a political trial. Yet the organized bar has no difficulty deciding that some hapless practitioner who mixed up his clients' funds with his office account should be disbarred.

Although parts of this book are written for an older lawyer about to encounter his first political case, most of it is premised on the more modest assumptions that the reader is admitted to the bar, speaks the legal language, knows his way around a law library, and is generally familiar with the mechanics of criminal procedure, though not of courtroom procedure. It is very much to be hoped that the reader, assumed to be facing a serious political trial, has at least defended a few ordinary criminal cases.

This book is written from a state-court point of view, because I think the need is greater there. Many procedural references (and some footnotes) are to California law, a point which I hope does not prevent the main points from having their intended usefulness in other jurisdictions; e.g., when I refer to a preliminary hearing as a way in which a felony case may arise, I assume the reader will translate that term into the analogous procedural step in his jurisdiction.

There seem to be three general ways that a trial lawyer can write about what he does. One is to wait until he is sure he has passed his prime, and then write about how he used to win them when he went to court regularly. That has the advantage of safety, because adversaries can no longer club him with the knowledge. The difficulty is that by the time this kind of writer gets around to it, his own techniques have become somewhat obsolete and his memory for how he really used to analyze things has probably gotten rather poor. His book will be anecdotal.

A second method is limited to those who write involuntarily, i.e., they achieve such success they are beset from every quarter to tell how they manage it. Most of these people respond by giving lectures chock-full of detail on what the statutes and local rules of court have to say about time limits, number of copies of briefs, et cetera. They mention not a word about method, of course.

A third way is what I have attempted here: to write while the impressions were fresh in my mind, and to tell all the relevant details of my work methods and tactics. The difficulty has been that it was necessary to write while still using them in court. Since I was writing before the juridic dust had settled, nervousness became the test of whether the advice being passed along was valuable. The more worried I became while writing, the more sure I felt that I was probably on the right track.

Acknowledgments. I am grateful to Leonard B. Boudin, Esq. (New York), Leonard I. Weinglass, Esq. (Los Angeles), Charles R. Nesson, Esq. (Cambridge), Charles E. Goodell, Esq. (New York), and Delores A. Donovan, Esq. (San Francisco), and H. Peter Young, Esq. (Los Angeles) for use of some of the instructions they requested when they defended the Ellsberg-Russo case [appendix D-4]; to Edward Carl Broege, Esq. (Newark), David Kairys, Esq. and Mr. David Lavine (both of Philadelphia) for the instruction on government overreaching given by Judge Clarkson S. Fisher in the Camden 28 case, which they defended [appendix D-3]; to the office of Mr. Robert G. Eckhoff, Public Defender of Santa Barbara County, for making available some of their jury instructions used in curfew cases in 1970–71 [appendix D-1]; that office defended so many curfew cases they no longer know who wrote the instructions quoted here, but feel that acknowledgment should be made to Russell J. Cosgrove, Esq. (San Francisco), and Robert D. Taggart, Esq. (Los Angeles).

I am particularly indebted to: the late L.B. Conant, Esq. (Los Angeles) for patiently talking me out of some bad courtroom habits in my younger days; his ebullient and gentlemanly style of defending public utilities has since served as a model for defending men and women—I don't think much of it would have come to me naturally; Woodruff J. Deem, Esq. (Salt Lake City, formerly District Attorney of Ventura County California), who, when asked to lecture on trial techniques, one afternoon years ago, generously delivered a boxcar-load of insights and tough admonitions on how to defend people—memorable advice from a prosecutor, for which some scattered footnotes in this book are small recompense; my friend James R. Westwick, Esq. (Santa Barbara) for advice in many hard cases, which has become so intermingled with my courtroom experience that I could not sort it out even for footnotes; Robert Cipes, Esq. (Santa Barbara) for suggesting that I write this book—it would not have been started otherwise; Ms. Jeanette Prickett for patience in typing and proofing, and for encouragement; several persons too shy to be named here, for criticizing parts of the manuscript; my editor, Tom Costner, for courage in undertaking his part of this book, for continuing advice, tactful deletions, and patience during revisions when a writer is supposed to keep hands off page proofs; his assistant, Rick Beardsley, and my son, Charles, for sweat and tact in working the manuscript into publishable condition; and most importantly my wife, without whose humor and fire this book would not have moved very far.

John M. Sink

Santa Barbara, California
February 1, 1974

TABLE OF CONTENTS

Chapter 1

Two Kinds of Political Trials

Chapter 2

Preliminary Advice About Being Retained in a Political Case

Chapter 3

The Lawyer's Personal Relations with Clients and with Other Lawyers

Chapter 4

Building the Defense Case
(General Rules and Necessary First Steps)

Chapter 5

Using the First Results of Early Spade Work to Increase the Odds Favoring Success in Trail

Chapter 6

How to Evaluate Relative Trial Preparations and Use Trial Timing as a Weapon

Chapter 7

Second-Round (Extensive) Discovery of Prosecution Evidence

Chapter 8

Preparation of Proposed Jury Instructions

Chapter 9

Final Preparation of Defense Witnesses

Chapter 10

Selecting a Fair Jury; Trial by Judge or Jury; The Choice of a Judge

Chapter 12

Opening Statements

Chapter 13

Things to Watch for at the Beginning

Chapter 14

Cross-Examining Prosecution Witnesses

Chapter 15

Putting on the Defense Case

Chapter 16

Final Argument

Chapter 1

TWO KINDS OF POLITICAL TRIALS

SYNOPSIS

§1.01 Introduction

An important thing about defending political cases is to know the cardinal difference between cases in which the accused makes no bones about the fact that he committed a crime, but says he did it for political reasons; and cases in which the accused is charged with something that he says he did not do, and it appears he is being prosecuted for political reasons. In the first kind of case the accused has been acting against his own legal interests (busy getting himself convicted of something), and in the other kind, the prosecutor is continually acting against *his* interests (overreaching, to get a conviction).

Appreciating the difference between these two kinds of political trials should be understood as a chiasmatic perception, at the fusion point of how a particular case ought to be tried, and how a particular lawyer would like to try whatever case he happens to be in. Since recollecting which kind of political case he is trying will inform several of the lawyer's major decisions during trial, the distinction rates extra attention here.

§ 1.02   The Admitted Crime Intended as a Political Protest

Assume a hypothetical crime done for political reasons: the defendant visits his local recruiting office after hours, arriving immediately behind a chunk of paving ballast. He steps through the shattered storefront window, turns on the office lights, and annoints random files with animal blood and paint thinner while striking occasional matches. His ineffectual fire is reflected in the faces of a growing ring of bystanders when the police arrive. He tells them, perhaps unnecessarily, that he started the fire because he opposes the most recent undeclared war in South America.

There is no secret that this defendant violated several ordinary, non-political statutes. He is prosecuted, but not for political reasons. The prosecutors, having no choice, can be expected to conduct themselves coolly at the trial. They may, of course, actually hate the defendant, and their animosity may be such that even if he had been somewhere else that night, they would have prosecuted him anyway. But they need not do that. They can respect the law; it makes the prosecution easier. It was the defendant who was carried away by passion, who committed felonies under circumstances the law does not recognize as a defense.

The difficult part of this defendant's trial is that his lawyer must defend him by making the jury see things the way the defendant saw them. If he can make twelve of them do that, they may (conceivably) acquit him, or at least limit his almost ineluctable conviction to a lesser included misdemeanor or to the least odious of the five felonies for which he was indicted.

This is an unusual kind of case in which the lawyer's narrow access to his client squeezes him into methods not otherwise worth considering. When a lawyer defends a case on the basis of his client's political ideas rather than acts—by asking the jury to acquit, despite what the law says, on account of their conscience and their sympathy—it should be because his client left him no choice and no way to invoke traditional rules more suited to acquittal.

For every political trial which has to be defended the hard way, by making the jury see through the defendant's eyes the admitted act, there are nine others that can be handled successfully by more traditional methods. The reason they are not always handled that way is that the remaining nine lawyers tend to lose sight of the fact that the one lawyer (in the example mentioned above) is doing his best to prevent his client from being a martyr; they do not see two kinds of cases, but only one kind which—it seems to them—subsumes ten martyrs. Too often they cannot (or will not) understand that what is an acceptable defense in one kind of political case is red-handed self-abuse in the other kind. Most political cases *are* the other kind (described in the following section). The difference stems from a reliable proposition: prosecuting attorneys, rather than defendants, tend to be the persons most swayed by passion in a political trial.

§ 1.03 The Disputed Crime Which Is Prosecuted for Political Reasons

Assume the same recruiting office is burned, but in this example the job is done, if not professionally, at least effectively and by someone who did not stay around to get caught. There are no proud statements in the morning papers about vital records surviving the embers. A lot of people watched the fire. It lasted a long time. Nobody knows who set it. Radicals and photographers (amateurs and police) gathered in their usual symbiosis. The results include a lot of black and white photographs, some color movies and a few hundred feet of jerky videotape. An amazing number of radicals can be identified.

This was of course an overtly political fire; but no one is holding press conferences to explain it. If a poll were taken, most of the community would certainly agree that this was arson, and that they disapprove of arson. On the other hand, it would be hard to frame questions to assess their real feelings, which—like the fire—are "political" and more divergent than a poll would suggest. Some people have very ambivalent feelings about the fire.

Feelings within the district attorney's office will probably not be ambivalent; but that does not necessarily mean there is going to be a political trial. That depends on the integrity and common sense of the district attorney and law enforcement officials. It may well turn out that the persons assigned to investigate and prosecute this case approach the job as they would approach any other felony, by acting on the most reliable evidence which can be found, and (within the limits of human reasonableness) prosecuting persons who appear guilty and convictable, and on just those charges which are strongly supported by evidence. Approaching it in this way, the prosecutors may try the case as an ordinary criminal trial, directing their proof to what the defendant is alleged to have done, rather than by proving that he has expressed political ideas (or associated with political persons) thought to be unacceptable in the community. If the case is actually investigated, prepared, and tried along these conventional lines, there will not have been a political trial, even if the crime itself was intended as a political act, even if the prosecutors dislike the defendant, even if they are wrong as to his guilt, and even if the trial results in an acquittal.

On the other hand, the charged feelings which produce political crimes always tend to polarize and excite those people in the community who are most susceptible to polarization. One may find that law enforcement personnel and attorneys working in the district attorney's office are especially prone to this contagion. Whether they are allowed to give in to their feelings depends on how well those departments are actually being run. If the departments are subjected to strong central control by persons dedicated to impartial enforcement of the laws, then individual members will not be humored very far in their personal feelings, particularly those who might like to have a pogrom.

Some chiefs of police and some district attorneys would not stand for the kind of political investigation or political trial which this book is all about, notwithstanding that they have no sympathy for radicals, dissidents, pacifists, or ecological causes. The prevalence of duty and self-restraint over hot-cheeked opinion is the way it ought to be; but unfortunately, that is the way it happens all too rarely.

Events of the last four years have shown that conditions favoring political trials are easy to come by. If it happens that the Justice Department of the United States contains a paranoid element bent on prosecuting political dissidents, then there is no need to *wait* for political fires or bombings, and nowhere is safe. The Justice Department taps telephones, and sometimes prosecutes phony conspiracy cases.

In state courts, political trials do not usually happen except in response to political crimes or at least political gestures; but the ingredients of local political trials are pretty widespread. All it takes is a sheriff or chief of police too weak to control his own department, and a prosecutor conscious that sooner or later he must run for re-election, whose financial backers are afraid of radicals. It is not actually necessary that the district attorney or sheriff hate persons of differing political views. Weak leadership is enough, in law enforcement. Any would-be storm trooper who wants to get assigned to the case can manage it, and one helps another aboard.

Once a political trial *does* emerge, it is quite important to understand the psychology at work among the prosecution. They will be thinking not in terms of prosecuting the guilty and defending the innocent, but of retaliation. Their feelings will tend to be somewhat elitist: they will have isolated themselves and become righteous and aggrieved. Too good for the world, and the world against them.

This prosecutorial psychology (which wells up from the lower levels of law enforcement) may resemble that of occupying troops in a hostile country. *We* have been hurt, *they* must be hurt. The guilty parties are one problem; but "they" are the main thing. "They" are not limited to dissidents, but may come to include the whole penumbra of persons not actively hating. If the atmosphere is *really* charged, the prosecution may come to feel that the group they distrust includes not just the courts and the radicals, but the whole permissive population, in fact everybody but law enforcement people, and not all of them. They must be shown that when something like this happens (in our example, the fire), somebody sure as hell pays for it.

None of this prosecutorial feeling is expressed—in fact, it would undoubtedly be denied—but reality emerges in the investigatory methods to be followed. These methods will differ importantly from those followed in other kinds of crime.

In a political prosecution, ordinary criteria for scanning evidence will not even be considered. Informers will be sought where they can be found, and they will not be informers previously used or tested. These informers will be the fringe who most covet attention; people who are not accorded much recognition on the street, where they spend so much time; people who can be persuaded that they saw this person or that person. It is not even necessary to look for most of these informers; they will knock on the door.

Photographs of known local radicals will be ready for showing. These photographs will be fairly and equitably mixed with photographs of radicals from nearby communities. Detectives will deal them like an endless hand of solitaire, and without keeping notes of the interviews. After several sessions with each witness, photographic identifications will have been made. A list gains accretions. At a certain point, the grand jury is convened. The indicted are not the ones on whom ordinary, reliable evidence would have centered; they are, oddly enough, people whom the prosecutors and police most want to hit.

In the minds of the deputy district attorneys working on this case, it is just a weak case, much too weak for a preliminary hearing. But the important thing is that it *is* a case. The category implies that deficiencies are merely technical.

The resulting prosecution will be pressed with political vigor only: vigorous, one-sided investigations, and a vigorous refusal to compromise. Most names will *not* be dropped from the indictment. Deals will *not* be offered. And the people who make these implacable decisions will *not* try the case themselves. Newer men will be assigned that task. And, as will be noticed later, not all the detectives who worked on the case at one time or another will wish to have their names linked with it.

This prosecution psychology is political, and having political momentum it will not be deterred by petty discouragements, e.g., the discovery that several of those indicted have air-tight alibis: they were attending a civic dinner with the district attorney on the night in question, or answering roll call in some jail at the critical hour. Those persons may be dropped from the list of the actively prosecuted. But self-criticism takes shallow root among saviors.

This kind of political prosecution rests on weak evidence because of the manner in which it was organized.

This weakness means almost every witness and most links of the prosecution case will be vulnerable to powerful evidentiary attacks and arguments, all of which are seasoned —even orthodox—in criminal trials. This fact makes the judge the natural ally of the defense.

The combination of weak prosecution evidence and the (to them surprising) alliance between the judge and the defense means the prosecutors will be driven to substitute bombast for logic and to try the case as a political trial instead of a criminal trial. Not only will the prosecutors be working beyond their emotional balance point, but the *rate* by which they lose balance can be grossly accelerated by means of causal circles. The results are almost unbelievable.

For example, the more obvious it becomes that the prosecutors cannot bolster a flaky (mendacious) witness, the more important it seems that they raise their voices. When they find themselves shouting, it seems only natural to suit the subject matter to the tone. The more overt their attempts to try the defendant's political ideas, instead of his acts, the easier it is for the defense to make the judge rebuke them in the presence of the jury. The sorrier the prosecutors feel for themselves, the less their restraint against lashing out, first at the judge (they become martyrs), then at the "permissive" traditions of the criminal law. The more they demean themselves in the eyes of the jury, the shabbier their witnesses seem, and the harder to rehabilitate (the more flaky) and so on around again.

This kind of case is great for the defendant's lawyer —a glorious case. The wonder is that so few are tried this way. The reason seems to be that so many young defense lawyers—usually the only ones who will defend these cases —are too bent on middle class martyrdom to let the prosecutors assume that role. Preventing the prosecutor from martyring himself is foolishness, and that is the reason for this long introduction.

Chapter 2

PRELIMINARY ADVICE ABOUT BEING RETAINED IN A POLITICAL CASE

SYNOPSIS

§ 2.01 The Economics of a Single Client

A meritorious political case is good for a lawyer apart from money. But one meritorious case will be followed by others. There is no use discriminating against the second, or the tenth. The lawyer should remember that the reason he is here to accept any political case at all is that he has so far afforded to be here. So if he is to be around next year, to take that year's political case, it will be because he was able to pay his rent meanwhile.

The lawyer cannot pay rent unless his clients pay him. Once into a political case he may forget he *has* other clients; and he will lose some of them. It is not clients in general who should pay for a political defense, but the political client, or at least someone on his behalf. Perhaps every third one will pay a little less, and every tenth one, nothing; but the lawyer should not develop illusions or rise above himself on the scale of charity.

The public defender can help. If there is no public defender, the court will appoint a lawyer to defend an indigent defendant, and the state will pay that lawyer. The court will be pleased if anyone volunteers. One should. When the state pays for the defense, however modestly, more than half of its enormous threat to the political defendant has been disenvenomed. They cannot bankrupt him.

The lawyer should remember that in political trials, and particularly when he is emotionally involved—which is to be hoped—he will be working dangerously near *morality*, and should be on guard against it. Moral persons will not wish to pay their lawyer when the trial is over; the difficulty being in part that they *are* moral: the lawyer's work is only successful at best. Success equals acquittal, acquittal is justice, and why should anybody pay for justice when there are so many moral demands on his pocketbook?

Decide what it will probably cost to defend the case, and get that much money in hand before appearing of record. Incidentally, the lawyer should not agree with his client that his retainer is all the fee he will ever hope to get. Rather, he should have it understood in writing that he will receive reasonable fees for whatever he must later do. Whether the lawyer intends to refund any part of his retainer upon various contingencies, e.g., the unforeseen dismissal of an indictment, is to be discussed and agreed. That agreement should be written and signed. If the client is unable to pay what may turn out to be a substantial balance, someone else must be found beforehand. That person should not only be financially responsible, but also a signatory to the fee agreement.

An idealistic lawyer who feels driven to evaluate his contribution in economic terms (whether he did it all gratis) should refrain from doing so in those terms. Instead, he should consider what he did; whether he committed enough of himself to doing it, whether it had to be done, whether anybody else would have done it at all, and whether he did it well. Housman's epitaph for mercenaries, "What God abandoned, these defended," [1] is not a description of unworthy men and may be as good a one as a political defender should wish. Seeking to defend clients without visible cost to the rest of the universe seems a little unreasonable.

§ 2.02 Mass Arraignments: Being Retained and Giving Advice Without Accepting a Retainer

The lawyer must be particularly careful while getting involved in riot cases. Since political prosecutions usually follow "disorders," and since mass arrests mean mass arraignments, there is a substantial chance that problems peculiar to riot cases will make their initial appearance at a mass arraignment. A defense lawyer walking into one of these will encounter demands he will meet in no other situation. Much depends on thinking them through correctly, the first time. An improvidently accepted retainer is especially difficult to rethink.

The atmosphere at a mass arraignment is charged, and the lawyer need not suppose he will be immune to common feelings. Such an arraignment will probably *not* take place in familiar surroundings. There are too many people. A mass arraignment in an American court may happen in some hangar-like room, too cold and ill-lit for any funded governmental agency to make regular use of it. If so, usual courtroom conveniences will be out of the question. The magistrate, in that case, will be found behind a government-issue desk. There may not be enough chairs. The loudspeaker system may not work. Many trappings of justice will be gone; but more importantly, their unobtrusive, steadying effect on the magistrate and other court personnel will also be absent. The typical magistrate will be attentive to the requirements of the guards, but startled and distracted by anything the lawyers say to him. His *tendencies* will be to (1) set bail too high; (2) use his position to coerce the accused to plead guilty by announcing his bail policy, while allowing the district attorney to announce *his* intention to ask ten dollar fines for all who plead guilty. This metamorphosis from the magistrate's usual personality may create special needs for legal advice in the courtroom and problems in accepting a retainer, and it foreshadows problems affecting trial.

The sight of large numbers of people under guard, including some who may be friends, will create feelings for which there can be no adequate preparation. These feelings will be aggravated by the large number of uniformed law enforcement officers present for the purpose of herding people about and standing over them. They are not the usual court attachés, nor do they take their directions from court attachés. They are arrogant, bullying, and conspicuously armed. They look on the accused with hatred. They may well refuse the men and women water and access to toilets for hours on end; they intend all the discomfort and humiliation which they inflict on people being arraigned. The magistrate will be afraid to intervene. These acts will be denied later; law enforcement authorities will conduct public relations campaigns later, but this is how it will probably happen.

A defense lawyer working in this situation is well advised to keep his mind on what he is doing, remembering there is a right and wrong way to do everything. The more there is to be done, the more important to do it right. A handy rule is, start from where you are.

The traditional legal view is that a lawyer has no business here unless he is present on behalf of an existing client, and he talks only for that client unless the court appoints him to talk for others. Another view (the one followed here) is that the lawyer will not turn his back on other persons who ask his help or who need it and are not being given a chance to ask for it.

Considerations with regard to existing clients are simple: find the client, and wait for his or her case to be called. If the charges laid on the client are all misdemeanors, either plead not guilty to all charges, or ask that the matter be continued for a reasonable time to make an investigation. The question whether to split a plea at this time is critical for the lawyer who knows that the charges against his client include one or more common to all persons being arraigned, and to which the client may wish to plead, e.g., unlawful assembly, and also one or more political charges unique to the client, and which are fraudulent, e.g., resisting an officer. (The problem of splitting these charges, pleading to some and trying others is discussed in §§ 5.02[3] to [8]. However, if any felony is laid against the client, then, all other considerations aside, it is imperative that a plea of not guilty to the felony be entered immediately, and a preliminary hearing within the statutory time *should be demanded.*

This is true because a preliminary hearing greatly enhances the odds in favor of defeating the felony charge; it should be remembered that, in a political prosecution, there will be no deals on felonies. The reason that the early hearing works in favor of later acquittal is that the police have not had a chance to remember how many times they filled out arrest reports describing things that never happened, which (according to their reports) are supposed to have happened at the same time in many different places.

The outstanding characteristic of mass arrests has been an enormous willingness to lie in preparing routine police reports. The lawyer should remember that it is quite likely that most of the persons being arraigned were arrested in some form of sweep, and that the officers who laid hands on them passed them around to other officers who decided among themselves which one would sign as the arresting officer and what form of imaginary events would be described in the arrest report. When passions have cooled, and notes are exchanged, it may be found that apparently some officers were arresting a number of different people at widely separated points at about the same time. The officers and prosecutors themselves may realize this, if given time. They should not be given an excess of time. An early preliminary hearing favors the defense.

Looking beyond those whose legal relation as clients existed before this arraignment, it is unhappily true that the lawyer may find friends sitting among the accused. These friends may indicate that they wish the lawyer to represent them. Depending on the hatefulness of the guards, they may not be able to communicate that wish except by a look. The meaning will be clear. The case may be accepted by the same channel. But to keep this channel of communication open, the lawyer must be in a position to see faces. The lawyer can move about; persons in custody cannot. Therefore he should move to the necessary places, and look at every face. Some lawyers fear any appearance of soliciting business like a lone woman in a bar fears being thought a pick-up. But the lawyer here should get this nonsense out of his mind. This is serious business. To the friend desperately trying to catch his eye, the assurance that the lawyer is there and will remain until his case is called can be a considerable comfort, probably the best thing that will happen to that friend for the rest of the day.

The lawyer's real problems arise neither from existing clients nor from friends whom he will represent for a nod. They concern requests from other persons.

There will always be persons there in need of help who are not clients or friends, who may or may not be someone known to the lawyer, but who unequivocally ask for representation. As to these people, the question is not whether to help them, but how. It is rather important *not* to make a formal appearance on behalf of any of these people at this time, for several reasons. First, depending on the circumstances, the advice they actually need can be imparted face to face. That advice should be to the point. This is not the place to take a case history. Anyone who asks should be told he has a right to a lawyer, and since there has not been time to obtain one, he should ask the court for a reasonable continuance so that he may be represented prior to his arraignment. For some reason, many people in this situation will prefer to do it the other way around: they will want to know how they should plead, right now, and they will get their lawyer later. They should be told to plead not quilty, to demand a jury trial, and not to waive time (assuming this jurisdiction imposes a time limit for trials). This advice can be given quite properly to those who ask it, and it should be given forcefully and often.

A more serious problem may emerge from the loudspeaker system. It may happen that confronted with all these citizens in custody, the district attorney extends a blanket offer. Several hundred people awaiting due process of law may suddenly be advised by a booming voice that all those who plead quilty to such and such a misdemeanor, when called to the table, will have other charges dropped, will be let off with a ten dollar fine, and told to go home. They may also be told the bail will be fifteen hundred dollars for their typical misdemeanor.

The lawyer who represents but one or two clients, and has already talked to them, may perhaps listen to such an announcement with adamantine cool. But the lawyer who knows he is going to represent one or more persons present with whom he has *not* yet been allowed to speak, may feel his blood rise. He should in this instance act on the hot impulse. The correct action in this situation is that *some* lawyer should request equal time to use the microphone. The public defender is the most suitable lawyer to do this; but it must be done immediately.

Whichever lawyer is handed the microphone should

point out that what he has to say will be said on behalf of all defense lawyers present; he should then go on to state the basic things which the magistrate and the district attorney may have omitted to say: that all of those about to be arraigned are innocent until proven guilty beyond a reasonable doubt; that each of them has an unconditional right to counsel before entering a plea; that each person has the right to a speedy jury trial, the right to remain silent, and the right to summon witnesses on his behalf and to confront his accusers. He has the right to testify or not, and failure to testify cannot be held against him. The lawyer should stress that pleading guilty to any crime is a serious thing and should never be done without the advice of counsel; that anyone in doubt should request time to get his lawyer and will be allowed to make necessary phone calls even from jail; that every person has a right to reasonable bail; that the public defender will be appointed for persons who cannot afford a lawyer; and, finally, that as a practical matter, any person who wishes to make his plea prior to retaining a lawyer would be well advised to plead not guilty and request a jury trial.

The foregoing is a short list of things that a defense lawyer can do for clients and others caught up in a mass arraignment, including those whom it would not be advisable to represent then or later. There are strong reasons why one should not accept many cases in this situation. (By "accepting" a case we mean making a formal appearance of record.)

The reasons why a retainer should not be accepted indiscriminately, i.e., not as often as the lawyer will wish under the emotional stress of a mass arraignment, are worth remembering.

First, accepting several cases without knowing the facts will probably involve the lawyer in a conflict of interest, much to be avoided.

Second, promiscuous acceptance of cases will put the lawyer at the mercy of the presiding judge for a period of six months to a year. That judge may be regarded as a hostile prince in a small fiefdom where the lawyer is going to be spending a lot of time. A presiding judge can determine whose cases will be severed and whose will be joined. The lawyer may find himself defending fifteen clients in the same trial on the grounds that all the defendants committed misdemeanors at the same time, and hence there are common questions of fact and law that justify a common trial. A case involving fifteen defendants can last as many weeks. If it happens that these defendants were accepted without adequate fee arrangements, the presiding judge has the power to inflict bankruptcy on the lawyer. To look at it another way, the lawyer may be confronted with fifteen consecutive trials, back-to-back. They may be separated by reasonable intervals, but the sequence of trials is also determined by the presiding judge, and it may not turn out to the lawyer's liking.

Accepting a case without knowing anything about the facts—because of emotional considerations, for example—amounts to a commitment to try an unknown case. When there are several of these unknown cases, some will later be found less meritorious than others. Some may be rotten from the defense point of view. But they all take roughly the same amount of work. Any lawyer worth his salt will prepare his cases, in part, by means of personal commitments, a process sometimes described as giving a piece of himself. That process is costly. Doing it too often and for the wrong cases can make a good lawyer temporarily ineffectual (though it has no effect on a bad lawyer), and unable to do justice to the cases which he has a chance of winning. There is nothing mysterious about this. It takes time to prepare cases for trial. The lawyer cannot be preparing a good case while he is trying a bad one. It is not true that it all comes out the same if trials are spaced a few days apart. The lawyer should limit himself to those cases that ought to be tried, and space *those* cases out.

A further reason against promiscuously accepting

even worthy cases is that acceptance may preclude the appointment of the public defender, with all his financial and investigative resources. If the public defender's office is good, or close to good, this is an important consideration. In a trial of several defendants the only investigator available to any of them may turn out to be the public defender's investigator. Surveys, diagrams, photographs, and other exhibits cost money. The public defender's office has a little; the public defender should be allowed (and requested) to participate where there are indigent defendants. The accused may not like this because there is the negative status attached to even a good public defender. Minority groups especially tend to regard the public defender as an institutional sellout. Clients and co-defendants should not be humored in this delusion, in jurisdictions where it is a delusion. The lawyer should bear in mind that he is a better judge of the quality of the public defender than most of the people who talk about public defenders, minority people or not.

There is another consideration against accepting too many cases where money could be found to pay the lawyer's fee for representing several defendants. For example, five defendants may be facing trial together. Assuming no conflict of interest exists, the public defender may have three, the lawyer may already have one, and he may be asked to represent the other as well. Assume there is enough money available for this last defendant either to hire the lawyer already in the case, or some other good lawyer. It may be worth everybody's while to bring another lawyer in. Before the case is over, the two lawyers presently in the case may be glad they had a third.

§ 2.03 Representing Groups of Popular Defendants

Special considerations apply to groups of popular defendants. These problems will probably arise from a mass arraignment; they will walk in the door several days afterward. These defendants will probably be out on bail before the lawyer meets them. They will have entered their pleas of not guilty or will have gotten continuances for that purpose.

The main point about them is that they are being prosecuted together, and they are not ordinary citizens caught in a mass arrest. These defendants are singled out by the authorities because they are thought to have organized the demonstration in the first place. If others are charged with misdemeanors, they are charged with felonies. They may think of themselves as planners; the authorities think of them as conspirators. Whether they are charged with conspiracy or not, the prosecutors will go after them vindictively. The defendants have a sense of group solidarity.

By the time the lawyer meets them, they may already be known as a group and referred to by their number. They are shopping for a lawyer, or a combination of lawyers, and they propose to use some of the funds which they are collecting for this purpose.

The emotional consideration here is that although the lawyer may or may not sympathize with the avowed purposes of this easily identifiable group, he will probably find strong rapport with some or even all of them. The lawyer may also be caught up with the popular feeling and more than willing to be identified publicly as the lawyer (or one of the lawyers) representing this group. He should remember three things before stepping into that role, however.

First, it is usually a poor idea to represent more than one of these defendants at a time. There is no use saying it is all right, that at first glance a conflict of interest is not suggested. It is amazing how fast these conflicts are magnetized to the lawyer who represents two clients. He learns something in confidence from one of them, which helps one and hurts the other. After that, it is impossible to justify using that information and impossible to justify not using it. The lawyer in that situation is somewhat like the snake who ate a melon and then squeezed part way through a knothole in a fence and ate another melon. Quite possibly he can get out of his problem, but he will have to digest his way through it; and meanwhile, he is at a terrible disadvantage with respect to the rest of the world.

This does not mean that the lawyer who represents one of a group of defendants should automatically seek to split his client from the others for some precious little hypothetical advantage, so as to disrupt what would otherwise be a smooth group defense. In almost every case, to do that would be an assinine obeisance to individual representation, required neither by rules nor common sense.

Two lawyers (representing different clients) can usually decide without any difficulty whether minor differences should be buried in the common interest. When they discuss their recommendations with their clients, each client can work out with his own lawyer whether to go along in the common interest, or to go separately. The fact that a client is able to make that decision after talking to his own lawyer, who represents only him, lends considerable moral authority to whatever they decide. That would never be true, however, if there were only one lawyer between two defendants. A lawyer talking to himself is unable to arrive at a *joint* recommendation;[2] and even if his conclusions are the same as those he would have worked out with a brother lawyer, he will certainly not look the same when explaining the results to two different clients, one of whom will be hurt by the conclusion he reached. The one who is disadvantaged will not think well of the lawyer later, but with separate lawyers, each client will know that he shares responsibility for decisions in which he concurred.

With two lawyers, each can point out very candidly that some value should be ascribed to the continued wholehearted cooperation of the other; but one lawyer alone cannot barter his goodwill between two clients.

Incidentally, in a group trial, most decisions will be made in favor of a common defense. There will *be* very few problems about splitting off, for the simple reason that group defendants do not agonize very much over technical conflicts of interest. The truth is, many supposed conflicts of interest are the creatures of lawyers, not clients; clients will probably not put up with that kind of nonsense, once it is properly explained to them. In most instances, they will tell the lawyers to act for the common good. On the other hand, the lawyer cannot help having received certain kinds of legal training any more than people can help having many other kinds of disability; the lawyer's own tranquility is important, not only to him but also to his clients, since his mental operations are tactically important to the outcome of the case.

For these reasons, even though a group of defendants may not share the lawyer's special wish to have other lawyers in the case, he should explain to them why that arrangement will enhance their own participation in making decisions as well as their responsibility for the results, and that in the long run, the presence of other counsel will substantially improve the odds favoring success in trial.

The second thing to watch for is that group defendants—agreeable as they usually are—have ambivalent feelings about lawyers. They may regard lawyers as class enemies. Lawyers have an interest in their fees, and that fact alone gives them adversary status. It should be noted very carefully that we are talking about something other than the normal reluctance of an individual to part with money. It may very well be that some of the group come from well-to-do families. But particularly if this group is composed of young people, they may have developed, long before this happened, a conscious reluctance to spend money on themselves.

Third, while they have a little pot of money which they intend to use to hire "a lawyer," they also have other uses for the same money. They may not intend to talk about these other uses, or about their reluctance to use all their money on their personal lawyers. All this has nothing to do with being ungenerous, it is just that they did not arrive at their present situation by accident. They may belong to a political group which has objectives wholly unrelated to a lawyer's personal welfare. Their present money is *not* from parents or friends. Part of it is the nickels and dimes of persons sympathetic to their cause. But most of it is likely to be proceeds of concerts and rallies organized by well-known names in their peer group. There were strings attached to *that* money. The defendants almost certainly have moral commitments to use some of their funds to help the people who helped them, or to help other persons in a similar plight.

The ability to raise money on behalf of popular defendants is a thing of the hour. That part of the public having the same outlook as the defendants will soon find its attention distracted by other causes. When this happens, it also may be found that none of the group defendants ever had a lasting interest in assuring that money should be provided for their defense. The group may soon be out of nickel-and-dime money, the only kind they had at the outset. This does not mean that other sources of money for the defense of the group, e.g., their families, are not available; but it is certainly true that those sources are best looked for at the outset, not months after the case is accepted.

An outstanding trait of group defendants (young ones) is that they have little idea of how much it will cost to fight their case. If money has not been discussed frankly, at the outset, and before their lawyers accepted the acclaim of defending this popular group, then a later difference of opinion between lawyers and clients will cause their relations to deteriorate very fast. For example, if $1,500 is needed for an investigator in the middle of a six-week trial, the lawyers may have to ask the group for $1,500. The answer may well be, "We gave you $1,500." If the lawyers then begin talking for the first time about the difference between legal fees and out-of-pocket costs, they will only stigmatize themselves as class enemies.

Lawyers who isolate their clients in this way are being unfair to their clients and will ruin themselves. They will make the clients withdraw essential rapport from them, and, to the extent that any one of the clients feels that fund raising is a group problem, he or she will then decide that it is someone else's business. (This dissociation from money problems is a phenomenon unique to group trials. A lone defendant is realistic.)

The result may well be growing disinterest, and eventually a sullen suggestion that the clients, having been imposed upon by their own lawyers, have no recourse but to plead guilty to whatever charges have been laid against them (though innocent)—if the lawyers' consciences will allow them to do that.

The lawyer must avoid the interesting position of financing a long trial out of his own pocket (probably impossible) while seeking to regain the favor of his client. The only way to avoid it is to talk things through at the outset.

§ 2.04 Considerations Affecting Use of Money Raised on Behalf of Popular Defendants

The following is simply a list of considerations which ought to be explored thoroughly by the defendants and lawyers who are in the case or who may be in the case. Needless to say, the discussions on this subject should be done with everybody present. The talks should be absolutely frank, within the limits of mutual respect, and law-

yers in particular should concentrate on telling what they
know about the situation, without assuming any sort of
pontifical role. As with many other discussions which will
happen during the litigation, persons other than clients and
lawyers should be politely asked to leave, so that every word
is not only private, but privileged.

There are two main goals. The first is to have these
discussions early on, and to make sure that they are
thorough and candid. The other is that some sort of agreement or consensus must emerge from the discussions.

The lawyers should tell what they know about the
possible length of the trial, *including related proceedings*.
It is not a good idea to offer estimates as to the probable
length of the trial because these estimates will probably
be wrong. A lawyer who has not previously done a number
of political trials will tend to underestimate the length of
this trial, with disastrous results.

If this is going to be a serious political trial, the
lawyer who really wishes to estimate its length should consider the available information about similar political trials,
whether or not in his jurisdiction, and how long they lasted.
If the estimate comes out less than one week plus an additional week for each defendant, perhaps the lawyer should
ask himself to justify *why* his estimate is less than that.
That is a conservative rule: any complications at all should
extend the estimate by half. It is much better to face the
shock at the time of making a fair estimate, rather than part
way into the trial.

The lawyers should discuss legal expenses, meaning
their own fees, roughly how these are figured and why they
are figured. The clients may well be at least as intelligent
and sophisticated as the lawyers, although their own training may be in other directions; lawyers should remember
that fact when talking about their fees, and should discuss
money in terms of reality rather than in terms of fee income
goals laid down by bar associations. For example, it is

ridiculous to tell a client, or anyone else, that a lawyer of average competence is "worth" such and such per hour; on the other hand, an explanation of the lawyer's own expenses, his rent and the salaries which he has to pay, will not be wasted.

The lawyers should also discuss out-of-pocket costs, with particular reference to the facts in the case before them (which will be glimpsed, not known at this time). One lawyer working for one client may personally locate and interview, say ten to twenty witnesses. But with a number of defendants having common trial problems, the number of people to be interviewed may be considerably larger. In other words, a good investigator will be needed. There should be a frank discussion about why he will be needed and what his probable cost will be. This discussion should by no means be abstract; the lawyers should check beforehand to make sure that the one or two investigators whom they may know and trust would be available and on what financial terms they may be employed.

Other things to be discussed include various types of photographic expense. It is amazing how many photographs can turn up in a riot case. The prosecution has virtually unlimited funds to make prints. They may mark 100 or more black and white prints as exhibits. It might as well be understood now that if identification at the scene of the crime will be a trial problem, and there are 100 photographs, many of them showing twenty or thirty identifiable faces, it is mandatory for the defense to have copies of all photographs, blown up to at least the same size as those used by the prosecution. There must be no nonsense about that since many hours will be spent examining those photographs. Eight-by-ten black and white prints cost money. Lawyers participating in this discussion should know how much such prints cost, and they should mention that cost. The prosecution will probably have movies. The defense would do well to get a print of each movie the prosecution has. It is important to make sure that after the lawyers get through with wrestling discovery motions and orders in court, and finally get an order compelling the prosecution to share all the photographs presently in their possession, there must be money available to take advantage of the order. Otherwise, the most valuable part of the discovery proceedings may be lost.

If videotapes are involved, these will doubtless remain in the possession of the television stations who own them. Private screenings of videotapes are hard to come by. It may be necessary to rent a machine for that purpose. That will be an additional expense, as will the drayage for moving the machine about.

Often there are unexepected expenses lurking in the interstices of predictable ones. The prosecution may run its movie, and the defense may already have a copy of the film, but an issue may develop in court as to what is shown on certain frames. All the prosecution has to do to raise such an issue is to screen the film and stop the projector on certain frames that show a particular vignette that seems attractive to the People's case. If the defense wishes to dispute what the prosecution says the film shows, the only way to do it is to have an enlargement made from the movie film frame.

This may sound simple because everybody knows such enlargements are well within the reach of commercial technology. But a few enlargements of this kind will entail somewhat more trouble and sweat than most persons would expect, and may also cost an extra $100.00 or $200.00.

If the case involves expert testimony of any sort, no trial lawyer will have to be reminded how *that* is obtained.

There will be miscellaneous expenses such as long distance telephone calls and even travel costs for the investigator, witnesses, or lawyers. There is no substitute for experience in estimating the cost of litigation.

The lawyers should agree on a generous but honest estimate of the probable out-of-pocket costs of the lawsuit. Out-of-pocket, in this sense, excludes lawyers' fees.

Another obvious subject for discussion which might otherwise escape being talked about is the actual amount of money on hand. If the group has $2,000.00 or $5,000.00 on hand, the amount should be discussed and everyone should know what it is. Also, it should be known at this point whether all of this money belongs to the group, or whether in fact some of it belongs to some other group. If there are strings on the money, including any moral commitment to use part of the money for some other purpose, the existence or nonexistence of these obligations must be discussed at the outset. If in fact any part of the money belongs to someone else, it had better be separated and paid over to them now, so that no misunderstanding can later arise as to ownership of the funds.

If other sources of group money are available, these should be discussed, realistically, at the outset.

A major decision is whether the money on hand (which belongs to the group), plus any money which is certainly and immediately receivable, is or is not substantially equal to the out-of-pocket costs of the defense. It will never be equal to the attorneys' fees. The clients will know about their money, the lawyers will have a better idea of the probable costs, and they must come to an understanding on this point.

While discussing whether their money will even cover their anticipated out-of-pocket expenses, lawyers and clients should confront the question whether the group which has been indicted together will actually be tried together.

From what little is known about the People's case

(and that will not be much at this point), is it likely that substantial conflicts of interest will develop among members of the group? If so, will such conflicts justify an effort to split the cases for trial? If a motion to sever is made, what is the likelihood of its success in this jurisdiction at this time?

These are hard questions to answer because so little can be known at this point about the factual nature of the trial. But an effort to answer them must be made. If it seems that a joint trial is likely, then certain other assumptions are relatively easy. For example, barring sharp conflicts of interest among the defendants, it is usually a safe assumption that in a joint trial any investigation or expense which helps one or more of the defendants (i.e., which destroys or weakens some portion of the People's case) will to some extent help all the defendants. This is true because the defendants will inevitably defend as a group despite the particular efforts of the lawyers on behalf of their own clients. There *will* be a group spirit notwithstanding that the case against each defendant in the eyes of the law is a tub sitting on its own bottom; the lawyers will work together even while they are working separately. All of this simply means that a large slush fund devoted to out-of-pocket expenses of the defense is probably a good idea.

Assuming that the money on hand plus the money expected roughly equals the out-of-pocket costs, the clients and lawyers will certainly wish to consider whether all available funds should be held and disbursed for that purpose. If the money is not enough to pay any substantial portion of legal fees on behalf of any individual defendant, outside expenses may be the best possible use for the money which was donated to all defendants.

While the lawyers are thinking that it would be a good idea to have litigation costs covered in advance, the clients may be advancing other ideas entirely. Assuming there are no strings to use this money for any outside group, there may nevertheless be strong feelings among the clients that some of it should be used on behalf of individual members of the group because of expenses or misfortunes known to them, in connection with this litigation, which are not common to the whole group. Whether these possible uses for the money are mentioned or not, there are still other problems to be thrown into the pot.

What happens if the case is dismissed or unexpectedly terminated in any manner before the "litigation money" has been used for litigation purposes? This could happen in a number of ways: the trial could end sooner than expected; the expenses could be less; or there could be more money than had been figured. If none of the money has been used for legal fees, there will be a problem whether to divide it equally among clients to be applied on their own lawyer's fees, return it to the donors, give it to somebody else, or whatever.

In most situations, it will be well beyond the capacity of a group of defendants to raise enough money to pay legal fees for all their lawyers. Unless one or two very rich people are interested in conducting a fund raising drive, and guaranteeing any deficit, then other means have to be found. Individual defendants, their families, and friends will probably be able to find funds and credit to hire several lawyers, on some kind of terms acceptable to the lawyers and themselves. It is almost equally certain that in any group of defendants about half will not have that much money or any access to it. This means that public defenders or court-appointed lawyers are going to be needed.

It is absolutely imperative to understand the relationship between the money now on hand and the availability of the public defender and court-appointed lawyers to members of the group who need them. The usual requirement for getting a court-appointed lawyer is indigency. Therefore, the lawyers will consider carefully and discuss frankly with the defendants the precise significance of this money and its availability for legal fees, with respect to whether any of them can be represented by the public defender. Needless to say, there will have to be a candid disclosure to the court if and when the court is requested to appoint a public defender or any other lawyer on behalf of any of these defendants.

Disclosure will have to include the amount of money, the terms under which it was received, the terms under which it is held, and its availability for legal expenses on behalf of the indigent defendant who is requesting the court to appoint the public defender to represent him. The main point is that a candid disclosure should be made. It will almost certainly be true that a pro rata share of what-ever portion of the group's money *might* become available for legal fees would not be nearly enough to hire a lawyer for any one of them, including any indigent members. Assuming an arrangement to use some part of the group money for legal fees on a pro rata basis, e.g., contingent on there being money left over after paying all the out-of-pocket expenses from a slush fund, it might be sufficient from the court's point of view if that contingency plan in-cluded a pro rata reimbursement of the public defender (or whatever state fund had been used to pay court appointed lawyers). On that basis the court might be quite willing to appoint the public defender at the onset. When handled this way the possible availability of leftover expense money should not prevent getting the valuable participation of the public defender.

In any case, whatever arrangements are worked out between defendants and lawyers during this conference about money, those arrangements should be the subject of total agreement. So far as the relation between clients and lawyers is concerned, that arrangement need not be in writ-ing, and it need not be excessively formal. But it certainly should be definite enough that everybody knows what has been done. It should be clear at the end of this meeting how much money there is, who will hold the money, how it will be used, whether it will be sufficient, *and who is responsible for getting the rest of it.* Equally important, the atmosphere at the end of the meeting must be such that the problems can be discussed freely and wihout self-consciousness, if it is necessary to do so, in later meetings involving lawyers and clients.

Footnotes

[1] A. E. Housman, "Epitaph on an Army of Mercenaries," *The Collected Poems of A.E. Housman* 144 (New York: Holt & Company, 1940).

[2] Not if he has a healthy personality, as we have.

Chapter 3

THE LAWYER'S PERSONAL RELATIONS WITH CLIENTS AND WITH OTHER LAWYERS

SYNOPSIS

---

§ 3.01 Advice on Relations with Younger Clients

A prerequisite of defending political cases is love for the clients, or at least for the kind of people whom they represent. A lawyer who believes he is helping the people he loves will not only do the necessary, but do it in a way which is acceptable to them. Half of these problems will be solved before they arise, since the people involved will always stand on firm ground in relation to each other.

Since relations with clients are founded as much in affection as in duty, the term "clients" in this chapter is not limited to the narrow, traditional meaning of one's own client. It includes not just the lawyer's personal clients in his political cases, but other lawyers' clients who are being defended in these same cases, in group trials. Apart from the occasional problem of conflict of interest, they are *all* the lawyer's clients.

Candor is important with younger clients. Most lawyers have a personal inventory of shopworn mannerisms which are used, more or less unconsciously, to keep clients at a distance. These mannerisms were presumably acquired for dealing with older clients. In dealing with younger clients it is especially important that anything which tends to inhibit honest discussion of the case problems be discarded. It is important for the lawyer not to exaggerate differences in age between himself and his younger clients, either failing to appreciate how much they understand (patronizing them), or ineptly attempting to close the gap by adopting their mannerisms and vocabulary. It is rather important not to talk down to younger clients, *not* to make thoughts simpler or easier to understand.

This does not mean the lawyer should inject a lot of legalisms into the conversation; on the contrary. But when he has something complicated to tell the clients about the case, that is just the way he should lay it out for them. If the lawyer's normal English vocabulary is just a little on this side of longer words rather than basic English, then he should generally talk in longer words. He should talk naturally even when he thinks that not all of these words are necessarily familiar to the clients. If they want him to explain something, they will say so quickly enough.

It is better to let the clients interrupt and ask for an explanation than for the lawyer to appear to get down on his hands and knees to yell in their ears—a posture that strongly suggests that the lawyer regards them as mental pygmies. They are not; moreover, they will be looking for attitudes like this in a new lawyer, and so the lawyer would be well advised to look for them in himself first.

Another thing about the lawyer's choice of words is, he should *not* attempt to use words which are commonly used (or assumed to be used) by the age bracket of the younger clients when these words are not ones which the lawyer would use himself. The lawyer should use the words which he is expected to use, and not make himself foolish by awkward endeavors to use other words which are probably no longer in style anyway.

This rule is so important that it seems advisable to lean a little backward in order to comply with it. The lawyer may, for example, have defended a number of narcotics cases. But if he happens to discuss marijuana with a group of younger clients, it would be better to call it marijuana than any of the other words that might occur to him. This is especially true if the clients are calling it something else.

No one will think less of the lawyer for using basic English words, but they would certainly be jarred if he attempted to use their words and used the wrong ones. They will understand him better in his own skin, and in this sense, he should never attempt to minimize age differences. This general rule is especially poignant if, in addition to age difference, the lawyer is caucasian and some of the clients are black. His chance of using black English adroitly is close to non-existent.

As a general rule, if what the lawyer has to say to his clients involves a little self-revelation, a touch of personal philosophy, he should say it for what it is worth in the discussion, rather than withholding that part of his message, which he might normally do among many of his contemporaries. Younger clients are generally more open in their dealings. It will be hard for them to trust someone who is not as open as they are.

The lawyer should refrain absolutely from promising results in any of the many court proceedings which comprise a trial. He can only promise effort, and should keep talk about that to a minimum. Clients will always understand why it is impossible to promise a particular result. (Older clients understand this as well as younger ones.) Most clients will secretly despise bombast. It is well to adhere to this rule against promising results at all times and circumstances because when the lawyer has honored this rule without exception, he will never feel bad later about not being able to remember what he said.

Another critical point in dealing with younger clients is the moment when they criticize the lawyer's peers. They will have considerable information and strong opinions about judges and other attorneys. As relations between the lawyer and his clients get on a firmer footing, their conversations will occasionally be laced with these opinions, few of which will be favorable to the subjects. These comments should be received either as a token of improving relations (trust) or as probes.

If the lawyer disagrees with these views on the ground that the subject is a friend of his, then he should be careful to point out that the person *is* a friend. That point will be received with understanding, and it will turn off the criticism without embroiling the lawyer and clients in a discussion of every single feature of the friend's practice or social conscience which may have aroused the clients' notice. After all, this may well be a friend who would never have defended these clients (and may have been *asked* to— one does not always know). Of all the things the lawyer and clients can discuss, the subject of this friend's professional merit is probably the least fruitful.

If the lawyer disagrees, not because the subject is a friend, but because he has information the clients do not have, he should mention that information at the same time he disagrees with them.

The point is, the lawyer should *never* give the impression of putting down his clients because they have presumed to criticize someone the lawyer's age, solely because of the age difference. That kind of put-down is obviously corrosive to good relations; more than that, the lawyer who feels an urge to stifle criticism of his own personal set of friends and established institutions should reexamine his mental attitude. He will have difficulty in defending a political case honestly, quite apart from what his clients are thinking.

§ 3.02 Advice to Younger Clients Regarding Their Appearance and Demeanor in the Courtroom

Regardless of normal style of living and dressing, all younger clients facing a trial do in fact look to their lawyers for advice on courtroom dress and demeanor. It is important to assure them, whether they ask it or not (many will), that no one will be expected—or even allowed if the lawyer has anything to say about it—to make any substantial change in hair length on account of the trial.

If hair is normally worn long, then it is important that it remain long. This point is of moral value to the client because he cannot really face the difficulties and uncertainties of the trial except on the basis of being his own person, of not having made any serious personal compromise as a price of admission. Hair length is serious. There is also a special tactical consideration here.

The prosecution will have at least one photograph of the defendant with long hair—the mug shot, taken at booking. At the outset of trial, the prosecutor will wish to use this malefic photograph for the straightforward purpose of degrading the defendant in the eyes of the jury. The lawyer should have no difficulty blocking that manuever (see § 13.02), but only if—right now—he prevents the defendant from cutting his hair or beard.

The lawyer should explain that any defendant who makes a significant change in his hair length or beard before trial will give the prosecutor a chance to twist his motives. The prosecution will simply argue to the jury that the defendant cut his hair to prevent identification in court, from a consciousness of guilt, but that fortunately his deceitfulness has been exposed by this honest prosecution photograph, taken at the time of booking, et cetera.

Of course a defendant who cuts his hair makes that mistake for the relatively innocent purpose of ingratiating himself with the jury. But it is a mistake which can only be corrected by putting him on the stand; and anything at all which leads the prosecution to suppose, *right or wrong*, that they know whether a particular defendant is going to testify, deprives the defense of an important, subtle, tactical advantage (see § 15.09). Details of personal appearance other than hair length are less important but very much worth discussing.

On the subject of clothing, the lawyer should advise whatever changes are necessary and he should do this immediately since the clients will be present at various court appearances well in advance of the trial. His advice to the clients should be for each of them to consider his own personal spectrum of clothing. Everybody has a spectrum except those who have only one set of clothing. (The lawyer should not be dismayed to find such a person as a client: he—this client is never a woman—may have compensations of character for such a sartorial deficiency.) In any case, the client should be invited to consider his or her own wardrobe, and appear in court in those items of clothing which lie toward the straight end of the scale.

One slight exception may be helpful: if a man has no coat, shirt or tie, but could borrow some that he feels good in from some friend (not the lawyer), and would not feel embarrassed by borrowing these items, he should be asked to wear them. This is true even of items of clothing which are not (for what are perhaps delicate reasons of taste) normally thought of as well matched. Levis, a brown sport coat, an old blue shirt, and a patterned silk tie are absolutely acceptable and the lawyer should not even think otherwise in his own mind, regardless of how he picks his own clothes. They are acceptable because the conglomeration is natural in the sense of including naturally borrowed items, and it seems to be what it is. A jury will know this and will not hold it against a defendant dressed in this way.

On the other hand, it is certainly not suggested that the client who has a slightly more conventional array of clothes should go out and borrow the items mentioned above, or mismatch his clothes unnecessarily, simply in order to achieve an image which would not be natural to him; the jury will know that they are being imposed upon, without being told, and that knowledge will hurt the defense.

Girls should be advised immediately to wear bras to court. The lawyer should tell them that if they do not they will distract the judge and the jury, which is the truth. The young lady who says that there is not a bra on her campus should be told to borrow one from her mother, which will end the discussion. It will be found that girls will wear bras on advice of counsel. They should also wear skirts if they have them, although this is not as important.

Needless to say, all clients should wear shoes to court, and if necessary, they should be argued out of their objections to this no matter how strenuously expressed. The lawyer should simply tell the clients that the jury which is finally selected will undoubtedly be composed of people who, in the back of their minds, very much wish to meet the defendants half way, and expect only a modest gesture in return. The shoes, the bras and so forth are no more than gestures in this direction.

The way the clients behave in court is of course more important than the clothing they wear. The lawyer must advise them how to act, if possible, before their first appearance in court. But only an inexperienced lawyer would leave it at that. It is quite important for the lawyer to keep an eye on the clients throughout a trial and to advise them about their demeanor whenever it is necessary. This advice should be given when all the clients are together, but only in a private place, and preferably at the end of the day, when tensions are somewhat relaxed.

In general they should be advised to keep poker faces in the courtroom, as far as possible. They should not sneer at the prosecutor or raise an eyebrow at any ruling of the judge. They should not talk about the case in the corridors nor on the sidewalk outside the courthouse, nor in the courtroom loud enough for the bailiffs to hear. They should be told that the bailiff or bailiffs seated near them must inevitably feel themselves on the prosecution team and that, no matter how much they come to like the clients (it is surprising how well some bailiffs get on with some defendants), they will nevertheless feel duty bound to report to the prosecutor anything material that they overhear. Therefore clients should be scrupulous not to place this temptation before the bailiff.

Clients should be advised that if it is necessary to whisper something in court, the correct way to do it is to let most of the air out of the lungs so as to eliminate sibilance and to lean very close to the ear of the other person. Courtroom acoustics may be funny so that a whisper can be heard in an unexpected corner of the room, and if the lawyer knows about this (which he should if he knows his business) clients must be informed.

They should be told not to pass notes. This is vital, and is a thing which some clients find irresistible. They always want to pass notes to the lawyers. The type of client who does this is nervous, articulate, and seems to find it impossible to sit still or keep away from the counsel table. Such a client should be absolutely required to sit still and keep away from the counsel table, and all other defendants should be asked to encourage him or her to do this. With a real note writer, no admonition from a lawyer, standing by itself, will keep him in his seat. But he must be made to understand that those actions in the presence of the jury speak louder than any other evidence in the case, and that even if conspiracy is not one of the felonies charged against the defendants the jury will understand clearer than words can say that this particular defendant could not keep his nose out of any mischief that was going on at the time and place involved, if there was any way for him to be there. If allowed to run about the courtroom like a squirrel, he will certainly convict himself and will probably weaken the defense of several other persons associated with him. If prescription drugs are needed to solve this problem they should be sought.

If the clients are young men and women, some of them will probably be fairly close to each other. There will be very strong psychological pressures on them not only to sit together, but to touch each other during the course of the trial. This is true because each knows the other is threatened, and the source of that threat seems to be the source also of normal social inhibition against sexual contact in public. In order to oppose and defy this rather intangible threat, a hand on the thigh may seem the best thing. The lawyer should treat this situation with understanding, but he should not let the sun go down on it. When the defendants are together, and things are somewhat relaxed, he should tell them very aimiably that the hand on the thigh will have to stop, not because affection should not be demonstrated, but because this gesture in this context tends to defeat the objects of affection. Sexual closeness which tends to send the other person to jail is self-defeating. Not only that, the situation endangers other defendants not involved. This is the kind of thing which the defendants themselves know already, in a way; but they cannot give that knowledge full value until they are made to confront it by a person who is not hostile. If the lawyer has any rapport with his clients, then he can solve this problem by five minutes of candid discussion. The lawyer certainly owes it to his clients to help them solve the problem in this way before it becomes a matter of principle. It may be very hard to get them to do what they should do in their own self-interest if the situation is allowed to drag on until a bailiff sees it going on and says something to the parties involved in the courtroom. Their sense of pride will be aroused and it will be ten times as hard for the lawyer to persuade the clients to act in a way which, unfortunately, a bailiff has already said they should act.

It should probably be unncessary to add that defendants should not put their feet on a courtroom bench, whether or not court is in session. If this happens during a session, the lawyer will probably not realize it until after the bailiff has spoken to the client about it because the bailiff will be in a better position to see this and cannot fail to notice it. Although the lawyer may feel considerably less sympathy for the client in this particular situation he should nevertheless follow a similar procedure of explaining to the client, privately, why he must not put his feet on the bench again. These things are not that serious provided they do not happen twice and provided the jury was picked with care.

§ 3.03 General Rules for Getting Along with Other Lawyers in a Group Trial

This discussion concerns group trials in which a number of defendants, represented by several lawyers, are facing serious political charges. The assumption here is, the defendants are not only prosecuted for political reasons, they are also lumped together for political reasons, and accordingly they have a sense of group identification and cohesiveness. These assumptions cover most group trials and serve to exclude only the rather theoretical situation in which two or three political defendants might be tried together who never met each other before, who detest each other, and who draw nothing from shared ideologies or the sense of facing a common enemy.

The need for defense lawyers to get along with each other is axiomatic in all types of trials. However, the need for unity seems more poignant in a political case than it is in an ordinary action for money damages. The possibility of going to jail together is a genuine bond; by contrast, the quiet maneuvering of a possible money judgment into the lap of somebody else's insurance company makes for only poker feelings among the participants—multichaired but lone-handed camaraderie.

Of course it is always true that each lawyer has his client and is solely responsible for that client's interest as against the whole legal world, including the interests of co-defendants; this rubric is also well known. But any perceptive lawyer will realize that where several political defendants are tried together, each client *has* an interest in the security of his or her co-defendants: political defendants tend somewhat to stand or fall together. If the defense succeeds in breaking up a prosecution attack on one defendant, that success helps all. This is true for both tactical and ideological reasons.

Tactically, any defense success tends to make the prosecution look sick. Moreover, beating off an attack on one defendant, by preventing him from being tarred, also prevents the prosecution from cleaning their brush on the remaining defendants. In an ideologic way, the jury inevitably tends to identify all defendants in a group trial as being on the same side. Although the longer the trial the better the jury gets to know individual defendants, the jurors understand perfectly well that every defendant is closer to every other defendant than any of them is to the prosecution. Most important, the defendants (under our assumption) have a strong sense of group identification, which they tend to strengthen as the trial goes on. *They will resent technical thinking by their own lawyers which tends to create unnecessary or unrealistic differences vis-à-vis each other.*

All of this simply means that defense lawyers should be generous in interpreting the common interests of their clients; to the extent that the lawyer's own client has a special defense or interest which is different, necessary, and to any degree antithetical to the interests of the others, the lawyer must, of course, pursue that interest on behalf of his client, but while he is doing this righteous thing he should be tactful, humble (not vaunting himself too much because of what he is doing in the name of ethics), and sincerely respectful of common interests.

The following are some of the facts which tend to split lawyers in a group case. Especially at the outset, attachment to one's own client will be strong. Knowledge of the facts of the case, the good qualities of other lawyers, and the special ways in which they can help each other, will all be future things, probably underrated. At the outset the lawyer may feel a particular need to justify his individual fee, which was just received or agreed upon with the client's family. While he does not wish anything ill on the other defendants, somewhere in the back of his mind may be a little thought that if there should be a general legal disaster, and his own client emerged unscathed, then the lawyer himself would be an object of awe (like Ishmael, "I only am escaped alone to tell thee" [1]). This is not a noble thought, and therefore presumably natural.

Also, trial lawyers are without exception notoriously egotistical. This fact enhances the possibility of conflict, even when all are drinking at the same waterhole. Especially then. Trials themselves tend to produce tension and exacerbated nerves, a fact which does not have to be explained to those involved.

There are differences in skills among trial lawyers, and differences in the rate at which skills become evident. As the lawyers get to know the clients better, it is probably true that all of them share a wish not to appear individually inept in the eyes of the group of clients, who are seen as arbiters. (This particular factor, discussed below, is probably a stronger influence for unity than for divergence.)

There are also possible differences in motivation among the lawyers present. Commonly, the motivation of the lawyers is the strongest unifying influence among them, but where the motivation is erratic, that difference can be destructive. For example, consider the following two hypothetical lawyers.

Type *A* lawyer was brought into the case by the family of one of the defendants. He was formerly a member of the district attorney's office; in his private practice he has built a reputation as an effective litigator, within the foot sound of his former office. In other words, he is known for political influence with the district attorney. His practice includes but few criminal defense cases because his heart is not in that sort of work; but when he does them, he gets charges dismissed. He accepted this retainer solely because of political ties with the defendant's father. He actually dislikes the kid, and moreover distrusts not only the co-defendants but all the other defense lawyers, whom he presumes to be radical though he has never known any of them very well. He will not get to know them now, either, but will see to it that relations are relatively superficial. His *tendency* in this case will be to arrange a cop-out. This is true because (1) he does not wish the defense to prevail, since that would affront his conscience; (2) he does not know how to defend this kind of case; (3) his main strength lies in existing relations with the district attorney's office; and (4) he intends to retain those good relations long after this case is over.

The danger of this kind of lawyer is that he will impair morale among the defendants by splitting off one of them (his client) for an exceptionally conspicuous and lenient cop-out, which would never be offered to any of the other defendants. The possible results are that the other defendants will wonder whether their own lawyers are as dedicated to principle as they say they are, or whether they are simply unable or unwilling to work out appropriate deals. They never doubt that they are innocent of the particular things for which they are about to go to trial; but they have very little trust in the system, either. They wonder if it would not be much better in the long run to be realistic, put up with the outrage of pleading guilty to something which they and the prosecution know very well they did not do, and get on with their political lives. These feelings are particularly dangerous because a lawyer can only fight the case for a client. He certainly cannot do much to imbue the client with a willingness to have that fight made.

While the foregoing describes what may happen, the more probable result is that the Type *A* lawyer will simply withdraw from the case and leave his client to be represented by other counsel. This will happen because his rapport is with the family and not with the client. On the other hand, if the influence of the family is strong, particularly if the client is a young man and the Type *A* lawyer is a friend of his mother, then he will probably cop-out. Other lawyers cannot properly interfere with this process, but they can certainly talk to their own clients to minimize the consequences.

The other hypothetical lawyer, Type *B*, may have been retained by some rather conservative group having an interest in one or more of the defendants and a strong influence with the family of one of them. Through that family the group arranges for this lawyer to take part in the case. The motivation of the sponsoring group (and the Type *B* lawyer) is quite simple: this particular defendant is *naive* as are most of the other defendants; they will all be imposed upon and exploited by a group of radical lawyers who have come to represent them.

The interesting thing about the Type *B* lawyer will probably be that he has no effective political power in this situation. That is interesting because in any other situation he certainly would have widespread contacts and he would be listened to. It may surprise him that when he makes overtures to the district attorney's office in *this* kind of case, he gets no response at all. The fact is, the district attorney's office will see the Type *B* lawyer, in this situation, as naive and out of his depth. They know him to be a moral and upright man; but he was never a deputy district attorney. What would he know about politics, or about radicals?

Another interesting thing about the Type *B* lawyer is that, given a little time, he will turn out to be a good man to have around. His own attempts to solve things in his own way will be an education to him. He will come to appreciate some of the problems of defense lawyers in a political case. After that, his contributions may be intermittent and unpredictable, but probably valuable. He is, after all, a moral man; and for some reason, in a political trial that fact must be weighed equal to a considerable amount of relevant experience, even though his own experience may have been limited to diocesan affairs.

The following factors tend to unify defense lawyers. First, they are all there (excepting only the theoretical Type *A* and *B* lawyers, who are aberrant) for a proper reason. They were all chosen by some client or clients, and they are all there to protect their own. The pressures of the case will be felt, but those pressures will fuse them. Where lawyers' egos are a problem, the situation is very well known to them. Most trial lawyers know that they have egos, know that the others also have egos, and learn to make allowances. Lawyers are familiar with trial nerves, and have sociable methods of assuaging them at lunch and after court.

The most important means of ameliorating bad feelings, however, will be the defendants themselves. This is one thing that seems unique to political cases: a group of defendants will have an astonishing awareness of clashes among their own lawyers, even when the lawyers take care (as they think) to have their confrontations out of their clients' earshot. A group of intelligent clients will take measures to correct this situation just as speedily as the lawyers take measures to correct their habits of dress in court. The lawyers should not be at all surprised to find themselves called to a group meeting and informed that all of their clients are rather concerned about the fact that they seem to be indulging their egos and otherwise doing things inconsistent with a proper defense of the case. This may come as quite a shock to the lawyers the first time it happens because lawyers tend to regard themselves primarily as samurai whose personal differences derive from a code which no one else would understand. They do not like to be told how to fight by a bunch of farmers who were lucky enough to hire them. All of these illusions can be shaken down in short order, however, if clients are sensitive to their own interests. In this sort of confrontation, the clients actually have an impregnable position.

The cardinal rule for lawyers who wish to get along with each other is never to say the unforgivable thing. They must remember that they are in this case now, and tomorrow they are still going to be in this case, together. (See also § 11.10, Getting Along with Other Defense Lawyers while Picking the Jury.)

Footnote

[1] Job 1:15; accord, Herman Melville, *Moby Dick*, Epilogue.

Chapter 4

BUILDING THE DEFENSE CASE
(GENERAL RULES AND NECESSARY FIRST STEPS)

SYNOPSIS

§ 4.07 **First-Round Discovery of Prosecution Evidence**
  [1] **The Shortcomings of Usual Discovery**
      Practice and Motions
  [2] **An Expanded Discovery Motion**
  [3] **Further Tactical Advantages of Making**
      the First Discovery Motion as Soon as
      Possible, and of Obtaining the Discovery
      Order by Means of Contested Hearing

---

§ 4.01 Getting Maximum Help from the Client

The lawyer should interview his client as soon as possible after accepting the case. It is assumed that some kind of interview was already done before accepting the case, as the basis for accepting it; but that kind of interview was probably not sufficient. The main interview will be much more thorough.

The lawyer should set aside enough time so that this interview can be finished in one session, if possible. Even in a simple case a minimum of two hours should be allocated. Probably the best way is to schedule the interview in an open end position, with no conferences or court appearances following. Other persons should be carefully excluded, especially parents of student defendants. Mothers who make a habit of running their sons' lives are not the only offenders, although it is suggested that women like this should not even be encouraged to occupy a chair in the waiting room while this interview is going on. They should be encouraged to busy themselves on the other side of town, that the interview may run along more smoothly. Fathers are also to be kept out, in this situation, because even fathers who understand the ways and differences of their own children turn a cold eye on their children's friends, and the client's friends will almost certainly be involved in the case.

At this first thorough interview with the client, the lawyer should request the client's permission to run a tape while the interview is going on, and he should explain why. The reason, of course, is that the lawyer is properly interested in hearing the whole story, including every nuance of expression. That requires absolute attention to the client, including watching him with a closeness which is not consistent with taking serious notes. This is true even if the lawyer was a good note taker in law school. These reasons should not be put to the client just that way, because so much scrutiny would make him self-conscious. It should be enough to say that the lawyer is not very good at taking the kind of notes he needs from the conference, and he does not wish to interrupt the client every minute or two; the tape can later be transcribed by someone in the lawyer's office on a semi-verbatim basis. The lawyer should explain that this will enable him to get on with the case without repeating the conference two or three times to pick up things he missed, and for that reason, unless the client really minds, he would like to use the tape machine. Clients understand this problem, and as a general rule, show no concern at all about the tape.

Needless to say, the lawyer should use a long-playing cassette-type machine and it should be in excellent working order. In view of the importance of this interview, there should be absolutely no carelessness or chintzing on the recording. If the machine runs on batteries, they should be new ones. The quality of tapes varies considerably with their price; the tape used for this interview should be top quality. The lawyer should be familiar with using his machine, and if it happens to be one in which the tape automatically and silently comes to a stop when it has run its course, the lawyer should ask the client to help him keep an eye on the tape, or take some other precaution to make quite sure that, in the middle of the interview, a vital fifteen or twenty minutes is not spoken into a dead microphone. It should be unnecessary to add that an office-type dictating machine is absolutely unsuitable for this purpose because, as a general rule, their magnetic tapes or belts have to be changed so often that the interruptions would seriously hinder the course of the interview.

The use of the tape machine does *not* mean that the lawyer should take no notes at all. On the contrary. Since the interview should be somewhat non-directive—meaning that the client's recollection should be encouraged to run along with a minimum of interference—he will be referring to people by their first names. The lawyer will naturally want their full names and addresses, etc. Rather than interrupt every minute it is well to make some notes, and then interrupt at some natural breaking point to go back and pick up all the loose strings. In order not to lose the context the lawyer must remember that while his tape is a far better source of information it may still be several days before the typed summary can be completed. Two hours of running tape is a lot of typing, particularly from cassette-type equipment, which is often incompatible with the usual office equipment (foot control, earphone, etc.). There will be things the lawyer wants to do about the case in the meantime and he simply cannot sit around waiting for the perfect copy. Therefore, he should have fairly accurate notes as to names, addresses, dates and times, to the extent that he will need such information in the time between the interview and the completion of the typed notes.

Among other things to be discussed in this interview should always be the forty-eight hour period which brackets the actual arrest, or if the arrest was substantially later than the events in question, then another forty-eight hour period bracketing those events. In other words, at critical points, the client must be told to go back to the day preceding that event, and state as well as he possibly can every single thing he did from the time he woke up that morning. Similarly, the running account of detail should be continuous not only through the event itself (whether a riot, arrest, or whatever) but a full twenty-four hours beyond when the action stopped. It is amazing the number of relevant details that will be turned up in this manner which might otherwise escape attention.

The main objects of this interview are to find out what the client was doing before, during, and after all the critical time periods and who are potential witnesses. By going through it, and then going over it again, the lawyer should see that the client's memory is brought to bear repeatedly on critical points: known or readily ascertainable time references. These should be corroborated by the client's best estimate of time intervals between various events.

The final point of this interview is to put the client to work again, immediately, on relevant problems. Since there will now be a list of potential witnesses, he should be asked to verify their present addresses. Many of them will not have telephones. The lawyer should remember that (if he follows these recommendations) he will personally be going door-to-door looking for these people, and it will save a great deal of his time if the doors he knocks on are the right ones. With students particularly, apartment numbers are vital. Also, it is well to learn at the outset, with reference to as many witnesses as possible, the names of various third persons who probably know where these witnesses are if they are not where they should be.

Another thing the client can do is firm up the actual times it took him to do certain things which he has described in the interview. He can probably do this by going over the same ground, at about the same time of day, using the same method of transportation as before, only this time with a watch. He should be requested to do this as soon as possible, making careful notes, and report these to the lawyer promptly.

A final thing the client can do is begin to help the lawyer prepare to defend the client against disastrous cross-examination (should a decision later be made that the client will testify) based on things the client has said or written. Many clients in political trials will have contributed articles, both signed and unsigned, to various newspapers or other publications. They may have been interviewed as well. They will know when and where they did these things. They will *not* know how devastating some of these things can be in court. Surprisingly, the client may assume that the lawyer has read all of these things and needs no particular assistance in finding them. Actually, this is a dangerous assumption. There may be a lot more of these published statements than the lawyer knows about, even if he is a regular reader of the publication. It is quite important that the client, *with the help of friends in that publication*, be put to work on an exhaustive search for every single article that fits into this category. Copies should be gotten, indexed, and included in the lawyer's evidence file, and he should take the trouble to read them attentively and with no interruptions, not only when they are received in his office, but later on during the trial.

It is rather important that the client *not* be asked to contact witnesses for any purpose other than to verify their addresses and to say that his lawyer will be in touch with them. This is true because, first, clients are not always supremely tactful in dealing with their peers (even sympathetic peers), and they may very well say something to the witness which lends itself to misinterpretation; second, when any one of these potential witnesses later testifies in court, he will be asked on cross-examination who was the first person to approach him in connection with this case. If the answer is the defendant, that information may smell a little funny to the jury. But if the answer is that the lawyer first approached the witness, that is natural, and it will be understood as natural by the jury. Keep the clients away from the witnesses.

The natural conclusion from all of this is that the

first contact with witnesses, and all other important contacts with witnesses, must be made by the lawyer in person. Contacts by an investigator are not just second choice, they are more accurately thought of as fifth choice, there usually being no second, third, or fourth choices.

§ 4.02   A Mosaic Method

This is a more difficult method of proof than the ordinary ones, but it is the only way to deal with a lying police officer. Several things should be noted about lying officers. First, if there are three or four officers present at the moment when the defendant is supposed to have done something violent to one of them (which he did not do), it is obvious that the prosecution will depend on one or possibly two officers who are willing to lie in order to convict the defendant; but the point which is often overlooked by the defendant's lawyer is there are several other officers who will *not* be willing to lie about what happened. It may well be that only one is willing to lie, while at most one other will shade his testimony to provide some corroboration. The other officers may simply say that they were not in a position to see what happened or did not have the opportunity to see because so many other things were going on.

The lawyer should not overlook the real significance of this important difference in testimony. The lawyer should remember that the officers who will not lie, for moral reasons, are governed by two decisions: they are not going to lie about what happened, but they will not overtly contradict an officer who will. The lawyer who is already angry about the officer who lied should not allow himself to be resentful over this relatively trivial omission. He should remember, rather, that the difference between these officers has opened a wide gap in the prosecution case, probably invisible to all except himself, which has decisive potential on behalf of the defendant.

He should also remember that this potential is absolutely meaningless unless he finds and produces the necessary evidence to prove that the lying officer is indeed lying. The fact that other officers were ostensibly looking the other way, even though they had good reason to do so, will be meaningless until there is a substantial amount of evidence which destroys the testimony of the lying officer; *then* the fact that other officers were looking the other way means something.

A lying police officer probably cannot be impeached by the testimony of any defendant. Police officers make better witnesses in the eyes of the jury because most jurors tend to think that society owes an unspecified moral debt to individual officers, and these jurors further tend to believe that the individual officer has no personal stake in the outcome of the case. The defendant, on the other hand, is always suspect; the theory seems to be, who wouldn't lie to save himself from conviction? There is no point in deploring this situation at length. Counsel had just better remember that if success depends in any way on the defendant's testimony, the defendant will lose. That does not mean the defendant should not testify, but it does mean that very strong defense evidence must be found and brought before the jury, whether or not the defendant testifies.

This is certainly one of those sensitive points in the trial when the lawyer must keep in mind which type of political case he is trying. If this is a case where the defendant did what the prosecution said he did, and the lying officer is lying about some point not strictly material to guilt or innocence (about some aggravating circumstance), then what follows has very little application. But in any case where the defendant, for political reasons, is wrongly accused of doing something which he did not do, e.g., resisting arrest, and where there *are* other witnesses, the following approach will be decisive for the defense.

The mosaic approach to proving a defense case is

based on this simple consideration: while there is no magic number of witnesses needed to overcome the testimony of one lying officer, there is a *watershed* at about the number of six or seven witnesses. More are desirable, but that is where the terrain starts sloping toward acquittal. There will probably be *no star defense witness*, for the simple reason that in most situations like this nobody other than the defendant was in a position to see very much of what happened, and sometimes even the defendant was a bad observer (because he or she was being knocked or thrown around). Of course, this is not any kind of unfailing rule, but generally most witnesses will not have seen much of the action, and many will have seen only a fleeting part. Each one sees only a little thing, and that part will probably seem to the witness relatively insignificant. All these parts put together, however, add up to the truth.

The lawyer investigating in this situation must remember that he is really looking for pieces of a mosaic, and when he finds a witness who saw part of it, he should assure that witness that what he saw or heard is important. He must also be scrupulous not to take the edges off what the witness has to say by suggesting that he modify his memory to agree with some other witness. The great value of this method of proof is that people *do* see things a little differently even when they are looking at the same thing. That is a matter of common sense. When defense witnesses tell what they actually saw, without making concessions to any theory of the defense lawyer or to each other other—but tell it just as they felt they saw it—then after a while the jury *knows* what happened. The jury also knows from its experience in life that people do see things differently. That is a truth that is entitled to an important position in the defense closing argument, and there will certainly be a jury instruction to the same effect.

After the sixth, seventh or eighth witness testifies to some part of what was seen, the jury loses its expectation that sooner or later there will be some star witness, and acquires instead an understanding of what really happened. The jury feels a growing bond of common sympathy, of sharing an experience with each successive witness. In this way the natural, little mistakes of various witnesses are cancelled by the collective memory of the group, and they do *not* deflect the jury's understanding of what happened, but instead lend confirmation.

The lawyer should remember while going from door to door that he is looking for tiles, and that at the end of the defense case there is going to be a mosaic.

§ 4.03 How to Look for Witnesses and What to Do When You Find Them

[1] The Importance of Remembering Which Kind of Case

The lawyer's approach to the problem of looking for witnesses will be determined by how well he appreciates what kind of political case he is trying. If the case involves an admitted crime which was intended as a political protest, then the thrust of the defense will be to make the jury see things as the defendant saw them, and, it is to be hoped, view his act sympathetically. A major part of this defense has nothing to do with witnesses; it will begin with a heavy battle on venue, which in turn is linked to a major battle on jury selection. Large parts of the defense may be brought out on cross-examination, relatively little by direct testimony of persons other than the defendant. The value of eyewitnesses to the defense will vary widely under the aegis of conceded facts and intended arguments. The value of eyewitnesses in that case may be small.

But if the case involves a disputed crime which is prosecuted for political reasons, the value of eyewitnesses is overwhelming. It would be senseless and stupid for a defense lawyer to approach trial preparation in *this kind of case* by neglecting eyewitnesses, simply because he prefers the agreeable exercise of shaming a jury into a better understanding of his client. The defense lawyer who does this has planted himself in a losing position before he ever starts, since it is logically indefensible to suggest that the law must be bent a little to allow a sympathetic defendant to escape the consequences of a crime which he committed, and at the same time to argue that he never did it at all. There may be several defense arguments at the end of the case, and they all need not be consistent; but there is room for only one main argument, and that argument should be logically impeccable.

When the defense is that the defendant did not do it, then the first main problem may be a psychological one, belonging to the lawyer. He must get rid of any supposed advantages accruing from: (1) the burden of proof being on the prosecution, and (2) possible testimony by the defendant. The lawyer must also rid his mind of resentment concerning the political nature of the prosecution, and bend every effort toward finding evidence establishing firmly that the defendant did not, in fact, do the crime.

[2] Sources of Witnesses

Finding witnesses is a pleasantly amorphous problem and not one that should ever be viewed in terms of checklists. The checklist approach tends to pay off in terms of small satisfactions based upon running through the list. Actually the thing is to find witnesses. Clients should be the most important source of names of witnesses. Also, since the client will probably have been doing whatever he was doing in the presence of a few friends, they may be potential witnesses, and if not, they can probably be very helpful in locating other witnesses.

If the case involves a civil disturbance of any kind,

there may well be some form of information center. If students were involved, this is very likely, indeed. Such a center will probably have come into existence before the lawyer got into the case. Volunteer workers at the center will have collected information about who was arrested, who was injured, and all kinds of valuable miscellany. A student information center will be potentially a source of great benefit to the defense, and also a potential disappointment if its services are not used promptly and well.

The lawyer should remember that written statements collected by an information center may be the best statements that he will ever get and the best source of fresh information and of witnesses. Some people who have written things down in the heat of the moment would never come forward voluntarily or make themselves readily visible to an investigation conducted later. Approximately half of the best photographs taken on the spot will have found their way into the information center within a week or two after the riot. On the other hand, one takes these things as he finds them.

The volunteers who run the information center do it entirely on the passion and energy of youth. They keep odd hours and they do not lock the doors. Access to their files may often be had by walking into a large unoccupied office at any hour of the day or night and pawing through open files. The lawyer should not allow himself to express criticism to anybody about these casual ways; he should be grateful that the information is there at all. At the same time, he should be aware that the search for statements and photographs through the information center's files is a project in itself. At different times, he may have to ask several agreeable people to search through the files to find things for him.

For some reason, it helps if the lawyer makes these requests personally—which probably means going out to find one or more people who know their way through these files, who actually work in this office. It does not necessarily pay to send the client to the information center with a request that all statements and photographs be turned over to the client. It probably will not happen that way. The client is, after all, only another person, like the hundreds who have contributed statements to the center, and like the obnoxious few who have already begun to paw through the files and to take things without asking. The client may be invited to leave the premises, and if that happens the lawyer should not take it amiss. He should simply go and do his own talking.

Another thing the lawyer should do quite early is go to where the event happened. The first time, it might help to go with the client and have things pointed out and explained. Another time, which should be soon after that, he should go without the client and see what he can find out from the people who would normally work in or around that place or pass through it, and who therefore might be witnesses. He should tell them who he is and why he wants to know, and simply go from person to person asking if they happened to see a certain thing. People will respond to the lawyer doing this, and he will find that if he expects to be taken at face value, he will be.

A thing which seems to satisfy those who wish to be helpful to the lawyer, and who persistently suggest this, but a thing which rarely produces any good, is to post small cards or notices in various places around where the action happened, inviting witnesses to phone the lawyer. On the other hand, if there is a small newspaper, such as the student paper, which is likely to be read by potential witnesses, then ads *should* be placed there from time to time. Often the paper will donate space, and that helps on a tight budget. In the same way, a student radio station will be glad to broadcast a discreet request for those having information to get in touch with the lawyer at a certain phone number. The mere fact that the paper and the station carry these messages is an endorsement that the information is needed by a friendly lawyer. Both of these media will probably produce results.

Of course, once a witness is located and the initial contacts made (discussed in the following sections) that witness may well be the source of leads to other witnesses.

[3] When and How to Look for Witnesses

Do it at night. Students as a general rule cannot be found in the daytime. The same considerations that govern dress and speech in dealing with young clients clearly apply in looking for witnesses in the same age bracket. In short, appropriateness in clothing and speech means what would normally be conducive to relaxation on the part of the lawyer, what is natural to him. Affected clothing and affected speech are deadly handicaps.

[4] Initial Contact with Witnesses

The initial goals in dealing with a witness, the things to try to do on the first contact, are to identify him, to establish rapport, to learn what he saw, to find out if he is liable to prosecution himself, to learn whether he is willing to testify, to find out if he knows of other witnesses or the existence of photographs, and to *move on*.

Identification includes not only his name and his local address, but also whatever second address he may have, and—quite important—the name and address of some person who knows where he would be found if he is not in his usual place.

Establishing rapport is mostly a matter of finding rapport; i.e., telling the witness that one is a lawyer representing such and such a person should do something positive for the relationship, and if it does not, the lawyer should be very sensitive as to why. The lawyer's message to the witness, not all of which is overtly spoken, is simply: "This matter is urgent; there is a need for anybody who saw any part of what happened to come forward and tell what he saw. What may not seem important to you may be quite important alongside similar statements from other people. [An explanation of mosaics will be very helpful.] Nobody remembers everything the same. You are not expected to alter your impression of what you saw to fit any preconceived notion. As to the outcome of the case, no one has a crystal ball, but we feel some confidence."

The main points, of course, are what the witness saw and heard, and what the witness did not see or hear, which requires more probing, but which probably would have been seen or heard if it had happened. If a statement has already been obtained from the information center, signed by this witness, of course, he may be shown the statement now. However, if he *is* shown the statement now, an important tactical decision has been made, consciously or not, which really should be thought about beforehand.

That tactical decision arises when the lawyer is in a jurisdiction where the witness may be asked on cross-examination if he has read any statement to refresh his memory before testifying, and where, if the answer is yes, the defense may be required to produce that statement for inspection while the witness is still on the stand. Where that rule is in effect, the act of showing this witness his own statement (which he has presumably not read since he filed it at the information center) would be sufficient to trigger the production of that statement in court. There may be good reasons why that statement should not be produced in court.

One reason is, the prosecution probably do not even *know* about the information center. Suppose that about midway through a ten-week trial the prosecution discovered for the first time that there was an information center containing many statements and photographs about all kinds of events relating to recent civil distrurbances. While it may be assumed that the lawyer by that time will have cleaned out the information center by obtaining the statements relating to this case, there is still the little matter of statements relating to other political cases, some of which must still be defended by the lawyer or his friends. For that matter, statements which the lawyer has not yet seen may still be arriving at the information center. Finally, if the center is well organized, someone will have taken over the job of coordinating and indexing all known statements. There will be copies of every statement which the lawyer has in his possession and which came from that information center. Many copies will relate to defense witnesses who have *not yet testified*. That is something to think about before gratuitously inviting the attention of the prosecution to the existence of that center.

Another possible reason for not wishing to produce the statement in court, apart from the danger of giving away a source of defense witness statements, is that this particular statement, involving the witness who is standing before the lawyer, may contain something particularly distasteful to the defense. Most witness statements will not contain any such thing, but the time to think about this problem is before showing the statement to the witness.

If the decision is *not* to show the statement to the witness, the lawyer should simply explain that he was able to contact this witness in the first place because of the existence of such a statement (if that is the reason), that he has the statement and is quite familiar with it, and that there is a rule in effect which says that if the witness takes this occasion to examine the statement, it will have to be produced in court. The lawyer should then explain that this may not always be in the best interests of the defense, and that as a practical matter, the witness almost certainly does not need to read the statement. The lawyer should then proceed to ask him questions about the case, including but not limited to what is in the statement, and not necessarily in the same order of subjects. The lawyer should do this *without suggesting to the witness that the lawyer is reading the statement during the interview.* To suggest that he is reading the statement would be little better than handing it to the witness and telling him to read it himself.

Fortunately, there is no real difficulty in conducting a witness interview without handing over the statement or making direct reference to it. The lawyer's natural questions concerning events should be adequate to bring out the witness' story; and, since the lawyer does know what is in the statement, he can always ask for enough details to draw the witness over the same ground, without being obvious about it. It is surprising how closely people do remember the same facts that are in their statements, often using some of the same words, without having reviewed the statements. That is true, at least, if the statements were properly taken. It is just a matter of the witness refreshing his memory, something he can do for himself, and can do almost as well by the process of recollection as he could by reading. Not exactly as well, not perhaps as to time references, or who else was in the car, but almost as well.

Assuming that the decision is to *show* the witness the statement, and that the witness has *asked* to see it, the witness should be told that the lawyer has already read the statement and does not wish him to memorize it, but only refer to it if it helps refresh his recollection. If the witness then wants a permanent copy of his statement, the lawyer should agree to send him one promptly, and he should do that. As a general rule, witnesses should not be pressed to take copies of their statements because they do in fact tend to memorize things.

A vital consideration at this point is whether the witness himself was involved in some crime related to the one being prosecuted against the defendant. If this was a riot case, the question is whether this witness was throwing rocks. He must be asked that *now*, in private, and not in the presence of other persons who would have to remember both the question and the answer when they in turn are asked about it on cross-examination. It is important for the lawyer to think about what he is doing in this first interview, and to remember that there probably will be a second interview and that there will be considerable time devoted to witness preparation. Final witness preparation will have to be done in groups (see Chapter 9); that cannot be done on an individual basis and cannot be done now. One of the things told the witnesses in preparation will be that if asked on cross-examination what was said during the preparation conference, they can and should tell all. It would not be very helpful to the defense if defense witnesses admitted that many were called but few were chosen, and that those not present in court were confessed rock throwers. Counsel should have thought about this, quite hard, before interviewing the first witness, and such thoughts should never be far from his mind.

It is a hard question to answer, what to do when an important potential witness turns out to be a rock thrower. The answer is that in almost every case, the witness should not be called by the defense. Anyone who doubts this should ask himself what the probable effect on the jury would be if, at the close of the prosecution rebuttal evidence, some officer came forward with a large crowd scene photograph showing one of the defense witnesses with his arm cocked in the act of throwing a rock, or, for that matter, if one of the arresting officers simply testified that he saw a particular defense witness throwing rocks.

A counter consideration (one in favor of calling such a witness, anyway) may be that he has already been arrested and charged. If the trial is over (regardless of whether he was acquitted or convicted), and if there is no motion for a new trial pending and no appeal pending, then the fact that it is over may be a point favoring the use of this witness in the present case. But that is only true if he did not take the stand in his own case and deny throwing the rock. If he testified in his own trial that he did *not* do the particular act in question, he cannot be put on the stand in this one for the purpose of repeating that perjury or for the purpose of inviting the prosecution to impeach him now, when they may not have been able to do it the first time. On the other hand, if this witness was acquitted without taking the stand, there may be no legal harm in taking the stand in this case, and admitting (if asked) that he was a rock thrower.

But he will still *be* a rock thrower, and for that reason it would still be extremely disadvantageous to put him on the stand in the present case; but in some rare situation in which his testimony is desperately needed, the fact that he was acquitted protects him from further prosecution for the same rock throwing, and the fact that he did not deny it in his own case will protect him from the accusation of perjury when he admits it in this one.

If this witness is awaiting trial on a charge of rock throwing, it would be cruel and stupid to call him as a witness in the present case, knowing that cross-examination will probably raise the question of what the witness was doing while all that was going on, and knowing that his testimony might be construed as a waiver of the privilege against self-incrimination. There is no point in bringing a witness close to destruction in order to defend someone else's case. In no event should the rock thrower be called against his wishes, or against the advice of his own lawyer, or without it; and, like any other witness, he should not be allowed to take the stand for the purpose of testifying to something contrary to what he has already told the lawyer in private.

During the first interview with any witness, it is important to establish his willingness to testify, but it is not important to hand him a subpoena. He may, of course, be subpoenaed on the spot, but if that is done, the lawyer should take the necessary additional time to explain why the subpoena is needed (see § 9.06 [1]) But that is something more readily explained to a group of witnesses than to one. A group will understand, but one person thinks, "Why me?" Although handing out subpoenas at the first opportunity may seem a reasonable and businesslike thing to many lawyers, rapport with witnesses is more important. Trust and mutual support are always more important than subpoenas, and so subpoenas should be used only in a way consistent with trust.

An important exception occurs when the lawyer is interviewing a younger person who is sympathetic to the defense but whose parents—who are present during the interview—are adamantly against the lawyer and everything he stands for. In this situation the lawyer may only get one interview and he had better use it to lay the subpoena on the witness, and at the same time explain why. If a hostile parent is sitting there throughout the interview, it may be a good thing to lay the subpoena on immediately, and not make it sound too casual. A hostile parent will probably be less obstructive to the ends of justice *after* a subpoena has been served on a witness, since the question of the witness' appearance in court is more obviously a matter involving the court and the witness, and less a matter with which the hostile parent wishes to interfere. If the subpoena is not served immediately in this situation it may be hard to serve at all. Once it is served, the lawyer can probably discuss the case with this particular witness later, on the telephone, at the university or somewhere. It is rather important *not* to ask critical questions of this witness in the presence of a hostile parent since it will be fairly clear to the parent what the lawyer is interested in, and then the parent may later hammer at the witness to get him to change his testimony until he really does not know what happened.

All witnesses should be asked, during the first interview, what they know about other witnesses, and particularly what they know about photographs. When proper notes have been taken, the lawyer should thank the witness for his time, and explain that he has to move on rather promptly, which is certainly the truth.

§ 4.04 The Importance of Finding Defense Photographs, and Early Precautions to Preserve Their Maximum Value as Evidence

[1] Definition of Defense Photograph

For purposes of this discussion, "defense photograph" means any kind of photograph which has been discovered solely through the activities of the lawyer or some other member of the defense team, or has otherwise come into the hands of the defense under circumstances justifying the expectation that it has not yet come to the knowledge of the prosecution. Unfortunately, this does not mean that a defense photograph cannot come into the possession of the prosecution before it is actually used in trial, if it is used in trial. But if that happens, its usefulness to the defense may well be destroyed .

[2] The Enormous Importance of Defense Photographs Which Tend to Impeach Prosecution Witnesses

As noted before, there is a watershed at about the number of six to seven witnesses, which is approximately the number of defense witnesses necessary to offset the effect of one lying cop. That rule of thumb is far more reliable if the witnesses are corroborated by at least one good photograph which impeaches the lying cop. The effect of even one such photograph is cataclysmic, provided it is used correctly (see § 14.05). This is true because the photograph not only shows that one particular officer has lied on the witness stand; more importantly, it shows that the six or seven or more defense witnesses who contradicted him were indeed telling the truth. This kind of photograph not only incriminates the lying officer (who will never be prosecuted for lying), but makes a fool of the deputy district attorney who spent so much time trying to show, on cross-examination, that the defense witnesses were perjurors. One or two good photographs like this, sprung from ambush after the whole prosecution has been morally committed to the truthfulness of a single cheating witness, will destroy most of the moral position of the prosecution.

While one officer who lied on the witness stand may be followed by any number of officers who are telling the truth as well as they understand it, the jury will not forgive the prosecutor for embarrassing them by inducing them to believe, even tentatively, an officer was candid, when actually he lied. While there may be other prosecution witnesses, it will be the same prosecutor who calls them to the stand and asks them questions under direct examination. That is why any defense photograph which impeaches a prosecution witness is killingly important.

[3] There Are Many Photographs in a Political Case Although the Lawyer May Not Believe It

While the following discussion may not apply to some kinds of political trial, e.g., a conspiracy trial where the disputed overt action is alleged to have occurred behind closed doors, it is certainly true of all cases involving riots and public disorders, and the more numerous cases which occur against the backdrop of recent disorders, where the police are indulging in repressive measures against a certain segment of the population, having suspended the constitution for a week or two with the permission of county authorities. Most of the participants in these disturbances, and most of the persons who view them with sympathy from the sidelines, are young people. Among these students, younger faculty members, and other persons are a large number who own cameras and know how to use them. One does not often have occasion to think how many cheap and efficient cameras there are in our society, how many excellent cameras there are, and how many people are more than just passingly acquainted with the use of cameras.

This part of the American public now knows something about the relationship of courts, civil disturbances, and law enforcement agencies. They know that police often club demonstrators and bystanders, and that a letter to the editor about it later will be totally ineffective. They also know that complaints to the police department will never result in a criminal prosecution of a police officer for beating or mistreating any person involved in a political demonstration, and that such a complaint will sometimes result in police harrassment of the citizen making the complaint. Also, this part of the public is generally aware, that local government officials, particularly boards of supervisors, city councilmen, and judges, increasingly blame any and all citizens who dissent from their own views for anything which is done *by* any dissenter, or for that matter, anything done *to* any dissenter by the police. Finally, most of the younger portion of the public knows that following any arrests in a civil disorder, the only "redress" open to citizens who have been beaten by the police or arrested without cause is the hope that they may not be convicted of the crimes charged against them, rather than the innocent expectation that something will be done to the officers involved. They know their own testimony as to things they see is relatively useless alone. (They do not know the value of their own testimony in combination with other witnesses.) And so, without anyone telling them, they have turned instinctively to the use of the camera.

The defense lawyer trying a political case for the first time may not have heard of this transmutation of respect for the legal system into a belief in photography, but the significance of this trend is so important in defending a political case that a new lawyer should accept what is said here about the existence of these photographs and how to use them and not use them, whether he believes it or not, without any question at all, except in the light of his own later experience.

Some of the most valuable riot photographs will seem to have been taken by a combat photographer. In fact, they may have been taken by a young man of outwardly retiring nature, whose personal appearance (when one finally meets him) can only be described as inconspicuous. The nerve is not related to the appearance. His photographs may well have been taken right on top of the action, at an unbelievably close range, say six, eight, ten, or twelve feet from where two or more officers were beating someone with batons, while a whole crowd of bystanders were afraid to come closer than 50 feet. The camera he used will typically have been one of excellent quality, rather appropriate to his courage: a spring-loaded device capable of shifting its own film and taking successive action photographs as fast as he pressed the trigger—five or six times in the space of two or three seconds. He will *not* have been seen by the officers, for reasons which are never entirely clear. But whatever the reasons are, of the fifty or so persons present within a few yards of the scene, only a few will remember that anyone took photographs; the lawyer himself may find it baffling that, of all the witnesses he interviewed, this is the one whose personal appearance he could not later call to mind.

Other (and equally valuable) action photographs may turn out to have been taken by women. For one reason or another, women seem less likely to be on the street with a camera. If they are on the street, involved in the action, they will probably not have a camera. But a woman in an apartment overlooking the scene is someone else entirely. She may in fact be there for reasons of her own, related to introspection, as opposed to plunging down the stairs, and her evaluation of the civil disorder which unfolds in view of her balcony may well include some appreciation of what will be happening in court the following week. There is no question of her being able to handle her delicate photographic equipment in the midst of the turmoil below, but she can manage from the balcony.

This young woman is especially important as a source of photographs in those situations in which the police have already beaten, gassed, and intimidated all the people off the streets. In short, a curfew. When matters reach the point that police are dragging persons out of private homes and bending them over automobile hoods in order to beat them more conveniently, the situation will be that no one will get on the street at all, not even the combat-photographer student who would have been able to take pictures from the edge of the crowd. In this situation, the young lady with the expensive equipment will not be found standing on the balcony, because she knows that if she were standing there she would be dragged down and beaten too. She will be standing back in the darkness of her apartment, with a tripod. The pictures she may get, even under the most adverse lighting conditions, may be of unbelievable value later on in court.

While the kind of photographs described above are not the only kinds of photographs the lawyer will find in his investigations, they do typify defense photographs. They differ in subject matter and in spirit from those which will later be produced by the prosecution. For one thing, prosecution photographs never show officers beating citizens; their cameramen are never there when the citizens are living those portions of their lives. The prosecution photographs are usually taken from store front balconies or upper level offices, with press-type cameras. They often include color movies of bad definition, and in cases of night demonstration, a great number of black-and-white crowd scenes. While there is no special benefit in characterizing all of the prosecution photographs, it is noteworthy that when viewed in large numbers from a number of cases, they show a recognizable trait, much as the individual frames of a motion picture will eventually show that it was made by a particular director. The common theme of prosecution photographs is that they were taken *not* with the view of seeing what happened, on the spot, or close up, but rather with a view to establishing *who was there,* at some general event which it was already known would happen. They sometimes suggest an eye-in-the-sky viewpoint, even though it is only the view from the justice department window. (For the defense uses of prosecution photographs, see § 5.01.)

To summarize, in a riot or civil disorder there are always more photographs than the prosecution knows about, and probably more than have been discovered by either side when the trial is over. These photographs can be taken, and often are taken, under seemingly impossible conditions by reason of violence or failing light. The lawyer must never allow himself to assume or accept somebody else's opinion that there were no photographs, or no more photographs, for any of the usual foolish reasons: "There couldn't have been a photographer there, they would have beat the shit out of him," or "If there had been one there, my client would have seen him," or "Nobody could take a picture there, there was hardly light enough to see as it was."

§ 4.05 Some Thoughts on Photographer/Witnesses

A characteristic of persons who take photographs made available to the defense is that (compared to the defendants and possibly most of the other witnesses) the photographer witness tends to be relatively straight in his political thinking. The high degree of skill necessary to take many of the photographs in question is not always consistent with radical political activism, since photography is to some extent a solitary hobby, demanding time and attention to mechanisms, emulsions, and catalogues. This turn of mind does not always go with a burning social awareness.

On the other hand, this witness is a person first, and a photographer by taste and avocation; he unquestionably sympathizes with his age group, although he expresses his feelings rather differently. Most photographers will not only make their films available to the defense, but they are happy to make prints and will even enlarge them. Some of them are so altruistic in this respect that they will refuse any compensation for doing this, even the cost of the print paper. They have a universal wish to keep their negatives, and the lawyer should never argue about the negatives. Photographers (including amateur photographers) feel about negatives the way some writers feel about manuscripts, the way some dogs feel about bones. There is no need to intrude.

The lawyer will have to give some consideration to the following points in deciding (or reconsidering) whether to call the photographer as a witness.

The photographer witnessed the events which he photographed (although he may not have noticed every detail which appears in the prints), and he personally witnessed other events which he did not photograph. On the other hand, his photographs can be used without him, but not the other way around. It is possible to place the photographs in evidence without having the photographer testify at all (or even be identified) provided some other witness testifies that each photograph is in fact an accurate representation of the scene as it really was at that time and place. But it is not to be expected that the photographer could testify as a witness without being required to produce all of his photographs on cross-examination.

This partial severability (the ability to use the

photographs without the photographer) is very important if it turns out that the photographer was also a rock thrower (an unlikely development), or a person otherwise liable to in-court identification and subsequent prosecution for some alleged crime. Severability is also important if this particular photographer has other photographs, besides those which the defense would like to use, which would be hurtful to the defense. And finally, severability matters if, through some unfortunate happenstance, the photographer has already destroyed negatives which were taken about the same time as the photographs which the defense intends to use, even though there was no evil purpose in doing so.

If he has other photographs which are hurtful, he would be made to produce them on cross-examination, and the defense would (justifiably) be made to look sick for not having produced the harmful photographs in the first place. Therefore, a decision to call the photographer as a defense witness is equivalent to the decision to produce all of his relevant photographs on direct examination, rather than leaving the bad ones for the cross-examiner. (It would be unbelievably stupid to gamble on the prosecutor's failing to ask—that would not pay off even once out of a hundred times.) Similarly, if the photographer has destroyed *for any reason* any negatives related to these events—and that includes negatives from the same roll of film, even if they were taken two months before the riot, and were overexposed—a strong argument will be made that he destroyed them because they were harmful to the defense; since they are in fact destroyed, there will be no conclusive way to rebut that argument.

So if the photographer does have other photographs which are hurtful, or if he has destroyed negatives, but he also has one or more photographs which the defense wishes to use, the lawyer may be well advised to use the photographs but not the photographer. This can only be done with aplomb if the photographer's identity remains reasonably secret, and should only be attempted if the good photographs are important enough to the defense to justify the risk that his identity will be found out in any event, and that he will be subpoened into court.

If the photographs *are* used without the photographer, the prosecution will still have one last argument: "Where is the photographer?" While this might seem a dangerous argument from the defense point of view, it is not really very effective, because it sounds like sour grapes. After all, if the photographs which were used were good enough to justify the risk, they probably destroyed the testimony of one or more prosecution witnesses, and in that case, what does it really matter who took the pictures? The best defense counter to the absent photographer argument is simply to ignore it.

Whether the photographer actually testifies in the case or not, his recollections of what he saw and of what he has heard since the events may still fullfil the expectations applicable to any potential witness. For example, he may well refer the lawyer to other witnesses, and, much more importantly, he may refer the lawyer to other photographers. This is particularly important because photographers seem to know each other, and one photographer is much more likely to know whether other photographers were present than is any other witness. This is true regardless of the fact, if it happens to be a fact, that the only people taking photographs were amateurs.

[1] Special Considerations Affecting the Interview of a Photographer/Witness

The first principle here is that the photographer should be interviewed separately from the other witnesses. His identity may already be known to several potential witnesses, but there is no need to propagate the knowledge. On cross-examination, any other witness interviewed with this one will have to remember each and every interview prior to testifying, and who was there. If any other person testifies he was jointly interviewed with the photographer, it may be safely assumed that the identity of the photographer will become public knowledge about five minutes after the cross-examination of that witness begins. Of course that will be embarrassing if the photographer's photographs have been used in evidence, but, for one reason or another, it was not feasible for the photographer to testify on behalf of the defense. It will be embarrassing even if the photographer is not later subpoenaed by the prosecution, and even if the reason for not calling him as a defense witness is *not* brought out. It will be embarrassing just because there was testimony about his being interviewed. It is easy to ignore insinuations about an absent photographer, if that is necessary (although it is sometimes devastating to call him as a defense witness, see § 15.07), but there is no justification for not calling a photographer who is proved to have been interviewed.

Apart from anything else in the interview, the lawyer *must get one print of each and every negative taken by the photographer in connection with the case. This includes a print of every shot on any roll which contains a shot relevant to the case.*

Another point is the lawyer must *ask the photographer if any print made in connection with this case has been cropped.* This is vital, because even if cropping was done for some innocent reason, an argument will certainly be made that this witness tampered with the photograph, thus impugning the entire defense case. An innocent reason might be a misplaced sense of tidiness, e.g., enlarging a 35 mm negative to an eight-by-ten inch print, where it does not fit, and leaving out some of the picture rather than making a slightly smaller enlargement and trimming the unused top and bottom of the print paper. A not so innocent reason would be that if the print had been made without cropping, it would have shown some friend of the photographer doing something in violation of the law.

The lawyer must explain to this witness why the existence of *any* cropped print would tend to impeach the photographer's testimony, whether or not the reason for cropping involved any of the defendants in this case, and even if the reason was totally innocent. If this interview establishes that one or more prints have been cropped, the lawyer should unhesitatingly advise the photographer to destroy all cropped prints in his possession, and, if there are any in existence which are not in his possession, the photographer should try to recover these prints by every proper means. And when he gets them—provided the negatives are still available—he should destroy the cropped prints. On the other hand, the lawyer should advise the photographer *not to destroy any negative related to this case, and not to destroy any negative on any roll of film related to this case.*

The lawyer should carefully number and catalog all prints received from each photographer.[1] The numbering is done by attaching small *removable* labels such as five-and-dime stores stick on their items. The numbering should contain a numeral and two letters, the numeral to fix the sequence in evidence, one letter to designate the source of the photograph (the particular photographer) and also the date received, the other letter to show whether this photograph is known to be available to the prosecution. These labels should be easily removable when it comes time to use the photograph in evidence.

It is important that the sequence of photographs be established with the help of the photographer, since he will retain the *uncut* negative roll from which the prints are made. The sequence on the roll of course determines which was taken after which, and so the lawyer should ask the photographer to examine his negatives and line up the prints accordingly. And the lawyer should label and number his prints in the same sequence. Needless to say, the film should remain uncut so that if there is any question about it later, or any question about whether some shots from the same roll were mislaid or destroyed, that can be settled by reference to the uncut negative.

This is not a very hard procedure to follow. The goal is that later on, when the lawyer has a great many photographs, he will know what *all* the photographs will look like which any particular photographer will produce in court when, on cross-examination, he is asked to produce all the pictures he took.

In interviewing the photographer who has made a movie, the considerations are slightly different. The difference is, in dealing with a friendly photographer the lawyer more or less has to insist on borrowing the original negative (the movie film itself), or on having an immediate copy made of the entire film. The anomaly is that the lawyer must be more careful to do this and more insistent about it in dealing with a friendly photographer than he might be in dealing with a relatively hostile television station manager in possession of similar film. The friendly defense witness who has taken movie film is more likely to harm the defense by losing some vital part of his film, despite all his good intentions, than an unfriendly photographer.

An unfriendly photographer can be subpoenaed to produce his film in court, and once subpoenaed he will not dare destroy it since he is quite sure that the lawyer's attitude toward him is every bit as unfriendly as his own, and that the lawyer will have no compunction about making considerable trouble for him if anything happens to the evidence. But the friendly photographer has other friends.

One of the other friends will probably be an older and more professionally oriented photographer than the witness himself. This person may live on the forest floor of an arboreal society, not caring much about his clothes or the condition of his living quarters, but he lives for the time he will complete the documentary film to which he devotes every spare hour and moment.

Social disorders are not just the subjects of political trials, they are also the subject of documentary films. Of course this friend's best sources of the necessary footage are the photographers he knows, from whom he borrows it. While he is every bit as sympathetic toward the plight of a political defendant as the photographer witness who shot the film in the street, he needs the film for a different purpose. If the lawyer waits very long in obtaining the film from the photographer who shot it, the documentary film maker will get it; the film will then travel to the particular laboratory where his cutting and editing is done, which may well be in another city (he can only use it at night, through the courtesy of other friends because he could not possibly afford to rent the laboratory during its business hours), and there, during the long hours and frenetic activity of some Saturday night to Sunday morning, footage which would have been quite valuable to the defense will be left on the cutting room floor simply because it lacked relevance to the documentary being made at the time. It will be lost forever, and no amount of regret will retrieve it.

Although the defense can be hurt in this way by people who mean well but do not take good care of their film, this loss can be anticipated and prevented by (1) borrowing the original film for use in the trial and keeping it in a safe deposit box, or (2) obtaining a complete and exact duplicate of the original film, made by the photographer or under his direction, and by having the photographer run both films and qualify himself to testify that they are exact copies, so that it does not matter later what happens to the original. Of course, if the lawyer borrows the original film, he *must* explain carefully to the photographer at the time of borrowing it, that he needs it because he may have to use it in court and because he cannot afford to make a duplicate, and that if the film is actually used in court, the lawyer will try later to obtain a court order releasing the film so that it can be returned to the photographer when the judgment becomes final. He should also state candidly to the photographer how long that might be: a year or two, depending on the jurisdiction. And having done that, he should take care to make good on that promise, even months after the case has receded into memory, for better or worse.

Other things which ought to be explained to a photographer witness, besides the things which must be explained to any witness (see §§ 9.06–9.07), are the following. If he is needed to testify in court, he must bring *all* negatives and prints which he took which relate to this case. The negatives should be uncut, the prints uncropped. If there is any question about not printing a picture because the negative was sloppy, the picture should be printed anyway, so that a jury can see the actual result of a sloppy negative. The photographer should not destroy any negative merely because it is something which, under other circumstances, he would not bother to print.

Similarly, the photographer must not be angry if the prosecutor questions either his prints or his honesty. On the contrary, he should be prepared to maintain his equilibrium in the face of such accusations, and, he should be quite familiar with the process which he followed (if he did it himself) in developing and printing these photographs, so that he can explain it clearly to the jury. Most photographers have a natural talent for these explanations. They are glad to explain it to a jury.

The lawyer should point out that his own questions to the photographer on the stand will be (if this is the case) rather limited. The important questions with respect to each photograph are (1) whether the photograph is a fair representation of the things shown in it, and (2) whether the photographic print is free of any intentional distortion.

The latter question is not necessary for admissibility but it is advisable as a matter of common sense.

If the photographer did not develop or print the photographs himself, but sent them to a laboratory for that purpose, the lawyer should go over as much as the witness remembers of the details about where he sent them and when, and when he got them back. Again, the lawyer should mention that he will ask the witness what might otherwise seem a silly question, which is whether the photographer gave any special instructions to the laboratory regarding the preparation of these pictures, or whether he simply sent them in for developing and printing in the usual course of business without special instructions. There is no magic wording for those questions, except that they should be natural, but the main thing is to advise the witness in advance that the point of these questions is to assure the jury that he did not go out of his way to have the laboratory do any tricky things to the negatives or the prints, so as to create some form of intentional distortion of the picture.

One of the most important things to be discussed with a friendly photographer witness is whether he intends to share his photographs with the prosecution. Of course, if the photographs in any way impeach the prosecution's case —and even if they do not—as a matter of general principle the lawyer does not wish the photographer to do this. The subject should not be brought up by way of asking the witness whether he would *like* to do that or whether he intends to. At some point, the lawyer should make it perfectly clear that, although the witness may, if he wishes, present these photographs to the prosecution, he is under no legal obligation to do so, and that if he does, he will probably hurt the defendant very much since some of the prosecution witnesses will be able to slant their testimony to get around the photographs. But—and this is the main point—the photographer will inevitably be asked on cross-examination why he did not go to the district attorney with these photographs.

The photographer undoubtedly *has* a reason. The lawyer should not suggest a reason. He should only tell the photographer that he will be asked why he did not offer his photographs to the prosecution, and that between now and the time of the trial he should think out his reason, and think of the words he will use in stating it. The lawyer need not even ask him what his reason is, since it is essential that it be his own. When the lawyer tells the witness there is no script for the witness's testimony, the lawyer must mean it. The lawyer can rest relatively easy on this point, that there *will be* a reason why the witness did not wish to take the photographs to the district attorney, and that when the reason is given on cross-examination, it will be a good one and the jury will understand it—provided that the lawyer has not spoiled things by injecting himself and his own views into the witness's testimony.

[2] Absolute Necessity for Nondisclosure of Impeaching Photographs or Movies

Once it becomes clear that the lawyer has found one or more photographs or movies which directly impeach some prosecution witness, it is absolutely imperative that he keep his mouth shut about it. These photographs can be devastating, but only if used in court, with the advantage of total surprise. They should be used in cross-examining the lying witness, and they should be sprung from ambush (see § 14.05). If the existence of these photographs is revealed, or even hinted at, to the prosecution beforehand, for any supposed advantage—such as the worthy motive of persuading the prosecution to dismiss the case—then the lawyer who does that should not kid himself. The result will not be what he hoped; rather, the witness who was lying, and who would have been impeached by this photograph, will go right on lying. The only difference is that now he will find a way to explain the photograph in advance and, because the explanation *is* made in advance, it will be believable. The witness who has been denying that he beat up somebody, if he knows the photograph shows him beating up that person, will be in a position to remember that he did in fact, under very great provocation, have occasion to do one particular act of violence which he regrets very much, and that one thing will just happen to be what is shown in the photograph.

A lawyer who shoots off his mouth about the photograph he has in his file will probably live to see that photograph become a sort of prosecution exhibit corroborating a remorseful (and not entirely unsympathetic) confession of human weakness on the part of the main prosecution witness. And it should not be doubted, if an impeaching photograph is revealed after a political prosecution is underway, that the prosecution will go right on with the political case. They will only do it better.

Defense lawyers who waste their emotional energy regretting a system which permits political trials are especially prone to the probings of deputy district attorneys. The latter often present themselves, in casual encounters during the early stages of a case, as overworked but basically sympathetic persons who have just been handed a file, who have very little information about the case, and (being a little surprised at the apparent intensity of the defense lawyer's feelings) would just like to know, on a man-to-man basis, if there is anything which they ought to be told, which might indicate that the case should be dismissed.

This, of course, is blatant fishing. But if the defense lawyer happens to be young and too concerned about the work and hazards of trial, or older and too inclined to talk things out as a means of avoiding conclusions, he may find himself reaching into his file for the photograph. Actually, there are many things a lawyer can say to the prosecutor in these relaxed situations, but talking about the photograph is not one of them. The lawyer should not only keep the photograph secret, but not let on by so much as a smile, or a meaningful silence, that if he wished to, he could say otherwise.[2]

The lawyer must not only keep the photograph secret from the prosecution, he must be rather careful about his friends. If there are several lawyers in the case, the lawyer should avoid mentioning the existence of a really impeaching photograph to any other lawyer, unless he already knows on a basis of personal experience that the other lawyer is perfectly closemouthed. The lawyer can (and should) reveal the existence of this photograph to co-counsel as the case gets on, when all the lawyers know each other a little better, when the trial has started, when the temptation to talk the prosecutors out of it has diminished, and when each of them has burned off the private urge to go his own way. But not now, not for a while. No tactical or personal consideration justifies blowing an opportunity to cross-examine a main prosecution witness with an impeaching photograph.

Of course, the photograph may be used *indirectly* at a preliminary hearing (see § 5.03), but only in the limited sense that the lawyer will have it in his mind (not his hand) when he encourages the lying witness to say it all again, under oath, and allows him to leave the stand under the impression that he could not possibly be impeached.

§ 4.06 Getting Access to Public Domain (Prosecution) Photographs and Tapes not Available to the Defense Through Ordinary Discovery Procedures

[1] Why this Evidence May Not be Available, Even Though "Public"

"Public domain" evidence includes newspaper photographs (published and unpublished), television film footage and videotape footage (some of which was broadcast, but most of which was not), and tapes containing on-the-spot reports broadcast by local radio stations. This evidence may be thought of as prosecution evidence, because the prosecution will have gotten there first.

The district attorney's investigators and other investigators will already have examined the newspaper photographs, screened the television footage, and possibly even listened to the radio tapes before the defense lawyer got into the case.

These investigators will have used friendship, influence, cajolery, and intimidation not only to examine these items, but to borrow the more important ones, e.g., movie film and videotape. They may very well have gone over this footage at great leisure, and then returned it to the television station, for example, for safekeeping, without (at this point) having made copies of their own. They have their own reasons for doing this (see §4.07 and § 7.01–7.02).

The defense lawyer may not find access so easy. The press is rather reactionary; and, as a general rule, newspaper photographers are skittish about going to court. Newspaper management has small use for political defendants, whom they suspect of seeking to exploit the press for their own benefit. Most requests by the defense lawyer will be referred to the city editor, or the television station manager, and may well be refused unless something is done to make it possible for their sense of fairness to function more freely.

[2] A Need for Speed

The lawyer will have to move fast with regard to public domain evidence, and he must not suppose that the ordinary means of discovery, applicable to evidence which is actually in the possession of the People, will be of any help. The reason is, a discovery order (see § 4.07[1]) will cover only those things which the People have in their possession or subject to their control; if they have taken care *not to get* possession or control of public domain photographs and tapes, the discovery order will not touch these items—nor can it possibly operate against third persons who are not associated with law enforcement. The latter are not "parties to the action."

If the lawyer makes the mistake of assuming that everything which the prosecution has seen will be turned over to him, or even preserved for use at the trial, he may be making a *big* mistake. For example, many newspaper photographers regard the negatives as their own property, especially negatives which were shot but not used by the newspaper. Photographers change jobs frequently. They sometimes take negatives with them. Similarly, videotapes are part of the stock-in-trade of television stations, and they are often erased shortly after use.

The prosecutors will of course, seek to preserve movie footage and videotapes for their own later use, but they will arrange for these things to remain in the hands of their owners. Any evidence which they do not want (because it does not fit the prosecution case) may well get lost simply because no one appeared to want it. Even the evidence which *is* preserved in this informal way may not become available to the defense, until the prosecutors actually choose to spring it during the trial. This is true because of their secret option as to when they will take possession of this evidence.

The prosecutors know very well there will be a discovery order in the case, and that in fact there may be more than one such order before the trial. So they simply elect to make their copies quite late. If they take them after the first discovery order has been complied with, they will be under no obligation to share that evidence with the defense, unless this happens to be a jurisdiction in which a running discovery order is permissible. In the absence of a running discovery order, there will be no obligation at all for the prosecution to give a copy of this film to the defense, or make their own copy available to the defense, unless a second discovery order is made (discussed in §7.01). Not only that, the prosecution may take advantage of the fact that most trial judges are lax, sluggish, and reluctant in making or enforcing discovery orders against the prosecution. In a jurisdiction where this common situation prevails, the prosecution may not only arrange to receive valuable evidence quite late in the case, they may also ignore one or two discovery orders, and then generously "comply" with the last discovery order by making a mass of prosecution evidence available to the defense on the evening before trial, or even during trial. Since prevention of this abuse lies primarily with the honesty of the prosecution, there is no sure cure with respect to evidence solely within the knowledge and control of the prosecution; but with respect to public domain evidence, a better path may be sought.

[3] Getting Early Access

It is not enough for the lawyer to preserve public domain evidence until the time of trial; it is even more important to examine this evidence before trial, and if at all possible, to secure copies for private examination. The solution is a subpoena duces tecum *for some hearing short of trial.* Of course it would be possible to subpoena this evidence for a trial date, where that has been set. But if that is done, the newspaper or television station will not produce the evidence *until trial;* meanwhile the prosecution will continue to have private access to it, while the defense may or may not have access.

The ingenuity of counsel will supply hearings to which the subpoenas duces tecum can be made returnable. The following are some obvious examples:

(1) The preliminary hearing, when that is available, in which event the evidence is simply adduced as defense evidence;

(2) If local law permits a deposition (under that name or any other) when an important witness is about to leave the jurisdiction, then it may well happen that an important witness *whose testimony requires these photographs or videotapes for purposes of illustration* is about to leave the jurisdition, and so his deposition may be taken in court, and this evidence subpoenaed there to facilitate it; or

(3) There may be a dispute between the lawyer and the prosecution in connection with a routine discovery motion, as to the amount of evidence presently available to the prosecution; the evidence can then be subpoenaed into court, along with the persons who own it (the station manager) to prove that it has already been available to the prosecution on an informal basis, and to request an immediate order that it be made available to the defense. That order may be granted or denied, but meanwhile the items subpoenaed should be marked as exhibits and offered in evidence *in support of the motion.* If it is denied, a writ can be sought to reverse the denial, as an abuse of discretion; and while the petition for the writ is pending, the exhibits

in the trial court should be designated as part of the record supporting the writ application in the appellate court. This keeps valuable evidence in the hands of the clerk and out of the local television's shredder, no matter how much the lower court judge would like to help it get there.

The lawyer should not let things go on the basis of the subpoena duces tecum, however. One reason is, once that has been served, the newspaper or television station has a strong reason to make the evidence available to the defense on an informal basis, the same as has already been done for the prosecution. *They should be encouraged to do this. Another reason is that if they are not persuaded to make it available informally, the subpoena may be quashed.*

But after the subpoena has been served, and before the hearing (when it is most likely to be quashed), the lawyer has an excellent opportunity to improve the defense case. This is true because the news media not only dislike political defendants, they have a general dislike of subpoenas.

It is not my recommendation that the First Amendment rights of the press be eroded in order to defend political prisoners, that procedure being something like opening the seacocks in order to clean out the bilge. With that premise in mind, what is said here is *not* meant to apply to (1) information or notes concerning news sources of reporters, or (2) notes, recollections, or recordings of news source interviews or communications. What follows applies *only* to photographs and videotapes showing what was actually happening at the scene of an alleged crime.

Of course these categories are not mutually exclusive, and a situation is not inconceivable in which a particular on-the-scene photograph might compromise a confidential news source; in such a situation, I can only suggest that the lawyer defer to a bona fide First Amendment objection and solve his own legal problems by other channels. But that situation will probably never arise in the experience of a lawyer defending political cases.

The real problem—extremely common with a small town reactionary press, and with network news staffs dominated by little plastic super patriots—is that the media have a lot of photographs which they already have made available to the prosecution, under the table. Rather than admit all this in the courts, most conservative newspapers and television stations would much prefer to make the same evidence available to the defense, but also under the table. This easy option combined with their knowledge of how they are going to look when they have to own up to it in court— how they have already supplied photographs to the district attorney—awakens their sense of fairness.[3]

In dealing with the local newspaper or television station, the lawyer should remember that his main object is to get early and convenient access to the evidence, not to initiate a second-front legal war against the media. Probably the lawyer should not take the initiative in telephoning the newspaper or television station after the subpoena duces tecum has been served, even though he has talked to them several times beforehand. To do so at this point would seem cynical even to newspaper management. It is much better to wait for a telephone call from the newspaper's attorney.

When this telephone call comes, the lawyer should remember to behave circumspectly. He should remember beforehand that the newspaper's attorney will present himself as defending the First Amendment, although nothing in his practice has brought him (knowingly) in touch with it; and that he will be conscious of representing his most important clients (newspaper owners), and of being under the surveillance of the really important members of the community (he will tell them every word afterward). The newspaper attorney will never have experienced any curiosity about criminal law, and so will have no feel for it now.

The lawyer should remember that when he receives this telephone call, there are two ways he can handle it. If he handles it in the way which comes naturally, he will be privileged to go into court when the subpoena duces tecum is returnable and fight both the deputy district attorney and the newspaper attorney at the same hearing, with a fair chance that his subpoena will be quashed. But if he handles it the other way, with one eye to his problem instead of his preference, then before the conversation is over it will simply be a question of how many copies he wants.

§ 4.07 First-Round Discovery of Prosecution Evidence

[1] The Shortcomings of Usual Discovery Practice and Motions

Discovery in a political case differs somewhat from the usual practice in other criminal cases. The usual practice varies among communities, but it commonly consists of a telephone call by the defense lawyer to the deputy district attorney, advising that he is defending the case and requesting copies of police reports and whatever else may customarily be open to discovery and inspection in that particular jurisdiction. This is a sloppy method, and will not do in a political case or, indeed, in any serious criminal case.

Similarly, the normal kind of discovery motion is totally inadequate. The normal discovery motion may be defined as one which asks for a court order compelling the prosecutor to disclose whatever prosecution evidence he is required to disclose in that jurisdiction. It is inadequate because it aims at an order addressed to the district attorney, thereby ignoring the realities of law enforcement practice.

The truth is, the district attorney's file is the wrong place to look for evidence; at any particular moment, it contains only a fraction of the People's case. Since the defense lawyer will have to overcome the People's case, it is quixotic for him to level his lance at the district attorney's file.

Almost all of what a defense lawyer is entitled to see under the law is to be found in the hands of law enforcement agencies. The prosecution understand this perfectly well, and they see to it that most of their case remains in the hands of law enforcement agencies and never finds its way into the district attorney's file (where it would be vulnerable to a defense discovery order) until after the trial has begun, if then.

The futility of ordinary discovery proceedings is especially poignant in political cases, since these cases (even more than narcotics cases) are likely to involve multiple law enforcement agencies, more than one level of agencies, e.g., federal, state, and county, or a mix of military intelligence agencies.

The aggregate prosecution evidence in a political case may well consist of investigation and arrest reports from several sheriff's offices and city police departments, in addition to similar reports from state and federal law enforcement agencies, both civilian and military. Because of their penchant for the clandestine, the state and federal agencies will have taken more care than local agencies to cover their tracks. The defense lawyer may not even know that their reports exist. They will certainly not be found by telephoning the district attorney for a "copy of the police reports" a few days before the preliminary hearing.

Not only do whole law enforcement agencies submerge themselves in order to escape defense attention, it is also true that individual officers of the local sheriff's office or police department invariably keep whatever notes and memoranda they have relating to the case in their own personal possession; they know far better than to give these to the district attorney's office. Similarly, fingerprint reports and various laboratory reports, which normally originate from local law enforcement agencies, actually move with great slowness toward the prosecutor's file. They get there, but sometimes not until after "discovery" has been completed.

Under the "normal" way of discovering things, many defense attorneys pretend not to notice these phenomena, or when they do notice them, they tend to pout about the fact that their friend, the deputy district attorney, does not *demand* that local law enforcement people give him their reports on time. There is a better way for a defense lawyer to get the information he is entitled to receive; it is not a method engendered in camaraderie. But since the prosecutorial animus of a political trial is dictated by law enforcement agencies, the following is the only sensible method for a defense lawyer to use.

[2] An Expanded Discovery Motion

The motion should be a formal, written one even though oral motions may be popular in this jurisdiction. The motion itself should specify an order directing "the People" to permit discovery as stated in the motion; and it should specify that *the motion is addressed not merely to the knowledge and possession of the district attorney of that county, but to those of all law officers, agencies, bureaus, departments, employees, and attorneys associated on the side of the People in prosecuting this particular action.* (For a sample of this motion, adaptable for general use, see Appendix A.)

It should be noted with care that while the motion speaks of an *order* addressed to all these different people, the *motion* is made within the context of the particular criminal action, and is therefore directed against (and served on) the prosecutor in that case. The motion is *not* to be served on all of the law officers, agents, agencies, etc., who are referred to in it, for the simple reason that they are not "parties" to the action. The parties are the People and the defendant. The People are represented by the prosecutor, and his opposition in court at the time the motion is heard should be considered sufficient. The others will know about the order later, after it is made. (The order, not the motion, will be physically served on them.) To serve them with a notice of motion would only make matters a little harder when the motion is heard, since most judges would be startled and frightened to be confronted by angry and bewildered chiefs of police, etc., in the middle of a hearing on the discovery motion.

The matters requested in the motion should be quite specific. The People should be required to make certain things available to the defendant's lawyer no later than a certain date and hour. It is advisable to make this time rather short, since it is probably not going to be complied with anyway. Since the motion will be set for hearing on a particular date, the requested order should require compliance within a short period, say, by 5:00 P.M. on the date of the order, or 5:00 P.M. on the day following the date of the order.

Counsel should bear in mind that, as a point of drafting, the compliance deadline should be fixed with reference to the *date of the order*, not the date of the hearing. Hearings are sometimes continued before they are ruled on; if the original motion requested an order to be complied with by a certain date, and the order itself is not made until after that date, it will of course be necessary to frame the order in terms of a new date. That may sound like nothing, but having to change one detail may be very undesirable if, for example, the court is in substantial agreement with the defense lawyer and grants the entire motion out of hand as soon as it is called for hearing (after being continued to a date later than originally noticed), or if by some prosecutorial slip the motion itself is not opposed at the later hearing. It is surprising how many times complications will spring up if counsel is not prepared to capitalize on success by handing the court an order ready for signature which is based entirely on the original motion. If the defense lawyer has to mention the fact that the deadline for compliance with the order must be refigured, he may have to go back to the deputy district attorney in order to get a *stipulation* on that detail; that particular stipulation may not be so easy to get when it is presented all by itself. The result of a trivial oversight in drafting the motion may well be the loss of two important weeks before the final order is signed.

The subject matter of the motion will be whatever is allowable in that jurisdiction. The following are extremely desirable items, some of which may ordinarily be overlooked if the discovery motion is too unassuming:

(1) Notes, memoranda, and reports made by any law enforcement officer, agent, or investigator for the People, in connection with any crime charged against the defendant in this action and/or *any other alleged crime or event which the People contend proves or tends to prove any element of any crime charged in this action whether or not it is incorporated in any official report;*

(2) Names, addresses, notes, and statements of any persons (not just police officers) who claim to be witnesses to any transaction which the People contend proves or tends to prove any element of the crime charged in the action;

(3) Those *statements* of persons claiming to have any relevant information to the prosecution *or defense* of the case, specifically including people who claim to have identified the defendant, personally or by photograph; and

(4) Laboratory or scientific reports, signed or unsigned.

In addition, the lawyer will, of course, want duplicates of all photographs and/or slides relevant to any element of the crime, including those used in any identification procedure, and specifically including mug shots. With these he will wish to have a list of names and addresses of those persons who took the photographs. Similarly, the lawyer will wish to have a written list of those persons identifying each photograph which has been shown to any witness in the case. Also, the lawyer will wish to have a duplicate (not just a transcript) of any tape containing a statement relating to any crime involved in the case. He will want to examine the real evidence relevant to the case, and he will wish to view any videotapes involved.

An important point about the discovery motion is that, particularly when discovery of the scope outlined here has not previously been allowed in this jurisdiction, the motion should specify with hyaline clarity that copies of all of these things are to be made available to the defense lawyer *at his expense*. The reason is that the prosecution will prefer to have these things available only for inspection. The prosecutors know perfectly well that convenience is at least eighty percent of the value of all their evidence.

If the defense lawyer has to come to the district attorney's office and sit across the desk from some deputy (or investigator, or secretary) and copy all the witness statements in longhand, he will get very little benefit from his notes. There is not time enough in the world to handle discovery on this basis, and counsel should not tolerate any discovery procedure which traps him in that position. The defense lawyer cannot testify, and therefore, to name a single objection of enormous importance, would not be able to impeach any prosecution witness on the basis of his own pencilled notes. What he needs is a photocopy of what the prosecutor has, and under no circumstances must he settle for anything less.

The prosecutor's main card (in opposing this motion)

is simply the matter of county budgets. All judges understand budgets more than budgets need to be understood; therefore, the prosecutor can be expected to argue that even if the People have to turn their pockets wrong side out, in the sense of sharing evidence, their limited budget simply does not countenance any legal disbursement for the purpose of making copies of evidence to be given away to defense lawyers. Furthermore, doing it for one would mean doing it for all, and the flood gates would be open.

The simple answer to this, of course, is that the defense lawyer should not ask for anything at the expense of the People. He is prepared to pay cash for whatever duplication expenses are involved. If the People say they cannot make photographic prints for the defense lawyer, he will pay for them. The People will then have to say they cannot have prints made, which is ridiculous. Similarly, the People will not wish to use "their" photocopy machine to make copies of witness statements. But photocopy machines are susceptible of simple cost accounting; everybody knows that photocopy machines are available in stenographic offices, even in public libraries, and it is no secret that pages can be reproduced by this method for so many cents per page, in any given community. The defense lawyer will simply offer to pay the going rate for the number of pages he gets.

If movie film has to be duplicated, the lawyer will have no objection to the choice of the district attorney's office: whatever outside laboratory they wish to use, they can send the film to that laboratory, and get it back from that laboratory, and a copy will be made for the defense and the defense lawyer will pay for it.

All of the foregoing is true, even if the defense lawyer happens to be a court-appointed lawyer. After all, he will be entitled to some form of reimbursement for his costs later on. Any and all of these necessary expenses will then be paid for by the state, even though the district attorney says that the state cannot afford to pay him for these things. There is simply no point quibbling about these anomalies, the point is to swamp any and all objections on the subject of money. The defense lawyer's real difficulty is always in getting an adequate discovery order. Getting money may be difficult, but it is always less difficult than persuading a court to make the right order. Therefore, the rule is pay for it, but get the order.

At the hearing of the discovery motion, particularly if this is the first such discovery motion in this jurisdiction, counsel should be prepared to make concessions. The district attorney may feel somewhat menaced by this kind of order (see Appendix B for a form of discovery order). He may request many variations, most of which will not hurt the defense. He may, for example, quite reasonably ask that compliance with the order (on the part of various law enforcement agencies) shall be made through his office. In other words, he may wish to prevent the situation from arising in which various law enforcement agencies are responding directly to the defense lawyer. While that is a better position from the defense point of view, it is not worth two minutes of argument. The law enforcement agencies are not going to give the defense lawyer anything in the way of cooperation, whether they deal through the district attorney or directly, so there is no point in arguing about this.

The district attorney may wish to have more than forty-eight hours in which to comply. Fine, if that is how the wind blows. The defense lawyer should gauge his arguments with a view to main values. These are as follows: (1) the order should be broad in scope, so that it will operate on all the law enforcement agencies and personnel involved —not narrow, so as to touch only what the district attorney chooses to have in his file at any given moment; (2) the order should be quite definite as to when compliance is expected; and (3) compliance should be required within a matter of several days after the order, not several days before trial. These are the main things. Details can be subject to much give and take.

After the order is made, it is of little or no value so long as it is only entered in the minutes. It must be signed in its most formal mode. The defense lawyer should have prepared an order for the judge's signature. If the judge modifies the order while granting it, the lawyer should give high priority to drafting a written order which complies with what the judge said in court. If it is customary to show this order to the prosecutor before presenting it for signature, the defense lawyer should do this, in person, without delay. He should then see that the order finds its way to the judge for his signature. Once the order is signed, the lawyer is finally in a position to build the defense case.

The next step is to obtain a number of certified copies of the order. In addition to whatever method is used for serving a copy of the order on the prosecutor, e.g., service by mail, a more formal ritual is appropriate for the law enforcement agencies. It is imperative that the defense lawyer serve a certified copy of the order on every law enforcement agency that has or may have any connection with the case. Counsel should not be finicky about this. And as to every agency, the order must be served on the top man in that agency, not on any "custodian of records." This is not civil litigation. There are no operative rules such as those controlling the production of hospital records. If the order is served on any person less than the chief of police or the sheriff of the county, counsel may be sure that the order will be evaded because it was not served on the "right" officer. Chiefs of police, however, cannot afford to evade these orders, and they will not do so. On the other hand, when it is known that particular officers have knowledge of the case (the arresting officers, without exception), every single one of them should be served personally with a certified copy of the order, notwithstanding that their superior has already been served. Every informer or other nonpolice agent known to have cooperated with the prosecution should also be served.

Proof of service should be filed in the case. Counsel should never be in the position of having to look around in the middle of trial for some piece of paper that shows that a particular agency was served with a copy of this order, but did not comply with it in time. That piece of paper should be in the court file, and not anywhere else. While the original discovery order necessarily remains in the court file from the moment the judge signs it, there is no limit to the number of certified copies. Every police agency gets served with a certified copy, and every time service is effected, the process server signs an affidavit stating that personal service was made on such and such chief of police, on a certain date and hour. These affidavits should be attached to still another certified copy of the order (to show *what* was served), and the resulting packet should be filed in court at an early date. That packet is the "piece of paper" which does it, if there is ever any question.

As with everything else the lawyer files in court, there should be a counterpart in his own file, complete in every detail, including photocopies of every affidavit of service. If the time comes to accuse the prosecution of evading the discovery order, in court, any sloppiness in keeping up the office file may be disastrous.

When all this has been done and evidence begins to flow in, counsel should meticulously note what is received, from what persons and agencies, and the *date* each item is received. An impeccable filing system will have to be used to account for evidence, otherwise counsel may not know later whether or not he was imposed upon in terms of delayed compliance with his discovery order.

Having gone to all the trouble of getting this discovery order, the lawyer should not sit back passively and allow the resulting evidence to accumulate. The main value of early evidence is early use. By using the fruits of this discovery order, and other investigatory methods discussed above, the lawyer can do a number of things to strengthen the defense case between the time of the initial investigation and the time of trial.

[3] Further Tactical Advantages of Making the First Discovery Motion as Soon as Possible, and of Obtaining the Discovery Order by Means of a Contested Hearing

An additional advantage to making this motion early (besides getting the information while fresh) is to help the prosecution place themselves as soon as possible in noncompliance with the resulting order. They are not going to comply with it anyway, without being forced to the wall, something not always possible. On the other hand, the lawyer may need a short continuance of the trial date. All that is necessary to put him in that position is to be engaged in trying another political case which lasts twice as long as anybody thought it would. When he comes out of that case, his other political cases are going to be jammed back to back, and the presiding judge may force him to go to trial without being prepared. If there is any chance to obviate that problem without resort to the desperate measures otherwise necessary (see § 6.04)—in other words, if there is a reasonable chance that a motion for a continuance will be honestly considered and ruled upon—that motion should be a strong one (see § 6.03).

The strongest ground for a short continuance is that the continuance is made necessary by the actions of the other side. In most situations, such activities (e.g., procuring the absence of a defense witness) would be so bizarre as to be extraneous to any logical thought. There is no use looking for them.[4] But one such ground so commonplace as to be generally relied upon is that the prosecution have impeded defense discovery. There will have been an order, and they will not have supplied one single piece of evidence in response to it, because nobody yelled in their ear. That is a wonderful ground for a continuance provided the stubborness of the prosecution is very noticeable, i.e., it has been going on for some time. That is a special reason why the first discovery motion should be made early. To give them a lot of time to disobey it.

Another great advantage of an early discovery motion and one which is often overlooked is that every motion entails at least a nominal hearing. By subpoenaing prosecution witnesses to testify at this hearing and by insuring that a court reporter is present (if there is any doubt about it in that court), the lawyer can obtain valuable transcripts of testimony—little depositions in advance of trial.

Most discovery motions in the past have, for some reason so dim as to be almost imperceptible, depended solely on the affidavit of the defense lawyer—and in some cases on one signed by the defendant himself—setting forth the extent of his ignorance of the prosecution case. This has been thought to be the fundational limit for discovery orders. While for a long time and in most jurisdictions the prosecution appear to have been negligent of their clear opportunities with respect to those affidavits which the defendant signed (to throw them in his face when he testifies in trial), it is also true that most defense lawyers have been equally remiss.

It is not so much a matter of proving what the defense lawyer does *not* have; everybody knows about that. A more fruitful field is, what do the prosecution *have?* As a prelude to getting a court order for the production of police radio records or interview notes which the police have *not* previously supplied to the prosecution (and which the prosecution are preparing to tell the court they do not possess), there is no substitute for subpoenaing the records and the officers directly into court to testify as to how many records there are, who made them, at what hour and date they were produced, and where they now repose.

Copies of the records can even be marked as exhibits and made part of the record in the case.

A great deal of interesting testimony can be forced out into the open in this manner. This is especially true if (the recommended procedure) the lawyer first sets the motion for hearing on a date certain, and then explodes his subpoenas and subpoenas duces tecum as close as humanly possible to the motion date. The interval between the service of the subpoenas and the hearing of the motion should be the exact number of days which the lawyer judges is the minimum necessary for the records to be gotten together or for witnesses to be called away from other duties. This may be one to two days for persons, and three to five days for records, all depending.

It helps to set these motions for hearing on a Monday, if that is possible, and to see that most subpoenas are served on the preceding Friday. By the time the officers who receive these subpoenas decide that they should check with the prosecutors before testifying on Monday, the prosecutors will have gone on their weekend. That will mean there are a lot of unprepared prosecution witnesses on the stand on Monday morning, which is the way it ought to be. That is the way something can be learned.

As soon as the hearing is over, the lawyer should privately approach the court reporter and request an immediate complete transcript of all the testimony that happened that morning. He should remember to tell the court reporter to leave out the arguments of counsel and any extended dialogs between counsel and court: one has to economize somewhere.

When the transcript is received, the testimony of each witness should be indexed separately (for individual indexing methods, see § 5.03). These indexes will later be combined with other indices for possible use in cross-examining the witnesses who testified at the hearing when they were not prepared (see § 14.01[2]).

Footnotes

[1] For an excellent discussion of how to organize evidence, see Robert D. Raven and Howard M. Downs, "Preparation and Organization of Trial Materials," in *The University of California, California Civil Procedure During Trial* 11 (1960).

[2] See *Hamlet*, Act 1, Scene V, lines 172–180.

[3] It is a matter of passing note that this kind of newspaper/television station is not really interested in protecting news sources. They will leave that to the *New York Times* and the *Washington Post*. If push comes to shove they will not only throw their news sources to the dogs, but their reporters as well.

[4] Events of the last few months suggest that *no* governmental misconduct is so bizarre as to be extraneous to a political case. This part of the text is already outdated. Unfortunately, the lawyer must now look for and expect to find things as bad as procuring the absence of a witness.

Chapter 5

USING THE FIRST RESULTS OF EARLY
SPADE WORK TO INCREASE THE ODDS
FAVORING SUCCESS IN TRIAL

SYNOPSIS

§ 5.01 How to Use Public Domain and Other Prosecution Photographs and Tapes in Preparing for Trial

[1] When to Get Copies and When to Economize

[a] Prosecution Materials

As a rule, the lawyer should get one copy of every photograph, movie, and tape which the prosecution have in their possession. The same rule would be true of video-tape if the defense had that kind of budget; as matters stand, it is unlikely that even the prosecution in a political case will have that much money. This rule (of obtaining copies) should be followed even at the expense of some financial sacrifice. It is *not* true that access to view or audit prosecution material is the same thing as having copies.

The only exception to this rule occurs when the lawyer is sure that particular photographs which the prosecution have obtained (and which he has a right to duplicate by virtue of his discovery order) are in fact exact duplicates of photographs already obtained by the lawyer, e.g., prints made from television footage or newspaper negatives which the prosecution obtained *after* the defense has managed to get the same things.

The most significant thing about a duplication of prosecution and defense photographs is not that the defense saves money, but the possible tactical implications of the duplication. The lawyer should look carefully for signs of selectivity and emphasis in the prosecution's particular form of duplication. For example, if 16-mm. television footage has been copied by both sides, but only a portion of what the defense copied was also copied by the prosecution, the lawyer should have it quite clear in his own mind why the prosecution chose that small portion of film for their file.

It should go without saying that the lawyer will look not only for selectivity but also for emphasis in the prosecution duplicates. If both sides have a dozen black and white prints made from negatives taken by a particular newspaper cameraman, all of them eight by ten except that the prosecution has selected four of them for greater enlargement, the lawyer will have no practical choice but to obtain enlargements of those photographs of at least the same quality and dimensions. And if the defense has obtained 100 feet of 16-mm. footage from the television station, and the prosecution have done the same, but have gone further and enlarged several of these frames for eight-by-ten prints, this is not the time for economy; an alarm bell should go off in the lawyer's mind. That bell should not be stilled until the lawyer has got copies of the same enlargements and examined them with his client, and until the full significance of these enlargements has been understood (which may turn out to be a misinterpretation by the prosecution).

Whenever duplications are found between defense photographs and prosecution photographs, whether or not the duplication leads to further work, getting enlargements or whatever, it is quite important that the lawyer's own evidence index should reflect unmistakably that particular defense photographs are also in the possession of the prosecution. This information should be lettered, coded, and included, not only in the index, but on the particular label on each of these defense photographs in the evidence file. The evidence index should be immediately updated to reflect the date the lawyer became aware that the prosecution had duplicate photographs, and how he acquired this information.

The index should show the date on which the photographs were physically received by the defense, and other pertinent information, such as the manner in which copies were prepared, the date on which the negatives were made available for copying, and whatever else is known about who took the photographs, when and where and what the subject matter is thought to be.

All of this can be extremely important if there is a question in the trial whether the prosecution has been holding back material evidence from the defense in the sense of not handing over evidence *at the time* required by an existing discovery order. The fact that the photographic evidence was held back may not be apparent at the time it is made available to the defense; that fact may emerge only when the prosecution witnesses are being cross-examined during the trial.

A prosecution witness may be forced to admit that he turned over certain photographs to the prosecution on a date which happens to be before a particular discovery order was made, and the photographs may not have been made available to the defense until a month or two after that discovery order. By that time, during the trial, the *reason* why the prosecution cheated on the discovery order, as well as the fact of their cheating, may be apparent. The lawyer's notes should be conscientious enough, and thorough enough, that he can unhesitatingly prepare and sign an affidavit on the basis of his evidence index, to support whatever action is necessary in the middle of the trial.

[b] Public Domain Materials

Movies found only in the public domain present easier problems than those already copied by the prosecution. A television station may have shot a great deal of footage, only part of which is relevant. The lawyer should view that film at the television station, accompanied only by his client and possibly an associate, both carefully briefed not to talk indiscreetly in the presence of studio personnel. It may be that hundreds of emulsion feet were used on events related to the case, but which seem in no way relevant to the trial. The lawyer can make arrangements with the station to have some laboratory duplicate as much or as little of this film footage as he wishes.

The lawyer can afford to be a little selective about what he copies, provided that all of the following are true: (1) money is a problem; (2) the lawyer is absolutely certain that what he is omitting is irrelevant; (3) he makes notes concerning the part that was not copied, so that if the trial situation makes this footage relevant in an unexpected manner, he will remember what is there and where it is; (4) a trial subpoena duces tecum has already been served on the owner of this film, so that it will be available if needed at the trial, and will not be destroyed in the meantime; and (5) the prosecution have not ordered a copy of the omitted portion. On these assumptions the lawyer may be selective, but it is better to be generous to himself by taking more instead of less.

Prints of still photographs present even fewer problems. The rule here is to get one of everything, and the lawyer should do this, rather than think about reasons to excuse not doing it.

General principles are especially appropriate in deciding on copies of public domain photographs, since decisions here may be hard to change. Identification is usually a problem in photographs. A good magnifying glass is not as good as a well made blow-up. Also, the lawyer should not skimp on near duplicates. If a photograph is a duplicate, then it is only that; but if there are slight differences, it may be extremely unwise to consider the two photographs as being the same thing and order only one of them. One may show something the other does not. One may be a slightly cropped version of the other, or both may really be the same photograph, cropped differently. There may be an important time sequence change between the photographs. Since photographs are chosen in haste and examined at leisure, the decision should always be to get the most photographs possible at the earliest time possible. Economize on size if necessary, rather than selection. Better to limit the risk to not seeing something which is actually in the photographs, since that risk can be offset by looking at the photographs again and again, then to risk not having the right photograph at all.

It will probably not be feasible to get duplicate videotapes, although duplicates can be made. Duplicate videotape is expensive; and let alone that expense, the lawyer will probably never be in a position to afford the videotape machine necessary to screen the film. If he *can* afford these things, then of course the videotape should be treated on the same basis as movie film.

[2] Special Uses of Movies and Videotapes

These should be viewed as soon as possible, and several times. There are two general purposes in viewing them, and each should be served by one or more viewings. The first purpose is to see what happened, i.e., whether the defendant or any codefendant is shown doing something which the prosecution claim he did, and, if so, whether he is identifiable from the film. This can only be done by viewing *in the presence of the defendants.* Needless to say it will have to be a private viewing. If videotape is involved, it is not wise to arrange such a viewing at the studio of the television station. A studio technician will inevitably operate the equipment, and other persons may wander in during the viewing. It is quite important that what is said during the viewing should be confidential and privileged. If a videotape is involved, a video machine should be rented, transported to the lawyer's office or some other private place, and it should be operated by the lawyer or someone else on the defense team. The machines are easy to operate.

During the screenings, every effort should be made to preserve some account of what is observed and said by the clients. They know where they were, and they are the persons who can best identify themselves and each other. If necessary their comments (with their permission) should be tape recorded, and correlation to the film footage or tape footage should be noted. The lawyer will probably benefit more from the sound tape than by trying to take notes in the dark while observing the screen. Also, the lawyer should see to it that when film is being viewed, the machine is one which is capable of stopping on a certain frame, backing up, and moving forward in slow motion. At critical points that will be the only way to see what really happened. Certain things may show on only two or three frames and then be gone, and if those frames are not run one at a time, critical events may never be perceived.

The second purpose of viewing films and videotapes concerns the lawyer only. He can do this without his client present, and probably better without him. This purpose is simply to form his own impression of how the film will look to the jury, and how it will probably be used by the prosecution. It is amazing how very different defendants look when photographed on the scene than they do sitting in the viewing room or in court. The lawyer will have to see, and remember, what kind of impressions will be made when the film is shown, if it is all shown. As a corollary, the lawyer will have to decide how much of the film the prosecution will wish to use. Parts of it will be obviously relevant, parts inflammatory or irrelevant.

The lawyer may assume that if inflammatory things are in the film, the film will be offered in evidence early in the case. The whole film will be offered by the prosecutors without any discrimination. The lawyer will have to be well prepared at that point not only to make his objection in advance, out of hearing of the jury, but also to state to the court how much of the film he thinks can properly be shown, how much should not be shown, and why. He should know the running time and approximate footage involved, as well as reasons for his objections. There is no way to do this except by careful private preparation, viewing the film. This is best done alone.

[3] Use of Still Photographs

The problems with still photographs are essentially the same as with movies, except that they may be better viewed on an individual basis. It is not necessary to have group meetings of defendants in order to do this, but it is important that every defendant in a group trial should examine every photograph. It is also important that the photographs be numbered and catalogued, with a sticker or label on each one showing its number. The number should, as far as possible, follow a chronological or other logical pattern of organization. Otherwise it will not be feasible to keep track of photographs, even for purposes of showing them to clients, since the numbers are necessary to provide a frame of reference for what was said about the photograph.

[4] Use of Mug Shots

The lawyer will want to get copies of the booking photographs for several important reasons. If the defendant was beaten at the time of his or her arrest, the booking photograph will probably be the only evidence to prove it. By the time the defendant got out on bail and had time to consult a doctor and be photographed by friends, the bruises probably became etiolated or they vanished altogether. The mug shots will show them unmistakably.

This is important because the police will not explain the beating. The police who hit the defendant will almost always deny that they hit him at all, rather than attempt to contrive persuasive reasons for having done so. Such reasons will often be hard to come by in view of the size, age, or sex of the defendant, or the otherwise admitted fact that several officers participated in the arrest simultaneously, thus making a protracted struggle unlikely. Also, there will have been several officers present and in a position to see what happened; most of them will not lie about this, and their testimony that they did not see the defendant struggling will make it somewhat harder for another officer, who *is* willing to lie about the details of the struggle, to do so. Also, most witnesses to an arrest, other than officers, will remember that they did see the defendant just before his arrest and at that time he did not have the bruises shown by the mug shots. This combination of testimony sometimes makes mug shots an invaluable tool for showing who is telling the truth.

Another reason for wanting mug shots is that they serve to refresh the defendant's memory of what clothing he was wearing at the time, if there is any doubt about that. Deputy district attorneys brood over mug shots; they like to cross-examine witnesses on what they were wearing (should the defendant testify, a material point), and also to cross-examine defense alibi witnesses on what the defendant was wearing. Conversely, a badly prepared prosecution witness who claims to have seen the defendant where he was not may be conveniently impeached by questions as to what the defendant was wearing, since the mug shots make the point without the defendant having to testify himself, just in order to describe his clothing.

Another reason for wanting mug shots is that they show whether the defendant has made any change in his personal appearance since his arrest, such as shaving a moustache. Counsel should certainly be informed by his own client about this, but nonetheless, nothing does it like a photograph to satisfy the inquiring mind.

Should it happen that the defendant *has* changed his appearance in some important respect, since his arrest, the lawyer may be sure that the point will be brought out and the jury will be advised that the defendant deliberately changed his appearance in order to prevent later identification; in that case, the prosecution will probably attempt to put the mug shot in evidence at the beginning of the trial, in the hope that its inadmissibility will not be immediately apparent to the defense lawyer. It will be, though, if the lawyer has seen the mug shot (see § 13.02).

This prosecution move may be coupled with a more serious one: the defendant may have been arrested before, and the particular mug shot offered will be the one taken at the first arrest. Since this mug shot will be dated, the jury needs no prologue to understand that the defendant has a criminal record. Once that picture is in, the damage is done. Needless to say, having succeeded in getting that photograph into evidence, the prosecution would never argue the defendant's criminal record out loud, but the photograph would be passed among the jury, and shown again in final argument. Of course the foundation for this type of evidence is somewhat twisted: the relevance of a photograph taken at a prior arrest, when offered to show the appearance of the defendant at his second arrest (the one for which he is being tried), would necessarily depend on the booking officer's testimony that the defendant looked that way at the time. Since the defense lawyer will have made himself aware of all of the mug shots in the case, he can easily handle this matter by a motion *in limine* (to insure that no such picture will be offered during the trial), or by a timely objection to be argued out of the presence of the jury.

Cross-examination of the authenticating witness will

reveal that he has another photograph taken at the time he actually saw the defendant, one which contains a built-in placard showing the date of the second arrest. This evidence would expose the offer of the earlier photograph as a sham. While the offer of an item of evidence known to be inadmissible is of course a violation of professional ethics, it is more important for a lawyer to be looking for it to happen than it is for him to classify the exact degree of malfeasance.

A political prosecution itself should be such a shock to any system of ethics as to render minor transgressions like this almost meaningless.

§ 5.02　Plea Bargaining

[1]　What Is Meant by Plea Bargaining

Plea bargaining is the arrangement by which a person accused of crime agrees to plead guilty to a particular charge in return for assurance that punishment will be confined to agreed limits, and that any other actual or possible charges will be dropped. Such an arrangement is made initially with the prosecutor, since only he can agree to dismiss an existing charge or not to file a pending one. The judge may have the last word about sentencing, but the prosecutor's recommendations are heavy. As the judge sees things, it is important for the prosecutor to tough out any public criticism. But the area of the prosecutor's importance may suffer from one great exception, which is particularly noticeable in political trials.

When pattern charges are filed against a great number of people, the same charges against each person, and all of the charges arise from a single course of conduct so that they amount to nothing more than statements of the same offense, two legal features emerge. First, the defendants are in a position to plead guilty to *one* of those charges, and the judge (without the prosecutor's approval) may sentence for that count, and, having done so, *must* dismiss the remaining charges. This is true because of a corollary of the rule (discussed infra) that a person cannot be put in jeopardy twice for the same act. Second, the judge can decide what the sentence will be on that count, without any assistance from the prosecutor. Seen in this perspective, the prosecutor's say-so depends on the political value of his recommendations to the judge, and also on whether the prosecutor has charges which are not subject to the double jeopardy rule, i.e., charges as to which he has the last word with respect to dismissal, so that the defendant and the judge cannot settle that particular matter between themselves.

Plea bargaining was, until recently, regarded as a dubious practice involving trial counsel, which the judge would discuss only in the privacy of chambers. Many a defendant has been required to stand in open court, with sweat prickling on his brow, and disavow any hope of leniency in return for the plea he is about to make, while his lawyer, the prosecutor, and the judge asking the questions were all perfectly aware that the sentence had been agreed upon in advance. Now, however, some honest judges are coming to insist that all plea bargains, and the facts and circumstances justifying them, be stated in open court and subjected to court approval at the time a plea is entered. Plea bargaining is respectable.

There is nothing wrong with plea bargaining from the defense standpoint, provided the defense lawyer is better informed about the case than either the prosecutor or the judge, and provided (in a political case) that he views the process as a trial weapon rather than a substitute for trial.

[2] The Importance of Remembering Which Kind of Political Case Is Involved

[a] The Admitted Act Done for Political Reasons

There is little if any point to plea bargaining in this kind of case. A political defendant who admittedly violated the law for reasons of conscience, as a personal declaration, will probably not be interested in any kind of deal regarding his sentence. The defendant in this kind of political case necessarily regards his public trial as a benefit, one of the things he gets in return for going to jail. The trial (as he views things) not only vindicates his sincerity, it is probably the only way at his disposal to force a disputed statute or policy to operate in its harshest, most mechanistic mode. There can be no discussion or thought of leniency while issues of guilt and innocence are still being determined at the trial. Thus the hated policy which lies behind the law will not be allowed to look benign as long as the trial continues. The political trial will temporarily put within the reach of an individual other resources which are normally denied to everyone except very large corporations.

Corporations can buy time on television and in newspapers, and they can also hire expensive advertising firms to influence public opinion. A trial is less controllable than an advertising agency, but indirectly offers greater public exposure than could possibly be paid for, even with a very large amount of money. A political trial is slow and therefore reinforces and multiplies whatever statement it imparts to the public. While the nature of this statement is the result of an averaging process, a sort of backing and filling by machinery pushing from one side and then the other, some form of message inevitably emerges. A political trial is a legal event occurring in the real universe and, at the same time, an unappreciated ritual proceeding by formulated steps. While important in the grey and white tones of prison days, a political trial is also a form of acting out, in which the audience knows itself to be powerfully involved.

In the admitted-act type of political case, plea bargaining is ruled out not only by the trial's innate necessity to the defendant, but also by the extent to which the prosecution count on a political trial to reach their own goals. Prosecutors tend to use these trials to run for re-election. They use press conferences and press leaks. These are easy cases to win from the prosecution point of view, and there is no shortage of prosecutors willing to win them on these terms and claim credit as if they had worked at it. A typical prosecutor will want to clock up as much political mileage from the proceedings as possible, in his own behalf.

This ritual pleases both the prosecutor and the defendant and makes plea bargaining unlikely. After all, a plea bargain might be dispositive of the whole case.

[b] The Disputed Act Prosecuted for Political Reasons

When the case is entirely based on disputed acts, plea bargaining cannot occur, because the prosecutor cannot offer an acceptable deal. It would not be acceptable for the defendant to plead guilty to even one misdemeanor, however "low-grade," which he did not do. But the situation is quite different where the charges contain something which the defendant can properly and advantageously admit.

[c] Mixed Cases

For purposes of this discussion, a "mixed case" is one in which there is a particular pattern of major and minor charges. In this situation, the major charge will be a felony (or misdemeanor) which the defendant did *not* do, but which is prosecuted for political reasons. The minor charges will include a misdemeanor (stated in several counts, amounting to the same thing) which the defendant *did*, and which he typically did in common with a number of other people. In this situation, which is encountered fairly often in demonstration cases, plea bargaining is not only possible, but may be extremely important for the defendant.

[3] Why a Partial Deal May Be Available in a Mixed Case

[a] A Typical Example of a Mixed Case

Assume that the defendant was one of the ring leaders of a large political demonstration, and that defendant and the other ring leaders were arrested along with about 300 other people. Everyone arrested is charged with the several misdemeanors usually laid at the feet of those who oppose majority wishes in public, e.g., unlawful assembly, failure to disburse, "riot," and "rout." (It should be added that "riot" and "rout" in this context denote any illegal assembly, not necessarily one at which dust was raised; illegality typically stems from stepping on the grass in front of the main office of some corporation.)

Assume the defendant, like everyone else arrested, is charged with these four misdemeanors; the difference is, however, that having spotted the defendant as one of the ring leaders, the police arrested him by clubbing him to the ground. In order to cover this assault, they inevitably charged the defendant with assaulting them. Assault on a police officer is a felony. This felony is a political crime: it never happened, and it will be prosecuted to the fullest extent that the district attorney can manage. The one or two officers who did the clubbing will lie about it, and will swear any number of times that the defendant actively resisted arrest, kicking and striking at them continuously, while they themselves used only necessary force to subdue him. They will deny that he was kicked or clubbed at all. The other officers will say they saw none of the close action.

In this example, a birds-eye view of the political charges will reveal that about 300 people are charged with a set of four misdemeanors, while five or six of the 300 (the real and supposed ring leaders), including defendant, are charged with felonies arising from the manner of their arrest. Assuming that the remainder of the 300 were well advised at the time of the mass arraignment (see § 2.02), about two-thirds of them will have pled not guilty. The district attorney or the presiding judge, who may be regarded as substantially on the same side of the fence, have a serious trial scheduling problem.

[b] Why a Partial Deal Becomes Available

In order to solve their scheduling problem, the district attorney and the court will in some manner offer a deal to the 300 or so persons who are charged with misdemeanors. Since they know very well that the four misdemeanors relate to a single course of conduct, and are in fact only different statements of the same offense, they are (in most jurisdictions) bound to realize that under the double jeopardy rule, a person convicted of all four misdemeanors can be punished only for one. There is nothing to lose in offering to dismiss three misdemeanors for a guilty plea to one.

The deal offered will be no jail and a moderate fine; in one form or another (it changes from week to week) the deal may include a suspended jail sentence or probation for a couple of years.[1] In its probation phase, the deal may be sweetened by a reminder that in this jurisdiction the misdemeanor involved is one which can be expunged following completion of a term of probation, however short.

This deal will be offered to the defendants at large

because of their sheer numbers. It would not have been offered to this defendant separately, and indeed it may not be offered to him now—or the offer may be withdrawn as to him only, should it appear that he may benefit by participating in the deal.

[c] Timing and Manner in Which the Offer Is Revealed

The first and probably best form of this offer will be announced at the mass arraignment. This will happen because at that point the prosecution is most disorganized, and is faced with the largest number of arrested persons. The prosecution and the presiding judge would like to get as many guilty pleas at that point as possible. The deal then offered will be in its absolutely sweetest form, probably something like a $10.00 fine and no probation.

One difficulty here is that general considerations against accepting it are manifest, while the special reasons which make this deal desirable from the point of view of a target defendant may not be apparent so early in the case. A reason against accepting the deal (as to the other 300 defendants) is that participation in the demonstration was a political act. The persons being arraigned have already suffered most of the physical and mental abuse which the police can inflict on them as a penalty for political dissent. They will have suffered violence, isolation, and degradation from the time of the demonstration until the arraignment, but at that point *most* of this abuse will be behind them. The only effective counter at their disposal is to require the state to do the balance of the proceedings properly, i.e., to have a full-dress trial for every defendant, either individually or in groups.

The district attorney and the presiding judge will, of course, expect to punish anybody who insists on a jury trial, by inflicting harsher sentences for those who go to trial than they did on those who plead guilty. This is judicial extortion, a practice for which the law has not yet bothered to formulate a remedy. Most judges wish to retain the privilege of extorting guilty pleas while important members of the real estate syndication bar and the entertainment bar find the practice amusing. The answer to this may be a class action to compel the trial court (by mandamus or prohibition) not to inflict any harsher sentence after a jury trial than the same court meted out to the other persons involved in the same protest demonstration who pled guilty, without a trial, unless the trial court could show a substantial (and honest) reason for imposing a harsher sentence.

For the lawyer who is defending a mixed political case, and who is in the unusual position of *knowing* that for various reasons (see § 5.02[4]) this partial deal is a desirable one for his client (a target defendant), the arraignment is probably the best time to take advantage of the situation. This is true because the offer will undoubtedly not be linked to any kind of probation. A week or two later, when the deputy district attorneys have had more time to look at films, they may begin to realize why the arrangement would benefit the target defendant, and they will withdraw the offer as to him. Assuming the iron is hammered while it is hot, the results will be as follows: (1) the target defendant will plead guilty to one misdemeanor, for which he will pay a ten-dollar fine; (2) the three other misdemeanors will be dismissed; and (3) he will plead not guilty to the felony charge and will proceed toward trial on that charge.

If such a deal is not overtly stated at a mass arraignment, it will certainly emerge in the pattern of light fines actually imposed at that time for those who plead guilty. The deal will then become more or less formally extended by the time that other arraignments are held following the first mass arraignment, i.e., on the date to which all arraignments were continued which were not completed at the time of the mass arraignment.

The formalization of this offer is more or less inevitable, since there *will* have been a pattern of light sentences at the mass arraignment, and there will still be a lot of trials depending on the postponed arraignments. The mechanics of such an announcement are simple. The presiding judge may announce his sentencing policy in open court. Or deputy district attorneys may be heard extending the offer informally to their counterparts in the public defender's office and to defense lawyers in general. If a hypothetical defendant is past the arraignment stage when the offer becomes formal, the lawyer will nonetheless hear the offer in other cases, and indeed it may be extended to other persons in a consolidated case involving his own client.

[4] How a Limited Plea Bargain Can Be Useful as a Trial Weapon in a Mixed Case

Vigorous spade work in the early stages of trial preparation will show whether there is any advantage to a limited plea bargain. Whatever advantage there is will be beautiful, once uncovered. For example, assume that in a mixed case the defendant is charged with a felony which he did not do (battery against a police officer), and four misdemeanors which he actually did (unlawful assembly, failure to disburse, riot and rout). In this hypothetical, the pragmatic *reason* why he is charged with a political felony is that the police beat him up because he was a ring leader of the demonstration. Prompt investigation of the case will probably produce movies and videotapes of the demonstration, and many other photographs. While the prosecution possess or have access to many of these photographs, they move (for all of their zeal) with a slower dynamic. All they have in the way of personnel to scrutinize these films are narcotics officers and third-rate informers, and they are attempting to organize many cases at the same time.

The lawyer has the help of his client and all of his client's friends.

What the lawyer may find (and it is to be hoped that he will be the first to know) is this: some of the most remarkable shots in the color footage, the ones that are really close up, well-focused and composed, show the defendant standing on the steps, or on a car, or in a space cleared specially for him, addressing a crowd with cupped hands, rolled newspaper, megaphone or a bullhorn. He is leading it. Other frames may show an anguished member of the establishment, some vice dean, bursar, or police commissioner, exhorting the demonstrators to be reasonable; standing right at his elbow with bullhorn slung carelessly at his side, a crooked smile relieving his tired features, will be the defendant. He has obviously just exhorted the crowd to be quiet so that the straight man can be heard, and he is smiling because he is about to deliver a short, blunt, and very clear version of why the demonstrators are there, and he is going to say it to the dean with words he will enjoy remembering, and which will please his three best friends (co-defendants) who are standing behind him. The film may not have a sound track, but the videotape does, and anyway, the dean and his colleagues remember the words. They promised themselves at the time they would do that later in court, and the only satisfaction they got that day was the thought of testifying about it later.

When the lawyer has seen all this he will understand immediately the advantages of a partial plea bargain in this situation. The reason is, the prosecution are allowed to use these films at the trial and they can capitalize on public resentment of the people who organized this particular demonstration. The prosecution can use emotions generated by these films to swing the jury toward block convictions, not only of the four misdemeanors which the defendant did (which are amply proved by these films) but *also of the felony of battery of a police officer*—which is *not* on any of these films and which the defendant did *not* do.

For purposes of this discussion, the serious charge is assumed to be a felony; it need not be. It might be instead a heavy misdemeanor—but it certainly must be a crime for which the prosecution intends to send the defendant away for a full year, and one as to which no leniency can be expected.

A crucial point is, the films are relevant and admissible *only* in connection with the four basic misdemeanors. There is absolutely nothing in the felony which relates to the facts leading up to defendant's arrest; and with any kind of vigor at all the lawyer could prevent their use in support of the felony count, if that count stood alone.

Under these circumstances, the defendant may be well advised to let persons who have nothing else at stake but misdemeanor sentences test the constitutionality of misdemeanor statutes. The lawyer by contrast knows he is going to trial on a felony, and that if his client is convicted, probably the judge and certainly everybody else in the penal system will believe the defendant actually did the felony and will treat him accordingly. The lawyer *must* eliminate these films from the felony trial, since defense of the felony is seriously jeopardized by them.

This situation is sufficiently serious that the lawyer should be willing to *plead* to one of these misdemeanors, if absolutely necessary, even without a plea bargain, just for the purpose of clearing the field for the felony trial. That being so, he should certainly recommend a plea bargain which does the same thing and limits the sentence for the misdemeanor.

Needless to say, the lawyer does not approach the plea bargaining problem by telling anyone else that he wants to keep the films out of the case, or that he would be willing to plead without assurance as to the sentence. But it is well to keep the scale of values firmly in mind when actually bargaining.

[5] The Mechanics of Bargaining

The lawyer should try to put himself in the position of picking up and accepting an offer from the prosecution, rather than suggesting the plea bargain himself. In other cases the lawyer may have to take the initiative for a desirable bargain, but in a political case such as the demonstration case, where calendar pressures force the prosecution to make their offer to the defendants at large, it may not be necessary for the lawyer to suggest anything. It is important for the lawyer not to seem to take the initiative since the general frame of mind of the prosecution seems to require them to spend more time and energy picking over anything the lawyer offers, than in preparing for trial. The lawyer will know with which particular prosecutor he must deal; and if that person has reached the point of extreme suspicion about anything suggested by the lawyer, then the lawyer should consider the interview carefully, making sure that it takes place under relatively relaxed conditions and always in the presence of some other person before whom the particular deputy district attorney would like to appear as a hail-fellow-well-met. This third person should be one sympathetic to the lawyer's position, with whom the prosecution have their own reasons for maintaining good relations. The best candidates for this role are friends of the lawyer who often defend criminal cases, but who are not conspicuously identified as defending political cases. The main points of the discussion are as follows: first, that the prosecution have extended a particular offer respecting the four misdemeanors to the whole world, and everybody knows it; second, no matter how much the prosecution say about the character of the defendant—in the light of his having bitten, kicked, and struck the harmless police officers—they will still be free to go to trial on their cherished felony charge.

[6] What to Do if the Necessary Plea Bargain Is Withheld as to this Particular Defendant Only

If the prosecutor withholds a plea arrangement which the lawyer needs in order to defend against the main charge, and the same plea arrangement is being offered to other defendants, the lawyer must not lose patience. The prosecution are probably acting more out of animosity than wisdom, and so it is necessary to be patient with them at this point. They are refusing the plea arrangement because they hate a "cop kicker"—at least the lawyer should hope that this is the only reason—and not because they really sense the importance of the films. They will sense it later. Meanwhile, some tactful leverage may be helpful.

A group deal is a plea bargain offered to (or demanded by) a number of defendants, on the basis that all must participate or the bargain will be withdrawn from (or rejected by) all. Its ethical significance is that if the lawyer had two clients involved in a group deal, and if their interests conflicted in the slightest with respect to that deal, their conflicting interests would preclude his negotiating it. Its moral significance is principally that if a number of defendants are charged in the same case or related cases, and the prosecution wish to make a plea bargain with some or all of them, it would seem immoral for the lawyer representing an excluded defendant to undercut the position of other defense lawyers by seeking to jam the negotiations or by abusing his role in them so as to prevent those who wish to negotiate from participating in the plea bargain.

The tactical usefulness of a group deal consists entirely of leverage. There is nothing unethical or immoral in a group of defendants deciding on their own not to accept a plea bargain unless an excluded defendant is brought within the terms of the offer. In a consolidated case in which a group feeling has occurred among the defendants, their attitude may well be that a plea bargain offered to one must be offered to all. The state of negotiations should be discussed by lawyers and clients together, in the same vein as money matters and other things lying close to the common throat. Once they understand the situation, the defendants may supply the unanimity needed to lever the prosecution off of their chosen square, unpinning the excluded defendant and bringing him or her within the terms of an offer despite the original wish of the prosecution to restrict it.

If a desired plea bargain cannot be negotiated, with or without the help of other defendants and their lawyers, an alternative remedy is severance. The lawyer may try his hand at severing the defendant's case from any others with which it may have been consolidated or filed. The only thing to be gained by severence (to continue the example of inflammatory films) is that at the trial, only close-ups of *this* defendant could be shown, not other close-ups which may be worse. But large crowd scenes, showing what the defendant was participating in, will almost certainly be admissible because the misdemeanors are still in the case, along with the felony. Unfortunately, the lawyer cannot reasonably expect (in this hypothetical case) to sever the defendant's own misdemeanors from his felony charge, since they will almost certainly be too closely related to warrant separate trials. Assuming this to be so, there are still remedies.

[7] Alternative Procedure for Achieving Substantial Benefit of Plea Bargain Which Is Not Made Available to Target Defendant

Where a favorable plea bargain has been effectively denied to the defendant, all considerations switch from whether the prosecution will acquiesce in a particular result, to whether the lawyer can force that result. The main considerations now are legal ones, and to a lesser extent they involve judicial personalities. The considerations are as follows: (1) whether conviction of one of these misdemeanors really blocks further prosecution on the others; (2) whether conviction in this sense requires sentencing in order for the blocking to take place; (3) whether the procedural stage of the case is such that the lawyer can guarantee (or at least reasonably hope to insure) that sentencing will take place prior to the trial of the remaining felony; and (4) whether the available judges who could pass sentence on the misdemeanor at this stage of the case can be relied on to exercise human reasonableness.

The lawyer approaching this problem without the benefit of recent familiarity and experience in this area might well be advised to start with these assumptions and distinctions. The Fifth Amendment provision, ". . . nor shall any person be subject for the same offense to be twice put in jeopardy of life or limb . . ." is there, and it applies to state prosecutions,[2] but in the opinion of some, it is rather ineffectual, owing to the narrowness of the federal "same offense" requirement,[3] and also the uncertainty of its application to successive prosecutions by different governments.[4] It is there, but no one can remember when that particular clause was interpreted in a way which helped anybody who was accused of a crime. Ironically, more puissant guarantees may be found in state constitutions or in state statutes designed to implement them.[5] These statutes may be found lying across each other like a pile of pick-up sticks, producing bizarre results which may help or hinder the parties to criminal litigation.[6] The lawyer should focus his research and judgment on the problem whether, in his jurisdiction, the courts labor under the self-imposed rule that where a defendant has been convicted of one crime, all elements of the second crime must be found among the elements of the first crime in order for prosecution of the second crime to be barred; or whether they operate under the more liberal rule that where a single, indivisible course of conduct results in breaking several laws, conviction of any one of those crimes will bar further prosecution with respect to all of the others. This distinction is quite important because we are dealing with misdemeanors. It is rather uncommon to find one, let alone several misdemeanors, all of whose elements are encompassed within the elements of some other misdemeanor. In other words, if the courts follow the narrow rule (that only included offenses are barred), what follows will probably not work at all; if they follow the liberal rule, there may be something to be gained.

The second focal point for serious research (assuming the first is surmounted) is the distinction that, in order to bar further prosecution for the same crime under another name, the essential stop is a conviction of the basic crime. In this sense "conviction" probably means sentencing, not merely a guilty plea. In other words, the defendant in our hypothetical case is being prosecuted for four misdemeanors, notwithstanding that all four of them relate to the same offense. Assuming he were convicted of all four in the same legal proceeding, he could only be sentenced for one. That stage normally occurs at the end of the trial, however, far too late to be of any use in blocking evidence in the felony case. By the same reasoning, the mere fact that defendant had pled guilty to one misdemeanor would not block further prosecution on the other three (because he had not yet been sentenced), thus leaving open the door for all the bad films and other evidence to be used at the combined trial of those three misdemeanors plus the felony. The point is, for this arrangement to achieve the necessary end, the defendant may have to be sentenced for one misdemeanor before the felony trial begins, so that he will have achieved dismissal of the three remaining misdemeanors and thus blocked the introduction of films pertaining only to those misdemeanors. This raises a question, can the lawyer guarantee such an early sentencing for that one misdemeanor?

The answer would seem to be, if it is necessary for this case to go through a lower and an upper court, he may be able to guarantee sentencing; but if the case exists entirely in an upper or a lower court he may not. If this case began with the filing of a complaint in a lower court which has jurisdiction only of misdemeanors, *for possible disposition of misdemeanors* and for the holding of a preliminary hearing as to the felony, and if the case then moves up to the trial court for the trial of the felony count, plus any ancillary misdemeanors which remain at that time, then it may be possible to do quite a lot in the lower court, even without the cooperation of the prosecutor, or, in fact, without the cooperation of judges.[7]

But if the whole case begins with an indictment filed in the same court which will try the felony, or if the charge which the lawyer is worried about is a misdemeanor rather than a felony, so that all the misdemeanors are scheduled for trial in a lower court, then the lawyer cannot guarantee sentencing prior to trial without some help from judges or a concession from the prosecution. This is true because it is possible for the judge in the single court which has jurisdiction of all the counts to take a guilty plea on one misdemeanor and postpone sentencing until he finishes the entire case. That result, of course, would preclude the plea, since there would be nothing to gain (it would not be possible to stop the use of the bad evidence) and much to lose (the admission contained in a guilty plea).

The conditions necessary in order to force the substantial equivalent of a necessary plea bargain may be summarized: (1) the client is charged with a crime—usually a felony—which he did not do; (2) he is also charged with multiple misdemeanors, which all amount to a single misdemeanor, which he actually did; (3) the misdemeanor is sufficiently related to the felony that all misdemeanor charges would be tried in the same proceeding as the felony; (4) the prosecution can easily prove that the defendant did the misdemeanors; (5) known evidence in the misdemeanor case is so inflammatory that it would seriously jeopardize defense of the felony case; (6) the defendant understands the need to block the evidence in the felony case, and the risk entailed in pleading to the misdemeanor; (7) the prosecution will not voluntarily dismiss the extra misdemeanors in return for a plea to one of them; (8) applicable law is such that conviction and sentencing as to one of these misdemeanors would legally block further prosecution on all the other misdemeanors; (9) the case is presently lodged in a lower court, where a plea to one misdemeanor will require some judge in the lower court to pass sentence, before the case is transferred to the upper court for trial of the felony.

The last requirement may be dispensed with, provided the judge will agree (probably with the prosecutor's consent) that if the defendant pleads guilty to one misdemeanor, he will be sentenced *immediately*, regardless of other options. The judge alone may be able to sever one misdemeanor from others, for this purpose. But if the misdemeanor is joined to a felony, the active cooperation of the prosecutor may be necessary, in order to refile the misdemeanor separately from the felony, to set it up for sentencing.

If all of these formidable conditions have been checked out like the lines on a trapeze, then the lawyer may trust his weight to the structure.

The next step is to shop for judges in the lower court. This is a common-sense matter which should be familiar to everybody who tries criminal cases. Judge shopping simply means getting the case before the right judge for the purpose of changing a plea from not guilty to guilty. How to go about this? The procedure does not require much ingenuity, and is entirely a matter of local knowledge. It helps to have friends on the bench and in the clerk's office, so as to know who would be amenable to a reasonable sentence in a case like this, who has been called out of town to sit as a relief judge in some other jurisdiction, who is on vacation, and who thinks the prosecutor has been pushing political cases too hard. Surprisingly, those prosecutors who will fight tooth and nail against a plea bargain in this situation may be more or less acquiescent in bringing the case before the right judge because they do not feel they can properly oppose everything.

Once the case is before the right judge, it may be well (depending on the informality in this court) for counsel to go into chambers and explain their differences and what is about to happen. By this time, the lawyer should be satisfied that he is dealing with a reasonable judge. The plea is then changed in open court, and time for sentencing is waived. This procedure should result in a reasonable sentence, notwithstanding anything the prosecutor may say at this stage. Immediately after it is pronounced, the lawyer should move to dismiss the other three misdemeanors, and he should have ready a short lucid brief which a child could understand, as to why dismissal of the other misdemeanors is now mandatory.

An alternative to risking a possible misunderstanding of the law by the judge may be found (where there is such a statute) in a conditional plea.[8] In other words, the plea of guilty to one misdemeanor can be expressly coupled with the condition that the other three should be dismissed. By this procedure it is still necessary for the judge to decide that the other three counts should be dismissed (or else he will not accept the conditional plea), and so the same brief and the same legal reasoning will have to be adduced at the time of a conditional plea. For the judge who is not quite sure of himself in legal matters but knows the calendar is full, this alternative procedure may reassure him that he is doing the right thing. Of course, the use of a conditional plea will not in itself persuade the judge that he is doing the right thing. That is the lawyer's job.

[8] The Advantage of Speed in Using Early Discovery Returns to Nail Down a Plea Bargain

Information has a special value while it is fresh. If there is going to be an agreement in the form of a plea bargain, this agreement is only possible during such time as the lawyer knows why he needs the agreement (to block inflammatory misdemeanor evidence which might otherwise be used in the felony case) and while the prosecution do not perceive or fully appreciate that reason. The fact that there is such an interval of time simply means that the lawyer is fortunate enough to be one step ahead of the prosecution; as in any other race, it is only a short wait until even the loser passes the same point on the track.

The longer the lawyer waits in attempting to reach the agreement he wishes, the more likely that the person with whom he is dealing (or the person to whom that person answers) will appreciate what is going on, and the plea bargain will become impossible. This is especially noticeable because if the lawyer initiates plea bargaining at a very early stage, he may well be dealing with opposite numbers in the prosecutor's office who only try lower court cases.

As a general rule, these people are easier to get along with, looser in their thinking, and much more likely to deal. Their egos are not involved in the outcome of felony trials. Some of them may be more experienced and better lawyers than some persons technically above them who try felony cases. It is worth remembering that in a large prosecutor's office which is engaged in political prosecutions, the internal system promotes the rise of those more zealously devoted to political prosecutions. The fact that a deputy district attorney can survive in such an office, with trial experience, and not move into the felony trial department is a point in favor of dealing with such a person. But the only chance to deal with him is to catch him early in the case.

Assuming there is to be a deal, and that the deal will be made with more favorably inclined personnel in the prosecutor's office, then while the case is still in the lower court, the lawyer may be able to leave an essential part of the deal unstructured. If the lower court deputy lacks authority, that may be the only way to solve the problem. An important detail like whether a term of probation will be six months or two years will be found totally unmalleable if the lower court prosecutor has to get authority from his superiors. They always want long probation terms. On the other hand, he may feel that he already has authority to leave that matter to the sentencing judge without consulting his superiors. This is all right, provided the right judge does the sentencing. And a lower court deputy will be more likely to go along with the necessary judge shopping. The necessity of finding the right judge is a further imperative for early action.

In judge shopping, the available judge opportunities may be thought of as a sort of fanciful number, which is the product of the number of suitable judges multiplied by the days remaining before the prosecutor's office becomes fully cognizant of what the lawyer is doing. The sooner the process is begun, the better; it may also be true that as a class, lower court judges are more reasonable in sentencing for misdemeanors than are sentencing judges in courts of general jurisdiction who happen to find themselves passing out sentences for misdemeanors. It is offered as an unprovable hypothesis that lower court judges, because of the number of petty cases thrust upon them, particularly the fact that they see so many drunks, may have a slight tendency to downgrade the procedural rights of defendants in the trial process, but conversely loosen up for sentencing. Some of them feel too busy to apply correct rules of trial procedure, and they do not believe in the efficacy of long sentences. So if there cannot be a deal with the prosecutor covering everything, or if there cannot be a deal at all, the lower courts will provide a rich oriental market for judge shopping.

[9] How to Consider a "Final" Offer for a Plea Bargain

The caption for this brief discussion is perhaps misleading. If there is really a good offer—even one made just before trial—its virtues will be apparent in the light of trial preparations, and no one will really need advice on what to do. The kind of offer we are talking about however looks a certain way just because it is made immediately before trial.

This offer is often presented as a "final" one. Some deputy-prosecutors spend a lot of time and energy preaching about the unsullied record of their office for never improving a final offer. This claptrap should be treated as such, even though it may be historically correct. But the offer, like any other, must be looked at.

When the client asks the lawyer for his advice about this offer, the lawyer may find unhappily that the thing seems evenly balanced. But one should remember *why* it seems balanced. The same offer would have seemed unbalanced were it made at any other time. When the lawyer's mind is distracted, and the pressure is on, his judgment will be warped. Human nature being what it is, it will probably be warped a little bit in favor of accepting something that should not be accepted.

It happens that the uncertainties of the trial always seem most menacing just before the trial begins. So if the offer looks balanced under these circumstances, that point alone is probably sufficient grounds for rejecting it. Things seeming equal, nobody can go far wrong who kicks the offer out the door and commits his case to trial.

§ 5.03 The Preliminary Hearing

Although the purpose of a preliminary hearing is supposedly to enable the magistrate to determine whether there is sufficient evidence to justify holding the defendant to stand trial for a felony, the real considerations are somewhat different. As a practical matter, most magistrates go through the motions of a preliminary hearing because the law requires them to, and not because they are prepared, under any foreseeable circumstances, to throw the case out at this stage. Most of them are not even aware, seemingly, that they have a legal duty to weigh evidence and the privilege of disbelieving a prosecution witness. They conduct preliminary hearings as if any amount of evidence—never mind how small—is enough to justify a felony trial. This judicial attitude has completely altered the purpose of preliminary hearings.

The lawyer defending a political case has the same goals at the preliminary hearing that he would have in defending any other criminal case. These are as follows: (1) where it seems likely that one of the prosecution witnesses intends to give perjured testimony and that the prosecution will rely on it, and the lawyer also knows he has an unassailable means of impeaching these lies, e.g., a photograph not yet known to the prosecution, then the lawyer must compel this witness to do his lying in the preliminary hearing, nailing down the lies so that he cannot possibly reconcile them with the impeaching evidence should that evidence become known before the trial; (2) in all cases, the lawyer must learn as much as possible about what the prosecution testimony will be, honest or otherwise; and (3) he must observe how the prosecution witnesses behave in court and what kind of impression they will make on a jury.

Preparation for the preliminary hearing requires a thorough reading of police reports and other evidence which the prosecution will have previously made available to the defense (for discovery motion procedure, see §4.07). The lawyer should subpoena every police officer and prosecution witness who had anything to do with this case, to require their attendance at the preliminary hearing.

Needless to say, the lawyer should *not* plan to put the defendant on the stand at the preliminary hearing, nor should he call any real defense witnesses. This is true because as everyone knows, there is nothing to be gained and everything to lose. The magistrate is not going to release the defendant no matter what defense evidence is adduced, but if any defense witness testifies, the prosecution will have it all down in black and white, and will share in the enormous new advantage of knowing what opposing witnesses are going to say. That advantage should accrue only to the defense, and accordingly, all witnesses summoned at the preliminary hearing as defense witnesses will in reality be hostile witnesses. This procedure, sometimes referred to by angry magistrates and prosecutors as a "fishing expedition," is in fact above legal reproach. The reason is, the defense has an entirely different understanding of the facts, a different version of what happened, than the one suggested by the prosecution.

If all the prosecution witnesses told the truth, the defense case would be proved. Truth-telling is an unarguable goal, and necessarily so in the contemplation of the law, since the law supposedly believes that a preliminary hearing has as much chance of coming out in favor of the defendant as it does in favor of the prosecution. If every "defense" witness proves a disappointment to the defense lawyer, those may be predictable disappointments, but not ones which should preclude him from trying to get the truth out of them and from learning as much as he can about the case.

Legislatures presumably intend the defense to have some leeway for purposes of discovery at a preliminary hearing, since the statutes compelling the magistrate to swear defense witnesses at a preliminary hearing typically do not limit the defendant's right to call them by requiring him first to make some kind of offer of proof.[9]

Since all witnesses at the preliminary will be adverse witnesses, the lawyer will be cross-examining every one of them. *Before the testimony begins, he should ask the magistrate to exclude all witnesses from the courtroom and order them not to discuss their testimony with each other until the hearing is completed.*

Prosecution hostile witnesses will testify first, and their cross-examination will be limited to the scope of their direct examination. When the lawyer calls the hostile defense witnesses, he will certainly be allowed to treat them as adversaries to the extent that he is allowed to examine them at all: in that situation, the only proper limit should be relevance to the charge before the magistrate.

In cross-examining these prosecution witnesses, the lawyer must necessarily follow a different pattern of questions from those he would ask in a real cross-examination. This is true because a real cross-examination is designed to question, impeach, limit, and throw a different light on the previous testimony of the witness, in order to persuade the jury that the witness was mistaken. But since the magistrate is not going to be persuaded of any such thing, there is probably little to be gained by directly attacking the witness' credibility at the preliminary, except as may be implicit in nailing him to his story; the only result of impeaching him now will be to teach the witness how to look after himself at the real trial.

Standard cross-examination techniques often put the witness on his guard and result in short ambiguous answers interspersed between long admonitory questions, quite the opposite of what is desired in a preliminary hearing.

Instead of following his natural path of cross-examination the lawyer should utilize what would otherwise be regarded as an incompetent style of cross-examination: he should take the witness over all the same ground again, the same things he just testified to, but in more detail. This may be painful for any other lawyer within earshot, and it will annoy the magistrate, but no matter.

The lawyer should remember how the questions and answers will look in print—or more accurately, how they will sound when read out loud to the jury—since that is how they are used to impeach. For example, assume the lawyer anticipates a certain police officer will lie at the trial about something that happened at the time of the defendant's arrest, and he hopes to impeach him (at the trial) with a photograph of what actually happened. Assuming further that this particular officer is not among those called by the prosecution at the preliminary, he should be called by the defense. If he is going to lie, he must be made to do it *now*, and in such rich detail that he could not tell even the approximate truth at the trial without being impeached by what he said at the preliminary. By the time of trial he may have learned of the impeaching photograph. His normal pattern under those circumstances would be to slant his story so as to be more or less consistent with the photograph (see §§4.04 and 14.05). In order to prevent the witness wriggling off, he must be totally committed to a detailed statement of his lies at the preliminary hearing.

Then if he wants to change it at the trial, the transcript of the preliminary hearing, in lieu of the more devastating photograph, will be there to impeach him. Assuming that it is the transcript, the lawyer will have to show it to him at the time of trial, and ask him to read it to himself, and then obtain permission from the trial judge to read the impeaching testimony to the jury. The lawyer should conduct his preliminary examination with that in mind, so that what he later reads to the jury will be devastatingly clear.

In order to achieve clarity, the lawyer should never ask questions at the preliminary hearing in a hurried or sophisticated manner. He should *not* subtly curry favor with the magistrate by seeming to move things along briskly, nor reach any kind of facile understanding with the witness, the prosecutor or anyone else, by using in-group references, by making knowing assumptions, by leading the witness along to get over dull parts or by using in-group words. All of this may be tempting to the lawyer's ego, but it makes terrible reading in front of the jury.

Instead, a better way is to ask the witness a lot of calm, small questions, leading him in meticulous detail to state whatever it is that he is going to say. The questions and answers should be so simple and free from ambiguity that a child could understand them. The testimony should be that of the witness and not the lawyer. If the witness is going to lie, he is going to do it. The lawyer need not fear that something will go wrong. He should simply follow a flat, orderly chronological development of testimony, with nothing left susceptible to two interpretations.

The lawyer should make it a point to ask the witness to draw necessary diagrams and sign them. The lawyer should be very careful about where the witness points on his diagrams while he is testifying. If the witness points to something, the lawyer should state out loud for the record where he is pointing. Things on diagrams should be labelled, houses, streets, et cetera. There should always be a North arrow. And if the witness nods, shakes his head, makes some personal gesture, the lawyer should always be there to note for the record that this has occurred, to ask the witness to speak out loud, or to ask the prosecutor if it is not correct that the witness has just made a gesture with his hands indicating a distance of about two feet.

After the witness has said whatever he is going to say, and has totally committed himself to his lie, the lawyer should resist the temptation to go back and give him a chance to say it again. The next time something may go wrong, and once is enough if it was done right. Rather than being greedy the lawyer should concentrate on an unobstrusive transition to another subject. In other words, once the witness has done it, so that impeachment is certain, the lawyer should not delay his next question for any purpose. He should *not* lean over and whisper to an associate, stare out the window and sigh deeply, close his notebook, rapidly turn pages as if looking for a new subject, or in any way signal that something important to the lawyer has just been completed. He should go smoothly to the next question. And it is always well, assuming that the prosecutor has not noticed what has happened, to continue the questioning just long enough that the magistrate and prosecutor are somewhat tired of hearing the witness testifying, so that when the lawyer stops his cross-examination, the natural response will be to excuse the witness without redirect.

It goes almost without saying, then, that at the preliminary hearing, the lawyer has nothing to gain by confronting such a witness with anything which tends to impeach his lies, even though the evidence available for this purpose is prosecution evidence. For example, if the witness has just lied by saying that the defendant was not beaten at the time of his arrest, and the lawyer has a secret photograph showing him being beaten, the lawyer should let it go at that. He should not make a big thing out of asking the prosecutor to hand over his copy of the defendant's mug shot, which shows his face black-and-blue, just so he can score some cheap point off this witness before the magistrate. The magistrate does not care. But the witness will have an opportunity to reconsider what he just said. And if the witness is not very witty, the prosecutor will ask for a recess, and the two of them will go into the prosecutor's office and discuss matters. The result is not going to be an abatement of the criminal prosecution. The result will be redirect examination on points that were raised in their private discussion in the office. The lawyer who allows this to happen will regret it.

One salient thing about preliminary hearing transcripts is that they are not subject to correction after the fact. Lawyers become inured to changes being made in civil depositions, before trial; but that cannot be done with a preliminary hearing transcript. The only way the witness can save his testimony at the preliminary hearing is to correct it while he is on the stand, and so, of course, anything which unnecessarily encourages or allows him an opportunity to do this is foolishness.

After the preliminary hearing is over, there are still two important steps which are often neglected. One is, the lawyer should take his notes back to the office and *immediately* dictate a memorandum to himself, describing the personal characteristics of each prosecution witness whom he has just cross-examined. He should take the time to do this right. Any impression, information, whatever, whether apparently relevant or not, is grist for this mill.

These impressions should be written with a view to the problems which the lawyer will be facing at the time he reads this memorandum, in trial. At that point, of course, the lawyer will have nothing to say about the order of prosecution witnesses, but must be ready to deal with all of them, in any order. He will have to remember, then, how they behave on cross-examination, whether they seem accurate or evasive, whether they have winning personalities, and whether they can be pursued into areas which are not familiar to the lawyer but which open up at the time of trial. The lawyer will have to know how much to expect of himself, in cross-examining each witness at that time. These notes, therefore, should summarize the lawyer's opinion of the witnesses' effectiveness with a jury, as it seemed at the time of the preliminary hearing. It is important not to restrict or edit this memorandum; the lawyer should dictate anything at all that comes into his mind about each witness who testifies at the preliminary hearing. Restrictions imply that the writer knows what will be relevant. But the lawyer cannot *possibly* know at that point everything that will be relevant at the trial. Every remembered foible should go in. This kind of memorandum is best written within half-an-hour after the hearing. Twenty-four hours seems to be the next best plateau for memory. After that there is a real loss (see §14.01).

The other thing to be done is to index the transcript. This means a separate index for each witness, neat, topically organized, and typewritten. The lawyer should do the organizing himself unless he has a skilled legal assistant who can do it better. Each index is organized by subject matter. The person preparing the index starts with a skeleton of topics, or subjects which logically delineate important parts of the witness's testimony and at least some of which will probably apply as well to the testimony of others, for comparison and future correlation. (See § 14.01[2] for a discussion of how these simple indices are later used to make combined indices.) The indexer reads through the transcript of that witness's testimony, making quick notes under each topical reference, showing the page and line of every reference and adding and revising topics as the job proceeds. Having compiled these notes, he rearranges them and dictates the index so that all references under a given subject are summarized under that subject, preferably in chronological order as they relate to real time under that subject, i.e., as they relate to real events rather than in the order that they appear in the transcript.

Anything in the transcript which tends to impeach should be signaled for rapid location by italics or underlining. Internal contradictions in the transcript are signaled in the same way.

When the index is finished and typed, the lawyer should recheck with extreme care, making sure that everything relating to impeachment is summarized with perfect accuracy in the index. It is rather embarrassing to go through the mechanics of impeaching someone in court, and then start to read the offending passage, in reliance on an index prepared some time before, only to discover that the witness actually said something slightly different from what the index says and quite consistent with his present testimony. This will not happen if the index has been checked.

Footnotes

[1] Before any plea bargain is accepted which involves probation or suspended sentence of a political defendant, the lawyer should be quite sure whether the prosecution intend to request—and whether the court intends to require—any restriction on political activity during the period of probation or suspended sentence. Such restrictions may be unconstitutional, and will certainly be extremely distasteful to the defendant. See, e.g., In re Mannino, 14 Cal. App. 3d 953, 92 Cal. Rptr. 880, 45 A.L.R. 3d 996 (1971); People v. Arvanites, 17 Cal. App. 3d 1052, 1061–1064, 95 Cal. Rptr. 493, 498–500 (1971); Annot., "Propriety of Conditioning Probation or Suspended Sentence on Defendant's Refraining from Political Activity, Protest or the Like," 45 A.L.R. 3d 1022 (1972).

[2] Benton v. Maryland, 395 U.S. 784, 23 L. Ed. 2d 707, 89 S. Ct. 2056 (1969).

[3] See, e.g., Comment, "The Double Jeopardy Clause: Refining the Constitutional Proscription Against Successive Criminal Prosecu-

tions," 19 U.C.L.A.L. Rev. 804 (1972); Note, "Twice in Jeopardy," 75 Yale L.J. 262, 267–277 (1965).

[4] See, e.g., W. Schaefer, "Unresolved Issues in the Law of Double Jeopardy: *Waller* and *Ashe*," 58 Cal. L. Rev. 391 (1970); Note, "Successive Prosecutions by Two Soverigns After *Benton v. Maryland*," 66 Nw. U.L. Rev. 248 (1971).

[5] *Compare*, Cal. Const. art. I, § 13; Cal. Penal Code §§ 654, 687, and 1023 (West 1970); People v. Bauer, 1 Cal. 3d 368, 375–378, 461 P.2d 637, 82 Cal. Rptr. 357 (1969); Kellett v. Superior Ct., 63 Cal. 2d 822, 825–828, 409 P.2d 206, 48 Cal. Rptr. 366 (1966); Neal v. California, 55 Cal. 2d 11, 18–21, 357 P.2d 839, 9 Cal. Rptr. 607 (1960); People v. Johnson, 5 Cal. App. 3d 844, 847, 85 Cal. Rptr. 238 (1970); People v. Greer, 30 Cal. 2d 589, 598–601, 184 P.2d 512, 517 (1947); People v. Marshall, 48 Cal. 2d 394, 398–408, 309 P.2d 356 (1957); A. Kahn, "Double Jeopardy, Multiple Prosecution, and Multiple Punishment: A Comparative Analysis," 50 Cal. L. Rev. 853 (1962); M. Bruce, "Double Jeopardy v. Double Punishment—Confusion in California," 2 San Diego L. Rev. 86 (1965); *with* Minn. Const. art. I, § 7; Minn. Stat. § 609.035 (1969); Note, "Multiple Prosecution and Punishment of Unitary Criminal Conduct," 56 Minn. L. Rev. 646 (1972); *and with* N.Y. Const. art. 1, § 6; N.Y. Crim. Pro. Law §§ 40.10, 40.20, 40.30, and 40.40 (McKinney 1971); Note, "Double Jeopardy Provisions of the New York Criminal Procedure Law: Variations on a Federal Theme," 38 Brooklyn L. Rev. 748 (1972); Comment, "Double Jeopardy: Constitutional Requirements and the New Criminal Procedure Law in New York," 22 Syracuse L. Rev. 969 (1971).

[6] However, no one should give up on the matter of double jeopardy, even if his state constitution does not seem to provide any protection. Even in states where it seems presently conceded that the state standards are no higher than those of the federal constitution, there may be room for maneuver, owing to confusion in the cases. See, e.g., N.C. Const., art. I, § 17; Note, "Multiple Punishment and the Same Evidence Rule," 8 Wake Forest L. Rev. 243 (1972).

[7] But the lawyer should be extraordinarily careful about reaching the conclusion that a guilty plea to a misdemeanor at or before the time of a preliminary hearing (in the lower court)—in connection with a felony count with which the misdemeanor has been joined—will automatically require sentencing to take place in the lower court. For example, the rule in California may be that joinder of a misdemeanor to a related felony for purposes of a preliminary hearing does not invoke the power of the municipal court (where this hearing occurs)

to sentence for the misdemeanor, but rather places the judge of the municipal court in the role of a magistrate and nothing else, so that he has power only to hold a preliminary hearing, and to certify the felony to the superior court or not, with the misdemeanor riding along. See, R. Bein, "Implementation of Kellett's Command: Joinder of Misdemeanors and Felonies in Superior Court," 7 San Diego L. Rev. 1, 19–21 (1970); accord, People v. Newton, 222 Cal. App.2d 187, 189, 34 Cal. Rptr. 888, 890 (1963); People v. Hardin, 256 Cal. App.2d Supp. 954, 961, 64 Cal. Rptr. 307, 312 (1967).

[8] See, e.g., Cal. Penal Code §§ 1192.1, 1192.2 (West 1970); 1192.4 and 1192.5 (West Supp. 1972).

[9] See, e.g., Cal. Penal Code § 866 (West 1970).

Chapter 6

HOW TO EVALUATE RELATIVE TRIAL PREPARATIONS AND USE TRIAL TIMING AS A WEAPON

SYNOPSIS

§ 6.01   Important Assumptions

Three important assumptions for this discussion are as follows: (1) there will be constant pressure from the presiding judge to try this political case (and all other political cases the lawyer is currently involved in) as soon as possible and prior to some statutory or court-imposed deadline; (2) the defendant has the sole power to waive this time requirement (not the prosecution); and (3) the presiding judge himself will probably oppose any attempt by either side to continue the trial date. This kind of pressure may arise from a statute which requires the prosecution to bring a criminal case to trial within, for example, sixty days, or face a mandatory dismissal, and which makes every judge in the state available for temporary transfer to a court which is in danger of falling behind.[1] A similar requirement may be imposed by court rule. Moreover, at the time of writing this book, it seems evident that there is a rising tide of judicial impatience with any kind of trial delay. While this unofficial platform of conservative judges may derive, as some suspect, primarily from impatience with the exercise of individual rights in criminal cases and a reluctance to "waste" judicial time on criminal matters while important property rights get frosted in the legal cooler, nonetheless one small result of judicial impatience is that it has already begun to generate a reliable pressure toward trial. This pressure, though certainly not intended to assist political defendants, can be used for that purpose.

The lawyer should look for ways to utilize this pressure, as if it were wind or current or any other reliable natural source of energy. The lawyer can then hope to establish a superior rate of trial preparation, get well ahead of the prosecution, get just enough small continuances to peak his preparation at the time of trial, and drop the case on the prosecution for immediate trial. However, it is well to remember that the comparison of judicial impatience to a natural force is not an idle thought. While it may be used (as just described) to great advantage in the context of a single case, this same pressure can be the mechanism for extreme judicial abuse where one lawyer is defending several political cases at the same time and has not time enough to prepare them all. Since the damage there consists of lack of time, and since the traditional legal remedy (a writ) takes up more time than it saves, the workable remedies for this abuse are few and desperate, and require a special stomach (see § 6.04).

If the assumption about pressure for an early trial is *not* true, however, then what follows as to timing is probably irrelevant. This is so because if the trial is delayed for very long, then no matter what the prosecution case load, the defense can never be sure that the prosecution have not finished most of their preparation for this particular trial long before the earliest trial date which the defense can inflict.

§ 6.02 How the Lawyer Should Assess his own Trial Preparations; And Why he Should Plan to Use a Notetaker in Court

What follows is not an argument against method, but a suggestion that method should adjust itself to the hidden strengths of a political case and seem outwardly a little more eclectic than orderly. The lawyer's viewpoint should be there is only *one* case here—even in the sense of two cases within a single trial, the prosecution and the defense case, there is really only one—the defense case. The realities of the defense case subrogate many of the neat, generic terms often used to describe trials and which tend to get in the way of legal thought. In other words, this case is not part of a continuum which includes cases the lawyer prepared in his trial practice seminar in law school, and the personal injury cases which he may have prepared for the edification of some older lawyer. It follows that what is important now are the elements of the defense in this case; time is necessary to develop them, and priorities must rearrange themselves accordingly.

It should be fairly apparent by now that one of the important strengths of a political case is the fact that the dynamics of trial preparation greatly favor an earlier preparation and a better use of time by the defense. The fact that the defendant is being prosecuted for political reasons puts his case near some of the nuclei of moral thought which are about to be accepted or denied by society. The sight of the law being perverted to send the defendant to jail is enough to cancel the reluctance of almost any one whose help is worthwhile. Not only the defendant and his friends, but many dedicated and intelligent people will know what kind of case this is, and they will help with information, ideas, and advice, and without any particular regard to their own convenience. This is the strength of a political case, and it is rather astonishing—once the lawyer has come to know this phenomenon—ever to think of a political case as being something related to other cases. The lawyer involved in some other kind of case can practice his whole professional life and not get the kind of cooperation he will find in one political case. This means that in preparing a political case for trial, the lawyer, although he has many places to go and many people to see, can move among people like a fish in water.[2] The prosecution cannot.

In assessing his own trial preparations, the lawyer should decide early (and continually assess) whether the situation is such that the defense has the advantage of a more dynamic and faster built case, and when he is satisfied that he does enjoy this advantage, he should place considerable reliance on exploiting it, rather than indulging in a pedestrian and somewhat mindless pursuit of a perfect check list. Similarly, the lawyer should view deadlines, particularly pre-trial conferences and trial dates, not as obstacles or sources of menace, but as trial weapons—things which can hurt the prosecution and which can be moved a little bit to hurt them more.

This is not to say that checklists are unimportant, or that things on these lists do not have to be done; they probably do have to be done. But many of the things which have to be done *can* be done in a hurried way or even in a *messy* way, between nine o'clock and midnight on the second day of trial, for example, and where there is pressure, then perhaps that is the way these things *ought* to be done. In order to do things right, the lawyer may have to war against certain professional attitudes, the origins of which are obscure.

One of these handicaps is an idealized perception of the trial advocate as a waxen figure who is perfectly prepared on every aspect of his case before it even has a chance to start, and who, presumably, has nothing to do thereafter except act his role. That is said not to be the best way on the stage, and it is certainly not the best way in court. Another unfortunate professional tendency is the wish to stand one step removed from the client in the case, doing things not for the ends which are sought but to avoid criticism for not having done them. The greater the fear of criticism, the longer the pedestrian march toward a sterile and irrelevant trial.

If trial preparation should be thought of as some kind of race, counsel should remember that the rules are different. It is not the first to finish who gets the trophy. *The secret rule is, if the loser finishes the race at all, the race is cancelled.* That means that something must be done by the winner immediately upon crossing the finish line which will prevent the arrival of the loser. What will effectively prevent the prosecution from crossing the finish line is to build the defense case as strong as possible and faster than the prosecution build theirs, and then to make the case come to trial just *before* the defense preparations have peaked. This will mean that certain trial preparations must go forward after the case has entered trial. This overlap of the trial and preparations will be hard on the defense, but if things go well, it will be impossible for the prosecution.

Of course it is never wise to assume that the prosecution are incompetent, or to underestimate an opponent. That is not necessary; part of the lawyer's mind can always expect competence from the prosecution. But there are differences in the dynamics of trial preparation, those differences do count for something, and in the long run it is wise to value and even bank on the lawyer's own energy and resourcefulness because these are things which he can to some extent control.

From the beginning to the end of every trial the lawyer should have a notetaker in court. If he has only one secretary, she will be the notetaker, and if he has to close the office while the trial is going on, that should be done. Matters are much easier if he has two secretaries. One will attend in the morning and transcribe her notes in the afternoon while the second is taking notes, and so on.

Since daily transcripts are such a rarity and a luxury in real trials, there is no substitute for notes. The lawyer is not going to get very much in the way of his own notes, unless he is an exceptional advocate. Lawyers who think they can manage alone are simply unacquainted with the difference between their notes and what they could get from a notetaker. The notetaker should be instructed to leave out everything superfluous and almost all comments from the bench, but to get down exactly what the witness says. The important thing here *is not to attempt any kind of verbatim transcription.* That is what court reporters are for and that is why they are months behind. The notetaker should neither interject silly partisan opinions nor decide to leave something out, but should simply put down what was said, leaving out all the pick-and-shovel work of how it was extracted. Four or five questions directed at where a witness was at a certain time can be reduced to one terse sentence in narrative form.

The notes will be meaningless until they are typed. They should be roughly indexed, and the indexes should be brought up to date at least every week.

The purpose of these notes is not only to record

testimony, but also to facilitate finding that testimony in the court reporter's notes. Therefore, every page of transcribed notes should make quite clear the date (and day of the week), whether it was morning or afternoon session, whether before or after a recess, which witness was on the stand, and whether the examination was direct or cross, re-direct or re-cross. These are the terms in which one looks for later testimony if it is imperative to have a verbatim transcript from the court reporter.

If the notetaker recognizes that something is really vital, he should type it in italics. The lawyer should read these notes regularly and make marginal annotations, particularly emphasizing argument points as these begin to emerge.

All of this does not mean the lawyer should not attempt to take notes himself. He certainly should because the notetaker's notes are not going to be typed up until the following day; but it is a great comfort to know while taking scratchy notes that they need only serve for the immediate future, and that one's own notes need only be relied upon to facilitate decisions which are being made right now, with the actual testimony fresh in mind.

It is amazing how many trial lawyers still think they can rely on their own notes. At every trial, much of the important material, which would have helped one side or the other, goes down the tubes simply because the lawyers cannot remember. Judges know because they take notes. But that is their book.

§ 6.03 The Psychology of Small Delays

On the assumption that there is judicial pressure for an immediate trial, the defense lawyer may well need one or two small delays (a week at a time) in order to finish trial preparations. If that is true, he must take care to see that he gets these extensions. The lawyer must provide himself with enough time, whether the presiding judge wishes him to have it or not.

The lawyer should ask for no more time than he really needs, otherwise he will be giving the extra time to the prosecution. Since whatever extension the defense gets will be bought at the price of increased judicial vindictiveness, it would be doubly unfortunate to pay this price in order to confer some undeserved benefit on the prosecutor.

The lawyer should expect that the presiding judge will hear his motion for a continuance on the basis, which the judge will probably not quite come out and state openly, that the judge feels the lawyer is slothful, inattentive, and bent on delaying the case so as to frustrate the ends of justice (a speedy conviction), at the expense of his own client (who apparently has a right to be convicted).[3]

Assisted by these little weather signals from the bench, the prosecutor will need no advice on how to set his sails. He can be relied upon to state quite openly that the defense is dragging its feet, the court has a large backlog of cases, and that the time has long passed when court administrators and taxpayers can be expected to put up with this sort of obstructionism, especially when the courts have gone so far (a reference to a pendulum is usually inserted at this point) in granting rights to defendants. This argument may not be logical, but it seems especially pleasing to prosecutors who may not be very well prepared for trial themselves at that moment. It enables them to cover their own weakness while heaping scorn on the defense, and gives them a feeling something like running a finesse at cards. The lawyer can see this on the face of the prosecutor, and it may be as good a clue as he will get.

Knowing all this is going to happen, the lawyer should see to it that his motion for a continuance complies with the letter of the law and all the rules of court, whether they are being strictly enforced on other people or not.

If a written motion is necessary in order to continue a criminal trial, then the lawyer's motion will be in writing, notwithstanding that it may be customary in this court for such motions to be made orally. If he needs an order shortening time, the lawyer will be well advised to get it, and not rely on the willingness of the prosecutor to ignore the fact that he only had eight days written notice of the motion when the rule requires ten days, even though it may happen that such motions are customarily made and argued without any notice at all.

The motion should be supported by an affidavit, signed by the lawyer, and it should be a good one. The affidavit should not reveal how much the lawyer is actually doing by way of trial preparation in *this* case. That would tend to spoil the purpose of the continuance. Rather the affidavit should dwell on the reasons why the lawyer needs more time to prepare for trial. There will be no difficulty about this, because the lawyer *does* need more time. A favorite subject for such affidavits is the lawyer's current work load, meaning cases other than this one in which he is now involved or has been involved since this case came on for arraignment, with particular stress on criminal cases as opposed to civil. Other points to be mentioned are as follows: (1) the lawyer has encountered obstructionism in *this* criminal case, such as the necessity to make a discovery motion (the lawyer would have made it in any case, there is always a necessity); (2) the fact that the prosecution have dragged their feet in complying with a discovery order; and (3) the fact (very common) that the prosecution have only partly complied with a discovery order and have promised or otherwise delayed compliance with respect to several particular things that they are required to do (see § 4.07).

There are always reasons for a necessary delay, and a number of them can usually be laid at the feet of the prosecution. They should be laid there in strong language and very plain English, in this affidavit. This kind of affidavit should contain an absolute minimum of legal expressions. The draftsman should favor short words and tough sentences, with names and dates. In the weather cycle of judicial abuse, this motion will provoke only a summer shower; even so, it is no time to be mealymouthed.

Unless the jurisdiction is one which provides for last minute pre-trial conferences, or other similar trip-wire occasions designed to set off motions for a continuance, a court may indulge in the archaic expectation that counsel set these motions for hearing on the same day the case is set for trial. The defense lawyer in that situation will feel the strain more than the prosecutor because the prosecutor is in the position of being able to consent to the motion openly if he chooses. Therefore, if it is possible to calendar a motion for a continuance on any date earlier than the trial date, that is the way it should be done. But in any event, the lawyer should bear in mind that the correct attitude for him is to do little or nothing to dispel the impression that he is (at least to some extent) stumbling along like an animal on the highway of justice, obstructing through traffic. He cannot persuade the judge otherwise in any case, and in fact that impression works as much in the lawyer's favor as against him. A judge's dislike for any lawyer is always tempered with a judicial theory that "lawyers will be lawyers," meaning, in a vein of judicial self-pity, "what can you do with them?" Judges can see the promised land, but they can do just so much to lead the peoples. Furthermore, the prosecutor may succeed in talking himself into a belief that the defense is afraid to try the case, that it has no particular case at all, and that it just does not want to face up to reality. The result will probably be that the motion for a continuance will be granted once or even twice. Everything that happens at the first motion will be aggravated at the second.

The desirable states of mind after the granting of

the defendant's motion to continue the trial date are something like the following: the judge should feel that he had little or no choice but to grant the motion—after all it was in order (but just wait until next time!). The prosecutor should feel that the defense, as in so many other cases, is simply stumbling around, and he should be glad of an opportunity to get back to doing those things which he has been doing instead of preparing this case for trial. The lawyer should be glad that he made it and aware that he has just enough time to complete his preparations as the trial begins, provided that he works on it full bore.

When the case does come up for trial, the absence of another defense motion for a continuance makes a point which could not have been made orally at the prior hearings. The lawyers simply answers, "Ready for the defendant," and looks at his watch. If it is necessary to say anything, the lawyer need only add that this is the date and hour reserved for the trial, that the defendant has a constitutional right to a speedy trial, that he is ready for trial, and that he has not been served with any written motion from the prosecution asking for a continuance. The prosecutor in this situation may have misled himself as to the likelihood of another continuance. The lawyer, needless to say, will not have made any representation that there would be another such motion. The result will probably be—no matter what the prosecutor thinks about it—that the case will be sent to a trial department for immediate trial.

§ 6.04 How the Lawyer Beset by a Hostile Presiding Judge May Occasionally Use a Pre-trial Conference to Destroy Two or More Cases

[1] A Word on the Limitations of this Section

What follows is offered for possible use in some variation or other, in what are sometimes called the lower courts, or more accurately, the cockpits. These are courts in which misdemeanors are tried—and in some jurisdictions only low-grade misdemeanors; they are not courts of general trial jurisdiction. They do not try felony cases. They arraign a lot of drunks on every Monday's calendar and, while their judges labor under difficulty and may do their very best to engender respect for the law and legal procedures, a broad stream of chaotic facts continually works against them. Once in a while one of them will give up the effort to look good, in favor of survival. Having shucked the impediments of pride for the balance of his time on the bench, such a judge will call to mind nothing so much as a man in the rapids, stretched by the current and hanging on to a muddy limb. He is a political judge, who can only handle his case load on the basis of ruling according to innate bias.

Every one who works in these courts feels the pressure of standing waist deep in that cold river. The law may be the law, but personalities matter a lot in these courts— more than in other courts; as it works out, whoever counts too heavily on what the law says may find himself getting edged and jostled into deeper water.

Attorneys who spend a greater proportion of their time in the lower courts than do others who practice there (nobody gets completely away from there) are the ones who impose their current values on day to day dealings. These values sometimes stress rather direct matters; these are expressed in terms of hitting hard, but what they mean is, hit first. Conduct in the cockpits is different from conduct in other courts, and seasoned lawyers are obliged to adapt to their surroundings, like it or not (in other words, revert to primitivism), rather than spend their whole professional lives taking appeals from lower courts.

There is going to be some kind of pre-trial conference in the cockpit. It may be known as a "settlement conference," a "trial setting conference," or some other name. Its central object is to find out what cases can be settled in chambers, and which ones are going to trial. Under crowded calendar conditions (the assumed state of affairs), cases will probably be set for trial in bunches, on a trailing system, even if that is not the ordinary procedure in that particular court.

Because of the closer relationships among judges and lawyers in these courts, and the special role of the ad hominem in their proceedings, what is suggested here is not something that could be reasonably considered under pre-trial procedures in courts of more general jurisdiction, or in most cockpits for that matter, under normal conditions. But we are assuming a backlog of political trials, and blood is up.

[2] The Difficulty with Pre-trial Conferences

The reason present pre-trials are so bad is that most of the lawyers attending are acting out some version of their stuffed-shirt behavior patterns. Defense lawyers tend to be a little shy with judges, at least at close quarters. Once they all sit down in chambers for a conference, judges tend to be paternalistic. Prosecutors spend more time with the judges. Generally they can manage a little bonhomie. All the law-yers present in these surroundings (the book-lined walls, the certificates of military service, the work-piled desk where the judge reaches his difficult decisions, a man alone) are stimulated to be more conscious than they might other-wise be of their status both as officers of the court, and as members of the local bar association. It seems to be a healing time, when a lot of bruises dealt and received outside that room are subtly stroked and soothed.

While all this is going on, what may be thought of as the Steppenwolf aspect of the lawyer's personality, if there is one,[4] is bored out of its mind, and may be conceived of as lying on the floor, eyes closed in what it has come to fear may be terminal ennui, enduring the bad air until the civilized persons finally get through what they are doing and open the door. That is too bad because more can happen at a pre-trial than usually happens, things might involve the lawyer at atavistic levels.

[3] The Common Problem of Multiple Cases for Immediate Trial

Assume that the lawyer has got himself in a bad situation, either because he did not heed the admonition in this book (see § 2.02) against taking on too many political cases at the same time, or because he could not help himself. For example, he may have just completed a trial that lasted ten weeks and was only supposed to last five. If so, his trial calendar may be in a state of extreme distress. Assume he has five or six political cases, all jammed together for immediate trial in the cockpit, some of them already trailing for two or three weeks.

In this situation, the basic assumption of the preceding discussion (that time works in favor of the defense, since the defense can prepare cases faster than the prosecution) is reversed. While the lawyer was living out his ten-week trial, another prosecutor, who was not involved in that trial, had more than enough time to prepare at least one of these cases which are now at the top of the calendar.

Moreover, the lawyer has become identified in the minds of the presiding judge and the prosecutor's office as one of the lawyers defending radicals. The result may be that the presiding judge dislikes not only the defendants, but the lawyer also. It may not always be true, he may get over it later, but that is the way he feels now. It is not uncommon in this situation that the very next case for trial involves a target defendant. That is the reason it *is* the next case.

The prosecutor really has it on for the target defendant, and he has a lot to say about why there should be no further "delays." Of course the prosecutor knows very well that continuances previously granted were mandatory ones, since the lawyer was actually engaged in a jury trial. None of those continuances could therefore be classified as any sort of abuse of the court's patience or its calendar, on the part of the lawyer. Nonetheless the rhetoric sounds good to the prosecutor. It sounds good to the presiding judge, too, because many things that are unfair make good listening.

Assume further that the presiding judge knows very well that the lawyer has not had much time to prepare for trial, but, because of the judge's personal feelings, he intends to throw the lawyer headlong into trial on all of his pending cases, just as fast as he can do it—which happens to be immediately after the next pre-trial conference.

In this situation, the presiding judge's feelings may be strong enough that they will get the better of him, not merely in what he is trying to do but in how he does it. In order to effectuate his anger, the presiding judge will be guided by the suggestions of the prosecutor. After all, if he is going to crowd the defense lawyer, he must do it in the right way.

Assume finally that all of these pending cases will appear for pre-trial at the same time, in the same pre-trial conference, and that this court is one which uses some form of trailing system for trials. In other words, a certain number of cases will be set for trial on *the same day,* to be tried in sequence, one following as soon as the preceding one is finished. That is a trailing system.

When these conditions exist, the lawyer should take steps to set the stage for the pre-trial conference, which will be different from most.

[4] Setting the Stage for the Pre-trial Conference

The lawyer will attempt to get a continuance well before the pre-trial. But his attempt in this instance will be quite different from the one just described (see § 6.03).

In this case, the lawyer is absolutely sure that his continuance will be denied, and, because of his desperate situation, he actually wants it to be denied, but denied only in a certain way. The reason he wants it to be denied is that the motion for a continuance applies only to one case. This is the target case, the one the prosecutor is most hot to try, the one which now is at the top of the pile. Of course the motion could apply to all the pending cases, since the lawyer has had no chance to prepare for any of them. But there is a reason why it only applies to one case.

A second major consideration (besides the fact that this motion is going to be denied) is the universal rule that when a trial judge hears and denies a motion for continuance, no appellate court in the world will disturb his ruling, since it is impossible to persuade an appellate court that a lawyer had a good reason for not being ready when his case was called for trial. To persuade the appellate court to upset the denial of a motion for a continuance, the lawyer would have to produce overwhelming evidence and arguments that the denial was an abuse of discretion so grievous as to require immediate intervention. But since the lawyer is desperate for lack of time, and since efforts by other people to get writs in these situations have uniformly failed, it seems most ill-advised to lavish what little time remains in seeking some appellate writ based on the fact that a formal motion for a continuance was made, argued, and denied by the trial court.

But that is not the only way. The rules are usually quite different if the trial court *refuses to hear the motion at all.* In other words, granted the trial judge will deny the motion, it makes all the difference whether he heard the motion, or refused to hear it. If he heard the motion, his ruling will stand no matter what he does or what his reason. But if he refuses to hear it, that may be something else entirely.

Consequently, knowing what the result will be, the

lawyer should present his motion (1) with a court reporter present, and (2) under circumstances likely to produce an angry outburst from the presiding judge. This is serious business. The lawyer will *not* be able to file a motion in advance, and still get that angry outburst. He will have to select an occasion with some care, and then orally ask leave to make the motion, to file an affidavit and written brief for a continuance, in the hope that what he does will be thrown back at him in great anger. It probably will be.

The lawyer should use the ensuing dialogue to shape this oral ruling to state very clearly that the lawyer wishes to present a motion and to file a supporting affidavit for the purpose of continuing this particular trial (the target defendant's trial) on the ground that he is not ready, that he has good reasons for being unready, and that the court will not let him do these things or listen to anything he has to say. This can be accomplished in a rapid exchange, and once this is done, the lawyer should *shut up*. He should take the first opportunity, within about sixty seconds, to change the subject or, better yet, get out of the courtroom. The refusal to hear the motion is enough. The record should not be trampled upon, nor the court presented with opportunities to reconsider its hasty language.

The next step in setting the stage for pre-trial is to file a petition with the next appellate court for an immediate order prohibiting the trial of this case for a reasonable period of time, e.g., thirty days, on the ground that a motion for a continuance was not heard. Refusal to exercise discretion. If it is necessary to stop trial preparation in order to prepare this petition, then that should be done. The petition for the writ should be prepared fast and filed immediately, and every reasonable supplementary step—including conversations with appropriate clerks in the court where this petition is filed—should be taken with vigor.

The lawyer should satisfy himself that the petition is good, and that the writ stopping the first of the series of trials will probably come down before the trial date. *Then* he is ready to go to pre-trial.

[5] A Sample Solution to the Multiple Case Problem

When this particular pre-trial conference starts, a number of files will be on the judge's desk. Among them will be cases *A, B, C, D,* and *E*—all the cases the lawyer does not want to try. *A* is the one with the target defendant, the one the prosecutor wants most of all, the case he intends to try first.

Once they are all seated in the judge's chambers— lawyers, judge, and clerk—interesting things can happen. For example, the judge may start the proceedings by mentioning that he has a pile of cases on his desk, and is it correct that the lawyer is defending all of them?

The lawyer will certainly agree that he is; and the lawyer may ask, rather casually, whether the prosecutor who is sitting there is prosecuting all of them. That is a perfectly reasonable question. If the answer is not known already, then it is well to ask.

Assume the answer is *yes,* the prosecutor is the same prosecutor assigned to try *A, B, C, D* and *E.* His mind is primarily on *A,* which is the first one up for discussion.

To continue the Steppenwolf analogy a little farther, the lawyer has learned that the prosecutor has been assigned to try *all* of these cases, and has observed that the prosecutor's attention seems primarily engaged by case *A.* The lawyer should resign himself to the fact that this pre-trial is going to be different; and an aspect of his personality that usually has little to say in pre-trial conferences will probably have something to say now. The wolf-half may be thought of as getting up off the carpet to stretch, his yellow eyes being finally wide open. He has begun to appreciate what it is that he will have the privilege of doing. The ensuing dialogue should be somewhat along the following lines.

JUDGE (*Guardedly, holding the file of case A, and looking at the lawyer*): "I suppose you're going to be ready for trial on Monday?"

LAWYER (*Animal half*): "Well, at the moment, it *looks like* there's nothing I can do to avoid it." The purist will not even say, "It *seems* there is nothing I can do to avoid it," because it does not *seem* that way to him. It only *looks* that way to others. The judge may look at the lawyer for a further explanation, but the lawyer simply looks back, smiling. (The wolf part is rather vain about his even teeth.)

It is quite important, of course, that the lawyer do nothing to mislead the court. For example, he must not say "Yes, I will be ready on Monday," or anything like that. They all know his petition for a writ is still pending, and the purpose of the writ is to postpone the trial. But there is no need to talk about that now because the writ is not actually down yet, and because the purpose of a pre-trial conference is to mollify injured feelings. It certainly appears at this point that the judge and the prosecutor have won. The lawyer has reason to think they have not. That is his business. No trial judge ever believes that a writ is going to come down stopping a criminal trial. The rest is simple.

JUDGE (*Magnanimously, holding up file B*): "Well, if you're going to be in trial on this one [case A], I suppose you'll want a new date on these others?" (please note, not new dates).

The implication here is that the judge is, after all, rather a good fellow: now that he's won his point, having set up case A for the prosecutor, he can afford to smooth things over and give the lawyer, say, another week on the other cases. It is absolutely essential not to go along with this.

While this dialogue is unfolding, it may be that

the stuffed-shirt aspect of the lawyer's personality is silently sweating blood, thinking something like, "Jesus Christ, I will never stick my face in this goddamn court again!" What is spoken out loud will be more like this:

LAWYER (*Animal part, very agreeably*): "Actually, I'm just not authorized to waive time on any of those trials . . . it's just that . . . well . . . my clients seem to think I've been *dragging my feet*. Put them down for the same date. Trailing."

JUDGE: "That's the order."

At this point the lawyer (animal-half) fixes the clerk with a long look. This is to be sure that the minutes are being recorded correctly. If there is any doubt about this, the lawyer will ask the clerk later, not now. What he wants to know is, that the minutes say in black and white that case *A* is set for trial on a certain day, and that *B, C, D,* and *E* are set for the same day, in a trailing sequence.

The lawyer continues preparing case *A* until he knows that the writ is coming down. When it does, he will see that it gets served on the trial court and prosecutor. As soon as the writ is served, of course, the trial of case *A* will be frozen. But there is no hurry about this. Without actually suggesting to anyone that the wheels can move a little slower, the lawyer will be very sure that this writ gets served at about five o'clock on the evening preceding the trial date. That is the time it is pushed under the door in the prosecutor's office, and that is the time it is handed to the clerk of the cockpit.

It is even better if it happens by some chance that the trial date is a Monday. The writ can be served on Friday evening, and this way the prosecution technically have three days notice, which really means nothing at all because they rarely work on weekends.

Trial preparations will be radically affected on the defense side. What follows is going to be mostly bluff, but

it cannot be entirely bluff. In this situation, before the writ
was issued, some work was done on case A. As soon as the
writ is issued that work stops. The lawyer then devotes himself to spreading his attention among four cases. Assuming
he has a reason to think that B and C will be the first ones
called, he should prepare himself to handle at least a day and
a half of trial in either case, whichever should be called first,
come what may. As to D and E, it is important that some
work be devoted to them, so that trial could be started on
those also, should the order be jumbled.

It is absolutely essential that while carrying out these
rather desperate preparations, the lawyer should sit down
separately with his clients, A through E, and explain to
each of them what is at stake, what is being risked, and
what may be gained. He should obtain their consent for he
cannot take this on himself.

On the morning of the trial date, the lawyer appears
with his clients, and answers, "Ready for trial," whatever
case is called first. It should be anticipated this will be a
cold morning in court. Case A will not be called because
the writ has finally reached its target. When B is called,
the lawyer's demeanor is one of absolute confidence. After
all, the prosecution put it on first, and in any event, the
lawyer is ready for a day and a half. That is probably more
than the prosecution are ready for. Police officers in political
cases may be willing to testify, but it is often true they come
from scattered locations. No matter how willing they are,
they cannot appear by magic. Often they are out of touch
with their home stations, they may be on a holiday, or in
any case, they may be living in some other city. There will
be a jury panel waiting, and the prosecutor will have to say
he is ready to go or he is not. It is quite likely that he will
not be, and this likelihood is greatly increased because the
court is a lower court, so that the normal expectation for
time spent picking a jury is short. The result will probably

be that the prosecutor, having answered, "Ready," at pre-trial conference, must confess to the court that he is not ready at all.

The court will be disgusted, but not in a position to take its anger out on the defense lawyer. The result will be a dismissal, voluntary or otherwise. As soon as this occurs, the next case in order is C. It is less likely that C will be ready. C will be dismissed, with even less arguing. Then the tempo will increase, so that D and E are dismissed almost before they are called.

When the foregoing solution works, it works drama-tically. It is not at all unlikely that three to five cases may suddenly disappear from the court's calendar in the space of an hour. It is assumed that in this jurisdiction, a misde-meanor, once dismissed, may not be filed again.[5] These dis-missals will then be as good as acquittals.

The lawyer should send each successive client out of the building and home, as fast as possible. As soon as he is done with what he is doing, he also should get out of the building and go somewhere else, preferably far from a tele-phone. This is to prevent any last-minute change of heart, some claim that witnesses can, indeed, be found after all, that this case or that one was not really dismissed, that its dismissal is not entered yet, or some other chaotic thing that might emerge from the cockpit. The important thing is to walk out the door and not look back.

Of course, sooner or later case A is going to come up on the calendar again, the only survivor of the original five. *The lawyer had better be ready for trial.* And if this happens to be his first appearance in the same court after his great adventure on the trial date, then he can expect some judicial unpleasantness concerning his role in what happened.

The lawyer should say as little as possible. While this gale is blowing, his general position should be some-thing like this: "I am sorry you feel that way. I am an innocent man. The record will substantiate that I misled nobody. And I do not think it would be very fruitful for me to review the matter here."

Footnotes

[1] See, e.g., Ariz. Rev. Stat. Ann. Rules of Criminal Procedure, Rules 236, 238 (1973); Cal. Penal Code §§ 1050, 1382 (West 1970); Fla. Stat. Ann. Rules of Criminal Procedure, Rule 3.191 (Supp. 1973); Ga. Code Ann. §§ 27–1901, 27–1901.2, 27–1902 (1972); Idaho Code § 19–3501 (1948); Ill. Rev. Stat. ch. 38, § 103–5 (1971); Ind. Rules of Crim. Proc., Rule 4 (Ind. Ann. Stat. (Burns 1973)); Minn. Stat. Ann. § 611.04 (1964); N.Y. Crim. Proc. Law § 30.30 (McKinney 1971); Ohio Rev. Code Ann. § 2945.71 (Page 1954); Okla. Stat. Ann. tit. 22, § 812 (1969); Va. Code Ann. § 19.1–190 (Supp. 1973); Wash. Rev. Code Ann. § 10.46.010 (1961); and W. Va. Code Ann. § 62–3–21 (1966).

[2] "The people are like water and the army is like fish." Mao Tse-Tung, *Aspects of China's Anti-Japanese Struggle* (1948).

When things are going really well, the lawyer may feel like a whole school of fish.

[3] "Conviction delayed is conviction denied." My wife's annotation.

[4] There should be one in there somewhere, if Hesse's onion view of personality is correct. H. Hesse, *Steppenwolf* (B. Creighton trans., J. Mileck and H. Frenz rev. 1936) "Treatise on the Steppenwolf," 46–75, at 69.

[5] E.g., Cal. Penal Code § 1387 (West 1970); N.Y. Crim. Proc. Law § 210.20(4) (McKinney 1971); see, also, Ariz. Rev. Stat. Ann. Rules of Criminal Procedure, Rule 238 (1973); Fla. Stat. Ann. Rules of Criminal Procedure, Rule 3.191(h)(1) (Supp. 1973); Ga. Code Ann. §§ 27–191, 27–1901.2 (1972); Ill. Rev. Stat. ch. 38, § 103–5(e) (1971); Wash. Rev. Code Ann. § 10.43.010 (1961); and W. Va. Code Ann. § 62–3–21 (1966).

Chapter 7

SECOND-ROUND (EXTENSIVE) DISCOVERY OF PROSECUTION EVIDENCE

SYNOPSIS

---

§ 7.01 The Second or Third (Nth) Discovery Motion

[1] Pragmatic Reasons Why Repetitive Discovery Motions Are Better Than a Running Motion

The advantages of a repetitive discovery motion, as opposed to a running motion, are very apparent in the give and take of trial. Theoretically it might seem to be that things ought to be the other way around. Of course, "repetitive motion" means a series of two or more discovery motions which are made and argued (if the jurisdiction is one which still requires argument on this kind of motion) successively, at different stages of the case. Ideally, the last one should be heard immediately before trial and should require compliance no later than the day before trial.

A running motion is a discovery motion which is made, argued and ordered only once, and which by the terms of the order requires the prosecution to supply everything in certain blanket categories, making the evidence available to the defense from time to time as it becomes available to the prosecution, without the necessity of any further order.[1]

Many lawyers would instinctively prefer the running motion, not only because of reasons of economy (it only has to be argued once), but because it seems to meet a professional yearning for reform. According to this view, the prosecution are obliged to provide certain things for the benefit of the defense, and that being so, why should the defense even have to make a motion for discovery? One motion is bad enough; anything beyond that affronts the sense of procedural justice. That may be, but defense discovery is really not that strong a plant. It is, more often than not, the product of court decisions and not statutes. And everything that is added to the scope of defense discovery brings with it more strident demands that the defense be required to turn its pockets inside-out for the prosecution, a totally unacceptable price.

Until the defendant's right to discovery is embodied in statutes—with large teeth in them sufficient to make the prosecution honest, and so that the defendant's right to discover may be said to have reached a level of public acceptance requiring it to be taken seriously by every district attorney—defense lawyers should remember that their right to discovery actually lies in a gray area of the law. It is enough to get the courts to grant a discovery order; but they are probably not going to enforce the order. Enforcement will be the lawyer's biggest difficulty.

Most trial court judges will probably refuse to grant

a running discovery order. More importantly, when asked to make one of these orders, they will experience a strong revulsion to the whole idea of discovery. This cuts entirely too close to the adversary system; i.e., if the prosecutor is required to produce things as fast as he gets them, that means to a large extent he is working on behalf of the defendant. This is thought to be intolerable. For that reason, the lawyer should not be too clever while arguing for the first, second, or fifth discovery motion. In other words, he should not brightly point out to the judge that he is accomplishing the same result as if he had a running discovery order, by means of repetitive intermittent motions. Actually, the repetitive motions are not that difficult for the lawyer. He can mimeograph parts of them, so as to reduce the drain on his own office staff (and increase the work load of the court's, geometrically). It would be boundless stupidity to point out how close these motions are to a running motion, in view of the judicial dislike of the latter, for the simple reason that if an antagonistic judge thinks about it, he may not grant any further discovery motions at all. Easier to file ten discovery motions than to get one writ.

The main advantage of successive motions is simply that they make it much more difficult for the prosecutor to evade the operation of the first motion. If the first motion happens to be a running discovery motion, the prosecutor will know very well that it will not be enforced according to its terms. If he complies with it at all—always doubtful— he will arrange to do so with a great flourish, in the presence of the jury, after the trial has started. At that point, about ninety percent of the value of the evidence has evaporated.

Furthermore, because he will have arranged *not* to have any office records reflecting the date that he received the items of evidence which he makes available to the defense after the trial starts, it will be very difficult to show bad faith on the part of the prosecutor. This is cheating, and the way to prevent it is to subject the prosecutor to several previous trip-wire experiences.

These experiences will be successive discovery orders, and, since each order will be directed to the prosecution, and will state with great clarity that as of a particular date, the prosecution are required to produce certain things which they have in their possession at that time, it will be impossible for them to continue cheating with a clear mind. Moreover, they will quite sensibly understand that when these orders are made, some gesture of compliance must be made for each order.

This need for gestures means that some evidence will be produced each time a discovery order is signed. It will become extremely hard for the prosecutor to hold things back when he has to remember that each and every thing he produces on one of these occasions may contain cross-references or reflections of something else which he is holding back. The successive orders show that the defense lawyer means it, while the steady accretion of orders makes for a show of judicial purpose which even a judge will have to respect. Furthermore, getting evidence in a steady stream enables the defense to structure its own records and cross-references so that when something late *is* received at the time of trial the defense lawyer can immediately compare it to the whole body of evidence which he has previously received and know whether or not cheating has occurred. This is true because his index will reflect the date of everything received from each source.

[2] Automatic Advantages Arising from Mere Repetition

As previously noted, the prosecution will probably receive the bulk of discoverable police reports, summaries, photographs, and other things of interest *after* complying with the first discovery order. To some extent this is natural.

It takes time for them to locate all the photographs which they will use, to find informers, and to summon witnesses, show photographs to witnesses, and prepare reports showing identifications made by witnesses. Chemical analyses and fingerprint reports always take time, and such things are not normally receivable until some time after the date when an early discovery order should have been made. In addition, however, the prosecution may have arranged to evade the effect of the first order, without actually disobeying its terms, by *not* having certain things in their possession at the time of the order. In other words, having acquired access to certain things in private hands, e.g., television station videotapes, the prosecution may have borrowed and returned those things prior to the discovery order. These items are disqualified from discovery, since the prosecution could argue that they did not have possession or control of the things at the time the order became effective.

By the time of the second or third discover order, however, many of these things will have actually been received. Things not actually received will have been mentioned in reports, and one way or another the defense will have found out about videotapes and things which had been available to the prosecution, even though not possessed by the prosecution. Furthermore, special things such as wire taps may show up directly or indirectly, as may detective reports and "intelligence" summaries received by the prosecution from other agencies. All of these things will be picked up by successive discovery orders.

[3] Evidence Peculiarly Susceptible to the Second or Third Discovery Motions

By the time of the second or third motions, the defense should know the identities of main prosecution witnesses. Informers are of intense interest. If the prosecution case turns on the work of some volunteer citizen or part-time undercover agent, not previously known to the defense, that fact will certainly become apparent after the defense has digested the results of the first discovery order. The whole case may turn on successful impeachment of such a witness. Special efforts are needed.

The most important question about a witness of this kind concerns his criminal record. The defense is entitled to know if he has a rap sheet and what it shows. The defense must be informed of every arrest and conviction sustained by such a witness. The prosecution has this available through its teletype. And, although the trial judge would probably have been reluctant to make a blanket order at the time of the first discovery motion, requiring the prosecution to supply rap sheets of every person claiming to have knowledge of any fact in the case, the situation is very different at a later stage.

Half-way through trial preparation, the defense can point to existing police reports which show that the testimony of certain persons will be highly material, and of much greater importance than the possible testimony of many others. As to these people, the lawyer can readily draft a paragraph or two for his own supporting affidavit, showing the ability of the prosecution to get rap sheets, his own inability, and the materiality of the testimony of these witnesses. Therefore, any discovery motion but the first one can and should contain demands for information concerning arrests and convictions of all prosecution witnesses other than those obviously unimportant (for a suggested form of second discovery motion, see Appendix C).

The other great benefit of later motions is that by the time they are made, it may become apparent that other law enforcement agencies, besides the ones previously known, have been involved in the case. Because these agencies were not known before, they were probably not served with copies of the original discovery order. They are known now, however, and they should certainly be served with copies of this order and later ones.

[4] Form and Content of Repetitive Discovery Motions

Any discovery motion after the first one should repeat the same broad demands for generally described items; every single thing described in the first motion should be described in all the others. The only difference is the date of compliance. Like the original motion, each successive motion has an early date perferably described as a date within forty-eight hours after the making of the discovery order, at which time the prosecution are required to comply with everything contained in the order. It should be noted carefully that the second motion aims at items in the possession or subject to the control of the prosecution, other than those previously made available to the defense, *not* merely to those received by the prosecution since the earlier order. The second order should cover everything received to date and not already produced. In other words, if the prosecution have been holding back, not delivering something which they should have delivered at the time of the first order, that refusal should violate both orders, the second order being not limited to things recently received. This arrangement might be helpful if it comes to a showdown, since the prosecution will have been placed on notice every time an order was made, that its entire file was subject to review for the purpose of complying with each order.

Successive motions should aways demand arrest and conviction records of prosecution witnesses, based on a specification of the supporting affidavit showing why those things are necessary.

Like the previous orders, repetitive orders should be served on all agencies and all officers then known to have been involved in the case. That is of course a lot of process serving. But then this is a criminal case, and service of process is gratis.

§ 7.02   Other Forms of Extensive Discovery Not Involving Discovery Motions

Once into a political case, the lawyer should make careful private inquiries as to the existence of other criminal cases of a political nature which involve the same officers (especially arresting officers) or the same lay witnesses. He should make inquiries among lawyer friends, among his client's friends, in the clerk's office, through ad hoc citizens' committees which may be serving as a clearing house for information, through underground newspapers and student radio, and through other "friendly contacts:" this means officers who are known to be friendly and who will probably have to be contacted through intermediaries.

When other similar political cases are found, the lawyer should follow through by asking the defendants and the lawyers in those cases to be sure and get police reports. He should then ask to be allowed to read these police reports, whatever the disposition of the other cases. These reports, where relevant, should be copied, indexed, and placed in the lawyer's file.

Of equal importance, the lawyer should make it a point to get copies of transcripts of grand jury hearings or preliminary hearings in these other cases in which the same witnesses testified who will testify in his case. These should be extensively compared to each other and to similar testimony in the lawyer's own case, and cross-indexed (see § 14.1[2]) for means of impeachment.

If testimony comes to the lawyer's attention which would be valuable in his own case, but it happens that such testimony was not reported by a court reporter, the lawyer should take the time to locate one or two good witnesses to that testimony. One of them will probably be the defense lawyer in that case. The other should be the judge presiding at the time the testimony was given, assuming he can remember what was said.

The lawyer should especially look for (in a demonstration case) testimony which shows the officer claims to have been in two, three, or five places at about the same time, some of them being rather distant from the others. This situation is common in demonstration cases. It is common because officers arrest people first and pass them along, and then decide later who is going to sign as arresting officer and what the charges are thought to be. The lawyer will be looking for this pattern as well as anything else grossly inconsistent with anticipated testimony in his own case.

Once these things have been sifted and important evidence found, the lawyer should of course keep it secret. He should then take the trouble to cross-reference his own notes on the particular witnesses to be impeached by this evidence to show what the evidence says, where it is in the file (its number, etc.), and how it is to be used. When a large amount of impeaching material accumulates, control over the evidence is critical.

Finally, when impeaching material has been found which relates to another case, the lawyer should find the time well in advance of the trial (there will not be enough time during trial) to prepare *and lay aside* necessary subpoenas. If a police report in another case is needed in order to impeach an officer, or the court reporter's notes in another case are needed for that purpose, but have not been typed up, or if the court's own file in a related case will have to be produced, then the necessary subpoenas and subpoenas duces tecum should be prepared in advance. But in order to preserve secrecy, they should not be served at this time. To file an affidavit supporting the subpoena duces tecum would be to let the cat out of the bag.

These subpoenas may or may not be necessary at the

time of trial, but if they are, they should not be served until after the officer has testified in the other trial who is to be impeached in this one.

Footnote

[1] The running discovery order is well established in federal criminal cases. See, Fed. R. Crim. R. 16(g).

Chapter 8

PREPARATION OF PROPOSED
JURY INSTRUCTIONS

SYNOPSIS

§ 8.01 The Need to Prepare Instructions Early

For reasons discussed later (see § 12.01) it is imperative to have a set of proposed defense jury instructions in hand so that they can be submitted to the trial judge no later than the time required by the local rules of court, and in any event before opening statements. More importantly, preparing jury instructions brings the legal issues into sharp focus. The lawyer should have it fresh in his mind what it is he is trying to prove before he briefs his witnesses.

§ 8.02 Why the Preparation of Defense Instructions Should Be Regarded as an Ongoing Process

Defense instructions should be regarded as a kind of stew which is important to have on the fire. Things can be added from time to time, and it is always available for serving. Before the trial, the lawyer discusses its ingredients with his friends, passes around samples, adds things perhaps at their suggestion, and generally nourishes himself (and indirectly, his witness) from the hotch pot. When the trial begins, he uses the stew to great advantage to inform the judge what he is going to be doing before he starts doing it.

Jury instructions should always be regarded as an ongoing thing, of which there is always one completed sample, capable of immediate filing and use if nothing better can be written. But these instructions are never quite the apotheosis of the defense case. Probably no jury instructions are going to be that good; they should be looked to for nourishment, not perfection. Because of their imperfections, the critical jury instructions (those proposed specifically for this case) should be regarded as draft, even after they are filed with the court.

The reasons are simple: the law regarding political crimes will be changing, especially during times of political trials; to regard the rules as static is to misunderstand them. Furthermore, as all trial judges and lawyers know, trials produce factual surprises. The case is rare in which a few more instructions should not be requested immediately prior to jury argument. The lawyer should plan to do this himself and expect the other side to do the same.

The only way he can have the necessary feel for both the instructions and the continual fight over which instructions will be given and which not—a fight which may go on intermittently in the judge's chambers even after final argument (see § 16.01[3])—is to regard the instructions not only as malleable, but as susceptible of improvement and vulnerable to loss. Instructions are not fixed until a legal verdict is in.

§ 8.03 General Description of Contents of Defense Jury Instructions

First off, there are going to be the standard items for inclusion, those instructions which the lawyer knows and loves, the ones that pertain to criminal trials and crime in general, the ones which he habitually includes in every criminal case which he defends. Everybody has a list, which makes it easy to start the job. These basic instructions are grizzled friends, analogous to the garrison of a border town, and one of the most notable things about them is the speed with which they put themselves together; they will form up before the whistle stops blowing, and if the mind is an observer standing apart in pre-dawn darkness, it is comforting to hear the small scrape of steel butt-plates on the cobblestones. These instructions are the friends of a hundred close moments. The lawyer has quoted them to juries many times before. But they will not be enough, by themselves. They must be reinforced by authorities specifically invoked to deal with particular charges in this case.

It should not be necessary to draw an open-sided polygon in the dust, or mutter a prayer backwards. But at the very least somebody is going to have to spend some hours in the law library and reach out his hand for his dictating equipment. These modest efforts merit some attention.

The challenge to draftsmanship comes not in the instructions relating to criminal trials nor to crime in general (the old friends mentioned above), but in those which will stand toe to toe with the political crimes laid against this defendant. Opportunities will vary with the type of political charge.

If the political crime happens to be a low grade misdemeanor or local ordinance, e.g., unlawful assembly, failure to disburse, or violation of curfew, there may be few reported decisions in that jurisdiction interpreting the statute, and no form-book instructions for a jury. Curfew especially is apt to be imposed by a county ordinance, a local administrative order, or possibly by some edict under martial law.

Prosecution instructions requested under this type of ordinance or edict will probably be very simple and misleading. Their instructions will always include one in which the judge reads the edict to the jury, and says that anybody who violates this edict is guilty of a crime. The defense needs an instruction to wipe out this bad impression.

The method here is simply to examine the ordinance which the defendant is supposed to have violated, and break it down into component elements. The defense should normally offer one instruction which points out that in order for a violation of this ordinance to occur, the prosecution must prove each and every element beyond a reasonable doubt and to a moral certainty, and that the elements of this particular offense are one, two, three. This instruction should be followed by a supplemental instruction (intended to be read immediately after the first one) which advises the jury that if such and such a state of facts existed (these being the facts on which the defense is actually based) then the defendant is entitled to an acquittal of this charge.

This type of instruction is sometimes known as a "formula" instruction. But when the judge refers to an instruction by that name, it means he is going to refuse it. Formula instruction is a pejorative. Therefore the lawyer should stop a little short, in drafting the instruction, of writing a real formula instruction. The way to do it right is to leave out all the silly detail, but make the instruction turn on a relatively general description of what it is the defendant hopes to prove. This somewhat divorces the instruction from the recognizable testimony of this witness or that one and seems to impart to the instruction a legal nature (good) as opposed to a factual one (bad). (Examples are to be found in Appendix D.)

Assuming that the political charge is an ordinary felony or felony-misdemeanor of the type commonly used by police to cover up police misconduct, e.g., "resisting arrest," the problem must be solved in substantially the same way. But there is one difference. The difference is that there may be form-book instructions available to the trial court (because of the more serious nature of the crime), and, in a jurisdiction where this charge has been used as a cover charge in so many cases that some of them have already reached appellate courts, and where form-book writers are especially sensitive to the trends of decisions, there just *may* be a form-book instruction which hints that the defendant has certain rights in this situation.

The presence of the form-book instruction means that the lawyer must bracket this charge with approximately three requested instructions. The first two will be exactly as described above: a defense instruction which breaks the charge down by elements and reminds the jury that the people must prove each and every one (not all of them, but each) beyond a reasonable doubt; and one which subtly states the defense involved and tells the jury that if it is proved the defendant is entitled to an acquittal. *Defense instructions are of course requested in writing. These two instructions must be indicated as first choice instructions because they will be better than the one that comes out of the form book. The way to do this is to request the form-book instruction, assuming it somewhat favors the defense, as a second choice instruction, marking it with an asterisk and indicating that this (form-book) instruction is requested as an alternative to be given only if the court refuses to give both of the other two.* This designation is absolutely essential to preserve the point on appeal; since three instructions are requested on the same point, and one of them (the form book one, which is the least desirable) is approximately equal in breadth to the other two, an appellate court would be very quick to say that the trial judge was within his rights in picking that one, the others being merely redundant, and that the lawyer waived his objection on appeal by not designating a first choice. First and second choices should always be clearly labelled.

Another form of drafting opportunity occurs where the defense against the political charge is basically an orthodox defense, but because of outrageous police or governmental conduct, the defense itself must be stretched beyond existing legal boundaries in order to mean anything. The only example that comes to mind is entrapment. (A unique and successful example of this form of instruction is to be found in Appendix D.) This kind of instruction is one which, if it were denied and the defense lost, might eventually find its way into an appellate opinion, and if the appellate court actually adopted it, would make a drastic change in existing law. On the other hand, if given in the trial court, it will probably result in an acquittal (as did the one quoted in Appendix D), and in that case, there being no appeals from acquittals, defense lawyers simply have to find these forms where they may, and remember where they read them.

Another form of drafting opportunity arises where the political crime (rather than the defense to it) entails a stretching of existing rules, e.g., the defendant is being prosecuted for theft, when what they really mean is "theft of government secrets," thus extending the statute to cover something it was never intended to proscribe. Drafting defense instructions in this situation is both a great challenge and a great opportunity for the defense lawyer. (Examples of such instructions prepared, but not given, are included in Appendix D).

Particularly with respect to problems of the types just mentioned (where the defense or the accusation requires some stretching of the law) careful research will usually show that the law is in a state of wild flux, well frothed with dicta and holdings. This is a situation that contains large opportunities for green-water draftsmanship.

There is absolutely nothing to be lost by asking for favorable jury instructions. This is a line of communication direct from the lawyer to the judge. The jury never hears about it, and so if the judge rules against the lawyer, denying some of his requested instructions (and thus setting up an appeal), that denial has cost the lawyer nothing with the jury. That is true of very few other confrontations with trial judges, and the lawyer should make the most of it.

§ 8.04 A Suggested Method of Drafting Instructions

The usual starting points are the particular statutes the defendant is supposed to have violated. The lawyer should unfailingly review the cases construing these statutes for about the last year, even though it may happen that he is generally familiar with them. He should pay special attention to recent decisions which have not yet found their way into the permanent volumes of the reports.

While reading, the lawyer should ask himself if it is *right* (not "reasonable") for this statute to be interpreted and enforced as the prosecution seek to do in his own case. When standard form books are available which are indexed to criminal statutes, the lawyer can glance at the currently accepted instructions on these statutes. But he should not dwell on them. What he should do next is simply draft instructions as he thinks they ought to be given in this case. The first draft of anything like this should be done as carefully as possible, as if that might actually be the thing submitted to the court, since bad drafts are especially difficult to work from when doing jury instructions.

Then, with draft in hand, the lawyer can start the familiar process of looking for the best authority to support the draft, and in view of whatever constitutes best authority, he should make some adjustments.

The cases considered will of course be those of his own jurisdiction in the first instance, but jurisdictions vary widely in the speed with which they loosen up the statutes commonly involved in political trials. This is because more political trials happen in one place than in another.

In many states, it may happen that nothing extraordinary has been decided under a particular statute for one hundred years. The lawyer should think where the cases *are* going down which will draw this *kind* of statute into litigation, and enlarge his research accordingly.

Finally, while doing this reading and while redrafting his instructions, the lawyer should check with friends who happen to be defending the same kinds of political cases. Jury instructions (and supporting authorities) should be swapped and circulated, since anything that helps one helps all. If the lawyer feels he has no friends currently engaged in this line of work, then it is a good idea to start making friends by telephone with people who are; if there is a public defender in the community it should be a true fact that the lawyer has an institutional friend there. The public defender should be defending some of these political trials. Allies are where allies are found, and this is an excellent time to find them.

§ 8.05 A Note on the Form in Which Handtooled Instructions Should Be Presented

Every handtooled instruction which is offered to a trial judge ought to be supported by the best authority the lawyer can muster, as if there were no court of appeal. The need for brevity in trial courts eliminates that portion of the brief which lies between the citations. In other words, on the face of every instruction requested by the defense, there should appear a strict list of authorities directly in support of that instruction. But no argument, no explanation. The only ornamentation allowed is that the order of cases be strictly construed by accepted standards of scholarship, notwithstanding the judge's and the lawyer's own level of attainment and the time available.

When constitutional provisions are invoked (which they had better be, should an appeal be necessary) then both federal and state constitutions should be cited with particularity. All statutes whose sections are subject to constitutional attack by reason of a possible adverse ruling on the jury instructions should be cited and noted as unconstitutional to the extent they would preclude the requested instruction; all cases should be correctly identified as directly supporting, supporting by analogy, supporting the general proposition, contra or whatever, using the familiar signal citations commonly accepted for that purpose.[1]

When cases are cited, of course the particular page on which that holding occurs should be mentioned. When time permits at all, both official and unofficial reporters should always be cited, even in cases where the lawyer is sufficiently familiar with the judge's library to know that only one and not the other lies within the reach of his hand. This also means, particular page references to both reports, not just the official one. These small details do take time and in the press of exigency may seem less than worthwhile, but they have their place.

In trial courts these things are matters of taste, and in appellate briefs they are necessary ornamentation, but they have a way of stopping the trial judge's (or any other legal reader's) attention just when it is about to fly off on some cheap, easy, and habitual tangent of reasoning. To use them is to meet the trial judge on his best level, or where he ought to be. Failure to use them is to patronize him, no matter what his scholarly attainments. There seems to be no middle ground.

Footnote

[1] *A Uniform System of Citation* (11th ed. 1967) (a/k/a The Harvard Blue Book) is not actually harmful to health, although some feel further research is needed before repealing the statutes preventing its general use in the profession.

Chapter 9

FINAL PREPARATION OF
DEFENSE WITNESSES

SYNOPSIS

§ 9.01   Importance of Preparing Defense Witnesses

Most of the witnesses called by the defense lawyer will be friendly witnesses. By "friendly" witnesses, we mean the ordinary usage of that word. There may be other witnesses known to be hostile, a custodian of police records for example, to whom the lawyer will necessarily send a subpoena, and whom he will meet for the first time in court. These witnesses are not on the same side as the lawyer and have no interest in discussing the case with him before they appear in response to the subpoena. Nothing that is said in this section concerns hostile witnesses.

Friendly witnesses are the sum and substance of the defense case. Preparing them to testify is so important that there is no question that the lawyer will do this himself even though the friendly witnesses were originally contacted by an investigator or an associate. The lawyer should remember that preparation of these witnesses is so important that it ranks with jury selection and final argument—things that really cannot be compared with each other and each of which, mysteriously, always seems to be more than half the case.

§ 9.02   Purpose of Preparing Defense Witnesses

The purpose of *preparing* friendly witnesses is to prepare them for direct and cross-examination and to establish rapport with them. The purpose is *not to interview them together,* since they will have already been interviewed separately before this conference, and will be interviewed separately afterward.

§ 9.03   Setting up Conferences

The best time to brief witnesses is about a week or ten days before trial. They can, of course, be briefed at any time before they testify, but a very important part of the process is allowing the witnesses time to think over what has been discussed so that they can reorganize it in their own minds. Since much of what they are told concerns their role as witnesses, they urgently need opportunities to review their testimony in their own minds, including probable lines of cross-examination in the light of their newly recognized relation to the jury. This means time to sleep on it, and a minimum of two to three days seems to be essential.

The briefing will have some beneficial effect for a long time, but some of its benefit is definitely lost if the interval between briefing and trial is more than about three weeks.

If there are more than six or eight defense witnesses, it will probably be necessary to have more than one briefing session. In order to conserve the lawyer's time, it is rather desirable that he explain the procedure to several people at one time, rather than individually. The process will probably take an hour and a half to two hours, in any case, whether there is one listener or many. The group to be briefed at any one time may number from three or four to a dozen or more, the main requirement being that they be able to sit down in a small group so that the lawyer can talk to them all without raising his voice or losing personal contact.

Careful thought should be given to the selection of persons comprising the group. If there are many witnesses in the case, some of them will testify on different subjects. For example, it is *not* a good idea to have all those witnesses present for a single briefing who will testify on a particular point, if it is possible to have a heterogenous group. The reason is, they will all be asked on cross-examination whether they discussed their testimony with anyone. One question will lead to another and they will inevitably be asked about this conference and who else was there.

If it appears that all persons testifying on a particular point, which has hurt the prosecution, were briefed at the same time, the prosecutor will of course suggest and argue to the jury that they all got together and "agreed" on their testimony. This argument can be disarmed in a number of ways, but one of the best will be the simple fact that one or two persons whose testimony hurt the prosecution the most on a particular point were in fact briefed with four or five other people who did not testify on that point at all. Since the lawyer will be organizing these groups himself, he can control the outcome of that line of cross-examination, and he certainly should.

Other considerations in selecting persons to attend are quite simple. If there is a photographer who has taken photographs which are to be kept *secret* (see § 4.05) that photographer should be briefed alone. The reason of course is that if he is briefed with anyone else, it may by some bad chance happen that the other person is forced to reveal on cross-examination, or conceivably is subpoenaed by the prosecution and forced to reveal *as part of the prosecution case*, that he or she was briefed along with a certain photographer who seems to have taken some pictures. The result may be a spoiling attack by the prosecution, spearheaded by a subpoena duces tecum whereby they drag all the photographer's prints into court before the defense case is developed, or (at worst) as part of the prosecution case and before testimony is given by the witness who was to be impeached and surprised by those photographs. Premature discovery of the photographs may impair the lawyer's opportunity to destroy the testimony of some lying prosecution witness who had otherwise been perfectly well set up for impeachment by these photographs. This bad result is far less likely to happen if the photographer witness is briefed privately even though his photographs can and should be shown to all defense witnesses who will testify to events shown in those photographs (see § 9.04).

The client should be absent from all of these briefings. The defendant can add nothing to anything a witness remembers, and in fact, most witnesses will resent his presence. The jury may also resent it when they hear about it.

However, if other persons happen to be present during some part of this briefing, that is no particular concern of the lawyer, provided it is obvious that his friendly witnesses know any other person who happens to be there, so that the group is composed only of friendly persons. After all, nothing that is said here will be privileged and none of it should be hampered by unnecessary secrecy.

The place chosen for a witness briefing is also rather important. The place should be convenient to the witnesses. If most of them are students, it may be that some classroom, lounge, conference room, corner of the student center or academic lawn may be the best place. The house or apartment of any of the witnesses is equally suitable. The main requirements are that the place be quiet and reasonably free from distractions.

The lawyer should remember that rapport is as important as the information which he is to give the witnesses. For that reason it is usually a good idea to avoid holding these meetings in the lawyer's office. The surroundings in a law office only tend to remind the witnesses that the lawyer does other things besides this case, and tend to reinforce and stress differences which the lawyer would prefer to eliminate. These little difficulties will be augmented by others more subtle. The lawyer's office may be something which certain witnesses will have trouble finding. The lawyer will have no control over the arrival time of any witness, but if someone is late in arriving at his office, there may be a feeling that it is the lawyer who is detaining the others while they are waiting for the absent member. This feeling might not arise at all if the same group is seated on the floor in somebody's house.

Also, it is important to the lawyer to know his witnesses and to try to get to know them better. He will get considerable help from the surroundings if he goes where they live, but none if he sticks to his own office.

Finally, nobody is going to wander into the lawyer's office. That may be unfortunate, because persons wandering into witness conferences sometimes turn out to be other witnesses, which happens to be why they "wandered in." They may know still other persons who will not be very far away if the lawyer has gone to where the witnesses are. But if they are all sitting around the lawyer's office, the mention of a new person, who might be a witness, becomes something to do tomorrow.

The time of the meeting is also important. The hour should be at a time when everyone is somewhat relaxed. On weekdays that will probably mean shortly after dinner. Saturday morning is not at all a bad time for witness conferences provided proper allowance is made for when everybody actually gets out of bed (as distinguished from when they say they will). One needs to finish the conference without breaking up anyone's weekend, which probably starts about noon. In any case, the lawyer should take care that his own schedule has left the witness conference open-ended, i.e., with no appointments immediately following.

§ 9.04   What to Bring to Witness Conferences

The lawyer should bring all the photographs which he intends to use in the defense case, including secret photographs. (There is one caveat, however: if this jurisdiction is one which requires the production on cross-examination of any *photograph* used to refresh the witness' memory, in addition to *writings* used for that purpose,[1] then it becomes a very serious question whether to risk premature revelation of the photograph, or to risk having a defense witness seem unfamiliar with it at a vital moment in trial.) The only thing missing with respect to secret photographs will be the photographer. It may well be that even the photographer is known to those present and the lawyer should not make a fetish of not discussing who took the pictures. On the other hand, there is certainly no reason to discuss it unnecessarily. The main consideration here is that a likely question on the cross-examination of these witnesses will be, "Who was there at your witness briefing?", not "Has anybody been telling you the names of other possible witnesses, and if so what did they tell you?"

The reason for bringing all the photographs in the first place is simple: the prosecution will lash out at any photograph which damages them. The only really promising line of attack on a defense photograph—basically an unimpeachable thing—might turn out to be that the photograph *is unfamiliar to defense witnesses*. A prosecution witness caught lying by a defense photograph will of course say the photograph was doctored, but nobody will believe him. If a defense witness says he never saw what is depicted in a defense photograph however, that is something else.

Unless all defense witnesses have had an opportunity to examine photographs relating to things which they had an opportunity to see, in advance, there is a distinct possibility that some witness will panic under the stress of cross-examination and give an incorrect answer. This would certainly be an undeserved break for the prosecution, and is one which the lawyer can preclude. It is more important that all defense witnesses be familiar with defense photographs than to lay undue stress on the need for secrecy.

The lawyer should also bring along a calendar to show what day of the week various things actually happened.

Witness statements and newspaper clippings, however, should be *omitted* (see § 4.03[4]), unless this is a jurisdiction in which it is not required on cross-examination to produce every writing used by a witness to refresh his recollection. Even in those happy jurisdictions the lawyer should always caution a witness examining these things not to reshape his own impressions to match something just because it is in writing. These are aids to memory, nothing more. But like aspirin, they are a welcome palliative for the nervous mind who needs a newspaper clipping to assure that all this did indeed happen on a certain Tuesday.

The lawyer should always bring a subpoena packet for each witness who will attend, and one or two extra packets without names. A subpoena packet consists of an original and one copy of the trial subpoena (completely filled out and issued by the clerk) requiring the attendance of the witness on the first day of trial, plus an original and one copy of an agreement by which the witness agrees to appear upon reasonable notice by telephone at a time other than that specified in the subpoena (see Appendix E for a sample agreement).

Preparation of these papers should be a normal procedure in the lawyer's office; if he keeps an office manual, the preparation of subpoena packets should certainly be part of that manual. In order to avoid needless shuffling of papers when the lawyer has important things to tell witnesses, the subpoena packet should be put together in a rather finicky way: the four pieces of paper related to each witness should be arranged so that the original subpoena and the original agreement are stapled together, and the copy of the subpoena plus the copy of the agreement are stapled together. The two pairs should be marked in some obvious way, such as by attaching a small piece of colored tape to each pair, say red tape to designate the originals and green for the copies. The two pairs can then be put together with a paperclip.

The point of doing it this way is simply that when the lawyer has explained what he wants done with the subpoenas and agreements (discussed infra), he can simply hand them to each witness, or pass them around, with the request that everybody fill out the agreement and return the red tagged papers to the lawyer, each of them keeping his green copy for his own use. This way, even if the lawyer's eyes are not good or the light is bad, and even if (as usually happens) when the meeting breaks up, the lawyer is talking to one or two people while a number of others file past him and hand him papers, he will still probably end up with the correct papers, and so will the witnesses, without any particular strain or fetishism about it. In the way of the world, that is achieving quite a lot.

At the beginning of the conference not everybody will be there. The lawyer should use this time carefully. Most witnesses want to know how the case is coming and when it probably will come to trial. The ones who came to the meeting first will be the most anxious to know this. The lawyer should explain it all, even though he knows he may be explaining it again before the evening is over.

Particular witnesses (again, among those most likely to come early) may be concerned about how they will place the date of these events. This is true if the events happened two weeks before, or two years. There is no substitute for friendly relaxed discussion of this subject, since the witnesses probably cannot discuss it so easily with a lot of other people. Other people, not involved in this case, do not share the witnesses' concern. It usually takes only a few minutes to revive common recollections and tie things down with reference to other dates. The calendar (and possibly newspaper clippings) which the lawyer brought will be of some help at this point. Finally, the lawyer should be attentive to the witnesses themselves. They are, in a sense, his people and he should not fool himself into thinking that there will be time enough to know them as well as he would like. This is one of those times when the lawyer can come to know, or remember, what they are doing, where they are working, how some of them feel about the others, and who is living with whom.

It is usually advisable to wait until everybody who is coming has got there. While a great many younger witnesses may say with some pride that they do not wear watches, have never understood about time and so forth, i.e., that they live without direct connection to any chronological drive shaft, the fact is that after a certain point they do not like to sit around and wait any more than anyone else does. They will appreciate it if the lawyer remembers this without their having to tell him, and even more if the lawyer shows consideration for their time *without talking about the value of time.*

It is all very well to remember that the total waste of time is the product of the number of people present times the actual delay, but there is no need to make any bright comments about it. Similarly if somebody who has kept them all waiting walks in finally, and if the lawyer feels a sense of grievance about the delay, he would be well advised to get it out of his head, not merely to conceal it. As likely as not, the tardy one will turn out to be one of the most helpful witnesses, compassionate in outlook and attentive to feelings and needs of the people who have been sitting around waiting. Not everybody thinks the same about time, or attaches the same significance to being a little late.

§ 9.05 Something the Lawyer Should Watch For While Briefing Witnesses

While the lawyer is explaining things to his witnesses, part of his mind should always be on the lookout for that rather uncommon creature, the smart-ass witness. This is the one who, while the lawyer is talking, is always interrupting with some long question, which not only shows that he has been thinking about the question instead of listening to what is being said, but also indicates that the witness really considers himself a sort of competitor for the role of his own adviser. Surprisingly, there is a real chance of overlooking the potential danger of this kind of witness because there may be nothing unpleasant about his manner, and little enough to suggest the consequences of his testifying. If he escapes detection, it will be because he appears quick, intelligent, and able to grasp explanations before they are finished. His quickness exists only in his interruptions, which have a certain hardness around the edges. These interruptions suggest that he understands all of this and much more, and they are especially notable for their frequency. If one listens closely to what he has to say, it will usually consist of: (1) some status-conferring encounter in which he bested some hapless attorney—usually in a way which seems to take points off all lawyers; (2) something that was said much earlier in the briefing, so far back as to raise the question whether he has been listening since then; or (3) a question so long and so nearly irrelevant as to make it evident that he could not possibly have been listening.

In this situation the lawyer should try to tone him down gently, and point out that he should be listening. At the same time the lawyer should answer his question or point out that he will come to it in a few minutes. If this does not work, the next best thing is to answer his many questions pretty much in the order he asks them, but only

206 / POLITICAL CRIMINAL TRIALS

briefly, and without disrupting the normal flow of the presentation.

It is actually rather easy to advise witnesses in a group provided one does it in an even-handed manner, using the same general order of topics for each session. It is far more important to prepare the other witnesses for their experience in court and to tell them all the things they have to be told, overlooking nothing, than it is to rearrange everything to suit the order of questions of this one nervous individual. That is what he will have to be told if he does not draw the conclusion for himself.

After the briefing session is over, the lawyer will have to think very hard about whether to call this person as a witness, and it is rather important to understand the nature of the problem. It is *not* that he did not hear, since, if absolutely necessary, he could be briefed again, all by himself. The real problem is his smart-ass attitude which was manifested once, and will be manifested again all through his testimony in court. Any reasonable doubts should be resolved against calling this person as a witness.

§ 9.06 A Chronological Explanation of What the Witness Should Expect

[1] About Subpoenas

The lawyer should begin by explaining about subpoenas. He should state immediately that at the end of the session he would like to hand each person present a subpoena, and he would appreciate it if they would accept it as a favor to him, and that he will certainly not subpoena anyone who does not wish to be subpoenaed. He should then proceed to explain why the subpoenas are important to him. Innate in this explanation are principles that lie at the center of the case and so the lawyer should explain things immediately, directly, and carefully.

This is a political case, as they all know. The defense is confronted with testimony of police officers, including (if this is the case) one or two who will be lying. While disproving their testimony is difficult, it is not (as was once thought) impossible. The defense in this situation has worked very hard to find a number of ordinary people, each of whom has some knowledge of what happened. Probably no one of them will have been in a position to see more than part of the action, and there will certainly be no "star witness." They may see things differently and remember them differently, and they will have to testify the best they can on the basis of what they remember, without any concern as to differences. Nonetheless, when enough persons have told what they know of the case, the jury does begin to understand what happened, and they will understand who is telling the truth. This kind of case therefore requires a considerable number of witnesses, even though their individual testimony may be short and limited in subject matter.

The need to put on this kind of case in turn creates scheduling problems for the defense. While the lawyer will make every effort to avoid having the witnesses spend unnecessary time in court, some overlap in scheduling is essential. In other words, if his first witness is to be called at ten o'clock, and he expects the testimony to take about twenty minutes, he may schedule two witnesses at ten o'clock (in case one of them is late) and two more at 10:20, and so on. He will not be asking all the witnesses who will testify on a certain date to be present at ten o'clock that morning, for example, but he will schedule some overlap in order to prevent an interruption in the flow of witnesses. Nevertheless, there will be interruptions.

The lawyer should stress that despite good schedules and the best of intentions, it happens in almost every case that owing to changes in the tempo of the trial (e.g., the prosecution waive cross-examination of two successive witnesses), there will probably be at least one occasion when the lawyer will call for his next witness, and there will be no witnesses in the corridor at that moment. For some reason this always seems to happen immediately after a recess, so there is no graceful solution to it.

When this happens, the lawyer will have to tell the judge, in the presence of the jury, that he seems to have misplaced some of his people, and that he needs a few minutes to find them. Actually, the witness may have had a flat tire, or may be wandering around the courthouse looking for the trial department. No matter. The lawyer still needs a short delay to find his witnesses.

He should explain to them now that when this happens, for whatever reason, the next thing he hears from the bench will be an inquiry as to whether he had subpoenaed the missing witness. If the answer is yes, then the judge will, at worst, admonish the lawyer in the presence of the jury to be more careful about scheduling. But if the answer is no, it is quite possible that a judge who regards his ego and authority as more important than a just result in this case— and there are such judges—will simply tell the lawyer that if he has a witness to put one on, and if he does not, then the defense case is over at that point, and if there is no rebuttal, the lawyer should get ready to argue in about three minutes.

In order to avoid having the defense case at the mercy of a hostile judge, it is imperative that the lawyer be able to say truthfully that all of his witnesses are subpoenaed. For that reason, as a favor to him and to save him this embarrassment and risk, he would very much appreciate the persons present accepting subpoenas at the end of the conference.

The next thing the lawyer should tell them about subpoenas is that although the language is quite formal, telling them to come to court at a certain day and time, or face penalties, *the subpoena does not mean what it says.* In other words, they are not supposed to be there the first day of trial, but rather to come at a more convenient time, which will be worked out by telephone as the day draws near. They can count on at least twenty-four hours notice, sometimes a good deal more than that. The worst thing that they could do is to come to court on the first day, because the lawyer will be picking a jury and witnesses could waste hours and hours sitting around the corridors. Nobody expects them to do that.

In fact, by custom (and by statute in some states) [2] witnesses are able to reach an agreement with the party who subpoenaed them to appear at a time other than the time indicated in the subpoena, and this agreement will not only stand up in court, but also the witness will be expected to comply with the agreement rather than the letter of the subpoena. As a matter of fact, the lawyer has a mimeographed form which he has used for a long time, and one of them is attached to each of these subpoenas. He should explain briefly what is in the packet and what to do with the red and green copies.

At this point, the lawyer might as well pass out the forms or have the witnesses pass them around. They can fill them out while he is talking if they wish.

[2] There Is Not Going to Be any Script

The lawyer should advise the witnesses what he is going to discuss and not discuss, and in what order. He should tell them that he is going to talk about what to expect in court, what will happen and how it will be. But he is not going to go over testimony of any individual witness at this time. Indeed, there is no script for anyone's testimony.

The lawyer should stress that the basic rule for testifying is to let the chips fall where they may, and that this is more than a well-worn adage. He should tell them that they will not be in court to serve as advocates in any sense, but to tell what they know about the case as well as they remember it. It is understood that there will be differences among them in their testimony, but that these differences are personal to the witnesses and valuable to the integrity of the defense, and that they must simply do their best and not worry too much about how their testimony fits in. The lawyer need not add, but it is a fact they would not *be* here if their testimony were fundamentally out of phase with reality as the lawyer understands it, since each of them has been interviewed separately prior to this meeting, and since the lawyer will already have exercised his prerogative not to call as a witness anyone whose testimony appears to be completely screwed up.

The lawyer should stress that merely because the defendant and the witnesses may have something in common, e.g., they are students, or all younger people, does not mean that anyone is going to ask them to slant their testimony or knock the rough edges off.

Occasionally a witness will already have asked the lawyer before this discussion began, just what it is the lawyer wants the witness to say. It might be a good idea for the lawyer to remember now, for the benefit of the others, what he has just told the other witness, which should be substantially this: "I want you to remember what happened and tell it as well as you remember it. Don't make up anything." The lawyer should make this point clear without belaboring it, but at the same time he should remember who asked him that question; later he should carefully reexamine the question whether to call that person as a witness at all.

The lawyer should explain that it would probably be easiest to describe court proceedings chronologically, as the witnesses will experience them.

[3] Arrival at Court

The lawyer should remind everyone that the case is up for trial on a certain day, and he should say what the odds seem to be that the case will actually go to trial on that day. If the jurisdiction is one in which cases trail from day to day, he should explain what that means, and he should give his best present estimate of the span of days during which defense witnesses will be needed. The lawyer should then explain with particularity what court the case will be tried in, and while he does so, he should take nothing for granted. He should tell them where it is, with reference to surrounding streets, and should distinguish any other court buildings in the vicinity. It may happen that some of the witnesses have attended other trials involving their friends; whether this trial will be in the same court, or not, is a necessary reference point. In areas where the witnesses would normally arrive at court by car, the lawyer should explain where to park. In other words, he should describe the less expensive parking lots and (where this condition exists) where a car may be parked on the street all day. The point is—he should tell the witnesses the reason for his concern— if they come by car they must not leave the car in a two-hour parking zone because then they will be nervous all through their testimony in court, far out of proportion to the cost of a traffic ticket.

The lawyer should stress several things. First, the time when each witness is scheduled to arrive outside the courtroom, which will have been arranged by telephone the day before, will not have much built-in margin for error. The witness should try to be on time. Second, the witness should consciously arrange matters to avoid subjecting himself to any unusual stress which will make him angry, or which will complicate his natural nervousness when he arrives in court. He should know where the court is, allow enough time to get there, avoid any concern about parking, and (discussed below) deal with any unusual problems in the corridor in a way protective of his own calm. Third, he should begin a careful blackout of conversation concerning this case as he approaches the courthouse.

[4] Silence Is Golden

The lawyer should not only remind the witnesses that they should not discuss the case in the corridor or on the street around the courthouse, but also explain why this is desirable and difficult. The closer one gets to a courthouse, the more likely the persons standing around will be members of the prospective jury panel, prosecution witnesses, plainclothes police officers, or girl friends of bailiffs. Judges' secretaries also talk a lot.

More important, when a prospective juror manages to hear something in an elevator or standing on a corner waiting for a traffic light, he places enormous value on whatever he heard or thought he heard; he will clutch that to his heart and take it straight to the jury room, where he will confide it at some point in the deliberations when it best serves his own views, and whatever he thought he heard may seem more important to him, and to two or three other jurors, than any sworn evidence to the contrary. Stolen information seems especially prized. Consequently, the witnesses should be impressed that it is extremely important not to say anything that touchs on the merits of the case anywhere within sight of a courthouse.

This admonition is fairly easy to remember going *into* court because the time before testifying is the time when a witness will probably be most self-possessed; coming *out* of court, however, everyone is gripped by an ebullient feeling of liberation, behaving rather like shaken champagne, and at that time it seems extraordinarily hard for most people, including lawyers, to keep quiet about the case. That is the time to be most careful.

The dangers of talking too much are broader than just talk on the subject of the lawsuit. Witnesses should be told that if they normally use the word "pig" in their working vocabulary, they should try to avoid using that pejorative, and others like it, around the courthouse. The lawyer should stress the reason for this advice: if the witnesses are overheard, the use of these words will work to the benefit of the prosecution because it will suggest the existence of a strong bias without revealing the personal reasons for it, casting the witness (in the mind of the juror) as a caricature of himself, but unfortunately, without the witness having the opportunity to realize that he is being viewed in that role. The result may be that his testimony is disbelieved, which would be a considerable loss to the defense.

While advising witnesses to be careful how they talk outside of court, it is a good idea to mention their companions. Many witnesses come to court with somebody else. The other person will have been brought along as a friend and companion, a source of moral support when the witness is feeling nervous. This person will always share the witness's known convictions, but he or she will not have been briefed, and more likely than not will be a far more provocative talker than the witness. It is not unusual that this companion—who is not a witness in the case, never briefed, and is trying to bolster the witness's courage—will say more about pigs in a single hour spent in the courtroom corridor than most student activists would say through a bullhorn in the course of an afternoon's demonstration.

The only defense against this liability is to advise the witnesses that their companions may be like that, and ask them to remember to talk to their friends in advance, to shut them up before they go to court. They should all learn to cultivate the skill of talking at length about the weather.

While it might be thought that this is the logical time to tell the witnesses what to wear in court (discussed in [19]) that is probably the least important problem of testifying. To put it in its proper place, the lawyer should quietly drop the subject to the end of the discussion, mentioning it almost as an afterthought, along with gum chewing.

[5] Problems in the Corridor

The lawyer should next tell the witnesses that when they actually arrive outside the courtroom they should remember not to walk straight in. The reason is one about which the lawyer's secretary will be reminding the witnesses later by telephone, but he should tell them now. There is a rule almost universally imposed in trials, at the request of either side, that witnesses will be excluded from the courtroom until after they have testified. The lawyer should describe this rule to the witnesses, and state frankly that even if the prosecution do not request this rule, he will do so himself, so that it seems virtually certain that the rule will be in effect when the witnesses arrive.

There will probably be a sign on the door, placed there by the bailiff, stating that all witnesses are to remain outside until called. However, the bailiff sometimes forgets to put this sign on the door, and it is possible that a witness might simply walk in and sit down and listen to the trial for a few minutes because the sign was not on the door. The witnesses should be advised to wait outside regardless because if they walked in and sat down, a hostile trial judge might decide that they were "disqualified" from testifying on behalf of the defense, which would hurt nobody but the defense.

The lawyer should describe the corridor and its discomforts as accurately as the witnesses will experience them. If the place is cold he should tell them so they can bring sweaters. And then he should discuss what to do if somebody walks up and tries to interrogate them on their role in the case.

The lawyer should tell them it is entirely possible that some plainclothes person, obviously a cop, will walk up and say something rather familiar or insolent such as, "I wonder what you're doing here? Do you want to tell me about it?" The lawyer should state frankly whether this is something which is likely to happen or something which is only a remote possibility in this jurisdiction, but all witnesses should be advised what to do if it does happen, regardless whether the lawyer thinks it will happen.

The witnesses should be told that in this situation they are not required to speak to anybody, and should not talk about the case. That part is quite easy to remember. The important thing is how they phrase their refusal, not because the cop can do anything to them, but because it is imperative for a witness in this situation to keep his calm, and not walk into the courtroom in the after-flush of recent anger.

The witnesses should be advised to give the matter of phraseology a little thought, to be able to say things in their own words, but that a good way of handling the situation is something like this: "I'm sorry, but I'm called here as a witness. I don't think this is any concern of yours." Or, "I don't really mean to give you a short answer, but I'm here as a witness. I think I will say it all in the courtroom." That sort of reply will terminate the conversation; and if the lawyer ever finds out that anyone actually has been molesting his witnesses, he should go straight into the chambers of the judge, with a court reporter, and terminate that sort of harassment by the prosecution. His attack will be pleasurable and successful; but for the present, the main thing is to advise the witnesses what to do if confronted with this not uncommon situation.

[6] Entering the Courtroom

At a certain time the bailiff will come out and call the witness's name. At that point the witness will get up, enter the courtroom, and walk up the aisle, around the counsel table, and enter the witness box, which is located between the judge and the jury. The lawyer should explain at just what point during this walk the witness will be interrupted by the clerk for the purpose of being sworn: whether this will happen in mid-stride, as in some courts, or after the witness is seated.

The witnesses should be told that at some point between entering the door and reaching the witness box, there will be a quite predictable moment of shock at the fact that there is a jury in the box, notwithstanding that everyone knows this is a jury trial. The lawyer should explain why the surprise is likely, and how the witness should try to feel about the jury, regardless of first impressions. The surprise will happen because the jury will be looking at the witness, and no amount of preparation is quite adequate to that encounter.

But the lawyer should stress that they are looking at the witness because they have heard a number of witnesses already and they are acclimated to the fact that each new witness comes through the door. Naturally they will be watching to see what the next witness looks like. The fact that the jury is silent is intimidating, but of course they have no speaking part. They are not hostile.

The lawyer should explain, in describing the first encounter with the jury, something of what the witness's own attitude toward the jury might be. First, the witness should *not* regard the jury as a "cross-section of the community." If the witness did that, in the climate of a political trial, he might have a good deal lower opinion of the jury than he ought to have. The lawyer should explain that he will have had a hand in picking that jury, and that they will not be what they seem. On the contrary, assuming he has a reasonable panel to work with, they will be a group of jurors at least ten of whom he likes, and two as to whom he has no particular adverse feelings (see § 11.09); the numbers may vary, depending on the number of peremptory challenges available in that jurisdiction. If the witness were confined with those people for any period of time, say, on a bus trip, he would almost certainly establish some rapport with several of them.

But they will not seem that way when the witness walks in the courtroom. Because our society is largely an urban one, the jurors will be wearing their urban masks. We are all conditioned from childhood to have a rather impersonal look encountering strangers in the street; if anyone looks at anyone else with a halfway intelligent expression, the other person is quite sure that he is odd, or at least about to ask them for a handout, or say something else equally unwelcome. So the jury will be wearing their masks, but things are not what they seem.[3]

[7] Predictable Psychic Problems During the First Three Minutes

A certain amount of nervousness is inevitable at the outset of testimony. The witnesses should be told what it will feel like, and how to deal with it. Most witnesses will experience some of the following symptoms, which are quite important to alleviate in advance.

After being surprised by the known fact that a jury is present, a witness may experience some perceptual disorders. For example, the room may seem slightly larger than it really is. The witness may be surprised if he returns to that room on some other day, not as a witness, to see that it is really rather small and ordinary. Walking toward the witness box, he may not recognize the lawyer, even though, as the lawyer assures him, he will be there and will see that the witness finds his way to the right chair.

Once seated, many people experience a rather strong urge to return to a fetal position. Shoulders tend to curl forward, the head wants to come down, and knees tend to press together to protect the genital area. Knowing this is going to happen, of course, the witness should plan beforehand to do the opposite. He should make it a point to sit up straight, with the shoulders back, and see that his head is raised. The lawyer should explain that it is desirable to guard against the instinct to curl up, for the simple reason that if the witness's head goes down his voice will be directed into the witness box, the jury will not be able to hear him very well, and the whole purpose of his being there will be defeated.

The lawyer should also advise the witnesses, at this point, of two fundamental rules for talking in court: The witness should speak a little louder than he thinks necessary, and a good deal slower than he thinks necessary. This is because all witnesses tend to pitch their voices too low, and nervousness makes them talk a little faster than they normally would.

Even the normal pace of conversation is too fast for a courtroom. The lawyer should explain that the jury is taking in a great deal of information in a short time, and there are twelve of them, and they have to get it. The need to talk slowly is not derived from any mental slowness on the part of the jury; they are being required to sort things out as they hear them, which is different from ordinary conversation, and they are also obliged to concentrate for longer periods of time than people generally do in other modes of activity. It is important to help the jury in this mental work since there is no other way for the defense case to be understood except by helping them understand it. That is why defense witnesses should be persuaded to talk louder and slower. (This advice may also serve as a useful reminder to the lawyer, to do the same thing while he is advising these witnesses, since they are laboring under the same difficulty which the jury will be required to face.)

There are certainly different degrees of importance in the things the lawyer tells the witnesses, so it is rather helpful to them for the lawyer to point this out. In other words, if everything the lawyer says about testifying is presented as equally serious, then sitting there and listening to it becomes first a responsibility and then a burden. So it is a good idea, for example, to point out that if the witness should forget and talk too low, or if he talks too fast, or his voice drops or his head comes down—if he does any of *these things*—it will not really matter so much. This is true because the lawyer will be standing at the far edge of the jury box while asking questions of the witness, just so he can make sure that every member of the jury can hear. If the witness drops his voice, then the lawyer will simply point out that he should talk louder. The lawyer can easily do this, but things will certainly go smoother if he does not have to do it.

The witnesses should understand that they are probably going to be nervous while testifying in court. It is not only normal to be nervous in this situation, the experience is almost universal. Certain perceptual changes and subjective feelings should be expected, and the lawyer should prepare the witnesses by explaining to them what they will experience, even though the experience is rather hard to describe. He should then explain how to deal with it.

For example, acute nervousness in court may involve slight alternations in depth perception. As noted above, the courtroom may seem cavernous; the lawyer will be asking friendly questions of the witness, but almost certainly he will seem to be standing a little farther from the witness than he really is. A kind of tunnel vision is common in this situation. The lawyer should demonstrate that this means exactly what the word implies: there will be a narrowing of the sector of peripheral vision. There may or may not be a little diminution of color perception. Because of the closeness of the jury and the fact that they are all looking at him, the witness may experience a definite impingement on what can only be called his personal space. Students who have taken sociology courses will be familiar with this concept although they may not have thought of it in terms of courtroom proceedings or stage fright. It is simply that every culture evolves a strong—but unstated—concept of the proper zone of space around an individual person, which may be thought of as "his." This space determines how close people stand to each other when carrying on a conversation on the street, how close a man and a woman will stand while talking at a party, whether business will be conducted across a desk or by people facing each other in chairs, and so forth.

While individual members of society do not ordinarily think about these rules and no one can define them very well, the fact is that when they are violated (e.g., when someone stands closer than is expected or permitted, or when a needed desk is absent from a business conversation) the people involved may become quite uneasy.

This is relevant to the plight of the witness, not because anyone will actually be physically closer than his arm's reach, for example, but because the entire jury is closer than he wants it to be. It may well be that the nearest juror is ten feet away, but no matter; the *feeling* will be that the witness's own personal space is encroached upon, driven in upon him in a way which would be very hard to articulate. His sense of personal space has collapsed around him like a blanket, and somehow that feeling is acutely related to a diminution of awareness, loss of peripheral vision, and inattention to detail such as color.

The lawyer should explain that, fortunately, there is a workable remedy for stage fright, at least insofar as it affects witnesses in court. The special virtue of this remedy is that it involves only one step, so there is no procedure to to become jumbled or forgotten; to have thought of it at all is to have done it already. And by a happy circumstance, this remedy requires only a conscious reversal of one of the less obvious symptoms of nervousness, tunnel vision. This is one of the reasons the lawyer should take the trouble to explain what the symptoms are like.

The remedy is, the witness should simply let his sense of awareness—his consciousness of being present in a particular place—go out to the limit of visibility, which in this case will be to the three walls of the room. To have thought about that is to have done it. Once it is done, the witness will automatically have included the entire room and everyone in it within his own zone of attention and awareness; he will be as much aware of the jury and everyone else as they are of him. He will no longer be particularly troubled by the fact that people are looking at him, but rather he will be able to relax, look back at them, and take his place in the train of things. Once this is done, the signs of tension in his voice will immediately smooth out, his heartbeat and breathing will swing back to normal, and if he has been sweating, while it is true that the sweat on the brow will not miraculously disappear, he will have the satisfaction of knowing that he is not sweating any more.

Many people have their own cures for nervousness, and some of those present may have better ones. In fact, the lawyer is poor indeed if his own circle of friends and acquaintances does not include at least one anthropologist who has lived with aborigines, and who can relate other methods for calming the mind in bad surroundings.

All of these methods are of course highly subjective. While they are all of interest, in a witness briefing it is only necessary to offer one. There are a great many other things to talk about. The lawyer can at least assure the witnesses that many other defense witnesses, in other cases, have found this home remedy efficacious. By explaining it to these witnesses now, the lawyer provides each of them with a single-handed means of achieving composure in court. They will be grateful for it because testifying in court is a scary thing and they need all the help they can get. The long-term steadying effect of this simple procedure on witness after witness is enormously important to the defense case as the trial goes on.

[8] How the Direct Examination Will Seem to the Witness, and Why He Should Exhibit Warmth

The lawyer should explain that since he is calling the witnesses as his own witnesses, he will be the first one to ask them questions in court. He will probably begin by asking each witness his name, where he lives, how old he is, and what he does (if a student, then what year and in what department, and if employed, a very brief description of what he actually does). The witnesses should expect these questions and should understand the reasons for them.

One reason is to help the witness find his voice level and give him a chance to remember to talk a little louder and a little slower than he might otherwise do. The answers to these questions are quite important as a prelude to the witness's testimony, since the jury has an extremely limited opportunity to get to know each witness. Anything they can learn about him will serve to answer some natural questions which are posed in their minds, and, along with many other things, serve to help them know what kind of person the witness is. These are the easiest questions to answer; going through them at the outset will afford most witnesses an important margin of time in which they can dispel the last bothersome symptoms of nervousness.

The lawyer should reiterate that there is no such thing as a script for testimony by any witness; i.e., he will not sit down and say, "I will ask you such-and-such a question, and your answer should be thus-and-so." On the contrary, the witness should simply listen to each question and answer it as well as he can, letting the chips fall where they will.

The lawyer will only say that his general pattern of questions in cases of this kind is chronological, and that he will ask them in effect what they saw, heard, and did. It is important, though, that they understand something about the form of the questions which the lawyer will be asking.

Since the witnesses are regarded in the law as "friendly witnesses," the lawyer will not be allowed to ask them leading questions.

He should explain briefly that a leading question, while its exact definition is somewhat hard to come by, can be defined with considerable accuracy as a question which can be answered yes or no. In other words, the lawyer would not be allowed to describe a certain event, and then ask in effect, "Isn't that true?" That would be a case of the lawyer testifying, and the witness acquiescing or agreeing to the testimony, and, of course, it would be no way to arrive at the truth in a situation where the witness and not the lawyer actually knows what the witness saw. The lawyer should explain that during a direct examination, which is the name for the process during which he is asking the questions, he is required to ask *nonleading* questions. A nonleading question is simply a question which admits of several possible answers, and gives the witness an opportunity to make up his mind and explain matters in his own words.

The lawyer should mention that because of the odd, almost awkward sound of a nonleading question, the witness may find the lawyer's question somewhat disconcerting. While testifying, the witness may hear a little voice in the back of his mind asking, "For God's sake, doesn't he know what happened, even *now?*" The witness will wonder about this because in ordinary conversation anyone who really knew what happened would not be asking these rather annoying questions which by their nature seem to make the other person explain a lot of things which ought to be obvious to the two of them. The lawyer should ask the witnesses to bear with him, nonetheless, and to take the time to explain these obvious things.

It is important that the lawyer stress one very desirable feature of testimony from his own witnesses, which has nothing to do with the substance of their testimony. He should tell them that if at all possible, if they can remember to do it while he is asking questions, he would appreciate their coming on rather *warmly*. When answering his questions, it would be very helpful to the defense if they would use a few more words than the minimum necessary, and say what they are going to say with an ample quantity of their own choice words and expressions. If they can remember, they should try to avoid terse answers, those which sound afraid to come out and are bitten off at the root. The reason is important.

In order for the jury to understand what is said, and in particular to understand what kind of person the witness is, they have to have more than the bare minimum of information. A great deal is conveyed to the jury by the witness's choice of words. Furthermore, when extra words are used, albeit they may be technically redundant or superfluous to a tight-minded critic of the English language, nevertheless, the more there are, the less chance there is for ambiguity to creep in. It is worth remembering that the jury has a great deal of mental work going on at the same time, and there are twelve of them. They all cannot possibly absorb information at the same rate. Anything which improves the clarity and quantity of information imparted from the witness to the jury is very much to be sought after, and the lawyer should take the time to explain this to his witnesses again, even though he has just said substantially the same thing in advising them to talk louder and slower than they would prefer to do. After explaining this, the lawyer should add, however, that some people simply find it impossible, because of the strangeness of their surroundings and their natural nervousness at testifying, to add anything other than the bare bones of their testimony. If this is the way it is with the witness, he or she should not be concerned; it will be the same testimony in any case. The main thing is to get it to the jury; it is only that if they *can* remember to come on warmly, that fact will enhance their own credibility, at the expense of the prosecutor, who will try to impeach their testimony, and it will greatly assist the defense.

[9] Misinterpreting the Lawyer's Questions

The lawyer should mention at this point that there seems to be an unfortunate disability which afflicts a certain proportion of friendly witnesses, perhaps as much as a third, and for some reason is impossible to forecast whom it will strike. This affliction is that, after the witness has begun to testify, he is suddenly under the delusion that the English language means something else in court than it means in the outside world. An example will be helpful.

Assume the case is not even a criminal case, but happens to be one involving an automobile collision at an intersection. The person testifying is an eyewitness to the accident. After he is sworn and a few preliminary questions answered, he is asked something like this: "On January 2, at about 9:00 A.M., were you standing at the corner of State and Figueroa Streets?" The lawyer may point out that although the question must be classified as a leading one, the point of this example is that the question has been asked and that its meaning is rather plain. But the witness does not hear it that way. A whole series of thoughts flash through his mind. The thoughts go something like this: "This is terribly serious business. I am under oath, ringed with enemies. They want to tear out my bowels. If I make any mistake, any mistake at all, it's perjury, and so I'm not going to get out of here safely unless I answer each and every portion of every question, every single nuance, with absolute, uncanny precision. Now. He just asked me was I on the corner of State and Figueroa Streets. Actually, the corner is the intersection of two imaginary lines which are the extensions of the curb lines of State and Figueroa Streets. These lines intersect in space. The intersection is definitely a right angle. The curb line, however, is actually curved. It curves back away from the intersection point by at least a couple of feet. And as for me, I was standing on the sidewalk, at least two or three feet back from the curb. Therefore, the answer has to be, *no*."

Of course, all of that went through the witness's head in about one millisecond. The only part that was audible was, "no." The lawyer should explain to the witnesses that this happens rather often. In other words, everybody in the courtroom will know that the witness must have been on this particular corner at the time in question, or else he would not be in the box. He certainly did not grow in the box, and someone must have interviewed him and thought that he was there to see the accident, or they would not have even called him. The witness knows that too, but what should be a "yes" comes out "no."

The lawyer should explain that when this happens, it is a little embarrassing for him, and that he certainly is going to start asking a lot of leading questions in order to re-establish rapport with his witness. That experience from the lawyer's point of view is rather like throwing a line to a small boat in a heavy sea. It is hard, cold work, and nobody is going to make it any easier for him. As soon as the opposition realize that the witness is in difficulty, which under the most favorable of circumstances will occur at about the second leading question from the lawyer, they are quite properly going to start interdicting the dialogue with valid objections. The lawyer will, of course, get it all straightened out, there is no doubt about that. But he will be bruised and aged by the process.

The moral of this story, as the lawyer should explain to his witnesses, is that the English language has the same meaning in court that it has outside, i.e., the witnesses should not infer any secret, weird meanings from his questions just because there is a lawsuit going on.

[10] Cross-Examination: The Philosophical View

The first thing to remember about cross-examination is to instruct the witness not to be angry at the idea of being cross-examined. Of course, it is quite correct to refer to cross-examination, in one sense, as "a necessary part of the adversary system." It might be equally correct to refer to it as a necessary part of any criminal procedure which depends on human testimony. The main difference between an adversary and a non-adversary system with respect to cross-examintion would probably be the identity of the person doing the cross-examining.

The lawyer should explain that under our adversary system, each side is privileged to bring on witnesses and other evidence to support its view of what happened, and the opposing side is privileged to throw a different light on that evidence, if it can. In general there are only a few ways in which a different light is thrown on a witness's testimony, by cross-examination or any other means. One is to show that the witness was not in a position to perceive what he now says that he perceived. Another is to show that he does not remember very well. A third is to show that he is not testifying very accurately or well, because of bias, inaccuracies, slanting, or whatever. Another is to show that while he is more or less testifying truthfully, there is a supervening fact which entirely changes the meaning of what he said, e.g., it is true the defendant's car was found a block from the scene of the crime, but it was stolen the day before that, from a police impound lot.

The reason each side is privileged to do all this is to make it easier for the jury to know what happened. Therefore the witnesses ought not to be offended at the general idea of cross-examination. It works fairly well for both sides, and the lawyer likes to think that he gets more out of prosecution witnesses on cross-examination than the prosecution ever get from his.

[11] Practical Suggestions About Being Cross-Examined: Handling Ugly Questions

All of this is not to say that cross-examination will be pleasant. The fact that cross-examination is philosophically acceptable is simply another tool in the witness's arsenal. Actually, despite the fact that cross-examination may be done in a gentle way, it will probably be offensive. The witness being cross-examined will feel anger at the prosecutor. This is a natural feeling, as much to be expected as the witness's earlier nervousness on entering the courtroom. This anger will happen because the prosecutor will be overtly antagonistic, attempting to disparage the witness's testimony in areas where he probably knows the witness is telling the truth, and because his innuendos will be unpleasant and his questions persistent and pig-headed.

The witness, at some point in the cross-examination, may very well feel a definite urge to push a knife right into the prosecutor's viscera. This is true even if the witness is a gentle person, e.g., a young woman who spends her time working with handicapped children. The anger and the wish are natural, but there is a *right* way and a *wrong* way to do everything.

The wrong way is to get flushed in the face and lash out at the prosecutor. All the words that naturally occur will probably be wrong words—sarcasm will fail, angry wit will miss by a wide, irresponsible margin. It is no good to say any of the following (or remarks like them):

"Where did you go to law school?"
"You must have learned your manners on television."
"Do you think you're Perry Mason?"
"I came here to tell the truth but you won't let me."

None of these outbursts will enhance a witness's credibility in the mind of a jury.

The right way to handle this is to smother any discourtesy in kindness. The witnesses must be advised that when they are being cross-examined, sugar would not melt in their mouths. The lawyer should explain, if that phrase is not endemic where some of the witnesses were brought up, it simply means that their outward manner should be kindly, agreeable, and even sweet to the saturation point. That is why sugar would not melt in their mouths. The reasons for doing this are (1) to sublimate and get some use out of anger, when anger is inevitable, and (2) to assist the jury in giving correct value to the testimony.

If there is one thing juries appreciate and respect, it is overt fairness in a witness; they see so little of it. All of this is best illustrated by a completely extraneous example. The questions which cause sudden flashes of anger are usually the ones which are both insulting and which cannot be answered cleanly on a "yes" or "no" basis anyway. In order to avoid having the witnesses hung up on some other aspect of the question chosen for an example, it is well to use one that does not directly relate to anything in the case before them. The apotheosis of this kind of question is, "Have you stopped beating your wife?" This *kind* of question will probably produce anger, especially in conjunction with what will have gone before it. While there is no script for dealing with this sort of thing, and everyone must do it in his own words, *a good way* to handle this sort of question is substantially as follows:

Q: "Have you stopped beating your wife?"

A: (*Allow the question to hang in the air for what is referred to in the theatre as "one beat." This is so everybody is quite sure he heard the question right. Then, beginning, very sweetly*) "Well . . . I never did beat her, you know, and so it would be rather difficult to *stop* beating her. . . . Because I never did beat her, you see. . . . I wonder if there is some *other way* you could ask that question?"

The beauty of this is, the witness has said it twice: He never *did* beat her. At the same time, he has been so extraordinarily helpful and kind that it seems he almost climbed over the witness box to come down and help the prosecutor frame a more intelligent question. That is generally how it should be done.

Of course, it is easier to handle that question the first time than the second, but in the normal course of cross-examination, the prosecutor may suddenly return to the topic with, "You never did tell me. Have you stopped beating your wife?" The reason that is not so easy to handle the second time is that the witness may have decided, quite correctly, that he handled it very well before, and may not expect another bout with the same loaded question. However, it is only another opportunity:

> Q: "Well, you never did tell me. Have you stopped beating your wife?"
>
> A: "Well . . . as I thought I testified a minute ago, I never did beat her. . . . I really don't know *how else* to answer your question."

There is a subtle point of phraseology here that is rather important. The witness might just as easily have said, "There's no other way to answer your question." The reason that is a less desirable answer is simply that when they hear it, the jury will instinctively ask themselves: *"Isn't* there really some other way to answer that question?" That reaction separates them from the witness, their minds are going in all directions, and if they find the answer, they will think a little less of the witness. There is a touch of arrogance about the notion that the witness perceives, and tells everybody, that there is no other way a question can be answered.

It is a little *better* (because it contains a trace of humility) to say, "I don't *know* how else to answer your question." That arouses quite a different response. The jury might very well be thinking then, "Neither do I. How the hell else *are* you supposed to answer that question." And if they do think of some way, they at least will not feel that the witness needs putting down.

This general rule (using kindness to smother discourtesy) is applicable to all situations in cross-examination. But it also helps to know about certain particular problems which will almost certainly arise during an ordinary cross-examination in a political case.

For example, each witness will probably be asked whether he discussed his testimony with anybody else before coming into the courtroom. This question is usually asked in a somewhat more unpleasant manner than the lawyer will just have used in describing it matter-of-factly for the witness. The question will be asked in court in such a tone as to suggest that if the witness *has* discussed the matter beforehand, he has committed treason against the sovereign; if they can find two witnesses to corroborate, he will go to the block.

Of course, the answer to the question is yes; but the point is *yes without embarrassment*. Everybody knows that the witness has discussed his testimony before appearing in the witness box. Absolutely everybody in the courtroom knows that. They know very well that witnesses do not appear in the witness box by spontaneous generation, they are called there, and the only reason they are called there is because someone, probably the lawyer trying the case, has interviewed them carefully beforehand and decided that their testimony is material and helpful. The judge knows this. The lawyers know it. And the jury certainly knows it because they have heard every other witness in the case being cross-examined in the same way and everyone has given the same answer. The jury is actually bored by this questioning after the second or third time. The only point in asking the question is to scare the witness, because once in a while, if a witness is not prepared for the question, he just may panic and stumble into denying that he discussed his testimony with anybody. If he does that, everybody will know the statement is untrue: a few people will pity him, and nothing he says after that will be believed.

The moral is, when asked whether he has discussed his testimony with other persons, a witness should not only say yes, but *say it with élun*. The lawyer should advise the witnesses not only to acknowledge freely the fact that each of them has been interviewed and attended this conference, but also to answer any questions the prosecutor may ask concerning what the lawyer told them at these interviews or this conference, including the very things he is telling them now. He should invite them to look around, to see who else is there, to remember their names, and this date, and what is being discussed. The lawyer should stress that they are entirely free to describe anything about this conference which they remember, to tell anything the lawyer has told them. He should add, of course, that he hopes they will remember that among other things he said "Let the chips fall where they may."

Of course, the question about whether a witness has discussed the matter can be asked in a wide variety of forms. As with other things, there is no script. The question may for example be, "So you all got together and *agreed* upon what your testimony would be, right?"

The lawyer should suggest to the witnesses that if the question is asked like that, they should not be too quick to agree with everything in that question. Part of it is true, and part of it is not. It is true that lawyer and witnesses are discussing court procedures and problems regarding testimony in general, with special reference to cross-examination. But the suggestion that all of the witnesses gathered together to *agree* on their testimony is something else. The word "agree" strongly implies a purpose of altering testimony, of making it up and rubbing off the genuine inconsistencies, with a view to preparing an agreed story, setting up some bogus defense, i.e., "Now, I'll say this, and you'll say that." Actually, that is not at all what the lawyer and witnesses are doing.

Although the lawyer has interviewed the witnesses before this occasion, individually, and will certainly do so again, individually, the primary purpose of this larger meeting is not to review or compare testimony. The lawyer should conclude this portion of the discussion by suggesting firmly to the witnesses that each of them consider privately how to phrase his or her answer to the question whether they got together and agreed on their testimony, should that question be asked. The lawyer is not going to suggest any particular answer to it.

The example just described ("So you all got together and agreed on what your testimony would be?") is a very common type of cross-examination question. This is the kind which contains a strong element of truth and something else entirely phony, in which the cross-examiner invites the witness to agree indiscriminately with the whole proposition.

This brings the lawyer to the second major rule which he has to offer his witnesses (the first one being to meet arrogance with courtesy). This rule has to do with how to answer "broken stick" questions.

[12] Some Unorthodox Advice Against Brevity, and Why this Advice Is Essential in a Political Case

A broken stick question may be thought of as a sort of sloppy, ill-conceived compound question which is intended not to inflict any kind of clean wound on the defense case, but to penetrate and then break off in a splintering manner so that considerable surgery is required to remove the pieces.

A lawyer inexperienced in meeting these questions might assume that they can all be dealt with by a timely objection that the question is compound or assumes facts not in evidence. While that may be theoretically true, the way of the legal world seems to be that few lawyers know how to ask qustions that are not compound, and while judges (most of them could not do it either) may sustain a certain number of objections on these two grounds, they will only do it as a pat on the head—as gesture toward law school days—and then they will get pretty testy and cut off the objections, not the questions. They know that if prosecutors were required to try their cases without asking compound questions, most of them could not try a single case; and prosecutors do nothing to discourage this view on the part of judges.

The lawyer need not discuss all that with the witnesses, but in order to plan his case on the plane of reality, he had better have it very clear in his own mind that the only adequate defense against this kind of question is adequate witness preparation. By and large the witness is going to have to defend himself because the lawyer cannot do much to help, and the lawyer will look bad in the eyes of the jury even attempting to do that. Although the lawyer must and should sell the logical validity of his objection to the jury whenever he is obliged to make one, nevertheless, there are one or two objections that probably cannot be sold, and compound question is one of them.

It has become orthodox advice in both civil and criminal cases, in the sense of what law students are taught to instruct their witnesses, that the witnesses should always strive (on cross-examination) to answer questions tersely—to limit their answers and not to volunteer information beyond what the questions absolutely require. The reasons usually given for this are that unnecessary information will suggest lines of inquiry to the cross-examiner which he might have overlooked if left to his own devices. Unnecessary words tend to be a channel for ill-thought-out abuse from the witness directed at the cross-examiner, and judges are likely to slap down a wordy witness, embarrassing him in front of the jury. The truth is, this orthodox advice has become obsolescent and dangerous in the context of a political case.

The correct rule ought to be that the witness being cross-examined in a political case should answer questions rather fully. The reason is that the only great danger the witness faces is the particular type of question referred to previously (broken stick), the question that contains some premise which is more or less true and another which is palpably false, the witness being invited to agree with the whole proposition. The prosecutor asks this type of question because he knows perfectly well if he broke it down into smaller questions, the false part would be immediately apparent to the witness, and the witness would not agree with it. He counts on a coaxing tone of voice, a protracted cross-examination, the natural wish of the witness to appear agreeable and reasonable in the eyes of the jury, and fatigue. When these things combine to make a witness agree more and more with little statements made by the prosecutor, the time rapidly comes when the witness will agree with almost anything. *Once the prosecutor has got the witness to agree with something containing a phony statement, there is no use telling the jury in final argument that it was really the prosecutor talking and the witness agreeing. At that point, the jury will not see that it makes any difference.* Meanwhile the prosecutor will be arguing that the witness *said* a particular thing or several particular things which are damaging to the defense case. That is when the defense lawyer knows what it is like to do legal surgery when he urgently needs that time (and its innate opportunities) to win his case.

Therefore, the correct rules for defense witnesses in a political case are as follows: (1) listen to the question; (2) notice whether it is a question which contains a part which is true and also a part which is false; (3) whatever needs to be agreed with, agree with it; (4) whatever needs to be denied, deny it; and (5) *use a full supply of words to make it clear both that the answer is in two parts, and what the answer is with respect to each part.*

The great danger of a "brief" answer is, the answer tends to go all one way or the other. Sooner or later, fatigue has a terrible effect on short answers.

The witnesses must be told that the reason for this rule—to use more words and not fewer—is that they will probably come across to the jury much clearer and be understood better than if they try to edit their answers. Individual choice of words and use of idiom help the jury immeasurably to know what sort of person the witness is. If they know, that knowledge will favor the defense.

Since the witnesses have already been told not to bandy words with the prosecutor and not to vent their anger overtly there is no particular danger that by using too many words they will get into an argument. The words used in this manner will be used for the purpose of amplifying and clarifying testimony, not with any petty object.

Finally, as part of this rule, witnesses should understand that they will require enormous patience. *The witnesses should be mentally prepared to answer one more question than the prosecutor can ask. They must not be in any hurry whatever to get out of court. They are going to sit there. It is their place, in the witness box; they really do not wish to be any place else. Their last answers will be as courteous as their first.*

[13] Estimating Time and Distance

The lawyer should alert the witnesses whether or not time is critical in this case, and at approximately what points time is most in question. The witnesses may be asked on cross-examination to estimate time or distance. Assuming the witness has testified that a certain thing happened at a certain time, the cross-examiner may wish to move that time later, either to coincide with other contentions of the prosecution, or simply for the sake of moving it, to make one witness radically inconsistent with another.

The lawyer should point out that a favorite technique for doing this on cross-examination is to ask the witness to pinpoint the time of some event that happened perhaps an hour or so before the main event, and then to take him step by step through various things which happened prior to the main event. The witness is asked with respect to each of these separate things approximately how much time elapsed while that thing was going on. The cross-examiner never invites the witness to add up all those estimates of time, because he knows perfectly well that they will total more time than can be contained between the two fixed time estimates. To point out the inconsistency to the witness while he was still in the stand would be to give him an opportunity to correct his estimates. So the witnesses should be fully instructed as to how this cross-examination technique works, and how to destroy it.

An example will be helpful. Suppose the defense contends that a particular event, say, an onslaught of police against demonstrators (or the onslaught of demonstrators against a bank), which is important in the outcome of the case, actually occurred at about 7:30 P.M. This might be material for a variety of reasons, e.g., in relation to the time of a curfew a half an hour later, or to an alibi good for that time. Suppose this witness has testified that his best estimate of the time is actually 7:25 P.M. (This is well within normal deviations, since when a number of people testify about the time of an event which they all witnessed, their own estimates will often deviate half an hour from the real time, most of them falling within about fifteen minutes plus or minus.)

Assume the prosecution want to move this time later. The cross-examiner will first inquire where the witness was during the hour or two preceding this event. Suppose he had dinner somewhere, say, in a university dining commons, at a definite time. He may testify that he always ate early and that the doors were opened at 6:30, and so he must have eaten between 6:30 and 6:45. That is quite definite.

The cross-examiner will then inquire where he went next and with whom. If he went back to his room, they will go over the distance together, and the witness will be asked to estimate how long it took to get there. After considerable discussion about the distance and whom he met on the way, he will be asked to estimate the elapsed time before he got to his room. The normal tendency will be to overestimate. He might say twenty to twenty-five minutes. He will then be asked what was the first thing he did when he got there, and the next thing, and so on. All this will seem like normal testing of a witness's memory. Actually, the purpose of the inquiry will be to impress the witness with the number of things he must have done, to further promote his overestimate of time. He will again be asked about how long it took to do those things, and he may say fifteen to twenty minutes.

The witness will then be invited to remember the next segment of his activity, which may be a detour to the bathroom or someone else's room to borrow a book, and all of this will be gone into and further estimates added up. Assume the further activities total ten to fifteen minutes. He will then be taken along his route from there toward wherever the incident happened, and invited to explain where he was going (the innuendo will be he was going to participate in a riot or some other *illicit* project), and the witness's natural reaction will be to remember very clearly that he had some quite specific and innocent business, say at the bookstore; he will be invited to go along, mentally, over the same ground, and will be asked how long *that* took. Another fifteen or twenty minutes may be added.

At some point, perhaps, a detour occurred and further ground was covered, which brought the witness within the necessary distance to see and hear the matters concerning which he testified on direct. He will be asked about that time as well.

The aggregate of all these time estimates may well be an hour and a half after he left the dining commons, which would quietly move his testimony as to the main event from 7:25 P.M. to some forty-five or fifty minutes later. There is nothing wrong with this method of cross-examining—in fact from a cross-examiner's standpoint it is good practice. But witnesses should be told about it. The antidote, of course, is that any witness who is going to testify as to time should be advised during the briefing session that before testifying, he should go back and *physically walk through all of his movements between the last known reference point of time, and the time of the main event. He should clock himself. If he drove somewhere, he should arrange to have the same car or a similar car parked at the same place, and he should carefully note how long it took him to do the various things he did. The witness should then total this all up in the privacy of his own quarters, well in advance of testifying. If he still thinks the main event happened at 7:25 P.M., then he had better revise his estimate as to when he left the dining commons, or how long he took in doing various other things, and get it all straight in his mind.* This is not done with a view to having the witness fudge on the actual time he spent doing these things; the point is to make the witness face up to something which he may be legitimately cross-examined upon, and if that changes his time estimate of the main event from 7:25 to 8:00, all right, the lawyer had better know about that before the witness testifies. It may be that the lawyer's own understanding of when something happened is wrong. He will only get it right in his head if all of his witnesses take considerable care in arriving at their time estimates. The main point is to prevent the witness from making some mistake on direct examination and then having to switch it all around in cross-examination. If the cross-examination would have produced a more accurate time, then let the witness testify to that time on direct. When a number of witnesses set about checking out their own memories in his way, there will still be a considerable spread of time estimates, even after all the dust has settled. But it will be a smaller spread, and, more importantly, all of the defense witnesses will be able to defend themselves against this common pattern of cross-examination. It does not mean that they are all correct, it just means that they are all honest.

Most people are not very good at estimating distances. Those that are adept probably know who they are. It is very common for witnesses to underestimate the length of automobilies, the width of streets and so on. All witnesses should be advised that if they are asked to estimate distances, and if they know that they can do it, all right, go ahead and do it; if they are doubtful, they certainly should not guess about distances. In this connection it is very helpful for the witness to return to the scene of the incident a few days before testifying, and take a fresh look at it. It may look different to him then. This is not to say he has to go about with a tape, measuring things, because most witnesses will not take that trouble and it seems a little unfair to ask it of them. But they can look.

The lawyer should point out that if a person has a fairly clear mental picture of what the distance is, and particularly if it is a small one which will fit within the courtroom, the best way to answer a question about distance is not to estimate it in terms of yards or feet (where the witness may be at a great disadvantage), but simply to say "I don't know in terms of feet, but I think it was about as far as from here to there [pointing to some other person or object in the courtroom]." That will leave it for the lawyers and the jury to decide what the actual distance was. Needless to say, if the distance is one which helps the defense, the lawyer will translate the witness's reference points into an accurate statement in terms of yards or feet, and get either a stipulation or a ruling that this measurement is what the witness meant, which will find its way into the written record.

In terms of time and distance, it is particularly important that the witnesses understand that there are many questions to which the only appropriate answer is, "I'm sorry, I don't know." These are the questions to which the witness does not know the answer. If a witness does not know it, he does not know it, and no amount of badgering should make him agree with the cross-examiner. There is no obligation to appease the prosecutor.

By way of example, the lawyer may invite the witnesses to suppose that the lawyer had asked them for a loan. If they had said no, that should be it. If he came back a few minutes later and made the same request, they would not feel embarrassed about saying no again. If he did the same thing five times, it would be ridiculous, but it should be obvious to anyone that the answer would still be no. It is rather like that on cross-examination. The cross-examiner may attempt to wheedle some kind of estimate in terms of minutes, seconds, feet or yards from the witness, and if the witness really is unable to answer the question in those terms, then the witness will just have to resign himself to saying so any number of times.

The lawyer should explain that if the process goes on too long, he will ask the court to stop that line of questions, but he cannot always do this during the first four or five times on cross-examination. The lawyer will have to be the judge of when to intervene, because that happens to be one of the little arguments a lawyer cannot afford to lose. He cannot seem over-protective with respect to his own witnesses, and so, if something stupid and obnoxious is going on, the witnesses should know that the lawyer will be aware of it, but that he may deliberately allow it to go on until such time as the jury is annoyed and the court is annoyed, and then he will jump in, make an objection, and get the prosecutor slapped down.

Meanwhile, the witnesses should understand that they are expected, within reason, to maintain their serenity and look after themselves. Along this time it seems appropriate to mention, but only in terms of what would be obvious to the witnesses anyway, that they must never *under any circumstances* turn to the judge and say, "Do I have to answer that?" Similarly, they should not look across the room at the lawyer and ask the same question. If the question is one which the witness really should not answer, the lawyer will be in there with a quick objection. If he has not seen fit to do this, the witness should go ahead and plan to answer the question, since anything else would make it appear that the witness is seeking to hide behind the judge or to assume the role of an advocate and make some kind of argument as to whether the question was proper. Both of these positions would be totally untenable. The lawyer knows the witnesses would not do any such thing, but he just mentions this point in passing.

[14] A Warning Against Suggestibility

While on the subject of common cross-examination experiences, the lawyer should advise the witnesses of a rather uncommon but sometimes very effective technique. This is to suggest to a witness that, because of the nature of the thing which he witnesses, there must have been certain things which happened, and which therefore he must have seen, although actually he does not remember seeing quite that many details. The point of this technique is to make the witness go a little too far, and to isolate him from other witnesses, for having seen something that did not happen.

An example of this technique may be helpful. Assume that a number of witnesses have testified concerning violence at the moment the defendant was arrested. According to their various recollections, they generally agree that he was roughed up, but differ as to the nature and extent of the violence. One or two may have testified that he was struck with fists. One or two may not remember that, but thought they saw him being kicked. Another person may have seen a billy club drawn, but not used. A couple may have seen it used but not have been close enough to see where the blows landed. Assume this witness saw the club used, and saw the blows strike the defendant.

The prosecutor may, during the course of a long cross-examination, produce a similar billy club in court. He may walk around idly slapping his hand with it, and generally demonstrating to everyone that the club is indeed rather large and heavy. He may walk over to his end of the counsel table and suddenly slam it down on a book, hard enough to make the table jump, and the other lawyers as well. While doing these things he may gradually cover the topic of the beating and what the witness saw. And after the demonstration on the table, he may ask the witness whether he *heard* the club strike the defendant. The witness at this point feels quite sure that he must have heard a thing as loud as that; he agrees. The next question may well be, "Well, I suppose you saw the blood splatter, too, didn't you?" The witness then agrees with that also, a club as heavy as that would naturally make blood splatter.

At about that point, it may be that the witness goes too far. Not only did the other witnesses see no blood, but it may be that the defendant himself, though not clear on the nature of his beating, knows and will later testify that there was no blood. Of course, this witness is allowed to leave the stand under the impression that all went well in his cross-examination. But inevitably he will be referred to during final argument as the witness who saw the blood splatter. He will have been successfully and correctly impeached.[4]

The moral of all this is, whatever the witnesses saw, they saw. And if they had an impression of something, they can testify that they had an impression of that. They should be very careful not to allow the cross-examiner to lead them into saying that they *saw* something when, in truth, they only suspect that they *may* have seen it.

At this time it would be appropriate for the lawyer to stress again that in order to testify about a point, it is not essential that the witness be so sure on the point that he would risk his life on it. There are different degrees of certainty, and the witness should make clear in his testimony what he is *sure* about, what he is *unsure* about, and what he has an *impression* of. This is so that if it later turns out he was mistaken on some minor point, the jury can also consider that the witness himself had said he might be mistaken on that point. His testimony on points as to which he was more sure may even be entitled to greater weight *because of that small mistake.* This is true because it is an indication of probity to warn the jury about parts of one's testimony which may be mistaken. It is the witness's concern for truth and his candor which are important, not his infallibility.

[15] Why This Event Is Recollected and Others Are Not

Most witnesses will be asked on cross-examination why this event is recollected and others not. They will be asked what they did on the day before the incident in question, and the day after. They probably will not remember very well. The lawyer should explain that this failure of recollection is normal, but at that same time, this type of cross-examination is perfectly proper; the prosecutor is entitled to show, if he can, that the witness's memory should be equally as faulty for the events in question, as it is with respect to those immediately before and after. The reason the prosecutor probably cannot make his point is simply that for each witness there is some reason why a particular event stands out in memory. It may not be a reason which calls to mind the whole day, it may only illuminate the moment when certain things happened.

The lawyer should not suggest to the witness what these reasons are, but merely point out that it is perfectly normal to remember outstanding events, and since the witness may well be asked what made these particular events memorable, he should give some consideration to how to phrase a personal answer to that question. The answers are going to be individual, they are not going to be the same, and it is particularly desirable that the witnesses do this on their own.

[16] Witnesses Are Not Advocates

The lawyer should remind the witnesses that it is especially critical during cross-examination that they let the chips fall where they may. They do not have responsibility for the case and should not feel that they are carrying any part of the case. Consequently if a truthful answer seems to hurt the defense in some way, that is not the concern of the witness.

It is important that the witness should concede what has to be conceded in good grace and not make a big thing of it. The witness should not be visibly reluctant to concede a point (which usually is not that important anyway). His attitude will be imparted to the jury quickly, and they will respond to him as an unskillful, though perhaps sympathetic advocate, and they will mark down his testimony for being partisan.

In this connection, it is very usual for a witness to be asked either indirectly or outright whether he is biased in favor of the defense. If the defendant happens to be a young person or a student, and if most of his witnesses are in the same category, there will be a short period of questions drawing the witness's attention (and the jury's) to the obvious fact that the witness and the defendant have certain things in common. The prosecutor will then ask whether the witness has any sympathy for the defendant, or whether he or she is a friend of the defendant, or some other witness, or whether the witness has a particular wish with respect to how this case should come out.

Depending on the relationships involved, it might

be absurd for a witness to attempt to deny this bias. The witnesses should be briefed carefully that *there is nothing abnormal about bias, and when it is there it should be admitted.* The testimony is not going to be discredited for that reason, but if they deny an obvious favoritism for the defense, no one is going to think the better of them for that. However, as with many other things, there is a right way and a wrong way to do it. The right way is something like this:

> Q: "Do you have any feeling as to how you would like this case to come out?"
> A: "Yes, I'm afraid I do."
> Q: "You would like for the defendant to be acquitted, wouldn't you?"
> A: "Yes, I do feel that way. *But I have tried to answer all of your questions as honestly as I possibly could. And what I said today is the truth.*"

The virtue of handling the question in this way is fairly obvious. The jury respects fairness and honesty in the witness above everything else. It is perfectly honest to admit bias when bias is present. On the other hand, all the pleasure has been taken out of this little victory, from the prosecution's point of view. The witness will have made a rather favorable impression at the moment this question was put. And the prosecutor will not dare to mention the question and answer in closing argument, if he knows his business, because when the jury thinks about the admission of bias, they will inevitably think about the other statement that was coupled with it—"What I said today is the truth." The prosecution will then be seen as seeking to obtain, at the expense of honesty, some cheap advantage when none was there. This is one of the few instances when it is well to advise witnesses that it is quite important that they answer a certain type of question in a particular way.

[17] How to Have Witnesses Correct Mistakes

The witness should be cautioned what to do if it becomes apparent that he has made a mistake in testifying. First, if the witness *has* made a mistake, his mind will probably be flooded with the recognition of that fact, so that there is no doubt about it. This is quite different from a niggling feeling that something may be wrong, or a general sense of malaise. Once the witness is aware of the mistake and is still on the stand, he may very well wonder what he is supposed to do. Is it perjury to have made a mistake?

The answer is, the witness should simply wait for the next question. Instead of answering it directly, he should say something along this line: "Look, a minute ago you asked me so-and-so, and I testified so-and-so. I thought that was correct at the time. I now realize I made a mistake. What actually happened was this. . . . *May I correct my testimony?"*

The virtue of this is, the witness has already corrected his testimony before asking permission to do so, and has done it kindly—who would refuse a request like that, even if they could?

If it should happen that no further question is forthcoming, the witness should simply say (to the judge), "Before I go, I would like to correct something I said a minute ago. Is that all right?" On receiving an affirmative answer he should then go ahead and do it.

There need be no concern about jury reaction to any effort to reach the truth. They will love and will almost embrace a witness who takes this much trouble to set matters straight. They will not hold it against him, but will certainly think the more of him for it.

This is not intended as any sort of insinuation to the witnesses that it would be well for theatrical reasons to make and then correct some mistake. On the contrary, most witnesses will not have to do this, and with any particular witness, it should only happen once.

[18] How Witnesses Should Behave When Asked to Examine Photographs

At this point in the discussion, the lawyer should pass around those defense photographs which he intends to use and which are relevant to what these witnesses will testify about (see § 9.04). He must advise them that the prosecution may have other photographs, and that the defense for that matter may still discover other photographs, all of which may find their way into evidence by the time the witnesses are cross-examined.

The prosecutor may ask each witness to examine anywhere from a dozen to a hundred photographs, including crowd scenes and mug shots, and to state whether the witness knows anybody shown in those photographs. The lawyer must explain to the witnesses that when this happens, they must *really* examine each photograph, and do it with care. If they happen to recognize someone in that photograph, *they should say so without hesitation.* If there is someone in there they are reasonably sure they recognize, but because of the angle or the lighting they cannot be certain of the identification, then they should say that the *image looks somewhat like such-and-such a person, but because of the angle or lighting they cannot make a positive identification.*

The witnesses will feel a natural reluctance to identify anyone they know under these circumstances because, unless they have been told about it beforehand, not having an opportunity for an extended reflection on the matter while on the witness stand, they will be afraid that any identification will put some friend in jail. This danger is rather remote. The police have other means of identifying people in photographs apart from testimony in court, and in any case it is almost always true that whatever prosecutions result from political demonstrations involve arrests made on the spot, not arrests made months later as a result of something which turns up in a trial. Finally, photographic identifications do not as a rule supply more than a portion of the evidence that someone in the photograph was engaged in a violation of the law. The natural fears which the witness might have of implicating a friend are therefore probably groundless.

On the other hand, there is a strong reason why the witness should not be embarrassed or frightened out of answering this question truthfully. There may very well be somebody in one of those photographs who, by rights, should be known to the witness. A friend or former roommate may be lurking in the background of some crowd shot. Other witnesses may have identified that person already. *The identification may have been made several times before the witness takes the stand, and the jury in that case will be waiting to see if the witness is honest and fair where friends are concerned,* or if he will commit perjury on the spur of the moment.

So, if the witness examines these photographs in such a hurry, or becomes so rattled that he overlooks finding someone he ought to find, his testimony will *not* get the benefit of any doubt in the mind of the jury, nor should it. If he fails to spot somebody that he should spot, he will not only discredit all of his own testimony on other matters, but he will jeopardize the testimony of other defense witnesses.

The correct procedure when shown photographs in cross-examination—particularly if the prosecutor shoves a pile of photographs in front of the witness at the end of a long session—is for the witness to take a deep breath and sit back as if he had all the time in the world. He should take considerable time to examine each and every photograph, and when he sees someone he should say so; and when he thinks he might recognize someone, he should say that, and explain at the same time the degree of certainty or uncertainty which he feels.

Finally, having identified one or two persons in a particular photograph, the witness should not assume that is all, but examine it further, and continue to go through all the remaining photographs at leisure. The witness should understand that if the prosecutor begins to show impatience, that is only *because he has very much hoped that the witness could be hurried into making a mistake.*

It is of course a corollary that when the situation occurs in court, the lawyer will see to it that the witness is *not* crowded, that the prosecutor is *not* allowed to stand directly behind the witness looking over his shoulder, and that in general all unnecessary pressure toward a hasty examination of photographs is prevented. The lawyer should tell the witnesses beforehand that he will do this. That is the way photographs are to be examined, and every witness should begin to prepare himself for this experience at the time of the conference.

[19] Advice Regarding Witnesses' Dress and General Appearance

Advice previously given to clients at the outset of the case on the subject of dress and appearance (see § 3.02) should be repeated for the benefit of witnesses. Young men should *not* make changes in their hair length for the purpose of testifying in court. Although witnesses certainly feel less compulsion to make such concessions than clients do, nevertheless it is a fact that many will offer to do this. And the lawyer should explain that this would be inappropriate, and as a moral matter it should not be done.

However, clothing *is* a matter in which some adjustments can usually be made. Girls should be advised to wear bras, so as not to distract the jury.[5] They should also be advised to wear skirts rather than slacks.

Young women as a general rule do not need much advice on how to dress other than, possibly, those points.

This is not to suggest that all women are equally endowed with clothes sense, only that women pay more attention to clothes, including the kinds they do not wear ordinarily, and therefore need less advice than men on what kind of clothes to wear.

Unlike some men, women are not fanatical on the subject of dress. They are more interested in knowing what is expected than in crusading for something; e.g., regardless of what a girl wears in her day-to-day life, which may consist entirely of a gauze chemise, if she is quietly advised to dress a little on the straight side, she will manage.

With men, things are a little different. A young man adopting an aggressively simple life style may go some distance for principle, giving away clothes which would have been very acceptable in court. He may revise much of what he properly knew about clothes. Therefore, the lawyer can suggest to men (which is easy to do when addressing a group), what he would never suggest to women (in a group or otherwise), which is that it may not be an entirely bad idea to borrow something from somebody else.

Witnesses of all sexes should be advised that it will be helpful if they consider their own personal spectrum of dress, and choose clothing a little on the straight side of their scale. But in the case of men, a direct suggestion should be made that shirt, tie and a coat of some sort be found. This suggestion should be coupled with the warning not to wear anything which makes the man feel uncomfortable, particularly something borrowed which makes him uncomfortable. The shirt, tie and coat are not that important. But if it is all the same to him, and if he can manage it, that is the way he should come to court. It does not matter to the jury what goes with what, as long as the effort is made.

If the lawyer has any question that some of those present may not wear shoes to court, then he should make it clear that shoes are necessary, but he should do this as tactfully as possible. He may do it tactfully by advising witnesses that if any *friends* of theirs wish to attend any session of court (which is quite likely) juries *do* make a kind of association between people who are obviously of the same age or life style, in this case the witnesses' friends being associated with the defendant. So the lawyer would be grateful if they would mention to their friends not to be too relaxed, i.e., they should wear shoes and not do anything out of the ordinary, such as talking loudly or putting their feet on the courtroom benches.

It is usually also helpful to mention something about chewing gum. Nervous people chew it, and sometimes nervous people forget and come into court to testify chewing it.

[20] Concluding Comments as to a Witness's Self-Image and Role

Everyone from time to time sees himself in one role or another; some people never see themselves without one. Prospective witnesses inevitably will devote considerable thought to the trial, and long before they testify they will (if unassisted) arrive at widely scattered versions of what their roles should be. These self-images are liable to be smashed in a rough cross-examination: the witnesses may come to see themselves as the prosecutor sees them, mean and dishonest. Probably the most important single thing a lawyer can do in briefing his witnesses is to give them such a clear understanding of their own function in court that their role will weather any cross-examination.

The lawyer should advise the witnesses that if he himself were about to testify, he would consider his own role something along the following lines.

First, this is quite a serious business. The witnesses will be in court for a serious reason. The reason is, the adversary system of deciding guilt and innocence depends entirely on those persons actually coming into court who have some knowledge of what happened, to impart that information to another group of people who have *no* knowledge of what happened. The two groups are essential to each other and to the system.

From the initial fact that the witnesses will come to court for a serious reason, and the second fact that the jury will have been chosen for a corresponding, and equally serious reason, it follows that *we* will have to come into court for a serious reason. The "we" in this instance is the witness himself and the jury. The judge may be included in that group if the witness wishes, but it is not essential. The witness and the jury are there to discharge an extremely serious obligation as citizens and to make the system of justice work.

It is an odd fact, like several others commonplace in court proceedings, that once a witness has mentally drawn a line around himself and the jury, in effect establishing an in-group in his own mind, that information is instantly imparted to the jury. It is rather like the lawyer's own experience in arguing a case: as long as he is looking any member of the jury in the eye, it is the same as if he were looking all of them in the eye. When he looks out the window, that breaks it, and he must re-establish rapport. No one knows exactly why that works, but the phenomenon is well known. By similar channels, when the witness perceives himself as a member of an in-group which includes the jury, the jury will feel rapport toward the witness. They could not, of course, articulate this—they would not if asked, say, "Ah, yes, we are an in-group, and our group includes this witness." But the witness and the jury are a step closer together, and everyone else in the room has drawn back a long step.

Age differences offer no obstacle to this kind of rapport, as party behavior occasionally shows. The witnesses may recall parties involving people of mixed ages. Quite often there is one younger person, who usually arrives late, who plunges into the mass of humanity with glass in hand,

and swims around until inevitably he or she pulls up along side the particular individual whom a sociologist would undoubtedly have identified as the senior or most prestige-laden individual in that gathering. A conversation then ensues, which will be conducted on the level of the senior individual.

If the same younger person were plucked out of that party and suddenly dropped in to a different party involving other unknown persons, much the same thing would happen. It would happen simply because that is the way the younger person—and the perstige-laden individual also —takes his pleasure (or minimizes his boredom) at that kind of party. It is certainly an interesting phenomenon to those who notice it, and it is a perfect example of how little age matters when conditions are right for in-group identification. The witnesses should be advised that they will have no trouble establishing this feeling with the jury, for the simple reason that the relationship will be a true one (derived from both being there for a serious reason), not something the witnesses will have made up in their heads. It helps a little in retaining this rapport if the witness singles out one or two members of the jury with whom he feels a natural rapport; if he makes it with one, he has made it with all.

The lawyer should remind the witnesses at this point that the witnesses' identification with the jury—the line which is mentally drawn all around the witness and the jury—does *not* include the lawyer. He is not there for the same reason.

This identification (and the omission of lawyers from it) has an important consequence: the witness stands in a firm position, and is better able to meet unexpected situations than any amount of specific advice would enable him to do. Also, a subtle contrast is created and made apparent to the jury.

The contrast is, anyone else in the courtroom who is there for some less serious purpose, i.e., playing some relatively shabby game, will be discerned as standing on quite a different footing; by as much as he works at what he is doing, by that much he will back himself off from any possible understanding with the jury. It is important that the cross-examiner be left no other role than to back himself off; and he will have none, once the witnesses understand their own roles.

§ 9.07 Conclusion of Briefing

The lawyer should of course ask for any questions which have not already been put to him while he was talking. At the same time—not everyone will stay for what follows—he should ask for everyone to complete filing out the agreements to appear at a time other than that specified in the subpoenas, which he had passed out at the beginning of the meeting. He should remind them to keep their own copies (green tabs) and return the originals (red) to him at this time. The last thing he should mention is that his office will be in touch with each witness when the case begins, to arrange a date and time for his appearance, and that if anyone has questions—or has to leave town unexpectedly—he should call the lawyer at the number which is shown on each copy of the subpoena.

§ 9.08 Summary of Expected Results

At the conclusion of every witness briefing, the lawyer should be conscious of the specific, hoped-for results, both as a yardstick for what he has just done, and a prelude to the next witness conference. The witnesses who were just briefed should have been thoroughly indoctrinated to trust their own memories and themselves, to eschew petty confrontations with the prosecutor, and to meet the jury more than half way. They should be in a good position to outlast most forms of cross-examination.

Having done this with some witnesses, the lawyer should remember that he must do it with more. Because these witnesses are being well prepared, the lawyer will be able to rely on using them not just two or three at a time, but in larger numbers; in short, a mosaic pattern of proof. That is worth the repeated efforts and long sessions at night.

The lawyer will not always feel in top form through-out every hour of the trial. There will be days when he is tired, and times when he has other trial problems on his mind. But apart from how he feels, effective witness preparation will have a considerable steadying effect on his case, and therefore on him. As the defense case gets stronger, it gains momentum. Prosecutors cross-examining these defense witnesses can be expected to get weaker, at least in their own eyes, tired of repeating patterns which have proved ineffectual, so that they become ineffectual in their own eyes, and even somewhat boring to the jury. (The jury at this point will probably not be as hard on the prosecutors as they will be on themselves.)

Partly as a result of this witness preparation, it is not too much to hope that conspicuous self pity on the part of prosecutors will emerge later in the trial, which will burst out in the form of irrational insinuations against defense witnesses as a class. The prosecutors would not have wished to make these statements at the beginning of the case, nor would they have dared to do so.

Finally, because the judge must inevitably make some movement toward the defense of witnesses who are unfairly disparaged, even if his movement is limited to sus-taining defense objections, a continuing result of good wit-ness preparation will turn out to be ill-concealed and only half-smothered aggressions by the prosecutors against the judge. (At that point, the jury really does turn against the prosecutors.)

The main task of the defense lawyer, from the outset of trial proceedings, will be to set a sufficiently moral tone ("let right be done"), so that when such outbursts happen, these devolutions of the prosecution will be intolerable to the jury.

Footnotes

[1] *Compare* the general rule that writings used by the witness before testifying, to refresh his memory, must be produced for inspection by the cross-examiner. E.g., Cal. Evid. Code §771 (West 1966); Papajesk v. C. & O.R.R. Co., 14 Mich. App. 550, 557, 166 N.W.2d 46, 49 (1968); State v. Grunau, 273 Minn. 315, 331, 141 N.W.2d 815, 826–827 (1966); State v. Hunt, 25 N.J. 514, 530–531, 138 A.2d 1, 6–9 (1958); State v. Deslovers, 40 R.I. 89, 104–105, 100 A. 64, 69–70 (1917); McCormick, *Evidence* 17–18 (2d ed. 1972); 3 Wigmore, *Evidence* § 762 (Chadbourn rev. ed. 1970); 98 *C.J.S.* "Witnesses" § 362 (1957); Annot., 7 A.L.R.3d 181, 247–251 (1966); Annot., 82 A.L.R.2d 473, 567–569 (1962); *with* authorities indicating that photographs are among the things which may be used to refresh recollection. E.g., 3 C. Scott, *Photographic Evidence* § 1523 (2d. ed. 1969); accord, 3 Wigmore, *Evidence* § 758 (Chadbourn rev. ed. 1970).

[2] E.g., Cal. Code Civ. Proc. § 1985.1 (West Supp. 1973); Cal. Penal Code § 1331.5 (West 1970).

[3] The phenomenon of "urban masks" in the courtroom, and various points made elsewhere in this book (e.g., the value of rudimentary speaking skills, the need for a sudden-opening defense argument, the importance of reminding the jury in argument of earlier promises, and some introductory thoughts and phrases useful for that purpose, were memorably expounded by Woodruff J. Deem, then District Attorney of Ventura County, California, in a lecture sponsored by the Continuing Education of the Bar Program of the University of California. I think that was in about 1962.

[4] I am indebted to William E. Poulis of the Santa Barbara District Attorney's office for a rather brilliant piece of cross-examination which is the basis of this example.

[5] Should styles continue their present swing, a girl wearing a bra may become more distracting to a jury than one without. *Alternis vicibus.* Advice to witnesses must vary accordingly.

Chapter 10

SELECTING A FAIR JURY; TRIAL BY JUDGE OR JURY; THE CHOICE OF A JUDGE

SYNOPSIS

§ 10.01 Insuring the Opportunity to Select a Fair Jury (A Representative Panel)

[1] The Common Error of Underestimating Jury Selection

It is a fatal mistake for a lawyer defending a criminal case—let alone a political case—to assume that jury panels are some kind of phenomena of nature which have to be accepted on the way to important engagements. Jury panels are not like the weather; or at least if they are, the lawyer should remember that there are weather makers.

No matter what the urgency to begin the trial or how strong the defense case, the lawyer must remember that he has nothing more important to do than to ascertain what kind of panels are being drawn for criminal juries in cases going to trial just before his case, and particularly, what kind of panel he has drawn.

A great many defense lawyers are ambushed at this stage of the trial because they do not clearly recognize it *as* a stage of trial, i.e., something which demands complete attention, energy, and courage. This is because criminal lawyers have traditionally regarded themselves more as a part of a system than as persons competent to correct its malfunctions. For the most part we have not been effective in defending clients against social onslaughts built into the trial system. These ambushes are serious business.

Jury selection is one of three dominant aspects of trial, each of which is so important (successively) as to equal the entire case; the other two are witness preparation and argument. Just as no amount of skill at cards can overcome a stacked deck, almost no amount of legal skill and no foreseeable luck will overcome a stacked jury panel.

The term "stacked jury panel" is not meant to sound melodramatic, such as the modern equivalent of Jacobite agents in the pay of a continental power, bribing and poisoning their way to membership in the King's petit juries. Something more commonplace exists: an arrangement between the jury commissioner and the judges by which a great number of persons who should have been included in the jury panel were never drawn at all, or were excused by the jury commissioner, for questionable reasons before the panel was sent to the trial court. The missing persons are easy to identify. They will be the young ones.

Based on the age breakdown of the total population, it seems reasonable to say that in any fairly chosen jury panel in the United States, persons under thirty-five should outnumber those over thirty-five. Young men and young women in their twenties and thirties should be conspicuously present and scattered throughout the panel. To the extent that is not true, the panel is suspect.

Should the lawyer find himself looking at a panel of forty or sixty prospective jurors whose average age appears to be about sixty, with a few if any members under forty, then it is absolutely certain he is dealing with a stacked jury panel. Someone has purposely screened out the elements of the community capable of acquitting in a criminal case.

None of the persons present will have bribed their way into the jury panel and none will have promised to vote for convictions; that point is sufficient for the judge, who is about the same age as the panel members and may even have friends among their number. The judge will see nothing wrong with this panel and will use the weight of his office to press the case forward into trial. But the defense lawyer should understand from the marrow of his bones that a jury drawn from a panel like this (made *entirely* of older people) probably will convict anybody of anything, and will not acquit anybody. Most of them are there in the expectation of being amused.

The behavior of older people in large groups, i.e., when they comprise ten out of the twelve members of the jury, is to nod, smile and wish to be fair. Regardless of what kind of people they were when they were young, on the last day of trial they will settle down and do what they always knew they were going to do, vote *guilty*. This is not necessarily the way older jurors will vote when there are only one or two among twelve; but when the entire panel is old, that is what they do. It is important to understand that they are not voting against their youth. Inside each of them is a younger person, and these younger people are probably as variegated—contain almost as many defense jurors—as if the entire panel were younger. They are going to vote for conviction, though, because the prosecution represents authority and they know they are going to bow to it. Rules like the presumption of innocence call for an inner struggle even to apply the rules to the evidence, and they do not have the strength for a fight—in their own minds or with other jurors who have announced their intention to vote guilty. Many of them were potentially good jurors, once, but in large numbers they will not do.

What happens to the lawyer who tamely accepts an older jury panel seems (to an observer, the lawyer may not realize it at the time) somewhat like an unarmed man stepping into a dark alley, about to get beaten to the pavement by four or five thugs armed with baseball bats. That is not pretty to watch or contemplate, but that is what will happen to him if he allows such a panel to take their seats without challenge.

[2] Minimum Standards in Jury Panels

In evaluating jury panels, the lawyer should remember that the standards applied to a jury panel are quite different from those applied to individual jurors sitting in the box. The panel as a whole is certainly not going to be made up of persons every one of whom is individually acceptable to the lawyer as a member of the jury. It is not necessary that they should be; that is what peremptory challenges are for. What *is* necessary is that the panel should be sufficiently representative of the entire community, including defense jurors and prosecution jurors, that by the intelligent exercise of the legally available number of peremptory challenges, the lawyer can be sure of a fair jury in the box with (it is to be hoped) one peremptory challenge left over.

Although this is a political trial, the standard of fairness which the lawyer expects from his ultimate jury should be no higher than what he could obtain in that community with that number of challenges for an *ordinary criminal case.* Another essential is that the lawyer have sufficient opportunity to ask questions of the jurors himself, under some procedure or pretext, so that he is able to establish communication and receive feedback from persons in the box: he must know how to exercise his peremptory challenges.

It is important to know what a normal panel looks like in a particular community. Lawyers who have tried a number of criminal cases will know what a normal draw looks like if it has not been improperly screened by the jury commissioner (e.g., by taking it on himself to excuse all the young women with baby-sitting problems). The lawyer will have to form his opinion on the basis of his own experience. The judge will always tell the lawyer that he thinks the panel is a normal one for that community. But the defense lawyer's opinion will have to dominate his own actions. The lawyer is not there to be a good guy.

If the panel is a bad one, the lawyer must approach the bench *with the court reporter present* and challenge the entire panel before the first name is drawn and state his reasons bluntly and to the point. This may seem an unfortunate thing, since most lawyers like to start trials on some basis of amiability with the judge. In this situation, however, amiability would be bought at too high a price.

At this kind of bench conference, the lawyer may anticipate that the judge will politely disagree with everything he says about the jury and will wish to brush the challenge aside without even making a record on it. The prosecutor on the other hand will be surprisingly pleasant; and why should he not be, looking at this panel which God and nature have sent him? Many prosecutors are so pleased at the sight, they are temporarily inarticulate. The lawyer should be deterred by none of this, but should state his objection politely and firmly and ask that the jury panel be excused from the room and a hearing be held on the qualifications of the panel in their absence.

The lawyer will be much better prepared to do all this if he has made it his business to learn what kind of panels his fellow lawyers have been drawing in that court during the last month. The more he knows about it, the closer he will come to the strongest possible proof that the jury panel was unfairly selected.

[3] Attacking a Stacked Jury Panel

The lawyer should bear in mind which of the two main kinds of political cases he is about to try, since that determines his ultimate relationship to the jury. If the act itself is disputed and the prosecution is politically motivated, he will take a fair jury, one that he likes and can work with, which contains the necessary number of young people, quite apart from other conspicuous deficiencies such as lack of members of the same race as the defendant. On the other hand, if the act is admitted and was done for political reasons, the lawyer will have special problems with the jury; he will want to make them understand somehow what the defendant had in mind, to view things from inside the defendant's skin, and for this purpose he may be willing to spend enormous effort to get a jury of the same race, individual background or outlook as the defendant.

The method of attack is simply to uncover a subpoena and a carefully drafted subpoena duces tecum for the jury commissioner, requiring him to appear immediately in the trial department and answer questions about the method of selection employed by him and to bring records showing the approximate numbers of persons called for jury duty, the sources of jury lists (telephone books, etc.), and facts relevant to the imbalance of this particular panel, as compared even to his own annual figures.

In the case of the elderly jury, the central facts are

the ages of the members of that particular panel, the ages of persons called in general, and the standards by which younger persons have been excused from jury duty.

Touchstones include the following: nonstatutory standards for excusing prospective jury panelists from appearance for jury duty, e.g., financial hardship on younger men who are employed for hourly wages and are not paid by their employers while serving on jury duty; the fact that young mothers with one or two children cannot afford baby-sitters for more than one or two days, and consequently wish to be excused from any jury duty other than the shortest possible trials (traffic cases); and the fact that the local judges may and probably have authorized the jury commissioner to exercise his own discretion in excusing these people from any jury duty or (a common alternative), in assigning them only to jury duty in justice courts or the like, quite apart from what the law says on the subject of jury excuses.

The pattern to look for is an arrangement whereby thousands of people are routinely excused from jury duty *without coming into court*, according to some set of standards or plan which vests a broader discretion in the jury commissioner than the law intended, but which has the sanction of local trial judges. Such a policy may be oral or in writing. If in writing, it should be subpoenaed. If it amounts to an understanding, the jury commissioner may not wish to admit it, but he certainly will admit under vigorous cross-examination that he does excuse people for these reasons, that he has excused hundreds or perhaps thousands for these causes, and then he eventually will be brought to the point of having to say *why* he feels authorized to do this. The judges have told him he can.

An essential part of any serious attack on a jury selection such as this is to call a sociologist, preferably from a local university to testify that on the basis of local population studies and in view of the median and average ages of persons eligible for jury duty in the community, a representative panel should contain a certain proportion of persons in particular age brackets. This attack can be mounted effectively only if the sociologist testifies further that a jury of predominantly older people (referring specifically to some of the same age brackets) is more likely to convict than a younger one.

At present, appellate courts are not inclined to the view that an old jury is an unfair one; [1] and as long as that is their feeling, the lawyer's objection stands little chance in a trial court. That does not mean the objection is wasted, quite apart from appellate results.

When the jury commissioner has been put through the wringer and the facts about his understanding with the presiding judge have become public knowledge, common sense may have its day, appellate courts notwithstanding. The jury commissioner may change his ways voluntarily. Panels in the next case called for trial—and maybe even the next panel in *this* case—may look substantially better. No one likes to seem unfair.

Although the lawyer will be forced to take the first panel despite his objection, he still has his challenges for cause and his peremptory challenges, and these may suffice to run through that entire panel, and so afford a chance to see the next one. Or, there may be a flu epidemic. Or, if the prosecutor is not very careful, there eventually may be a mistrial (see § 14.10). If the defense lawyer remains cool, much can be done. One always has some kind of arsenal.

§ 10.02 Considerations Affecting the Choice of Judge or Jury

[1] Nature of Choice

This discussion is based on the assumption that under applicable local rules, the defendant may waive his right to trial by jury, provided the prosecution also waive their right to trial by jury. A stipulation is assumed to be necessary for this joint waiver, and the question is simply whether, in a particular case, the defendant would be *willing* to waive a jury trial. To put it another way, in the situation where the prosecution would be willing to waive the jury, how should the lawyer feel about having a judge try his political case?

[2] Considerations

In almost any foreseeable situation the lawyer should take a jury trial, and all doubts should be resolved in that direction. In the rubble and dust under a political case there should always be certain pilings, and these are where the footings rest. The lawyer should remember that, appearances notwithstanding, one of these pilings is the community's strong elements of common sense and fairness, even if it is known as a conservative place or commonly thought of as one having a limited outlook. This is true even where a local newspaper or television newscaster has been fanning coals. It is usually true—and always unappreciated by prosecutors—that partisan television coverage serves to project the prosecution's own feelings on to the community, rather than to change underlying feelings. That is why prosecutors often expect the political defendant to move for a change of venue. For the same reason, most prosecutors expect jury selection to go all their own way, at least when trying the first of a series of political cases.

The fact that partisan news media probably had less effect than the prosecution think may be quite important. It is necessary to the lawyer not to share this view (that partisan coverage will help the prosecution), but instead to approach prospective jury panels as if they contain fair and sensible people, friendly to the defense; if he cannot do this, the lawyer's own relationship with the jury will be warped, and with that disadvantage it would be impossible for him to defend the case correctly.

Doubts about the fairness of the community will also affect local judges, who will *to some extent* share the prosecutor's view that the public is inflamed. Judges will sense pressure, and either because they overvalue the opinions of newspaper owners or overestimate the effect of these opinions on the public, they will attribute to this pressure a magnitude which would not really occur in a jury room. This means that judges are less likely to be fair than they might be at calmer times.

The third reason why a misappreciation of community fairness can be important is that it makes prosecutors overconfident.

Assuming the lawyer has taken care to provide himself with the opportunity of picking a fair jury, he may well be the only one at the trial who understands that a fair jury can be selected, and that it has a composite personality. When juries are well picked, they are relatively *stable* from case to case in the same community. The lawyer will of course devote his attention to separate personalities when picking a jury, and he will think of individuals in planning and delivering his final argument, but these are other phases of the case. In deciding beforehand whether the trial will be a jury trial, he must think in terms of this composite personality.

A jury trial is *not* a gamble in the sense that trial before many judges is a gamble. A jury is something the lawyer can count on, and there would seem to be no rational exception to the rule that the jury you know is always better than the strange judge whom you do not know. And because a well-picked jury is inherently fair and reasonable, its composite personality is—for most political cases—far better than the personalities of judges whom the lawyer does know. A well-picked jury has automatically cancelled out many of its human biases and idiosyncrasies; the lawyer can count on that as a fact, even though he has no idea what those biases and quirks are, on a seat-by-seat basis. But with a judge, the lawyer only can rely on the fact that those biases and quirks are *not* cancelled out. The problem (with the judge) is to decide whether the lawyer has found them all. Few people are good at finding them all.

Trial judges tend to be unfair in political cases because they do not question the reasonableness or constitutionality of repressive political laws, nor will they listen to any suggestion that an ordinary criminal statute is being prosecuted for political reasons. Judges see themselves as ordained to enforce any and all laws, and to enforce these "impartially." They do not seem aware that, insofar as criminal laws are concerned, there has already been a process of selection before any case reaches court, so that their entire legal universe (the laws they are enforcing impartially) consists of cases which the district attorney has already decided to prosecute, and never includes the ones which he has decided not to prosecute.

For a trial judge, it is only necessary in order to activate his sense of fairness that a case should be brought before him; at that moment his sense of professionalism is engaged, and he will look to the enforcement of the laws, one law being enforced as well as another, no partiality being shown to any law, and no special consideration being given to the defendant.

A jury is different. A jury may take the same oath to enforce the law impartially, but it will consult its own conscience and it will certainly listen to the lawyers. When push comes to shove, judges will do neither of these things.

Another reason why judges are not suited to try the question of guilt or innocence in political cases is simply that they have no vascular system to bring them feedback from the community. This is true because judges lead isolated lives. Once appointed to the bench, a judge tends to withdraw from casual friendships and generally makes himself unavailable to people who would tell him how to decide cases. He naturally misses quite a lot, and he will never be found cooling his feet in the private, responsive well-springs of community consciousness.

While people in general may identify with some political defendants, that kind of identification is done on the basis that it is their own business. They do not think about it too much, or talk about it except to close friends. Prosecutors, television newscasters, judges, and (apparently) many poll takers are generally unaware of such feelings.

People who are aware of basic reasons behind the political prosecution will to some extent share the defendant's sense of helplessness in the face of the law. No judge ever feels helpless in the face of the law.

Citizens who serve on juries are the same ones who answer public opinion polls, consistently checking off answers under the attentive gaze of the poll taker, adopting phrases which a part of the public is expected to adopt. But the poll taker is not their close friend.

Judges are not prone to these little lapses from candor; judges say what they think, and they are in a position to look for disagreement with a punishing eye. They are simply not aware that people sometimes think differently from what they say, and have such feelings that, if the questions had been asked a little differently, or the facts stated more fully, or if they were answering their own poll, the answers would have come out very differently.

The main thing about a jury is that it is willing to help a political defendant, provided it is challenged to do so, and provided the lawyer shows the way to provide this help. Jurors will not think up this help for themselves, but they are ready to help if the lawyer will lead; when properly invoked, in the right case, they will move a great distance and act with great authority.

A judge, apart from being an isolated member of

society and having no sense of these feelings, certainly does not look to any lawyer for guidance; and if he does, it will not be to any defense lawyer.

A judge may be slipshod and unfair on questions of guilt or innocence because he tends to solve these problems in a technical way (has there been an infraction?), and because he figures he can always make it up to the defendant by giving a lenient sentence or putting him on probation. Typically, when a judge's sense of *unfairness* has been aroused in a political trial, his response will *not* be, "This act should not be a crime," nor will it be, "This case should be dismissed." Rather, his reaction will be something like this: "This case should never have been prosecuted as a felony— at worst it was nothing more than a misdemeanor [of which the defendant is *guilty*]."

Judges identify themselves completely with court- room decorum. They identify political defendants as sources of disruption, as a challenge to a judge's authority. A judge usually feels that he is nothing if not a presence and a power in the courtroom. In his own eyes, he is not separable from his dignity. A defendant who may be raucous—or worse yet, have raucous friends—is a threat to that dignity.

Juries do not spend a lot of time brooding about their dignity or the force of their presence in a courtroom. They may not like a disruptive defendant or spectator in the courtroom, but they are certainly not threatened in a pro- fessional sense by anything like that (it's the judge's prob- lem), and so they do not fear courtroom disruptions in advance. They cannot project those fears onto the defendant in any fear-hate relationship.

As between judge and jury, there is a great difference in the *effect* of the judge's rulings. In a political case of the type where a disputed act is being prosecuted for political reasons, the lawyer can anticipate that some important evi- dentiary rulings will be vigorously argued in the presence of the jury and decided against the prosecution. *The effect on the judge* of having to make such rulings is actually very slight, i.e., even if an inexperienced prosecutor turns on the judge and reproaches him in the presence of the jury, the judge is more likely to decide the question of guilt or innocence according to his habitual frame of mind. After all, he is a professional judge. He may vent his anger at the prosecutor, then or later, possibly by some personal communication to the prosecutor's superior, but that will not help the defendant.

A jury feels otherwise about these rulings. Witnessing the same events in open court, the jury will resent the fact that the prosecutor has taken these rulings in bad form. They will resent the prosecutor turning on the judge, and they *will* react against him when deciding questions of guilt or innocence. Since these rulings are virtually assured in this kind of political case, this jury reaction against the prosecution can be relied upon, and it is an overwhelming plus in deciding whether a jury trial is necessary. This is a main reason why, all other considerations aside, the jury should be chosen.

Another point is that in a jury trial, the defendant always has what is fondly called "two shots at it." The jury can acquit, and if they do not, the judge can grant a new trial. But if there is no jury, there is only one shot at it, and and when the result of that shot is examined, the lawyer will probably decide that it would have been a very difficult shot to make in any case. When it comes to acquitting, there seem to be few liberals on the bench. Judges—being harshest when they are most professional (impartially enforcing laws), isolated from the community and sensitive to its supposed biases—are simply not people to be trusted with a request to acquit. The only exception to this rule might be a particular judge before whom the lawyer has personally tried one or more political cases in the past (with juries) which the lawyer *lost*, and after he did so, this particular judge went out of his way to tell the lawyer that if he had tried that case by himself, he would have acquitted. If the lawyer has actually been told that, and believes it, and is about to try another case very like those, then everything that has been said above about the advantages of juries should be re-evaluated. And after re-evaluating everything, the lawyer would probably still be well advised to take the jury.

§ 10.03   Choosing a Judge to Preside at a Jury Trial

[1] The Relative Importance and the Mechanics of "Choosing" a Judge

The process of selecting a judge to preside at a jury trial is of trivial importance compared to the selection of a jury; which is all well and good, because in most situations the lawyer will have relatively little say in the selection of a judge. If selection of a trier of fact is something like committing yourself to unknown waters, then the rules of jury selection offer sophisticated steerage and power mechanisms sufficient to sail an ocean. In picking a judge, the decision is probably going to be whether to go in swimming or not.

When the lawyer can count on the equivalent of a peremptory challenge [2] available for use against at least one judge, without stating or proving any grounds for using it, that challenge can prove invaluable. It is especially effective in a court having ten judges or fewer. The lawyer will know them all, and as against the still considerable chance of getting a less desirable judge than the one assigned, one challenge may be a source of comfort, and all that is really necessary. But in a larger court, with ninety judges available to try criminal matters, one challenge may be less helpful; there may be too many unknown judges, including the one assigned.

There are other more helpful ways of influencing the seemingly random event which determines which particular judge will be assigned this jury trial. In a large court, the only effective way of having anything to say about it is to be on very good terms with the presiding judge, i.e., the judge who makes the assignment to a trial department. If the lawyer's relationship with the presiding judge happens to be a good one, it will probably follow that the lawyer's own particular preferences and needs in terms of judicial personalities will be known to the presiding judge, without anything being said about it, and if the relationship is *really* good, these needs may be met. Lacking this relationship, there may be other ways.

If the lawyer does *not* have a good relationship with the presiding judge (and even a good relationship will be chilled when the lawyer is representing political defendants), he should at least have friends in the clerk's office, and in particular in that portion of the clerk's office which keeps track of calendar assignments. If there is a particular judge the lawyer would *not* care to try this case before (e.g., because of his sentencing habits), the lawyer may be able to bring this case to trial (or not bring it to trial) in such a way that the trial coincides with that judge's vacation or his attendance at some judicial conference, or occurs when he is engaged in a sixteen-week jury trial which has just begun. However, it should be noted that these simple devices, and others like them which will occur to the lawyer in the context of a particular situation (e.g., associating an undesirable judge's ex-partner as co-counsel, in order to disqualify him by reason of the relationship) offer only a negative choice. By using them, the lawyer may be able to influence who will not try the case.

After taking a realistic view of these limitations, the lawyer should attempt to provide himself with whatever information there is concerning the judges who *may*.

[2] Strange Judges

After mass arrests the local courts will not have enough judges to try all the political cases. Local judges will be augmented by strange ones assigned from other jurisdictions. These should not be viewed necessarily with discomfort. These judges will probably have been selected by some statewide judicial council; if so, they are probably more experienced than some of the judges locally available.

Assuming that the jurisdiction enjoys a shortage of judges, these persons may have been called back from recent retirement, in which case (the retirement list being a long one) it is to be hoped that they were selected on the basis of long criminal experience. If it happens that way, the lawyer may have the interesting privilege of trying some political cases before rather distinguished judges whom otherwise he would not have seen again on the bench. Among strange judges, the odds favor seasoned and well-tempered men, rather than the occasional aberrant whose authoritarian personality characteristics have driven him to a high place. Simple inquiries will show who is coming.

It goes almost without saying that in making inquiries about strange judges, the lawyer should take care to get a sample of what his *own* opinion might be if he practiced in the home jurisdiction of the strange judge. It is all well and good to telephone a friend in that place and get his opinion, but it may be grossly misleading. The friend may happen to be engaged in other legal pursuits than defending criminal cases or political cases. He may belong to the same club as the judge, and they may lunch together.

Asking this friend's opinion might be a double mistake. He might try to put in a "good word" with the strange judge, mentioning the lawyer's name. That might have unknowable results, most of them unpleasant. And he might succeed in selling his own friendly appraisal of the judge to the lawyer. The lawyer should simply bear in mind that everyone is popular with someone; the judge's family probably thinks highly of him.

The lawyer should ask the opinion of at least two practicing lawyers in the jurisdiction where the strange judge presides (or presided), whether he knew these lawyers before or not, and the persons asked should be engaged in the same type of legal work as the lawyer himself. Since this problem involves a political case, the lawyer should make sure that he is talking to people who defend political cases; if it seems that there have been no political cases in that community, the lawyer will have to satisfy himself that these are people who are experienced in criminal cases and who would be likely to defend a political case if one occurred in that area.

It will not take even two minutes on the telephone to explain the problem to these lawyers, and the result will be two opinions which could not be acquired in any other manner. The lawyer will want to know, at a minimum, how the judge behaves in areas where he can hurt the lawyer or his client the most. Is the judge a man who lets the lawyers try their own case? Does he hog the jury selection process, spreading his ham personality before a captive audience? Will he interrupt the lawyers when they are asking questions of the jury panel? Does he hate lawyers? Will he in fact try to prevent them from asking any questions of the jury panel? Does he have special eccentricities regarding the rules of evidence, or special zones of arrogance in which he manages to reprimand and humiliate lawyers in the presence of a jury? And, assuming the worst, how is he on the matter of sentencing? The lawyer should learn as much as he possibly can in the time that his advisors are able to talk about the matter; the foregoing is not any sort of definitive check list.

[3] Psychological Quirks of Conservative and Liberal Judges in Political Trials

The special requirements of a political case throw unexpected lights on conservative and liberal judges. In order to switch on these lights it is only necessary to remember what it is that a judge can do for a political defendant. He cannot be trusted to acquit him, since people seldom do what they cannot do. But he can be expected to apply orthodox rules of evidence—which will generally operate in favor of the defendant—and to do so without tiring in the dusty, repetitive exchanges which continually recur in the presence of the jury. It is very desirable that the judge should make these rulings not only without faltering (because they are so numerous), but also without seeming to blame the defense lawyer for the necessity of making them. In short, the judge must have his inner reasons for making the necessary rulings and they should be reasons in no way related to what he regards as the role of a defense lawyer.

If it comes out this way, the judge will be a valuable adjunct to the jury, a factor increasing the odds in favor of acquittal. While there is no documentation on this point, it is offered as a highly subjective reading that a good conservative judge may be more desirable in a political case than a liberal judge.

A conservative judge usually seems more resigned to the display of purely human emotions in connection with his rulings. His mind is on other "values." Along the same line, a conservative judge seems to expect less in the way of support from lawyers, and nothing at all from the defense lawyer. He has no sense of political identity with a liberal or a radical lawyer. Consequently, he has no sense of "betrayal" if it happens to be the defense lawyer who is differing with him on a point of law.

A conservative judge seems to draw on entirely different personal resources in making rulings touching the procedural rights of defendants. It is not just that he is less sympathetic to defendants than a liberal judge; he does not want to be *indebted* to them. It seems very much as if a defendant's procedural rights are thought of by a conservative judge as being the defendant's *property* rights. If that is not the way he would put it, it is at least a good model of how he thinks. The defendant is probably going to jail anyway. Many of them have. So why have a lot of people brooding in jail because you took something away from them? If one is going to sentence them to jail, better to owe them nothing. If a prosecutor persists in attempting to get rulings which would cheat the defendants of these rights, that is his job, but the rulings are going against him like it or not.

A liberal judge suffers from no sense of indebtedness to defendants. If anything, he may feel that a defendant would be a bit grateful to him for being liberal, come what may, and that while he is at it a lawyer representing a political defendant should in all cases be supportive of the judge and grateful to him, their minor differences being, actually, the fault of the law. While a liberal judge may feel sympathy for the defendant (or more accurately *concern* for him), the dangers are as follows: (1) the liberal judge senses his own role as basically hopeless vis-à-vis the appellate courts—an attitude which often leads him to say, before making an adverse ruling, that although the question is an interesting one there is nothing he can do about it, and so the lawyer had better plan on appealing; (2) in making rulings on objections and motions, he may feel that he understands the spirit of the law a little better than others— although somehow his approach, coupled with his undoubted reading of the cases, often turns out to have considerable bite for defendants.

It is possible that a liberal judge typically sees himself as more of a *position*, as less of a role than other judges. Therefore any defense argument on points of law is apt to be received as an argument against the liberal judge rather than against the prosecution.

On the other hand, if the conservative judge is an extremist or a police judge at heart, considerations will be different. This is the kind of judge who will sign a search warrant for any officer at any time, and endorse it for service by night if that promises inconvenience to the house-holder; and he shouts at defense lawyers. He is so over-bearing he embarrasses even prosecutors.

When considering this kind of "conservative" judge, the lawyer will have to estimate his own personal reactions. This person can be a *good* judge, a *valuable* judge for the defense, but only if the lawyer handles him in a certain way. By surmounting this judge's bellicosity and snottiness with his own self-respect intact, the lawyer will stand much closer to the respect and affection of the jury. The lawyer can take no nonsense from this judge; he cannot defer too much to him, or let him overrun the lawyer or the defendant. Normal courtroom manners sometimes touch on the ob-sequious, and so manners must be re-examined for this kind of trial. The lawyer must act correctly and firmly, without appearing to be drawn down to this judge's level.

The lawyer must be prepared for a bad five or ten minutes at the beginning of every case, when this kind of judge has started on his usual course of abuse and while there still has not been quite enough time for the jury to be totally alienated. Those are the bad minutes, but once through them (at the beginning of the jury selection process) the lawyer can take the jury as his friends, and saddle the prosecutor with the onus of having this damned fool for an ally.

Assuming the lawyer can handle it like that, he may actually *prefer* this judge over a "real" one. It helps a great deal if their personalities match, both parties doing what they want. The lawyer wants to win, and there is a great deal of masochism in this kind of judge. It is only necessary to look at his face during the defense argument, if one can spare a look for small pleasures at a time like that.

On the other hand, if the lawyer is too young and has not yet attained confidence in handling himself, there is no use subjecting his client to the risk that this kind of judge will run all over the two of them. The lawyer must be in a position to make a moral claim on the loyalty of the jury (not a tentative request). However, this assurance is easily acquired, and only the very new lawyer need beware of this problem. Two or three successful trials should solve it.

§ 10.04 Summary

The main thing is to insure that the local jury selection machinery produces a steady flow of representative panels. This means panels from which fair juries can be chosen, with ordinary skill and luck. If this situation does not exist at the time a political case comes on for trial, the situation must be corrected before a trial starts. If a series of political cases are coming up for trial, and fair panels cannot be chosen, every effort must be made to correct the situation as soon as it is discovered, even if the discovery occurs in a trial which might otherwise be regarded as the least important of the series.

Meanwhile, the presence of a system which produces stacked jury panels must never be considered as a factor favoring the choice of trial before a judge rather than trial by jury; rather, the jury panel situation must be corrected before any consideration is given to the alternative of a judicial trial. This is true because any form of acquiescence to jury tampering is the same as consenting to the subversion of the jury system and, incidentally, the lawyer's own effective disbarment as an agent capable of defending a political case.

Once the flow of reasonable jury panels is assured, the lawyer may give consideration to trial by judge rather than trial by jury, but in almost every imaginable case he should prefer trial by jury.

The lawyer will probably enjoy very limited means of influencing the selection of a judge to try his jury case. However, to the extent he has any influence, the lawyer should hope for a judge of sufficient character to make correct rulings on motions and evidentiary problems under extreme, repetitive pressure from the prosecution to do otherwise. It seems probable that in many situations, a competent conservative judge is more likely to do this than a liberal one. The lawyer should also prefer a judge who will allow the trial lawyers reasonable latitude in conducting their own case, since anything which tends to cramp the presentation of evidence or diminish the lawyer's rapport with the jury will to some extent harm the defense.

Although leniency in sentencing is a favorable consideration in choosing a judge for any criminal case, to the extent that a judge known to be lenient in sentencing also happens to be a judge who will diminish the defendant's chances of having a fair trial, he should be discarded; it is absolutely essential that all efforts be laid toward winning the case and all reasonable risks should be taken to that end. Possible leniency is a consideration that (given this choice) has to go under.

Footnotes

[1] See United States v. Olson, 473 F.2d 686 (8th Cir.), cert. denied — U.S. —, 36 L. Ed.2d 970, 93 S. Ct. 2291 (1973); People v. Hoiland, 22 Cal. App. 3d 530, 534–537, 99 Cal. Rptr. 523, 526–527 (1971); cf. Hoyt v. Florida, 368 U.S. 57, 7 L. Ed. 2d 118, 82 S. Ct. 159 (1961); but cf. Alexander v Louisiana, 405 U.S. 625, 641–642, 31 L. Ed. 2d 536, 92 S. Ct. 1221 (1972).

[2] Cal. Code Civ. Proc. § 170.6 (West Supp. 1973).

Chapter 11

PICKING THE JURY

SYNOPSIS

§ 11.01   Importance and Feasibility of Picking a Fair Jury

Picking the jury is one of the three political trial stages which are so important that each of them is, in defiance of rules of logic, equal to the whole case. (The other two important phases are witness preparation and final argument.) In other words, if witness preparation is done adequately, it is possible to win the case; if not, it may be close to impossible. Assuming the best in witness preparation, it is still possible to win with a well-picked jury, but if the jury is not picked well, then no matter how successfully everything else runs at the trial, the expected victory will always be in jeopardy and may at best be marred by unnecessary compromises in the verdict. As often happens, it may be absolutely impossible to win—almost regardless of the evidence—just because the jury was chosen without adequate attention. And, of course, if everything goes well with the witnesses and the jury, the entire case will be on the line again during argument.

Jury selection is intimately linked to witness preparation and to final argument. Witnesses who have been briefed
along the lines recommended (see Chapter 9) are in fact
witnesses prepared to respond to a jury of a certain type.
They need a jury that wants to see old-fashioned justice
done, that has no serious bias against the kind of person
represented by the political defendant (or his witnesses),
and is prepared to respond to fairness and candor. Similarly,
the argument will be geared to a relationship between lawyer
and jury which is established at the time of selecting the
jury. This relationship does not depend upon "indoctrinat-
ing the jury" on points of law—at least not in the usual way.

Picking a fair jury is not very difficult provided the
lawyer keeps in mind exactly what he is doing, does nothing
without a reason, and takes pains not to fool himself. The
process demands the use of arbitrary rules and subjective
insights, with an unnatural ordering of importance which
gives priority to arbitrary rules (see § 11.05[1]). But mainly
jury selection demands that the lawyer give it the time and
attention it deserves.

Thoroughness is not always easy under current conditions, since opinion makers in the legal profession talk so
much in public about the need to speed up trials. They conduct courtroom experiments and issue press releases describing the actual number of minutes used to pick an average
jury by method A and method B, and they conduct seminars.
Notwithstanding all that, the lawyer will have to decide
that he *will* take the necessary time, and he *will* do this
right, regardless whether this means he will have words
with the judge, or whether he will be asked to serve on the
Criminal Procedure Committee next year. Accelerating trial
procedure is not a defense lawyer's concern, and anyone
who lets these pressures touch his mental processes while
picking a jury should admit to himself that he may not be
in a good frame of mind to try a political case.

§ 11.02   Preparation for Jury Selection

The function of preparation is to remove certain mechanical impediments (the framing of questions) so that on the morning trial begins, the lawyer can keep his mind on two important realities. The lawyer must keep his mind on the jury, not just looking at them, but seeing them. And the lawyer must bear in mind his position vis-à-vis the jury and the prosecutors. This will be a moral position and therefore especially difficult to occupy under pressure and while operations are going on. However, there is the convenience that a moral position occurs in one's own mind, and can therefore be occupied in advance. That is the way it should be done. A certain tranquility of mind is important.

To attain this tranquility, the lawyer should do his special preparations no later than the night before. These preparations are personal and highly subjective. For those who have no set routine, the following suggestions may do until more personal procedures are found.

Most trial lawyers have accumulated a list of questions to ask prospective jury members in criminal cases.[1] It helps to copy this in *longhand* the night before the trial. Copying it is not something the lawyer's secretary or anyone else can do for him; the point of the exercise is to draw the lawyer's attention once again over the familiar questions. While copying them, he gives himself a chance to think which ones apply particularly to this case and which ones might well be left out, and to remember which have received a storm of objections in several previous cases and may possibly need rewording. It is helpful if the list is a fairly long one, containing more questions than the lawyer will ever use. In order to gain the full advantage of this particular form of preparation, *it is not even necessary that these questions be the ones which the lawyer actually uses in court.* But having copied them, the lawyer will have an ample supply of usable questions in mind. (The list itself can be put in his trial book, and it should not be referred to in court.)

This is a simple procedure, quite adequate for "simple" cases, i.e., those devoid of the flash-points which often occur in criminal cases. If this particular political case will for any reason involve *extra* emotional factors, e.g., the attitude of Jesuits toward the state legislature, the efficacy of various psychiatric methods of therapy, homosexuality, or mental retardation, then some thought must be allocated to writing special questions for the jury.

These will be first and second level questions, used to touch and isolate members of the panel who may be affected by these issues, especially those members of the panel who will not admit to any bias in response to general inquiries and general descriptions of the case.[2]

Being completed in hours of relative quiet and with the trial looming immediately ahead, these drills go as far as can reasonably be expected toward insuring that the lawyer will make the necessary inquiries. And they are not very demanding, since copy work, at least, is done by rote. When the jurors begin to answer these questions, reality lies not so much in what they say, but in how those words are said, and in what thoughts and feelings lie behind them. The lawyer's mind must be among those thoughts and feelings, not on how to phrase his next question.

§ 11.03 Exactly What a Lawyer Is Doing When He Is Picking a Jury

In political cases, the lawyer will either be picking the jury alone (representing the sole defendant, or possibly representing all the defendants during this phase of the trial only), or he may pick the jury in cooperation with other defense lawyers. This section concerns acting alone, which is the way it will be most of the time. The lawyer who has it straight in his own head what he is doing and how to do it

will find it relatively simple to do the same thing in cooperation with other lawyers (see § 11.10). In picking any jury,
the lawyer must immediately pre-empt a moral position
(which he will hold throughout the case), and then proceed
to pick a jury of people that he likes. In doing these things,
he must be guided by the cardinal rule, "Don't fool yourself."

In pre-empting his moral position, the lawyer should
tell the jury directly (e.g., by questions on voir dire), con-
firming it by many nuances of language and gesture and by
his demeanor in court, (1) that the lawyer trusts the basic
fairness of the criminal law and expects the jury to apply it,
(2) that the jury's role is a hard one, but worthwhile, and
(3) that the lawyer intends to try this as an old-fashioned
criminal case. By not very subtle innuendo, the lawyer
should suggest that the prosecution have no stomach for
morality, and that consequently the prosecution intend to
try this case on an illegal basis, evading the law: i.e., they
intend to try it as a political case.

The lawyer should pick a jury which the *lawyer*
likes, for *himself*. He should not attempt to pick one for the
defendant, i.e., he should *not* try for a jury of people who,
for one reason or another, might be supposed to favor the
defendant, nor should he indulge in the regrettable practice,
sometimes recommended in textbooks, of attempting to pick
a jury containing a maximum number of persons who are
supposed to have some reason for being antagonistic to the
prosecution.

To attempt either of these things is a bad mistake,
since it amounts to doing something in the presence of the
jury without a reason. This is true because to pick a jury
on the basis that it will like somebody else (the defendant),
or dislike somebody else (the prosecutor) really amounts to
keeping a juror on the basis of reasons which the juror is
supposed to have, but which the lawyer cannot sense
directly. As a basic rule arbitrary judgments of this kind

should be used only to *strike* jurors, not to keep them; *keeping* is something which can be done only because of affirmative reasons which the lawyer can read face to face with the juror. The lawyer would not be presumptuous enough to suppose that he could select a spouse for the defendant, and he has just about as much business selecting a juror for him.

Similarly, anyone who approaches jury selection with an eye to finding persons antagonistic to the prosecution is steering a self-destructive course. It is easy enough to find people basically antagonistic to the prosecution, but the results of keeping them in a political case will more often than not prove disastrous: e.g., the lawyer might suppose that truck drivers get a lot of tickets (some of them do), and that consequently they are antagonistic to the police. Suppose he succeeds in keeping a particular truck driver on the jury whose robust complexion suggests correctly that he has got more than his share of traffic citations from coast to coast. It is likely that he harbors negative feelings toward traffic officers. But a more important consideration is that he belongs to an occupational group which is presumptively set against political defendants, and those feelings are far more important to him than traffic tickets. He may be the foreman of the jury, and when the jurors have convicted the defendant, he will have a laugh about it—he may even use that story to ingratiate himself with the next five traffic officers who give him tickets!

It is safe to say that any defense lawyer who keeps a juror on the basis of supposed antipathy to police officers, and for no better reason than that, is doing a very foolish thing. The only conclusion to be drawn from the fact that a juror does not like police is simply that the prosecution may be afraid to keep him and may well strike him first, so that the lawyer's own strike for this juror should be set at the bottom of his strike list.

The advantage of picking a jury of people whom the

lawyer likes is simply that they will like the lawyer in return. Having arrived at that state of rapport, the lawyer and jury can then agree that the defendant—whether the jury has actually accepted the defendant or not—is really a person who is entitled to acquittal. The lawyer should remember that the defendant is not trying this case, although to anybody not responsible for his safety, he is "the most important person in the trial."

In keeping this necessary perspective, it helps for the lawyer to remember that he is really picking the jury as an essential safeguard for his own witnesses (they have been prepared to meet a fair jury), and for the purposes of his own final argument.

That argument will be one whose elements are known to the lawyer even at this time. It will be flat in places and emotional in places. The lawyer must keep that in mind *now*. When emotional moments arrive in the argument, the lawyer is going to be inside out for the jury. The lawyer will probably not be able to achieve that necessary intimacy in the presence of cold people, let alone those he might suspect of hating the type of person he is. Since the lawyer is going to have to get to the jury then, he had better pick people right now that he can get next to at the outset.

With all of this in mind, and the final admonition that the lawyer must not fool himself under any circumstances, it is time to take a look at the first jury panel.

§ 11.04   First Encounter with the Jury Panel and Initial Evaluations

On the first day of trial, a panel of prospective jurors may or may not be present in the trial department before the case is called. While the timing of their arrival is variable from court to court and among departments within the same court, the panel will generally arrive when the judge is not there. This is true because even if the judge prefers to hear motions or have a pre-voir dire conference before summoning the panel, i.e., even if he is warmed up, he will seldom remain on the bench for their arrival. And so it often works out that whether the panel was summoned before or after these preliminary matters are dealt with, there will be a period when the panel is seated in the courtroom, and only the lawyers, defendant, and court attachés are present. Everybody is waiting for the judge, who is probably on the telephone. This common situation presents excellent opportunities and a few minor pitfalls which are often overlooked.

It is obviously important that the first impression the defense makes on the jury panel should be a favorable one. This impression should also be quite open and absolutely free of anything that could be mistaken for devious conduct. For example, it goes almost without saying that the lawyer, his client, and the lawyer's notetaker will arrive together. The client and the notetaker will know and will recently have been reminded of what the seating arrangements will be.

There is the small question whether the client sits with the lawyer at the counsel table. In some courts this is permitted and expected, and others it is not. In many courts it is optional: the client may either sit at the table with the lawyer or sit in a chair nearby. In either case, he will be within the rail, not in the section reserved for the public (which in this instance is occupied by jury panelists). If the defendant is the only defendant in the case, and he is permitted to sit at the counsel table under the rules of court, that is probably the place to seat him. As between lawyer and defendant, the defendant should be seated closer to the jury. Of course, if there are two or more lawyers on the defense side, almost no courtroom table in the world is going to be ample enough for their notes. In that case, the defendant will have to sit somewhere else, since as everyone knows, people defer to papers.

The defendant will of course have been provided with a notebook for his own use, which he will bring into court. Since he will be nervous, the defendant may need to have a ballpoint placed in his hand at the last minute. The purpose of giving him the notebook is to enable him to respond intelligently to the lawyer's questions about the jury panel, which the lawyer will ask during recesses and from time to time. The defendant will understand that he is expected to help in the process of selecting the jury, and that he is to keep notes for his own use in whatever fashion he chooses, while the process is going on. He should understand there will be no whispering or note passing during the session.

He should also be told that although he is a participant in the process and will be consulted, and that the jury will not be accepted without his final approval, nonetheless, he should not be surprised if it turns out that he has very few firm opinions on the various panelists. It is surprising, but true, that many defendants have no reaction to prospective jurors, or at best, have reactions to only a few. On the other hand, those reactions are valuable. The defendant will notice things the lawyer will not have noticed; some defendants are extremely observant and their help would be worth paying for. As for the others, they have a clear right to be consulted. There is little need for the lawyer to worry about a strong divergence of opinion with his own client. In most instances, clients simply offer their views on the jury because they are asked, and in case of differences, gladly go along with their lawyer's judgment; for the rare case in which a client has a strong feeling of antipathy for somebody whom the lawyer would prefer to keep on the jury, it seems reasonable that the client should be humored to the same extent as another lawyer would be humored in that situation (see § 11.10). If the lawyer wants to keep a person and the client wants him off, the lawyer *may* conceivably excuse that juror, provided, among other things, that there are enough challenges. If the lawyer wants a person *off*, he goes off, no matter what the client thinks. It is the lawyer's jury.

It is important that lawyer, client, and notetaker all arrive together, not only for the first session, but for all of them. This is true because the lawyer and client are going to be spending a lot of time together. They should lunch together, and in the rare situation when they do not, they should arrange to meet elsewhere and return to court together. It is important to create an understanding, from the first moment of the trial, that lawyer and client are together, in their own minds and in those of the jury.

As a corollary of this, the lawyer should have little association with persons on the prosecution side, albeit some of them may be friends of his in the outside world. The lawyer will not, for example, seat his client and then go over and exchange pleasantries with the prosecutor or some plainclothes policeman who is in court. The lawyer will have very little to say to the bailiff, as a matter of fact. The lawyer will not be found bending over the prosecutor's chair to inquire if the latter has a hangover or for any other piece of camaraderie. He should confine himself to minimum, terse pleasantries, at a distance.

This is not to suggest that the prosecution do not exist, but it does mean that from the defense point of view there is no such thing as another case before the court. Although the prosecutors are sitting there, they are really there as representatives of a case which does not exist. This point of view is obviously not to be stated out loud to anybody, but it should underlie everything the defense does.

The reason why the notetaker must arrive in court with the lawyer and defendant is very simple. The notetaker is not allowed to sit inside the bar, and accordingly, will have to be somewhere in that portion of the courtroom reserved for the audience. That means sitting among the jury panelists. They tend to be somewhat suspicious, and if it happens that there is any ambiguity at all about the identification of the lawyer's notetaker, someone who later sits on the jury might remember that he or she exchanged pleasantries with a stranger in court or in the corridor, under the impression that the other person was a prospective juror, and was later shocked to learn that the stranger was associated with the defense side. To avoid this, the lawyer should go a little out of his way to make the identification clear, not just by walking into court with the notetaker, but by conferring with him in recess, and possibly having him come forward at some moment (but only once) to hand the lawyer an envelope or a file. While not everybody will be concerned with the identification of the notetaker, this minimal activity will be sufficient so that if the subject is later discussed in the jury room, two or three of those present will be able to state with finality that there was nothing funny about the notetaker, and that in fact, they were aware of this person's existence and activity from the very moment the trial began.

Seating arrangements at the counsel table are also quite important. In almost every court, some rule will determine where the prosecutor sits and where the defense lawyer sits in a criminal case. The usual arrangement is that the prosecutor is closer to the jury, on the theory that he has the burden of proof, and on the underlying assumption that being closer to the jury helps him discharge his grave public responsibilities. It is very much to be hoped that this *is* the arrangement in court, since sitting closer to the jury does nothing of the kind. If there is any choice about it, the defense lawyer should prefer the seat farthest from the jury box. There are several advantages to being there, most of which relate to the all important beginning of the case.

Some feel the best position for picking a jury is the end of the counsel table (the short side), so that the lawyer can look directly at the jury box while keeping a profile toward the waiting jury panel. There is a definite advantage to the lawyer in being seen as an individual person, in emerging from anonymity as soon as possible.[3]

While the end of the table may not always be feasible, for example if the courtroom is too small, sitting stolidly at the counsel table with one's back to the waiting panelists only preserves anonymity. The lawyer's profile does make him real for the jury, whether aesthetically pleasing or not. This is not egoism, but something to be done.

If the lawyer is not in a position to sit at the end of the table without causing a stir (he must not under any circumstances ask somebody else to move a table in order to make room), virtually the same result can be achieved by turning his chair more or less sideways so as to watch the jury box while facing approximately parallel to the table.

The advantage in being farther from the jury is at once apparent. The range of visibility from this greater distance includes the vital part of the courtroom; the same view from closer to the box does not. In other words, the lawyer will be able to see the entire jury box and a portion of the room occupied by waiting panelists. He will have a much better sense of who is friendly to whom. The postures of persons occupying the jury box are quite important, and it is well to know all the time who is glancing at whom to share a look of disgust at the last question asked by the prosecutor.

Also, from a position farther from the jury box, the lawyer watching the jury will experience much less distraction via eye contract with individual panelists than he would if he were practically on top of them. A lot of close eye contact is not to be sought during moments when the lawyer is not asking questions of a panelist. This does not mean he should not look them in the eye, on the contrary, but it does mean he should not do it in a way to make them self-conscious. From a little farther away, the lawyer can watch the whole jury and make no one self-conscious; from ten feet or less, it is quite a different story.

Another tactical advantage accruing to the far end of the table is the ability to keep the prosecutor more or less under control while he is attempting to work with the jury. As long as the prosecutor is forced to stand between the lawyer and the jury, the lawyer's presence will be almost as much with the jury as that of the prosecutor; the lawyer can measure the reactions of anyone on the jury to the prosecutor, and at the same time keep track of what the prosecutor is doing. The fact that the latter has his back to the lawyer changes nothing.

On the other hand, the prosecutor will not be in a position to see what the lawyer is doing. If there is to be any exchange at all (and there will be, although much of it will be unspoken), the prosecutor will be upstaged, since any reaction to the lawyer will require him to turn his back on the jury. A crucial aspect of this geometry is simply that the lawyer can see unerringly what reactions by individual jurors are really being made to (or meant for) the prosecutor; this advantage is readily apparent in the courtroom though not easy to visualize elsewhere. The prosecutor, standing closer to the jury, is inevitably the focus of sharply converging lines of attention (from various points in the jury box), all of which are apparent from where the lawyer sits.

The situation would not be the same if their seats were reversed. If the lawyer were closer and the prosecutor standing behind, the lawyer still would not be able to see the prosecutor's face (since his attention will be mostly on the jury), and he would not be able to decide whether certain individual reactions are actually intended for the prosecutor or for himself.

It might be supposed that much of what has been said above about seating arrangements would come to nothing if, when his own turn to examine the jury came, the lawyer got up from his chair and moved toward the jury box, standing as close as the prosecutor's chair or even

closer. As a matter of fact, that is the recommended procedure (see § 11.06[3]). But it is not at all disadvantageous,
for the simple reason that while the lawyer is doing this, he
is working more or less cheek and jowl with the prosecutor,
who is *still* seated too close to the jury to derive any advantage from the experience. In other words, the advantage
does not happen if both lawyers are quite close to the jury,
even if one of them is a foot or two closer; it only happens
when one of them is seated some distance away, such as the
length of a long counsel table.

Although seating at the counsel table is important, it
is certainly nothing to make a fetish of, and if it turns out
that the far seat was up for grabs but the prosecutor got
there first, the lawyer should take his seat closer to the jury
as if that were the most natural preference in the world; if
that is the worst thing that happens to him that day, it will
be a great beginning for the trial. Nothing is worse luck
than steadfastly having your own way in a lot of little
things.

[1] A First Look at the Jury Panel

Once the lawyer's portion of the counsel table is
arranged in a reasonable semblance of order (which is important, because he must not be seen scrambling for things
once the judge enters the courtroom), and while waiting for
the judge's arrival, it is time to take a look at the large number of people who have arrived in the courtroom and who
are seated, waiting to be called as prospective members of
the jury.

The method here is very simple: *take a look at them.*
Unfortunately, many lawyers fail to do this rather obvious
thing, since, because of diffidence or inexperience, they feel
that the eyes of the jury are upon them, and that as lawyers
they are expected to play a particular small-muscle role,
i.e., they should be consumed in bending over their papers,

and preferably conducting some kind of serious, whispered conference either with their client, another defense lawyer, or (worst of all) somebody on the prosecution side. All of this is self-destructive.

The lawyer is *not* in the presence of the jury, he is rather in the presence of a large number of people who understand that they may be called for jury duty, but who (at this point) have no sense of group identity or cohesiveness, or in fact of any of the authority which resides in the conscious knowledge that one is actually a member of a jury in a particular case. These people, including those who have served on juries before, are in surroundings which are basically unfamiliar to them. They look to the judge for guidance, and the judge is not there yet.

Of course, they are aware of people seated at the counsel table and will be somewhat curious about the case. But they certainly do not have any personal expectations which require that the lawyers at the counsel table ignore them. They feel (if they think anything at all about the lawyers) that the lawyers are more at home in these surroundings than they are (which had better be true!), and they will not resent it if a lawyer looks at them from time to time. That is exactly what the lawyer should do.

Naturally, he should not do this in a way to draw attention to his action, or indicate any display of arrogance. But it is most important that in looking them over, the lawyer should *not attempt to ingratiate himself by any gesture*. In other words, it does no harm at all for the lawyer to quietly turn his chair a little toward the jury, and survey the room, part by part, not dwelling on any particular individual for more than a moment. While he is doing this, the lawyer will be well advised to eschew any particular expression; no childish smile should engage the corners of his mouth, and nothing about the eyes should suggest that the lawyer expects that he will soon stand revealed as some kind of shining knight, the recipient of every good wish.

It is better just to look and see who is there, and let the rest take care of itself. People do not mind being looked at in this way, provided the lawyer is not belligerent about it, and provided his attention does not linger too long on anyone.

The lawyer will be looking for the usual obvious things; the advantages in doing the looking in this fashion are that the method is direct rather than surreptitious, and that the lawyer is getting the information immediately, so that he has more time to think about it. The lawyer will know whether he has a good panel or a bad one, whether the panel includes a representative spread of age groups, or is heavily weighted toward old people, whether the distribution of men and women is normal (women slightly predominating), or whether men outnumber women by 3-to-1 (a stacked panel), and whether there are persons present whom the lawyer knows, including perhaps some half-forgotten, disgruntled client (see § 11.10).

The most important thing to look for during these candid eye-to-eye examinations is a hard look. In plain English, the lawyer should look first of all for a hard look from anywhere in the room, and he should remember who gave him that look. He should check from time to time, and, inevitably, he will find that the persons who have hard eyes for the defense table are almost always indulging in the same stare, every time the lawyer looks at them. It goes without saying that these people will not serve on the jury, no matter what is said in response to any question. The lawyer will just have to save that number of peremptory challenges as long as they are still in the room.

The important thing about looking at them *now* is not just to identify them, although this may be the only way to know the full intensity of their feeling; another advantage is that after several eye encounters, these people know perfectly well that their animosity has been noted and understood. Once they realize that their feelings are in the open, their better nature will come somewhat to the front, and many of them will be rather anxious to state their bias to the court if they are called into the box, without waiting to have the lawyer drag it out of them. Assuming that a jury panel of fifty people contains five of this kind, matters will probably go very differently depending on whether the lawyer identifies them immediately or whether he keeps his back to the jury and waits to find out about them after they are called into the box.

If he waits until they are in the box, their hostility will have grown considerably, and they will not be the least bit ashamed of it. Moreover they will have heard other jurors being questioned, some of whom will have fought rather skillfully to maintain their positions in the box. Of these five hypothetical jurors, it is possible that at least four of them will change their minds and do their utmost to remain in the box, *merely because they did not have to make the decision to stay in the box until they got there.* In any case, their animosity should be sensed once in the box, but that means the loss of four peremptory challenges to get them out.

On the other hand, if the same hypothetical five bad jurors had been caught giving dirty looks to the lawyer or the defendant several times before they entered the box, it is quite likely that three or four of them will have thought better of the whole thing before they were called, and will seek to excuse themselves as soon as possible on the ground of admitted bias; their example will encourage the others to do the same. If events go this way, the lawyer may not have to use more than one peremptory challenge on the whole group. The difference between using one peremptory challenge and wasting four of them unnecessarily is a stunning difference, one that rubs shoulders with victory and defeat.

Another thing to look for in scanning a jury panel (besides dirty looks and former clients) is who is seated with whom. It is not expected the lawyer will have a mental photograph of the whole room as the result of one look, but after several quiet examinations he should have a pretty fair idea of the seating pattern of fifty or sixty people. This impression grows as the case gets under way. After several recesses and after a number of people have been excused, it should be very obvious who is sitting with whom.

The lawyer will also want to know who is spending his time reading, who is pointing things out in the court-room for the benefit of whom, and who is dressed in what clothing. The latter point is helpful to know if the notetaker should later inform the lawyer at lunchtime that the lady in the green plaid skirt had something outrageous to say about him. If the lawyer gets this information when he is about to return to the courtroom after a late noontime recess, with both sides having a couple of peremptory chal-lenges left and considerable pressure from the bench to pick the jury, then it is really helpful for the lawyer to know where that lady was seated, and if she is now seated in the box, then who among the remaining panelists not yet called has been spending time with her. These are not things to be memorized, but if the lawyer has done enough looking, he will *know*.

[2] While the Case Is Being Explained to the Panel and Before Individual Members Are Called to the Box

After the judge arrives there will be the usual busi-ness of calling court to order. The judge will get into that right away. Normally his next steps will be to make some explanation to the jury panel as a whole concerning the nature of the case, and to introduce the defendant and the lawyers. The defendant will have been prepared for this; when introduced, he will simply stand, face the jury panel with a neutral expression, remain standing for only a moment, and then sit down. The lawyer will do the same when his turn comes. There will be no smiling as far as the lawyer is concerned, or any particular attempt to make any-thing out of this. He will already have been looking at the jury, and will not use this occasion to do it again.

As soon as the judge starts explaining the nature of the case, the attention of the entire jury panel is at once shifted to the judge. The lawyer can again move and observe things, and while this is going on, he may proceed with what almost amounts to the gift of invisibility, provided he makes no sudden moves. This is important, because there are things to be seen and heard while this process of explaining the case goes on. It is surprising how many times there will be an audible intake of breath, or even an "ooh" from one or another point in the room. Furthermore, this explanation will absolutely put the mark of authenticity on any hard looks in the room, and it will draw forth hard looks from those who did not appreciate what the case was about previously, but would really like to see the defendant burn now that they are beginning to understand. Not only can the lawyer locate the source of any little outcries, but he can also register individual reactions of *other persons in the room who may have heard those same noises*, who may be of the opposite frame of mind, and who may even be dis-gusted by those noises, and the sources of all extant hard looks.

The best way to pick up these things is to have casually turned somewhat in the chair before they happen, not necessarily enough to be looking right at the panel while the judge is talking, but far enough that it only takes a slight unobtrusive movement of the head for the lawyer to scan the room. He should check the entire room from time to time while the judge is talking, but not stare at the panel continuously, since that would be offensive to the panel, like anything else that is overdone.

On the other hand, it does not hurt at all for a jury panel to sense that it is being observed in a polite way, since the panel *expects* to be observed and tested, and anything less than this is a pointless incitement to behave like spectators at a Roman circus. In short, when the case is being explained to the panel for the first time, it would be a very poor idea to let them receive the news behind the lawyer's back.

The third thing the judge will probably do (besides introducing people and explaining the case) is to make a general explanation to the panel of how long the case is expected to last, and to invite a show of hands from those who feel they must be excused now, by reason of personal inconvenience or hardship. When this procedure begins, it is not really the lawyers' show. The judge supposedly will handle it. If he knows what he is doing, he will hear excuses and release persons whose service on the jury would entail genuine hardship—all without involving the lawyers. Similarly, the judge should courteously explain to the first panelist whose excuse does not quite measure up, just why it is that he cannot excuse this person: (1) jury duty entails some sacrifice for everyone; (2) others there probably will suffer inconveniences no less pressing than his; and (3) if he excused one person from jury duty for such a reason, he would have to excuse them all, which the law does not allow. This is how it should go, and as long as the judge is conducting himself properly, the lawyer can simply remain a silent spectator, keeping track of who are removing themselves from the panel.

If things go normally, several of the hard-eyed people will remove themselves in this manner, simply by selling the matter of their personal inconvenience to the court; in fact, the reasons which they are now explaining to the court may have contributed to some extent to the overt hostility they radiated toward the defendant before the judge ever came into the room.

However, even the best of judges has weak moments while listening to the continual, familiar pleas to be excused. Sooner or later, he is going to invite the lawyers to stipulate that a certain person may be excused, and at that point, important tactical considerations apply.

The lawyer should of course monitor all of these excuses and rulings very closely, and be prepared to participate when the judge suddenly invites a stipulation. With experience the lawyer can almost tell when this is going to happen. Those with the strongest reasons to get out of jury duty will probably have spoken up first. Those with less certain reasons will have waited a little longer, but encouraged by the success of the first two or three people to leave the room, they come forward more or less as a group, all motivated by a sincere desire to get out of jury duty, and all rather doubtful about succeeding (with good reason).

It is important to sense about how many of these excuses are going to be forthcoming, not just from the number of hands raised at any moment, but from a general awareness of what is going on in the room. During this process, *there will begin to emerge a group self-conscious ness on the part of the jury panel.* This consciousness certainly has not been present before now. If the lawyer has forgotten the particular sum which the state pays the jurors for their daily attendance in court, he has been guilty of a small oversight; he may be sure the jury panel has not forgotten it. Every single one of them knows what they will be paid for their daily attendance, and there is no one in the room who has the slightest reason to regard that sum as adequate compensation for a day's time.

This is not to say that mercenary considerations are uppermost in this group consciousness. People generally are willing to do their duty, but nobody likes to be left holding the bag, and that particular unwillingness will come rather rapidly to the fore in the mind of the jury panel as these less worthy excuses are being heard and considered. It is imperative that the lawyer be attuned to these conflicting feelings (civic duty versus personal affairs) and bear in mind that he is going to ride only one of them during this trial. The lawyer's horse is civic duty.

Accordingly, a good general rule when asked to stipulate that a juror may be excused on some weak pretext —one which seems a little weak to the lawyer, and which he also feels will *sound* weak to the members of the jury panel—is this: Treat the problem as a seriatim matter, the first or second examples of which will not affect the lawyer much, but which, after about the third excuse, will either hurt or help the defense case very considerably. It is best to appear rather passive on the first and probably the second such excuse, stipulating without comment that the person may be excused as the judge has impliedly requested the lawyers to stipulate. After that—and the moment requires careful judgment—the lawyer should disapprove any further excuses in mild but unmistakable language.

The reasons for this rule are fairly easy to define. There will be a number of people who want out on the basis of weak excuses. These are not defense jurors, for the simple reason that they are poorly motivated toward jury duty (by definition, these are people with weak excuses), and it would be a poor bet to expect any of them to place great value on reasonable doubt or other duty-related instructions which favor a defendant. The question, therefore, is how to get rid of them without hurting the defense.

Letting one or two of them go will be easy enough at the outset because the lawyer's own participation (joining in the requested stipulation to excuse them) really is not being stressed at that point. The jury panel may not realize the first one or two times it happens that the judge is really asking the lawyer's permission to excuse people whom the judge *would otherwise not excuse himself*. The lawyer needs a little time to form some impression of how many of these people there really are in the room. One or two stipulations will provide this time.

Depending on economic conditions in the community and the accuracy of the jury selection system (the administrative machinery which has brought these people into the courtroom), there may be five or six out of a group of fifty who are willing to try their luck on bad excuses. If they are all able to get away with it, however, the morale of all the remaining persons in the panel will be damaged: they all would *like* to be excused, and some of them will secretly despise the lawyers for being pusillanimous in approving weak excuses which they themselves have as yet been too proud to offer. They are about to decide that the lawyers are downgrading the system of justice.

For these reasons, the defense lawyer cannot yield very far to the temptation to be a good guy. Potential defense jurors will simply not put up with it; they will lose respect for the defense in advance if there is any showing of a lapse of principle on the part of the defense lawyer, i.e., they will not let him come to them later as a person who is completely serious about the values and sanctity of the legal process, when they have seen him acquiesce in a series of trivial evasions of jury duty. Many of those who do not raise their hands have better excuses than those who do, but they are staying out of a sense of duty. These people ultimately are defense jurors, since they are the only ones capable of according respect to the instructions regarding reasonable doubt. The lawyer must maintain identity with these people (whose hands are *not* raised) from the first. That consideration is far more important than getting rid of the few people who wish to be gotten rid of anyway, most of whom will manage to disqualify themselves later without the necessity of using peremptory challenges.

It follows that the lawyer should not worry too much about offending the four or five people who are not going to get off with easy excuses after the lawyer puts the brakes on this process. Some of them will later profess extreme bias in the case in order to get out anyway, and in any event it is by no means sure that the prosecution appreciate that these jurors are undesirable to the defense; it often happens that the prosecution will generously use one or two of their peremptory challenges on these people, under the mistaken impression that someone who does not want to be on the jury will be bad for the prosecution. If worse comes to worst, the defense lawyer may have to do it. But these people are basically not worth catering to, and the only real question is how to refuse the requested stipulation in a graceful way.

The answer is simply to withhold approval of the stipulation without actually throwing it back in the judge's face. The lawyer should share the unspoken disapproval which will be present in the room, but he should not flaunt this disapproval or attempt to make much of it. A little diffidence goes a long way, providing its meaning is understood. The lawyer should simply rise and advise the judge that although he appreciates the inconvenience described by the panelist who has just addressed the court, he would feel a little uncomfortable entering into the stipulation to excuse that person from jury duty, since jury service entails some sacrifice from everybody, and there are probably many other persons in the room under similar inconveniences. If one were excused it would be only fair to excuse them all. Although the lawyer does not wish to single out this particular person, he really does not feel he should make this stipulation, but instead would prefer to leave the decision entirely up to the court. Those are the main points, however they are phrased.

It is important to remember always that in a courtroom situation the lawyers have an almost unconscionable advantage over everybody else, and they should be scrupulous not to embarrass jury panelists unnecessarily, even the hard-eyed ones. Panelists are not there by their own choice, with rare exceptions ('volunteer jurors" are discussed below in § 11.06[6]).

A last point to remember about the problem of putting a stop to easy excuses is simply that this particular courtroom action has a double significance; not only will failure to do it hurt the defense case, but doing it will help. Therefore while the manner of doing it is a little touchy and in that sense a little dangerous, this is not one of those things to be left for the prosecutor. There are other things which the defense lawyer may consider touchy and dangerous and which he hopes the prosecutor will do for him, such as challenging a bad juror who happens to be a member of some minority group (see §§ 11.07[1] and 11.08), but this is not one of those things. A distinct advantage accrues to the person who puts a stop to easy excuses, so if the lawyer senses that the prosecutor is about to do this, he should be sure to do it first.

[3] While Individual Panelists Are Being Called to the Box

A second major opportunity to assess jurors (the first one being while the judge is absent) occurs when they are called to the box. This opportunity is most often neglected by people unaccustomed to jury trials. They are much too busy writing things down in their notes. The lawyer should school himself *not to write anything at all*, until there is nothing else to do but write.

It is very illuminating to see the expression on a panelist's face at the moment his or her name is called by the clerk. One can only see that by looking. The lawyer will not be looking *for* anything in particular, just looking, more or less like a photographic emulsion. If the juror's mouth turns down, or he asks his neighbor to keep his coat, or hands back a book which he had borrowed, these things should be remembered.

How a person walks to the jury box says a great deal. People walk confidently, gracefully, painfully, heavily, with manifest self-consciousness or manifest self-possession.

Normal traits are somewhat exaggerated when a person is the center of attention. It is important to be aware whether the juror limps, of course, and to start thinking about whether the limp is congenital or possibly traumatic.[4] In general the lawyer should note whether the juror's large muscle and joint activity seems normal. The lawyer will know without running through any particular checklist whether this person is generally comfortable in his or her body, and for that matter whether the juror is accustomed to walking to the front of a room for the purpose of addressing a group.

Usually the bailiff will be directing each panel member where to sit, a piece of information not always obvious to persons unfamiliar with courtrooms. The bailiff will almost always do this in a low tone of voice. Some people will not hear it, or will be too nervous to understand what the bailiff says, or even to think. A few people do sit down in the wrong chairs out of sheer nervousness. A more subtle point arises when the box has already been filled, but a juror is called to fill a seat just vacated by a peremptory challenge. This usually involves climbing over other jurors. Human anatomy being what it is, and chairs being designed accordingly, there is usually only one way to do this, which is with the back toward the seated persons over whom one is climbing. But there are certainly differences in *whether* one person climbs over another. Shy ones sit in a wrong chair, e.g., one reserved for alternate jurors, rather than climb across other people to reach the right chair. And there are differences in *how* one climbs over people. Some will do it with awareness of the people who are being climbed over, with a sort of diffidence; others treat them like mannequins. Some are so large that a little physical contact with the persons they are climbing over is inevitable; they may take this in stride, and even like that physical contact. Some are squeamish. Some people being climbed over are very squeamish about physical contact and withdraw themselves rather tightly to avoid it, and what they are doing shows on their faces.

A good deal can be sensed about who is going to pursuade whom later on, in the jury room, just by the way people arrange themselves in chairs (which way they lean, or whether they sprawl). The lawyer will get none of it, however, if he is busy writing his notes during this important sequence.

The correct way is simply to watch for the juror's initial reaction, then to put a finger at his name on the jury list so that it cannot be forgotten even if another name is suddenly called, and then to spend the entire remaining time watching the juror all the way into the box. At the moment the juror is seated, and looks up to take his bearings in the room, the lawyer, who will not wish to seem a person who stares at jurors, will just have devoted himself to his notes. If the clerk calls another name before the first juror has been fully seated, as some nervous clerks do, it is no matter. The lawyer can write the first name rather rapidly, spot the second name, and watch both jurors with no particular difficulty. Knowing the importance of doing things this way makes the job very easy. Once twelve of them have been seated, the lawyer can go back and correct his notes so that they are totally legible and accurate.

While he is doing this, the judge will probably be talking to the jury about something or other. There is almost always time to get the notes in order before the lawyer is called upon to say anything to the jury panel. If not, the note problem is automatically solved anyway; the client has been taking notes, and the lawyer's own notetaker has been taking what are presumably infallible notes. The lawyer's own notes need only be sufficiently good that when he talks to a juror, or exercises a challenge against some juror, he knows to whom he is talking. Minimal reliance on his own notes leaves the lawyer free to do things which only he can do.

§ 11.05   Things the Lawyer Should Have in Mind Even Before the Jurors Are Questioned

[1] Arbitrary Decisions

There are generally two ways that a trial lawyer can decide whether he wishes to keep or exclude a prospective juror. This has nothing to do with effectuating these decisions once they are made. Problems of how and when to exercise challenges are discussed elsewhere (see §§11.08 and 11.09). These two ways are arbitrary and intuitive decisions.

What is called an "arbitrary" decision in this section is simply a decision to exclude (never to retain) a person, based entirely on general information. By "general information" is meant information that places an individual in various kinds of categories, but stops short of any intuitive information about him. This kind of information is so obvious that the judge will elicit most of these facts during his introductory examination of jurors, and the rest is easy to get. It includes the juror's age, his occupation, whether he is married, his spouse's occupation, and whether he has children or grandchildren; it includes also where he lives, the extent of his prior jury (or grand jury) experience; and of course it includes his acquaintance or association with persons actually involved in the case, and with the kinds of persons and problems involved.

The advantages of an arbitrary decision concerning a prospective juror are quite different from the usual results of snap judgments about people in general. For one thing, the information which the lawyer acts on is reasonably accurate and, within its own special category, reasonably complete. People just do not lie about their residence or occupation. They will not be asked about their age or general health, since these will be apparent. As to their associations with police officers, people are generally quite satisfied with their own selection of friends. They will by no means be apologetic or mendacious, and will at worst only tend to softpedal somewhat an answer which might cause them to be excused from jury duty.

The significance of some of the information being supplied is of course quite obvious, but there is no way that most jurors could share in some of the rather personal inferences which lawyers draw from these seemingly general facts, a point which makes such information intrinsically reliable.

The special strength and weakness of an arbitrary decision about a juror is simply that the decision is made without reference to what the lawyer sees when he looks at the juror. An arbitrary decision to exclude a certain person may be at war with the lawyer's own intuitive feeling about that person, but for reasons discussed later (§ 11.05[3]) the arbitrary decision should probably prevail because if it does the lawyer is a lot less likely to fool himself, the greatest danger in selecting jurors. Of course the weakness of an arbitrary decision is that it takes no account of the person, and so it is unarguable that when rejecting this person and that person on the sole ground of occupation, the lawyer will once in a while do an injustice to his own case. It follows from this that whatever the rules which lead to arbitrary decisions, they had better be good ones.

The legal world is full of little rules of thumb for picking defense jurors in a criminal case. Unfortunately, these little rules gain by accretion, somewhat like a rolling snowball, since the children who roll them will leave nothing lying around. Probably the better way to view these rules of thumb is just see them all as obsolescent. No such rule should ever be used by a lawyer unless he has good reason to believe it is valid at the time. To pick a jury on the basis of reasons popular with a prior generation of lawyers is, in effect, to be doing something without a valid reason, a very unwise procedure. The following are offered as a beginning list of biases, for the lawyer who has none of his own, good under existing circumstances and for purposes of political trials, but not necessarily good for every kind of criminal case, and not good for long.

First, the defense does not want real estate brokers or anybody who is married to one. It is of course possible that among all the real estate brokers in a given community, there may be one or two who are well known as liberal or radical persons, whose names are publicly identified with radical causes, and who have dried their feet south of the Rubicon. They will be at war with the other brokers in town, and the lawyer will know about it. As to these one or two brokers only, the rule does not apply. (And of course these will not be allowed to sit anyway, since the prosecution read the papers too.)

Equally unacceptable are "ranchers" of one kind or another; this rule is (like the one pertaining to brokers) so strong that it covers anybody who belongs to a ranching family, who lives on a ranch, or permanently works on a ranch in any capacity at all, no matter how menial. In this context, ranching is something of a frame of mind, not a strict definition. It includes anybody who is inclined to think of himself as a "rancher" or "planter," i.e., anybody devoted to making money out of stock or agriculture. It is surprising how many people with a few acres of avocados regard themselves as "ranchers," and they are, too, so far as the lawyer is concerned. In the western states citrus ranchers are numberless. For purposes of this discussion, the term "ranchers" includes actual ranchers, self-styled "ranchers," "planters," and big-time farmers. It does not include that diminishing breed of farmers who till the ground with their own labor; no opinion is expressed in this book as to them.

All of these people described as "ranchers" live their lives in a state of enormous rectitude vis-à-vis political dissenters, and as it just happens, their bank accounts depend on cheap labor. If the lawyer meeting some of these people in the jury box finds them agreeable, straight-forward, Attic or otherwise representative of bygone virtues, he should make a mental note to shake hands with them in the corridor and get himself invited for a barbecue sometime; but to accept one of these people on the jury would be an act of legal insanity. It is worth repeating: this rule bars also the rancher's foreman, the foreman's wife, and absolutely anybody who finds it congenial to live on the same spread with ranchers.

Under present conditions, the defense in a political case should generally avoid people actively engaged in trades, not just hard-hat construction workers. This rule covers everybody in the construction industry, whether licensed building contractors, estimators, accountants, equipment operators, or persons operating businesses which lease equipment. These people dislike students and political dissidents of all ages, and any lawyer who is not aware of this by now had better start believing it. These are people most likely to fool a new or inexperienced lawyer who is relying primarily on advice from ten-year-old textbooks on jury selection. This is true because in a political case they will unfailingly act on their political biases, not on some other kinds of biases which they were supposed to have. To repeat an example cited previously, a truck driver who has accumulated many traffic tickets might be regarded by some as a "defense" juror because of his accumulated resentment toward traffic police; but for him any reason may be good enough to convict a political dissident. Similarly, if the political defendant is a young woman and not bad looking, the telephone repairman in the jury box may give her the unabashed eye, obviously entertaining fantasies, and according to some that fact should be a point in favor of keeping him on the jury. But these fantasies are probably sadistic. He will smash her case if he possibly can, and he must not be given the chance.

People who have lived in the county for an appreciable period of time are bad defense jurors. The amount of time obviously varies according to the region of the country, but these will be the people who are known as "old-time residents." Easy reasons for this fact are hard to come by, but these persons are set in their ways, or at least more so than people who have not lived there quite so long, and they have no use for universities, students, or dissidents. They have no particular stomach for change.

This bias is especially marked among members of an ethnic group which has been in the community for some time but has only made it financially within the last two generations. While any landed property owner can be regarded as a poor choice for a defense juror, a member of an identifiable ethnic minority who has attained land or professional status, but who is not yet secure in his own mind, is probably the most biased of all. He will probably excuse himself, but if he does not, the lawyer should do it for him.

Friends (and to some extent relatives) of law enforcement personnel are not acceptable on the jury. As a rule of exclusion, this is a rather short one, but some common sense must be used before the rule applies. The rule absolutely applies to exclude persons who are friends *or merely acquaintances* of the sheriff, the chief of police, or the district attorney. It also applies absolutely against those who have any degree of personal friendship, i.e., more than a nodding acquaintance, with any policeman or deputy sheriff of whatever rank. The rule also applies against jurors who number more than one policeman or deputy sheriff among their friends or acquaintances, no matter how much the relationships are deprecated by the juror. Of course it applies to anyone whose father, children or siblings are law enforcement officers. And needless to say, it applies to anybody who was ever a law enforcement person, regardless of whatever else may be said.

This rule does *not* necessarily apply to the juror who

simply happens to be acquainted with a law enforcement officer (or more likely, the latter's family) merely because they live more or less in the same neighborhood. Common sense dictates that in this situation the relationship will have to be explored, and it may turn out that this is not the time to apply an arbitrary rule at all—this relationship is merely something to remember in forming an intuitive opinion as to this juror.

Also, the lawyer cannot afford to indulge this rule uncritically with respect to relatives of police. There are far too many of them, and in many cases the relationship does not matter at all. If the juror has a brother-in-law or a cousin in some other part of the country who happens to be a law enforcement officer, that fact alone is no reason to invoke this rule. Closer relationships are also subject to discriminating judgment, but only where circumstances require it.

The lawyer would never, under any circumstances, accept a policeman's mother on the jury, but if he is confronted with hard decisions and is short of challenges, he might once in a while accept a policeman's wife. The lawyer will have to do that with great care, and entirely on the basis of subjective readings and his own estimate of the people remaining in the room who have not been called. Women see their husbands differently than mothers see their sons. If they have been married for at least four or five years, if she has a mind of her own, if strong subjective feelings (discussed infra) indicate that she might be a good defense juror, and particularly if the agency which her husband works for is not directly involved in the case, then the policeman's wife may possibly be a good defense juror. The responsibility of deciding to keep her is a heavy one, and makes a heavy demand on the lawyer's sense of rapport and his sense of hers. The decision to keep her probably can never be taken if there are two or more lawyers on the defense side, since there would not be enough of that feeling to sustain both lawyers.

People who work for insurance companies and have any contact with claims adjustment should not be accepted. It should be remembered, however, that insurance companies employ many kinds of talent, and women in particular who work for insurance companies may do things wholly unrelated to claims work. On the other hand, men who work for insurance companies (casualty insurance, not life insurance) pick up attitudes—possibly related to some gender identification with the company's liability to financial claims—which makes them antagonistic to criminal defendants. They should not be accepted. This rules of exclusion applies even more vehemently to persons who work for claim adjustment firms, and to their spouses.

Many insurance adjustment firms are small, and it is quite common that what is now a well-established firm was, until five years ago, a strictly mom and pop operation. The fact that a woman in the jury box says her husband is a claims adjuster is not merely a statement of spousal employment—it may well be the statement of a dominant and not very silent partner who until recently did all the typing and filing. One should ask her about this.

While there may seem no rational explanation for a rule barring insurance personnel and insurance adjusters (because they do not seem directly related to criminal prosecutions) this relationship of antagonism is quite real to anyone who knows anything about lawyers. For example, it is a simple fact that most lawyers who defend criminal cases, to the extent that they engage in personal injury litigation, almost invariably represent plaintiffs. Former prosecutors, when they find themselves in this line of work, almost always are counted among the partners and employees of law firms retained by insurance companies. A former deputy of the United States attorney's office will often gravitate to a particular type of downtown law firm, where he performs a certain function, i.e., he is the acceptable bully. These patterns and alliances are undeniable although reasons are not always apparent. These same patterns hold rather inflexibly that persons touched with insurance casualty adjustment are poisonous from the point of view of any criminal defendant, let alone a political one.

Another arbitrary rule is to exclude business executives in any line of work. They are persuasive people to the extent that they are successful as executives. It is especially important to strike them on an arbitrary basis without the slightest regret or second thoughts, for three simple reasons: (1) they are antithetical to the defendant's viewpoints; (2) they tend to become jury foreman and to organize juries in short order, not only to convict the defendant, but to do so cheerfully; and (3) most lawyers are duck soup for this kind of juror. Duck soup may not be a flattering self-image for anybody, but certain lawyer traits, interestingly diagnosed as resulting from psychological self-selection and various well-known pedagogic methods,[5] do show up in picking juries. A lawyer standing in front of the jury box making judgments on panelists is exactly the sort of person with whom a moderately successful executive is most adept at dealing. If a lawyer indulges in intuitive judgments and listens to the executive for about three minutes, the executive will know exactly how to talk him out of the peremptory challenge. The executive will gently sell himself in the image the lawyer seems to want, without too much effort. He may seem to the lawyer an unusual man of the world, accustomed to make decisions on the basis of information supplied to him by others, gentle, articulate, and not a person to be fooled by a ponied-up case or the blusterings of the deputy district attorney. All of this is nonsense. The man will ruin the jury if he is allowed to stay there. If the lawyer lets himself be flattered or cozened into permitting the executive to stay, his case will be in shambles before it starts.

The executive in fact belongs to a different subculture, and he has the ways and mannerisms of a lifetime lived differently. The only way to contend with him is to make an arbitrary judgment to reject him and then to stick to it.

Old jurors are not good defense jurors, where there is any choice. If it happens that the jurisdiction is one in which panelists serve for six months at a time, it will probably be true that everybody on the panel has some prior experience. But in other jurisdictions it may well be true that at least half the panel has never served on a jury, and the other half not more than once or twice. This allows some choice, which should generally be exercised *against* anyone who has served on a prior *criminal* jury. They have heard too much discussion of reasonable doubt, and they will turn off before the lawyer gets a chance to sell them his main defense.

Prior jury service is of course a mild sort of disqualification, having no part of the virulence which attaches to being a real estate broker, for example.

On the other hand, anyone who has ever served on a grand jury at any time in his life in any jurisdisction should be kept out of the box. This *is* a very strong prohibition, but there is probably no need to compare it to the other strong ones since any person who has been on a grand jury will be found to be disqualified on several other counts already, e.g., as a rancher or a business executive. Grand jury service, however, is a special disqualification, since members of grand juries become closely identified with the particular district attorney who leads them in their quest for justice. They never even see defense lawyers in a grand jury room. All they know is that they are serving God and their community by indicting everybody the district attorney says to indict; they really feel themselves to be in partnership with mighty forces, which just happen to be allied with the prosecution. These people are poison. There is just no use thinking about them.

Once in a while an unusually ingratiating person—usually a man—will show up in the jury box, who will fit no other arbitrary rule but this one: he must be excluded because he threatens to be a one-man jury. The reason the lawyer has to do it on an arbitrary basis is that he probably *cannot* do it on a purely intuitive basis. This fellow is just too winsome. He may be a little older, but with few signs of aging; he is courteous to the other jurors and all the lawyers, and he spreads a sense of well-being. He is attentive to the ladies seated near him in the jury box, he radiates compassion, and if one just probes a little deeper, he is thinking of running for public office. One cannot very well ask him if he is about to run for public office, but a few simple inquiries may show that he has been a candidate at least once for some minor office, and that it was in this community. He is thinking about running again. He is a kind of leader, a point which is evident not so much because he shows stereotyped leadership qualities, but because he is unarguably accepted as such by eleven other persons who have not yet even been sworn as jurors.

This kind of juror is exceptionally hard to dislodge once he has been on the jury for several days, which is exactly the position he is in when one at last recognizes him. He will have been there several days because nobody thought to challenge him, and so challenges will have been used all around him. This is noteworthy in a large case, where a number of lawyers have to more or less agree on what they are going to do for the defense. Everyday that goes on with this man in the box makes it less thinkable for anyone to challenge him.

The hallmark of this kind of juror is that when the lawyer analyzes his own feelings, he will find something close to *fear* to make this challenge. There is going to be a profound reaction among the remaining jurors, including friendly jurors; and if there are other lawyers in the case, there are certainly going to be some earnest discussions in the conference room before this juror can be challenged. But once he is recognized, the only possible solution is to challenge him, even if that means (in respect to this one act) stepping totally apart from the other lawyers in the case, and the clients as well. This is serious business and it has to be done. The alternative is to have a one-man jury, and that cannot be countenanced.

It should also be noted that when this dominant type of juror is finally challenged by one side or the other, there will be an almost physical change of temperature in the courtroom. A cold blast will be felt. And afterwards, a lot of tacit agreements between prosecution and defense —which no one may have thought about as agreements— will suddenly be ruptured. If a large number of challenges are available on both sides—which there probably will be in a large case—then the penalty will be that many friendly jurors, previously regarded as safe (because they had survived so many opportunities for challenge) will suddenly be thrown off the jury by the prosecution. There will be similar retaliations by the defense. There will be a kind of frenzy of striking people who otherwise would have stayed in the jury.

That is bad news from the trial scheduling point of view, since it may protract the jury selection process by a full week and in the long run make for a blander jury than was desired. But that prospect is no reason to leave the dominant juror in the box; he must go.

[2] Intuitive Judgments

These are the lawyer's personal feelings about how a prospective juror will actually work out. These feelings are based partly on the information available, but mostly they arise while standing close to the juror and asking questions; they are more related to insight than to information, and they have little to do with rules. Things will be known from the juror's age, appearance, dress, sense of style or the lack of it, and ways of dealing with other persons in the room. There will be answers to questions about occupation and so forth, the same things which may or may not have triggered some arbitrary decision to exclude the juror. Most importantly, things are revealed by the way the juror answers questions asked by the lawyer, dealing with the lawyer directly. Everything is grist for intuitive feelings, there is no need to be overly analytical as to the origin of one's own. The main thing in picking a jury is to be sure that there is enough raw material to generate intuitions (see § 11.06[6]).

Intuitive feelings are by far the more important of the two general methods for picking jurors. This is true because, of the first twelve persons tentatively placed in the box, purely arbitrary decisions will account for only four or five of them in an average draw. The lawyer will always be choosing among the others and comparing them to the panelists not yet called into the box. All of this selecting is done by intuitive judgment; if the lawyer cannot do this really well, he is not going to end up with an adequate jury.

The only thing to remember about intuitive judgment is the seeming anomaly that while intuition is far more reliable and more important than arbitrary judgment, to use it right, one has to subordinate intuition to arbitrariness. This is true because with intuition, first impressions are usually the right ones; the longer one reads these impressions, the less reliable they are.

Normal courtroom pressures tend to accelerate the empanelment of a jury. These pressures arise from fatigue, self-consciousness (about asking repetitive questions), discouragement at the quality of the panel which is slowly passing through the jury box, and mounting concern as the number of peremptory challenges drops and the threat of an uncontrolled choice becomes more real. All these things tend to warp a lawyer's judgment and push him toward accepting particular individuals who happen to be presently seated in the box.

As it often happens, some of those individuals should not be allowed to stay there, but for competitive reasons they want to stay. They will make themselves agreeable and they will see to it, after watching each other answer questions, that to the extent it is humanly possible for them to do so, they will give the right answers. All of these things tend to warp intuitive judgments, although none of them and no combination of them is sufficient to destroy early impressions, *if* the lawyer remembers to place special value on these impressions.

For all of these reasons, whoever is using intuitive judgments has to take special care—must in fact use particular mental force and self-discipline—in order to provide a finite area where his innate abilities are allowed to function near their best levels. In other words, the lawyer will have to have an established set of priorities which controls the way decisions will be made in picking the jury. He must be able to rely upon these priorities regardless whether he is fresh or tired, and in the face of all kinds of judicial conduct.

[3] Suggested Priority

The following is a sturdy and simple list of priorities which will work well enough, and is offered for the benefit of anyone who lacks his own, until he can work out something better.

As a general rule, arbitrary decisions to exclude people from the jury should be followed as far as they are applicable, regardless of intuitive feelings. Nobody should ever be kept *on* a jury because of any arbitrary judgment, but any number of people can be thrown *off* juries for arbitrary reasons. The lawyer can look at the first twelve people in the box, and on the basis of general information, he can probably exclude a few of them because of their occupations, friends and associates. When the arbitrary rules require someone to be excused from the jury, that decision should be made immediately and the lawyer should *adhere* to it, regardless whether he later gets good little vibrations from these same people. To that extent, arbitrary judgments should prevail over intuitive ones.

Of course, this does not mean that the people who are to be excluded on account of some arbitrary rule are necessarily the first ones to be struck when it comes time to use peremptory challenges (for the order of strikes, see § 11.09[2]). But it does mean that in the lawyer's mind, there has been a firm decision that those people will not remain on the jury.

The majority of panelists will be unaffected by any arbitrary rule, and to choose among these, the lawyer simply uses intuitive judgments, with special value being placed on early impressions.

There is one situation where intuitive judgments necessarily take priority over arbitrary ones. This is where the lawyer only has a few peremptory challenges, and the jury draw is so bad that there are more people remaining in the box who ought to be excused, purely on the basis of arbitrary rules, than there are challenges remaining: e.g., the lawyer has three peremptory challenges, and there are two real estate brokers, a rancher, a recent member of the grand jury, and the mother of a policeman all seated in the box. The fact that this is a regrettable problem does not mean it does not have to be dealt with ("solved" is too strong a word), and in choosing the least of evils, the lawyer will have to use intuitive judgments. There is a wry consolation in knowing that no matter what the lawyer does with this problem, it makes little difference.

[4] Timing of Decisions

It is a good idea always to have in mind a tentative list of who will have to be struck from the jury panel by one side or the other, and who the lawyer hopes will stay. One should always know who are the next two or three people he would most like to get off the jury, and in what order, and whom he intends to strike next.

The time for exercising challenges will come soon enough, and when it does, there is no controlling whether the prosecution will exercise their turn promptly or wallow in indecision. The time for exercising one's own challenges always comes rather suddenly, and it is obviously important for the lawyer to know what he wants to do at that moment. If he does not know, then he will sit there, and even if he is thinking about something else, every person in the jury box will suspect that he is thinking about striking that person, and they will all resent it. It is important to be prompt about exercising challenges.

Also, if the lawyer knows at all times whom he wants to excuse, whom he wants to keep, and exactly which people he is uncertain about, then he always has a good idea of how close he is to having an adequate jury (see § 11.09 [3]). This information, coupled with a continuing awareness of who is still waiting to be called to the jury box, and how many challenges each side has remaining, will keep the lawyer appraised of whether he can make it.

§ 11.06 The Lawyer's First Questions to the Jury Panel; Beginning the Final Argument; and Getting Information and Impressions Needed to Make Decisions

[1] Insuring the Opportunity to Address Questions Individually to Members of the Jury Panel

It is extremely important for the lawyer to be able to ask at least a few questions of each individual member of the jury panel, including not only the first twelve seated in the box, but each successive person who fills a vacancy on the panel. This contact between lawyer and jurors is thought by most lawyers to be an essential part of jury

326 / POLITICAL CRIMINAL TRIALS

trials, and is traditionally respected in most states, although not of course in the federal courts. At the time of writing this book there is a movement afoot, however, sponsored by some bar association leaders and appellate judges, aimed at reducing the participation of lawyers in criminal cases. Although this movement is ostensibly aimed at "stream-lining" jury selection in civil cases, where the worst backlogs occur, it has begun to slop over into state court criminal procedures.

As matters stand, most trial court judges are reluctant to exclude counsel from the jury selection process, notwithstanding the fact that they may be egged on to do this by appellate courts. As the encouragement from above becomes more intense, trial judges will probably divide into those who will and those who will not exclude defense counsel from participation in the questioning of prospective jurors. As this development unfolds, defense lawyers may have little choice but to seek legislation (writs of mandamus will not do it) in order to prevent the loss of their right to question jurors. But writs, appeals, and legislative hearings are time consuming and in no way compensate for adverse jury verdicts.

As long as there are only a few judges who attempt to exclude the lawyers from the jury selection process, the willingness or unwillingness of a judge to do this should be the strongest criterion applied in the "selection" of judges (see § 10.03). In other words, the lawyer will not confront this problem for the first time at the beginning of the jury trial, but rather will have done everything possible to have the case assigned to a judge who will *not* interfere too much in the jury selection process.

[2] Introductory Comments to the Jury Panel

When the lawyer's turn comes to ask a few questions of the jury panel, he should start with some remarks directed at the panel and all the prospective jurors who are seated in the courtroom. The whole purpose and tone of these remarks should be warm, relaxed and reassuring (in complete contrast to the way the lawyer has been looking at the panel while they were being called into the box).

In order to avoid precipitating a premature onslaught from a hostile or strange judge, the lawyer should begin his remarks rather carefully. Since he wishes to do his actual voir dire as close as possible to the jury box, and since some judges will attempt to interfere with that rather natural wish, it is important either to (1) divert the judges attention, and sooth him so that he will not attempt to interject himself, or (2) put him in such a position that if he does so he will look bad in the eyes of the jury.

For these reasons, and to be heard in the courtroom, the lawyer should begin his comments somewhere near his own chair, rather than walking the length of the counsel table to the jury box before speaking. Also, while his remarks are mainly addressed to those in the box, he will have to turn from time to time while he is talking to make sure that his voice reaches the farthest corner of the room. It is imperative that he do this, not only for the obvious purpose of being heard, but to head off interruptions from the bench inviting the lawyer to speak up. It is particularly important to speak slowly.

The lawyer should remind the jury panel who he is and whom he represents, even though he was introduced within the past two minutes. He should tell them that what he is about to say is really said on behalf of the prosecutor as well as himself, and that *we* would like the jury panel to know that while the questions will be rather personal, they are not being asked with the intention of prying into the jurors' affairs. The reason is that it is important to the moral force of the decision which is reached at the end of the case that both sides should have agreed, before the case began, that the jury was chosen as fairly as possible. And so the point of the questions will simply be to assure both sides of the lawsuit that the jury is a fair one. There are certain questions that *must* be asked, and are going to be asked, but they will all be asked for that reason.

Since the defense lawyer in a political case is the one more threatened by a bad jury draw, he will probably be the one reading the jurors more intently. He may be the one who exercises more challenges, and if so he will certainly be the one who is identified as forcing the selection process. If both sides had ten challenges and the defense lawyer stopped at four, it is likely (in most cases) that the prosecution would do about the same. The defense probably cannot be that casual, but will usually come closer to its limit. The jury panel will sense this forcing relationship before long, as soon as the prosecution accept the panel and the defense does not; for that reason the lawyer must protect himself now against the onus of being too picky, of prolonging a tedious process.

The lawyer not only needs understanding, he also needs some candor from the jury and relaxation with them. He *cannot* do this all at arm's length, he *must* enlist them to share in the values which underlie his search, even though it is one for their own weaknesses. So it is a good idea at this point to stress that on some subjects, everybody has *feelings* (*not* "prejudices"). The universal existence of some form of prejudice is a point not debatable in the privacy of an honest mind. The lawyer should go on to say, however, that there is no stigma attached to these feelings; actually, the only bad thing a prospective juror can do is conceal them. The fair and honorable thing is simply to acknowledge one's feelings even if not directly asked to do so, and if that means one does not sit on the jury in this particular case, well "God bless you, sit on a jury in some other case. We will appreciate your honesty." It is important for the lawyer to be absolutely reassuring while explaining this, to speak informally, to say it and mean it, and really to sell the idea that an honest admission of "feelings" is a commendable thing which one can do with good grace, and walk out of the room with thanks from every corner.

The lawyer should maintain everybody in the room within the scope of his remarks, and at the conclusion of them he should be standing rather close to the jury box. If some lectern or movable podium has been placed there at the wishes of the judge, he should (for reasons discussed below) be standing away from it, and oblivious to it. After all, the lectern faces the one direction, but the lawyer was talking to everybody.

Most hostile judges will refrain from interrupting remarks of this kind. However, a very hostile judge may be pitched overboard by his apprehension that the lawyer is stealing his show. A judge like that is going to make an ass of himself through the whole trial anyway, and it is especially appropriate that he should begin by interrupting a speech such as this. These remarks are intended to be so soothing and nonpartisan that any little Caligula who interrupts to tell the lawyer to get on with his questions to the jury is going to look bad. If it is going to be that way, better to have it overt and obvious from the beginning, and to have it begin on something that does not involve any particular point of law.

This is why, if the lawyer senses the judge is boiling with hostility, likely to spill over on the defense end of the table, he should never be deterred from making this particular approach to the jury panel, but the contrary. That is why, with a very hostile judge, the lawyer should be especially mindful *not* to give the judge either of two seemingly reasonable grounds for interrupting him. The lawyer should pitch his voice quite audibly, to prevent being told to "speak up"; and the lawyer should begin his remarks near his own end of the counsel table, to prevent an interruption on the ground that he has got so near the jury box he has backsided the judge and therefore become inaudible.

[3] How Close to Stand While Working With the Jury

This is one of the most important things in the trial: the lawyer should stand as close as reasonably possible to the persons who occupy the jury box, while he is asking them questions. Assuming no interference from the bench, he should generally stand close enough to touch the jury box, at a point somewhere near the middle. Moving around a little may help to keep one relaxed, which is good because the lawyer should be generally outgoing while talking to the jury. It is important to be very openhanded in giving impressions to the jury during this process, as to what the lawyer is like, and how he expects to treat the jury. The more of these impressions he gives at this time, the stronger and more reliable will be the reactions of the panel members. If he keeps himself covered up, they cannot really see him, to like him or dislike him, and so he cannot read in their faces now what will be written there later. In this way the lawyer will certainly fool himself.

If there is a lectern provided, it is a good idea to avoid it. This is true notwithstanding that a younger lawyer may feel a strong wish to use the lectern—it is especially true if he feels that wish. There is always a pressure felt by anyone getting up to speak to a jury, but it is felt rather acutely by younger lawyers; they naturally wish to retreat into the role of professional men [6]—teachers in fact—and they feel a considerable easing of tension once they step behind the lectern. Similarly, an older lawyer whose main line of trial experience has been defending civil lawsuits may have become quite habituated to the use of a lectern, since it suits those cases so well.

All of these little tugs should be disregarded. One step behind that lectern will almost certainly kill off any chance of establishing rapport with the jury at this time. The lawyer is not a teacher addressing a class; he is certainly not there to tell the jury what it must do; and if he feels exposed to something without the lectern, so are the individual members sitting in the box. They do not have lecterns. This will not be the only time during the trial that the lawyer and the jury will share that element of exposure.

If the courtroom is one in which the judge *likes* to have lawyers use the lectern, perhaps because it has a microphone and he is hard of hearing, the problem is easily solved. The lawyer can stand beside the lectern, with his arm affectionately on it if need be, and he can pull the microphone over so as to solve the judge's problem. But there should be nothing between him and the jury box.

The rationale for all of this advice is hard to explain except in terms of pragmatic results. Jury trials are highly personal things. Tension, unease and personal contact are the inseparable companions of a successful defense. Also, there does seem to be a kind of short-range radar in human relations, by which it is possible for human beings to pick up many impressions and impulses from one another when they are in close physical proximity, which would be missed if they were a few feet farther apart. This is really the main reason. The lawyer will be standing there in front of the jury box, and he will know things about the people in the box like he knows his own name, as clear as daylight, while there will be people seated ten feet farther away, in the same room, including his own client (and the judge) who do not get any of these impressions. They have no idea how much information the lawyer is getting, or what he is up to. The immediate presence of the jury is a rich matrix of impressions, and they get impressions of the lawyer on the same scale. This is a good way to exchange impressions and draw conclusions. There seems to be no substitute.

[4] A General Method for Questioning Panel Members Individually

The main point is that they *are* to be questioned individually, not broadside, as long as the lawyer has a choice. There is absolutely nothing to be gained by standing in front of a jury box and addressing good questions in a dumb way, by asking them of the panel as a whole. This is cold, stupid, and absolutely never to be done except under the compulsion of a court order. The truth is that when questions are asked in this way, of the group, the individuals sitting in the box not only are reluctant to answer, they hardly feel addressed at all.

If anyone doubts that he has only to ask a general question of the panel in two ways, and then add up the responses and see if they come to twelve. For example, ask the whole panel if there is anyone persent who is related to a police officer. There may be two hands. But if the next question is, is there anyone on the panel who is *not* related to a police officer, there will be only two or three hands, or none. For the most part, the panel is not involved enough to answer, at least not at that time.

If this pattern of questioning is the only one allowed or followed, some of the jurors may eventually respond, later, who should have done so at the time. After the jury has been sworn, someone may timidly raise a hand and say that she has been thinking about an earlier question (asked about an hour and a half before) and has decided that she *is* related to a police officer, since her brother is on the force. Other members of the panel may be harboring similar qualifications hardly less killing than that.

The fault is not with the jurors, who are not mendacious by nature, but with the asinine notion that broadside questions are as good as any other. The lawyer should always ask individual questions unless blocked by a court order, and when that happens he should occasionally sprinkle the record with instances of double questions like the one mentioned above, noting after each question the number of responses, and informing the court after each such episode that he is genuinely confused as to the meaning of these contradictory negative responses; he should then specifically request permission to ask individual questions, to clarify the situation. The judge may not like that approach, but that is unfortunate; broadside questions are the special pet of prosecution-minded judges, and pleasing them is bad for the soul.

The next main thing of course is to question jurors by name. If the lawyer feels he cannot do it the other way, notes may be used for this purpose, but if notes are used, they should be only for names—not to remind the lawyer what questions to ask. The lawyer should be scrupulous to maintain eye contact with the juror while asking questions, and *keep his own eyes wide open.* He should pronounce words carefully, giving the consonants full value. He should speak slowly, and loudly enough for the judge to hear.[7]

The lawyer's questions for different panelists will be roughly the same in content, although they need not be in the same order. There is no reason to be self-conscious. After awhile the jury panel may react to the monotony of repetitive questions and the lawyer will of course know that. But the reaction will be sympathetic boredom, not to be mistaken for the other kind, and it does not last.

There is no magic about the order in which individual members are questioned. While the lawyer may very well wish to jump around (from one row to the other, picking at random) doing so makes it harder to be sure, after a long voir dire, that one has actually asked questions of everybody. There is little to be gained by jumping around, even though the pattern is *not* random and the lawyer has no difficulty keeping it straight in his own mind. The panel members are not going to sleep in any case, and there is no need to keep their attention by this artificial device.

On the other hand there is a strong reason *not* to jump around: it is important to the lawyer that each member of the panel should feel sure that once the questioning is past him, his speaking lines are temporarily over. As long as the lawyer is jumping around, it will not be clear to the jury that he is really asking questions of one person at a time only. They will suspect that he may intend to come back and ask further questions of various members; from where they sit, it is impossible to be sure what the lawyer is doing. They do not even know each others' names yet. The difficulty is that if they think they are all on the spot at the same time, they will all keep their urban masks firmly in place. They will all remain on the alert, a highly undesirable state of affairs for the lawyer.

It seems better practice to go right down the line, giving a tacit assurance to each person that after his or her turn has come, that will be that. This way, when the lawyer gets a smart-assed answer from some juror—which is bound to happen once in a while—the others will be relatively relaxed; they will know that their turn has already passed, or has not yet come. At that moment, the lawyer can understand more about a jury panel than he could learn with an extra hour of questioning, simply by noting out of the corner of his eye who is pleased by the smart-assed remark, who thinks that was a clever little thing to say and secretly admires the courage of the juror who said it, and on the other hand who is on the lawyer's side. If the lawyer has been asking questions straight down the line, he will have no difficulty getting this reading; if he has been jumping around, he may not get it at all.

[5] Questions to Set the Case and Begin the Final Argument

There are a few questions that have to be asked of every single juror, including those whom the lawyer has already decided to strike. He must ask these questions in order to set up the jury for the final argument, extracting a serious promise from each person who will ultimately sit there. These promises will give the lawyer leverage to make the jury take the law seriously, and to offset the fact that the prosecution case goes on first. He must ask these same questions of those whom he is going to strike because failure to do so would clearly give away his intentions in that secret matter.

Since the final argument is going to begin with a reference to the time when the jury was selected (see § 16.04[3]), the lawyer must now frame these questions with the opening portion of his final argument in mind. It is suggested that these mandatory questions for individual members of the jury panel include the following.

1. *If you serve as a member of this jury, would you make every effort to keep an open mind about the case until it is finally submitted to the jury?* The juror will undoubtedly answer, yes. But instead of being satisfied with the first yes, the lawyer should take the occasion to explain what he means, not just to the persons in the box but the entire panel seated elsewhere in the room. He will only have to make this explanation once, unless an entirely fresh panel is later sent to this department. The explanation is, when we say "until the case is submitted to the jury," that is really much longer than a person might think. First the prosecution puts on its case. Then the defense puts on its case. Then the prosecution and the defense may wish to put on further evidence. The juror is expected to keep an open mind throughout all of that, and that is not all. The lawyers then argue the case, first the People, then the defense, and then the People. After that, the judge will instruct the jury on the law. Only then will the case be "submitted" to the jury, and the jury will at that time be allowed to discuss the case and begin to draw conclusions. It is very hard to keep an open mind throughout all of these proceedings and until the case is submitted to the jury, particularly since, as in this case, that may require (whatever period of time the lawyer estimates). The juror will find it hard to do, but he will be expected to do it. So the question really is, bearing all of that in mind, will you make every human *effort* to keep

an open mind until the case is finally submitted to the jury? Having got a second yes from his panel member, the lawyer can safely include the short version of this question among those asked of each successive jury panelist.

2. *If you serve in this jury, would you judge the case entirely on its own evidence, and not on the basis of any guess-work or speculation?* Once in a while this question can be supplemented with one on the subject of keeping political views out of the case (discussed below), but the question of political views is primarily for the tone of the case, not something to be laid on every single person in the box.

3. *If you serve on this jury, would you take the law exactly as Judge Hardtack gives it to the jury at the end of the case, regardless of whether, in your own mind, you might feel that some part of the law is wise or unwise, or whether you may not have been familiar with parts of the law before?*

This has to do of course with reasonable doubt, but in an indirect way. The difference here is, this question can be laid on every member of the panel and the judge will not object to it at all. He rather likes to have his name mentioned, and can certainly find no fault with the notion that the jury will accept the law from him. Of course the lawyer will also be asking questions about reasonable doubt, but in order to avoid being accused by the judge in the presence of the jury of attempting to teach them the law, the lawyer should be well advised not to attempt to teach them the law, at least not blatantly.

Besides the above questions which should be asked of everybody, the reasonable doubt question should be used with discretion, say on every third or fourth person who is questioned. This of course is not because reasonable doubt is less important than the things mentioned above. On the contrary, it is undoubtedly the most important part of the defendant's case.

The problem at the beginning of every criminal case is how to drive the concept of reasonable doubt into the jury without getting called down for doing so. For this reason, it is suggested that the reasonable doubt question be triggered primarily where something about the juror's personality actually raises the problem: it is not at all a bad thing to lay this question on someone whom the lawyer has already decided to strike, because it clearly signals to the rest of the jury, after he is gone, what the reason may have been. The question may be phrased something like the following: *Among the principles of law which Judge Hardtack will give to the jury at the end of this case will probably be the well-known rule that a defendant in a criminal case is presumed to be innocent unless proven guilty beyond a reasonable doubt. Would you have any personal reluctance or mental reservations about applying that rule in this case?* If there are any real doubts about this, the lawyer may well follow the question with another along the following lines: *Do you belong to any organization or group that has among its purposes that of changing established rules of procedure in criminal cases?*

Another necessary but intermittent question in a political case concerns the exclusion of personal views from the trial. That can be accomplished with a question something like the following: *I suppose like everybody else, you read local newspapers? Are you a subscriber of the [local newspaper]? And I guess that like everybody else, you sometimes watch television?* (It is a good idea to couch this rather gently, including the juror along with the rest of society, and mentioning that his television watching is only intermittent, since nobody likes to admit that he has nothing better to do than sit around watching television.)

At the time of this civil disturbance that happened last June, I suppose like everybody else you were generally aware of what was reported in the press and on television concerning those events? And I guess like everybody alse you probably had some feelings on the general subject of permissiveness, the police, and student demonstrations?

All right, if you serve on this jury, do you feel that you could set aside whatever feelings [not "prejudices"] you may have, as a voter or a member of society, on the subject of confrontations or whatever, and just decide this case on its own facts, and treat it as a universe within itself?

Do you understand that this is not any kind of "political case"? In other words, the universities are not on trial here, the police department is not on trial here, and we are not settling any kind of social issues in this case? Do you understand that? Would you just treat this case as an old-fashioned case, not as some kind of political case?

Obviously all of those questions are not meant to be nailed together and asked back-to-back of the same person. They are simply variations on a theme, the theme being absolutely essential to the conduct of the case: namely that this is a legal case in which the defense relies on traditional legal values. Conversely, anybody who tries to turn this into a political circus is bent on perverting the law. Anybody who attempts to try the defendant as a member of a group or a social movement, or who chastises the defendant's witnesses as members of a politically inferior class, is himself no better than a criminal. *It is absolutely essential to get this message over to the jury.*

The way to get it over is to ask these questions sincerely and thoroughly, and with the obvious (though tacit) approval of the court. The court will not wish to do anything but approve it, and consequently relations between the defense and the judge will improve steadily as this line of questions goes on. Every time the questions are asked, it is a further assurance to the judge that the defense is not planning a political outburst in his courtroom, and has no intention of attempting to humiliate him or to disparage the law in the presence of the jury.

While this alliance grows and these questions are

hammered home, the prosecution must necessarily sit there dumb, since their turn has not come. They have nothing to do about the growing liaison between the defense and the judge, and little enough time to reshape their thinking should that be their wish. When this line of voir dire has finally been completed, along with the other questions discussed below, there should be no ground at all on which the prosecution can stand. They are the people who came in here to try a political case, they are pretty hell bent on it, and as soon as they start doing it with their own voir dire they are going to get stoned. Actually, the only thing the proceedings lack is a convenient moment in which the prosecution might apologize for planning a political circus.

[6] Questions to Get Necessary Information and Impressions About Jurors

There is no special order to these questions. They may precede or mix with the other kind of questions, those designed to set the tone of the case and lay the foundation for final argument (described above). These questions (to elicit information) will supplement what the judge has just asked the panel, picking up exactly where he left off. If the judge inquired as to a juror's occupation, the lawyer should inquire about the occupation of the juror's spouse, about whether the juror has children or grandchildren and how many and—if the case is one which involves students— whether any of these children were ever students at the same university as the students involved in this case.

Incidentally, if they were not, it may not be a good idea to press general inquiries as to the extent of the education of various members of the juror's family. A juror may not be self-conscious about his own education or limitations, but there is snob appeal attached to education; detailed questioning as to how well the juror's offspring have been educated, under the prevailing social view that nothing is good enough, tends to draw down an inevitable pall of self-consciousness and embarrassment over any juror forced to answer these questions, probably more than he or she should have to handle. If there is something really special about the education of the juror's children, that revelation will often be triggered by simple inquiries as to whether they went to the particular school involved in this case. The answer may well be yes they did, but the juror made them live at home, which tells the lawyer all he needs to know about the juror's own impressions of the child's contemporaries (some of whom may soon be testifying in this case.) Or, the juror may say no, and by a tone of rectitude indicate that more and more of his children are attending college at a particular church school, or in a city which clearly imparts to the lawyer's mind the fact that they are attending a church school which is located there. That information should tell the lawyer a great deal about the juror without the need of asking the awkward question (not allowed in most courts), "What is your religion?" (But with evangelical fundamentalists, particularly young ones, a more frank line of questions is entirely appropriate: see § 11.07[3]).

Other obvious follow-up questions concern jury service. Of course, the lawyer will not inquire how the juror voted in some other case. But if the judge's own inquiry for example has already revealed that the juror has served on more criminal cases than the juror can remember, so that the decision has already been made to strike him, it may be a good idea to ask the juror how many civil cases he has sat on. This has a double value: it may turn out that the juror has sat on few or no civil cases and on a lot of criminal cases. The fact that this juror was going to be excused anyway is nothing beside the news that he is a "volunteer" criminal juror. A tactful question or two may confirm what is obvious, that he volunteers for jury duty in criminal cases.

That means the lawyer is dealing with a jury commissioner who keeps a special list of volunteers, and that he assigns them to criminal cases; in the whole history of man, there probably was never a defense juror who was included on a jury commissioner's permanent list of acceptable volunteers.

If the lawyer finds one *on his first panel*, that is bad news indeed, because it indicates an overtly stacked deck. The presence of one or two of these disreputable jurors in the third, fourth, or fifth panel might not be nearly as significant as their presence in the first one, because a later panel may be a small one, huddled up by the jury commissioner on orders from the trial judge, perhaps got together in the late afternoon to report for immediate duty because the trial judge was under the impression that just ten more warm bodies would be enough to satisfy the remaining peremptory challenges—these are still impossible jurors, but under certain circumstances one can expect to meet them. One should never meet them on the first or second panel when clearly there has been time for the commissioner to assemble an honest one.

The other valuable thing about pressing the inquiry concerning civil cases is that it gives the lawyer an opportunity for the time-honored question: whether the juror, in view of his experience in civil cases, would find it difficult to remember that in criminal cases, such as this one, the prosecution must prove its case beyond a reasonable doubt, the rule being otherwise in civil cases. The juror would of course say that he would not find it difficult at all, but the fact that the question was asked will suggest a simple reason, when this juror is later struck from the panel. That reason may be useful, because anyone watching the proceedings might think that in view of his prior "experience," this person would have made a "good" juror.

One line of inquiry which must be followed assiduously concerns the juror's acquaintance with the police. The judge will often have asked this question, but he will never have asked it adequately. It is not just the police that the lawyer is concerned with; he is concerned that the juror may be acquainted with police, members of the sheriff's office, assorted law enforcement officers, judges, members of the district attorney's office, other lawyers in town, and prosecution witnesses. For that reason, it is usually a good idea to frame the question broadly, something like the following.

Is there anyone among your family or circle of friends who is connected with law enforcement. . . , and by "law enforcement," I mean anyone who is a police officer, a deputy sheriff, a lawyer, a member of the district attorney's office, a judge, a bailiff, probation officer, or anyone connected with this line of work?

Any affirmative response should of course be followed up. The lawyer wants to know how close the relationship is. Has this deputy sheriff who is a friend of the juror's been a guest in the juror's house? Has the juror been a guest in his house? How well do they really know each other? If it seems the relationship is slight, the lawyer can leave the subject easily by an innocuous inquiry, whether there is anything in the relationship which the juror feels would make it difficult for him to be fair in a case of this kind, as distinguished from some other kind of case. The answer to that is almost invariably that there will be no problem.

Occasionally a juror will think that question over and bring it up on his own, much later, with a different answer. If this is going to happen, it will probably happen at the beginning of the next session of court, possibly the following morning, at which time the juror may well have relayed his problem directly to the judge. But the first time the question is asked, people seldom admit that there is anything about the relationship. If the lawyer senses there *is*, he must of course press the inquiry, but in a fair way, and not belligerently.

If the answer to the police question is uniformly no, the lawyer should ask related questions, but only if there is something in the juror's background which seems to make them necessary. For example, if the juror works in a bank, he or she has ample opportunity for contact with security guards in the bank, and if the juror works for an insurance company, much of the company's information concerning its claims may come from law enforcement agencies.

If the juror works for the telephone company or some other public utility, the lawyer should always inquire what division of the company that person works for. There are usually several, and it does not hurt for the lawyer to know the names of the three or four major divisions of his local public utility. The point is, he should ask the juror not only what his present job with the telephone company is, but whether he has ever worked in any other division; and in particular, whether he has ever had contact with the "special agents' office" of the telephone company (or whatever its local name is). These are the private police employed by the company, who spend a large part of their time catching persons who rob telephone coin boxes and the like. They are invariably former policemen, and it is part of their work to maintain close liaison with the local law enforcement agencies.

Friendship or acquaintance with anybody in the special agents' office is as virulent as friendship with the particular police officers expected to testify in this case— and often it may turn out to be exactly that.

Naturally the lawyer will want to know about friendship with prosecution witnesses. The best way to find out about this is one which varies considerably from what used to be regarded as the textbook solution. The correct way is simply to be so familiar with the results of one's own pretrial discovery efforts that the lawyer already knows who the prosecution witnesses *may* be, the total list of persons whose testimony against the defendant might be dangerous.

In most cases, this information will make it unnecessary to do what was sometimes regarded as a clever thing, i.e., ask the prosecution in the presence of the jury for a list of their witnesses, for the ostensible purpose of asking the jury whether any of them know any of those witnesses. The difficulty about this in a political case is that the response of the prosecution is never reliable in any event. If they later decide to call a witness whom they had not mentioned in their list, they will never be short of reasons for having omitted his name. But if the lawyer asks for a list in the presence of the jury, the next thing he is going to hear is a similar request from the prosecution for a list of all defense witnesses.

He may hear that anyway, but if he hears it right after making that request himself, he is going to look very bad if he refuses the list. Of course he *must* refuse in any event, since it would be stupid to give the prosecution any advantage in dealing with defense witnesses. It is much better never to ask for a list in the presence of the jury, and if the prosecution does so, brush the request aside with a simple statement that the nature of the defense depends on what evidence, if any, the People care to put on. This should be said with a straight look at the judge—to indicate that a cat fight is about to shape up—which will trigger the judge's impatience with seemingly fruitless quarrels among counsel. He will almost certainly react by telling the lawyers to get on with whatever they were doing, provided only that that the lawyer did not bring this on himself by asking for a list.

Having in mind the names of the main prosecution witnesses, the ones most likely to be called, the lawyer should dispose of them in a way which does *not* build up their prestige or entice the jury to await their testimony with expectation. This is one of the rare instances in which a broadside question is the only way.

The lawyer should simply ask one particular juror if he is acquainted with A, B, C, or D, since it is possible that they may testify in this case. When the answer is no, the lawyer should then turn to those in the box and ask whether anyone else in the box would have answered that question differently. Thereafter, as individuals in the box are replaced one by one, the lawyer will have to use his own judgment whether to repeat the names of these witnesses. He need not do this very often, since having said it once, and perhaps picked it up once or twice later, anyone who was seated in the room who really did know those people will have had a lot of time to think about it, and, in response to some general inquiry as to possible prejudice, will probably reveal that acquaintance.

There can be no definite rules about how often to mention the names of prosecution witnesses to a jury panel, since one must always do this kind of thing by ear. There is value in not mentioning the names, and great value in knowing whether the juror is acquainted with a prosecution witness. This is not life or death, since this particular problem concerns prosecution witnesses other than law enforcement officers. The lawyer will already have found out about them. As to other witnesses, some of the more dangerous ones are not only persons whom the lawyer is going to have to discredit, but persons who are almost certainly discreditable. The fact that a juror knows one of these people may very well mean that the juror has a low opinion of that witnesses' truthfulness, simply because he *does* know him. If the lawyer fails to uncover the fact of their acquaintance and the prosecution do likewise, the prosecution are as likely to be hurt by this oversight as the defense.

In some situations, a noted prosecution witness may be so thoroughly disliked among his circle of acquaintances that the lawyer will *not* ask the jurors whether they know him, out of pure hope that someone who sits in the jury will know him.

In asking questions about occupations, the lawyer should think carefully how they might involve a person with police: e.g., retail liquor dealers are at the mercy of police because their licenses may not be renewed or easily transferred without police approval; and motel owners depend more than most on police cooperation not only in dealing with unruly guests but also in keeping the neighborhood attractive to tourists. The list of occupations which bring a person in contact with the police is a long one. Every time the lawyer comes across a juror in one of these occupations, he should ask about contacts with police, the extent to which they actually occur, and how much they will matter to the juror in the context of this case. For example, if a motel owner (or more likely manager), reveals that he meets police officers from time to time when they come to the premises in response to his own complaints or requests for assistance, but he had not previously mentioned that fact when asked about his acquaintance with police (because he did not know their names and therefore did not feel "acquainted" with them), then he should now be asked the usual questions about acquaintance with police officers. One of these should be something like the following.

Well, assuming you sat as a member of this jury, and if it develops that after all of the evidence and the instructions of the court, the jury votes unanimously for acquittal, do you think that the next time you met one of these police officers, you might be a little bit embarrassed about that, or feel that you would have to make some explanation to him for your vote in the jury room?

If a contractor discloses (because he is asked specifically) that a large amount of his inventory is stored outdoors in relatively unprotected areas, that he values his business relations with the Sheriff's Office (while disclaiming any personal encounters with it), he might be asked whether anything about that business relationship would make it more difficult for him to be fair in a case of this kind than in some other case.

The answer to all questions of this kind will always

be, no. That is not the point. In the two examples cited above (motel owner and contractor), the decision will of course have been made to challenge these people in any event, since they are poison. But asking the question will lay it before the members of the jury who remain, that these little involvements with the police are important, and that the defense is being as careful as possible to select a fair jury.

There will be many times when the lawyer will ask questions concerning occupational involvement with police, will get the same negative answers, and will be quite satisfied with them; e.g., a telephone operator may have occasional business contacts with a member of the special agents' office of the telephone company (private police) and the relationship may mean nothing. If she is going to stay on the jury, it is well to ask her about it and let her think about it and realize that these questions are being asked with the tacit approval of the court and that the court and the lawyer mean business. Only when this is done can these relatively dangerous portions of a person's background be considered safe for purposes of trial, and only *then* when the lawyer is dealing with a relatively favorable juror.

There is of course another possible area of involvement between a potential juror and the police, and one which must be explored delicately. The question is, has the juror (or a member of the juror's family) ever been a victim of some crime? It is generally considered not a good idea to ask the question in those terms. It sets all the jurors thinking about the law from the viewpoint of the victim of the crime, whether or not any of them has been one. If the answer is yes, it may be a crime which the juror would be embarrassed to reveal.

The traditional inquiry is simply to ask whether there is anybody among the circle of the juror's family or friends (a group which obviously includes the juror) who has ever been a complaining witness in any criminal case. If the juror does not seem to understand what complaining witness means, the lawyer should explain that it means victim of a crime.

If the answer is yes, then the lawyer will have to explore it further, but his questions should aim at the conclusion, (whether it will matter), not the details. The reason for this is to spare the juror's feelings if the details are embarrassing. The juror may respond directly by saying that there is something there, that it *does* matter and that he would rather be excused because he does not feel he could be fair in this case. A question designed to do this might be something like the following.

Well, without going into personal details, is there anything about the situation which you feel might make it difficult for you to be fair in this case?

On the other hand, if it does not matter at all, the juror in almost every instance will respond by saying first that it does not matter, and second, by assuring the lawyer to the extent of supplying a few details. If the lawyer wants more he should ask for them.

The lawyer may very well want more details, especially if the juror feels quite at ease, and the lawyer senses that the juror has especially warm feelings for the law enforcement agency which got his stolen car back for him. These things may be followed up in a matter-of-fact way, and they should be.

§ 11.07 The Special Need for Careful Intuitive Evaluations of Stereotyped Defense Jurors

There are two general kinds of "defense jurors" who are often accepted when they should not be, and who can be harmful to the defense case far out of proportion to their voting power on the jury. These are members of minority groups who are under particular stress in the community, and young people.

It cannot be said too often that jurors can be *rejected* for arbitrary reasons, but nobody should be *accepted* because of an arbitrary rule. In any American city, blacks are still taking plenty of stress from the dominant white majority. They are invariably under stress from the police department, which has been selected (or self-selected) [8] as the instrument for keeping blacks in their place. Blacks are therefore often assumed to be natural defense jurors. Similarly, younger people have sometimes sponsored and energized political change, and sometimes they have been on the receiving end of police violence. Young people are a relief and a welcome sight to the defense lawyer when they appear in the jury panel.

The same reasons that make blacks and young people generally desirable on juries are the reasons which give them a disproportionate voice in the jury room. If there are only one or two blacks or young people on a jury dominated by older caucasians, then a great deal of trust has been placed in the mouths of those one or two blacks or young people. If they are *really* defense jurors, they will have only about the same standing as anyone else on the jury, because that is what they are expected to be. But if they turn out to be violently in favor of the prosecution, they will have far greater influence than the several defense jurors opposed to them, for the simple reason that they provide a cover for unworthy feelings in other people.

Any other person on the jury who is motivated to convict by feelings of bigotry or intolerance will feel an absolute license to do so. Why not? If there were anything to the defense case, the black, or the student would have seen it. Why not just get on with it, convict this defendant, and save one's own laudable charity for a more deserving case? The lawyer can argue all he wants to in favor of a liberal cause, but if the persons who are the natural beneficiaries of these arguments reject them, it is very hard to hold the defense case together long enough to *get it* to the jury. The defense lawyer had better not be wrong in accepting one of these jurors.

On the other hand, if the decision is to get rid of them, that may not be very hard. Prosecutors almost always fear these jurors, and they will always strike blacks. Moreover, if the prosecutor wants to keep a young person for some reason, that fact in itself is significant to the defense.

[1] When the Juror Is Black and the Lawyers Are Not

The lawyer has to remember several basic things that do not ordinarily occur to the non-black mind in this situation. For example, the black juror may actually be somewhat inclined to favor the defendant in a case of this kind. But strangely, that is not the controlling fact, for the simple reason that the juror cannot do his voting at the outset of the case, when it is relatively impersonal: he has to wait until the end, and by that time there has been considerable involvement between the lawyers and the jury.

Jury duty is not the most important thing that has happened to a politically aware black person in his recent memory, nor is the defendant's case the most grievous injustice that he can imagine. All his life he is putting up with things which he has no choice but to put up with or else oppose on terms that are very dangerous to himself; when he looks at the political defendant, he may well see the latter as a fool for biting off a piece of trouble when he did not have to. He may still sympathize with the defendant, but not as much as a white lawyer would expect him to do. Besides, while the white lawyer is arguing a liberal cause, the lawyer is probably going to expect the black juror to be particularly appreciative of his efforts. After all, we are on the same side, aren't we?

The truth is that a very different dynamic may be going on. The white lawyer is looking at the black juror for sympathy, but the black juror sees two white lawyers. One of them is a prosecutor, and the juror could hardly care less for the welfare of the prosecutor, but on the other hand, he does not really feel there is anything he can do to hurt the prosecutor. This is true because the prosecutor is basically a heartless son-of-a-bitch, and in every context in which the black juror has seen the prosecutor or his surrogates, the police, they have all seemed relatively impervious to harm. If wishes could kill them, they would be dead.

On the other hand, the other white lawyer is really getting vulnerable. The more he talks, the more he is getting involved. He is really laying himself open, and at the end of the case in his final argument he is making personal commitments and asking for the same from the jury. That is one white person who is in a position to be rejected and it will hurt, and the temptation to do it is very real.

The white lawyer should think about this, and remember that the situation between himself and the black juror is not totally unlike the relationship between white and black society in general: as long as a particular form of oppression goes on and the people doing the oppressing are unconscious of what they are doing, the ones who are being oppressed tend to be unconscious of the fact as well. But during the transitional time, when the ones on top are beginning to feel sorry about it and to make amends in some directions, the ones who have been on the bottom are most able to see and appreciate what they have actually been putting up with, and most likely to explode over things then being more or less corrected. It is also that way between individuals, and it seems to be human nature to throw more cruelty into a situation while there is still time, than one would have used when there was all the time in the world for emnity. The white lawyer turning himself wrong side out in the process of the final argument (the recommended procedure) may walk straight into this situation with a black juror; and both of them will regret it later.

The moral seems to be that under present social conditions, a white defense lawyer had better be extremely careful about accepting black jurors; he should only do it when he has the situation clearly in mind, and feels that notwithstanding these pressures, when it comes time to make his final argument (and the lawyer should visualize it and remember how it is going to be while looking at his juror) that it will still be safe to make that argument to this juror. If the answer is yes, he can keep the black juror.

[2] A Particular Type of Younger Person

In considering younger persons for inclusion on the jury panel it is important to keep one hand on the fundamental rule that youth is a very favorable qualification for jurors, from the defense viewpoint. Any lawyer who does not really believe that should perhaps stop right here, because he will have difficulty in keeping the rare exception in *its* somewhat smaller perspective.

But there are exceptions, and what follows is not intended as an admonition against young people on juries, only against the uncritical acceptance of all of them. Now and then the lawyer will find an extremely cold younger person confronting him from the jury box. This young person will generally be a man, but not always. He will not necessarily be a cold-eyed person, only cold. There is no need to look for these people since they will be immediately noticeable. What sets them apart if not their physical appearance, but their absolute lack of rapport with the lawyer and his client.

The thing that comes to mind when meeting one of them is that they are not good at faking objectivity. That is significant also, because it is not what one normally supposes about a juror who is cold or hostile—most jurors do not intend to fake objectivity when they feel hostile.

The only other outstanding characteristic of this type

of juror, which for some reason is characteristic only of young men in this category, is that he is surprisingly patient. All the details of his personal life which the lawyer has been able to elicit—few, but important—will indicate that this young man either has family responsibilities (he may have married too young) or has normal personal interests which place a premium on his time—that he should be working at his job which may not be paying him too much because of his youth, and which will typically not be a job with a very large company. He will be working in a smaller shop or possibly as a salesman, on a commission basis. His time will be a sacrifice, and yet there he will have been throughout the whole jury selection process, notable for his patience.

His hand will not have been among those raised when there was a market for easy excuses. On the other side, he was certainly not disapproving of those people who got off jury duty. If the lawyer received any impression of this juror's attitude before he entered the box, it may have been that the juror appreciated the sound economic reasons why other people were trying to get out of jury duty, but felt that for reasons of his own, he intended to stay.

When this person is in the box, the lawyer should by all means discover those reasons. The lawyer should, for example, stand fairly close to this person and ask his questions in the most relaxed possible tone. The lawyer should look directly in this person's eyes and smile, albeit the smile may have a cadaverous quality. It is not necessary to feel these things in order to do them. The response from this kind of juror will be exactly *nothing*. The response from almost anyone else will be at least an uncertain or self-conscious smile in reply. The lawyer should by all means try some of his questions having to do with things the lawyer values. Ask this person if he would have any reluctance to apply the rule about reasonable doubt. Explain the rule to him in a relaxed way and then ask him. Of course he will say that he will have no difficulty with that rule. But there will be a curious deadness to this dialogue.

Although once in a while the lawyer will be able to confirm his suspicions by a lucky shot, that will not happen in most cases. For example, the lawyer will probably draw a blank with questions about the juror's acquaintance with law enforcement personnel. But a follow-up question whether the juror belongs to an automobile racing club and perhaps in that connection is acquainted with some people connected with the police department (some police officers are actually very fond of well-tuned automobiles and motor-cycles in their private lives)—presented as if it were the most natural thing in the world for this juror to overlook such an obscure point—will occasionally draw a yes.

But in most cases, the witness's denials will be uni-form, and the lawyer will be left to make his decision on the basis of intuition. Certainly nothing about the juror's physical appearance is going to help. If longer hair is modish among younger persons in this community, this juror will have it; and in an age of mass produced young-person cloth-ing, his attire will be within the normal limits (although it will not be as extreme as some young people the lawyer may know).

It is generally a good idea to strike a juror in this category. If the lawyer needs an articulate reason, he should simply remind himself that this type of juror is in the same age bracket with younger police officers and is acquainted with them and talks things over with them. The lawyer may assume that sometimes a police officer may suggest to a younger person that since there are so many younger people trying to get on juries, perhaps someone in his particular frame of mind ought to make sure that he also gets on a jury in order that their common viewpoints should be better represented. The lawyer may further assume that a few of these young people may get carried away with the idea to the extent that they would give themselves a private license to lie about their true feelings in the jury box. Assuming these things, is it possible that the cold young individual sitting in the jury box got there in this manner?

The lawyer should excuse this person, and he will have to do it, because the prosecution will not. But he should never be heavy-handed about it or appear to doubt the juror's answers during the voir dire examination, or in any way seem to badger this juror. It is unconscionable to embarrass anyone called for jury duty; not only may the lawyer be wrong, but even if he is right, he will almost certainly be unable to demonstrate that fact to his own objective satisfaction or to that of any other person.

If the young person in this category is a woman, matters will be easier, although objective signs may still mislead. She will probably dress the same as other young women. She will appear as pleasant as those of her sisters who smile at the lawyer, but she will have no use for his client.

This mystery can probably be solved in seconds with a simple question about whether she dates police officers. The answer will be yes, and she will not be ashamed of it. It is a poor idea to ask too many questions of a juror of this kind, whether having to do with reasonable doubt or anything else. She tends to be defensive, sharp tongued, and given to smart-ass answers. Better to treat her briefly, with as much camaraderie as the lawyer can manage, suggesting by a smile and a few words that she might be a great little juror but that the defense does not wish to complicate her social life. That is the level at which she can be relaxed and momentarily disarmed, while the lawyer switches his questions to the next juror, and it is the easiest explanation to leave in the air for what the lawyer is going to do. At the first opportunity and with the best of good humor he will of course bounce her.

[3] Young Adults of Marked Religious Preference ("Jesus Freaks")

The main thing to bear in mind when evaluating these people is that the lawyer's own argument is going to bear heavily on the question of reasonable doubt. The lawyer's final appeal to duty (to acquit) is an appeal to law—at first glance an appeal to procedural rules, but actually an appeal to fundamental, sophisticated moral values. If this person's religion is of a fundamentalist variety—especially an evangelical group—then the juror may be very well qualified to understand this argument and act upon it. This will be especially clear if the law as presented in the defense argument is equated with morality, and in particular with Old Testament morality.

If the juror is active as an evangelist, that probably means standing on street corners. Young evangelists often seek young converts, and if it turns out that this evangelist has sought them out in student neighborhoods, as for example, by circulating through pool halls or parking some religious van at an intersection where students thrive, then better and better. An evangelist like this may be the only one on the jury panel who knows where these neighborhoods are.

The lawyer should remember that the obligation of persuasion is an obligation to meet the other person on equal terms. That is what the lawyer is doing, and common sense should confirm that the evangelist has been doing it also. Old evangelists can miss, because they may not be listening when dealing with younger types, but young ones have no choice at all except to mix it up or be rejected. Furthermore, it takes considerable guts to do this kind of person-gathering. Shyness, embarrassment, and rejection have to be endured. This work takes time and often it has to be done at night. The person who does this has to expect all kinds of abuse, among other responses. A person who thinks that highly of moral values will fight like hell in the jury room. This is a trait of character rare indeed, and certainly not one that is common among genteel persons of vaguely liberal "persuasions."

The lawyer who finds a young evangelist in the box has probably found a rare defense juror, and one moreover that the prosecution will not suspect. For that reason, the lawyer should lay it on rather hard, doing his best to establish rapport during the voir dire examination, first by finding out all about these evangelical activities, and second by asking if the juror would have any objection to reasonable doubt and so forth. This is safe. The reason it is safe is that most prosecutors think that anybody on God's side is on theirs. They work too closely with grand juries and not enough in the streets.

Clients may not like the idea of having a "Jesus Freak" on the jury, at least not the first time the idea is presented to them. But clients are not going to make the final argument.

§ 11.08   Challenges for Cause

"Challenges for cause" are those based on some narrow but obvious disqualifications, such as admitted bias, family relationship or deafness, and which are available to both sides without limitation as to number. They are of course distinguished from "peremptory challenges" (by that or any other name), which are strictly limited in number, so many to each side, and which may be exercised without any stated reason.

The judge will trigger most challenges for cause during his initial questioning of the jury, but since a judge does not "challenge" a potential juror, he may simply ask counsel for a stipulation that the juror may be excused, meaning that the challenge is so obvious it should be considered as made and acquiesced in by both lawyers. These

are clear-cut cases, in which a juror takes the first opportunity to say that based on what he has heard about the case,
he really does not think he could be fair. Of course it is better to take these people at their word by agreeing to the
stipulation, since to do otherwise involves inquiry into a bias
frankly admitted.

Such an inquiry (pressing for details) would be
stupied at this stage of the proceedings, because this bias
was something the judge not only uncovered, but which
he also endorsed by asking counsel to stipulate that the
juror be excused. Wanting to find out all about it strongly
implies that the lawyer who pushes the inquiry is only
interested in finding jurors biased in his own favor, hardly
a flattering light to stand under; moreover, this form of
inquiry sets the lawyer up for considerable embarrassment
—during the critical time when the jury is forming its
first opinion of him—should the biased juror decide to tell
why he feels biased.

There is all the difference in the world between the
situation in which the lawyer asks for this kind of embarrassment, and the situation where despite efforts from
all quarters to maintain a fair atmosphere, a juror who was
not asked his opinion suddenly vilifies the defendant. In the
latter situation the juror will be looked down upon by other
jurors, and his exit can only generate sympathy for the defense; but this is not true where the defense lawyer has
invited a tirade.

There are many situations in the courtroom that have
the potential to move, to affect the outcome of the case
and sway the minds of persons in it, but which just sit
there, without delivering their potential energy. But this
one will move; and it will move against the lawyer who has
been rash enough to ask a juror to explain his bias during
the portion of the case in which the judge was still conducting the voir dire.

That does not mean the lawyer should avoid asking people about their biases, only that he should not take unreasonable chances at a time when there is nothing to be gained. When the judge is conducting the voir dire, the dialogue between judge and jury will be pitched on a glassy slope. The judge's prestige is high, the lawyer's prestige is uncertain. The juror seeking to excuse himself is, in all likelihood, a prosecution juror and not one the lawyer would wish to retain if he knew all the facts. The juror seeking to excuse himself is doing a good thing and affords a salutary example to other biased persons who may wish to do likewise. All of these things argue for accepting the judge's suggested stipulation.

Quite a different situation arises when either (1) the judge is unfairly pursuing a potential defense juror by questions which he does not use on potential prosecution jurors, pressing him to admit a bias which is not apparent, and actually revealing some bias of his own; or (2) the prosecutor stumbles over something he regards as so good it will save him a peremptory challenge, and after some initial success in questioning a defense juror, he finally makes a challenge for cause. In both situations the defense lawyer will have to decide how far to go in defending the challenged juror, and he must know how to defend him.

Conversely, the defense lawyer conducting his own voir dire will feel that many (but not all) of the people he wishes to see excused from the jury should be excused for cause. This is important because there are seldom enough peremptory challenges.

If there is going to be an adequate jury, the peremptory challenges available to the defense are going to have to be augmented by a few successful defense challenges for cause; some people whom the judge passed over, and who did not identify themselves as biased, are going to have to be cornered into revealing their bias anyway, and successfully challenged by the defense for cause. The defense lawyer will therefore have to decide whether to do that and how to do it.

The processes of making and opposing challenges for cause are governed by the same considerations.

In defending against a challenge for cause, the first consideration is whether to do it, and that is a question which answers itself. Every now and then and to the lawyer's great regret there will be some obvious defense juror who raises his hand and, with what to the lawyer seems an excess of zeal flatly disqualifies himself by reason of bias. This is obviously a defense juror. It would be pointless to state the reasons in print, the lawyer will know them. And for this juror, there is no question of preventing him from disqualifying himself. He does not want to be on the jury because he is biased and that must be the end of it.

The considerations are very very different when it appears that the judge is unfairly belaboring a defense juror, or when the prosecutor has challenged any juror for cause who had not previously disqualified herself. In these situations, the answer to the question of whether to oppose the challenge must be, yes, of course the lawyer opposes it, and he should not be mealy-mouthed. The main thing is to *do* it and do it well, and not just to cave in because somebody seems to be bent on challenging an intelligent juror.[9] The lawyer should take this opportunity to align himself not just with this juror but indirectly on the side of the jury, in all these little engagements. While the lawyer is actually opposing a challenge addressed to one juror among a group who have not yet been sworn as a jury, it is probably wiser for him to think of it as defending the jury, and to move himself physically to the jury box and stand there, possibly with his arm on the rail, making the situation a little clearer to everybody. This will probably leave the prosecutor at the counsel table making his objections while seated (which many prosecutors seem to find a natural posture for the purpose). The prosecutor will be a little distance from the jury, and yet not so far as the judge. That is about where he should be, physically and conceptually.

While this recommendation appears inconsistent with what was just said about not seeming to want jurors who have bias in one's own favor, and not inviting damaging explanations of bias, there are cardinal differences: this juror is *not* one who has overtly broached the subject of his own bias with the plain intention of being excused from jury duty; rather he is one who seems at least to some extent capable of serving as a juror. He obviously would like to remain in the jury box, and is either being pursued by the judge on a line of questions which are beginning to look quite unfair, or else he is being pursued by the prosecutor, in which case the partisan motivation of the prosecutor is understood and need not be inferred from the questions. Finally, this juror is a potential defense juror, and the risk of a sudden onslaught—an unsavory revelation of why the juror feels biased—is entirely on the prosecution. These considerations make all the difference in the world.

The lawyer can mix it up, and he should. If he loses (the juror is excused by the judge), all the lawyer needs to do in order to solidify his quite satisfactory impression on the remaining jurors is simply to take the adverse ruling with good grace.

Usually it is essential for the defense to make several *successful* challenges for cause in order to win the case. Jury panels are not that good, judges are not that perceptive, and rarely are there enough peremptory challenges. Some jurors are going to have to be thrown out by challenges for cause, and the longer the jury selection continues and the more the peremptory challenges dwindle, the greater the emphasis on the defense lawyer's skill in effectuating challenges for cause.

While that rule may be fairly obvious, it is important to remember that it *is* a first rule, and accordingly it takes precedence over the second, which is that it is usually a very bad idea to lose when making a challenge for cause. The reason it is so bad is simply that when the challenge for cause has been made and argued, and the defense lawyer loses the argument, he not only looks bad in the eyes of the jury (because he has been unsuccessful with something he initiated himself), but the juror is still sitting there. He will of course have to be excused with a peremptory challenge, and the prosecutor knows that as well as the lawyer. The rest of the jury knows it too, and in this atmosphere it is hard to exercise the peremptory challenge later without seeming to be a disgruntled loser. To have to use a peremptory challenge under these circumstances (we are assuming the lawyer has not been rash enough to lose on a challenge for cause without at least one peremptory remaining in his box) and without any possibility of getting someone else to do it for him is harsh indeed.

To win the requisite challenge for cause, the first problem is to know when such a challenge has a reasonable chance of success, or in short, when it has been properly set up. One can go about setting it up without incurring any of the potential disadvantages of a bad challenge, and then one either manages to set it up or not; if not, it is a good idea not to make the challenge.

Knowing when the challenge is set for a favorable ruling obviously depends on how the judge rules on similar challenges—there is no substitute for knowing his predilections. But a good rule of thumb with strange judges is, the challenge will probably go (succeed) if the hostile juror has been led to say (and does not back down from it) that he has some feelings about this case concerning the way he would like to see it come out, and *that it would take a little extra evidence to offset those feelings.*

It is important to remember that having bias means nothing at all by itself, and a good many challenges for cause founder on that rock. If all the lawyer can get is a concession that the witness has bias, he has not wasted his time, because that fact alone is ample justification for a later peremptory challenge in the eyes of the remaining jurors; but if a challenge for cause is offered solely on the strength of the bias, the next thing the lawyer hears will simply be a question from the bench as to whether the juror feels he could nevertheless follow the judge's instructions regarding the burden of proof, and the answer to that will be yes, and the *next* thing after that will be that the challenge for cause is denied.

On the other hand, if matters have reached the point that a little extra evidence is needed, most judges will think twice about bullying the witness out of that statement, and the prosecutor will certainly look sick trying to do so.

Nonetheless, these matters rapidly degenerate to a level at which no one looks good. The juror who has said that it will take extra evidence to offset his feelings has, after all, only said that by way of agreeing with something the defense lawyer almost put in his mouth. (And one can be quite sure those words are not going to come to his mouth any other way.) Most people regard that form of admission as something a good deal less than a free statement, and rightly so. The juror will, in about 50 percent of the times this occurs, gladly change what he just said about extra evidence being needed. All that is required is a question from the prosecutor or the judge inviting him to say this. That question is usually forthcoming, but not always.

This means that as a rule of thumb, the juror who has admitted that extra evidence is necessary to offset his bias is a fair target for a challenge of cause, and the challenge will probably succeed slightly more than 50 percent of the time, but not much more.

Once the juror is in this category (set up for a challenge for cause, but not yet actually challenged), there is no mystery about the peremptory situation. Though he has not been asked to state the nature of his bias, it should be apparent. He is obviously a person whom the defense will have to challenge in any event. That means that the prosecution are not going to challenge him, whether or not a challenge for cause is attempted.

The decision should probably be to make the challenge, except that there are still two other considerations. The lawyer may have a feel for the situation by which he knows intuitively that losing this challenge for cause would hurt him in the eyes of the jury more than he should risk at this point. And, second, there is the matter of arithmetic. He may have only one or two peremptory challenges left, and he may have more pressing needs to use these on *other persons* still sitting in the box.

Those situations present a hard choice; from the trial viewpoint, it is slightly less evil to end up with this admittedly biased person on the jury than it is to end up having the same person on the jury *after having lost a challenge for cause against him*. But from an appeal viewpoint, the only way to upset a judgment based on erroneous rulings on challenges for cause is to *make the challenges* (and lose one or more) *and to have used up all the peremptory challenges*. This is so because with a unanimous verdict rule, no appellate court can evade its responsibility by saying that retaining a particular juror was harmless error, since, with all the peremptories gone, there was actually no other way to get at him except for cause. As every trial lawyer knows, this situation is only one of many in which trial tactics demand one thing, and appellate arguments wish for another; there is no way to handle these problems except to look at them squarely for one moment, make a decision one way or the other, and go on.

In this example, if the decision is in favor of appellate arguments—in other words, to risk a challenge for cause when there are no peremptories left, or none which can be used on this juror—then the lawyer had better squeeze the last ounce of what he can by way of voir direing this juror.

In other words, the lawyer will have to be creative, since the greatest danger of losing a challenge for cause primarily grows out of using only pedestrian questions. This juror had indicated some feelings in the case which will require evidence to offset them. The lawyer knows that, given an opportunity, the juror will probably change what he just said, and defeat the challenge for cause. Other ways to get at him will not be so easy to evade. In the hands of a really skillful lawyer,[10] a hostile juror may go through the whole charade, and then throw it in.

§ 11.09   Peremptory Challenges

[1] Mechanics

Peremptory challenges should be exercised promptly and firmly and with a minimum amount of nonsense. One should always have the next two or three firmly in mind so there will be no vacillation when the judge says it is with the defendant.

The actual mechanics should be direct. The lawyer simply stands, looks at the person to be excused, and says that the defendant thanks and excuses Mr. Brown. He should never refer to a juror by a number, since no one will know who is meant, and for that matter, numbering systems vary from court to court. The challenge should be done without apology or antagonism, as a necessary step, which indeed it is.

It is always a good idea to keep careful notes about the number of challenges exercised on both sides, not just by check marks, but by names. Unless the lawyer has the unusual gift of not making mistakes under pressure, it is also a good idea to check the box score with that of some other person in the courtroom, the client, the clerk or the bailiff, to insure that everybody's tally is the same. It would be a very bad thing indeed to exercise the last challenge thinking there was still one more remaining; but it would be even more embarrassing to exercise one more challenge than one actually had, e.g., an eleventh challenge when there were but ten. Rather than demonstrate to the twelve jurors how wrong he can be and make a personal enemy of one of them (who will remain on the jury, though unwanted by the defense, embarrassed among the other eleven) defense counsel should take the modest trouble of double checking his notes.

[2] The Order of Strikes

What follows is based on the assumption that peremptory challenges can be exercised against any of the twelve persons seated in the box, as well as replacements for persons challenged in a random sequence until the number of peremptory challenges is exhausted. In other words, both sides can skip around, and none of jury is "accepted" until all of them are accepted. Calculations would be a little different under a system in which both sides were nailed to the problem of accepting jurors one by one, so that after the first juror was "accepted" no peremptory challenge could thereafter be used against him.

Under the arrangement being discussed (that both sides can skip around in exercising challenges) a necessary corollary of the rule is that when both sides have passed, the peremptory challenges are terminated regardless of the number remaining unused on either side, and the jury is automatically accepted.

Under this random system, it is a good idea to take out the most obviously undesirable jurors immediately. There are two strong reasons for this, the first of which is so obvious that it might escape notice altogether. This may be thought of as the "refill problem."

The refill problem is best illustrated by a grossly exaggerated example. Assume the lawyer has ten peremptory challenges, and when he looks at the people in the jury box he finds ten bad apples. Of these, five are really *really* bad and five are only half-bad. Assuming that the lawyer made the mistake of using his first five challenges on the ones that were only half-bad, the effectiveness of those challenges will, of course, depend upon who are called from the remaining panelists to occupy those five vacant seats. Assume that the five *replacements* are also really bad apples. The situation now is, there are ten really bad apples in the jury box, and only five challenges remaining. That means there will be five really bad apples on the jury which is sworn, an intolerable count.

This dire example can be greatly improved if the lawyer uses his first five challenges on the really bad apples. When they are replaced by the same sort, the situation will be, of the ten bad ones in the box, only five are really bad, and five are half-bad; there will be five challenges remaining. The result of course is that when the dust settles, the jury will contain five people who are only half-bad, an enormous improvement. (When faced with this Pleistocene array one should think about the improvement, not the count; only a mistrial will make the breed extinct.)

The second reason favoring a general policy of striking the most obviously bad jurors immediately is that this procedure takes all the fun out of it for the prosecutor and tends to insure that he will do the same thing without fooling around. If the prosecutor follows this response (obvious choices immediately) the best that he can do is break even; if he follows any other course he will lose.

The reason is, if the prosecutor is *not* to exercise obvious choices, he must either pass or use his initial strikes on doubtful choices. If he passes, then the controlling rule is either that the prosecutor is compelled to announce his decision (i.e., strike someone or pass) before the defense does so, or vice versa. If the prosecutor goes first on each round and elects to *pass* rather than make a serious choice, within a very short time the defense will have eliminated the worst prosecution people without having lost any defense jurors, and may suddenly pass. The result will be the termination of peremptory challenges (two passes consecutively), with all of the prosecution challenges unused. This would of course be a considerable advantage to the defendant.

On the other hand, if the controlling rules require the defense to exercise the first challenge in each round, the prosecutor cannot be sandbagged in this manner because he can always start exercising his challenges after the defense has passed for the first time. However, by passing five or six times, the prosecutor has impliedly represented to those persons in the box that they are acceptable to the prosecution. By suddenly starting to exercise challenges late in the game, he will identify himself as having trifled with justice. The sticky residue of duplicity is not to be sought after.

If the prosecutor elects to preserve his standing with the jury by exercising *some* challenges, but not his most obvious ones, then he will certainly be taking chances. Not only will he be wasting peremptories, it is very likely that some of these doubtful choices will turn out to be people the defense would have challenged anyway. This is a magnificent bonus for the defense.

The result is that by exercising obvious challenges immediately, the defense can be reasonably sure the prosecution will do the same, and if it turns out otherwise, can penalize them heavily.

With most jury panels, the job of picking a good jury is far more difficult and challenging for the defense than for the prosecution; it is important that the defense keep matters under control and see them with a clear eye. It is always helpful to the defense to get an early feel for how well the prosecutor is picking jurors, and that consideration is especially important when looking at the people who have not yet been called to the box.

If the prosecutor is doing it badly, the defense will probably gain by continuing exchanges, picking up a juror here and there, and it may be worthwhile to run the challenges out to the last one, provided only that the remainder of the panel looks promising. But if the lawyer feels the prosecutor is picking them well (i.e., knocking off defense jurors that are not so easy to spot) then, unless the remainder of the panel is exceptionally promising, it may be well to stop the process short of the limit that will keep the mixture of people in the box from deteriorating. This essential feel for how the prosecutor is doing will probably come much sooner if the defense lawyer is able to decide early on whether things that are obvious to him are equally obvious to the prosecutor.

A single exception to the rule of making obvious choices first should be that if the defense lawyer has already made a challenge for cause which was *not* successful, it may be advisable to excuse that juror with the second peremptory challenge. To jump him immediately may suggest to some that the lawyer is a sore-headed loser.

All the defense strikes that fall within the possible area of the prosecutor's bias should be regarded as *secret* choices, no matter that they may seem obvious to the lawyer himself. For example, many prosecutors automatically strike blacks, without any consideration whether a black juror might be a prosecution juror. They never look and it never enters their minds. Assuming the defense lawyer had decided that a particular black juror would not be helpful to the defense (see § 11.07[1]), he should never strike that black juror while there is a chance remaining that the prosecutor will do it for him.

Similarly, many prosecutors automatically challenge Jews, presumably on the recommendation of outdated textbook writers. Some inept prosecutors have been known to do this by reflex action even in burglary cases, where the person challenged was a shopkeeper and the victim of many burglaries. There is no substitute for knowing the prosecutor's personal predelictions; but, in general, a strange prosecutor should be given credit for behaving like a bigot. He should be given every opportunity to do this, to take the full opprobrium of bigotry, to look like a bigot in the eyes of the jury and feel like one in his own mind. All of this can be accomplished if it is going to happen at all, only by holding back whatever challenges the lawyer might have been about to make himself on a purely intuitive basis.

In working with a less experienced prosecutor a competent defense lawyer can sometimes get the benefit of several prosecution challenges. In other words, he will have his own challenges (e.g., ten), and if he is very lucky it may happen that three or four of the prosecution challenges fall on people whom he would have challenged anyway. This may work out to be, for example, that the defense (having excused ten) gets the benefit of fourteen challenges while the prosecution (who also used ten) will get the benefit of only six. The fact that the prosecution may feel that they are getting the full benefit of their ten challenges is irrelevant, if in fact the defense lawyer is right in calling these shots as his own. If things are going like this, even a very bad jury panel can be purified.

[3] When to Stop

Although jury selection is highly subjective, apart from the arbitrary rules, there is a very interesting fact which affords the individual lawyer an almost objective standard for deciding what is a safe jury for the defense. The interesting fact is this: most trial lawyers can form an extremely reliable opinion as to what kind of juror is sitting in the box *during the jury selection process.*

After the jury is sworn, the lawyer and the jury are caught up in the dynamics of the trial, and the lawyer's estimate of the jury may become highly inaccurate. Most of the time the lawyer spends with juries is after they are sworn. When lawyers think about juries, and how unknowable they seem at times, they are mostly thinking about jurors during the trial and at the time the verdict comes back.

One tends to forget that over a period of time, *initial* evaluations of jurors are rather accurate. All that is necessary is for the lawyer to decide while picking the jury whether a potential juror is one whom he likes, whom he does not like, or about whom he has no opinion. That is easy enough since at every moment from the first, all potential jurors will be in one of those categories. After the lawyer has done his voir dire and while he is making decisions about strikes, most of the people in the box should fit into the category of liked or not, with no more than three or four regarded as unknowns.

The categories of persons whom the lawyer likes (whom he feels to be good defense jurors) and whom he does not like are reliable categories. That fact makes the third category (unknown) reliable as well: it is certainly neither of the other two. In trial after trial, the people whom the lawyer regards as good defense jurors will turn out to be just that, and the ones he regards as prosecution jurors will, if any of them are allowed to remain on juries, do extreme harm. These estimates are more than just a little accurate, they are extremely accurate, but they are *only* accurate while based on relatively slight information, i.e., before the jury is sworn.

It is probably true that if most lawyers were asked to size up their juries midway through the trial, these later opinions would be a great deal less accurate than their earlier ones. This ability to size up jurors early comes with a reasonably modest amount of experience; all that is necessary is to apply a private rule of thumb as to what kind of jury the lawyer will settle for. This guide will of course vary among lawyers, but there is no reason why any lawyer should be without one. For example, one might try to get a jury in which ten people appear to be good defense jurors and no more than two are unknowns. There should be no bad jurors in the box at all.

This selection presupposes that all the arbitrary rules have been followed, i.e., there are no real estate brokers or ranchers sitting in the box, and all persons intuitively regarded as bad defense jurors have been excluded. If those who remain are at least ten that are liked (who pass the intuition tests), and no more than two as to whom there is no intuitive reaction either way, that is (according to this view) an adequate jury, one which is capable of acquitting if the evidence warrants and one that can be talked to. This jury is also quite capable of convicting, but so are most juries put together by human intelligence.

Other rules of thumb would obviously be necessary, depending on the subjective level at which a lawyer regards an individual as a good juror. If the lawyer feels a good deal tighter as to who are good jurors, his rule of thumb might require only nine that are "good" jurors and three unknowns; if his approach is a little looser, he might need eleven or even twelve that are "good."

Whatever it is, however, experience will show what the lawyer's own rule should be. The main point is, the lawyer should have a number in mind, and just before accepting the jury, he should ask himself exactly how he sizes up this particular group of twelve. He should listen to his own answer, and if adjustments are necessary, they should be made now.

Once the lawyer has established his own rule and tested it to his satisfaction, it will tell him with amazing accuracy (but never total accuracy) just before he accepts the jury, whether he has got an adequate one or something less. If it is something less, then usually (but not always) he can assume that the jury he actually got is not capable of acquitting on reasonable evidence; that the best it may be capable of doing for him is a hung verdict on all counts, or perhaps on just some counts. That is a sobering, or more than sobering, assessment, and the lawyer should not voluntarily settle for that kind of jury if there is any way to avoid doing so.

On the other hand, if at any moment the lawyer looks at the box and finds that he has what is an adequate jury by his own standards, *that is the time to stop the jury selection process.* To insist on continuing it beyond this point by striking even one more juror is to do something without a reason—something not to be done in the presence of the jury.

§ 11.10 Getting Along with Other Defense Lawyers While Picking the Jury

As previously noted, a cardinal rule for lawyers working on the same side of the case, who wish to get along with each other, is not to say anything that is likely to prove unforgivable. This is not always easy, especially when the lawyers do not know each other very well.

Another helpful maxim is not to back another lawyer into doing something which he would regard as professional malfeasance—especially apposite to the question whether a particular juror will be retained against the strong personal wishes of one lawyer only.

The procedural rules controlling the process of joint jury selection may vary, but the principle of doing it by cooperation should be obvious regardless of the jurisdiction. Mechanical differences occur as to how one may exercise peremptory challenges. Local rules will (one hopes) afford an increased number of peremptory challenges (for prosecution and defense), where several defendants are being tried together. The rules may require that all of these challenges be exercised jointly (all of the defense lawyers concurring), that all be exercised individually, allocating so many to each defendant, or that they be allocated as a combination of joint and individual challenges on the defense side.[11]

But apart from whether the defense peremptory challenges are joint, separate, or mixed, it seems intuitively obvious that they should be exercised as far as possible on a joint basis. This is true because (to the extent challenges are exercised separately) if someone starts using too many separate challenges against the wishes of the others, another lawyer may retaliate, and if that happens it is a short degenerate step to where the defense does more harm to itself than the prosecution do. Similarly, failure to agree will paralyze joint challenges. It is very desirable that reason be the arbiter here.

Assuming reason is going to arbitrate, it is anomalous but true that there must be an absolute minimum of discussion about the matter. When several defense lawyers are at the counsel table, if they are working intelligently together, the most noticeable thing about jury selection should be that about nine out of ten defense challenges run off like a well-coiled line through a hawsehole, without a hitch. This is true because common sense dictates that even among a group of six or eight lawyers, three or four of them are going to be sufficiently experienced and well acquainted with each other to trust each other's judgment; and so although the challenges may be exercised right down the line, each lawyer speaking in turn, the dominant group will either trust each other to make their own challenges without prior consultation, or at most with a bare minimum, and that will be done unobtrusively.

The other lawyers at the table may not always feel as sure about what challenges to make, and nothing is more natural than to ask a colleague who is. Again there is no formality about this, no need to ask for a recess or to make a thing of it.

But it is also a matter of common sense that when a difficult choice has to be made, or when it may be approximately time to stop making challenges, the dominant group will realize this in advance, and there will be a general conference about it *in advance*. These conferences may occur several times a day, but they should be done during normal recess periods. It is a bad idea for the defense to request any special time to huddle over what challenge to make next, even though that is exactly what the lawyers are going to do. The times when they will have a real problem will probably not occur with more than one out of ten challenges. The question is how to go about reaching total agreement if that is possible, and if it is not possible, then to take whatever action is necessary with a minimum of damage to group identification.

Of course if reason is going to control the outcome of these confrences, the next question is, *whose?* If somebody has already been designated "chief counsel" then some of these problems may not arise. But "chief counsel" usually means chief counsel for a particular defendant who has more than one lawyer. The usual situation is that several lawyers are associated on the defense side, not because they are representing the same defendant or defendants, but because they are representing separate defendants. "Chief counsel" in this situation must necessarily be a dubious title because the lawyers are responsible to their respective clients, not to each other.

It is rather important that nobody should abuse the obvious need for reaching a general agreement, and it is especially desirable that no one do so in the name of his client. The representation that, "I am a reasonable man, but my client is stubborn," is not to be used among friends. Only a fool thinks that fig leaf will provide him cover. It may be regarded as something of an insult to the other lawyers for anyone of them to drag his client (or his client's opinions) into the conference room, saying in effect that his client knows as much about how to pick a jury as any of the lawyers. Presumably the other lawyers know their business and so this suggestion is not going to be conducive to a quiet conference. Most lawyers in this situation expect each of the others to keep his client in the background and to state his views as his own, regardless of the fact (if it is a fact) that his views were somewhat shaped by talking to his own client beforehand.

In addition to the large objective of keeping the alliance intact, there are many important little benefits to be gained from picking a jury by reason and consensus. By working together lawyers more or less pool their experience and in the overwhelming number of decisions to be made, the hunches, choices, and insights of experienced men will reinforce each other. If the selection process becomes protracted, defense lawyers can shift the burden from time to time so that somebody who has frankly gotten tired of the process or feels that he is boring the panel beyond the permissible limit and is temporarily unable to do anything about it can take a smaller speaking part; his friends can carry it.

Similarly, in the matter of actually exercising strikes, it is a delight to do it among friends. For example, the lawyer may have just gotten the worst of some exchange with a person on the jury, and it will be obvious to everybody that this juror will have to be excused. The lawyer who got the bloody nose will not wish to do this himself (he certainly would if he were the only one in the case), because that makes him look like a bad loser. Another lawyer can exercise that challenge, and letting him do so also makes the point to the jury that all the defense lawyers think this was a bad juror, not just the one who was questioning him.

One of the lawyers may find among the jury panel a former client whom he knows very well to be disgruntled. The reaction of the prosecutor to anybody's former client will be suspicion and puzzlement. The prosecutor (if he knows what he is doing) will inquire carefully about whether the client thinks well of the lawyer, well enough to save him using a peremptory. If a former client is really disgruntled he may express only good feelings about the lawyer—a baleful response to the lawyer's ears, since it seems only to confirm that the former client has a *reason* for wanting to get on the jury. Most prosecutors are wary in this situation, like an animal nosing around a badly baited trap. Almost invariably they manage to get little vibrations which tell them the true situation. How they relish it.

The lawyer is going to have to excuse his own former client, and everybody on the panel will know that there was something sour. This is embarrassing; there is no way to do it gracefully and no way to make an amiable reference to it later. But not if the lawyer is among friends. Once the matter is explained during recess, one of the lawyer's friends will excuse this juror with such suavity that no one will even wonder why it was done; so there will be nothing to explain. There is nothing wrong with lawyers scratching each other's backs.

Another small advantage of working smoothly among friends while picking a jury is simply that it affords everyone a better chance to watch the responses of members of the panel, while one of the other defense lawyers is asking questions. Not only that, but one lawyer can ask questions through another. What lawyer has not had the experience, immediately after questioning twelve jurors at great length, and after passing for cause, of sitting down only to think of some vital question that he should have asked one of the persons in the box? Well, if one of the lawyer's friends is about to stand up and begin *his* questioning, that question will still get asked.

It is a good idea to have an understanding among defense lawyers that nobody will be kept on the jury who is really hateful to any one of them. This is easy to say and hard to follow, because after a week or two of difficult jury selection every lawyer will have strong feelings about the members of the panel who are seated in the box. Defense lawyers will certainly differ as to who the "good" defense jurors are, and each of them will have favorites in the box. Some defense lawyers may still entertain fears and doubts about some of these same jurors. The better solution would seem to be, as long as there is an adequate number of strikes available and the judge remains reasonably patient, strike every juror who is unacceptable to any of the lawyers. This process uses up time, but in return for that loss the jury which is eventually sworn will substantially reflect the experience and skill of all lawyers on the defense side, even though it may be entirely possible that the jury would have been picked a week sooner, or might have been slightly better, had one of the lawyers kept quiet.

The wrong way to do it is to abort the striking process by means of trade-offs, i.e., one defense lawyer persuading another to accept one or two panel members whom the latter considers to be hateful, simply on the say-so of the first lawyer. That is bad enough, but a further difficulty here is that even if the first lawyer is "right" (he can only be right as to him), he is now going to have to make a deal. He will have to accept one or two that he does not like in return. The result will be an impossible jury, several of whose members have strong antipathy toward the defense for reasons which even they might not be able to express very clearly. Nobody gains from that situation except the prosecution. The correct way is not to *keep* both jurors by means of an agreement, but to *excuse* them both. This works as long as there are enough challenges remaining that no one is worried about the number. But when the challenges get close to the end, something will have to give. The lawyers should, if humanly possible, talk it out. Some deference in that situation has to be accorded the experience and skill of the person who wants to make the objection, and the experience and skill of the person who opposes it. Some consideration must also be given to the fact that if the parties have gotten so far along in the process that there are only a few challenges left, the twelve people in the box must not be *too* bad. At this stage, the argument in favor of making another strike should perhaps have a lot more going for it than a similar argument at any earlier time. It may not be worth damaging good relations among lawyers.

There is one exception, however. If at about this stage of the proceedings the defense lawyers have still not agreed that there is a "one-man jury" occupying one of the seats in the box, and if the lawyer himself has finally screwed up nerve enough to make a long overdue strike, then he had better do it. That is one thing that needs doing so urgently that it is worth disrupting everybody. It is to be hoped the disruption will be temporary. Counsel is going to hear quite a lot about it, nevertheless.

§ 11.11 Picking Alternate Jurors

After a twelve-man jury has been picked and sworn, it is a usual practice in any jury trial expected to last longer than a few days to pick one or more alternate jurors. The main thing about picking alternates is to use as much care in their selection as was used on the regular members of the jury. They will probably end up sitting in the jury. If a trial lasts as much as one week, there is a strong probability that at least one alternate will be used, even if there is no epidemic going through the community. If the trial goes two weeks or more, it is almost certain that at least one alternate will be used.

The selection of alternates usually goes faster than the selection of the jury proper, possibly because the lawyers are totally warmed up to their job, and partly because everybody wants to get on with the case. The number of challenges available for alternates will probably be small.[12] There is no chance to use those challenges on anyone but prospective alternate jurors.

The main differences in choosing alternates have to

do with the change in pace and in atmosphere. Things are not only moving faster, but there is always a sense of relief that the jury has finally been chosen. The jurors were under considerable strain until they were sworn; after that they are relaxed. There is a general good feeling in the courtroom. The atmosphere at this point usually is, the lawyers have picked a good jury, and are only interested in protecting it from interlopers in the form of unworthy alternates. The jury is very tolerant of questions addressed to prospective alternates. They are the original members of a rather exclusive club, and they are entirely sympathetic to any effort to raise the standards of admission. Their feeling is, fire away, and make those bastards answer truthfully.

Before the process of choosing alternates begins, it is essential to know the ground rules, if applicable rules of court leave anything in doubt. For example, if two or more alternates are being picked, and a certain number of challenges are allocated to each side for the purpose of picking them, it is essential to know whether all of those challenges are available for use on any particular seat, i.e., whether, if two challenges are available for two alternates, both of them may be used on the first alternate selected and none on the second, or whether it must be no more than one as to each chair.

The other important thing to settle is, assuming there are two or more alternates and *one* vacancy occurs in the jury, what process will be used to determine which alternate fills that vacancy? If it is understood in advance that the first alternate *chosen* will be the first one seated in the box, then more importance attaches to the choice of that alternate. The second may never be seated.

On the other hand, if the arrangement is that the names of alternates are to be drawn by lot or by some other procedure, when a vacancy in the jury occurs, then no alternate seat is any less important than any other. Which ground rule applies is not so important, but knowing which rule applies is vital.

§ 11.12 Relations with the Jury While Selecting Them and Throughout the Trial

There are a few more or less obvious rules about conduct in the presence of juries. It goes almost without saying that the lawyer should not take chances on being late for any court appearance involving the jury, and if by some mishap he is late, he should create an opportunity to say something about it immediately when the judge enters, or if he is so late that the judge is on the bench, immediately after he arrives in court. Any lateness at all means an apology to the court and jury, and that should not be deferred.

At any time when a jury or jury panel is leaving the room, it is usually a bad idea to become engaged in picking up one's own books and papers. Much better to let those lie as they are and to avoid any immediate conversations with anyone. This is a good time to watch the jury as they leave; whether they are still being selected or have become a sworn jury many weeks before, it is quite important to know how they leave the courtroom.

The lawyers notice who goes with whom, who has been knitting and reading, and whether they look at the defendant. One should always keep track of the number of smiles or occasional words bestowed on the defendant by the jury as they file out. Needless to say, the defendant, the notetaker, and anybody in the room who is associated with the defense (this includes any friends who may have dropped in) should be encouraged to remain seated and say nothing about the case until the last juror has disappeared. This tends to prevent partisan defense remarks from being overheard by individual members of the jury in the corridor, which can easily happen if one follows too closely, gets into the same elevator with the jury, or walks up behind them at the first traffic light.

If anyone on the jury *does* overhear private remarks by people associated with the defense, they may very well assume that the lawyer or his friends are trying to put them on, which is something to lose sleep over.

Footnotes

1 For helpful lists showing the kinds of questions asked in criminal cases, see, 1 M. Belli, *Modern Trials* 804–807 (1954); and *Minimizing Racism in Jury Trials* (voir dire conducted by Charles R. Garry) 19–41 (A. Ginger ed. 1969).

2 For a brief, excellent discussion of secondary questions, illustrating an area of the defense case which would justify their use, the kinds of information sought and how to employ the questions, see G. Stout, "Homicide," in 7 *Am. Jur. Trials* 586–587 (1964).

3 Id. at 580–581.

4 Id. at 578–579.

5 A. Watson, "The Quest for Professional Competence: Psychological Aspects of Legal Education," 37 U. Cin. L. Rev. 93 (Winter 1968).

6 Meaning the little social buffers sometimes used to insulate the legal profession and others.

7 W. Deem, see ch. 9, N. 3.

8 W.H. Ferry, "Is a Police State Emerging?" 115 Current 33 (Feb. 1970).

9 W. Deem, see Ch. 9, N. 3.

10 See C. Garry, N. 1, supra, at 90–94.

11 See, e.g., Cal. Penal Code § 1070 (West 1970) which allows the defendant and the prosecution ten peremptory challenges each (twenty each where the offense is punishable by death or life imprisonment); and § 1070.5 which provides that where two or more defendants are tried jointly, the number of challenges allowed under § 1070 must be exercised by the defendants jointly but that each defendant is also entitled to five additional challenges which may be exercised separately (with the prosecution getting additional challenges equal to the number of all additional challenges allowed defendants.) One method used in California trial courts is for the defendants to exercise the joint

challenges first, until these are exhausted or as long as they can be agreed upon, but also allowing the defendants to interspere separate challenges when (for the moment) they cannot agree on a joint one.

[12] See, e.g., Cal. Penal Code § 1089 (West 1970) which allows the defendant (and the prosecution) as many peremptory challenges to alternate jurors as there are alternate jurors called; if two or more defendants are tried jointly, each receives as many peremptory challenges as there are alternate jurors called, and the prosecution receive the same number.

Chapter 12

OPENING STATEMENTS

SYNOPSIS

§ 12.01 Two Important Preliminary Steps

The lawyer should be quite certain that his own requested jury instructions are filed with the trial judge well in advance of the time that opening statements begin. This is true even if local practice permits filing jury instructions at a later stage, after the trial has begun.

The reason is that the defense jury instructions will make the trial judge familiar with the legal outline of the defendant's case at the outset. The judge can read the cases cited in support of the jury instructions in the privacy of his chambers, when the lawyers are not around, before he is called upon to make any rulings on the points raised in the instructions. And, of course, as a moment's thought will show, *those legal points are going to be raised throughout the trial, and so all of them will be raised long before the jury is instructed.*

It is possible that certain legal points which will pitch

the case on one incline or another will be raised during opening statements. The prosecutor will probably make overt
moves in his statement designed to arouse latent bigotries
and political animosities, to isolate the defendant and
identify him with some class of persons whom it is safe to
vilify in court. (These convenient groups change at least
every generation, and recently every four or five years; they
have notably included black militants and "outside agitators," as well as communists, anarchists, German-Amer-
icans, Jews, slaveholders, abolitionists, Tories, and Catholics
at one time or another.)

By submitting defense instructions early, the lawyer
will have been able to supply any last measure of reassur-
ance which the trial judge may have needed that this is *not*
going to be a political circus—at least as far as the defense
is concerned—and (by innuendo) that the lawyer intends to
try the case rather than disrupt it. By giving that tacit assurance the lawyer removes what may have been a source of
anxiety for the judge, and lays a foundation for what should
be a growing rapport with him. This in turn increases the
likelihood that when the *prosecutor* breaks into vituperation,
the judge will slap him down in the presence of the jury.

Another important consideration is that during the
lawyer's own opening statement, if he has occasion to outline proof which depends on a particular line of cases, and
on certain instructions eventually being given to the jury,
the judge will be much less likely to interrupt the defense
opening statement or to sustain a prosecution objection to
it, for the simple reason that he will have had an opportunity
to read the cases. Since the judge will then know that the
lawyer's position is a respectable one, even if he is not fully
persuaded at this time that he should ultimately give the
instructions requested by the defense, he is certainly not
going to foreclose giving those instructions yet, or risk reversible error by disrupting the defense opening statement.

In short, by filing the requested defense instructions early, the lawyer substantially improves the odds that the prosecution's opening statement will go on the rocks at some point, and decreases the odds that the same thing will happen to his own.

The second important preliminary step is to request an order excluding all witnesses from the courtroom until after they have testified. This request should be made promptly and it is not a bad idea to make it in the presence of the jury. This kind of request is almost universally honored, regardless of which side makes it.

The defense has nothing to lose by this order. The lawyer will have taken great care *not* to have his witnesses compare testimony, *not* to have them change their stories to agree with each other, and his witnesses are *not* going to attend court more than an hour or so before the time they actually testify.

Even if the lawyer wished otherwise, it would never be practical for defense witnesses to sit in court to monitor testimony and cross-examination. Defense witnesses—including housewives and students—are all working people. It is not economically feasible for them to be there before they are actually needed. Only the state has money and malice enough to keep various agents stationed in the courtroom throughout a trial, attempting to soak up information about the case. The People's witnesses will be there (at taxpayer expense) trying to prepare themselves for cross-examination by watching each other testify, unless there is a court order preventing them. That order should *always* be requested.

There is a small psychological advantage in being the one to request the order, since the request clearly indicates to the jury which side is more concerned about perjured testimony; and when the judge makes the order, he subtly but effectively endorses that concern.

§ 12.02   While the Prosecutor Is Making his Opening Statment

The main thing to remember while the prosecutor is making his opening statement is not to sit there passively making little scribbles about it, but to make aggressive notes, and to have told the note taker to do likewise. Most lawyers in court draw a line down the center of the notebook page, making actual notes on one side and annotations, plans, and comments on the other. With the prosecutor's opening statement the lawyer should write on one side what the prosecutor is saying, and on the other side everything that occurs to him as to what the lawyer is going to do about it while the case is going on. Things will occur, and they should be noted as they happen.'

The big reason for getting it all down so carefully is that prosecutors are not usually that well prepared. They tend to exhibit an excess of enthusiasm and ebullience in their first apologia to the jury. They are more likely to do this during the opening statement than at any other time in the trial, and it hurts them more at this time than if they made the same mistake later. The reason they tend to become excessive at this point is that they have not had a very good speaking part during the jury selection. By a natural order of priorities, the important details of the case will have been first explained to the jury by the judge; after that, most of the meaty voir dire questions were asked by the lawyer for the defendant. (This assumes the defendant's turn was first.)

Now the prosecutor has his moment, and the psychological pressure is to justify his own feelings about the case (not really necessary, because these feelings will not have been articulted at this point), and to show that his proof is indeed formidable. Prosecutors tend to overdo opening statements; and they almost always have a lot to say about why they think the defendant is a bad person, as distinguished from how they intend to prove him guilty.

While taking notes it is, of course, not possible to know exactly how the prosecutor's words will prove useful later. But if the comparison of evidence at the end of the case to the evidence outlined by the prosecutor in his opening statement indicates that large areas were not covered, then it will be a pleasure in final argument to remind the jury of what the prosecutor said, and say to them, "And you never heard another thing about it." [2]

When the prosecutor resorts to unrestrained political vituperation, the defense lawyer should hold him back with telling objections, every time. There need be nothing polite about this. If the interruption is necessary at all, it should be done with enough firmness and vigor to bring the opening statement to a protracted halt. The lawyer should make the point that the prosecutor has started to argue his case, that he is saying things to the jury which are not proper elements of proof in a criminal case and which do not relate to any admissible evidence, and that he is attempting to make this into some kind of *political case.*

Things to look out for here are just what the lawyer might expect: smearing references aimed at guilt by association. If there has been talk in the community (for example the local police chief being quoted in the press) about outside agitators having caused unrest, then the lawyer can expect to hear this charge in the prosecutor's opening statement. If some noted radical has just made a speech in the community, then the radical's name will be dragged into the opening statement and linked with the defendant by some facile innuendo. Every time this happens, the lawyer should cut the prosecutor down, and insist on supporting rulings from the bench.

The judge will have to go along with the defense (although he probably did not expect such abuses and objections to be happening at this point) because he is a judge and because he intends to preside over a trial and not a political circus. The defense lawyer should actually use that phrase ("political circus") not only to remind the judge where his duty lies but also to stake out his own moral position in view of the jury and drive the prosecutor off it. That position is—*and this must be presented as the defense's own idea*—*this case will be tried as an "old-fashioned case," or like any other criminal case, or whatever one chooses to term it, but it will not be a political trial.*

It should be understood at this point that it is not just an orderly trial which is desirable for the defendant, but to have forced the prosecution to accede to an orderly trial. This is one situation in which it is not enough to arrive at a good result (an orderly trial)—it is of first importance to catch the prosecution off base, to reveal them as being *far* off base, and then to hammer at them so they are driven to defend their untenable position.

The desirability of jumping the prosecutor in the presence of the jury is particularly worth stressing because there is another way of accomplishing a similar aim, which is often used in other types of cases, but which would be far less desirable procedure in a political trial. That way is simply to go into chambers before opening statements, with a court reporter, and advise the trial judge that one's opponent is about to say something improper to the jury, and request an order (in limine) preventing him from doing so.

As everyone knows, this kind of secret motion might typically be used by a defense lawyer in a civil case if he feels that the plaintiff's lawyer is going to make impermissible references to insurance, or by a plaintiff's lawyer who feels (in a wrongful death case) that the defense lawyer will somehow mention to the jury that the widow has remarried.

It is suggested very strongly that in a political trial, a motion in limine—although it will undoubtedly work—is a poor substitute for having it out with the prosecutor in the presence of the jury.

The prosecutor's opening statement presents an excellent opportunity to show how deeply the two sides differ as to how the case should be tried, and to inflict an initial defeat on the prosecutor. Similar opportunities will occur during the trial, but probably none of them will be as excellent as the one which occurs in the opening statement; and that chance should never be wasted.

§ 12.03 The General Necessity to Make an Opening Statement for the Defense

The problem whether to make an opening statement is really a question whether to make it immediately after the prosecutor's opening statement. Of course the defense may "reserve its opening statement" until the beginning of the defense case; but for practical purposes that is the same as waiving an opening statement.

Political trials differ importantly from other criminal trials on this point. It is more or less accepted among the many good criminal defense lawyers that an opening statement should seldom be made, and only then for exceptional reasons, since the defense has much to lose and little to gain by making one. But in a political case, special considerations compel a different rule. In this kind of defense, the jurors— and the judge, too, for that matter—are, in effect, taken into partnership by the defense. They do not expect their partner to spend all of this time with his face turned away from them. The jurors do expect him to come out somewhat in the open and be aggressive.

On the one hand the lawyer knows that he intends to rely heavily on the presumption of innocence and the prosecution's burden of proof. But he should not behave throughout the political trial as if he were hiding behind these rules, even though he has certainly drawn them to the jury's attention. If the presumption of innocence is going to be of any real help in the final argument, the lawyer must meanwhile behave as if that rule did not exist.

This is not in what he says to the jury, but in the way he conducts the case. Of course he will not assume a burden of proving innocence, or imply to anyone that this burden is on the defendant. But the lawyer will not only have to attack the prosecution's case while it is being put on, he must also put on a very strong case of his own. The fight for the jury's mind is under way from the start.

All of this would seem fairly obvious, but there are psychological pressures which work on defense lawyers at this time, which tend to inhibit them from making any kind of opening statement. A certain amount of fear is quite natural. The lawyer may well feel that he has nothing to gain from making a statement (an habitual feeling), even though his mind tells him this is not true in this case. He may fear that his own lack of preparation—however well he has prepared his case—may cause him to say something now which will not be matched by proof. The prosecutor then will be able to say, "And you never heard another thing about it."

It is especially tempting to waive the opening statement because all trial judges expect all defense lawyers to do so, and they usually manage to present the question of an opening statement in a fatherly tone so low the jury can barely hear it, strongly suggesting to any bystander that, of course, the defense *may* make an opening statement but is not really expected to do so.

Finally, there is the strong fear of professional criticism. No defense lawyer who waives an opening statement was ever faulted for doing so by his brothers at the bar. If the lawyer feels he needs a little pat on the head from some friend in the courtroom, or even just a little sense of approval from courtroom hangers-on, all he has to do is waive his opening statement. Then he can tell his friends in the corridor that he is "trying a tight little case." Colleagues will understand that. But colleagues are not sitting in the jury box, and the jury will certainly not understand it.

The usual reason in favor of waiving opening statements is that they enable the prosecution witnesses to slant their testimony somewhat against the points which the defense wishes to make. But in a political case which has been prepared along the lines recommended here, the defense will probably hope the prosecution witnesses *do* slant their testimony, because the defense will be well enough prepared to make the most of it.

The defense opening statement will be especially helpful to the jury when the slanting occurs. It will show them why certain points are important, and will enable them to focus on those points quickly and to understand when someone is fudging. If they know what the lawyer is doing, they can share his concern, and so during those tedious times in the trial when the lawyer has a lot of hard cross-examining to do, because someone has slanted his testimony a little, the jury is more likely to understand, to sympathize, and to see things through the lawyer's eyes. They may or may not agree that the lawyer has made his point in cross-examination; but later, when the lawyer brings on his own witnesses, they will remember again what the prosecution witness was saying, and the cross-examination. This is worthwhile.

§ 12.04 Some Suggestions as to the Form of a Defense Opening Statement

The defense opening statement should be quite different from other kinds of opening statements, for several reasons. The main thing is to *make a statement*, and within reason the advantages to be had will be got simply by making one. Since the actual proof is a long way off, with the whole prosecution case intervening, it is something of a waste of time to go into detail.

The statement should be brief but never terse. The lawyer would be better off just to think of it as something else he has on his mind which he wants to tell the jury, and not, for example, as some special event possessing a separate reality from the case. The lawyer should ignore any lecterns in the vicinity; he should stand near the jury and talk to them directly. He should keep his tone low-key for those parts that deserve a low-key treatment, and, when he has strong feelings, it is quite all right to let those feelings come through in his tone of voice. Everyone knows that an opening statement is not a time for argument. But on the other hand, in covering the flat factual subjects that are proper for an opening statement, one can say the words as one pleases.

In general, the lawyer should be fairly specific as to *what* he intends to prove, but vague as to *how* he will prove it. To take a rather extreme example, if the defense is alibi, the lawyer shoud say so. He should not use the word "alibi," of course, because that word acquired all its current penumbra of meaning from 1930's movies. He should simply inform the jury that the truth is, the defendant was somewhere else.

If the lawyer feels reasonably safe, he may go so far as to say where and at approximately what times, but this probably is not advisable. It is quite possible—and it requires no special skill to carry this off—merely to tell the jury that at the time and place involved, the defendant was *not there*, and that no worthwhile purpose would be served by going into the details at the present time, of the testimony which will prove this fact.

If one has already retraced the defendant's actions, in this example, and knows for a fact that every single potential witness is a defense witness and has been thoroughly briefed, and can be relied upon (as a matter of personal choice) not to discuss his testimony with the prosecutor's investigator, then it may possibly be safe to go ahead and add a detail or two as to where the defendant was. But the lawyer will be well advised not to say even this much, if it happens (as it often does) that one or two of the potential witnesses to be found along this trail were so deviant from the anticipated testimony of the others that, in self-interest, the defense is not going to call them at all. In that case the lawyer should remain silent about where the defendant was. In any event it would be stupid to reveal the names of witnesses, trusted or not.

An experienced trial lawyer may find this kind of opening statement an unabashed, boldfaced antithesis of an opening statement—an almost stunning omission of information normally associated with opening statements. But that is only because the lawyer is experienced with more normal kinds of opening statements, and thinks of them as having a certain form and reasonable content. Compared to the careful, flat, enormously detailed and factual opening statements appropriate to personal injury cases, this kind of opening statement might seem laughable, but the humor is only in the comparison. In context, nothing about a short opening statement is disproportionate or out of keeping.

All the jury wants to know from the defense lawyer at the beginning of the case is, "If the defendant is innocent, what in general is the nature of your defense?" Once they have been told something about it, that is enough. The psychological pressure was to find out *something*, and that pressure has been eased. The jurors are not children; they know that it would be dangerous and unwise for the lawyer to tick off every single witness and every item of testimony at this stage, and they will certainly not hold it against him for omitting to do so. Of course the opening statement was short. But what was there about it inconsistent with shortness? The lawyer was not excessively formal; he did not address them from across the room in solemn tones, and he certainly did not utilize any lectern. These are the advantages of talking directly, of looking jurors in the eye from close range, and suiting words and style to the message. No one is going to stand up after the lawyer completes this statement (as they will at final argument) to draw attention to what they might regard as shortcomings in what he just said. For that simple reason, the lawyer can make any kind of opening statement he pleases. Better one like this than none at all, and better to be brief about it than to name witnesses.

A final caveat in making a defense opening statement is, never commit the defendant to testify, even though the defense proof may depend upon his testimony. What may seem perfectly safe at the outset of the trial may be impossible at the end. The lawyer does not know what efforts have been made or will be made to impeach the defendant on the stand. There is absolutely no point in assuring the prosecution that the defendant *will* be on the stand, because that is the same thing as assuring them that any and all efforts made to prepare impeaching evidence will be rewarded with an opportunity to use them. The lawyer will be much better off leaving that in doubt; this provides the prosecution with a continuing opportunity to make a mistake in allocating their investigative resources. They may not be prepared for the defendant when he does testify, or they may be prepared to the hilt, only to find out that he will not testify. That is all to be decided later.

If the final decision is that the defendant does *not* testify, it should be true then, as it is now, that the defendant's lawyer never said he would.

Footnotes

1 W. Deem, see ch. 9, N. 3.

2 Id.

Chapter 13

THINGS TO WATCH FOR AT THE BEGINNING

SYNOPSIS

§ 13.01 Introduction

This chapter is about things to watch for in some kinds of political cases while the prosecution witnesses are still testifying on direct examination. The lawyer should be prepared to jump on them immediately. The proper remedies are well-thought-out objections rather than cross-examination.

§ 13.02 Improper Use of Mug Shots

Mug shots (photographs taken for identification at the time of booking) can be expected to appear in the prosecutor's hand at the beginning of any political trial. There are two kinds: the one taken at the time of the defendant's arrest in *this* case; and one which may have been taken in connection with some prior arrest.

As to the mug shot taken at this arrest, there is usually no excuse at all for offering it into evidence. A certain type of prosecutor will suddenly have this mug shot on the counsel table in view of the jury, with the intention of asking one of his first witnesses (a police officer) if this is indeed a picture of the defendant.

Mug shots are demeaning. Few people who have been photographed in that situation looked normal in the photograph. This society is more picture-oriented than word-oriented; members of the jury have seen scores of mug shots in their life times, almost all of them on television or in movies, and every single mug shot they have seen was presented as the picture of a public enemy. Most of these presentations occur in television programs designed to glorify the police at the expense of various citizen characters, often portrayed as either simpering or selfish. Mug shots are shown to television victims for identification, and at the end of the program, another mug shot may flash the message that one more running dog has been dropped from the pack.

This conditioning lends mug shots an especially unpleasant impact and makes them a perfect tool for smearing a person whose trial is about to begin. That is why the prosecutor wishes to use them, and if he is allowed even to flash them before the jury, some damage will have been done which is very difficult to argue against with words.

Needless to say, in the absence of certain foreseeable considerations (mentioned below), the defense lawyer should jump the prosecutor at the first sign a mug shot is going to be offered.

The objection should go a little farther than just "irrelevant." The mug shot is intended to debase, and while a really accurate objection might be stated in scatalogical terms, everyone knows it is not customary to match the objection to the thought. "Inflammatory" will do. But if the prosecutor has managed to show the mug shot to the jury before "offering" it (because he knows the objection will be sustained), he should be cited for misconduct on the spot, vehemently and in the hearing of the jury. One bad turn deserves another.

The prosecutor's justification may be that the photograph is needed for "identification." This is a ridiculous contention and should not go unscathed. The witness who is supposed to make this identification is right there in the witness box, and the defendant is seated in the courtroom a few yards away; it is unthinkable (short of major plastic surgery—which has not occurred in most cases) that the witness would have to identify the photograph rather than the man, thus leaving it to the jury to compare the photograph to the defendant and make the "identification" for him. That is a ridiculous proposition, but that is what is implicit in marking the mug shot for identification.

If the defendant has changed his appearance since being arrested, e.g., by cutting his hair (contrary to good advice, see § 3.02), the offer of the mug shot is much more likely to succeed. The lawyer should offer to stipulate that the defendant is the same person who was arrested, in support of his objection. But there should be no talk of bad faith by the prosecutor, after a haircut. There may not *be* any bad faith.

There is one situation, however, in which the lawyer may have to respond differently, or even let the mug shot into evidence without objection. If this is a case in which the defendant was beaten by police officers, then the beating either occurred before the booking photograph or after. (There are instances of people who were abused *while* the booking photograph was being taken, but not in places that would show in the photograph.) Such a beating will be one of the issues in the case, and the lawyer will have mentioned it in his opening statement. If the beating was before booking, then either the beating was such as to leave some marks on the defendant's face which should have been visible at the time the mug shot was taken, or it was not that kind of beating.

If the marks are visible in the mug shot, the lawyer will want it in evidence, immediately, regardless of other considerations. He would offer it himself for the purpose of cross-examining various officers, if it were omitted; since he would do this anyway, there is absolutely no point in objecting to the mug shot merely because the prosecutor happens to offer it first. On the other hand, if the beating left no mark that is visible in the mug shot, the lawyer should consider offering a stipulation in the presence of the jury that at the time the booking photograph was taken, there was no mark visible on the defendant's face. The object of this stipulation is to concede the fact frankly and without attempting to cover it up, while at the same time arguing, also in the presence of the jury, that the reason for the objection is that the booking photograph will add nothing to the stipulation, but it is only intended to demean and embarrass the defendant.

Exactly to the extent that the prosecutor argues to put the mug shot in evidence anyway, notwithstanding the stipulation, he will be proving himself guilty of just what the lawyer said: attempting to demean the defendant. But the lawyer should only make that accusation against the prosecutor if, and just to the extent that, the prosecutor pushes to get the photograph in for an improper reason. It will not be improper except in the light of the offered stipulation. The beauty of this argument is that it is self-operating, something like an automatic brake shoe, so that the harder the prosecutor pushes, the more he burns himself.

The situation in which the lawyer may have to let the mug shot in—although it is not as helpful to the defense as it is demeaning to the defendant—occurs when the beating took place before the mug shot, which shows some swelling or bruising, but not as much as developed a few hours later. In this case a stipulation would be useless, because one cannot seriously offer a stipulation that the defendant was "slightly marked."

If he was not totally free of marks, the jury *should* see the photograph for whatever light it throws on the situation. (The defense can still prove the later bruising by other evidence, and if necessary, the medical reasons why swelling and black eyes take a little time to develop.) The mug shot will go into evidence, and the lawyer should not oppose it at all. If he does, on the grounds that it is demeaning or whatever, he is going to lose the argument, and worse than that, he will seem to be trying to suppress a piece of evidence merely because it is somewhat unfavorable. The trial may be full of unfavorable details, but they will mean relatively little if the defense accepts them (when it has to) with good grace.

For the case in which the defendant was beaten after booking so as to mark him or his clothing in places that would be shown on a mug shot, the lawyer will probably want the mug shot in evidence anyway as a "before" picture, to show that at the time of booking the defendant was clean and unharmed. That kind of photograph will have some weight, even though, as it often happens, there are no other photographs showing how the defendant looked afterwards.

Similarly, if the prosecution contend that the defendant had been engaged in some wild melee prior to his arrest, so that he should (according to their argument) have been bruised at the time of booking, and the mug shot shows the contrary, it should go in. And if it supports such a prosecution contention, i.e., shows dirt or bruises at the time of booking, then it is certainly going in anyway, and the lawyer should not oppose it.

Finally, if the beating occurred after booking, but was not the kind of beating which created marks which would show, if there is no prosecution contention of unrelated violence prior to arrest, then the mug shot is totally irrelevant, and it should be blocked by all the objections which would apply in a case where there was no beating at all.

The second kind of mug shot is the one that was obviously made in connection with a *prior arrest*. This will be self-evident from the shot itself, since the defendant will not only look at little different because of the lapse of time, but *the date on which a mug shot is taken always appears in the shot*. There is absolutely no excuse for offering such a mug shot, and its only purpose can be to show the jury that the defendant is a person who was arrested prior to the time of his arrest in this case. The innuendo is that he is an habitual criminal.

The lawyer should not only object to the photograph, he should take the court reporter and the photograph to the bench and quietly advise the judge of what it shows (this is *not* to be stated for the jury's hearing), and point out quite forcefully to the judge that the prosecutor is trying to introduce evidence of a prior arrest, in order to prove guilt of this crime by the insinuation of guilt of a prior one.

This kind of "evidence" is so inflammatory as to overwhelm about any conceivable argument the prosecutor might advance for introducing it. While saying all this to the judge, the lawyer would be well advised not to forget to glance back at the counsel table. If it just happens that the prosecutor has carelessly left the photograph face up on the counsel table in view of the jury, the lawyer should state that fact for the record, and while doing so, he should ask himself, whether at the conclusion of the jury selection process, he had an adequate jury (see § 11.09[3]). It is a better idea to remember one's own conclusion at that moment than to reassess it now. If the answer is that the jury did *not* seem adequate at that time—and particularly if this jury was chosen from a "stacked panel"—then the remedy is probably to move for a mistrial.

The stated ground for that motion will be that the prosecutor has already made a fair trial impossible by showing the jury a prejudicial photograph, and by doing so even before it was offered in evidence. The lawyer should cite the prosecutor for misconduct while he is at it. It is particularly important to comply with whatever ritual local practice requires in support of a motion for mistrial. For example, it may be necessary to do it in two steps: by asking the trial judge to admonish the jury to disregard the photograph as if they had never seen it, and then, by moving for a mistrial on the ground that the admonition was not strong enough, and that no other admonition could be strong enough to cure this particular error. Whatever is required should be done punctiliously.

§ 13.03 Inflammatory Film Footage

Everybody likes to go to the movies, and people serving on juries especially regard the prospect of a little film footage with expectation. They may examine still photographs with indifference, but ennui vanishes when the portable screen has been set up and the courtroom lights dim. Minds are unusually open for whatever impressions they are about to receive; even judges like movies.

For these reasons, movie footage showing scenes of riot and turmoil, which are sometimes shot (or spliced) to stress the steadfast services of some of the police involved, can provide the prosecution with much leverage to perpetrate unfairness or fraud against a defendant. It is not uncommon for a prosecutor to expect to show the jury, immediately after the case has begun, heavy footage of events that happened somewhere else, several blocks away, six or eight hours before or after the crime alleged in this case, simply because these events are linked to the defendant *in the prosecutor's mind.* This is a cheap and delusory practice but the temptation is sometimes too much. If one or more defendants are charged with inciting to riot, or participating in a riot, then the prosecution will probably wish to show all the footage they have of any disturbance anywhere in town on or about the date charged. If a building was burned in a civil disturbance, the footage may contain a ten-minute fixed camera shot of the burning building, in color. This is to impress on the jury the prosecutor's own theory that when private property has been destroyed, all bystanders (other than informers) are privy to conspiracy.

It may also happen that in a case where the defendant actually pled guilty to some misdemeanor prior to the felony trial for the sole purpose of preventing the introduction of movie footage which was relevant only to the misdemeanor, the prosecution will nonetheless try to slip it in, relevant or not, at the felony trial. The defense cannot allow this fraud to succeed.

The main point about blocking improper movie footage is that *it cannot be done effectively on the spur of the moment.* That is why careful attention to all prosecution movie footage is stressed as part of the early pre-trial preparation (see § 5.02). The lawyer must know before the footage is offered whether any part of it is properly admissible.

When the film footage is offered—or when it becomes obvious that the prosecutor thinks he is going to be allowed to show it to the jury without formally offering it in evidence—the lawyer should state his objection. This objection should be as strong as the facts warrant, e.g., the film is improper (and the prosecution knows it to be improper) since it relates to events other than those involved in this case, or (where this can be shown) the film was altered by splicing in footage relating to something else. The lawyer should ask the court to view the film and hear authenticating testimony before ruling. Any judge will be glad to do that, with the jury absent.

Selling the initial objection to the jury in this way lends some weight to the ruling which will come. The jury may get to see *some* of the movie, and even if they do not, this is one deprivation they will not hold against counsel.

When the jury is gone, the lawyer should ask the judge to require some form of authenticating, foundational testimony as to what this film shows. When an authenticating (prosecution) witness is on the stand, his testimony in response to questions from the prosecutor may be a little vague and unsatisfactory. The lawyer should clear it all up on cross-examination.

The way to do this is by making him run the film, *and by stopping the projector at every identifiable splice.* This witness will either be the cameraman or somebody else who was *there;* he should be asked separately with reference to each of these portions whether he took it (or witnessed the events directly) and what is shown here, and when it was taken (or happened). If he does not know from personal knowledge he should certainly not be allowed to speculate about it, or testify on the basis of hearsay. This kind of examination should be conducted rather tightly. If the cameraman/witness is not the same one who did the splicing, he should be asked whether he knows who did splice the film, and if that person is available. Assuming both answers are yes, this puts a heavy responsibility on the prosecution to produce the splicer. Once he is on the stand, other things may be learned.

For example, when the splicer takes the stand, the cameraman may have already pointed out that some of the footage shows unrelated events. The splicer should be asked whose idea it was to put these unrelated events in this particular film footage. It may be that one of the prosecutors or their investigators had something to do with this. Details should be brought out mercilessly. When it is all over there may be a very different smell about the film than that of hot celluloid.

In arguing the objection (with the jury absent) the lawyer must know how much, if any, of the footage is really relevant to the case, and whether it can be shown to the jury without imflaming the natural feelings of some of them in a manner which would be unfair to the defense. The lawyer will know this because he has studied the film. It is essential in arguing the objection to:

(1) Describe each portion of footage under discusion with some precision, e.g., the first forty feet of the first reel, a continuous shot of a burning building, with unidentifiable running figures and a view of a clock which reads 6:30;

(2) State the objections accurately and without rambling, relating them directly to the description of what the footage actually shows, e.g., the time is three hours wrong; and

(3) At a propitious moment if and when the argument seems more or less balanced and not otherwise, and not before then—and only in cases in which this is the fact—suggest to the judge that some parts of this film are admissible, describing *that* footage and those scenes.

At this point, the lawyer may point out that it would be possible to start the projector at a certain frame and stop it at a certain frame, and that the footage thus shown would be material and non-prejudicial.

If that kind of compromise (showing part only) is worked out, the lawyer should remember that this film is about to go into evidence. That means it will go in the jury room. Once the admissible footage is identified, he should insist that it be physically cut so as to eliminate the improper portions, and he should personally see to it that offending (not admitted) pieces of film are kept *out of the hands of the clerk* and put back in the prosecution brief case, where they belong. Failure to do this may well blow the whole case at the last instant. If the jury is allowed to take the uncut footage into the jury room with a camera and screen, everything may be in vain; and mishap is almost certain if the film is shown to them again during their deliberations by an operator supplied by the prosecution. It is much better to eliminate the problem by cutting out the improper parts of the film, rather than leaving them in and having to fashion some kind of makeshift solution later, after some wrong film has been screened.

§ 13.04   Inflammatory Tapes of Radio Broadcasts

Tapes of radio broadcasts are not quite as dangerous as movie footage, but they are certainly more dangerous than most ordinary testimony. Recorded hearsay has a special charm. With tapes as with movie footage, the lawyer will have taken early pains to analyze them.

The main thing about tapes is that the prosecutor may want to put in some excited radio broadcast by an on-the-spot witness. Some of this may consist of interviews with bystanders. Of course, what the announcer is saying and what the bystanders are saying is not only hearsay; as a rule, most of the people whose voices are heard will not be present in the courtroom as witnesses. Cross-examining them is impossible at the trial. As to them, the admission of anything at all which they have said on the tape is a total denial of the right to be confronted by persons testifying against the defendant in a criminal trial, i.e., a denial of his Sixth Amendment right to confrontation. The objection should be made and argued, of course, not only on the ground of hearsay, but that the offered testimony would violate defendant's rights under the Sixth and Fourteenth Amendments of the Constitution of the United States, as well as whatever state constitutional provisions may be involved.

As to the announcer, if he is not present in court, the same arguments work. If he is present, the proper objection would seem to be simply hearsay. There is nothing on the tape which he could not say as a witness, in court, so that he could be cross-examined at the time he said it. How this objection will fare will depend largely on whether the announcer's words on the tape are considered part of the res gestae.

This is a sticky argument and the best way to obtain a good result is to move in quickly by interrupting direct examination for the purposes of an objection (hearsay) and to request permission to ask a few questions of the witness on voir dire, in the absence of the jury.

These questions should have been thought out rather carefully. If the prosecutor does not quite realize what the turning point of the objection is going to be (some do not), a skillful cross-examiner *may* get this witness to acknowledge that although he was an excitable, authentic, and very with-it sort of reporter at the time of the event being described, he was also a cold and dispassionate observer, professionally able to set himself apart from things, if only momentarily, in order to say it right for his listeners. In other words, he said what he said carefully and did not just blurt it out (did not act under the spur of the moment).

Obviously all of this line of questioning has to do with emphasis; the lawyer should lead the witness a little toward the end of his spectrum where he conceives himself as weighing words, and away from the other end where he might equally conceive himself as hot-blooded and deeply involved in news where it was happening. By guiding this witness and watching carefully what he is doing, the lawyer *may* move him firmly out of the area of res gestae before the prosecutor becomes sufficiently turned on to make objections.

This voir dire is difficult, and doing it right is doing it briskly, since it *ends* on the first objection. Either the lawyer gets the witness to admit that he stopped and thought *before* he spoke the words on this tape—in which case the res gestae exception is out, the hearsay objection is good, the lawyer stops the voir dire, makes the objection, and it is sustained; or else the voir dire falters or stalls for a moment, the prosecutor demands to know where all this is taking us, the judge concurs and asks that the lawyer explain the object of the voir dire (with the witness sitting there), and there is not much hope of getting the witness to say anything right after that. Do it fast or forget it.

§ 13.05   Improper Attempts to Label the Case as Political by Means of Special "Titles" of Police Witnesses

The improper use of "titles" will occur at about the first or second question addressed to certain police officers. Normal introductory questions elicit the officer's name, the fact that he is a police officer, sometimes his length of service and the extent of his training (if these are relevant to the case), and whether he was working in a certain position or department on the date in question.

But with a certain kind of prosecutor in a political case, there will be another question (or at least an answer) concerning the particular unit to which this officer belongs, e.g., he is in charge of the sheriff's "Subversive Activities Control Section," or perhaps the "Major Crimes Interstate Conspiracy Intelligence Division" or some other such aromatic office. Of course, there may *be* some such organization, and the witness may be its founding and sole member. This gratuitous use of fanciful titles is pernicious since it amounts to a representation by the prosecution (in this case the sheriff's office) that, quite apart from any evidence in the case, this is indeed a "major" case, that there are law enforcement people whose daily service to the public takes them unquestioningly into dark paths of interstate conspiracy, and that pursuant to this public interest and despite all attendant dangers, they think this case ought to be prosecuted to a conviction.

This is very much the same as the prosecutor telling the jury in final argument that the jury is a "partner" in law enforcement; that overt kind of argument is not allowed, and neither should this subtle one be. The difficulty is what to do about it.

From a narrow, "evidentiary" viewpoint, the lawyer is at a disadvantage with that kind of answer. Revealing that the witness is not merely a detective but belongs to this particular "section" cannot usually be stigmatized as "non-responsive." It is responsive all right—to a question so innocuous that one could not have objected to it:

Q: Were you employed on that date?
A: Yes, I was.
Q: Where were you employed?
A: I was working for the Sheriff's Office as Chief of the Major Crimes Interstate Conspiracy Intelligence Division.

But tactically the lawyer enjoys a considerable advantage from his very careful discovery work (e.g., how people have been signing their intraoffice reports); and probably because of his acquaintance with some of the officers involved in the case, he will know which one or two of the prosecution witnesses actually belong to some such section, and who probably will be looking for an opportunity to tell the jury all about it.

This is probably another situation in which the lawyer has a perfectly good objection, as long as he makes it in front of the jury. This is probably not a good subject for a motion in limine. The reason is, the ruling will be close, so that some judges would sustain the objection and many would overrule it; but once the objection is made in the privacy of chambers, and a ruling is obtained, the best the lawyer is going to get out of it (if he loses) is the fact that he made his record for a possible appeal. In other words, having tried the objection in chambers, and lost there, the lawyer is not in a position to do it again in front of the jury. The judge would regard that as bad faith, and so would most trial lawyers. There is no need to goad a judge to anger, particularly in the presence of the jury, without any reason.

Probably a better way to handle this problem is to discount it somewhat in advance, i.e., the lawyer should acknowledge to himself that this witness is about to slip in some improper testimony which will hurt the defense a little, and that the objection (however made) is doubtful. Accordingly, the lawyer should proceed to make the objection for the jury in a way which will hurt the prosecution a little and minimize the damage to the defense.

Once the witness is on the stand, there are two ways to make an objection. The lawyer could take opposing counsel and the court reporter to a little bench conference, while everybody waits, and tell the judge that the witness is about to slip in some nonsense having to do with his job title, and that the defense wants a ruling preventing him from doing so. The most likely judicial reaction to this move will be a statement that the judge does not *know* what the prosecutor is going to ask the witness, since he is not a mind reader, and that so far there is no question pending to which an objection has been made. Most judges will send people back to the counsel table to proceed from that point as if the bench conference had never happened. This is somewhat *better* than doing it in chambers, in the sense that the judge has not foreclosed an objection which will now have to be made (which the lawyer will now have the privilege of making).

On the other hand, the jury has been kept waiting, and accoustics in courtrooms are generally such that it is no secret what the lawyers and the judge are talking about, despite the fact that they are huddling. However, the prosecutor will enjoy this little scene, and he will convey to the jury his satisfaction with the "ruling."

This kind of inconclusive bench encounter may serve to caution the witness in the box, who will certainly strain his ears to overhear it. It will also move the judge several inches toward a favorable ruling, when one is needed—in about one minute. This is because he has just said, in effect, "Don't bother me, there is nothing yet to rule on." And if one minute later there *is* something to rule on, then there *was* something to the original objection, and the judge will rule on it with that in mind.

After the bench conference, this piece of bad testimony is either blurted out by the witness, or if the witness has been turned off by what he overheard, he will be cold for the prosecutor and it will be necessary for the prosecutor to ask a direct question in order to elicit this information. If the witness blurts it out, the best response is a slightly rhetorical motion to strike, in which the valid ground is not the rhetorical one. The lawyer should move to strike that part of the answer having to do with being a member of the despicable subversive conspiracy control board on the ground that it was not responsive to the question (a valid ground on the assumption the witness blurted it out). Also, the lawyer should add *as part of the same motion* that the answer being striken was a deliberate attempt by the prosecution to insinuate their own opinions into the case, and imply to the jury that for reasons not related to any evidence, the present case should be regarded as a "subversive activities conspiracy case." This latter part of the objection is valid too, but it enjoys a far better prospect of success if it rides in on the coattails of "not responsive."

In most quick exchanges of this kind, a single ruling either approves or disapproves everything the objecting lawyer just said. Few judges, when sustaining objections by the defense in a criminal case, will stop to make nice distinctions, sustaining the objection on this ground and not on that. The result in this example is simply a judicial endorsement of what the defense just said about the prosecution making this a political case. This endorsement, needless to say, should be sought at every opportunity.

On the other hand, if the witness does not blurt it out, the prosecutor may ask for it directly. The objection here is that the answer would be irrelevant, and further that it would constitute an effort to mislead the jury (as discussed supra). Now the objection must stand on its own. If it works, fine. If it does not work, the prosecutor is still not going to look very good for having pressed that kind of a point; and if the objection is stated sincerely and the ruling is accepted in good grace, most or all of the prosecution's petty advantage will have been spoiled. Juries do not like to be diddled with in this manner, especially by public servants!

A special caveat seems appropriate here: this kind of objection (relating to a police officer's politically inflammatory job title) is a valid one, but it is extremely minor. There should be no more than one of these encounters in the course of the trial, and the lawyer should come nowhere near the brink of overdoing it. There may be fingerprint experts, chemists, pathologists, and in fact personnel of all kinds who are called into court as witnesses on behalf of the prosecution. They will all be stating their job titles, and for almost everyone of them, there will be no reason for objecting to their doing so.

Even if it happens that there are two or three political conspiracy persons called to the stand, and even if the prosecution should attempt to extract the same job title information from all of them, this particular objection should be argued with vigor only once. After that, it should not be repeated unless the lawyer was successful the first time, and even then should state his objection in minimal words: something like, "The same objection as was made with respect to the last witness, with respect to these imaginative job titles."

If the objection was overruled the first time, the lawyer should probably not chew it over again. It is rather important that the jury respect the lawyer's perspective and sense of values. They can understand an objection like this if the grounds for it are stated sincerely to them at the time it is first made, even though the objection is overruled. But they cannot totally identify with any lawyer who seems preoccupied with some grievance arising from an earlier ruling, and who sits there, so interested in renewing his prior objection to some minor point that he seems insensitive to the larger case unfolding in the courtroom. It is important not to do this, and not to seem to do it.

§ 13.06 Hearsay Evidence of What Officers Were Told in "Briefings"

In any case involving police misconduct, the prosecution will usually try to justify it in advance by some evidence of the officers' "state of mind." This is especially true if the incident involving their misconduct allegedly arose out of an attempt by them to stop some person for questioning (on grounds of reasonable suspicion) as distinguished from stopping him or her to make an arrest (where the requirements of probable cause are more strict). Instead of presenting this stop, or arrest, in the context of objective facts, the prosecution will sometimes try to present it on the basis that the officers involved had just been briefed by some other officers (who do not testify) and had been informed of a number of specific terrible things that had happened or were about to happen. And so, on the basis of this information, the officers did what they had to do in the interests of protecting the state (or because they "feared for their lives"). This kind of evidence (what another officer said) is of course hearsay of the worst sort, and is knowingly offered in defiance of the defendant's right to confront persons testifying against him. It is also stunningly irrelevant. When the objection is made, which it should be with vigor, there should always be specific mention of the Sixth and Fourteenth Amendments as well as specific provisions of the state constitution touching the right to confront prosecution witnesses in a criminal case. A trial judge may be inclined to vacillate over the hearsay objection when there is any room to argue "state of mind." But there is no answer to the Sixth Amendment argument except to sustain the objection.

It should go almost without saying that while making this valid objection, the lawyer should lace it with blunt, tough accusations that the prosecution is attempting to try this as a political case by injecting events which have nothing to do with it, through witnesses who are not called and cannot be cross-examined, for the purpose of prosecuting the defendant on the basis of his alleged or implied identification with persons not under indictment.

These points are also good, and in the long run (for the purpose of persuading the jury rather than winning a ruling on one point of evidence) the argument against a political trial is far more important than the one against hearsay. But as with so many other things, these arguments will fare better—will get the much desired judicial endorsement—when made in the company of an unarguable, prosaic, and relatively automatic objection such as hearsay/denial of confrontation. These are such major points that there is no danger at all of overdoing.

§ 13.07 Things in the Witness's Hand While He Is Testifying

The rule here is, *always* go look to find out what the witness is holding. For some reason, defense lawyers will sometimes sit at the counsel table while the prosecutor finds it necessary to stand beside his witness examining some

416 / POLITICAL CRIMINAL TRIALS

notes or tables which the witness needs (or they both need) while they are testifying. (Leading questions usually go with this performance.)

It is one thing to observe that a witness is testifying by the use of notes, and to save that fact for cross-examination and then demand the notes. But it is another thing to allow the prosecutor to go unaccompanied and stand beside the witness, the two of them poring over something, pointing here and there while the questions and answers go on. There should always be three people at the witness box when this happens, and the lawyer should stay there as long as the prosecutor does.

The reasons are obvious. If the witness is using notes, he is probably being selective, skipping things. And if the prosecutor is standing there, he is helping him do it. Similarly, if the witness is testifying about something on a page or in a photograph, it is not very fruitful to cross-examine him about it as long as he can say, "That is not what I meant. *This* is the person I identified, *over here*." And even while direct examination is going on, the lawyer can help things along by suggesting that while the witness is testifying about something he should mark it, or note specifically for the record his own description of where the witness is pointing on some document. All of this dictates being close.

Chapter 14

CROSS-EXAMINING
PROSECUTION WITNESSES

SYNOPSIS

§ 14.01 Preparations and Why They Must Be Kept in Perspective

Preparations do not necessarily mean that there is going to be a cross-examination; they merely assure that when a prosecution witness opens his month to testify, the lawyer has made adequate use of all previously available information, so that his mind is free to listen.

The lawyer may decide to cross-examine, to impeach the witness by other means, to use this witness to impeach another, or to set up a small point for use in argument. Or he may decide that the witnesses' testimony is not worth dignifying with cross-examination, or the witness is holding back something with the special intention of exploding it during cross-examination, so that the answer will be to avoid cross-examination or not to cross-examine on a certain topic.

Preparations to cross-examine are phenomena of the lawyer's personal history which happen to coincide with the appearance of that particular witness on the stand, *not* any kind of personal investment which has to be justified by public use. The inexperienced lawyer should remember that the mere fact of having spent a lot of time in preparing to cross-examine a certain witness does not mean he has to spend a lot of time cross-examining him, or for that matter, any time. When ready for use, preparations should be regarded as having ceased to exist, leaving the lawyer only with the benefit of them. They are a suit that he should wear without self-consciousness.

[1] Suggested Minimal Preparations for a Large Number of Potential Witnesses About Whom Little Is Known

In certain political cases, there will be a school of potential witnesses whose names and (in some cases) statements will have been fished up by the discovery nets. These are not the star witnesses for the prosecution, but persons who nonetheless could be called to the stand at any time.

While the case is in progress, the prosecution may be re-evaluating their testimony and reinterviewing them at night, but without the benefit of fresh, written witness statements. Nothing more will be handed to the defense, to indicate which of them will appear in court. In a large trial, perhaps 10 percent of these people will be called to the stand. Naturally, some minimal state of preparation must be maintained against this entire group at all times. And naturally, the big organizing problems concern materials received from the prosecutor.

Frequently, these will be people who volunteered information to the police that was not central to the subject of the trial. Perhaps someone on the prosecution side thought this information *might* be helpful in proving some element on a crime charged against one of the defendants. As to some of these witnesses, a short statement may have been taken, but it will not always be very indicative of what the witness could contribute. As to the rest, there may be only a brief memorandum from some police officer reflecting a contact on a certain date with a very short reference to what it was about.

Needless to say, the lawyer or his investigator will have made whatever efforts time permitted to contact these people, and so there should be defense investigation notes as to some. But most of those contacts will have been unproductive, either because the person refused to talk to anyone on the defense side, or because he could not be found at all.

The organizational plan here is extremely plain. As to each of these potential witnesses, the pieces of paper relating to that witness should be put together in a little packet with his name on it. All the packets should then be arranged in alphabetical order, or in whatever order the lawyer pleases, and these should be kept within arm's reach throughout the trial.

In a long trial, the lawyer should review these at night from time to time so that he is quite familiar with the modest contents of each packet, and knows, for example, whether his investigator can be expected to come back with more information about this one or that one. The lawyer can add his own notes, annotating and underlining things in whatever bright color pleases the tired eye.

These preparations are childishly simple, but as it happens they are sometimes neglected, apparently on the theory that with so little to go on, there is no point in getting it together. While it may be true that in most cases the little packets make little difference in the sense of adding usable information, not to have organized even this much is to face the witness with a knowledge of things undone, a sense of chaos at the elbow, and guilt. But to have organized even modest materials is to look at the same witness with serenity at the elbow, as much as if the lawyer had spent many hours organizing prolix information. Serenity, of course, if one has not been introduced to him in court, is a great murderer of hostile testimony.

[2] Standard Preparations Against All Known Prosecution Witnesses

[a] How Prosecution Witnesses Are Known

The lawyer will know the main prosecution witnesses because he knows his case, and having utilized discovery procedures to the fullest, he will have studied all of their witness statements, and noted how many times they were referred to in prosecution memoranda. His sense of the prosecution witness list is the result of his knowledge of the case at any given moment; but it is *not* the result of having asked the prosecution for a *list* of their witnesses. For reasons elaborated previously, the lawyer should not ask for a list of witnesses as such.

[b] Making a Combined Index for Each Witness

[i] Importance of Indexing

With a main prosecution witness, the problem is to index all of the available materials. It is to be hoped that these will include two or more transcripts, and several reports or statements. The general objects of indexing are to show: (1) where the witness has already contradicted himself; (2) what he has said on other subjects, whether obviously relevant or not, which may turn out to be contradictory to something he says in the future; (3) where it seems that he is vulnerable to impeachment from sources other than his own testimony; and (4) where it appears that his testimony may be useful in impeaching some other witness.

A combined index is not a difficult achievement, but it *is* an enormously powerful trial weapon. An index is a kind of machine offering mechanical advantage and a reservoir of stored energy, capable of producing more sudden results than an unassisted mind could generate on the spur of the moment. Putting one together is a pleasure for those who have used them, since anticipation makes the work go faster. The following section outlines a simple, workable technique for making a combined index.

[ii] Collecting the Transcripts

First, assemble copies of all the transcripts or transcript-surrogates which pertain to this witness. Available transcripts will be those pertaining to his sworn testimony on one or more of the following occasions: (1) before the grand jury; (2) at the preliminary hearing; (3) when he was subpoenaed and forced to testify in connection with some defense motion in this case; (4) at a prior trial of this case, assuming there was a mistrial, new trial or successful appeal; (5) in a related criminal case; or (6) in a related civil deposition. For any worthwhile prosecution witness, the lawyer should have seen to it that there are at least one or two transcripts.

In addition, any other papers of the following kinds should be included in the array of material: (1) a witness statement made by this witness; (2) a witness statement made by someone else, which contains a material reference to this witness; (3) a police report or interoffice memorandum, if this witness wrote it or was one of the investigating officers responsible for its contents—as distinguished from one which the witness "approved" but without personal knowledge of the events described; (4) a police report or memorandum written by some other person, which makes a material reference to this witness.

The foregoing lists are not definitive, but they cover the most important sources of material.

[iii] The Mechanics of Indexing

The next point to note about making a combined index is, who is going to do it? Basically, a combined index is an earthy little thing that serves the lawyer's personal needs, and which feeds upon and contributes to his knowledge of the whole case. The lawyer himself is the logical one to make this index. If it is true that "time does not always permit," perhaps the lawyer should reconsider that cliche before dismissing the entire problem to the desk of his legal assistant (if he has one). "Time does not permit," in this situation comes close to saying that time does not permit an effective cross-examination.

No matter how good his legal assistant may be, the lawyer is probably going to have to do the first part of this job himself (examining with precision what the topical categories will be), although parts may be left for others. But he should remember that he is the only one who is going to be using it, and when he does use it, his mind is going to have to be completely familiar with this index, moving very fast. The organization of the index and what the entries stand for should be as familiar to him as the touch of his own hand.

The first step in making a combined index is to have already made separate indexes of whatever transcripts are now in hand. If trial preparation has been progressing evenly, then transcripts will probably have been received from time to time, and each of these will have been indexed shortly after it was received.

Assuming the transcripts are already indexed, the rest is fairly easy. In most situations, it usually works out that testimony at different times and places covers substantially the same events, and so the topical outlines of existing transcripts will probably be identical as to all areas of overlap. This is the time to review the adequacy of the outline, however.

The indexer should make a larger outline of topical headings, which includes all the headings in any of the transcripts. He should then examine it in the light of other papers, such as witness statements and police reports, to decide whether the outline is really large enough and detailed enough to include everything which reasonably ought to go into it. If there is any adjusting and reorganizing to do in terms of headings, this is the time to do it. When the large outline is satisfactory, it is only a matter of transferring existing outlines to a combined one. This is rather like taking several decks of cards and melding them together by suits.

In typing the combined index, the lawyer and his secretary should arrange things so that all headings relating to any of the transcripts which belong under a particular subject head are vertically arranged under that subject head, in the same order (as nearly as anyone can tell) in which the events described actually happened. This is obviously not going to be the same order in which miscellaneous statements are scattered around in the transcripts themselves. Appropriate page and line references are collected in columns, one separate column for each transcript.

Assuming that separate indexes have already been made before this job is done, a good legal secretary can take much of the work off the lawyer. But experience shows that it is usually a *bad* idea to leave it to someone else to decide whether something is contradictory or impeaching. So a better procedure is probably for the lawyer to sit down with dictating equipment, after he has decided on the shape of the larger outline, and to summarize not only how he wants this combination put together, but exactly what testimony is contradictory to what; if something is contra to another entry, he should make that decision himself (since he is going to rely on it in court) and he should specifically dictate what entry should be typed under what other entry, what will be designated as contra, and what is important enough to merit italics.

While doing this particular chore, the lawyer should re-read every witness statement and police report for items contradictory to the transcripts, and whenever he finds one, he should dictate an appropriate entry for the index, in italics.

In order to keep things under control, entries of this sort (relating to witness statements and police reports) should be inserted by simple references and only where they are particularly relevent; i.e., it will *not* be necessary or helpful to clutter the multiple index with a lot of vertical columns labeled "page" and "line" with respect to some witness statement that appears only once or twice in the entire index. (At this point it might be helpful to look at a sample page from a combined index—see Appendix F.)

The process of making a combined index is somewhat harder if the various transcripts have not already been indexed separately. The easy way out is just to index them separately, have those indexes typed up separately, and then proceeded as described above.

But those who have a flair for doing things directly will find a shorter method. The way to do this is to sit very still in the middle of the night, utterly free from distraction or interruption, and make compendious notes from one transcript after another, organizing all the notes under common headings, keeping in mind very carefully what one is doing, and then, in cold blood, picking up the dictating equipment and dictating the finished combined index. But if the phone rings once before this is completed the whole thing may collapse in shambles.

[c] A Written Summary of Early Impressions of the Witness

At the end of every combined index it is usually helpful to reproduce in a succinct form the lawyer's early impressions of this witness. In order to be really helpful this notation should be limited to what the lawyer wrote *at the time*. In its best form, this memorandum is not a summary of present recollection, but rather a reproduction (or summary) of notes recorded *then*, while the experience was still fresh (see § 5.03).

In deciding whether to attack the witness in areas where he can only be impeached out of his own mouth, it is important to remember his own personal manner of lying, what he does when he is about to lie or is actually doing it, what his self-image seems to be, what he will bring up (though not asked), and what he thinks throws credit on himself. The lawyer's early notes on these subjects are gold.

[d] An Advance Note as to What Cross-Examination Should Hope to Achieve

It is sometimes helpful for the lawyer to write out a note to himself concisely stating what seems (at the time of writing the note) to be the reasonable object and limits of cross-examination. This is certainly part of keeping things in perspective.

If the witness is probably going to be persuasive with the jury, and yet his testimony is really not all that important, the lawyer may be well advised to take some precautions against his own hunting instincts. The fact that the jury likes the prosecution witness is something which is going to wear on the lawyer at the time of trial. This situation can be foreseen almost as well as it can be seen in hindsight, if the lawyer has met the witness, and there is no reason not to take a simple precaution. After all, if the lawyer's best perspective of the entire trial indicates that the witness's testimony is harmless, and if the jury likes the witness, it may be that the object of cross-examination is to skip it entirely and get rid of him.

On the other hand, if a preview of the witness indicates that even though his testimony is not very harmful, his self-confidence may tend to add momentum to the prosecution case, the lawyer may wish to set out some small stumbling blocks to break his stride and at least change his breathing a little. For example, the combined index may reveal two or three insignificant contradictions in things the witness has said. In their small way, these are golden. They are golden because it is only necessary to ask the witness the same questions, and whatever he says, another answer contradicts him. These things may not be even worth mentioning in final argument, but with a certain type of egotistical witness, they are detrimental to his self-confidence. If the lawyer plays these small trumps immediately, it may be just sufficient to take the edge off the witness's self-confidence.

The lawyer can ask him in a very nice way if he did not previously testify thus and so, and the witness will read the transcript to himself, and he will have to admit that he did. At just this point, it may be possible to ask the witness one or two marginal questions as to other things (where it is *not* possible to impeach him), and the reward may well be "I don't know," even though the witness certainly does know. If the lawyer stops at just this point, he has certainly prevented this witness from adding momentum to the prosecution case, yet he has not risked a bloody nose by attacking the witness on grounds where he is right and where he can look good.

This sort of cross-examination has for its goal something very unambitious; on the other hand, the total of these little achievements in a long trial is a substantial benefit for the defense. The point is, this kind of cross-examination can well be *planned* in advance because it is so limited. The lawyer will know his own personality and his own work methods best; if he is one who can benefit from a little written admonition to himself, that is what paper is for.

There are many other things which should be noted in this memorandum, even though some of them may be so obvious that none seems necessary; e.g., whether a police officer testifying as a prosecution witness is to be treated substantially as a defense witness (see § 14.03), and relied upon in final argument. The fact that such an argument lies ahead is quite important in cross-examining the witness. If the lawyer forgets and goes after the witness hammer and tongs as if he wanted to convict him of perjury, then he is not going to sound very sincere in final argument when he adopts this witness's testimony. It is the argument which must control the cross-examination, not the other way around. This should be remembered now, and *noted* now, before the cross-examination starts.

Similarly, it may be that this witness should be asked something important even though he did not testify about it on direct examination, to set up an argument or to impeach some other witness. For example, the witness may be a police officer who saw the defendant arrested, but did not see him thereafter. If the defendant was beaten at a stopping point on the way to jail, and if the results of the beating are clearly visible in the booking photograph, it would be an excellent idea to ask this witness whether he saw the defendant being put into the police car, handcuffed, and if so, whether there was anything unusual about his appearance at that time. It is very easy to slip this kind of question in during the course of cross-examination, but it is also very easy to forget it under trial pressure.

Finally, it may be that this witness is vulnerable to impeachment on some collateral ground. It may be a prior inconsistent statement or anything else classified as "collateral." The lawyer should know whether, under the local operative rules, he has to do something preliminary to impeaching this witness on the collateral point, e.g., (1) specifically ask the witness about the statement, with appropriate identification of time, place, and persons present or (2) skip the foundation but do something else instead, such as asking the judge not to excuse this witness from further attendance when he finally leaves the stand. Whatever it is going to take in order to get at this witness on a collateral matter should be carefully noted so that it will not be overlooked.

§ 14.02 The Volunteer Witness Not Sufficiently Involved to Be an Informer

[1] Characteristics of his Personality

This kind of main prosecution witness (more often a man) tends to have certain characteristics worth looking for, which if found may explain his dangerous and otherwise unaccountable testimony. Since these characteristics and their explanation will decisively shape the defense argument, they should also actuate the special cross-examination which sets up that argument.

This kind of witness may come from the same stratum of society that includes the defendant and many of the defense witnesses. Their paths may have crossed before. He may even know some of them; but if so, they will probably know each other as acquaintances, not friends.

When this witness is an older man, he may be encountered as capricious and querulous; and in that case his motivation may seem eroded. Young or old he suffers from an overriding need to gather attention to himself, especially the favorable attention of law enforcement people. If he is young, he may be a firm believer in education or other kinds of self-improvement; and he may include among his ambitions the wish to be a police officer. The reasons for this goal may (for other people) be as variegated as the human condition, but for this witness, the feelings actuating it—and many other things in his life—may be thought of as misguided romanticism.

For instance, if this witness is young and a ladies' man (he may not be), he probably will not think of himself as *merely* a ladies' man; he has to be something closer to James Bond. If discovery reveals that he had some minor brush with the law, it will probably turn out to be innocuous; but while someone else's innocuous brush may have involved a moving traffic violation or public intoxication, his is more likely to involve some mix-up with a woman, or having a firearm at the wrong time or place or without the right permit. This witness may in fact own a lot of firearms, but that feature of his personality will not be particularly noticeable because he will always have an acceptable reason. He collects them, or he has a job or a residence in the country which makes firearms appropriate. His romantic self-image makes them *necessary*.

This witness is always auto-suggestible; he can deceive himself far more than most people. He does not come into court to lie; and that point may be *vital* to understanding his motives and through him the case. He testifies because he manages to believe it all. He has probably believed many similar things in his private life.

If this witness is an older man, some of his acquaintances may think of him as a person not to be trusted, which just means that his misstatements were never disappointing enough to arouse antagonism. But if he is younger, he may have told a few tall tales. These were not necessarily iniquitous, but unfortunately they were tales told rather convincingly by one adult to another. Some of his acquaintances who were told these stories (and believed them) may not have been amused at all. They may have been disgusted when they learned the cold facts, may have found these episodes (in context) discontinuous from normal adult intercourse, and privately may have written off this witness as a "pathological liar." (The use of these potential character witnesses is discussed below.)

His definitional attributes are that he is a main witness, a volunteer, and that he can be impeached, usually out of his own mouth. Because they did not know what they were getting into, the prosecution will have mixed feelings about him. But they will take measures to protect him at this point.

[2] Characteristics of his Testimony

This witness sees important things that did not actually happen. He is always a percipient witness, always involved, always the person who went just a little out of his way because he thought something was about to happen.

His description of his own motives has a curious, flat quality. On direct examination, he will always stress his precautions (his activities are very dangerous and romantic) and imply that he is in a better position to recall events now; i.e., he knew it was important when he saw it happening and, in fact, he was there for the purpose of seeing it. His laudable interest and his special training on how to observe things (this witness almost always has some special training somewhere) are sufficient in his eyes to give his testimony special reliability. The prosecution are taken with this notion too, and they will always bring it out on direct examination.

The witness's difficulty is that he not only sees people who *were* there, he also is inclined to see people who were *not* there. These are target people. The witness knew at the time he made the identification that "law enforcement" wanted to get the ass of these target people. Consequently, he places persons on the scene in such numbers that inevitably one or two of them can later prove—even to the satisfaction of a prosecutor—that they were not there.

Moreover, this witness sees target defendants doing

things and hears them saying things which add up to outrageous crimes. These are crimes which the prosecutor believes happened, and for which he wants convictions more
than he wants the fingers on his hands. It was by making
these impossible identifications that this particular witness
got the attention of the prosecution.

[3] Significance to the Prosecution Case

Typically this witness is the *cause* of this action being
filed. The prosecutor chose to accept his testimony in order
to have a case, because he would incriminate target defendants nobody else would incriminate. If his testimony
were subtracted from the case, it would never have been
filed.

Although the witness is subject to psychological
hazards which were apparent—or should have been apparent—to the first police officer who interrogated him,
nonetheless, the prosecution accepted the risk of using his
testimony. Because of their own suspicions of this particular
witness, the prosecution will typically have taken this case
before a grand jury rather than exposing him to cross-
examination at a preliminary hearing. The prosecution's
fears have now been confirmed: discrepancies have emerged
which they wish very much had been apparent before he
started telling it to the grand jury. If this were any kind of
case but a political case, the prosecution would dismiss it
entirely. But it *is* a political case, and they are not going to
back down. They have decided to brazen it out.

On account of their great concern about this witness's lapses, the prosecution will attempt precautions, e.g.,
mentioning this witness in the opening statement as a hero
the defense will try to villify, or portraying him (while on
the stand) as a person constantly in danger.

Although the prosecution will see that he does not
come to court carrying a weapon of any kind, they may ask

him a few questions showing that he has a license to carry a concealed weapon. The innuendo is that he lives such a dangerous life, informing on people, upholding property rights, that he has to have this privilege. A secondary innuendo is that the defendants and their friends are persons who would kill a man of this caliber in cold blood. For final argument, the prosecutor cannot wait to say that this witness was dealt with unfairly, and that despite all the things the defense tried to do, "they could not discredit him."

[4] Importance to the Defense

This witness not only requires a special sort of cross-examination but he will also influence the extent and form of cross-examination of many other prosecution witnesses.

[5] From the Cross-Examiner's Viewpoint

Cross-examination will probably pivot on knowing in advance that this witness can be materially impeached by his own prior testimony. He will have said things that were wrong; by the time of trial everybody will know what they were and how easy it will be to prove them wrong. When this typical situation occurs, these points are well known to both sides and indeed they are the reasons why the prosecutor is overprotective of this witness. For example, some other defendant may have been prosecuted on the identification made by this witness. Later the identification was found to be so wrong (because of an iron alibi) that the case had to be dismissed. So this witness is either going to have to admit that he made a bad identification or stick with his private fancy that he made a good one and face overwhelming proof to the contrary. That kind of impeachment is often possible with this type of witness.

Another point about the witness is that he has been thinking about his shortcomings for at least two months before trial, and thinking about what he is going to say when he is asked the obvious questions. Despite everything, he is nervous and apprehensive when he takes the stand. Although he cannot be attacked with any degree of surprise (on these points), that does not really matter.

The second controlling consideration (besides the certainty of some impeachment) is that this witness radiates apprehension. The jury will know, the moment he enters the room. It does not matter that he is overcontrolled, it is just that he is so caught up in apprehension that it is impossible for his situation to be a secret for even a minute. This feeling has a considerable potential, since it is going to be transmuted by the jury into sympathy or distrust.

When he takes the stand, there will be an electric feeling in the courtroom, which was building from the opening statement. Most prosecutors are heavy-handed in dealing with witnesses of this kind, and will have imparted to the jury a special feeling about this witness (fear). They will have said this is a man who is doing his duty, and that he will be taking his life in his hands by coming into court. The jury is not sure at this point. There is no need for them to hurry. The witness will be coming soon enough, and he is either an informer, whom people will secretly despise while pretending not to, or perhaps for various reasons he may deserve respect.

Then, when this witness finally appears, he is much more apprehensive and inner-directed than other witnesses. Maybe he fears for his life, as the prosecution imply. Or maybe he is just thinking in terms of personal, psychological problems only partly related to testifying. The jury does not have to decide all that now, while he is on direct examination; they will wait a little longer. They will wait just long enough for cross-examination to begin, and then feelings about this witness are going to jell.

This great unstable feeling—to sympathize with the witness or disbelieve him—lends special value to a prompt, apparently detached cross-examination which carries all of its obvious points on the front end. The cross-examiner will be successful only if he throws all these teetering impressions of the witness onto the side of distrust, and away from gratitude, and if he does this much immediately. The feeling should be, "Sure the defense is after this witness. But they damned well have a *reason* to be!" A certain coolness about it argues louder than any of the prosecutor's words that the defense lawyer is not crucifying this witness.

These considerations mean the witness should be helped to be his own worst enemy, should be put to work explaining things he cannot explain. They also mean that a long cross-examination is beneficial to the defense, because that will better impart the witness's psychological aura. The jury will get to know him.

It is also characteristic of this kind of witness that it would be a great mistake to let him off easily, in any sense. There is a constant temptation to do this, because the prosecutor will have said so much about how this witness is going to be crucified. He will utilize almost every objection during cross-examination to add a few words about crucifixion.

However, this nonsense should never be allowed to warp the cross-examination, to make the defense lawyer bend over backwards. In fact, this is an excellent example of the general rule that the defense lawyer should always view the case as if there *were* only one case, namely the defense, with the prosecution non-existent. Since the defense case requires a thorough job of cross-examining this witness, the lawyer should do it thoroughly, even though it looks like walking into a prosecution trap, seeming to make so much of things. Appearances to the contrary, the lawyer is perfectly protected against the prosecution trap (the accusation of crucifying an heroic witness). He is protected by his own cool demeanor and by the argument which he will make at the end of the case. His coolness will keep him away from sarcasm or other overbearing conduct which might generate sympathy for the witness. His argument will be not that the witness is a perjurer, but that he has fooled himself all of his adult life, was fooling himself when he made the prior inconsistent statements which impeach him now, and was probably fooling himself when he made certain other statements as to which he cannot be impeached. And although he is not a person to be hated, he is certainly not a person to be believed (see § 14.02[6][c]).

Another point to look for is vulnerability to impeachment by character witnesses. There may be two or three people among his acquaintances who have ample reason to believe this witness is a pathological liar, i.e., who can testify that they are acquainted with his reputation for truth and veracity, and that it is a bad one. Before deciding to use character evidence, however, one should remember an unwritten law: before this main prosecution witness— the subject of such protectiveness—can ever be impeached by character evidence, *he must first be impeached more directly.* Direct impeachment can come either (1) out of his own mouth (former sworn testimony which he now repudiates) or (2) partly out of his own mouth and partly from testimony of other persons (he refuses to repudiate his own former testimony himself, but other witnesses—preferably prosecution witnesses—do it for him). Often these conditions can be met. This witness typically *can* be impeached out of his own mouth on one or two material points. That being done, the door is open to character testimony about his truthfulness, to make up for the fact that it is not possible to impeach him on every single thing he says about every defendant. There *are* people who think this witness is a pathological liar, and they should get their say after the jury has begun to suspect the same.

Another characteristic of this witness is that he is deeply antagonistic to the defense. He may turn out to be the kind of witness sometimes referred to as a "squirrel," and he is always what may be thought of as a "splinter" witness.

Everyone knows that "squirrel" has been part of the trial idiom for a long time. It is sometimes applied to another person's client or a witness. The word implies a form of antagonism to the proceedings and to the lawyer using the term which suggests a small, light-boned, furry creature given to going out in high places, on slender support, full of clucking and taunting, and actually having a lot less substance or weight than he seems to. This kind of witness tends to make counsel react on the basis of the witness's personality, generally a mistake. Anyway, as those who observe them know, squirrels do occasionally fall. Parts of the cross-examination may be envisioned as a tree-shaking operation.

A "splinter" witness conceives himself as an advocate, and in a criminal case one identified with law enforcement. When a splinter witness is being cross-examined he will try to use each answer to elaborate on the damage he has already done, or to do further damage in a different way. This means that if his original testimony is thought of as inflicting a wound, it will never be a clean one. When the lawyer attempts to withdraw fragments from the flesh, they will not come easily or cleanly. These bits and pieces (answers) will always tend to break into smaller parts, each as troublesome as the whole. To the extent that a splinter witness testifies about something he claims to have seen or heard, he will never take it back. He will never admit error. In dealing with him, the lawyer must show him to be mistaken; he cannot make this witness agree that he may have been wrong.

To summarize the cross-examination characteristics of this witness, the lawyer should try to impeach him immediately (throwing the jury's feelings toward mistrust rather than sympathy); he should use objective methods (demonstrating untruthfulness rather than accusing the witness of it); he should be thorough; he should avoid personalities and particularly avoid reacting to taunts or gleams of personal arrogance from the witness; the lawyer should be courteous to this witness. At the same time the lawyer should block the witness's efforts to rehash (or splinter) his direct testimony. Where it is appropriate, the lawyer should do what he can to set this witness up for adverse character testimony.

[6] Some Suggestions as to Method

[a] Why It May Be Advantageous to Cross-Examine Immediately on the Strongest, Most Obvious Grounds of Impeachment

It is probably a good idea to nail this kind of witness down immediately by impeaching him on the one or two best known and most serious mistakes in his previous testimony. If this witness misidentifies somebody as having participated in this crime, or as having been present at a certain place—particularly some target defendant or personality in the local community—and if this witness was later made to take it back, or can be made to take it back during cross-examination, so that his defense of that identification would be hopeless, then that is probably the first thing to hit him with. He knows it is going to happen anyway, but if it is done immediately, the witness will not be half as well prepared for the experience as he would if it were delayed even three or five minutes, so that he has gotten used to being cross-examined. After all, he has been worrying about this for a long time.

Cross-examination is strangest at its beginning, so let it be then. An additional reason for using this material immediately is that the jury expects the lawyer to do so. Probably there will have been enough references by the prosecution to the fact that this witness may have made a mistake, but he is still an honest man, etc., and that he is going to be ill-treated by the defense. The jury will be looking for this, and the fact will diminish their attention on other points until their expectations are satisfied. This does not mean be theatrical; on the contrary, it means get to the point. The strongest reason for doing this is the likelihood that the witness will be evasive.

Both the lawyer and the witness will have been thinking about this cross-examination for months. But for the lawyer this is essentially a low temperature form of drill, not involving himself. Moreover this is something he has done many times in different courts and cases, in all kinds of surroundings and for varying stakes. If this is regarded as for blood, he has also done it for marbles and matchcovers. The process should not involve him much, and apart from differences in decorum, he could as easily do it standing on his head.

With the witness there is no such thing as an impersonal attack on his integrity. He *is* involved, but unfortunately for him, the chosen area of involvement is a prior inconsistent statement.

Both lawyer and witness know that the witness has only three choices: (1) he did not testify that way—did not say it; (2) he did say it, and it is *true* regardless of what is revealed during cross-examination; or (3) he did say it, but acknowledges his mistake. The first of these (he did not say it) is only a phenomenological thing—but he cannot really deny what is in the grand jury transcript or what he told a police reporter in a formal statement. Somebody's professional reputation rests on the accuracy of that transcript or that report, and he can be subpoenaed if necessary.

The second choice (he said it and it is really true) may seem equally ridiculous in context, but it is surprising how the witness's psychology will draw him closer and closer to that position, because of personal pride and self-pity

("That would be a wrong thing, and I do not do wrong things"). This witness will be drawn toward justifying himself even though he had originally decided to opt for number three.

The third and only rational choice on these assumptions is that the witness made a mistake. That is what the prosecutor has briefed him to say, that is the only sensible thing to say; but saying it calls for considerable aplomb and aplomb may be in short supply in the first two or three minutes of cross-examination.

The witness may be rattled just enough that in acknowledging his prior statement, he will recollect it a little differently from the way he said it. This it true even though he practically memorized the transcript. He will want very much to appear in a certain light, because the jury is real and has human presence, a thing that no transcript can match, even one still plainly visible on the prosecutor's table. The witness will want it to be that he said something a little more general than the specific mistake he actually made. Something a little more qualified than what is flatly in print, more reserved than he really was, something that would seem to say, even at the time, that he realized he might be wrong, something almost humble. Therefore, even if the witness has thought about it a great deal, and practiced his cross-examination with prosecutors, he will *tend* at some point to override what he said before, summarizing it rather favorably to himself, instead of facing up to it exactly. The lawyer certainly cannot count on this happening, but it may very well; it often happens.

When the witness acknowledges a mistake in terms slightly more favorable to himself then the truth, that small indulgence gives the lawyer a chance for a small, familiar tactical wedge. The wedge is not a big thing, but in this kind of set-piece cross-examination, progress is measured in little gains. The small wedge is the opportunity to use the transcript by reading it to the jury. This allows the lawyer to say the witness's original words, using the lawyer's inflections. He takes over the role of the witness and plays it for him again, just those few words from the earlier scene.

The lawyer will only be allowed to do this if the actual transcript says it differently from what the witness just remembered. But when that happens, the transcript should be produced and all the formalities attendant to impeaching a witness from a transcript should be followed to the letter. He should be asked if he remembers testifying at that time and place, asked to read the transcript, and finally asked if that is what he said. Page and line references injected into the record, the lawyer should ask permission to read the passage which directly impeaches the witness's version of his earlier mistake. It helps to do this rather coldly, remembering that the words are for the benefit of the jury. A lawyer reading a transcript should take care to read it slowly and distinctly, recalling his own advice to witnesses. This should always be done matter-of-factly and without any forensic attempts to use face muscles for the benefit of the jury. A little voice inflection does it.

The result of using the transcript when the witness had hoped it would not be used is simply to push him back a little from his prepared position, to demonstrate clearly that despite all preparations, things are not going that well. He may then become a little slippery, evasive, which is to be hoped for.

But if the witness takes the best position (yes, he said it, and now he realizes he was wrong) there is a right and wrong way to handle that. This witness is not in the happy situation of a defense witness who has been well briefed on what to do after he has made a mistake. Defense witnesses have been told how to correct a mistake while they are still on the stand. This witness is by definition a person who made his mistake some time ago. This is definitely *not* a case in which he made his mistake while testifying before the grand jury, and then corrected himself while still before the grand jury. This is *not* a situation in which the prosecution witness can point to something in the old transcript which is the same transcript where he made the mistake, and show that at that very time he corrected himself. If he could do that, one would not be impeaching him on the basis of that particular mistake.

This witness can be hit rather hard, even for a mistake he now admits, although he should not be hit in the way that might occur naturally to an inexperienced lawyer. The wrong way to do it is to *argue* with the witness. The right way is to decide in advance what the final argument is going to be, as to *why* this witness makes mistakes *in general*, and cross-examine according to that argument. This puts everything in different terms than those in which the witness is prepared to defend himself. The witness has in mind his own honesty and sincerity, and how good he must look even while acknowledging a mistake. The lawyer may have in mind that the witness made this particular mistake because of gross irresponsibility, but he may intend, after demonstrating that irresponsibility, to actually settle for a much milder argument, which is that the witness made this mistake and other mistakes *because* he was so well-meaning and sincere—the very traits the witness has in mind.

The *wrong* way to cross-examine the witness is to accuse him of perjury when he made his earlier mistake. A better way is to ask a few factual questions establishing that at the time of his prior testimony, the witness was well aware that it was serious, that it was under oath, that it was before a grand jury or in court, that before testifying he reviewed the relevant events in his own mind, and reviewed any earlier statements, that he intended to tell the truth, and that at the time he said what he said, *he believed it to be true.*

If the witness wants to stress that later on he realized he had made a mistake, a good line of cross-examination concerns the details of when and how he realized his mistake. This will be exceptionally difficult for the witness and he should not be allowed to slither out of it. It is very likely he realized his mistake when somebody in the prosecutor's office told him they had uncovered some stupidly obvious fact that made his position indefensible, e.g., somebody he placed at the scene of the crime was actually somewhere else in the company of a police officer.

The witness should be asked if he realized his mistake because someone told him about the evidence which proved him wrong. If he denies that this information was imparted to him at that time, he should be asked if he was ever told that, and by whom. This creates a definite opening for further impeachment of this witness via the person who told him. That person may very well be a police officer, but without the usual motive to lie; i.e., he will not be protecting another police officer but only a rather disreputable prosecution witness.

If the witness admits that he acknowledged his mistake only after embarrassing facts came to light, the situation will be completely satisfactory. This is true because, having first established that the witness took the proceedings seriously when he made his original mistake ("When you testified before the grand jury, you believed your testimony to be true, didn't you?"), and then throwing a dubious light on the reason why the witness later acknowledged that mistake, the lawyer will have created a strong innuendo that the witness was irresponsible, possibly even lying and that he never *would* have changed his testimony if the facts had not caught up with him. Since all this is implied, but not stated, there is no danger of going too far, of creating undeserved sympathy for the witness. That is the way to leave it.

In this way, the lawyer can take all the fun out of the witness's new-found sincerity, and may even drive him back from where the prosecutor told him to stand (sincerely acknowledging his mistake) onto the thoroughly shaky

ground where he still believes his original testimony. A witness will not often go back to this ground, but when he does,
it will not be logic that drove him there but the presence
of the jury and a deep need for self-justification. If this is
done, or when this has been established as impossible, the
lawyer should drop the subject of the witness's one or two
big mistakes and go on to less dramatic but more fruitful
grounds.

[b] Gearing Cross-Examination to the Argument

The lawyer should remember that while the type of
cross-examination described above may be personally
satisfying to the lawyer and to those associated with
the defense, the force of the defense actually lies in the
final argument; and judged purely by its usefulness there,
this particular portion of the impeachment process (contradiction of the witness by himself or other evidence) is
probably the less important portion. Although it is very important to show that this witness was wrong *once* in sworn
testimony—and therefore could be wrong *this time* in what
he says about the defendant—and that he is evasive, these
revelations are not nearly enough. After all, the prosecution
argument will be, sure, he was wrong once, but because of
all the other evidence in the case, you have to believe that he
is right in what he now says about the defendant. Good
prosecution arguments can be made in that direction, such
as: (1) everybody is human; (2) the mistake was unimportant; (3) he admitted the mistake, the man is obviously
sincere; and (4) he is corroborated by other little points in
the case.

What is still lacking at this point in the cross-
examination and must still be supplied, now or later, is
factual evidence explaining *why* his former mistakes are in
fact characteristic of his entire testimony, *reasons* why this
mistake should be regarded as symptomatic rather than

isolated, and *reasons* why this witness should be disbelieved right now, despite the fact that he may believe he is telling the truth. The difference between conviction and acquittal should not be allowed to ride on the question whether the jury believes this witness is deliberately perjuring himself. Much better to adduce facts sustaining the argument that he believes he is saying the truth and fooling himself as he did before. This argument must be strong enough to create a reasonable doubt in the minds of the jury. This part of the cross-examination, the one designed to get at these facts, the undramatic part, is the one lawyers tend to overook. The questions require a little spin, but that is not hard to apply.

The lawyer should lead the witness over those parts of his testimony which place him in the particular situations and positions necessary for him to have observed the things he says he observed, i.e., necessary for him to *be* a witness. The lawyer should quietly develop facts to support his later argument that this witness was *eager*.

For the case in which the witness became involved more or less on the spur of the moment (e.g., in an unplanned street demonstration), rather than as an informer, the lawyer should begin this portion of the cross-examination by backing off slightly in point of time, to reach that portion of the day when the witness's activity ceased to be usual and changed so as to encompass what later became the events of this case. There is always a point—usually a little earlier than the time span covered by the witness on direct examination—when the witness really began to volunteer himself as a future witness, either by remaining in some place longer than he planned or by going somewhere he had not intended to be. He changed plans; maybe he broke a date. The lawyer should go into this with the help of diagrams, being quite definite as to time and persons present. The purpose of all this is to show graphically how much the witness went out of his way.

Other means are also available both in cross-examining the witness himself and in cross-examining the other prosecution witnesses later used to bolster his good character. In dealing with the witness himself, it is a good idea to cross-examine in a way which makes him demonstrate out of his own mouth how eager he is to succeed in any job he undertakes. One way to do it is to lead him over ground where the subject matter makes him uncomfortable, where his own reactions are to stress unduly his "straight" or eager motives. If it happens that there was a reward offered in connection with this criminal prosecution, then a witness of this kind should always be asked if he knew about the reward.

Before cross-examining on this point, the lawyer should take care to provide himself with some physical evidence of the reward, e.g., a newspaper ad. Most rewards are published. The lawyer will need something tangible because the witness's reaction may be so negative as to make the judge doubt that there *was* a reward and to suppose that perhaps the lawyer is making it up. The witness should be shown the ad and asked if he read it, and if not, if he normally needs that newspaper. This kind of witness will recoil in horror from the suggestion that a reward would influence his testimony, which in turn makes him stress for the jury how motivated he really is to do the right thing. The lawyer should not lean on the implied accusation of informing for pay. This witness really would not do that; he is quite sincere in his denials. The lawyer will know that and the jury will certainly know it, and there is no use implying otherwise.

The heart of the matter is that the jury will begin to sense something else which may become the basis of a main defense argument: this witness is sincere all right, but all these moral protests are just a little bit too strong for a person who makes the rather unfortunate mistakes which have already showed up in this witness's testimony. There is something in his make-up that needs explaining, that relates to self-deception, to making these mistakes and not being able to face up to them.

If it turns out that this witness has an employment application pending with some law enforcement agency, he must be asked about that; this is absolute confirmation that he was trying to please someone and wished very much to please law enforcement people. This is a stronger piece of evidence than the witness's own declarations as to how sincere he is. Anybody can be sincere, but not everybody has a job application on file with the local police department.

Assuming the decision is made to impeach this witness by evidence of his bad reputation for truth and veracity, then there will surely come a time when the prosecution call their character witnesses in rebuttal. Usually these character witnesses (defense versus prosecution) cancel each other like spouses voting for opposite parties. But in this case something can be done to change all that.

The defense advantage comes in selecting one or two of these rebuttal prosecution witnesses and asking them how well they know the person and *why* his character for truthfulness is so good. They will say he was always a good man, right in there doing his job, satisfactory in every way and well motivated. His *attitude* was good.

Of course he has a good attitude, and in the defense argument he will be remembered that way, pleasing and eager to please: a volunteer eager to please the *police*, a point that goes far to explain some of those mistakes he made.

[c] Using the Witness's own Mental Distortions to Isolate him from the Jury

As he goes along the lawyer should sweep up details showing how this witness dramatizes himself. It is important not to be heavy-handed; nonetheless, one may not have to open too many oyster shells to find that this witness was *armed* at the critical time he became a witness; or conversely, that he was usually armed, but went out of his way to leave his weapon somewhere else for this particular occasion. It really does not matter which, since either fact is highly self-dramatizing. If the witness went out of his way to leave his weapon before going into the street, he will be glad to explain that he did so from professional fear that his weapon would be used against him by a maddened demonstrator. Whichever it is, this witness's mental attitude toward weapons, the fact that he usually finds it necessary to carry one, and the fact that he was thinking seriously of weapons in connection with the type of person represented by the defense witnesses will be distinctly unpleasant to the jury. This will jar. It would not jar the jurors if it were something they read in the newspapers, but they have already met the defendant, in court, and they are about to meet his counterparts and contemporaries.

[d] Setting Up the Witness for Evidence of Specific Incidents Reflecting Adversely on his Credibility

Pre-trial investigation may have turned up two or three bizarre incidents which detract from this witness's credibility, i.e., several of those approached concerning his reputation for truth and veracity may say not only that his reputation is bad but may go further and relate some extraordinary encounter with this witness when he told a completely fictitious story about something. They might add that he is a pathological liar and that they would be glad to cite their respective examples of his conduct as the basis for that conclusion.

Of course the general rule for impeaching a witness on the basis of his character is that he can be impeached only on the basis of his general reputation for truth, honesty, and veracity. Character witnesses may be called and asked if they are acquainted with this witness's reputation in the community for truth and veracity, and whether it is good or bad. The traditional rule prevents any inquiries as to reasons which the character witness may have for concluding that this reputation is good or bad, and bars evidence of specific conduct.[1]

As law students know, this is a wry situation in which usual courtroom rules are reversed, so that an important question of fact (whether the witness is to be believed) is proved entirely on the basis of hearsay, while those who have direct, personal knowledge of the facts are required to keep their mouths shut. The traditional rule is modified in some jurisdictions by allowing the witness's character for truth, honesty, and veracity to be proved by *opinion evidence*, in addition to proof by general reputation.[2] This variation adds little to the general rule, since a character witness who gives his opinion as to a person's truthfulness, honesty, and veracity will in every case turn out to be the same witness who, moments before, testified concerning that person's reputation for the same traits. His opinion adds exactly nothing to what he just said about reputation. The character witnesses mentioned in this example (who think the main witness is a pathological liar) would be capable of adding quite a lot, if the prosecutor would only ask them on cross-examination to state the reasons for their opinions. That will never happen in this world. No prosecutor would open that door, and nobody should hold his breath waiting for him to do so.

There is a right way and a wrong way to do everything. If there is a way to get this evidence *in* (evidence of specific misconduct, to prove mendacity as a trait of character) it will lie along a path which is overgrown to the point of wildness, and which normally might not suggest itself in the heat of trial. This path may be found in the difference between habit and character evidence, or in the acceptability of evidence that a witness suffers from some defect in perceiving or recollecting things; and it definitely lies along the line that a jury may be allowed to consider the nonexistence of some fact testified to by a witness, as tending to show the untruthfulness of his testimony, even though the subject matter is collateral and the purpose of the cross-examiner is to show that the witness is a person given to mendacity and therefore probably lying on more material points.[3]

The opening may occur without the lawyer doing anything at all to create it, i.e., the main prosecution witness may be so full of himself that at some point in his direct examination, he will stress how *careful* he was in doing certain things, to avoid making mistakes. If what he said could be construed as evidence of his own *habit* of being careful, the lawyer should ask himself whether the bizarre incidents (which his own witnesses are prepared to describe) would be evidence contradictory to this assertion of habit. If so, the job is virtually done.

If the witness proves suggestible during cross-examination, he can be led to embellish his earlier claim to good habits. This is one time when cross-examination should be conducted with an eye to a written trial brief (face down on the counsel table); it will probably be a very good idea, with a brief oriented to *habit*, to get the witness to agree that he was in the habit of doing certain things well. He will probably agree to having good habits even if he is not suggestible. He may then be confronted, point blank, with questions (discussed infra) in the style the lawyer finds most congenial, as to whether at certain times he has not deviated from these good habits, or suffered lapses from the good perceptions and memory to which he lays claim.

There are strong reasons why the matter of bizarre incidents should be brought out on the cross-examination of the main prosecution witness, rather than left solely for the testimony of character witnesses. The prosecution witness may *deny* the incident entirely, in which case he may be liable to double impeachment, once because of the incident itself (for example, an irresponsible accusation may suggest that he is an habitual liar, or a bizarre episode of another sort may suggest that he is unable to perceive or remember things correctly); and again because of denying the incident when, in truth, he should have admitted it.

Another reason for tackling this problem on cross-examination is that if by mishap the prosecutor's objection to this line of questions is sustained, better for the defense to have it sustained now, in the context of infringing the right to cross-examine the main prosecution witness, than to have the same ruling made for the first time in response to an offer of similar evidence from the character witnesses, whose testimony is relatively disfavored on appeal.

But before devoting serious thought to using evidence of bizarre incidents or other specific misconduct to prove the mendacity of the main prosecution witness, there is the all important consideration of getting the facts absolutely straight.

The lawyer must have interviewed the character witness who is going to testify concerning the incident in question. The lawyer cannot rely on the summary of an investigator or an associate. He must be completely satisfied himself, that the incident *as actually related* is serious enough to make a deep impression on the jury, that the character witness is prepared to testify with conviction, that the lawyer knows exactly what the character witness will say, that the lawyer did the briefing personally and uncovered no area of equivocation or unacceptable vulnerability by the character witness.

When the lawyer has served a "friendly subpoena" on the character witness and has prepared a small trial brief supporting the introduction of this evidence—and if writing the brief has not changed his opinion that the evidence is admissible—it is safe to cross-examine the main prosecution witness on details of this bizarre incident.

Even where this evidence of specific misconduct is admissible, the questions are not going to get by without some objections. Knowing that, and in order to preserve the judge's equanimity, so that the objections can be ruled on fairly, the lawyer should be rather deliberate about getting into the subject. It may not be feasible to get into it with nonleading questions, but on the other hand, the lawyer should not frame a question encompassing the whole story of the witness's bizarre falsehood, and then ask him to agree that he told it. If there is going to be an objection, the prosecutor must be given a fair chance to interpose it. If the objection of irrelevancy is made, the answer will be to file the trial brief, make a glowing offer of proof out of the hearing of the jury and argue the point vigorously on the brief and the offer.

When beginning to ask questions on this subject the lawyer should arrange his cross-examination so that other questions concerning other topics are immediately available to follow. This is so that if an objection is sustained to this line of inquiry, the cross-examination will continue past that point and gain ground in other areas rather than end on a weak note.

§ 14.03 The Unpaid Informer ("Expenses Only")

[1] When He Is Substantially Telling the Truth

When the informer told it like it was on direct examination, then presumably the defense is entrapment. This will be a case in which a criminal act was done, but it was done at the instigation of the government. The government will have grossly overreached its function of enforcing laws, by sending an agent (this informer) among the defendants for the purpose of suggesting that they commit some political crime which they had no thought of doing, or which (if they ever thought of it) they had already abandoned.[4]

In that situation, it seems reasonable to assume that

if the informer was acting not for pay but from a sense of duty, and was telling the truth on direct examination, he will also tell the truth on cross-examination, and might even make an excellent defense witness. If the court does not allow the evidence of entrapment at the time of cross-examination, it will certainly be necessary to recall this witness as a defense witness. In that event, many details of government overreaching and intervention should be provable by his testimony.

[2] When He Is Not Telling the Truth

In the common situation where an informer was lying on direct examination, but was not doing it for money (other than "expense money," discussed infra), the basis of cross-examination is the question *why* is he lying? That must be answered to the satisfaction of the jury, or the case is lost.

Among many possible reasons why a witness might be lying happens to be one which frequently arises with informers and which always presents a serious question of whether to cross-examine on the subject at all. This ground of impeachment is sometimes referred to as "hope of leniency," and the reasons why it is so dangerous are, (1) judges dislike it, and are prone to block this line of cross-examination in a manner calculated to embarrass the lawyer in front of the jury; (2) as a practical matter, there is an unwritten requirement that substantially *more* evidence be produced to make this impeachment stick, than the bare minimum necessary for admissibility, otherwise the jury will not accept it; and (3) there is a definite penalty for attempting this impeachment if it does not work.

[a] Hope of Leniency

Hope of leniency always arises in connection with one or more prior arrests. Assuming that discovery orders were complied with on anything approaching an honest basis, the lawyer will have learned this witness's arrest record. He will know the times, places, and dates of prior arrests; and if any kind of prosecution occurred, he may have been able to learn who testified at any hearings in connection with the prosecution.

When the lawyer is deciding whether to ask this witness questions about his criminal background, he should be prepared for a rather peculiar judicial phenomenon. It happens that the law is well settled that a witness can be cross-examined (and impeached by other evidence) concerning his bias and financial interest in the outcome of a case. This very elementary rule has been heavily applied in criminal cases to allow cross-examination on money payments to a prosecuting witness, as well as his possible expectation of leniency in connection with his past offenses. Judges presumably know these rules as well as anybody else, and that is why it is so surprising that when this line of cross-examination begins, many judges get extremely fidgety.

They will often interrupt without even waiting for an objection, demanding to know what is the materiality of this line of questioning. Otherwise intelligent judges will actually order this line of cross-examination stopped. There is no excuse for this, and no reason for the lawyer to anticipate it who has never seen it happen before, and yet it must be anticipated. This kind of judicial misconduct is of course reversible error. Once it occurs not much can be done about it until the parties are standing in an appellate court. If the lawyer has had a bad draw with the jury then of course this kind of judicial lapse should be stroked and cossetted, and put away in a jeweled casket to preserve its magical properties on appeal.

But since a political defense should be oriented toward acquittal rather than reversal and retrial, some measures shoud be taken to head off this judicial interruption before it goes too far. There are only two adequate countermeasures. The first countermeasure should have been taken long before the prosecution witness climbed into the box. Knowing that he intended to cross-examine in part on hope of leniency or financial interest, the lawyer should have included among his requested jury instructions one or two which tell the jury in plain English that in weighing a witness's credibility, they may consider (among other things) any financial interest which he may have in the outcome of the case, and any hope of leniency or favored treatment for himself which he may entertain in connection with some other prosecution (see § 12.01).

These instructions should not only be handtooled, but loaded with the strongest cases in the jurisdiction supporting this kind of impeachment in a criminal case. Since they were filed before the opening statements, the judge will have had an opportunity to go over them in chambers, and refresh himself on the cases. If he has any real problem about this kind of evidence, his normal reaction will be to call the lawyers to a private conference in chambers before the cross-examination begins, which virtually eliminates the chance of a bad ruling.

The second countermeasure is to have prepared a trial brief and a careful offer of proof, for use either in chambers or in open court, wherever the trouble begins. The trial brief should be tightly packed and should not exceed two pages, containing the same authorities that were attached to the jury instructions. At the first sign of trouble from the bench, the lawyer should file the brief and make an accurate, forceful offer of proof. The touchstones are: (1) the witness was arrested and prosecuted for some alleged crime; (2) the arrest was either in this jurisdiction or else, if it was in another one, this is evidence of cooperation between that law enforcement agency and the one prosecuting this case; (3) there was some disposition other than acquittal, so that "law enforcement" got some kind of advantage over this witness; (4) the disposition occurred at about the time the witness became involved in this case; and (5) the advantage is a continuing one, e.g., they dropped charges, but the statute of limitations has not run and the charges could be refiled at any time. The lawyer should of course specify in the offer of proof, that it is made for the purpose of impeachment on the ground of the witness's bias and in particular his hope and expectation of leniency in consideration of his testimony in this case. If the judge replies that he will not tolerate a "fishing expedition," the lawyer should point out how much of the information was obtained by discovery, from the prosecution, and then respectfully ask what the judge means by "fishing expedition."

If this line of action does not open the door for this fruitful form of cross-examination, there is nothing further to be said about it in the trial court. The main thing is that the offer of proof be thorough and powerful. If it is needed at all later, much will depend on it. If that offer is made right, and if it is needed later, it will strike any reader of the transcript that, as compared to the usual density level of pages before and after this passage, at this point the lawyer suddenly unloaded a great deal of specific information on the trial judge.

On the other hand, assuming evidence will go in, most of it will go in via cross-examination. The lawyer should see that it goes in matter-of-factly. The main value of this evidence is not its shock effect, which is *small*, but its usefulness in argument. This part of the cross-examination differs importantly in tone from the part where the witness was being impeached by his own prior statements. In *that* situation, a little impatience on the lawyer's part may not be harmful, if the witness is being evasive. No one admires an evasive witness. But in this situation, the lawyer is confronting the witness with something that may have happened a long time ago. A year can be a long time ago in this sense.

Whether or not the jury comes to share the lawyer's belief that the witness is in fact biased because of his expectation of leniency for this other offense, the fact remains, it *is* another offense, not something that happened in the courtroom or in this case. For that reason, a little impatience or any impatience at all is *not* permitted the lawyer. He should be as matter-of-fact as if he were weighing the matter himself, not yet convinced that the witness is so venal as to be influenced by a thing like that.

It should be clearly understood by anyone planning this line of cross-examination that he *cannot* just ask if the witness was arrested on a certain date and not prosecuted afterward, and just let it go at that. There are strong reasons here, that may not be apparent under the pressure of trial. Although a connection may seem quite obvious to the lawyer's mind, between this witness's prior arrest and his service to the prosecution, that connection is not going to be equally clear to the jury. The gap between the two events will be very real.

More importantly, in order for the jury to establish that connection, they would be called upon to *speculate* on the subject. The lawyer cannot rationally ask them to do that at the time of his final argument, when his own argument will depend entirely on the point that the jury has sworn to try the case on evidence, as opposed to mere speculation (the recommended procedure, see § 16.03[3]). In attacking this witness, the lawyer must therefore carry impeaching evidence far past the place where it looks like speculation.

A second hidden danger in this line of cross-examination is that the prosecution will say that the defense has "persecuted" this witness, and unless the defense is very careful, *this will be at least partly true.* It is imperative to remember that there is a big difference between what is legally admissible by way of impeachment—because it logically and qualitatively tends to impeach the witness—

and the amount of proof actually needed to square it with the jury for having used this kind of evidence at all. Impeaching an informer on the ground of his own hope of leniency is a dangerous business and it can be done successfully only in one way.

The lawyer must have his impeaching evidence completely in hand, and carry the jury with him at every step. There are other times in court when the lawyer may (or must) gamble on lucky shots, dropping a whole line of questions in return for a half-decent answer to one, and times when he cannot give the witness a chance to reconsider. That kind of nervous, sketchy cross-examination will not do when working in this area. To do it right, the lawyer has to ask all of the necessary questions in a workmanlike manner, giving the witness a fair opportunity to say it his way, but with sufficient preparation that if the witness turns on him, he can still prove all the material points by other means. *If it cannot be done in this manner, it should not be done at all.*

When asking about the particular crime for which the witness was arrested, it is a poor idea to ask for details of the alleged crime, even though they may be a little juicy (it looks like witness persecution). Much better to ask him the charge for which he was arrested, and the date and place of his arrest. The jurisdiction should be definitely fixed ("That's in this county, isn't it?").

The thing which derails most cross-examinations on the subject of hope of leniency is failure to nail down the connection. Minimum standards to prove a connection between the witness's earlier prosecution and his testimony in the present case should include the following kinds of evidence:

(1) The witness should have received some kind of favor, or break, in the disposition of his own case, and some official record should show that some police officer took affirmative action to help the witness

get that break, e.g., an officer recommended in writing that charges be dropped, or personally appeared in court and recommended to a judge that the charges be dropped, or was favorably quoted in some probation report or pre-sentence report which is on file in that case. The officer who did this should be available and subpoenaed, so that if the witness denies it, he will have to affirm it, under the prodding of the written evidence.

(2) The same officer (or his partner, assuming he is a detective) should be the particular officer who contacted this witness in the present case or took a witness statement from him (or the partner of the one who did so), and this participation is corroborated by a notation on the statement or by some other police record or inter-office memorandum; and

(3) The time relation between those events should be rather short, and totally consistent with the defense that one thing was in consideration of the other. If the witness had done a little informing from time to time in other cases, and this is known, then the time lapse can be extended considerably, since a continuing business relationship is then established.

If it happens that the witness was arrested in another jurisdiction, the minimum connecting evidence can be stretched very slightly, but not much. The connection should be that officers from both jurisdictions have been working on both cases. That may seem a tough requirement, but officers from neighboring jurisdictions frequently work together across county lines, while investigating political cases or narcotics cases. They do this because strange faces are less recognizable to the people they are investigating. Like lawyers, they scratch each other's backs.

In this situation, the minimum requirement should be that some officer associated with the prosecution of the present case was actually on loan to the other jurisdiction and participated in the witness's arrest at that time; he need not have been the particular officer who intervened on behalf of the witness when he got his special break in court. Alternatively, one of the officers from the other jurisdiction who participated in that arrest may be shown to have associated with officers working on the present case at about the time the witness himself got involved.

The foregoing rules of thumb are entirely subjective and pragmatic; weaker evidence would be legally admissible, but it would not be a very good idea to use weaker evidence, because making this charge and failing to put together respectable proof will most emphatically alienate the jury.

[b] How to Handle the Money Part

When his informing services in this case have been placed in context with his informing in other cases, the witness should be asked what money or other compensation he has received. For the amateur informer (the one who is not being offered illicit protection and larger sums) this often proves an embarrassing question. The amateur regards the money as blood money. For this reason, most law enforcement agencies dole it out as "expenses." It is not really for expenses, and the informer knows that. But it is not enough money that anyone can tell *what* it is for. He will not want to testify that he informs for that kind of money (and he probably does not), and so he will react by stressing his relatively straight motives and that he has his overhead. He will say he does this work as a public service.

Since this witness was probably motivated by something other than the "expense money"—e.g., hope of leniency, or possibly just a misguided nose for romance—it would be a serious mistake to stress the minimal sums paid him. The lawyer should *know* before cross-examination approximately how much the witness was paid for "expenses."

This is true because his second discovery motion (see § 7.01[4]) called for information concerning financial remuneration of certain obvious prosecution witnesses. The lawyer will have supplemented this information by serving a subpoena duces tecum on the custodian of records of the law enforcement agency for records showing how much money was actually paid. This subpoena will have been returnable on the first day of trial. The lawyer will have had these records marked for identification and left with the clerk, for the ostensible convenience of hostile witnesses (so as to let the custodian return to his duties). The lawyer should know how much money this witness has been paid without the need of asking him in the presence of the jury.

If the lawyer is still doubtful at the time of cross-examination, he should remember that in general this is no place to take a deposition, and accordingly should decide on the basis of everything else he knows about the witness whether he has been paid a lot of money or very little. In deciding, the lawyer should remember that most informers are *eager* witnesses, and that in all likelihood no law enforcement agency has ever seen fit to pay this witness very much money. They do not have to.

Where it is known or inferred that the witness has not been paid much money, the lawyer should limit cross-examination on this point to the simple fact that the witness has been paid *some* money. There are several reasons not to press ahead and establish just how little money it was. The controlling point is that cross-examination on this subject may conflict with the argument.

After all, doing it for money is doing it for money, and before this particular argument can be relied upon, the facts must show strongly that the witness would lie for these particular sums. This is probably not our witness. Stressing exactly how little money he gets will mislead the jury, since it suggests the lawyer is going to argue that this witness lies for small sums; and, to the extent that any of them feel that he *is* motivated by the money, they may feel sympathetic. Anyone who is engaged in such a mean activity as informing for that amount of money—or who (the prosecution's argument) performs such dangerous public services for such small returns—may seem merely a pathetic person, rather than (as he actually is) an unreliable one.

§ 14.04   The Informer Who Does It in Return for Police Protection

Once in a long while the lawyer may run across a main prosecution witness whose business *includes* informing, the only genuinely professional informer. He does it for money, but mainly in the sense of being given an opportunity to make his own. He is really an entrepreneur, and he has absolutely no use for radicals.

This professional informer is not going to impress the jury as sincere-but-inaccurate; he is probably not interested in ingratiating himself, but in protecting himself, and so his hostility may irradiate the courtroom. The jury will not like him. His testimony can also be destroyed, but not by the same methods. While the amateur can be cross-examined by a process thought of as tree-shaking, impeachment of the professional is more analagous to demolition.

The professional informer cares less than other witnesses about how he looks, an advantage to the lawyer. On the other hand, he will say nothing that helps the defense unless he is momentarily confused. The key to this witness is his enormous value to law enforcement. His local law enforcement agency not only knows all about the witness's illicit business, e.g., wholesaling aliens, or narcotics, but they let him do it and see that other ("cooperating") law enforcement agencies within the same metropolitan area do likewise. The special value of this witness to law enforcement, month-in and month-out, is the information which he is able to supply them about his own industry. Beyond that he is always in a position to set up various business rivals for arrest. (Most of the people he works with are vulnerable.) A perfect example of social symbiosis.

Every time this witness sets up a competitor for arrest, he does several things which benefit himself or the police: (1) he eliminates a competitor (probably a retailer with ambitions to move into the wholesale business); (2) he improves the market for his own retail outlets; (3) he gets paid "expense money" for his time; and (4) he makes the cops look good.

This witness derives a substantial part of his income from various law enforcement agencies. These payments are also designated as "expenses" the same as those made to amateur informers. But the comparison really ends at that point. When this witness gets expense money, he gets paid at a scale more commensurate with his status in business. The witness does not believe in doing anything for "nothing," although there certainly are larger considerations involved, and he knows the money is there. Nor would the officers who work with him wish to patronize him by small payments. If a true law enforcement accounting were ever made, it might be learned (to the witness's potential dismay and the surprise of some governmental agency) that he was the indirect beneficiary of some federal crime-fighting grant. The existence and scale of these payments—difficult to trace as they are—provide one of the very few avenues for corroborating this business relationship, assuming that a live witness can be found to testify about it first hand.

A witness of this type may volunteer to be a political informer, or his own law enforcement friends might, probably with some diffidence, ask him to perform that function. The witness's political views will be such that he would be glad to do something to purge society of dissidents. And this is how he will have found his way into a stellar role in a political prosecution.

Evidence of his funny relation to law enforcement

will be relevant to his bias as a witness (he has a financial interest in continuing to accommodate the prosecution, and hence in the outcome of this case) and, if the defense of entrapment is involved, also relevant to the agency relationship (he set up the defendant as he had set up so many others before, for the pleasure of law enforcement).

In cross-examining this witness as to his relationship to the police, it is not enough to get him to admit that he has been paid some money by way of expenses. He will not reveal how much it was. Doing the job right means subpoenaing records from the law enforcement agencies.

The really important feature of his symbiotic relationship to law enforcement is permission to run his own business; that provision, and the extent of that business can only be proved by the testimony of some former collaborator. The officers will never admit that they know the witness does anything illegal. The witness will deny it. The court will undoubtedly resent questions addressed to the witness along this line, unless there is something immediately at hand to back them up. The back-up can only be the rather brave testimony of somebody once close to this witness, who knows all about his illicit activities and the various benefits he gets from his relationship to particular officers, and who will testify about it despite the fact that the testimony is not only self-incriminating but dangerous.

Possible candidates for this far-reaching investigation will be former associates who were busted at the witness's instigation, and former girl friends who were dropped in favor of others. When the lawyer is fortunate enough to have such a witness ready, extraordinary measures should be taken to assure the safety of that witness. Moreover, before this witness takes the stand to impeach the informer, he or she must have been forced to consult an independent lawyer, and on the basis of that lawyer's advice, must have reached a decision to testify, self-incrimination notwithstanding. That lawyer should be in court when the time comes.

In a situation like this, threats against the life of the defense witness can be expected, and steps should be taken to make the transmission of those threats difficult. The witness should be put in a rather secret place pending the trial, free of access from former associates. Also, the lawyer should see that his own office is made more secure than usual against intrusions. Evidence, particularly tapes and notes relating to this witness, should be kept in a safe place.

Once the informer is attacked on grounds as serious as those just stated, the lawyer must be ready and able to finish the job. If he is not able to finish it, of course, the prosecutor will claim in his final argument that the defense was attempting to persecute or "crucify" this prosecution witness, this brave fellow who stepped from the shadows at such risk to himself.

§ 14.05   How to Use a Photograph Which Heavily Impeaches a Prosecution Witness

[1] The Kind of Photograph Involved

This has to do with the proper use of a photograph which is going to destroy a main prosecution witness. The lawyer will know the importance of this photograph because discovery procedures will have shown that a particular prosecution witness was so intimately involved in the action that his testimony is inevitable. If he did not testify for the prosecution, he could be subpoenaed and made to testify as a hostile witness. Also, he is nailed to a certain version of events at the heart of the prosecution case, either because he has already testified to that version or because he has committed himself to it in writing. The lawyer has a photograph which clearly shows the material part of this witness's testimony is a lie.

The impeaching photograph will show not just that the witness was fudging a little, but that he has totally committed himself to something important to the case which is palpably not true. The real question is not how to use the photograph so as to destroy a witness, but how to use it to destroy the prosecution case. Using this kind of photograph properly is not very hard, provided the lawyer has kept its existence secret (see § 4.05[2]). Doing the thing right is a source of real satisfaction.

An initial consideration is whether to use other photographs in cross-examining this witness or earlier witnesses. This is a small point, but the correct answer may be helpful. The answer depends on the temper and speed of the prosecution case.

Assume this is a political trial in which feelings run high, and in which the prosecution witnesses were making arrests in a whey-faced frenzy. If the trial follows sufficiently close to events (such as related trials) in which they have not doubted their own rightness or gotten any bloody noses, and if the particular prosecution witness against whom the photograph should be used is inclined to be a little hasty and lacking in insight or self-criticism (the lawyer's notes will be helpful in knowing this), then he may be subject to quick, mindless deviations when something goes wrong. On these assumptions, it may be a good idea not to use any defense photographs until this photograph is sprung on a main witness. A defense photograph may be disquieting to all the prosecution witnesses, prodding them to think along lines they should not be encouraged to consider.

On the other hand, if the prosecution have already begun using photographs of their own in support of direct examination, and *if the prosecution photographs are very similar to the remaining photographs which are in the lawyer's own file, other than the one which will impeach this witness,* then it does not matter much whether the lawyer uses his other photographs, or when.

[2] How to Decide On Whom to Use this Photograph

Use the photograph on the witness it will hurt the most, one who will lie about the things shown in it, and who is certain to testify on behalf of the prosecution. *This means that if two or more potential prosecution witnesses answer this description, but no more than one of them is really essential to the prosecution case, use the photograph on the first to testify; there may not be a second.* The photograph will not be one-tenth as effective if there is anything seemingly abnormal about the manner in which it is used. If the defense had a good chance to use it on a main witness and failed to do so, calling that same witness back later (as a hostile witness) and *then* springing the photograph on him would seem unnatural. It is better to have some prince of the prosecution come swaggering through the case, testifying about the interstate major subversive squad, sowing innuendos right and left like coins to the poor, and walk straight into this photograph and get busted flat on his ass, down on the first swing. That makes an impression, that makes a social comment, and nothing less does it half so well.

For example, assume the defendant is charged with resisting arrest. The prosecution evidence will probably be that he was detained in a courteous manner for questioning about some circumstance which, because of all the terrible things that were happening to police in that area at that time, constituted reasonable grounds for a stop. Or maybe he was being arrested for some misdemeanor. In any event, the People's case will be that the defendant, because of his ungovernable temper forthwith assaulted two or three of the arresting officers while calling loudly on his bearded, rock-throwing friends to come to his assistance. In this situation, the officers will *not* have denied that violence occurred; they will simply portray themselves as having used an absolute minimum of good, clean, reasonable American force to restrain this person. The prosecutor will portray this witness as heroic in the face of provocation. The word "obscenity" will be used often in his questions and the witness will quote to the impassive jury all the epithets of the day. Defense evidence will be that some rocks were thrown and some words yelled, but not until after an unprovoked beating began. An impeaching photograph in this situation is one which shows the defendant being beaten when he was helpless. The rare photograph with extra defense value will show clearly that there *were few or no onlookers,* no one jeering or throwing rocks, and where the witness said there was a mob, no mob at all, but just the officers and the defendant.

In this situation, the photograph should be used on the one or two officers who are shown in the photograph as inflicting this particular beating. They will have to testify, otherwise it would not be feasible to make a case of resisting arrest. This is not a case where the defendant is charged with something other than what happened at the moment of arrest, where other witnesses might carry the prosecution case. The ones who are going to carry *this* case are the ones who are going to feel this photograph.

This choice (to use it on the officers doing the beating in the photograph) should be adhered to no matter how many tempting little opportunities occur beforehand. And there will have been other officers around, and some of them may actually take the stand and testify that they witnessed the whole arrest and that it happened as the prosecution say. The photograph should probably not be used on them. This kind of photograph must be used on those who are most damned by it, not on those who (in the jury's mind) may have some slight excuse for lying about it, to protect their fellow officers.

On the other hand, suppose the defendant is charged with doing something not directly contradicted by this photograph, e.g., the photograph shows him being beaten during the arrest, but he is charged with violating curfew. The main significance of the beating is to impeach the testimony of the officers who did the beating (it goes to their willingness to tell the truth, since they have denied the beating in previous testimony, and to their bias, since they must dislike the defendant), but *they may not testify in the prosecution case.* Other witnesses may say they saw the defendant breaking the law. However, this same photograph will still be somewhat effective against any officer who was present and saw the beating or should have seen it *and denies that it happened.*

In this situation, the photograph *could* be used on the first officer who testifies about what the defendant was doing (violating curfew), and who also (1) denies that the beating occurred—says flatly that it did not occur, and he was looking all the time; or (2) evades the question of whether a beating occurred by saying he did not see it, but is forced to admit being so close that it could not have happened without his knowing it.

It is very important to remember that in this example, the defendant is *not* charged with resisting arrest. If he were facing that charge, the prosecution would have to produce the officers directly involved in the fracas and, in that situation, any *other* officer who should have seen the violence and says he did not see it should be regarded as a defense witness (see § 14.07). *An impeaching photograph should never be sprung on a police officer who is regarded as a defense witness.* Therefore, what will be said about springing the photograph on an officer who did not see the beating applies only when the defendant is *not* charged with resisting arrest, so that the nonobserving officer really *is* a prosecution witness with respect to the actual charge.

The photograph (whether used now or later) will be material to impeach this witness because it shows an unwillingness to tell the truth about something he must have known, certainly a point for the jury to consider in weighing his testimony on other things. But the problem is, since he says that he did not know about the beating, he may also claim that he does not know about what is shown in the photograph, and so the photograph will still have to be authenticated by others for the purpose of impeaching him. If there is any possible way to use it on the officers who did the beating, that is the way it should be used.

Rather than hazarding this important decision (whether to use the photograph on the first witness or wait for the right one), a little direct action may be necessary. For example, the lawyer might just ask the witness directly to tell the jury the names of the officers who actually arrested the defendant. He should then ask the witness if those officers are available to come in court and testify (e.g., they are not sick or on vacation). If the answer is yes, the lawyer should turn to the prosecutor and ask him in a clear voice if those officers are going to testify in this case (this is by no means the same thing as asking for a list of witnesses since, coming as it does right in the middle of the case, the response pretty well has to be yes or no, and not a counter request for a defense list). If the answer is yes, fine. Save the photograph for use on the people who deserve it most. If the answer is no, the lawyer should turn to the witness (having previously established how close he was to what must have been the scene of the beating) and ask him directly about the beating.

> Q: Isn't it a fact that Officers Strongarm and Headbust beat the defendant to the pavement at the time of the arrest, and that you stood right there and watched it and did nothing?

A: No.

Q: Have you discussed this case with Strongarm before testifying today?

A: I am not sure.

Q: Have you discussed it with Headbust?

A: I do not know, I might have.

Q: Did they tell you they weren't going to be called as witnesses because they beat the hell out of the defendant and don't want to testify about it?

A: No.

Q: Did they tell you that?

A: No.

Q: Well, they did beat him up, didn't they?

A: No.

Q: And you stood right there, didn't you?

A: I was right there and they didn't beat him up.

Q: They didn't beat him up?

A: No.

Q: If they had done that, you certainly would have seen it and heard it, wouldn't you?

A: Yes, I am sure I would.

Q: Did you see the defendant when he was being led to the police car [*walking to a diagram already marked by the witness*] when he was right about here? [*The place where the photograph was taken.*]

[*This is how it might go if the witness unintentionally admits having seen events which are about to appear in the photograph (Alternative 1)*]:

A: Yes.

Q: And you saw the defendant there?

A: Yes.

Q: What was he wearing? [*This is to authenticate the the photograph which clearly shows what the defendant was wearing.*]

A: I think it was a Pendleton-type sport shirt and

maybe Levi's. [*The witness has been studying the mug shot.*]

Q: And you saw Officer Strongarm?

A: Yes.

Q: And you saw Officer Headbust?

A: Yes.

Q: And there was a black and white vehicle parked [*indicating on diagram because this vehicle also appears in the photograph*] right about here?

A: Yes.

Q: And in this direction [*gesturing on the diagram a line of sight from where the photograph was taken*] there was an apartment with a balcony right about here?

A: Yes, I think I testified to that.

Q: Isn't it true and at just that point, Officer Strongarm knocked the defendant down and clubbed him when he was lying face-down in the gutter? [*this is shown in the photograph*]

A: No.

Q: You were looking and that didn't happen?

A: That's right.

Q: If you saw that happen, you would tell us about it, wouldn't you?

A: That never happened.

Q: [*To the Court.*] I have a photograph here which I would like marked as Defendant's next in order for identification [*and proceed to use the photograph as described in the following section*].

[*This is how it might go if the witness denies having seen these things (Alternative 2)*]:

A: No, I am sorry. I wasn't looking when they moved along there. Somebody threw a rock and it hit the vehicle right beside me and my attention was diverted and so I wasn't looking.

Q: I think you said you were fifteen feet away from the car when they brought the defendant to it?

A: That is about it.

Q: And you were certainly aware of what was going on behind you, weren't you?

A: I don't follow that.

Q: I mean, the rocks were being thrown because this arrest was taking place. I think you said that.

A: Yes, I think that is true.

Q: Well, you were concerned about getting the defendant in the police unit and getting out of there, weren't you?

A: Sure.

Q: And if the officers who were escorting the defendant to the police unit had needed help you would have given it, wouldn't you?

A: I don't understand.

Q: Well, that is what you were there for, to help effect this arrest?

A: Partly.

Q: And so it would be safe to say that you were partly aware of what was going on behind you, isn't that right?

A: Yes.

Q: And if Officers Strongarm and Headbust had stopped to slug the defendant and knock him flat on the ground and then club him about fifteen feet away from you, you would have heard that and been aware of that, isn't that correct?

A: Yes, but that didn't happen.

Q: If they clubbed him on the ground, right behind you, you would tell us about that, wouldn't you?

A: Yes, but that didn't happen.

In the second situation (Alternative 2), the decision should be not to authenticate the photograph by this witness. Since he has denied that he was looking in that direction, it is too easy for him to say that the photograph is *not* a fair representation of the events shown. The photograph would get hung up (marked but not admitted) and the prosecution would get to see it before the jury, and study it. In this situation, the photograph will still be used to impeach this witness's testimony, as evidence of his unwillingness to describe truthfully something which happened so close that he must have been aware of it, according to his own statements. But the person who authenticates the photograph will either be (1) one of the officers who actually did the beating, probably called as a hostile witness as part of the defense case; or (2) a defense witness who saw the beating, possibly the photographer.

[3] The Pleasurable Mechanics of Springing the Photograph

An impeaching photograph should be suitably enlarged, but not too much. Roughly eight by ten inches is usually big enough to do the job. Anything much larger than that would be conspicuous even in an envelope. Of course, as previously noted (§ 4.05[1]), the impeaching photograph must be an exact enlargement, not cropped in either dimension. For example, a 35-mm. negative should be blown up to an enlargement having the same proportions as the negative, which do *not* happen to be eight by ten inches. If a 35-mm. negative is enlarged to eight-by-ten print paper, there should be a lot of white at the top and bottom, otherwise it means the picture was cropped at one side or both sides. It is usually a good idea to have the negative at hand as well, although the negative will not be volunteered at this time.

If there are several defense photographs to be used in this trial, the lawyer should probably know them rather well, and when it comes time to use this one, he should pull it from the envelope without exposing the remaining photographs. When the time comes there will be no particular doubt about it. This will be the moment when, because the witness is finished answering in a very thorough way, the lawyer would either have to be content with the answer and go on to something else, or impeach the witness.

One should do it formally, and even if this trial department is one in which procedures are somewhat relaxed, the lawyer should be quite correct. The photograph will be handed to the clerk for marking, shown to the prosecutor, and if the judge is one who sometimes likes to see evidence before it is shown to the witness, it should be offered to him. All of this ritual is time consuming and it is good theatre.

When the photograph is entirely processed, it is simply passed up to the witness. The lawyer should ask him to examine it and to take his time doing so. It is helpful to ask the witness rather gently if this person shown in the picture is the witness himself, if this one over here is officer so and so, and if that person in a supine or prone position is the defendant. Then the lawyer should quickly ask the only essential qualifying question, as though it did not matter the least in the world, and that question will be, "Is this a fair representation of the situation at the time shown in the photograph?" *It is very important for the lawyer not to be belligerent with the witness, or triumphant or taunting.* The reason is, not merely that he will sacrifice some of the good feeling which this picture is about to engender, but that those tones of voice will warn the witness to fight back. He will usually be rather destroyed by the photograph and gentle ways are better. After all, the lawyer does want the admission that this photograph is a valid representation of the scene. Putting the question gently will almost always insure the necessary admission.

The next thing is simply to say that the photograph is offered in evidence. The prosecution are usually in a state of shock at this point and their reactions are minimal. There will probably be no objection at all. Once the photograph is in evidence, *the lawyer should immediately ask the trial judge if this would be a convenient time to pass the photograph among the members of the jury.* If the judge has seen the photograph in advance, he will know very well its significance, and he cannot deny that request. Since nobody else is going to be moving, the lawyer should simply take the photograph and hand it to the first juror and then go and sit down and catch up on his notes. It will take a long time for the photograph to pass among the jury, and nothing will be happening. But when that photograph has made its trip from hand to hand, the prosecution case will be destroyed. It is surprising how the whole mood of a jury changes after something like this. If they were serious before, they will be relaxed now.

The effect of using the photograph in this way is to destroy not only the witness, but everybody who endorsed him. The main victim is the prosecutor, who had vouched for this witness by calling him. The jury will not believe the witness any more, or the other witnesses who said he was telling the truth; but the main point is, they will not believe the prosecutor, in his final argument. The lawyer can use this collapse of confidence in his own final argument, provided only that he does it by analogy and not by direct reference (see § 16.03[5][d]).

The effect of this photograph is so strong as to obviate certain previous considerations of trial timing. For example, it might be nice if the lawyer could drop the photograph on the witness near the end of a session of court, and if things were really going well, on a Friday afternoon. These little points are usually regarded as favorable because the jury has a lunch recess, or possibly even a weekend to remember their very bad impression of this witness and the prosecution case, during which time there is no rebuttal at all. However, that kind of trial timing is of only microscopic value compared to what is really at stake in using a good photograph, and *the lawyer should on no account gamble for that small benefit.* There are some forms of impeachment which are sufficiently weak in themselves that they need the added benefit of good trial timing. But this kind of impeachment is killing and needs no further benefit.

On the other hand, there is one great danger in using the photograph, which the lawyer simply cannot afford to risk. That is the danger that at the moment the lawyer marks the photograph for identification, and before he hands it to the witness, the judge will call some recess. If the lawyer is straining for effect, trying very hard to explode this photograph just before lunch, or at the end of the Friday session, he is inviting a situation in which the judge has been waiting to go to the bathroom, or to telephone his mistress, so that he can wait no longer to get off the bench, and the very thought of taking an extra minute to mark that photograph will prompt him to declare that court is in recess.

If that happens, the next thing the lawyer sees will be the witness coming off the stand, huddling with the prosecutors, and all of them will be examining the photograph. They will go out in the corridor, have a lot to say about it all by themselves, and at the next session of court the witness will get on the stand, and no matter how tightly the lawyer had nailed it down at the previous session, he will be sick to hear what the witness has to say. This should not be allowed to happen. The best way to prevent it is to use the photograph on the witness when the lawyer is very sure that things are fresh and moving fast and that the lawyer will complete this passage without serious interruption. Do it after recess, and do not attempt to be too clever about it.

Another necessary admonition as to the mechanics is, do not hammer at the witness too much or become entangled with him after using the photograph. There are several reasons why, once the photograph has made its point firmly, the lawyer should not hack at the witness. The main object is to persuade the jury, not to degrade the witness; this flows from a basic premise of defending political trials, which is that there is really only one case involved—the defense. The prosecution case does not exist. So a strong main element of the defense case should never be allowed to become obscured or transformed downward into what might emerge as a personality attack on the witness. After all, any further berating of the witness at this stage shows lack of confidence in the jury (it patronizes them), and in the point being made. The meaning of successful impeachment is very large, but the limited dialogue which may follow between the lawyer and a sullen, resentful witness will not add much to the meaning already apprehended. In short, a successful impeachment will be much better exploited by the relatively broad references which can be made at a time of the lawyer's choosing and in his own words. This final, exploitative attack must be saved for closing argument, and even then it must be done with skill, and not necessarily from the direction the prosecution expects (see § 16.03[5][a][i]).

Of course, the witness will sooner or later recover and may well attempt to squirm out of what has happened. He may do this while still on the stand, having thought it over while the photograph is being passed among the jury. Or he may be brought back on redirect examination after some conference in the corridor. That matters very little, provided only that the photograph has already been passed among the jury. For example, even though the witness has just admitted (prior to the admission of the photograph) that the photograph shows the scene as it was, he may suddenly claim he is not at all sure it shows the scene correctly. The normal temptation at this point is for the lawyer to react with anger, real or feigned. This would be a mistake.

Nobody is fooled when the witness says something

like this. All the lawyer has to do is ask a few plain, flat questions which ineluctably compel the witness to clarify the nature of his accusation. The lawyer should simply ask what is wrong with the photograph or what is missing from it. He can conclude this short list with something like this: "Do you mean you're saying that defendant's Exhibit A in evidence is a fake?" The witness will probably say it *is* a fake, although he had not really meant to go that far.

The controlling considerations here are as follows: (1) the photograph is already in evidence; (2) the jury has already seen it; (3) other witnesses can always testify later that the photograph does show the situation as it was—this will be quite easy to establish since it does show the scene correctly, and several witnesses, directing their memories to details in the photograph, can establish that point overwhelmingly; and (4) the photographer himself is the one best able to react to the accusation of "fake." It often happens that his personality alone would be sufficient to discredit that charge, since he is clearly able to explain the procedures by which the photograph was taken (he will have the negative), and that nothing has been done to alter it.

Once it is quite clear that the impeached witness has made the accusation that the photograph is a fake, the lawyer should not encourage him to lecture or ramble on the subject of his accusation. Instead, he should quietly go on to another point in the cross-examination, preferably a very bland one, and as soon as possible, so as to allow nothing bad to happen, drop the witness.

§ 14.06 When to Skip or Drastically Limit Cross-Examination

It seems axiomatic that not all witnesses have to be cross-examined at any length and that many of them do not have to be cross-examined at all. The witness may have done no harm to the defense case. If he has done no harm, but has somehow added a little extra momentum or spin to the prosecution case by reason of his engaging personality, he can probably be jarred, and the edge taken off his testimony by one or two carefully prepared points having to do with minor inconsistent statements. The lawyer will then be in a position to stop the cross-examination as quickly as it started without giving the witness a chance to look good again.

For some reason, many lawyers find it impossible to skip cross-examination. The feeling seems to be, there has been some preparation done for every witness, and none of this is going to be wasted by silence. Also, some lawyers feel that not to cross-examine a prosecution witness is, somehow, to endorse his testimony by implication—as if there had been an unspoken challenge to cross-examine every witness. This is absurd. The lawyer's real job is to win the case, and incidental to that, to the extent possible, to exercise all the control he can exert over prosecution witnesses. Quite often what the lawyer will want the prosecution witness to do is simply to get up out of the witness box and walk out of the room. The way to do that, unglamorous as it may seem, is simply to stop the cross-examination or to say "no questions."

Incidentally, it is sometimes suggested by writers that a special forensic emphasis be given to this statement, i.e., "I have no questions for *this* witness." The tone—worthy of daytime television—is intended to stress the point for the benefit of the jury that the lawyer does not consider this witness worthy of cross-examination. It is probably a better idea to say the same words and skip the historionics. By the time the prosecution get to their first unimportant witness, the lawyer and jury will know each other better than that. If the lawyer overstates a nothing point, the jury will simply know that he is patronizing them. They will not care anything about the implied representation that the witness was unimportant, but they will resent being patronized.

It is especially important to omit, limit, or somehow defer cross-examination when it appears that the prosecutor can be forced into putting on an unprepared witness who happens to be his only available standby witness. There is a definite syndrome of observable things in the courtroom which signals this situation:

(1) The prosecutor is noticeably stalling in his direct examination of the witness now on the stand;

(2) The witness seems to be a nothing witness so that it appears that he might not have been called at all under normal circumstances, but may be serving as a stop-gap;

(3) The prosecutor has had several worried conferences with his secretary or investigator, who has found it necessary to enter the courtroom (they do not sit with him at the counsel table) and approach him by walking to the counsel table or by sending notes through the bailiff;

(4) The prosecutor has unconsciously looked toward the courtroom door through which witnesses emerge, even though there is an order keeping witnesses in the corridor; and

(5) There is an angry looking man walking up and down in the corridor (this is almost conclusive when it happens).

These points of course could be separately explainable in many different ways, but as a matter of common sense, they usually indicate that the prosecutor has experienced a perfectly normal interruption in the flow of witnesses, the same as the defense often does.

It may have just happened (somehow this situation often occurs in the morning) that one or two previously scheduled witnesses suddenly became unavailable. This made it necessary to bring on the next in line, who would not otherwise have testified for another day or so. That is why he is angry. He got orders from somebody to leave his job sooner than expected, and he is very interested in his day-to-day work. He may be a police officer stationed in some distant city. He knows very well why it is important for him to be back there on the job right now, rather than be dragged into town to testify in court about something that happened many months ago. He is irritated because he had to rush to get here, because his mind is on other things, because his immediate superior was rather curt about sending him here with little or no explanation, and because he feels that someone (probably the prosecutor) has fucked up.

Also, most importantly, he has not been briefed about this case. He has not been persuaded that the defendant is the devil. Give the prosecutor half an hour with this man in his own office and all of this will change. When this situation arises, the lawyer should decide whether he can get rid of the witness on the stand in time to force the one in the corridor in his place before the next break. Everything depends on the time and the judge's habits. If it is almost lunch time, probably this will not work.

But if there is something like an hour remaining, particularly if the situation becomes apparent immediately after a recess, then probably the lawyer should start using his objections to cut in on the long repetitive questions. He should be rather sharp and disinterested, and do everything he can to limit the rambling direct examination.

These objections should be short and any words said in support of them should be quite blunt. The lawyer should not get involved in any kind of wrangle over a particular objection, since that will serve the prosecutor's purpose as well as rambling testimony. Also, the tone of these objections will show the jury better than any histrionics that the testimony of this witness is pointless, and they will not expect any cross-examination. They will be grateful when the lawyer says he has no questions.

It helps a great deal at this point if the lawyer has

been able to learn the name of the witness waiting in the corridor. When the prosecutor gets up and starts to say something about being out of witnesses and needing a little more time (looking at the clock), the lawyer should interject that he supposes the prosecutor knows that Officer Fahrenheit has been waiting in the corridor for half an hour, and is it correct that Officer Fahrenheit is the next prosecution witness? The prosecutor can say whatever he likes to that, but has to say it in the light of certain knowledge that he is going to put Officer Fahrenheit on the stand either now or after lunch.

If the prosecutor blurts out that he has not briefed this witness, the lawyer should point out that it is just too bad, the witness will be under *oath* and presumably will tell the *truth*, and it is unfair to the defense and the jury to ask everybody to wait while the prosecutor *coaches* his next witness. This should be said without any hint as to how important it actually is to get that witness in the box now.

Once the angry witness is in the box, most of the damage he is capable of doing to the prosecution case will happen during direct examination. The lawyer should be very alert to leading questions and follow the standard procedure with them. This is, let two or three or four of them go by so long as they are unimportant, and then the first time a leading question gets near a vital area, stick the prosecutor with an objection, and remind the judge that the lawyer has been rather patient with these questions up to this point but that the witness must be allowed to tell his own story and the last question was leading and *suggestive*. The sustaining of the objection will endorse the whole speech, and the prosecutor will be closer to real trouble. He will now be dealing with an unprepared witness in the presence of an aroused judge and jury.

Officer Fahrenheit probably will say a few things that will help the defense, and when he does make a mistake, it will probably *not* lie in the direction of any previous prosecution contention. It really will not fit very well with the prosecution's opening statement. This witness's errors will all be extraneous (a surprise to everybody), but they will spread confusion among the prosecutor's arguments, something like wild elephants among an army of foot soldiers. When the time comes to pick up the pieces for final argument, the lawyer can pick up as much of this witness's evidence as seems corroborated by other people, and leave the rest for the prosecutor.

§ 14.07 Cross-Examining the Police Officer Who Was in a Position to Corroborate the Main Prosecution Witness and Fails to Do so

This situation typically arises when the main felony charged against the defendant concerns his alleged violence in resisting arrest and when, in fact, one or two of the arresting officers beat him up despite his nonresistance. Other officers who saw that happen may not be willing to lie about it, so they will not corroborate the testimony that the defendant was the aggressor. On the other hand, such a witness will not undercut his fellow officers (who did the beating) by directly contradicting them, and so he testifies he did not see it happen at all. Note that this is a case in which the officers who did the beating must and do testify.

Since the fact that this bystander-witness does not corroborate the main prosecution witness will have been picked up quite easily in trial preparation, his importance to the defense will have been obvious for some time and his cross-examination the subject of planning. Of course, the main thing is to put this witness in a position from which he must have been able to see and hear what happened, and must have been aware of it regardless of what he says. Usually there will not be much difficulty about this, since this witness is *not* motivated to lie about anything other than the one main point, that he did see what happened.

Even on this point, he is not deeply concerned with whether the jury believes him, since he is basically an honest person who would not believe anyone else giving the same testimony on that point, and he is reasonably confident that in this case the jury will understand why he is testifying as he does and will not blame him.

It is important for the lawyer to preserve that attitude on the part of the witness, since that is exactly what he wishes the jury to do. The lawyer will not blame the witness either. On the contrary, this witness's testimony is vital in final argument (see § 16.03[5][a][iii]).

The mechanics of putting the witness where he must have seen things are rather simple. Like all other witnesses, he should be asked to draw a diagram of what was happening and where he was. This witness should not be allowed to feel too threatened, except to the extent needed to keep him on the track. Some deviations by the witness are much less important than others. He may say that he did not see what was going on because of something else that was happening which distracted him. He should be cross-examined in some detail on that point, and asked to draw the positions of other various persons involved. It will be fairly easy to discredit that portion of his testimony by means of highly believable defense witnesses who will say that no such thing happened. Since the problem of whether he was really distracted can be solved so easily, there is no point in making a big thing of it in cross-examination.

The main feature of this witness's testimony is that he did *not see* what happened. This is the one part that will probably have been left unclear on his direct examination. If he did not actually say, during direct, that he *saw* what happened, then it is imperative that he be made to say during cross-examination that he *did not see* it. This negative part must not be left to doubt, otherwise his value as a defense witness disappears.

If the witness suddenly takes the position on cross-

examination that he *did see* the action, then he must be impeached immediately on that point, using the police report,
transcript of testimony at the preliminary hearing, or whatever weapon the lawyer has to push him off that untenable
position back to his original role of the man who saw no evil.
Such a drastic cross-examination will probably not be necessary, however, because of this witness's character. Basically,
he does not want to lie, and with the single exception of saying he did not see the beating, he probably will not.

This witness should be treated as a friendly witness
as long as he says he did not see what he must have seen.
The key to this cross-examination is that it is *not* done for
immediate effect, but for its effect in final argument, which
is analagous to a silent explosion. Because of the overriding
value of this witness as a "defense witness" during argument, his cross-examination should not be allowed to take
on emotional overtones, and the lawyer should not appear
to be scoring points in the presence of the jury. There is
always a danger that the witness will lose his head, turn
hostile, and start lying like the main prosecution witness,
forcing a different form of cross-examination and ruining
his usefulness in argument.

Also it is quite important not to give this witness a
chance to say something again (a second chance not to),
just to score an immediate point with the jury. Once he has
said that he was not aware of the critical action going on
(in our example, the beating), that is *enough*. Once he has
said it, there is nothing to be gained by asking him to say it
again, and much to lose. *If that point was clear on direct, it
need not even be mentioned on cross-examination.* All that
is necessary, then, is to establish those few facts which indicate that he must have seen and heard everything.

Since the lawyer wishes to take advantage of the
witness's moral dilemma, not punish him for it, he should
usher the witness off the stand in a way that dampens and
minimizes his testimony. To do anything else with such a

valuable defense witness, e.g., to accuse him of holding back to protect a fellow officer, would be stupid.

§ 14.08 The Urgent Need to Make Prosecution Witnesses Draw Diagrams

Many political cases turn on the jeweled bearing of whether a particular action happened in exactly the way the prosecution claim, what physical events led up to it, who was there, and who was (or was not) in a position to observe things. These physical relationships are important to the final argument, although they seldom seem quite so important while the testimony is going down. It is not enough to say that these physical relationships are merely susceptible of being diagramed—it is more accurate to say they cannot really be communicated except by diagram or photograph; and virtually nothing transmits as fast as a good diagram.

As a general rule, all prosecution witnesses whose testimonies touch an area of disputed action should be required to make some simple drawing showing their recollection of what happened, where they were, and where other people were at the time. If the witness's name is Sam, and he is describing the movements of a person named Fred, it may be helpful to handle things in the following manner. Have the witness mark the place where he was standing when he first noticed Fred. He should mark the place where he was standing S-1. He should then mark the place where Fred was standing at that moment, and label that F-1. He should then be asked to record his own movements seriatim, marking each place he went to as S-2, S-3, etc., and marking the corresponding points where he noticed Fred at each of those moments, using the same numerals to indicate the same moments. Anyone can look at the drawing and understand that when Sam was at S-3, Fred was at F-3 and so on. Sam's points can be connected by arrows indicating the direction he was going, and the same for Fred. This nails it all down, much better than a lot of unadorned anonymous little lines. These drawings should of course never be made on a blackboard, but on a big piece of butcher paper, using felt pen or crayon. These drawings can be very simple, in many cases only a few lines. The first two or three witnesses who are required to make these drawings should be asked to put in more detail, and to label things rather carefully. After that, it will be pretty clear where things were.

Each witness should do a separate drawing, although as a practical matter, little harm is done with two or three witnesses marking the same one, provided they use different colored crayons, and provided the lawyer states for the record that the witness is making a line or drawing a rectangle in a certain place with a certain crayon, so that— should it matter in case of appeal—the contribution of each witness can be sorted out from the record. Similarly, after doing an individual drawing, each witness should be asked to sign it. This is in addition to the usual formality of marking and offering the exhibit in evidence. The lawyer will be able to determine later from his notes which witness drew which exhibit by means of the clerk's numbers, but in the jury room, things will go better if each drawing bears its author's signature.

The drawing will always relate to the action which the witness is describing, so if there is any objection to any of these drawings, it can easily be overcome. A common objection from a new prosecutior is, lack of foundation. (The drawing is not to scale—he wants a surveyor.) The answer of course is that the drawing is not intended to be to scale, but is offered as illustrative of the witness's testimony, and as a means of understanding it. Drawings should not be offered, for example, on the relatively sterile ground of testing a witness's memory, an entirely different (and in my view misguided) theory which assumes that the lawyer is going to bring in some kind of surveyor's map or diagram showing everything as it really was, so that the witness's drawing can be compared to *that*. Presumably, the lawyer is not interested in testing a witness's skill as a map maker but in seeing that his testimony is properly understood by the jury, so that his testimony may be properly compared to other evidence in the case (rather than just his memory).

There are three general benefits from making prosecution witnesses draw diagrams. The first is, as a matter of common sense, the witness can only *be* in one place at a given moment, and he should be *put* there, so that in each juror's mind there is a common reference point, which says that at a certain time this particular witness's testimony places him right *here*, and at that moment he testified that certain other things were happening *here* and *here*. Unless the witness has been nailed down as to exactly what he is saying—in other words, if he is allowed to get away with just saying it in words—then inevitably different jurors will have different mental impressions of where he was at a critical moment. Some jurors may not have *any* impression of where he was, unless a drawing is made.

The result may be that in the jury room, two or three jurors who are inclined to the prosecution view of the case may continue to hold on for some time simply because they have different mental pictures of where the main prosecution witness was. One or two of them may have no impression of where he was, but are willing to give him the benefit of the doubt. It is very hard for these jurors to know that their interpretation of the physical facts is different from that of the other jurors, or, if that difference is laid on the table, to have any means of resolving it. The special benefit of having prosecution witnesses make drawings is that, after the drawings have been properly used in final argument, there cannot be any substantial difference of opinion as to where he said he was. *This simply means that the prose-*

cution witnesses will lose an important benefit they might have otherwise had, which is lack of particularity as to where they were when important things were happening.

While this point may seem to limit all witnesses impartially, three things make it very one-sided:

(1) With a mosaic pattern of proof there will be more defense witnesses; the exact location of any one of these is less important since others can confirm what he saw.

(2) The burden of proof is on the prosecution.

(3) Somebody on the prosecution side is going to be grossly misstating the facts.

The second major benefit of making prosecution witnesses draw diagrams is that the lawyer will also be asking defense witnesses to draw similar diagrams. Most of the diagrams drawn by witnesses on both sides will be amazingly similar. The repetition of these diagrams before the jury may give rise to a little boredom, but it will be friendly boredom. The jury's initial surpise that drawings are coming in with every witness ("God, we certainly know where that intersection is by now") becomes an area of understanding and tolerance by the time defense witnesses testify ("This child seems to have drawn the pool hall too far from the corner . . . but she's doing the best she can!")

The general effect of having prosecution and defense witnesses making similar diagrams is to stress how much they have in common. This is a high priority subject throughout the trial, since one of the lawyer's unstated problems is to destroy any notion that defense witnesses are a separate class. Since the defense witnesses will have been well briefed, they will meet the jury more than half way, and the jury will accept them. The fact that many prosecution witnesses seem to have remembered things much in common with defense witnesses (a point made clear by their respective diagrams) will have the subtle effect of seeming to draw some of the prosecution witnesses in the train of the defense evidence. This phenomenon is not to be proved objectively; but it is there, and it should be exploited by the defense in argument.

A third benefit of using repetitive drawings is that they serve to isolate important differences of testimony. Prosecution witnesses who testify to events that did not happen always tend to overdo it. With a crayon in hand, they will draw too much, over too wide an area. Since their reasons for misstating the facts are emotional, their drawing will be of the same quality. A drawing which does violence to the facts will not reflect a fine precision of mind. A few prosecution witnesses will have made their drawings like angry children. By contrast, numerous defense witnesses (and some prosecution witnesses) will have made drawings which differ from each other only as much as human recollection normally differs. These drawings come into evidence like ballots into a box; and before long there will be a strong trend against the prosecution. At some point when this trend has begun to bear them down, even in a case where there *are no* dramatic impeaching photographs, it will happen that certain prosaic defense photographs corroborate first this portion and then that portion of the defense drawings, while other photographs will show that certain sloppy features of the prosecution drawings do not exist. At some transitional moment which no one foresaw, the trend of persuasion accelerates; rocks begin to clatter down the scree and suddenly the whole field of view moves; there is a silent avalanche of belief like something viewed through binoculars and not yet audible, which can be wondered at but not prevented.

§ 14.09 Cross-Examining as to Time When the Defense Is Alibi

In establishing an alibi defense, the lawyer will already have determined the critical time span from the defendant's own recollection. This will be the time span during which the defendant can prove that he was elsewhere, by his own testimony and other evidence. This time span will bracket that in which the prosecution says he was present at the scene of the crime.

In cross-examining prosecution witnesses, it is important to nail down the prosecution's version of the time when the defendant was in the neighborhood. Most prosecution witnesses will not claim to have seen the defendant there. But there will always be prosecution witnesses testifying as to certain events closely related to the crime, whether or not they claim to have seen the defendant.

All of these witnesses (whether they saw the defendant or not) should be cross-examined as to the time of the main events. This is quite easy, since after a certain amount of testimony, the jury understands perfectly well what the sequence of events was, and so it is simple to pick one or two convenient reference point events and ask each witness when those things happened. These time estimates can be averaged for use in argument. It is amazing how estimates of many people, even months after the event, will group very tightly around a small spread of minutes. In a list of twenty time estimates, more than half may fall within fifteen minutes one side or the other of the average time. This point can be used very effectively in argument.

There is little profit in trying to influence the trend of time estimates for most prosecution witnesses, particularly those who did not see the defendant. The average of time estimates from prosecution witnesses will probably coincide with the average of defense witnesses. But there is one thing the lawyer must watch out for.

He must watch for the particular prosecution witness who *does* claim to have seen the defendant, and whose testimony as to time is radically different from that of other prosecution witnesses. While the average estimate can be relied upon not to drift too far from the facts, so that the average can actually be used in support of the defendant's own alibi testimony, there is always the danger that one aberrant witness will wipe out the benefits of averaging by (1) personally identifying the defendant as being at the scene of the crime, and (2) fixing the time as either earlier or later than the time span during which the defendant can best prove he was somewhere else. The danger is that if this witness is believed, it does not matter that other prosecution witnesses remembered the time differently. It is the lawyer's job to move this mistaken time estimate back into the right time span. The techniques are fairly simple.

If this witness has placed the defendant's alleged presence at a time *earlier* than the critical time span, the technique for moving it forward is simply to nail him down on the exact time of some event an hour or so before he allegedly saw the defendant and then lead him through the sequence of things he did, where he went, whom he saw, and what he did at every stage; and with respect to each increment, make him estimate the amount of time necessary to do that thing (this technique is discussed above in the section on briefing defense witnesses; see § 9.06[13]).

The lawyer does *not* ask this witness to total all those increments before he leaves the stand for the simple reason they will total far more than the hour or so which he thinks elapsed between the earlier event and the time he saw the defendant. The fact that they total a great deal more can be used effectively *in argument*, and would be spoiled if the witness were allowed to think about it (and then routinely deny it) while he is on the stand.

On the other hand, if the witness places the defendant on the scene *later* than the critical time span, the technique is obverse. The lawyer asks the witness to fix the exact time of some event which the witness supposes would be about an hour after he saw the defendant. The lawyer then takes the witness through everything he did from the time he saw the defendant until that time, asking him to estimate the time necessary for each step. Again, the witness is not asked to total those events while he is on the stand. They will, as a general rule, be found to total a lot more time than the witness thought. The lawyer can then point out in argument that since according to the witness's own testimony it took him two hours to do the things which he did between the time he saw the defendant and 9:00, it follows that his estimate that he saw the defendant at 8:00 must be disbelieved and the time moved back to 7:00, which just happens to be only ten minutes off what it should have been according to average time estimates of all other witnesses. This kind of cross-examination, coupled with this kind of argument, serves to put the aberrant witness's time estimate back where it belongs—right in the middle of the defendant's alibi period.

§ 14.10 Alertness to Cheating on Discovery

In cross-examining any prosecution witness, the lawyer should generally inquire if the witness has refreshed his memory from any statement or written document before coming to the stand, and if the answer is yes, he should ask to see it. The main thing here is, be sensitive to any reference (however indirect) to evidence which the prosecution were obligated to hand over by the terms of some discovery order, and which they may not have delivered.

When something like this turns up, the lawyer should cross-examine quickly and matter-of-factly to ascertain the nature of the evidence, where it is now, when the witness first saw it, who showed it to him, whether he knows the contents, and *how many times* (not whether) he has discussed this particular piece of evidence with the prosecutor. When the lawyer has actually turned up something like this, he should immediately go into chambers with the court reporter, and he should decide whether he wants to move for a mistrial or dismissal. If this was a case in which the lawyer had to settle for a less than adequate jury (see § 10.01[3]), this is the time to remember exactly what the lawyer's opinion was at the moment the jury was sworn and not, for example, what the lawyer was thinking about the jury five minutes ago. If the lawyer got a bad draw on the jury, this is the time and place to square it. Square it with a mistrial and do better with the next jury.

Footnotes

[1] McCormick, *Evidence* 90–93 (2d ed. 1972); 3-A Wigmore, *Evidence* §§ 977–979 (Chadbourn rev. ed. 1970); Witkin, *California Evidence* 1140–1141 (2d ed. 1966).

[2] See, e.g., Cal. Evid. Code §§ 1100 and 780 (West 1966); Witkin, *California Evidence* 1145 (2d ed. 1966).

[3] Cf. People v. Moses, 24 Cal. App. 3d 384, 396–399, 100 Cal. Rptr. 907, 915–916 (1972); 1 Wigmore, *Evidence* §§ 92, 93, 97 and 199 (3d ed. 1940); 2 Wigmore, *Evidence* § 375; W. Hale, "Some Comments on Character Evidence and Related Topics," 22 S. Cal. L. Rev. 341, 346 (1949).

[4] For example, United States v. Anderson, et al., Crim. No. 602–71 (D.N.J. 1973) ("the Camden 28") which ended in acquittals all around on May 21, 1973. See N.Y. Times, May 21, 1973, p. 1, col. 2. The defense lawyers in that case very kindly made available a copy of a rather important jury instruction. See Appendix D-3[b] herein.

Chapter 15

PUTTING ON THE DEFENSE CASE

SYNOPSIS

---

§ 15.01 Basic Considerations When Putting On the Defense Case

In order to put on a good defense case, it is necessary to understand what the total effort is supposed to be. This helps in doing all the smaller actions which make up the whole. The cardinal point is something mentioned from time to time in this book: the lawyer's outlook must be that there *is* only one case, the defense case. This is true although one happens to be in trial against the prosecutors and all of their witnesses. In the back of the lawyer's mind should be the tenet that the prosecution contentions lack the name of reality. It follows naturally that defense evidence should not be viewed by the jury as "relating" (or reacting) to the prosecution case. The lawyer's aim is to blank the prosecution case into nothing, rather than have the defense evidence descend to the level of separate squabbles with the main prosecution witnesses. The defense witnesses will contradict every material thing said by the main prosecution witnesses, in one way or another, but they will not seem to do so for that purpose, but only to tell what happened.

As a rule, the array of defense witnesses will contain no star witness—no one the mind will point to and say, *this* witness is a counterpoise to *that* main prosecution witness. But the effect of combined defense testimonies should be to reduce the prosecution case to nonreality (the condition of being disbelieved), almost without anyone realizing the moment when that happens.

It is important to avoid the appearance of strain, even though there will probably be more defense witnesses per fact to be proved than there were for the prosecution. Each defense witness will have some bits of information, and these will fit together. In following this mosaic method of proof, the lawyer should not be embarrassed by minor discrepancies in testimony among his own witnesses. These will happen, they are expected, and in fact the lawyer will have taken care to preserve these natural discrepancies rather than smooth them over. They are part of the defense presentation, not a cause for anxiety. The lawyer is going to get a jury instruction that minor discrepancies are a trait of human nature and, in argument, he will rely on them as an indication of honesty and one of the strong points of the defense. The jury will not feel any anxiety about this either; they hardly need to be told trivial differences are natural.

The lawyer should present his evidence briskly, to contrast with what was probably a long-drawn, agonizing, and dull presentation by the prosecution. Briskness is natural when one holds the cards, and the need for it puts a premium on scheduling defense witnesses rapidly, asking them simple, short nonleading questions, placing their drawings in evidence and getting them off the stand with style and élan.

The lawyer should be able to manage a little serenity along with his evidence. The actual presentation of evidence is only the tip of a work cone, which, after all, was fashioned before this trial started. Success in putting on the defense case will be largely determined by what has gone before; certainly there is danger when witnesses are going on the stand, and the unexpected is as real as ever; but the whole thing is energized. It moves itself. Do it with grace and let the results take care of themselves.

§ 15.02   An Important Preliminary: Keeping In Touch

The lawyer or his secretary will have been in touch with all defense witnesses from time to time as they were added to the roster. He will have been informing the witnesses with increasing precision of the approximate times during which they will be needed to testify. The method for doing this is important.

While the lawyer is in trial it is essential to have a secretary or someone else in the office who knows what the weather is in court, and exactly what to tell witnesses who telephone to find out how things are going and when they will be needed. If witnesses do *not* call in, this person must know them well enough to reach them by telephone, so that contact is made with all witnesses about once a week. Much of this telephoning must be done during the day because some witnesses cannot always be reached after court hours. While the lawyer may have his problems in court, his witnesses need to make their plans as well. They need to know when to take time off from work, whether they have to arrange for babysitters (testify in the morning or after school), whether they can take a three-day weekend or start on vacation next week, whether they can arrange to testify on their day off, how they are going to get to court (if they do not have a car), and where they will stay (if they are coming from out of town). It is essential to keep up with the steadily changing personal problems and requirements of defense witnesses, and to schedule their testimony with a minimum of inconvenience to them.

Keeping up with the witnesses also has the advantage of maintaining rapport, and of maintaining the lawyer's peace of mind. It takes very little to maintain rapport with friendly witnesses. They understand about the trial, and they only like to learn once in a while how things are going. In terms of equanimity, it is probably much more important for the lawyer to be continually reassured that the witnesses are there, that they remember him and know the case is still on. Lawyers in a long case are subject to a nightmare rather like the one about suddenly facing an examination for which one has somehow forgotten to attend classes all term. This trial nightmare is that an important witness, when asked to appear in court tomorrow, will suddenly say that while he *does remember* having once talked to the lawyer about the case, long ago, he had assumed the trial was over and had forgotten about it. Now he is waiting for the taxi and he is going overseas this afternoon.

Another reason for maintaining contact with witnesses is that they are always supplying names of new witnesses, whom they have thought of since they talked to the lawyer last, or whom he could not find. They have just run into them and they have written down some addresses. Preparing the defense case is an ongoing thing. There will always be new witnesses turning up, especially in a long trial, and there will always be first witness briefings for newly-found witnesses after the defense case has begun.

For established witnesses (those previously briefed), it is always essential to confer again just before they testify, preferably the night before. This briefing may be done over the telephone, or sometimes in the lawyer's office. The lawyer should go over the main points which he will ask the witness and be sure that he understands what the answers are going to be, *as of right now*. Some of these answers may have changed since the witness was first interviewed. He may, for example, have taken the lawyer's advice to retrace his steps, noting the time it took him to do certain things, and he will certainly have been thinking about the case rather intensively. Many important points are subject to modification at this time, and the lawyer had better find out what they are.

It is probably a poor idea to show the witness his previous written statement just now. The lawyer can use the statement himself in discussing things with the witness, but there is no use setting him up for a question on cross-examination as to whether he has refreshed his memory from any particular document. The lawyer would not be very happy to hand over his own private memorandum for use by the cross-examiner the next day, but that is exactly what may happen if he actually hands the statement to the witness now. (See § 4.03[4] for a discussion of the correct method of reviewing the facts with a witness in a jurisdiction where this tell-and-show rule prevails.)

As part of this interview on the night before testifying, the lawyer should advise the witness how the case has been going, and what the main points are which the prosecutor will try to get him to say. There may be patterns of cross-examination emerging—this will almost always be true in a long trial—and the witness should be brought up to date on the prosecutor's favorite techniques and questions. The lawyer may also have some things to tell the witness about the trial judge's idiosyncrasies.

§ 15.03 Looking After Large Numbers of Witnesses

In a political trial involving a large number of witnesses and particularly in a series of political trials, the lawyer will find a special need for someone outside of his own office who can help look after witnesses. There is usually someone around who can fill this need, and she (yes, usually a woman) will probably think of this job herself. Main requirements are that this friend be sympathetic to the defense case, that she know most of the witnesses from the context of her daily life, that she have a car and be willing to use it occasionally to help get a witness to court in an emergency. Above all, she must be reachable by telephone. It is desirable that she not be a witness, since all this work on behalf of the defense would give her a partisan coloring that could be used to impeach her testimony.

This kind of friend is invaluable in the very common situation in which a witness has car trouble on the way to court; or an out-of-town witness turns up without a place to stay; or the lawyer suddenly needs a witness, who doesn't have a telephone, to testify sooner than his previously scheduled time, and someone must immediately go to find him. These problems may well be beyond the capacity of the regular office staff, working under trial pressure. If the lawyer's secretary and notetaker are trading off— alternately taking notes in the morning and typing them in the afternoon—they will not be able to leave the office. It is refreshing that someone can be reached in these common emergencies who will be ready and able to solve them.

§ 15.04 The Mechanics of Scheduling Witnesses

To achieve a smooth flow of witnesses with minimum inconvenience to those standing by, the lawyer may find the following method helpful. Start the morning session of court with the first two witnesses on hand. If court begins at 10:00, both witnesses should be scheduled to appear in the corridor just before 10:00. The lawyer should schedule the third witness to appear in the corridor a short interval later. This interval will be the time the lawyer estimates the first witness will be on the stand. He schedules the fourth witness to appear in the corridor a short interval of time after that, which will be the time he estimates the second witness will be on the stand.

To pursue an example, if the lawyer thinks the first witness will be on the stand for twenty minutes, the second for thirty-five minutes, and the third for forty minutes, then witnesses #1 and #2 should be in the corridor at 10:00, witness #3 at 10:20, witness #4 at 10:55, and witness #5 at 11:35. The morning may be filled in this way.

The afternoon session should be planned on the same basis, to begin with two witnesses on hand, and with others scheduled as in the morning, the main difference being that the afternoon schedule must be more flexible. The morning schedule may well run over, making it impossible for all the afternoon witnesses to testify; or the morning may accelerate making it desirable to move one or two of the afternoon witnesses to testify before lunch.

The result of this system is that there should always be one more witness than necessary, if the lawyer's time estimates are correct. There is no substitute for experience in making these estimates, which means simply that the lawyer can do a better job in minimizing the inconvenience to his own witnesses when he has a feel for the way things are going in court.

It is interesting how this feel develops: the lawyer may not be able to explain *why*, and he is certainly not able to predict all the questions and answers on cross-examination. Nonetheless, the lawyer can mentally look at the clock when he pictures the witness getting on the stand, and ask himself what time it will be when the witness gets off, and the answer, remarkably, will be right.

Everybody knows that witnesses are often late getting to court; and it is also true that the prosecutor may get tired of the sound of his own voice and skip or drastically limit his cross-examination. It is foreseeable that these things will happen, although it is not very foreseeable when.

The lawyer must *not* keep running out of witnesses nor should he drag out a direct examination in order to cover a hiatus in the order of their appearances. The solution (described supra) is to have one on the stand and one in the corridor at every plannable moment; if the one in the corridor is late, or if the prosecutor skips his cross-examination of the one on the stand, a witness is always on hand, in the right order.

The lawyer should naturally be a little conservative in estimating time on the stand, so that in a sequence of several witnesses, they tend slightly to pile up, rather than stretch apart. The benefit (to the lawyer) is that if the one in the corridor is *very* late, and the prosecutor picks that moment to skip cross-examination, the next witness after that is really only minutes away, or may have come early. It may not be necessary to request a recess.

The lawyer should not find himself asking for a recess very often (although he will, notwithstanding everything). When it happens, he should not only *feel* embarrassed, he should make no bones about it. The jury should know it, and the lawyer's apology to the judge and jury should be quick and candid.

He should remind the judge immediately that the missing witness, though under subpoena, has apparently been delayed. (See § 9.06[1] for the need to subpoena even friendly witnesses to cover this contingency.) He should express regret at the loss of time and suggest if the next customary recess is near at hand that it be taken now; or if this is near the end of the session, perhaps it might be convenient to end a few minutes early, and start the next session correspondingly early, as may suit the convenience of the court. The judge will probably then ask the jury if it will be convenient to break for lunch fifteen minutes early, and come back on the same basis and, generally, it will be. When this happens, the lawyer should tighten his scheduling considerably (make the intervals shorter).

The more usual situation is that this system works fine. When it is working well, the witnesses should tend to back up slightly: by the end of the morning session there should be one left over whom the lawyer was not able to use during that session. If the prosecutor is really windy on cross-examination, there may be two or three left over.

One of the happy purposes that lunchtime serves is to adjust the afternoon schedule. The lawyer will have to decide what changes to make. These changes are not necessarily to push everybody forward in the same order as before. There will probably be persons scheduled to testify that day who have either come from out of town or who have used up hard-earned good will to be excused from work at this particular time. Naturally, these witnesses should be accommodated by putting them on the same day that they were asked to appear. If this means that other witnesses scheduled to testify ahead of them must be brought back the next day, that is probably the way it should be done.

Also, if there is a valuable out of town witness who has an airplane to make shortly after the end of the afternoon session, and if the lawyer particularly wishes to keep cross-examination of that witness on a reasonable leash, the lawyer may be well advised to see to it that the witness testifies in mid-afternoon, so that there remains enough time for a reasonable cross-examination and no more, and he should remind the judge and jury of the witness's problem when the witness first takes the stand. This enables everybody to see that the lawyer is proceeding briskly with his own direct examination (the same way he is asking the prosecutor to proceed when his turn comes).

There is no excuse for anybody dawdling through the direct examination for an hour or so, and then looking at his watch and asking his adversary to wrap up the cross in twenty minutes. That is not to be done; neither is the lawyer, however, to humor the perversity of some prosecutors who, when they hear that a witness has an airplane to catch at 5:00, automatically double the time of their cross-examination out of pure spite. That is why we suggest that when confronted with a prosecutor of this sort, the lawyer should not only announce the time problem at the beginning of his own direct examination, but should also begin it and conduct it with an eye on the clock, so as to allow time for reasonable cross-examination.

Then if the prosecutor dawdles, the lawyer can turn the heat on him during the last twenty minutes of the cross-examination and finally enlist the judge's aid in bringing matters to a halt. This will promote that desirable bad feeling between prosecutor and judge, which the prosecutor's general line of conduct in a political trial so often engenders anyway.

There are certainly many ways of dealing with the papers that go with one's own witnesses. A very simple and therefore very useful method is to have a packet for each witness. This packet may, for example, be held together with a paperclip and flagged with a piece of paper with the witness's name printed on it with a felt pen. This is all rather straightforward. The lawyer can deal them out (face down) on the counsel table, in ranks and files, something like the beginning of a solitaire game. Each packet will have the papers that pertain to that witness: his statement, the lawyer's notes, the original subpoena (plus agreement to appear).

Lawyers differ as to whether questions should be written out. Since he will have reviewed his files the night before, and probably again on the morning the witnesses appear, there should be little need of extensive lists of questions. If the order of witnesses changes, nothing could be simpler than to rearrange the packets.

For some reason, photographs seem easier to control (and much easier to keep secret) if they are all kept together in a particular envelope. So it is probably a good idea not to include photographs in these witness packets, even though, in the lawyer's plan, certain photographs are to be put into evidence by certain witnesses.

By proceeding with some such simple system, the lawyer can use up a number of witnesses rather briskly, with everything under control. The witnesses are all well prepared; sooner or later the time spent in preparing them will have its steadying effect. The case will move, the jury will center on the witnesses and the lawyer's personality can quietly fade from their notice. This gives to the defense witnesses the jury's undivided attention—which is no less than the witnesses deserve and entirely befits a workman doing his job.

§ 15.05 Suggested Rules for the Order of Defense Witnesses in General

With a large number, the order of witnesses will be controlled as much by their convenience as anything else. The main thing is that the witnesses shall have been well prepared. Beside that, order counts for *relatively* little, at least with respect to defense witnesses in general. (Special considerations affecting the defendant, his alibi witnesses, and certain other witnesses are discussed in §§ 15.06, 15.07, 15.08 and 15.09.) There are some general guides, but they are easy to overemphasize; the main thing about them is to keep them in perspective. These are intended as modest pointers, and not iron rules.

The first witness called by the defense should be a strong one and should have something important to say on a material point. It also helps if the first witness works in a

508 / POLITICAL CRIMINAL TRIALS

particularly sympathetic occupation. Other witnesses may be teachers, students, persons of widely differing tastes and activity; but if there is one who works with retarded children (and it is surprising how often among defense witnesses there will be several in this or comparable lines of work), then that witness is a fine first choice. Let the first one the prosecutor singles out—in the hope that he has a long-haired welfare freak he can isolate from the jury—be the one who works with retarded children.

Similarly, a witness with a recent military record which the prosecutor would envy may be an excellent first witness, provided the record is in sharp contrast with his present appearance and life style. Not only that, but get the record *in,* on direct. A little does it. One might think these things cannot often be arranged, but usually they can be.

There is a subtle value in contrasting a sequence of witnesses, e.g., men and women, or persons of straight political outlook interspersed with radicals.

There is a special value in a witness whose sex and occupation are refreshingly combined, and whose associations and political views stand in marked contrast to those of the defendant and possibly other defense witnesses. This combination is especially interesting if the witness also happens to be *good* as a witness, i.e., exhibits self-possession and poise. For example, an attractive young lady who is studying law (but not studying it to be a radical lawyer) may fit this category if the necessary part of her testimony will naturally reveal (e.g., because she was attending a particular meeting at the time she witnessed something) that in view of her associations, she would hardly have gone out of her way under normal circumstances to do anything at all for the defendant. If her testimony is also material on a point that really counts, and she is able to handle cross-examination well, then she is a strong witness indeed, possibly *too strong to use as the first witness.*

Some consideration should be given to using her as the last witness, or the last but one. This is especially desirable if there is a tentative plan that the defendant will be the last witness (see § 15.09), because the prosecutor may be faked out of position, deciding at the last minute that the defendant will not testify, so that he unloads some particularly difficult line of cross-examination on what he then supposes to be the last witness (last chance to use it). Something he had meant to save for the defendant. This will be a double pleasure to the lawyer if it turns out that the next to last witness is too much for the prosecutor, so that his cross-examination is not only misdirected but broken up.

From time to time there will be other defense witnesses who may be characterized as weak witnesses, simply because they saw only part of what they should have seen, because they are uncertain on some point, or because if pressed on cross-examination (or if not handled right on direct examination), they will say something which differs noticeably from the testimony of other defense witnesses. It is imperative not to attempt to change the testimony of these witnesses on such points; the only decision is whether to call them at all. If the decision is to call them, the lawyer will take the bad with the good. The question then will be whether to bring out the unfavorable point on direct, or wait to see if it turns up on cross. Either way, the witness is presumably worthwhile or the lawyer would not be calling him; regardless of whether it happens on direct or cross-examination, the witness will hurt the defense a little bit, while helping it somewhat. This kind of witness is a weak witness and should *always* be sandwiched between two relatively strong ones. A weak witness should not be left as a last witness for the day.

While it is certainly debatable how much importance the jury attaches to the last thing they hear (many trial lawyers feel the jury attaches no extra significance to the last thing they hear), nonetheless, a piece of bad news from a defense witness is hard on the *lawyer's* feelings. He may lose sleep over it and he should plan to make things as easy for himself as he can. Much better to round off the afternoon with a firm witness who puts things right.

§ 15.06 Special Note on the Positioning of Character Witnesses

Place them late. This is true because the defense case must stand on its own, and this kind of evidence does nothing to build the defense case. From the point of view that there is *only* the defense case, this is negative evidence. It has to do only with pulling someone down who is part of the prosecution case.

Rules are only rules, however, and notwithstanding that this is negative evidence, the lawyer *is* going to take out the main prosecution witnesses—that is part of what he has to do. So to keep the defense case in perspective, these witnesses should be assigned a rather minor role, late in the sequence. This means that a number of defense witnesses will have testified beforehand, lending the defense case considerable power and momentum, before this kind of evidence is worked in.

When they *are* put on, however, these witnesses should follow one another rapidly. This is true whether their testimony is limited to the witnesses' reputation for truth and veracity, or whether they are allowed to testify as to specific conduct, i.e., to events justifying their low opinion of the prosecution witness's character. When they follow each other, one after the other, the prosecutor may get goosey; if he does, he may blurt out in the presence of the jury that he wants an order limiting the number of witnesses who testify on this subject, offering at the same time to stipulate that if the next witness were called, he would testify that the reputation of the prosecution witness in question for truth and veracity is a bad one.

This is surprising to hear, but it happens, and may even happen after the third character witness, and there may not even *be* a fourth. This kind of outburst will be sweet to the lawyer's ears, because while the prosecutor may portray himself as a person interested in saving the court's time (he wants to be on the judge's side for once, and he hopes the jury is bored with these character witnesses), actually the prosecutor will place himself on the defensive in the eyes of the jury, as a person with something to hide. This role will be accentuated if the prosecutor has lately been fighting (understandably) to keep out evidence of specific conduct, as distinguished from evidence of reputation.

Another important benefit from grouping these witnesses together and placing them late in the defense case is that this arrangement allows much less time for the prosecutor to muster up favorable character witnesses to bolster his main witness. He can do it, of course, but now he will have to work harder at it, with less time remaining, and there will be other demands on his time which later on he might wish he had been more responsive to.

§ 15.07 Special Note on the Positioning of Photographers

It is quite important to hold this witness until late in the defense case. The reasons are more important than those mentioned above for the character witnesses, since these reasons concern the psychology of persuasion rather than mere tactics (whether the prosecutor will have enough time to find counter witnesses etc., none of which applies here).

By holding the photographer back, the lawyer allows all the main defense witnesses to put their evidence in first, which will build an extremely favorable climate for anything remaining in the defense case. After all, the main point is that the defense case is honest, and that things shown in this photograph happened that way. Usually a number of other witnesses can establish what happened, and could have done so even without the photograph. Let them do that first.

After they have testified very persuasively about what really happened, the defense case will have the full benefit not only of their evidence, but of the time spent in preparing them to testify and in getting a jury receptive to their testimony. The result will be that by the time the photographer appears, the jury already knows that what was shown in that photograph is true. There would be *no motive* to fake a photograph, since what is shown in the photograph is what actually happened.

When the photographer does appear, the allegation that this photograph was faked will long since have faded from the jury's concerns. The photographer will probably be an excellent witness, and he will have been especially prepared as to what to bring and what kind of cross-examination to expect. (See § 4.05[1].)

The photographer's sincerity, his straightforward account of how he took the photograph, how he developed the negative (or how he sent it to the drug store and got it back developed), how the prints were made and how nothing was tampered with—all this will be very persuasive evidence. More importantly, the impact of his testimony will be multiplied by the unstated point that the defense did not see fit to call this witness any sooner because there was no *need* to do so; the charge of "fake photograph" was *not* to be taken seriously, *not* something the defense had to feel concerned about.

The jury by now should feel that it was unnecessary even to call the photographer. It is a corollary that nothing else which that particular prosecution witness (the one who said this photograph was a fake) said under oath is to be taken seriously, either. By the time this photographer leaves the witness stand, the prosecutor will be embarrassed by the fact that his witness ever made the charge of "fake photograph." He will certainly have to drop it from his argument notes.

The situation might be quite different, had the lawyer called this photographer as his first witness, implying that he had to deal with that accusation before putting on the defense case, or worse yet, implying that all the following defense witnesses were somehow being produced for the purpose of backing the photograph rather than the other way around. This is one example in which the position of the witness *is* quite important.

The considerations here seem related to a curious phenomenon of argument in certain civil cases which has no analogue in criminal cases but the reasoning described above. In a certain kind of closing argument in a civil case, where the attorney has made a seemingly endless series of nothing points, and has only one rather mild point in his favor, the fact that he saves that mild point until near the end, and then mentions it *without attempting to play on it as being different from the other points makes it very effective.* This delayed positioning and low-keyed argument may shake a listener who was preparing to vote against him by suggesting that there must have been something after all to those dull arguments which went before, since otherwise the arguer should have been more enamoured of his one good point. Whether or not that is a valid rule in civil cases, it certainly controls rebuttal evidence in a political case, when defending against a charge of dishonesty on the part of the defense. Do it late, do it strong, and do not over emphasize it.

§ 15.08 Positioning Alibi Witnesses

If the defense is alibi and the defendant is being tried alone (not with co-defendants), then the alibi witnesses may comprise most or all of the defense case. That fact obviates any positioning problem. When there is a choice, the alibi witnesses should of course be last of all, except for the defendant (if he is to testify). This positioning requirement may be critical in group trials.

If several people are standing trial together, and only one has an alibi defense, then by agreement among the defense lawyers, his case should come on last. The alibi witnesses should come right at the end of the combined defense. This is absolutely essential, in order to leave little or no reaction time for the prosecutor's investigators. Once they know the details of the defendant's alibi, they will expend considerable work to break it down. They may have had little enough to go on until this time, but now they will try hard.

Three things will combine to defeat them: (1) careful preparation of those alibi witnesses who testify on behalf of the defense; (2) careful statement-taking from those few people who were *not* called as defense witnesses because they could not remember whether they saw the defendant or not (the statements serving to nail down that they cannot remember *whether* they saw him, as distinguished from not being able to remember *that* they saw him); and (3) minimal time for the prosecution to locate these people and try to convert them into prosecution witnesses.

If it happens in a group trial that there are two or more defendants with alibi defenses, their lawyers will simply have to get together and decide which alibi defense will go last and which will go next to last in the entire case. This should be done on the basis of where the more substantial disadvantage lies. The lawyers should discuss candidly whether either of them knows of a potential prosecution witness against his client's alibi, whom he is prepared to cross-examine but would rather that the prosecution did not find. If one of them is faced with the threat of having a nonwitness ("I do not remember whether I saw him there or not") being found and doctored into a prosecution witness ("I remember that I did not see him") then it seems sensible that he should have the relative advantage of going last.

§ 15.09 If the Defendant Testifies

This *is* an iron rule. If the defendant testifies, then he testifies last of all. The possible exception is that another witness may testify afterwards, if the subject of his testimony (including any conceivable cross-examination) is so remote from that of the defendant that he could not *possibly* say anything which would impeach the defendant. The reason for this rule is that if the defendant testifies at the end of the case, whatever discrepancies appear between his testimony and those of his own witnesses will seem benign. The defendant will be in the position of one who has been sitting there throughout the trial listening to all this testimony, and who now takes the stand to tell it exactly as it was, correcting (as may be necessary) certain understandable and minor mistakes made by his own witnesses. This actually will be the situation, and that is exactly how it should be presented and argued. But if by some mistake the defendant testifies in the middle of his own witnesses, and then one of them comes after him and testifies differently from the defendant, whether the point is material or not, it will seem that the defendant has been *caught off base by one of his own witnesses*. The prosecutor will have a field day in his argument, and this must never be allowed.

Equally important, a final decision as to whether the defendant will testify must be reserved until the end of the case. The lawyer must *not* represent to the jury at any time before the defendant testifies that he is going to do so. The lawyer may in fact change his own mind on this point several times during the course of the trial—he may have to do that—and he must be flexible. The thing to remember is, one can always tell the jury in final argument that it was not the defendant's fault he did not testify, but the decision of his lawyer, which would be true.

By putting on strong defense witnesses first and making the prosecution guess whether the defendant will testify or not, the lawyer forces the prosecution to hedge certain important bets and to spread their strength in ways in which some of it is bound to be wasted. From the prosecution's point of view either the defendant will testify or he will not. If he does, the most important part of the prosecution case will be to prepare an effective cross-examination for him. This takes many man-hours and much ability. If the prosecution do not know for sure that the defendant will testify (in other words, if the lawyer has refrained from making that promise to the jury), then they will have to make the decision of how much time to invest in preparing for cross-examination of the defendant, *without knowing whether the time will be well spent or wasted*. If they knew for sure that he would testify, the prosecution would go all out in preparing for cross-examination. As long as they do not, it is virtually certain that they will have to spread some of their time on other problems. They know as well as anyone that the defendant may not testify, and that there are other demands on their time in the same case. The result will be that the prosecution will spend some time preparing to cross-examine, and some time on other things, and whichever way the lawyer decides, some of their effort will have been wasted.

If the secret is *really* well kept, i.e., if the prosecution not only do not *know* whether the defendant will testify, but do not even feel they can make an intelligent guess, then an interesting psychological situation develops. The prosecutors will have some evidence which could damage the defendant considerably, and which they would much prefer to throw in his face at cross-examination; but it will be evidence of a kind which might legitimately be offered through the medium of some other defense witness. They can throw it at someone else about as well. As the lawyer gets closer to the end of the defense case, moving rapidly from witness to witness, the prosecutors may begin to sweat over their big decision.

If they gamble that the defense will testify, they have to abstain from using this evidence on any other defense witness. Their worry is that the next thing they hear is, "The defense rests." They may not be able to use their choice evidence *at all,* or at best do it with a broken back on rebuttal.

On the other hand, if they use it on some other defense witnesses, the evidence may be of only marginal admissibility through that witness, and that may look very bad. The temptation may suddenly be too much, and the long yellow pad slaps on the counsel table. The prosecutors suddenly throw their precious evidence in the face of the wrong witness. This is especially moving if it happens to be the last witness *but one,* the one remaining being the defendant.

The evidence may be something the defendant said or wrote about a subject of doubtful relevance to the crime charged against him. It might have been very telling with him on the stand, but addressed to anyone else (in this example) it is objectionable as hearsay, and a palpable attempt to smear the defendant. The lawyer's pleasure at scathing the prosecutors in the presence of the jury may well be mingled with other agreeable feelings: satisfaction that he has a strong witness in the box (he should have chosen a good one for this position), and considerable relief that his option is still open whether to put the defendant on the stand. The opportunity to rub the prosecutors' noses in their own mistake is doubly pleasurable when it provides the lawyer an opportunity to avoid one of his own. It would have been a mistake to have put the defendant on without uncovering this morsel from his past and discussing it with him; even now it might be a mistake to put him on at all—

depending on the evidence and the discussion. But fortunately there is time to decide.

§ 15.10 The Inadvisability of Calling Character Witnesses for the Defendant

The rule here is *don't*. The defendant has the right to put on evidence of his good reputation with respect to a particular trait of character involved in the crime charged against him, e.g., if it is a crime of violence, then he can present evidence of his reputation for peace and quiet. But according to the general rule, the prosecution may not inject this kind of evidence into the case unless the defendant initiates it.[1] There is no point in initiating it. Character evidence once in awhile may be helpful in certain kinds of criminal cases, where it is one person's word against another, where surrounding circumstances seem to throw little weight to either side, and where, from the nature of the crime itself, it seems important that the jury know what kind of person the defendant is. In those rare cases, a little character evidence may help.

In a political case, favorable character evidence would add exactly nothing to the defense case. The jury is already going to know much more about what happened than any character witness ever could know; when they have heard that much, they really do not care if someone comes in and takes the stand, who has no information about the case, and says (in effect) that he does not think the defendant would have done it because he is a nice guy. This will help not at all.

Moreover, the prosecution want nothing so much in the whole world as an opportunity to put on their version of the defendant's character. It is no answer in considering this question to think that the defendant is a good person, and therefore there is no such evidence available as the prosecution would like to find. This is by definition a political trial, and one absolutely certain ingredient of a political trial is that the prosecution have been energized by their hatred of the kind of person they suppose the defendant to be. They will probably find as many people who hate the defendant, who will testify to his "bad reputation," as the defense can find favorable witnesses.

The case must not be allowed to degenerate into a battle between slander and cross-examination, since cross-examination of character witnesses is notoriously difficult and unfruitful. It is an unsuitable job for the tool in hand— something like driving a railroad spike with a rattlesnake for a hammer.

If the lawyer finds himself even considering the use of character evidence on behalf of the defendant in a political case, that fact alone indicates that his thinking has taken a wrong turn, and he should go back and find the right one.

§ 15.11 Protecting Defense Witnesses Against Cross-Examination

The main thing to watch for is that the prosecutor will try to put words in the mouths of defense witnesses. The very fact that they *are* well prepared will drive the prosecutor in this direction; since the witnesses will not say what he wants them to say, he will, in effect, have to say it for them. The lawyer should listen attentively to the questions, and the first time he hears one which seriously misquotes the evidence he should stick the prosecutor with the objection that the question assumes facts not in evidence, or misquotes the witness's previous testimony. The lawyer should be sure that the question is serious enough that it counts; but when in doubt, stick him. This kind of objection not only tends to keep the prosecutor honest, it reminds the witness of what was said at the briefing, that it is necessary to sort out mixed questions, agreeing with what has to be agreed with, and rejecting what ought to be rejected.

A properly briefed witness will be able to do this anyway, but the witness should never be left to do 100 percent of the work. If a number of these questions come along, and even if the witness is doing a very good job of sorting things out, the lawyer should stick the prosecutor with objections regularly, to deter him from the practice. This kind of thing is too dangerous to leave it all to the witness, however well prepared.

A second main point is that the lawyer should watch for signs of fatigue, particularly when the cross-examination becomes prolonged. At the first indication of fatigue, on the part of the witness, the lawyer should break up the pattern of cross-examination. The first signs are *not* a tremor in the hand or a request for a glass of water. Generally, the first sign of fatigue in a witness is a kind of narrowing of attention, in which the witness gets more and more concerned with the prosecutor and less aware of other persons in the room. The lawyer can feel this readily, although the feeling is hard to describe. He can tell whether the witness is remaining aware of the jury, for example, and is directing answers to the jury or for the benefit of the jury. (This is not merely a matter of where he faces, physically.)

Although the witness will not be looking at the lawyer before every answer (having been briefed not to do this), there is considerable difference between the witness who is aware of the friendly lawyer's presence and of other people in the courtroom, and the one who is centering too much attention on the prosecutor.

The witness who is beginning to worry too much about the prosecutor usually begins to answer questions in a sort of rhythm. The pace of the questions is noticeably determined by the prosecutor, rather than by the witness's particular consideration of each question. This rhythm must be destroyed as soon as it is noticed. Anything at all will do for that purpose. A trial lawyer will always have potential objections running through his mind, most of which he will not use because they are too trivial or would tend to put the jury off. The lawyer should use them right now, and if no good objection occurs, simply ask to have the last question read back. It may very well have been asked and answered, an objection that is almost always appropriate in cross-examination, and is almost always overruled.

While making his objection and arguing it, the lawyer will give the witness a chance to collect himself. If it then develops that the prosecutor wants to work his way toward the witness box while asking questions (in a court which tolerates that practice) the lawyer should interrupt and ask that the prosecutor be directed to return to his seat or, at least, to the counsel table.

Needless to say, hovering over the witness should not be tolerated. The prosecutor may occasionally approach the witness and in most courts should ask the court's permission to do so. This will be for the purpose of handing an exhibit to the witness or of looking at some photograph or drawing together with the witness. But a certain type of prosecutor will do this, and then stand up slightly beside or behind the witness and continue to ask questions in that position. The lawyer should pull him down immediately by asking the court to direct the prosecutor to return to his seat and not to hover over the witness. Courts will almost invariably grant this request. Oddly enough, bringing the prosecutor back to the table tends more to deflate the prosecutor than it does to help the witness; most witnesses really do not care that much where the prosecutor stands, unless he threatens to get nose to nose with them.

It goes almost without saying that when the defendant is on the stand, the lawyer must be more protective, quicker, and snottier than he might be with any other defense witness. This is true because any slip on the part of the defendant will hurt the case and *continue to hurt it*, although a similar slip by another defense witness might not be serious at all.

If the defendant is being tried alone, the lawyer will of course have to take the risk of seeming overprotective of his own client, which is a small risk compared to the danger of letting something get by. However, if there are several lawyers at the defense table representing several defendants, the lawyer can go a long way toward dissipating this onus by having his friends make some of the objections on behalf of his own client. This shifts the disadvantage to the prosecutor for asking improper questions and prevents the lawyer from seeming too worried about what his client may say.

In a group trial, particularly one that has gone on for some time, one of the defense lawyers may have established a helpful rapport with the trial judge with respect to objections, so that his objections are more likely to be sustained than if they came from other lawyers at the table. This is the one who should make a few of the objections when someone else's client is on the stand. Lawyers should always scratch each other's backs whenever they can. No one resents it, and it feels good.

Footnote

[1] McCormick, *Evidence* 324 (2d ed. 1972); 1 Wigmore, *Evidence* §§ 55–57 (3d ed. 1940); Witkin, *California Evidence* § 329 (2d ed. 1966); see, e.g., Cal. Evid. Code § 1102 (West 1966).

Chapter 16

FINAL ARGUMENT

SYNOPSIS

§16.01 Essential Preliminaries to Assure a Narrow Target for the Defense Argument

[1] Conflicting Goals and Motivations of the Lawyers and the Judge

As the evidence draws to a close, the lawyers and the judge seemingly pull apart into a three-cornered configuration, each taking a noticeably different role from what he had shown before, each somewhat introspective and withdrawn, and each occupying a more professional relationship vis-à-vis the others than at any previous time in the trial. All of these changes have to do with the imminence of closing arguments. Everyone understands that the case is not going to argue itself, that the lawyers are going to have to argue it, and that no matter how well or badly things have gone for one side or the other in terms of evidence (and potential arguments), if one side makes a bad argument now, and the other makes a good one, the side with a good argument will probably win. That is a sobering consideration.

In this anomalous interval when witnesses are still testifying, but things are getting quiet in the interstices of the trial, there will always be an opportunity to make a motion or two, for conferences involving the lawyers and the judge, all of which happens in the absence of the jury.

Surprisingly, much can be done at this time to help the defense argument. The defense goals are to: (1) narrow the issues to be argued; (2) force the prosecution to reveal prematurely some of its main argument points; (3) get the judge to give advantageous jury instructions; (4) get a fair allocation of argument time between the prosecution and defense so that no one is imposed upon; (5) prevent the judge from dumping a lot of things on the lawyers to be done after hours, which would impede their argument preparation.

Decisions must be made now on: (1) whether or not there will be a motion for a directed verdict on certain counts; (2) the extent to which the motion will be argued in terms of real arguments and intellectual force on both sides, or whether sterile arguments should be used; (3) whether there will be a conference in chambers about jury instructions and what will be said there; (4) whether further instructions will be offered at the last minute or not; and (5) whether the trial judge will be humored in his usual request that everybody limit their arguments. In making all these decisions, it is important to understand how the goals and motivation of the lawyers and the judge differ, where they concur, and which (in a normal situation) can be expected to prevail.

The defense would of course like to narrow the issues as much as possible, by striking one or more of the counts so that not all the counts charged against the defendant will go to the jury. This is true because the defendant cannot be convicted of charges which are struck at this time, nor will he be penalized by having bad counts traded off against good argument points in the jury room. The prosecution naturally wishes to retain all counts, and to see the defendant convicted of as many as possible.

The trial judge—this *is* a three-sided conflict—is

somewhat in favor of seeing things come out the way his personal interpretation of the evidence indicates, but more importantly, he would like to see the jury shoulder the responsibility for all decisions, whether for acquittal or conviction. This means that in the normal situation, other things being reasonably close, the trial judge will deny any motion for a directed verdict. He confronts himself with the thought that while the evidence may be strongly in favor of dismissing certain counts, there is always (arguably) some thin evidence to the contrary, so that it would be a usurpation on his part to take the decision from the jury; the jury presumably will do the right thing and make a decision which will have greater moral force than any decision he might make.

Questions of timing usually present the closest identification of interests and feeling. The judge changes from a person keyed to rule on adversary problems of evidence to one touched by feelings. As a former lawyer, he probably appreciates that both lawyers in this case have come to the end of the case, that the arguments are terribly important to them and to the interests they represent. He would like to be reasonable with them, treating them as adults during what may be the only portion of the trial which enjoys this beneficence. On the other hand, he must suit the convenience of the jury, and he may want to promote the image of the judiciary as being fast moving, and, in any case, he would like to bring the case to a conclusion. At about this point, most judges will remember how it was when they were arguing cases and will instinctively approach the task of making one argument or the other. A judge will probably perceive the problem as a little tougher than it is (because the judge has not been thinking about it all through trial, as the lawyers have). He will decide that it is certainly a bitch, and he will be willing to make allowances for the lawyers.

A very few judges, however, who lack personal experience as trial lawyers or who are naturally malevolent, may use the conclusion of the evidence as an occasion to try to bully the lawyers into beginning arguments about ten minutes after the last witness leaves the bar. This is one time when the defense lawyer and prosecutor will automatically join forces to oppose such a judge. They have to make this son-of-a-bitch back down, so that matters can be concluded on a reasonable basis.

At the end of the case, all lawyers get extremely withdrawn, and they want nothing so much as time to examine their notes. Nobody wants to make a stupid argument. Nobody wants to be shoved before the jury on the wrong foot and be obliged to argue the case without time to put it together right in his head, without time to sleep on it, so that it comes out about 15 percent of what it should have been. Nobody likes to fuck up or be made to fuck up or, for that matter, to engage in a stumbling contest to see who can be slightly less ridiculous.

This community of feeling among trial lawyers is so strong that there is something like a widespread, tacit agreement not to interfere with argument preparation time. It seems perfectly acceptable to use trial timing as a weapon in other areas, e.g., to limit one's own cross-examination in the hope of getting an unprepared witness on the stand before lunch. In fact, one of the tenets of this book is the need to prepare (and try) the entire defense case on an accelerated basis in the hope of benefiting from superior methods. But for the most part trial lawyers do not sit around speculating which side would be hurt more if the arguments were all forced on a push-and-stumble basis. Everybody wants time to prepare his own argument, and that is that.

Accordingly the lawyer should certainly join the prosecutor in taking steps to assure that each of them has adequate time to prepare for argument. It is surprising how readily lawyers can make common cause against a judge who wishes to force a premature argument. They can do this without exchanging so much as a word, which is probably the best basis for these rare moments of cooperation. The lawyers have their ways. They have two general methods of positioning jury arguments: by arguing a motion, and by having a conference in chambers about jury instructions. These things are important for reasons unrelated to scheduling jury arguments, of course, but in the rare case where the judge wants "immediate" argument, they also serve the purpose of moving the argument to the following morning.

[2] Motions to Dismiss

At the end of the case, the defense usually has the right to move for directed verdict upon some or all of the counts. As a practical matter, this motion may only be arguable against one or two counts, out of a larger number. The argument has to be that there is no evidence from which a jury could reasonably convict the defendant of the particular changes involved.

These motions are of course quite difficult to win, owing to the reluctance of most trial judges to take responsibility for throwing out a count. If a trial judge doubts that the evidence is sufficient to convict, he would much rather have the jury return an acquittal on that count. He is not at all concerned with what may have to be traded for that acquittal in the jury room.

Since the defense lawyer *is* concerned about potential trade-offs in the jury room, any question as to whether to make this motion should usually be resolved in favor of the motion. This is not to say that there are no arguments against making a motion for directed verdict, particularly if the only reasonable target for the motion is a misdemeanor count which is included among several felony counts.

The argument against making a motion for a directed verdict on the only misdemeanor will be that if the jury cannot be persuaded to acquit on all counts, they may decide to do the next least harmful thing to the defendant, which would be to convict him of a misdemeanor while acquitting on the felony counts. Without a convenient misdemeanor at hand, they may instead convict him of a felony.

If the weakest count happens to be a felony, the argument against moving for a directed verdict on the felony might be that the felony count is so weak it will certainly be eliminated by the jury in any event, but it should stay in, for the time being, because all the wonderful arguments against that count will tend to bear down the whole prosecution case (by association).

While it is impossible to make general statements about a problem which always depends on a balance of facts, it is suggested that in almost every case, the arguments against making the motion will probably turn out to be a lot of precious nonsense. It should be one of the strong rules of criminal practice, that whenever a count can be struck on any basis whatsoever before it gets to the jury, it should be struck; the lawyer should not even bother to look back or give it a second thought. This is true because insofar as juries are concerned (as distinguished from appellate courts) weak points do *not* bear down strong ones with them. If the prosecution is caught with one count which is exceptionally weak, that fact may actually get in the way of the lawyer whose goal is to eliminate all of the counts. The reason is, a lot of trade-offs may occur in the jury room.

There is always the danger that after the lawyer has made his main argument against the really dangerous felony counts—the ones on which there *is* something to decide, the ones that could go one way or the other—two or three jurors who think of themselves as favorable to the defense will react to that argument by voting quite *hard* for acquittal on the one count which should have been thrown out anyway, while giving in (voting for conviction) on several counts where it really mattered, where their votes were needed. This danger can only be prevented by seeing that the rotten, weak counts never get to the jury in the first place. If the judge strikes the counts before he instructs the jury, it is not merely that the defendant escapes possible conviction on those counts, but more importantly, no one in the jury room can be tempted to sell out the defendant's case too cheaply by acquitting on just those counts.

Similarly, misdemeanor counts should always be struck when they are vulnerable. While it may be that lesser included counts offer a possible haven for the defendant if things go wrong in the jury room, it is probably more important to strike them. A powerful reason is, there is no way in the world that the jury can be insulated from the knowledge that certain counts have been struck. The indictment or information will certainly have been read to them at the outset of the case, and when counts are withheld from the jury, the judge will have to state that fact to them one way or another. While (like so many other trial phenomena) dismissals are susceptible of two interpretations, the better view would seem to be that a dismissal by the judge hurts the prosecution, in the eyes of the jury.

The point is often made that a jury may react against the defendant when a count is struck, on the theory that a directed verdict on one count strongly suggests to the jury that the other counts are valid. *But this is a political case.* One of the heavy timbers of the defense has been that the prosecutors rushed into court to get a conviction on any grounds and by any means, despite the defendant's legal rights. *Anything which confirms that position helps the defense.* A directed verdict on any count, even a misdemeanor, confirms it. In a political case, doubts should generally be resolved in favor of trying to get counts dismissed before they go to the jury.

The second advantage of arguing a motion for directed verdict (apart from the opportunity of having it granted) is flushing out prosecution arguments. The situation here is somewhat like a preliminary hearing, but with the shoe on the other foot. In a preliminary hearing, the prosecution must be sure to put on enough evidence to justify a trial, but will bend over backwards to conceal their main case. In arguing a motion for a directed verdict, the defense lawyer will have to commit enough argument to give the motion a reasonable chance in view of the likelihood of success; but regardless of the apparent likelihood of having the motion granted, the lawyer should not commit any of his main jury arguments at this time.

The jury is the whole show, and this only concerns something the judge is being asked to do, which affects only a part of the case, and which he is probably not going to do anyway. When kept in perspective, a motion for a directed verdict is nothing more than a preliminary phase of the jury argument, something designed to tidy up the field of operations before real action begins.

Actually, there is no need to commit any jury argument to this motion, because of the fundamental difference between arguments in support of a motion for directed verdict, and arguments to the jury. With the motion, the whole argument has to be that there is *no* evidence upon which a reasonable jury could convict. But in the main argument to the jury, the argument is that the jury *ought* to acquit, because of the way conflicting evidence should be interpreted, because of the absence of prosecution evidence where it was needed, because of the uncontradicted effect of defense evidence, and because of the presumption of innocence.

The argument for a directed verdict is necessarily aimed at a fraction of the People's case, since in the way of the world, it is not very likely that they will have gotten to the end of a political case without enough evidence to go to a jury on *some* count. The usual situation is that several counts out of a larger number have been left exposed to this motion by an unexpected turn in the way the prosecution evidence went in, by effective cross-examination of certain witnesses who disappointed the prosecution, and by the fact that certain counts were only marginal in the first place. The argument against those counts is, no evidence.

The main thing to remember about arguing this motion to the judge is that if he is going to grant this motion, he will probably think of it himself, before the motion is ever made. What he is going to listen for is not so much what the defense lawyer will say (continuing on the assumption he is going to grant the motion). The main problem being lack of evidence, he will listen mainly to find out if the prosecutor has anything to say, whether he can point to specific evidence supporting the charge.

If the prosecutor can point to anything, the motion will be denied. If he points to something that the lawyer thinks is not in the record, that is certainly a moment when the lawyer can do something for his client. He can use his superior notetaking system (see § 6.02) to find out the precise spot in the testimony where the prosecutor said the evidence went in, and if his summary indicates the prosecutor is fudging, call him on it immediately at the conclusion of the prosecutor's argument, or even interrupt him if necessary. It is then a simple matter to direct the court reporter's attention to the particular session of court, the witness, and the precise portion of the examination in which the evidence is supposed to have happened. The court reporter's readback will settle the matter. If the lawyer wins an argument addressed to the judge, he will probably win it because of superior notetaking, not superior arguing.

Although the lawyer will find little need to draw on his jury argument in support of this motion, *he should listen carefully to the prosecutor*, because the situation is not the same at all on the prosecutor's end of the table. The prosecutor's argument to the judge is going to be that there is so much evidence of the defendant's guilt on every count that there is no reasonable doubt of it. If this motion for a directed verdict is denied, the prosecutor is going to be arguing these same counts to the jury.

At the moment, the prosecutor is going to be rather desperate, *because even a judge who intends to deny the motion usually takes pleasure in concealing his intention until the moment of ruling.* As far as the prosecutor can tell *now*, the situation with respect to these counts must be treated as critical. The judge is *entertaining* a motion to dismiss. The prosecutor is going to lay on with everything he can, which means getting together every single thing in the record, which (to his mind) supports the charge, directly or indirectly. *The lawyer may have forgotten something in formulating his own argument, and before he goes to the jury and tells them how weak the prosecution case is on these points, it is a very good thing to find out whether the prosecutor has something really strong which the lawyer may have overlooked.* This is the time to find out. If the prosecutor has it, he will trot it out now. He is afraid not to. That is why the lawyer made this motion.

It goes almost without saying that the lawyer will take vigorous notes throughout the prosecutor's argument. Of course, the lawyer's notetaker will be there, as at any other session of court. But the situation *now* is, the case is coming to an end. The notetaker may or may not be able to catch up in transcribing notes on the closing testimony, let alone notes of an argument occuring only hours before the jury argument. The closer to the end of the case, the more the lawyer has to get it down for himself.

Of course, one incidental value of arguing a motion for a directed verdict is that it places a critical increment of time, which directly relates to the moment the jury arguments will begin, more or less within the control of the lawyer and the prosecutor. This argument cannot be made in the presence of the jury. So before the matter even starts, the judge will have had to decide when the jury is to come back. The longer the trial has been, the more difficult it is to assemble notes even to argue a motion for a directed verdict, let alone a jury argument. By testing the trial judge immediately before this argument begins, suggesting that a little time is needed to get notes together, and by making a reasonably generous time allowance for the motion argument, the lawyers (they are working together on this) can find out—if they do not already know—what the judge's attitude will be on allocating time for argument.

[3] The Absolute Necessity of Knowing What Jury Instructions the Judge Is Going to Give, Before Argument

Although certain jury instructions are common to all criminal cases, there will always be gross differences in the special instructions requested by the defense and the prosecution. Some will be handtooled and some will be boiler plate; but it will depend on the state of the evidence at the end of the case—what is actually in the record—whether they should be given. In most cases, the most important disputed instructions will be those especially drafted for the case by counsel, applying the most favorable interpretations of existing law—or the law as it ought to be—on behalf of one side or the other, as counsel see it (see §§ 8.03–8.05). It is imperative to know which of these disputed instructions are going to be given, which may still be given if they are modified somewhat, and which have been refused.

The lawyer will be relying on some of these instructions in his argument, but only on those which will actually be given. He will refer to the exact language of certain instructions during argument, so that when these are in fact given, that portion of the jury instruction process will constitute a continued phase of the defense argument.

As a rule, there will be no serious dispute with the judge on the point that all counsel are entitled to know what the judge is going to say before they make their arguments.

It is helpful if this point has been settled by statute; [1] in other jurisdictions, presumably, it is a matter of reason. The point is settled because if it were not already clear before argument began what the instructions would be, the lawyers might argue different versions of the law to the jury, which would lead to immediate and repeated interruptions by opposing counsel, with the necessity for the judge to rule on the spot. That would be unseemly, and since it would involve the same decisions by the judge as to what instructions he would give in any event, there is nothing to be gained and much to be lost by keeping the jury instructions secret.

Jury instructions are generally settled by a conference in chambers, while the jury is given a little holiday. Occasionally a judge will insist on doing it in open court, but the jury will still have its holiday. The procedure in chambers is probably better, since it can be done without a court reporter present. As a rule, everyone profits somewhat by the absence of a court reporter in these conferences.

The conference in chambers gives the lawyer his second opportunity to argue in favor of his own jury instructions. The first one was when he filed them, since he should have attached a written memorandum of authorities to the disputed instructions. The memorandum (see § 8.05) may prove decisive at the conference in chambers. The reason is, some of these instructions will have been drafted to apply existing case law, which will be carefully arrayed in support of those instructions; the others may be somewhat more advanced from the defendant's point of view, projecting favorably somewhat beyond the point of decided cases, and staking out advance positions for the defendant in those areas. The judge will certainly have read the authorities by the time of the conference.

As to the ones applying existing law, he will be forced to acknowledge outright that he intends to give them, or else come forward with some weak reason for not doing so. If he does the later, it may be helpful for the lawyer to press his argument in favor of the more advanced position, while deciding whether the judge's objection to those instructions, or his weak reasons for not giving the more conservative ones, have any merit at all. If they do not, the lawyer enjoys a considerable advantage in obtaining at least the conservative instructions, since it is rather hard for even a judge to maintain a stupid position during an informal discussion in chambers.[2] From the bench, an irresponsible judge can make his ruling and whack his hammer down and that is that. In chambers, he is closer to being accountable to somebody or something, if not the law.

On the other hand, if it seems that the judge may have some valid ground for objecting to instructions which the lawyer particularly wants, this is the time to decide whether little modifications can be made without doing serious harm to the instructions. The lawyer should take care to preserve whatever automatic objection he has, arising from the fact that he has submitted one instruction, and what is about to be given to the jury is only a modified version of that instruction.[3]

If the judge is responsible for the modification, the lawyer's right to the original instruction should be preserved for appellate purposes. In the jurisdiction where the defense has an automatic objection to all instructions not requested by the defense, including modifications of defense instructions, there is no need to do more. Where there is a need, the lawyer should say the magic words needed to preserve his appellate position, but he should do so with diffidence, with a court reporter present. After all, the main object is the jury. As long as the record is clear that the judge is insisting on whatever modifications are being made, and if the altered instruction is better than none, then the modification might as well be made and the instruction given.

The main thing to remember about most conferences in chambers that have to do with jury instructions is that they are a continuing cat fight. Set aside the problem of special defense instructions, the lawyer can always expect a carload of bad prosecution instructions, most of which will seem (under the circumstances) to have originated in some paranoid fantasy. These must be opposed according to the thoughts which naturally occur to the lawyer at the time. In many of these situations, the answer may be to see that the level of the argument is more or less proportional to the degree of outrage of the prosecution's instructions. This rapidly puts the situation out of hand, and in order to restore reason, the judge may start throwing them out wholesale (instructions, not lawyers) which is the measure of how they were conceived in the first place.

The result of all this should be a more or less fair set of instructions, containing a few of those prepared especially by the lawyer to reflect, at least in a conservative way, the maximum benefit which present law allows the defendant in resolving the disputes now in evidence.

There may also be an important secondary benefit. Assuming the lawyer was reasonably careful in drafting his requested instructions, and assuming also that the prosecution relied more on weight of numbers than on accuracy of citations, the judge should be left with the feeling that, of the counsel in *this* case, the defense lawyer is more likely to present solid instructions to the judge, whether or not the judge is persuaded to give them all, and that the prosecutor (in the matter of drafting jury instructions at least) is an agreeable but irresponsible bastard.

To the new lawyer, engendering this feeling in a judge may not seem like very much of an achievement. It is though. This conference is only the first round. What frequently occurs—especially with political cases, in which some of the instructions are necessarily unusual—is that the jury will come back after hours of deliberation, and ask the judge, what does this instruction *mean*? The instruction under scrutiny may well be a critical defense instruction which the judge insisted on modifying before he gave it, and which was the subject of concentrated oral argument.

At that time, the judge is going to have to decide what to tell the jury. In other words, he is going to have to give them a new instruction, clearer than the last one, on a pivotal point in the case. The previous discussion on jury instructions will now be resumed in chambers, only this time it will be quite clear that the result will determine the outcome of the case. Everybody will be tired, and tensions will be high. The judge will be somewhat on the spot and he will be looking for help from both lawyers. He will not be in the mood to listen to much, but he will be listening.

It is important at that moment for the defense lawyer to enjoy a substantial advantage over the prosecutor as a person whom the judge can respect and trust in drawing a reasonable jury instruction. The original conference on jury instructions with this judge—and in fact all such conferences with trial judges throughout a series of cases—should be conducted with this moment in view.

[4] Working with Other Defense Lawyers to Map Out Areas for Arguments: Allocating Argument Time

In a group trial, the defense lawyers will have to decide among themselves the order of defense arguments. Assuming lawyers are of approximately equal skill, defense arguments can be arranged in almost any order. However, since people vary a lot in what they are good at, even in the same field of endeavor, there is no particular reason to suppose that any group of lawyers will present a bland uniformity in the matter of arguments.

As with everything else in trials, there are preferred ways of arranging arguments—provided no one's ego is going to be hurt. All trial lawyers have strong feelings about arguments, and in the interest of human sensibilities, the group which has worked together up to this point will have to take full account of the feelings of its members. It probably *is* going to be important who argues in what order—that result is important to the case—but it is also very desirable that the lawyers reach that result by consensus, that they manage to sort themselves out with tact and consideration for each other's feelings. The following are suggested ground rules.

If there are only two defense lawyers in the case (or only two who will argue, by agreement of a larger number) then in general the one who is more at home with making an argument to the jury (i.e., the one who is "better") should go first.

If there are only two lawyers and they are about equal in skill, there may still be important differences in their usual ways of arguing. If one has a rather intense style and the other is low-keyed throughout his entire argument, then perhaps the intense one should go first. The reason is, intensity is an especially useful tool during the all important first three minutes—it helps get things done which can only be done then. Another reason is, a low-keyed man can follow an intense man without much difficulty. The low-keyed one will be rather welcome to the jury after what they have just been through. It does not work very well the other way around, though. The jury will wonder, why be so worked up about it?

If three or more defense lawyers are going to argue, considerations are the same. It is still true that the most experienced should probably go first, and that among lawyers equally qualified, the more intense one should go first. The last argument of the series is virtually as important as the first, but it is an argument particularly suited to a very experienced man whose style is always low-key. This is true because the emotional level of his argument is such that he can follow anybody; being experienced, he can anchor the whole line, adjusting and correcting for every single thing that has gone well or gone badly in any of the prior arguments, and if need be, weaving into his own argument every good point which every previous lawyer forgot to make.

With three or more lawyers, it matters very little about the sequence *between* the first and the last argument. Once these slots are filled, everything else drops into a natural order.

Another interesting question is, when several defense lawyers are arguing in series, to what extent should they agree in advance to divide the case? All that can be offered here are one or two general observations which *may* be helpful to lawyers faced with this problem. First, it may well be true that the only strict requirement of form that must be imposed on *one* argument, which need *not* be imposed on any of the others, concerns the first two or three minutes of the opening argument. Those minutes have to be used in a certain way, for the purpose of protecting the entire defense case, regardless of the identity of the client whose interests are technically being covered by the lawyer making that argument. It has to be done right then, and done on behalf of everybody. If it is not done correctly the first time, there is no corresponding opportunity during the first three minutes of any of the successive defense arguments, and the lapse would be more than just a little difficult to correct.

Another general rule seems to be, the only real danger in combined arguments is that something will *not* be said at all—not that it will be said too often. For that reason, it is rather dangerous to allocate whole areas among lawyers, so that certain areas are *excluded* from certain arguments. It is quite all right to allocate areas for purposes of emphasis, but that should not mean that other lawyers cannot step into those areas.

Of course there will be moments in a series of defense arguments when the jury is frankly a little bored, when they have heard it all before. That is all right, they are not going to penalize anybody for their being bored. Everybody is bored sometimes, and they do not get vindictive about it; so it is probably a better idea to accept the advantages of repetition—with everybody being sure that main points have been hit (or hit again)—than it is to risk leaving something unsaid.

A third rule may be that the opening argument should always include one or two extremely damaging arguments directed at main portions of the prosecution case, *even if those portions do not directly affect the client of the lawyer who is making the opening argument.* The jury expects a substantial part of the defense case to appear in the opening argument, and their minds will never be more receptive than during that argument. This opportunity *must* be used. For example, if the prosecution case depends largely on the testimony of two main witnesses (and with analysis, almost every case *can* be narrowed to a similar scale) then the lawyer making the opening argument had better see to it that before he sits down he has destroyed at least one of those witnesses. That is what he is there for. If he can manage to destroy two of them, that is fine.

The first defense lawyer to argue should destroy as much of the prosecution case as he conveniently can, and then, while he is at it, he should also say everything that has to be said on behalf of his own client. When he sits down, it should be understood that every other defense lawyer is free to make similar points—or the same points—on any of the same subjects which have already been covered.

The jury probably expects to hear arguments from all the lawyers in the case; the lawyers themselves have a deep need to make the arguments. There is really nothing to be lost by repetition, and even if it happened by some freak chance that *every* point made by three or four successive lawyers had been more or less covered before they stood up to argue, it is probably better for the defense case to have all those points made all over again. It is a way of vouching for something.

All of these arrangements among defense lawyers should be agreed upon in advance of the jury instruction conference, (which will probably take place in the judge's chambers). It is perfectly reasonable for the trial judge to want an estimate from each lawyer as to about how much time he will take in argument. He has to know that in order to decide when certain arguments will begin (so as not to prejudice either side unnecessarily) and in estimating when to give jury instructions. Most judges and trial lawyers agree that it is a poor idea to give a case to the jury late in the afternoon.

In making individual time estimates, one should be fair with the trial judge, but within the scope of genuine uncertainty, estimate a little on the high side. The only important thing here is, *never* agree to be limited to a particular number of minutes. Nine out of ten judges have no intention of cutting off the lawyer before the end of his argument; they would regard that as a very gross and unseemly thing. All they want is an honest estimate. With that tenth judge, one should be polite, but as tough as necessary. If the conference in chambers resembles some kind of showdown, then it is important to summon a court reporter and put it on the record. The lawyer should say very courteously that although his best estimate for argument time is an hour and twenty minutes (or three hours, or one day), still this *has* been a long case. The lawyer has been thinking about this argument since the case began, he has been organizing his notes, collecting his thoughts and condensing some of his ideas, and he will be doing that from now until the argument begins. The defendant's liberty depends on this argument, and the argument in turn depends partly on what the prosecution have to say in their opening argument. The lawyer has given the judge the best estimate he can, but he *does not wish to be bound by that estimate*. If it takes a little longer to say what has to be said, then he expects to cover all these points in his presentation to the jury, even if that means an argument of a different length than the one he now estimates. It may be longer, it may be shorter, but his duty to his client requires him to cover everything in his client's case which has to be presented to the jury.

Of course when the time comes, the lawyer cannot physically prevent the judge from disrupting his argument to the jury; but by calling a court reporter into chambers beforehand, he can totally dispel any representation by the trial judge (to the appellate court) that there had been some kind of contract or agreement among the lawyers. And then if the trial judge disrupts the argument, the lawyer should simply turn to the judge, in the presence of the jury, and state that he is not through with his argument and ask if the judge is ordering him to sit down. And if the answer is yes, he should explain to the judge (with or without the jury present, but with the court reporter there) that he is not through, and that he has several important things to say which must be said. He should estimate the time needed to finish and then ask the judge to (1) withdraw his order terminating argument, (2) explain to the jury that no prejudice was intended, and (3) allow the time necessary to finish. If the judge refuses, the lawyer should move for a mistrial on the spot. Fortunately, there are very few judges on the bench who are malevolent enough to force matters that far.

When time estimates have been made in chambers, there will be a question of how arguments in general should be allocated. In a group trial, the lawyers might as well face the fact that the arguments are going to start with an opening argument by the prosecution, and they are going to run along more or less continuously until they are finished. Once it is clear that the total argument time for the prosecution and defense exceeds one day, nice allocations between the two sides are probably out of the question.

In a case where the total argument time (prosecution and defense) is less than one day, most lawyers and judges would agree that the arguments should begin in the morning, or that in any event, they should be completed on the same day. It is a little unfair to split short arguments in any other way, i.e., by forcing the prosecutor to make his opening argument in the afternoon, while allowing the defense all night to think about it, or by forcing the defense lawyer to make his argument in the afternoon and allowing the prosecutor all night to think about his rebuttal. Most trial lawyers (not all) would be a little shy about asking for that kind of advantage, and most judges (not all) would be annoyed with anyone who did.

It is suggested as a matter of passing interest and as an unprovable hypothesis that even when this "advantage" is given to one side or the other, it really does not matter very much—the case is so full of detail, the obvious arguments are so well known anyway, and the deadening effect of studying someone else's argument is so marked, that one keeps looking for the great advantage, and gets only tired eyes.

§ 16.02 How to Organize the Defense Argument: General Suggestions as to Methods

[1] An Important Assumption

It is assumed that the defense argument will be positioned in accordance with what seems to be a universal rule: the prosecution, having the burden of proof, have the right to make both an opening and a rebuttal argument, with the defense argument sandwiched in the middle. Since the defense has but one argument, the prosecution are supposed to limit their closing argument to a direct rebuttal of things mentioned by the defense.

[2] A Matter of Perspective

The main thing to remember about the defense argument is that it is based on the case *as a whole,* not on what the prosecution may say in their opening argument. The defense argument should be planned at leisure, organized for maximum effect, and reduced to a written outline no later than the night before argument. By planning the argument based on the total case the lawyer exploits and multiplies the advantages accruing from a superior note-taking method (see § 6.02).

The argument should be organized with all evidence bearing on a single argument point (positive and negative) brought to bear on that point. The lawyer does not care who produced the evidence, or failed to produce it, except insofar as omissions of the prosecution may be given special impact.

It is a basic part of planning the defense argument that it will range widely and use material from all over; the defense argument will not directly relate to any specifics in the prosecution's opening argument. The defense argument is *not* involved in the limited scope of the prosecution's opening argument nor in its selective interpretation of the evidence. On the other hand, the defense argument will make thorough allowance for offsetting the *effect* of the prosecution opening argument—something that can be done without knowledge of its exact content.

[3] Helpful Work Methods

It is usually a good idea to review the trial notes at the end of every day, and to make marginal annotations (with a felt pen, or something equally obvious) wherever possible argument points occur. If the trial lasts more than a week, then part of every weekend should be set aside to review the trial notes for that week. The lawyer should have a section of his trial notebook devoted to ideas for possible use in argument. While the case goes on, he should have his secretary index the trial notes according to the names of witnesses and whether testifying in the morning or afternoon sessions, so that reasonably small portions of testimony can be found immediately.

When the time for the oral argument is getting close, the lawyer should make an effort to get things together in the evenings, rather than leave it all for the last night. On the other hand, there *will be* a last night, and that is probably the time when things are going to get done. The trick is to see that enough of the preliminaries have been done so that it is just feasible to complete the remaining work the night before the argument.

For those who have not settled on their own work methods, the following may be helpful. A convenient way of writing an outline for the argument is simply to follow the customary pattern for trial notes, and draw a line down the center of the page. The argument notes can go on one side, and afterthoughts on the other. The argument should be organized rather carefully; when the lawyer has taken a bad turn, and the notes do not read quite right, he should unhesitatingly go back and strike out the parts that feel wrong.

There will be too much argument to attempt originality in every part. For reasons discussed infra, it is probably a good idea to have an interchangeable, standard-form opening, common to all criminal cases. This may be written out in longhand at the beginning of each outline. In writing the main portion of the argument, it is sometimes useful to review notes of other arguments in other criminal cases. A successful argument from one set of facts will often find its counterpart in another. Old arguments may suggest new ones.

The conclusion of an argument (like the beginning) should be one with which the lawyer is very familiar. He need not write this out, he need not do anything about it, but having it ready to his hand enables him to continue working on the vital middle portion as long as energy is available. It is a good idea to stop well short of exhaustion. The mind goes on working anyway, once the problems have been clearly identified; in the morning, some other ideas may have developed.

§ 16.03   Form and Sample Contents of a Defense Argument

[1] The Special Importance of What the Lawyer Says at the Beginning

The most formative force shaping the defense argument is the *effect* (not the substance) of what the prosecutor will have said beforehand, not what the prosecutor may say afterwards. There is something almost magic here, buried in the psychology of the jury and the order of speaking: many lawyers plan defense arguments with their attention diverted from a serious danger to a comparatively trivial problem. They draft them with an eye to what the prosecutor will say in rebuttal, as if that were the real danger. This feeling often leads a defense lawyer to make a slow and cautious beginning of his own argument, building toward main points which he saves for the end, on the theory that by doing it that way, he gives the prosecutor less time to think about his response. This is a total mistake.

Most prosecutors can do relatively little damage in their rebuttal argument; they work under too great a disadvantage. By the time of the rebuttal, the emotional and intellectual climate of a courtroom has become attenuated almost to the point of desperation. Everybody will have heard what should have been everything in the case, and the jury in particular is not receptive to a lot of fresh ideas at that time. The prosecutor will then be under a strict injunction not to introduce new arguments in his rebuttal; if he attempts to do so, nothing is easier than to drive him through the floor with objections that are certain to be sustained immediately. Finally, when the prosecutor gets up to make his rebuttal argument, he will (if these recommendations are followed) just have received an unexpected damburst of emotion, which is going to make it rather difficult for him to respond even to logical arguments previously advanced by the defense.

The real danger lies in the opposite direction, in a predictable psychological drift toward conviction, which always sets in while any prosecutor is making his opening speech, and which is only partly related to what he is saying.

The prosecutor may not be aware of this drift; he may even think he is doing himself a favor by holding back some of his points in the hope that they will sound better on rebuttal. In some cases, the defense lawyer might be tempted to *write off* the prosecutor's opening comments as ineffectual. In actual fact, something is certainly going on, which can loosely be thought of as the result of the prosecutor's opening remarks, and which poses so much danger for the defense that the whole defense argument has to be organized to correct it immediately, at the risk of losing the case.

This psychological drift apparently arises from the jurors' original self-images, which were never directly invoked until this moment. The members of the jury originally thought of themselves as called by civic duty to enforce the law. By the time the prosecutor is getting up to argue, the case is practically over, the evidence is in, and the jurors understand that if the prosecutor has anything to say, this is the time for him to say it. This is the *first* time the jury has had a clear sense of how much these criminal statutes (the ones the defendant is suppose to have violated) are in their hands. The power to acquit or convict is the same as the power to write those statutes in the first place—as far as this case is concerned. That power is not going to be exercised without second thoughts, no matter how well the jury likes the defendant.

Oddly enough, the less the prosecutor has to offer in the way of argument, the more the jury will feel an urge to do it for him. If the prosecutor is inept, the jury will think, if this is the best the prosecution have to offer, what else could have been said? What is behind this prosecution that ought to be given weight even if it is *not* in evidence? More importantly, they wonder if those rules about the presumption of innocence really mean what they say.

All of this will be going on in the jury's mind, and if the defense lawyer makes the mistake of hearing only an inept prosecution argument, without sensing these unspoken responses, he will have done his case grave harm. The situation is like being in a small boat drifting on a lake on a pleasant day, with a light breeze blowing. A man sitting in the boat might not notice anything, but the air moves, the water moves, and things are not the same. If the boat has a glass bottom, the man might look down at the sandy slope a few yards below. He might see ripple marks in the sand, and be surprised to see them moving steadily under the boat. He may be in a trackless medium, but to something as real as the bottom, he is drifting. A criminal case is always drifting during the prosecution opening argument, whether that fact is apparent or not. It is drifting toward conviction, and the lawyer is going to have to do something about it.

This means that the lawyer's first remarks are the most important in his argument. Quintilian's beautiful explanation of how an advocate should begin an argument is worth remembering:

> "[H]e who has a speech to make should consider what he has to say; before whom, in whose defence, against whom, at what time and place, under what circumstances he has to speak; what is the popular opinion on

the subject, and what the prepossessions of the judge are likely to be; and finally of what we should express our deprecation or desire. Nature herself will give him the knowledge of what he ought to say first." [4]

The phrase "under what circumstances he has to speak" might be read as meaning, in the light of who will have spoken immediately before and will have just sat down when the advocate gets up to speak, and what will be the feeling of the judge [the jury] *at that moment.*

When the defense lawyer gets up to speak, he will have the jury's complete attention. He will have about three minutes in which to win the case.[5] This does not mean he must complete the argument in three minutes, it means he has two to three minutes in which to turn things around, stop the prosecution case once and for all, and induct the minds of the jury into the main channel of the defense argument. Unless he does this right off the top of his argument, the jury will withdraw a large measure of their attention and support, which will be extraordinarily difficult to reclaim later.

Slow-starting defense arguments—even though they turn meritorious later on—usually fail; this rule of thumb is reliable enough that one can slip into the spectator section of the courtroom during the trial of some criminal case about which one knows nothing at all, and listen to the first three minutes of the defense argument and form a fairly reliable impression as to whether it is still possible for the defendant to be acquitted.

[2] A Manner of Speaking

Everyone has his own manner of making arguments; those who have not yet settled on one may find these suggestions helpful.

The beginning should be immediate, direct, and extremely personal, said *to* the individuals in the box, not spoken *at* them. This is no time for any measured or mannered style of speaking. People who take themselves and their "speech" too seriously, rather than the case, come off pompous. Since any pause tends to swell like a heated raisin, it seems a good idea to prevent there being any, and to do this one may say the formal words which begin an argument while actually walking the last two or three steps to where he will stand.

It should go almost without saying, that the lawyer should move to a point close to the jury box, preferably close enough to touch it, and that he should avoid standing near any lectern, unless there is an unambiguous court order requiring lawyers to "use the lectern" in argument. And in that rare and stupid situation, the lawyer should stand to one side of the lectern so that nothing is between him and the jury. An arm resting on the lectern will satisfy the martinet who put it there.

The lawyer should stand naturally, and after he gets into his argument, he can move around. He should look members of the jury in the eye, ignoring nobody for long, and he should talk directly to them. The lawyer should make sure his eyes are wide open—this is just as important as looking the jury in the eye. He should also make sure that he gets his mouth open while he is talking, because if they cannot hear the words, there is no point in making the argument. Every syllable and every consonant should get full value. He should change his voice level, pitch, intensity, and speed from time to time. He should use inflections to convey meaning (nothing bores the jury like a continuous drone).

The main thing about the opening phase of the argument is that the jurors' minds are very much with the lawyer at this point. Their minds are working rapidly and they can assimilate information faster now than they can later. They are *listening* to what he has to say, and so it is essential that nothing go down haltingly, but that he talk directly to them, say what he has to say to *them* as if no one in this case had spoken before, as if there were no one else in the room.

It is helpful to use the same introduction in all criminal arguments. The same one will certainly apply in all of them, and its wording and easy delivery are far too important to leave to spontaneous composition.

[3] A Suggested Introduction

The introduction should be in the lawyer's own words, and these words must feel exactly right to him. Repetition in court (without notes) will show what is natural; notes can be revised to match what is said; and what is said can be improved from case to case by careful thought.

Some personal adaptation of the following may prove adequate:

May it please the court, counsel, ladies and gentlemen of the jury . . .

You may remember that at the very beginning of this case, you made certain promises and you took an oath as jurors. The time has now come to remind you of that oath, and also to hold you to your promises.

Your oath was to keep an open mind and not to decide this case until it was submitted to you. So if any of you has already decided guilty, then he or she has violated your oath as jurors.

It is quite important not to apologize (by any nuance of expression) for making that point. The lawyer should not drop his voice or hurry through it. Someone in the jury may have done that. Do not pause for effect, but say it to them and mean it when you say it.

Another promise was to follow the instructions which his Honor, Judge Hardtack is about to give you tomorrow morning.

Another promise was to decide this case on the

evidence and not on the basis of guesswork or speculation, and that promise turned out to be quite important. We will come back to that.

Another promise was not to allow any personal feelings about dissidents or students or permissiveness or the state of society to influence your judgment on the question of guilt or innocence, but that you would treat this case as an old-fashioned criminal case.

Another promise was to give the defendant the benefit of the rule that he is presumed to be innocent unless and until the People fully meet the requirement of proving every element of the offense charged beyond a reasonable doubt and to a moral certainty.

It is usually a good idea *not* to leave all these commitments hanging just on the basis of personal promises. People do not like to be committed like that. They probably feel in back of their minds that they had no choice but to agree with a lot of statements during the voir dire examination. And, their minds are *not* moved to total acceptance of of the presumption of innocence. Not just yet. It is at this point that many lawyers may begin to lose a jury, because they assume that the abstract notion of reasonable doubt is acceptable and attractive to them. This may help:

I am not going to put it to you just on the basis of personal promises, that you *said* it and now you have that personal obligation because you *promised*. As with everything else, there is a *reason* for the rule.

The *reason* is, it is harder to prove that you didn't do something than it is to prove that you *did*. For example, you may remember . . . something may have happened to you when you were a child . . . You may have been alone in a room, or you may have been with a playmate, and a cup fell out of the cabinet or a dish was broken. Maybe your playmate broke it, maybe you had nothing to do with it. And before you knew it, there may have been an adult in the room saying, *why* did you break the dish? And before you could say anything, perhaps the next thing that happened was that you were shaken until your teeth rattled.

It's harder to prove that you did *not* do something than it is to prove that you did, and that is the reason for the rule.

Also, you may be asking yourselves what is meant by "reasonable doubt." Of course you will be instructed on that by Judge Hardtack, and you will take your instructions from him, and those will be put to you in the traditional measured phrases of the law. I am not going to recite the one on reasonable doubt now. But in the meantime it might be helpful if we give you an example from everyday life, of our understanding of reasonable doubt.

We suggest that it simply means that if you think about this case a week from now, a month from now, or a year from now, and your first impression and recollection is that *right was done,* then the case was decided beyond a reasonable doubt. Or perhaps if you find yourself awake in the middle of the night, as I sometimes do, staring at the ceiling and thinking about things in general, and your mind suddenly comes on the subject of this case, and because your mind is tired, you have no mental defenses and you are not prepared to brace yourself for the recollection, and if *then* the first feeling you have about this case is that it was decided *right,* then it was really decided on the basis of proof beyond a reasonable doubt. But if the first feeling you have is "Oh God," then it was not. That is our view of reasonable doubt.

When this case is submitted to you, you will have to ask yourselves how this evidence looks to you in the light of reasonable doubt and moral certainty.

That is why I am here—to give you our view of the evidence. No one can tell you how you must decide anything in this case. You are the jury and no one can tell you that you have to do this or have to do that. No one can tell you; we can only suggest to you, and you have to decide how the evidence looks to you.

Before I start, I would like to suggest one thing. You are not in the position of a batter in a baseball game, who is standing at the plate and has to decide, right then, whether to swing at a ball, whether it is going to be a strike or not. You are not in that position.

You do not have to decide right now, while I am talking, whether my suggestions are meritorious or not. I may mention points that are important to me, and you may give them less value, and I may mention other things which you would value quite differently, and you may have in mind points that I do not mention at all.

I suggest that you take these ideas as we present them, and just mentally wrap them in brown paper and lay them to one side. Don't decide right *now* whether these are good points or not. *Later on*, in the jury room, when there is time to discuss it, unwrap these points and put them on the table, and give them whatever value you think they are worth at that time.

No matter how we approach this case, insofar as it involves [defendant], the most important, serious part concerns the accusation of [e.g., conspiracy, arson: the *main* charge (see next section)].

[4] Transition to the Main Crime Charged Against Defendant

This transition should be made very quickly because the jury has been expecting the main points of the defense argument and has only deferred that expectation because the lawyer had something important to say in his beginning remarks. But those remarks have made their point now, so the slightest faltering, or casting about for where to go next (perfectly permissible later) will risk losing the jury's attention.

This transitional part of the argument is the one which will have taken the most time to prepare, although very little time is required to *say* it. The immediate object is to lead the minds of the jury into the main defense case, at the same time destroying what may have been a natural impression engendered by the prosecutor, that somehow most or all of the prosecution evidence supports the prosecution case. Actually, it is seldom true that very much of it supports the critical points of the prosecution case.

For example, in a group trial, if this defendant's position is that he was somewhere else (i.e., alibi), the critical part as to him is whether he was present at the time and place of the crime. In a large trial, it may be that only one out of as many as fifty prosecution witnesses actually claims to have identified *this* defendant at the scene. If he is also a main prosecution witness (whose testimony damages many other people), *splendid*. This opening argument made for one defendant—but actually made for the whole defense— can then be centered on that witness, impeaching him with evidence from the entire case, contradicting him with all the alibi evidence concentrated in favor of this one defendant, capitalizing on mis-identification of this defendant as showing unreliability regarding other defendants, using mistakes about other defendants to reinforce his mistakes about this one—a damning, overwhelming interplay between general and particular. All of this depends first upon narrowing the issues, then upon concentrating the evidence. The purpose of the transitional phase is to narrow and concentrate.

In making the transition, the lawyer should identify the "main" charge against the defendant, explaining why (if this is the case) it actually hinges on only one fact issue or the testimony of *one or two witnesses;* he should then explain the law and the legal defense upon which he relies; and above all, the lawyer must start explaining to the jury *as he goes along* why this point or that point *favors the defendant.*

In a few kinds of cases, when the lawyer is explaining to the jury what is the main single issue they must decide, the explanation may *not* require any particular legal elaboration as to the nature of special defenses. For example, if the defense is alibi, it is quite obvious what the jury has to decide. If the charge is throwing a fire bomb at a police vehicle, and the defendant testified that he was present, but did *not* throw it, no elaborate explanation is necessary as to the nature of arson or certain arson defenses relevant to barn burnings.

But in most political trials, a careful legal explanation will be necessary for that portion of the law which states a main defense. This legal defense will undoubtedly be something that the jury would not know unless they were told, and they must be told immediately. They must be told *before* any discussion of the facts, so that they will know *how the facts fit in,* and why particular points fit into this lawsuit so as to favor the defendant.

It is absolutely imperative that the jury be kept fully aware of all the points that favor the defendant *as they are made,* so that they will share the lawyer's own sense of what is being accomplished as the argument progresses, so that they will go with him all the way.

The jury expects arguments for the defense, and they want them *now.* The fact that they have probably been sympathetic to the defense throughout the case only lends emphasis to this expectation. They may want to help the defendant, but they do not yet know how to help him.

The lawyer must tell the jury exactly what facts to look for in order to acquit the defendant, and then carefully lead them to find these facts. No one else is going to do it. That is why it would be a very great mistake to present things the other way around, e.g., by first trotting a lot of favorable facts before the jury in argument, and then surprising them with a little law at the very end; this might have the effect of making the lawyer look like a magician (in his own eyes) but overlooks the fact that it is the jury who are doing things.

The right way is to simplify the issues, state the law on which the lawyer relies, and then slam in factual arguments relevant to the law, which favor the defense, making sure that every factual configuration fits in before the next one is applied. It is exactly like building a wall.

Before identifying the main issue the jurors have to decide, the lawyer should first remind them what is the main charge against the defendant:

No matter how we approach this case, the most important, serious part of it concerns the charge of [e.g. arson].

This is true for a couple of reasons. First, arson is a very serious felony.

Second, the prosecutors have staked their whole case on this charge. They asked you to believe at the beginning of this case, in their opening statement that they would prove that Mr. [defendant] committed an assault at about 7:00 and attempted to commit burglary a few blocks away at about 8:00—those were Count I and Count II. *But the opening statement was the last you ever heard about that.* By failing to offer any evidence that he did either of those things, throughout the entire case, the prosecution have tacitly conceded that they never had any case at all in Count I and Count II. *They did not even mention it in their argument.*

That is what I mean when I say that they have

staked their entire case against this defendant on the accusation of arson which is Count III.

That is a point in favor of the defendant, because it means that the prosecution have not prepared their case nor stopped to ask themselves if their evidence resembled their accusations.

Similarly, the prosecutor has offered no explanation of [defendant's] alleged attack on Officer Headbust except the argument that he must have wanted to get away because he was already guilty of arson.

As you will be instructed, the crime of arson, as applicable to this case, means unlawfully, willfully and maliciously, and feloniously setting fire to a building. The prosecution has the burden of proving every element of that felony beyond a reasonable doubt.

But the prosecution cannot use *guesswork* to prove any part of it, only evidence. Either he poured the gasoline on the lathing or he didn't. If you find that he did, then find him guilty. If you find that he did not—in the light of reasonable doubt—then you must acquit him.

What I mean by *guesswork* is the idea that if the defendant knows what the word "pig" means, he must be guilty of arson. Or the idea that if he greeted people when he arrived where the crowd was gathered, he was actually fomenting a conspiracy and was somehow involved in what happened later. That is not the law, and that is not what this case is about. That is trial by rumor, not by evidence.

Everything relied on by the prosecution concerning the accusation of arson depends on the truthfulness and accuracy and impartiality of Officer Headbust. This is true because nobody corroborates his story that the defendant brought this bottle of gasoline and threw it into the recruiting office. The other officers [A,

B, C, and D] did not see *any* of this or any details which make the difference.

This is a point for the defendant, because it means that in flat contradiction, the defendant is corroborated and Officer Headbust *is not,* and equally important, it means that surrounding circumstances take on some weight. . .

The foregoing example of a transitional argument is based on a *simple* factual issue. In other words, this argument assumes that there is *no special legal defense,* i.e., the only necessary reference to the elements of the crime is to touch on them once and go straight on into evidentiary problems. The defendant either did it or he did not.

The situation will be very different if the defense is mostly a legal one, e.g., not guilty of resisting arrest by reason of self-defense. In this situation, the lawyer will have fought very hard to get the right jury instructions given, and now that he knows they *will* be given, they become the most important part of his argument. This kind of case cannot possibly be won except by bearing down hard on the legal elements of the alleged crime and the defense to that crime. This must be done in the transitional part of the argument. The lawyer must *never* jump into the facts first and leave the law for later—he must explain the law first, very clearly so that the jury will know, as they go along, what facts are relevant, and what facts must be accepted or regarded as unproved in order to acquit the defendant. It is no exaggeration to say that if the lawyer follows some other, cute little sequence, some friends on the jury will hate him for it.

The lawyer should write this part of his argument with the actual jury instructions spread before him, so that he can use language in his argument which comes from those instructions. He should explain to the jury what they are going to hear (first) in terms of the prosecution instruction. This is the one that says that doing a particular act is a violation of a certain statute, which is a crime. This instruction may also state that for this violation to occur, a particular element (e.g., a specific intent) must exist at the same time. The lawyer should hammer at that element, and tell them exactly what it is.

He should then go on and explain that on the *other* hand, the jury will also be instructed concerning a defense to that charge. The lawyer should stick closely to the defense instruction to be given, which, if it was well-drafted by him, will be written in layman's terms.

For example, if the main felony is resisting arrest (rather than arson, the previous example) and the defense is unreasonable force and self-defense, the lawyer might say something like this:

On the other hand, you will also be instructed that it is not part of any police officer's duty to use excessive or unnecessary force in arresting a person—in fact, an officer who does so commits a public offense—and under the law of this state, the person being arrested is entitled to protect himself against the officer's excessive force, and is himself entitled to use a reasonable amount of force to protect himself. If he uses no more force than is necessary, he does not commit this crime. In plain English, he is entitled to a verdict of not guilty.

In this case, defendant is charged with resisting, obstructing, and delaying Officer Headbust. If he did that, and had the specific intent to do that, he would be guilty of violating this section.

But if he did the very same actions, for the *purpose of protecting himself against the police,* then he is entitled to a verdict of not guilty.

Please remember that the prosecutor has the burden of proving every element of this crime beyond a reasonable doubt and to a moral certainty.

This part is absolutely imperative. The lawyer must

tell the jury *how* to help the defendant, so as to convert their good wishes into the intellectual means of effectuating them.

The next step, which recurs throughout this defense argument is *explain why this particular point is a point in favor of the defendant*. This thought should be expressed as often as possible, with respect to different points and different *kinds* of points—now is none too soon:

> This is actually a point for the defendant, because on the issue of self-defense, which is the only one you have to decide, the evidence is very clear, and it means you do not have to get involved in certain extraneous issues, such as whether the police were right or wrong in arresting the defendant.

At this point, the lawyer should be very careful to specify what tempting issues are *out*. This is the time to kill off the possibility that hours will be wasted in the jury room, in some absolutely irrelevant, tangential discussion, which could have been foreseen and quashed.

For example, if this is a case in which the defendant, long before the trial, pled guilty to participating in an illegal assembly, in order to go to trial on the sole issue of whether he resisted arrest, *this is the time to remind the jury that they are not to get involved in deciding what the defendant was doing there, whether he was right or wrong*. In fact, this is an excellent time to remind the jury that the defendant has already pled guilty to another (misdemeanor) count, and that they must not be concerned in that matter at all, but must instead trust the operation of the law to see that justice is done there. (There is no need to go into the sentence actually imposed in that court.) This can bring the lawyer back to his strong point, that the jury has only one main issue to resolve.

Having explained the law favoring the defendant, and having eliminated side issues, the lawyer should remind the jury *again* that it is the burden of the prosecution to prove every element of the offense beyond a reasonable doubt, including the burden of proving beyond a reasonable doubt that facts establishing this particular legal defense (the one just described) do *not* exist. A moment's thought will show this prosecution burden to lie in their duty to prove that the defendant did something "unlawfully" (or some word from the statute). "Unlawfully" means without a legal defense.

Having done all this, the lawyer is in the same position as where there was only one simple factual issue (example cited previously). This position is that *where careful analysis of the case justifies doing so*, the issues must be narrowed so that proof of the prosecution case depends entirely on the evidence of one or two main prosecution witnesses. The lawyer should be very sure that he is not overlooking something when he narrows the issues like this, but, as a general rule, that is the way the evidence will break. Not all of the prosecution evidence bears on the critical point. In a political case, the usual rule is that only one or two witnesses, and only a very little evidence really does bear on the critical point; the rest is *speculation*. And having pointed out to the jury the part that was merely speculation (e.g., the examples cited earlier in this section that the defendant knew the meaning of the term, "pigs") the lawyer can center exactly on the testimony and other evidence to be discredited.

At about this point in the argument, the lawyer will have used his critical two or three minutes of opening, and he will certainly have stopped the dangerous drift toward conviction resulting from the prosecution opening argument, which it was so essential to stop. At this moment, the lawyer should be getting to the guts of the prosecution case, which is exactly where he should be with this much elasped time.

[5] Some Suggestions as to the Conduct of the Main Argument

The object in the main argument is to do maximum damage to main prosecution arguments as soon as possible, then use that accomplishment to cast doubt on lesser prosecution arguments, and to reinforce lesser defense arguments, leading to the general conclusion that the presumption of innocence is hardly necessary in this case, since the defense could eventually prove innocence by a preponderance of the evidence; but that in any event, the presumption is decisive for the defendant.

The following are samples of arguments that are available for use in common situations.

[a] Where Testimony of Uncorroborated Prosecution Witnesses Opposes Corroborated Testimony of Defendant

[i] Mentioning the Conflict of Testimony

It is sometimes helpful when focusing a large number of defense witnesses against the critical part of the prosecution case, to refer to the major conflict of direct testimony, and then move into circumstantial evidence. There are several reasons.

First, the jury is most aware of conflicts in direct testimony. If two prosecution witnesses claim they saw the defendant doing something, and eleven or twelve defense witnesses testify that they were in a position to see and that he did no such thing, the jury is well aware of that conflict. Each of them has his own impressions of the witnesses, which, it is to be hoped, are very favorable to the defense. Each is also aware of any disparity in numbers between defense and prosecution witnesses. There may be more defense witnesses, as a result of using a mosaic pattern of proving things. But the jurors are also at the point of having to decide that a couple of prosecution witnesses, probably police officers, were lying, or at least badly mistaken.

At just this point, some lawyers begin to lose touch with the jury. They do this because they make two gross mistakes. The first mistake is to itemize all the testimony of all the defense witnesses, and invite the jury to agree that these are all nice people. Itemizing testimony like that will bore the jury out of their minds; and asking them to agree that defense witnesses are truthful is approximately the same as asking guests to applaud a recital by the youngest child in the house. The guests may have had a favorable impression of the child, but that is a wonderful way to ruin it. Second, it is even worse to point the finger at prosecution witnesses and say that they have been lying. The jury may decide that, but the lawyer must never say it.

It may be a good idea simply to point out to the jury that there is a substantial conflict in evidence. This will have been accomplished (in the example previously cited) by pointing out that the whole prosecution case depends on one or two witnesses, and that these witnesses are *not* corroborated by certain other prosecution witnesses. The lawyer will have pointed out that this situation favors the defendant, because the defendant *is* corroborated.

The lawyer may go so far as to tell the jury that they have seen the defense witnesses, and that they are entitled to form their own impressions of them. He should mention a jury instruction which sets out standards for judging the credibility of witnesses, one of which is the demeanor of the witness on the stand. This instruction will almost certainly advise the jury not to decide a factual issue on the basis of a mere plurality of witnesses, but rather on the basis of the greater persuasive power of the evidence; the same instruction will probably say that the jury is not free to disregard the testimony of a large number of witnesses out of whimsey or crotchet.[6] In short, whatever the jury instruction is going to have to say on the subject, the lawyer should say it first, in his own words.

He should conclude these references to the conflict of witnesses by pointing out that, while nobody can tell the jury that it must do this or must do that, the jury would be entitled to conclude that from the demeanor of the defense witnesses (apart from their number) that their persuasive power was great enough, that the testimony of each of them was not just a point in favor of the defendant, but more than enough to create a reasonable doubt, and to justify acquittal.

[ii] The Value of Surrounding Circumstances

It might be helpful to continue something along this line:

However, we are not going to leave it just on the basis of one person's word against another's, that you have to look at these witnesses and decide to believe this one or that one, by the color of their eyes, or just on the basis of their direct testimony.

Actually, there are two kinds of evidence in court, and as Judge Hardtack will instruct you, circumstantial evidence is just as good as direct evidence. At least it is in court. There is an impression on television that circumstantial evidence is bad, but legally speaking, it is just as good as the other kind.

In a case like this where there is a head-on conflict of evidence, there is a special premium on the small facts . . . the little facts . . . the ones that are not even noticed as a general rule. But as we all know, little surrounding facts are always there, and when one examines them, they *do* tend to corroborate one side or the other.

After all, somebody has to be right, and somebody has to be wrong. First you will find one fact, and then another, and these little facts will indicate what really happened, because they will be consistent with one version, and inconsistent with the other, and pretty soon, there will be a definite trend, and finally a tide of surrounding facts and circumstances, which indicates whose memory is better [please note, *not* who is lying].

The special virtues of this kind of argument are, first, that it is true about circumstantial evidence; and second, this approach affords the lawyer a means of talking to the jury about some things that were not very obvious to them until now. After all, the lawyer has had time to think about these "little facts." The jury has not. This is certainly an area in which the lawyer can tell them something, and they will listen closely.

Depending on how many little facts the lawyer has been able to assemble, it may be a good idea to use some of the very small ones first. This is true because if they are used later, they will look like nothing. With everybody's attention on them, they will get some value now. Also, they serve to create a little pause, a little tension, before the strong facts are produced. In this situation (where the prosecution witnesses are not corroborated) the greatest "small fact" that can be thrown in their faces is the *negative* fact that no one corroborated the main witnesses. If they were telling the truth, they would have been corroborated. A negative circumstance, but killing.

It is better to lead up to this big negative fact, and if possible, couple it with another big negative fact, assuming another can be found in the same case. Just before springing the negative facts, it may be helpful to use some personal, chatty little anecdote which has to do with the value of negative evidence. The one I like (described in [iii] infra) may be referred to as "barking dog."

It is time to take a look at the small facts. A lot of thought must be devoted to the subject of these small facts (surrounding circumstances); this means pouring over trial notes. Planning this part of the argument is time consuming. There is no other way.

For example, in a case in which defendant was surrounded by police at the critical moment, so that his actions are known only to himself and one or two of those officers, and other persons in the vicinity could not possibly see what was going on (and have not claimed to see it), then the "surrounding circumstances" (those preceding and following what could not be seen directly) will have to be facts testified to by scattered witnesses on one side or the other.

Typically these will be things the defendant said and did just beforehand. There will also be testimony as to where the defendant was, where other people were, and who moved where. Facts consistent with the defendant's recollection will be things indicative of his actual state of mind, things wholly inconsistent with prosecution claims.

Much of the favorable evidence concerning defendant's state of mind will come from defense witnesses. That is all right. They will not be contradicted, or most of them will not, because the prosecution will have finished their case before the defense case began. And in rebuttal, the prosecution never think or take the trouble to attempt to rebut small "peripheral" facts, such as what somebody said two minutes before the action. Their power to slant testimony and muddy water is not applied to this part of the case, and therefore this evidence is uncontradicted.

It should be presented just that way, as uncontradicted evidence. The lawyer can then say, e.g., that one of the facts which is not contradicted is that, the defendant was doing his best to pacify a crowd and move it out of the area rather than—what would be more consistent with his other alleged acts—incite it to riot. This is indicated by the fact that he said this, and that approximately seven witnesses have so testified.

[iii] A Barking Dog

Before introducing negative evidence, it is sometimes a good idea to change the pace and tone of the argument and make sure the jury's attention is there, while at the same time bearing down on the next point, which in this instance happens to be negative evidence.

[*after a definite pause—looking around, changing breathing—long enough to indicate a transition, and long enough to cause some concern that maybe the lawyer has forgotten what he is going to say next*] You know, I don't often get a chance to quote Arthur Conan Doyle to a California jury, but this seems to be the time, and so I think I'll do it.

I don't know if you read the Sherlock Holmes stories, but when I was a boy I did—I read them all. There was one—I think it was called, "The Case of the Barking Dog." At the end of it Holmes and Watson were sitting around discussing the case, and Watson said, "Holmes, how *did* you manage to unravel it?" and Holmes said, "Very simple, the barking dog." And Watson said, "But the dog *didn't* bark!" and Holmes said, "Exactly." [7]

And what he meant was, there was a dog there that *didn't* bark, and the *fact* that he didn't bark . . . I should have mentioned this was a burglary case at an English country house where they had dogs . . . well, the fact that he didn't bark meant that he knew the burglar, who turned out to be the dog's owner—a negative piece of information, but absolutely conclusive.

And in this case, there is also a dog that didn't bark; I mean, a piece of negative information which is also rather persuasive. That negative information is that although Officer Headbust testified the defendant assaulted him and also assaulted his partner, kicking and swinging at them and cursing them, they are not corroborated by a single other police officer. *And there were three other police officers standing within fifteen feet of them.*

You may remember that when Officer Oldbadge drew this diagram . . . I am referring to defendant's F in evidence . . . you will remember he signed it at the bottom . . . you will remember that he said the defendant was right here, and that his own partner Smith was over here, and that another officer was between them . . . and I think Officer Oldbadge indicated that his attention was momentarily diverted by something going on here . . . but actually, if you look at the photograph of the scene . . . this is defendant's G in evidence . . . you will see that in the direction Oldbadge was looking the nearest spectators were about seventy-five feet away and do not seem to be engaging in any kind of violence, and so it is a fair inference from these circumstances that if the defendant had been shouting and cursing and assaulting two officers right there as Headbust testified, then it is absolutely certain that these three officers would have corroborated Headbust. *If that had really happened, you would have heard nothing else but testimony from these officers from the beginning of this case to the end, and you have not heard one word out of them. Why is that? Because it didn't happen.* That is the only common sense explanation. It simply did not happen the way Officer Headbust testified in court.

This is a very strong point in favor of defendant and against the prosecution, because it means where there was a direct conflict of testimony between on the one hand, the defendant and three defense witnesses, and on the other hand, Officer Headbust, the defense witnesses were not only corroborated by the surrounding facts, they were also tacitly corroborated by the three police officers who were there and who failed to back up the prosecution case.

Once negative evidence has been explained and introduced as indicated above, it is a good idea to use whatever else is available in that category. If there are two rather strong examples in the same case, then probably the more subtle, or surprising one ought to come second. In the examples cited, the fact that officers failed to corroborate other officers may not have been the most obvious fact in the trial, but it can hardly have been a secret; many jurors will have noticed it well before argument. But something else, not quite so obvious, following on the heels of the first strong example may be devastating.

To continue with convenient examples, assume that as part of the same criminal case, the defendant is supposed to have been the member of a crowd who threw a homemade fire bomb into a deserted recruiting office. Assume it was a gasoline fire bomb, and that the defendant was arrested within a minute after the thing was thrown. There may have been much testimony about the alleged violence at the time of his arrest, but throughout the whole case there may not have been one single word on the subject of personal odors. If the lawyer was fortunate enough to think about it while the trial is going on, he was well advised to keep his mouth shut, and so, now that the time for arguments has arrived, the state of the record is there is not one question, answer, comment or innuendo on the subject of how the defendant smelled. This is a splendid example of an argument which, if the lawyer saw it coming, he should never have asked a single question about it. Now he can say something though.

Having discussed the barking dog and the other big example of negative evidence, the lawyer might continue with a couple of minor, preliminary negative arguments: that if the fire bomb had been thrown while the defendant was standing there, somebody would have heard the sound of breaking glass at that moment (but nobody did); that if he had thrown it at that moment, with other people standing near him, persons nearest him would instinctively have drawn away in fear of an explosion (but no one did). And then the lawyer might finish somewhat along this line:

And there is one more negative point that may be as important as anything else in this case. It is just this. Everybody knows from common experience that if you have a bottle of gasoline or a can of gasoline or any container with gasoline in it, and if you fool around with it or handle it for as much as a minute, no matter how careful you are, you are going to get gasoline on your hands, and it is wet, and it is gritty and it is smelly, and above everything else, your hands will smell of gasoline. Everybody knows that who has an outboard motor in the garage or a lawn mower or a spare can for the trunk of the car. It just gets all over the outside of the container and you can't handle it and not have some on you. You certainly couldn't handle a cola bottle full of gasoline and calmly carry it in your hand and walk through a crowd of people and get next to the recruiting office *and throw the thing hard enough to break and start a fire, and not have a little on your hand.* And the defendant, you will remember, was arrested within seconds after that gasoline bottle was thrown.

There was never one single word in this case about the smell of gasoline on his hands, and it certainly wasn't because they didn't handle him on the way to the police station. Think about that carefully, not one word about the smell of gasoline. And you heard the testimony about the handcuffs, the booking, the photographs, the *fingerprinting,* and the whole thing, and the booking process took two hours.

If he really touched that bottle, there would have been gasoline on his hands, and the officers would have smelled it in a minute, and you would have heard about how he had the smell of gasoline on his hands, and you would have heard about that from one end of this case to the other. Not one word! Does that create a reasonable doubt? That should be enough to acquit.

[b] Where Prosecution Relies On Flawed Testimony of a Principal Witness

In this situation, also, the transitional argument should have narrowed things considerably: (1) the prosecution case depends on this witness; (2) nobody corroborates his testimony as to crucial events (several prominent prosecution witnesses being named at this point, to lend emphasis to the fact that they do not corroborate this witness); (3) this lack of corroboration favors the defendant, who contradicted this witness, because it means that on the critical points, the defendant was corroborated by a number of other (defense) witnesses, while this main prosecution witness was not corroborated at all; (5) in this situation, surrounding circumstances become quite important.

In dealing with a witness in this category, it may be helpful to remind the jury not just that the prosecution have the burden of proving the crime beyond a reasonable doubt, but also that when the prosecution hangs their case on the testimony of one witness, the jury has the right to expect that this witness will be: (1) free from any financial interest or character trait which would lead him to "exaggerate"; (2) able to observe things accurately; (3) able to remember accurately; and (4) willing to testify truthfully and without slanting his story. The lawyer should add that the "surrounding circumstances" which are most important will be those which throw light on these points.

In a case where there happens to have been a reward offered, this witness will have been cross-examined about it, and will (predictably) have rejected the notion that the award would matter to him one way or another. If he went so far as to say that he *never even knew* about the reward, this is the time to mention it.

This sub-argument must be hit so as to give it a special spin. Possibly relevant circumstances should be: (1) the particular medium through which the reward was transmitted (e.g., a newspaper ad), producing the actual exhibit which shows the ad; (2) whether the witness read that newspaper; (3) whether there was anything about his line of work which reinforces the conclusion that he must have read the paper or otherwise have learned of the reward; (4) the date of the reward; (5) the exact dates on which this witness sought out the investigating police agency for the purpose of giving information or signing statements, which later resulted in his being a witness in this case; (6) the fact that the reward must have been known to the police officers with whom he had all these meetings; (7) the fact that his own character witnesses may have characterized him as eager or aggressive in his line of work..

The first conclusion to this line of argument should be something like, "With that much interest, how could he *not* know about the reward?" The lawyer should then immediately point out that this point (he must have known about it) favors the defendant because it: (1) corroborates a particular character witness called by the defense, who stated that this prosecution witness had a bad reputation for truth and veracity; (2) shows that the prosecution witness's memory is poor; (3) shows that he is influenced by a desire to please (representing his motives to the jury as better than human); and (4) touches the witness's veracity in this very case: *it is not that he knew about the reward, but that he denied knowing about it.*

This kind of beginning is helpful because it presents with some clarity and force a line of argument on which the defense can win (the witness is not a perjurer, but he is certainly fooling himself) and at the same time completely shatters the prosecution version of what the defense argument was supposed to be. According to that version, the defense was out to "get" this witness, to accuse him of perjury, and to accuse him of lying in the hope of getting the reward. This prosecution version is now seen to be crap, something disappearing into the past like bilge in the wake of a rapidly moving ship. There is no point in gloating about it, and, needless to say, the defense lawyer should not waste any breath on the fact that the prosecution said their witness was going to be treated one way, while in fact he is being treated a very different way.

By starting with a relatively small circumstance such as a reward, and using that as the introduction to this whole line of argument, the lawyer strongly implies to the jury that much more is coming, and more is. Having developed the prosecution witness's poor memory and willingness to please, the next question is, how to present the mistakes and self-contradictions in his testimony. On the assumption that his testimony contains at least one major, glaring example of mis-identification (a person who was actually having dinner with the district attorney at the time or answering roll call in jail) the jury will of course be waiting for a discussion of that point. But assuming other discrepancies can be found, it is well to keep them waiting a little while.

For example, in a large case, especially one involving a group of defendants, this witness may have been forced to admit in cross-examination that he actually identified quite a few persons as being present at the scene of the crime, most of whom are not prosecuted or involved in the case at all. Assuming that a few of these persons who were identified as being there have actually testified as defense witnesses, that they were not there, then this is the best time to mention them. This is the time to remind the jury that this witness, who is so eager to please, actually "identified" a large number of people on the scene of the crime. The exact number should be quoted. The lawyer should remind the jury that this witness identified Smith as *being* there, and was quite *sure* about it, but that Smith testified that he was not there. The witness also felt that Jones and Kelley were there, but they *were not*. This indicates that the witness is *suggestible* [for God's sake, not lying]. This is a point for the defendant, because it means that the witness, in his eagerness to please and to exaggerate, can persuade himself, and swear wrongly, that a certain person was there who was not there.

Having begun with lesser identifications, this is the time to mention the major one. The reason for doing it in this way is not just to create a little dramatic tension, although that helps. The major mistake that this witness made will of course have been the subject of protective measures by the prosecution. In other words, they will have produced evidence tending to show either that (1) this mistake may not have really happened, since according to some of their own evidence, the mis-identified person may *not* have been dining with the district attorney—perhaps he slipped out of the banquet and got to the scene of the crime, or (2) if the mistake happened, it was understandable.

When it comes time to discuss the major mistake, the lawyer will have to dispose of all the evidentiary trash which the prosecution will have gathered around it. He can do that in any case, and now is the time to do it; but it helps a great deal if just before starting the job the lawyer has reminded the jury of several other minor mistakes this witness made, which are very like this one. It helps because it shows that the witness is a person who makes a lot of mistakes, all the more reason that no one should doubt that he was guilty of this major mistake.

In discussing the major mistake, the lawyer should clean it up rather vigorously, and it is quite all right to be angry. Only in this instance, the anger should be directed at the prosecution or their efforts to cover up the mistake, and *not* (to be consistent with the approach being followed throughout this whole argument) at the erring prosecution witness.

Since the subject of the witness's major mistake is certainly one that everyone was waiting for, it is well not to stop right there. The lawyer should round off this argument by discussing a few other circumstances which also tend to discredit this witness's testimony. These circumstances may be of the following kinds: (1) it is a fact that human memory normally tends to diminish after an event, i.e., the longer it has been since something, the more people tend to forget details; (2) *this* witness seems to do the opposite—his memory improves after a passage of time. The need to please has that effect.

The need to please is oriented toward the act of pleasing, and so the person suffering from that disability will *add* things if that is what it takes to please. The lawyer should then mention several examples, carefully selected from the record: (1) he never told Detective Smith that such-and-such a thing happened (referring to a statement signed by the witness quite early in the case), "But he told you"; (2) he never told the grand jury that such-and-such a thing happened, or that it happened in that way, "but he told you." The lawyer should remind the jury that this is a point for the defendant because it means that this witness's word cannot be trusted.

A final developmental theme on the need to please should be, what does the witness do when confronted with a mistake? The answer is, he never faces up to it. He just goes right on. He hopes to please in three other ways, and so he sets about doing *those* things rather than admitting his mistake. The lawyer should supply two or three examples from the witness's testimony in court, *in which the witness may have been frankly correcting something which he had said before.* This is the way to handle that part of the witness's testimony in which he frankly admitted having made a mistake or two, and was seeking to correct it for the jury. Ironically, that may have been the best-advised testimony he gave during the entire case. The way to handle it is to point out that he was still trying to please (in this case, the jury) and that he was *not even contrite*. He was not really facing his mistake. He was just ingratiating himself. Otherwise, he would have given a more convincing explanation of why he made the mistake in the first place.

[c] Using the Photograph Which Heavily Impeaches a Main Prosecution Witness

When the lawyer is fortunate enough to have a photograph which destroys a main prosecution witness, and when he has successfully used that photograph in trial so that this witness *is* destroyed (see § 14.05[3]), then the photograph will have already done great things for the defense case. It is certainly going to be used at some point in the argument, everybody knows that.

Probably the only mistakes the lawyer can make with such a photograph are, to use it too soon, or to talk about it too much. If he uses the photograph too soon, it looks as if the argument is built entirely on the photograph. That is a mistake in its own right, because the jury has already seen the photograph, and they know how important it is. Whatever they need to know about it, they already know. So if the argument is going to be built on the photograph, the argument is something they do not need to hear, and they will start to think of it as a waste of time.

The lawyer who brings the photograph out too early probably does so because he wishes to talk about it; and when he senses the jury's attention drifting away, he will be impelled to talk about it more and more. All of this is a mistake. The degree of appreciation which the jury attaches to a good impeaching photograph lights the sky of the mind; talking about it afterwards is really like walking along kicking in a dusty road.

Once the lawyer starts to talk about it, and talks too much, the level of the jury's appreciation may very well (as to several members of the jury) come *down* to the level of the lawyer's words. Cicero could probably have managed that sort of thing, since he is known to have engendered feelings in his listeners similar to the feelings created by good impeaching photographs. Short of his gifts, however, it seems much easier to let a photograph which has been so successful in its first appearance quietly go into the jury room with the jury and continue its little representations in there.

This does not mean the impeaching photograph should not be used, only that it is better to use it later in the case, *and not appear to rely too much on it*. This may seem anomalous, since the photograph is, by definition, devastating. Nonetheless, the recommended procedure is to set about arguing the defense case almost as if the photograph were not there (although everybody knows it is). The thing should be done as if the case were not already won, as though everything depended upon milking the last drop of persuasion from every single fact and circumstance which can be brought to bear on the argument. Everything should be done as if the case were very much in doubt, *because despite everything, it may be*. Nobody has a crystal ball. Nobody really knows what is going to happen in the jury room; and knowledge of probabilities is one thing, but hubris is something else entirely.

The lawyer should view the argument—if he cannot persuade himself to be apprehensive—as a continuing professional test, and should approach it as seriously as if it were an Olympic, gold medal final event. After that kind of strenuous argument, when it finally comes time to use the photograph, it really does not matter very much how it is used.

The lawyer should simply present the photograph as, "Well, in the light of all these other points, the prosecution case is in shambles anyway, and so we probably don't even really need it, but after all there *is* the photograph." He should then produce it and walk slowly along the jury box showing it to the jury. It is true that in the matter of photographs, especially good photographs, much of what is said is not verbal.

Finally, the lawyer should remind the jurors that they can take it into the jury room with them, that if they want to see that exhibit referred to as Defendant's A in evidence, or any other exhibit, all they have to do is ask the bailiff.

[d] Where the Main Prosecution Case Rests on Circumstantial Evidence

In this situation, the transitional argument will have come to rest on a different beach. Issues will have been narrowed, as with the other examples; but instead of pointing out that the entire prosecution case depends upon the truth of one particular witness, who was or was not corroborated (and then proceeding to deal with the *witness*), the transitional argument will simply point out that the prosecution case depends upon a certain theory of circumstantial evidence. In other words, it depends upon giving a certain *meaning* to certain evidence.

Only very short steps are necessary to get from (1) an explanation of the law, to (2) a recitation of that part of the prosecution evidence which was most thoroughly destroyed by the defense, to (3) the conclusion that one was supposed to draw from the prosecution evidence, to (4) the defense evidence which destroyed those conclusions, to (5) the point that the jury would not have heard about any of this except for the defense, to (6) the conclusion that the prosecution are dishonest, and finally to (7) the conclusion that the prosecution are not to be trusted in other respects either.

An example may be helpful. Suppose that the defendant is charged with assaulting someone (e.g., an arresting officer at a political demonstration) by kicking him, and that the charge is especially hellish because at the time of the incident, the defendant was wearing heavy shoes with steel reinforcing in the toe, and that there has been some ugly prosecution testimony about how he went out of his way to own those shoes. Evidence warranting, an argument might go something like this:

[having just analyzed the elements of the crime charged, and the elements of the legal defense which will actually be given in defense jury instructions] How does that rule of law apply here? You well may ask.

Orville Orville—you remember him, he is the manager of the shoe store—testified that two weeks before this happened, the defendant came in the store and bought these shoes. He identified them as being the same ones the defendant was wearing that day. He said he remembered the sale. He remembered it because the defendant spent some time looking at shoes, and asked for shoes with metal reinforcing in the toes. He looked at what was in the display case and didn't find what he liked there, and so Orville Orville finally had to go up a ladder and get these work boots, which were part of his regular stock, but he never sold very many and they were way at the top of the loft.

So what? The *guesswork* is all *against* us, you know. The *guesswork* is supposed to be done by *you.* The guesswork is that the defendant bought these shoes in order to stomp somebody with them. *The guesswork is all one way. And the evidence is all the other way.*

You may remember the defense witness, Roger Stoutheart. He worked at the same shop as the defendant. You will remember this is a shop that makes metal products, light industrial goods. Roger has been working there two years. He was working there before the defendant started working there. As a matter of fact he did the very same kind of work as the defendant. This work involved delivering a lot of metal tools and dies, and moving them around the shop. These were oily and they were always being dropped on people's toes. There was also a lot of sheet metal around and part of his day to day work involved kicking against sheet metal.

Stoutheart testified that this work not only involved heavy shoes, but that shortly before this expedition to the shoe store, there had been an accident in the plant and their boss had come around and flatly ordered the defendant to get some hard-toed shoes, as a protection against industrial accidents.

Stoutheart told you that he himself owns two pairs of these same shoes and he showed you one of them. And he testified that when defendant went to the shoe store, Stoutheart went there with him, to make perfectly sure the defendant got exactly the same kind of shoes, which he did.

That is what I mean, the guesswork is all one way, and the evidence is all the other.

You would have never heard about that except for us.

From that point on, the recommended procedure is to take the entire prosecution case, main point by main point, and review prosecution "theories" as to what the circumstantial evidence is supposed to mean. At every possible juncture, the lawyer should preface that part of the prosecution theory by saying "The guesswork is that. . . ." After developing the theory a little further, the lawyer might simply ask, "But why guess? The actual evidence on this point is. . . ." This should be followed by a very clear statement of the defense evidence, or the defense version of the mixed evidence.

After ruining the most vulnerable prosecution theories in this manner, and before getting into ones where the evidence may be a little closer, it is well to remember who can be trusted in a close case. If the lawyer were to say outright, "We got the better of them on that point, and that one, and so pay no attention to their other points," his approach would be artless. A better way would be something like this:

Well, it is almost lunch time, and there are still some prosecution arguments to be discussed after lunch. But while I am still thinking about the shoes, there is one little thing . . . and it might be helpful to put it in terms of personal experience.

Suppose you had a friend that you hadn't seen for a while, and you ran into him on the street one day, and the first thing he did was to ask you for a loan of $100.00. And because he *was* a friend you would have been glad to loan him $100.00, except that you didn't happen to have it at the time. And so you had to tell him no. And then, a few days later, you may have learned that he moved out of town, and that in fact he had moved out of town the very day he asked you for the loan. And he never ever told you he was about to move.

If you ever met him again, how would you feel about anything he might tell you?

Well, in this case, the prosecution didn't even make an argument on the subject of the shoes . . . in fact, that is a felony count, and it seems that they are not even asking for any kind of a finding on that count. So at least with reference to that count, the prosecution has just moved out of town. They left their indictment, and they didn't even take their baggage, and they didn't tell you a thing about moving.

When we come to the next prosecution count, [*looking at watch*], which is Count II, that will be after lunch . . . they are going to want you to guess about some other things. They are going to want you to guess that . . . there is no use going into that yet.

After lunch, I will be glad to tell you what they want you to guess, and how the defense feels you should look upon this latest, rather *seedy* application for credit.

[*to the court*] Your Honor, I wonder if this would be a convenient time to take the noon recess?

[e] Where the Prosecutor Has Been Critical of Discrepancies Among Defense Witnesses

This problem is easily solved, and should be covered, in passing, near the end of the defense argument. The answer is, the jury is going to hear an instruction to the general effect that in assessing the credibility of witnesses, they should remember that it is very common for two or more people to witness the same event and to recollect it somewhat differently, and that innocent mistakes are by no means uncommon.[8] The lawyer should mention that minor discrepancies may be a hallmark of truthfulness, and that it is really for the jury to decide whether any discrepancies were minor or otherwise. An example is never wasted here.

The lawyer may remember a particular film [9] or some example from literature, in which a number of people perjured their testimony by agreeing to the same story, and it was obvious to everyone that they had done this, because they even used the same words and phrases. In fact, if certain discrepancies did *not* appear in testimony, the very uniformity of testimony might be thought of as grounds for suspicion.

[6] Concluding the Argument

At some point in his argument when he has covered every point that has to be said (and that will obviously include more points than are suggested by the bare-bones elements outlined in the preceding sections), there will be a change in the pace of the lawyer's thinking as well as his speaking, which indicates to him and to his listeners that he is near the end of what he has to say. It is a good thing for both of them to know it. The lawyer should immediately begin the concluding phase of his argument, and because they know this is coming, the jury will renew their attention. The end is at hand, and they will certainly stay with the lawyer.

Before actually leaving the factual argument, it may be well for the lawyer to remind the jury, in so many words, that he has covered a lot of points, that he has emphasized the ones which seemed important to him, and that when the time comes to review these matters at leisure in the jury room, the jury may well decide that some of those points deserve less value, and some more, and they may value things he never mentioned. At this point it may be helpful for the lawyer to say something along the line of what Sam Spade said to Brigid O'Shaughnessy in *The Maltese Falcon*.[10] Following the gist of Spade's reasoning, the lawyer can summarize a number of argument points, large and small, and remind the jurors that although they may not view all of these points in the same light as the lawyer does, "Look at the number of them." Having touched on the reasons, it is time to leave them and make sure the jurors will take their work seriously, as they promised to do at the beginning of the case. There is no need to talk about promises again. It is time to talk about reasons. The lawyer needs a small connecting thought, between where he left the facts, and the rather necessary, emotional conclusion of what he will say. That connecting thought may go something like this:

Well, I think I have covered most of what I had to say, but I have tried to be careful about that, because, as you know, the defense only has one argument. If I overlook something now, we never have another chance to say it to you.

I think if I were sitting as a juror, I might begin

to ask myself—and you must have asked yourselves—
whether these rather rigid procedural rules really mean
what they say. In other words, when you decide something according to the rules of reasonable doubt, and
when you apply the presumption of innocence, you are
being asked to do something very different from the
way we ordinarily think. People just do not think in
terms of whether something is proved beyond a reasonable doubt. If we want to go to the store, or decide
whether to get some gas for the car, we just do it, we
don't ask ourselves questions like that.

And so the thought must have occurred to you,
a little question whether this may all be some kind of
genteel game, in which the judge reads you instructions, but everybody understands that you are not
really supposed to apply them, that you are supposed
to go into the jury room and just do what you think
best. Let me tell you that the rules really *do* mean what
they say. You *are* expected to follow the court's instructions, even though we all understand that in some
ways this is like doing acrobatics. When the judge
tells you that you are to apply a presumption of innocence, he really does mean it.

It is not just this judge talking to this jury, but
when Judge Hardtack reads you those instructions
tomorrow he is really the present successor of a long
line of judges, and that line goes back for more than
nine centuries. Judges change, faces in the jury box
change, the lawyers change, and there are always some
of us standing here in our dark suits addressing a jury
such as you, but the system goes on. It is absolutely essential to that system that you should comply with
the rules that the court gives you. Otherwise it is
meaningless.

Following the court's instructions may be as
difficult a thing as you have done in a long time, but I

suggest that it may also be one of the most worthwhile things you have done, and I hope that—although it may be that some of you in the past have done more dangerous things for your country—this is as serious a thing as any of you ever have to do.

This is where the government comes in contact with the governed, or as an old advertisement use to say, "Where the rubber meets the road." The constitution means nothing at all in the abstract. It only has meaning when it is being applied by an actual jury. Our whole legal system has no reality except in the jury room. A good deal is expected of you.

From this point the lawyer should finish the argument with something a little above the ordinary in terms of thought and language, which is both personal to him and consonant with a jury's duty. It is not necessary to write something for the occasion. Literature has examples. What a lawyer says to one jury he may not wish to say again, or to another; or he may find himself saying essentially the same thoughts many times to many juries. It does have to be personal, and so the following is not cited with a suggestion that it be paraphrased or copied, but as an example of things the lawyer may feel, and therefore adapt for this necessary part of his argument:

It has been some years since I was admitted to the bar—more than I care to remember—and I don't often have occasion to think about it, but sometimes I do, and today is one of those times.

In California, you know, getting admitted to the bar depends on where you live. You take the bar examination, and then many months later you hear the results, and finally there comes a day when the people who are going to be admitted to the bar go to court.

There are two ceremonies. The first one is in the state court, and at that point the California

Supreme Court admits the new lawyers to the bar. Then you adjourn, and go a few blocks to the federal court, where they have a similar ceremony.

When I did it, I don't remember what happened in the state court, but I do remember what happened in the federal court. The judge who was presiding that day was Leon Yankwich, a senior trial judge for the United States District Court, in Los Angeles, and a well-known scholar, and on this occasion he had been thinking about something. He had been thinking about the book of Leviticus.

As you may remember, Leviticus is mostly a variegated collection of laws, some of which are dietary. He said that the basic philosophy of Leviticus could be summarized rather briefly—let me say there is no use looking for these words in Leviticus, because they are not there; they are a distillation or a summary of ideas contained in the book, and not a direct quote. He said that the essence of Leviticus was that in trying to establish courts, and a system of justice, what people ought to look for, and seek after is not just a court system good enough to mete out justice between, on the one hand, your brother, and on the other, your brother. That is too easy. You know them both.

What you should really look for and hope to get is a system of courts so perfect, that it will mete out even-handed justice between, on the one hand your own brother . . . and on the other hand . . . the stranger who stands within your gates.

So, do your duty. But approach it in that spirit.

[7] While the Prosecutor is Making his Closing Argument

There is not much to be done here except to remain still and listen to every single thing the prosecutor says. The lawyer should not make a point of looking at the jury or the prosecutor, or of visibly reacting in any way. The desirable posture here is not to spoil one's own argument by jumping up and down too easily. If the prosecutor becomes somewhat excessive, let it go by, but *if he steps out of line and seriously misquotes the case, or attempts to argue improperly* (e.g., on the basis of his personal belief in his own witnesses, or the fact that the jury is supposed to be a partner of law enforcement, any of those serious things) then stick him with another objection, and bring his argument to a stop to force a ruling on it. There is no point in letting him away with something.

Footnotes

[1] E.g., Cal. Penal Code § 1093.5 (West 1970).

[2] "Difficult but not impossible." (My wife's curious annotation. All she knows of judicial behavior in chambers is what she knows of lawyers.)

[3] With an automatic exception statute such as Cal. Penal Code § 1176 (West 1970), the defense lawyer is probably protected with respect to any modifications to which he does not stipulate. This should not inhibit the lawyer from participating in the all-important discussion of how certain defense (or prosecution) instructions are going to be modified, once it is clear that the judge will require modifications. The lawyer must not mislead the judge into thinking an original defense instruction has been withdrawn if it has not been; but that is no problem, since virtually all judges understand that the lawyers are intent on "preserving the record," and that modification at the court's insistence are, in fact, court's instructions.

[4] 2 *The Institutio Oratoria of Quintilian* 35 (H. Butler transl. 1933).

[5] The three minute estimate is that of Woodruff J. Deem, see ch. 9, N. 3. Three minutes may be a little on the generous side.

[6] An excellent instruction for this purpose is *California Jury Instructions Criminal* 41 (P. Richard ed. 1970) [usually cited *CALJIC* 2.22].

[7] Admittedly there is no literary justification for referring to the story in this mixed-up fashion. Conan Doyle would never give away a plot with a title like that, and it wasn't a burglary case. Holmes' reference to the dog was not really at the denouement and he phrased his remarks quite differently from those quoted in the argument. To set

matters right, see "Silver Blaze" in A. Conan Doyle, *The Complete Sherlock Holmes* 383, 397 (Literary Guild 1936). Still, the argument probably makes its point better with these loose references.

[8] Id. at 40 [usually cited *CALJIC* 2.21].

[9] For example, the film "Z" (director, Costa-Gavras, screenplay Costa-Gavras and Jorge Semprun, producers Jacques Perrin and Hamed Rachedi, 1969).

[10] What Sam said was,

"'Listen. This isn't a damned bit of good. You'll never understand me, but I'll try once more and then we'll give it up. Listen. When a man's partner is killed he's supposed to do something about it. It doesn't make any difference what you thought of him. He was your partner and you're supposed to do something about it. Then it happens we were in the detective business. Well, when one of your organization gets killed it's bad business to let the killer get away with it. It's bad all around—bad for that one organization, bad for every detective everywhere. Third, I'm a detective and expecting me to run criminals down and then let them go free is like asking a dog to catch a rabbit and let it go. It can be done, all right, and sometimes it is done, but it's not the natural thing. The only way I could have let you go was by letting Gutman and Cairo and the kid go. That's—'

"'You're not serious,' she said. 'You don't expect me to think that these things you're saying are sufficient reason for sending me to the—'

"'Wait till I'm through and then you can talk. Fourth, no matter what I wanted to do now it would be absolutely impossible for me to let you go without having myself dragged to the gallows with the others. Next, I've no reason in God's world to think I can trust you and if I did this and got away with it you'd have something on me that you could use whenever you happened to want to. That's five of them. The sixth would be that, since I've also got something on you, I couldn't be sure you wouldn't decide to shoot a hole in *me* some day. Seventh, I don't even like the idea of thinking that there might be one chance in a hundred that you'd played me for a sucker. And eighth—but that's enough. All those on one side. Maybe some of them are unimportant. I won't argue about that. But look at the number of them. Now on the the other side we've got what? All we've got is the fact that maybe you love me and maybe I love you.'"

The Maltese Falcon, in *The Novels of Dashiell Hammett* at 438 (Knopf 1965).

EPILOGUE

When the Verdict Comes Back

There seems to be no adequate preparation for the tension the lawyers feel while waiting for a jury verdict, and while it is being read. It is bad enough in some cases that a lawyer may feel he cannot live through it. With a little practice, though, he can.

It is to be hoped that if the general principles outlined in this book are followed, *and with a reasonable amount of luck*, that the verdict will be the right one.

APPENDIXES

APPENDIX A

Sample First-Round Discovery Motion

JOHN J. DOE
111 Elm Street
Santa Barbara, California 93101
Telephone: (805) 444-4444

Lawyer for Defendant

SUPERIOR COURT OF THE STATE OF CALIFORNIA
FOR THE COUNTY OF SANTA BARBARA

THE PEOPLE OF THE STATE OF CALIFORNIA,	No. . . . .
Plaintiff,	NOTICE OF MOTION FOR PRE-TRIAL DISCOVERY;
—vs—	SUPPORTING DECLARATION; POINTS AND AUTHORITIES;
. . . .,	ORDER SHORTENING TIME
Defendant.	

NOTICE IS HEREBY GIVEN that on . . . ., 197. ., at 9:00 A.M., or as soon thereafter as counsel may be heard, defendant will move for an order directing The People of the State of California to permit discovery as hereinbelow set forth; this motion is addressed not merely to the knowledge and possession of the District Attorney of Santa Barbara County, but to those of all officers, agents, agencies, bureaus, departments, employees and attorneys associated on the side of The People of the State of California in prosecuting the above-entitled action (hereinafter collectively called "The People"). Defendant will move for an order requiring The People to do the following with respect to things and information wholly or partly in their possession or subject to their control as of the date of the order made in response to this motion:

1. Supply to defendant's lawyer and otherwise make available to him things and information required by this order, according to the terms hereinbelow set forth, and complete all discovery required by this order to be completed by or on behalf of The People, no later than 5:00 P.M. on the date of this order.

2. Supply to defendant's lawyer, at his expense, one legible copy (by photostatic reproduction, or other method of comparable quality) of each of the following:

(a) Statements of defendant herein, written, typed or otherwise recorded, signed or unsigned;

(b) Notes, memoranda, reports or statements, written, typed or otherwise recorded, signed or unsigned, made by any law enforcement officer, special agent or investigator of The People, or by any informer (paid or unpaid) associated with The People, in connection with any crime charged against defendant in the above-entitled action or any other alleged crime or event which The People contend proves or tends to prove any element of any crime charged herein, whether or not incorporated in any official report;

(c) Notes, memoranda, reports or statements, written, typed, or otherwise recorded, signed or unsigned, made by any person known to The People who claims to be a witness to any transaction or event constituting part of or which The People contend proves or tends to prove any element of any crime charged against the defendant in the above-entitled action, or any person who has or claims to have information relevant to the prosecution or defense of this case.

3. Advise defendant's lawyer, in writing, of the fact and substance of any alleged oral statements by defendant in this case, including (to the extent known to The People), the date, hour and place of each such statement, the person or persons to whom made or present at the time such statement was made, and a full and accurate description of the contents of such statement.

4. Supply to defendant's lawyer, in writing, the names and addresses of all persons, whether or not police officers, known to The People, who have knowledge, or claim to have knowledge of any transaction or event constituting part of, or which The People contend proves or tends to prove any element of any alleged crime charged against the defendant in the above-entitled action, or who have or claim to have information material to the prosecution or defense of this case, including any person who identified or claims to have identified defendant either personally or in any photograph as being present at the scene of the events alleged herein.

5. Supply directly to defendant's lawyer, at his expense, or make available to him for copying, copies of all photographs, photographic slides and moving picture film pertaining to actions charged against defendant in this case, including all photographs shown to any alleged witnesses, or deliver such negatives, slides and film to the temporary custody of . . . . Laboratory located at . . . ., Santa Barbara, California, for the purpose of having said laboratory make and deliver to defendant's lawyer whatever copies he may order and pay for, the original negatives, slides and film to be returned to the custody of The People thereafter.

6. Supply to defendant's lawyer legible and complete copies of all scientific, laboratory or expert reports pertaining to this case.

7. Make available to defendant's lawyer by 5:00 P.M. on the date of this order, and from time to time thereafter as may be reasonably requested, for private viewing by said lawyer and defendant, any videotape recording which The People contend proves or tends to prove any part of any crime charged against defendant in this action.

8. To permit defendant's lawyer and experts designated by him no later than 5:00 P.M. on the date of this order, and from time to time thereafter as may be reasonably requested, access to real evidence which The People contend proves or tends to prove any part of any crime charged against defendant herein, and reasonable opportunity to measure, photograph, examine and test such evidence.

9. Supply to defendant's lawyer, at his expense, copies of any audio tape which The People contend proves or tends to prove any element of any crime charged against defendant herein, or make such tape available to him for copying.

10. Inform defendant's lawyer in writing whether any telephone or other conversations to which defendant was a party, or defendant's lawyer or any person working for defendant's lawyer was a party has been the subject of electronic or other eavesdropping by or on behalf of The People, and, if so, the date and time of each such telephone tap or eavesdropping, the identity of each person whose conversation was overheard, whether or not a recording was made, whether or not a transcript of any such conversation has been made in whole or in part, the identity of the person and agency participating in such telephone tap or eavesdropping, and the legal authority, if any, therefore; and further to make such transcripts and recordings available to defendant's lawyer for copying.

11. Supply to defendant's lawyer records showing any felony convictions including dates, places, and charges, available from the Bureau of Criminal Identification and Investigation and/or from the

Federal Bureau of Investigation or other law enforcement records sources, with respect to those among the following named persons who, to the knowledge of The People, have or claim to have information material to any element of any charge against defendant in the above-entitled action: [1]

. . . .

. . . .

. . . .

12. Supply to defendant's lawyer, with respect to any informer associated on the side of The People (paid or unpaid), in writing, the amount of money paid by or on behalf of The People to such informer in connection with his work in the above-entitled case, whether paid "for services," "for expenses," or for whatever stated reason; the time, dates, and amounts of payments; the name, business address, and official designation (if any) of each person known to The People who has or claims to have records or other information relating to the purposes, dates, and amounts of such payments made to each such informer.

13. Supply to defendant's lawyer a copy of any affidavit supporting the issuance of any search warrant which, as of the date of this order has been issued and served, or which, as of the date of this order has been applied for and refused, to obtain evidence which The People expect or expected to prove or tend to prove any part of any element of any charge against defendant in the above-entitled action; and a copy of any inventory of items seized pursuant to any such warrant.

This motion may be deemed severable as to objects and means of discovery mentioned above; may be granted on such other, further or different terms or conditions as are reasonable and just; and will be based on this notice, the supporting declaration hereinbelow set forth, the pleadings, records, files and documents in the above-entitled action, and oral and documentary evidence to be presented at the hearing.

DATED: . . . . , 197. .

. . . .
JOHN J. DOE, Lawyer for
Defendant

SUPPORTING DECLARATION

JOHN J. DOE hereby declares under penalty of perjury:

1. I am the lawyer for defendant in the above-entitled action.

2. Of the categories mentioned, only the following have been supplied to me as of the date of this declaration:

. . . .

. . . .

. . . .

. . . .

3. I am informed and believe and upon that ground state that The People have in their possession or subject to their control other evidence and information, including photographs, answering some if not all of the categories described in this motion, besides the items which have already been supplied to me. For example, the incident which is the subject of this action is alleged to have occurred on the evening of . . . ., 197.., in Isla Vista, California. According to the best information presently available to me, there were present in the immediate neighborhood of the alleged incident, at about that time, contingents of law enforcement officers from approximately six law enforcement agencies, namely: Santa Barbara County Sheriff's Office; the Santa Barbara Police Department; the California Highway Patrol; the Ventura County Sheriff's Office; the Los Angeles County Sheriff's Office; San Luis Obispo Sheriff's Office. According to this same information, officers present at that time and place included at least some officers from Santa Barbara County Sheriff's Office and the Los Angeles County Sheriff's Office.

4. Law enforcement agencies unfailingly make police reports in connection with events such as those alleged in this case. We have been supplied with only five reports concerning these events, all from the Santa Barbara County Sheriff's Office. We have not yet received anything from the Los Angeles County Sheriff's Office. Those records would normally be made in the usual course of events, and must in fact exist in the custody of the Los Angeles County Sheriff's Office even though, as we are informed by the District Attorney's Office, none of those reports has yet arrived at the District Attorney's Office. It is obviously necessary that some court order be utilized to obtain the early production of these relevant police reports from the Los Angeles County Sheriff's Office, and from such other of these law enforcement agencies as may also have custody of relevant reports.[2]

5. I believe it necessary in order to prepare for trial that I be afforded prompt and reasonable access to all such evidence and information available to The People, other than previously supplied, which meets the descriptions set forth in this motion.

6. I have previously made an informal demand on the District Attorney's Office for the categories of information specified in this motion, and more than five (5) days have elapsed since that demand; during that time, The People have omitted to supply such evidence and information, except as hereinabove itemized.[3]

7. Since time is quite important in the preparation of this case for trial, it is desirable that the discovery order be made as soon as possible; for that reason, I request that the statutory time for service of this notice of motion be shortened to permit service by hand/by mail no later than . . . ., 197. . .

8. I make this declaration in Santa Barbara, California on the . . . . day of . . . ., 19. . .

. . . .

JOHN J. DOE, Lawyer for
Defendant

POINTS AND AUTHORITIES

This motion is made on the authority of the following cases: *Engstrom v. Superior Court,* 20 Cal. App. 3d 240, 243–244, 97 Cal. Rptr. 484, 486–487 (1971) [criminal discovery not limited to evidence in prosecutor's possession, but includes that available at his request from other agencies in the criminal justice system]; *People v. Garner,* 57 Cal. 2d 135, 142, 367 P.2d 680, 684, 18 Cal. Rptr. 40, 44 (1961), cert. denied 370 U.S. 929 (1962) [defendant's counsel entitled to inspect, hear or copy all statements of defendant]; *Vance v. Superior Court,* 51 Cal. 2d 92, 330 P.2d 773 (1958) [recording of conversations of defendant and victim with police]; *Cash v. Superior Court,* 53 Cal. 2d 72, 75–76, 346 P.2d 407, 409 (1959) [recordings of conversations between defendant and police officer posing as accomplice]; *People v. Campbell,* 27 Cal. App. 3d 849, 854–858, 104 Cal. Rptr. 118, 122–124 (1972) [oral statements of defendant]; *People v. Estrada,* 54 Cal. 2d 713, 716, 355 P.2d 641, 642–643, 7 Cal. Rptr. 897, 898–899 (1960) [unsigned statement by prosecution witness relating to his own testimony]; *Funk v. Superior Court,* 52 Cal. 2d 423, 340 P.2d 593 (1959) [notes by officers on oral statements by prosecution witnesses]; *Norton v. Superior Court,* 173 Cal. App. 2d 133, 136, 343 P.2d 139, 141 (1959) [names and addresses of eye witnesses; photographs exhibited to them]; *Walker v. Superior Court,* 155 Cal. App. 2d 134, 139–141, 317 P.2d 130, 135 (1957) [laboratory report]; *People v. Renchie,* 201 Cal. App. 2d 1, 3–6, 19 Cal. Rptr. 734, 736–737 (1962) [notes in possession of police officers subject to discovery even if not

in possession of District Attorney]; *People v. Lindsay,* 227 Cal. App.
2d 482, 510, 38 Cal. Rptr. 755, 773 (1964) [real evidence]; *Yannacone
v. Mun. Ct. San Francisco,* 222 Cal. App. 2d 72, 74, 34 Cal. Rptr. 838,
839 (1963) [real evidence]; *In re Ferguson,* 5 Cal. 3d 525, 96 Cal.
Rptr. 594, 487 P.2d 1234 (1971) [felony conviction and commitment
to state hospital of main prosecution witness]; *Engstrom v. Superior
Court,* 20 Cal. App. 3d 240, 97 Cal. Rptr. 484 (1971) [felony convictions of prosecution witnesses; reports, memoranda or other information re arrests of prosecution witnesses for specific acts of
aggression]; *see also, Brady v. Maryland,* 373 U.S. 83, 87, 10 L. Ed.
2d 215, 218–219, 83 S. Ct. 1194 (1963) [suppression of evidence by
prosecution]; 18 U.S.C.A. §§ 2516 and 2518(8)(d) [service on party
whose communications have been intercepted, in the interests of
justice, of an inventory including the application or the order for
eavesdropping; the period authorized; the fact that wire or oral communications were or were not intercepted; availability of portions of
intercepted communications, applications and orders; and other mat-
ters]; [4] Cal. Penal Code §§ 1526, 1527, and 1541 [affidavits supporting
the issuance of search wararnts, and filing requirements].

Respectfully submitted,

. . . .

JOHN J. DOE, Lawyer for
Defendant

ORDER SHORTENING TIME

GOOD CAUSE APPEARING THEREFORE, time for serving
the foregoing motion is hereby shortened to permit service by hand
(or completed service by mail) on or before . . . . 197. . .
DATED: . . . ., 197. .

. . . .

JUDGE OF THE SUPERIOR COURT

Author's Footnotes

[1] The information sought by this paragraph is much more susceptible
to discovery in a second or subsequent discovery motion, since the
main prosecution witnesses will be better known at that time; however, to the extent that they are known now, this is the time to make
the demand.

[2] It is usually advisable in the supporting declaration or affidavit to

state *why* the lawyer feels that other reports exist which have not been made available to him. If there is any doubt about obtaining this order for not having alleged the facts with particularity, he should subpoena the custodian of records of every law enforcement agency involved, all subpoenas returnable at the hearing of the discovery motion. That will take up a little court time, but it is beneficial to the defense, and will settle the point that records answering most of all of the categories described in the motion do exist, and who has them. After a few experiences of this sort, most judges who like to quash discovery motions ("show me they have any of those things, because I am not going to permit you to just go on a fishing expedition") will think better of it and start bending over backwards to grant them without enduring that kind of proof.

[3] This paragraph is to comply with a local rule requiring a five day demand as a condition of making a discovery motion (Santa Barbara Superior Court, Rule No. 304). Such requisites can probably be met by sending the district attorney a mimeographed copy of the discovery motion which will later be filed, with a letter requesting the things and information specified in the motion. It is essential to avoid wasting the lawyer's time and that of his secretary by elaborate demand letters and other nonproductive gestures.

[4] See also, Annot., "Right of Accused in State Courts to Inspection or Disclosure of Evidence in Possession of Prosecution," 7 A.L.R.3d 8 (1966); Annot., "Withholding or Suppression of Evidence by Prosecution in Criminal Case as Vitiating a Conviction," 34 A.L.R.3d 16 (1970).

Sample First-Round Discovery Order

JOHN J. DOE
111 Elm Street
Santa Barbara, California 93101
Telephone: (805) 444-4444

Lawyer for Defendant

SUPERIOR COURT OF THE STATE OF CALIFORNIA
FOR THE COUNTY OF SANTA BARBARA

THE PEOPLE OF THE STATE OF CALIFORNIA, Plaintiff, —vs— . . . . , Defendant.	No. . . . . ORDER FOR PRE-TRIAL DISCOVERY IN FAVOR OF DEFENDANT

Defendant's Motion For Pre-Trial Discovery having come on for hearing on . . . . , 197. . at 9:00 A.M., before the Honorable . . . . , Judge Presiding in Department . . . . . , and . . . . , Esq., having appeared for The People, and John J. Doe, Esq. having appeared for the defendant, and evidence having been received, and good cause appearing therefore,

IT IS HEREBY ORDERED that the People of the State of California permit discovery as hereinbelow set forth: this Order is directed not only to the District Attorney of Santa Barbara County, but to all officers, agents, agencies, bureaus, departments, employees and attorneys associated on the side of The People of the State of

California prosecuting the above-entitled action (hereinafter collectively called "The People").

THE PEOPLE ARE HEREBY ORDERED TO DO THE FOLLOWING WITH RESPECT TO THINGS AND INFORMATION WHOLLY OR PARTLY IN THEIR POSSESSION OR SUBJECT TO THEIR CONTROL AS OF THE DATE OF THIS ORDER:

1. Supply to defendant's lawyer, John J. Doe, whose address is 111 Elm Street, Santa Barbara, California 93101, and otherwise make available to him things and information required by this order according to the terms hereinbelow set forth, and complete all discovery required by this order to be completed by or on behalf of The People, no later than 5:00 P.M. on ...., 197...

2. Supply to defendant's lawyer, at his expense, one legible copy (by photostatic reproduction or other method of comparable quality) of each of the following:

(a) Statements of defendant herein, written, typed or otherwise recorded, signed or unsigned;

(b) Notes, memoranda, reports or statements, written, typed or otherwise recorded, signed or unsigned, made by any law enforcement officer, special agent or investigator of The People, or by any informer (paid or unpaid) associated with The People, in connection with any crime charged against defendant in the above-entitled action or any other alleged crime or event which The People contend proves or tends to prove any element of any crime charged herein whether or not incorporated in any official report;

(c) Notes, memoranda, reports or statements, written, typed, or otherwise recorded, signed or unsigned, made by any person known to The People who claims to be a witness to any transaction or event constituting part of, or which The People contend proves or tends to prove any element of any crime charged against the defendant in the above-entitled action, or any person who has or claims to have information relevant to the prosecution or defense of this case.

3. Advise defendant's lawyer, in writing, of the fact and substance of any alleged oral statements by defendant in this case, including (to the extent known to The People), the date, hour and place of each such statement, the person or persons to whom made or present at the time such statement was made, and a full and accurate description of the contents of such statement.

4. Supply to defendant's lawyer, in writing, the names and addresses of all persons, whether or not police officers, known to The People, who have knowledge, or claim to have knowledge of any transaction or event constituting part of, or which The People con-

tend proves or tends to prove any element of any alleged crime charged against the defendant in the above-entitled action, or who have or claim to have information material to the prosecution or defense of this case, including any person who identified or claims to have identified defendant either personally or in any photograph as being present at the scene of the events alleged herein.

5. Supply directly to defendant's lawyer, at his expense, or make available to him for copying, all photographs, photographic slides and moving picture film pertaining to actions charged against defendant in this case, including all photographs shown to any alleged witnesses, or deliver such negatives, slides and film to the temporary custody of .... Laboratory located at ....
........., Santa Barbara, California, for the purpose of having said laboratory make and deliver to defendant's lawyer whatever copies he may order and pay for, the original negatives, slides and film to be returned to the custody of The People thereafter.

6. Supply to defendant's lawyer legible and complete copies of all scientific, laboratory or expert reports pertaining to this case.

7. Make available to defendant's lawyer by 5:00 P.M. on the effective date specified above in this order, and from time to time thereafter as may be reasonably requested, for private viewing by said lawyer and defendant, any videotape recording which The People contend proves or tends to prove any part of any crime charged against defendant in this action.

8. To permit defendant's lawyer and experts designated by him no later than 5:00 P.M. on the effective date specified above in this order, and from time to time thereafter as may be reasonably requested, access to real evidence which The People contend proves or tends to prove any part of any crime charged against defendant herein, and reasonable opportunity to measure, photograph, examine and test such evidence.

9. Supply to defendant's lawyer, at his expense, copies of any audio tape which The People contend proves or tends to prove any element of any crime charged against defendant herein, or make such tape available to him for copying.

10. Inform defendant's lawyer in writing whether any telephone or other conversations to which defendant was a party, or defendant's lawyer or any person working for defendant's lawyer was a party, has been the subject of electronic or other eavesdropping by or on behalf of The People, and if so, the date and time of each such telephone tap or eavesdropping, the identity of each person whose conversation was overheard, whether or not a recording was

made, whether or not a transcript of any such conversation has been made in whole or in part, the identity of the person and agency participating in such telephone tap or eavesdropping, and the legal authority, if any, therefore; and further to make such transcripts and recordings available to defendant's lawyer for copying.

11. Supply to defendant's lawyer records showing any felony convictions including dates, places, and charges, available from the Bureau of Criminal Identification and Investigation and/or from the Federal Bureau of Investigation or other law enforcement records sources, with respect to those among the following named persons who, to the knowledge of The People, have or claim to have information material to any element of any charge against defendant in the above-entitled action:

. . . .

. . . .

. . . .

12. Supply to defendant's lawyer, with respect to any informer associated on the side of The People (paid or unpaid), in writing, the amount of money paid by or on behalf of The People to such informer in connection with his work in the above-entitled case, whether paid "for services," "for expenses," or for whatever stated reason; the time, dates, and amounts of payments; the name, business address, and official designation (if any) of each person known to The People who has or claims to have records or other information relating to the purposes, dates, and amounts of such payments made to each such informer.

13. Supply to defendant's lawyer a copy of any affidavit supporting the issuance of any search warrant which, as of the date of this order, has been issued and served, or which, as of the date of this order has been applied for and refused, to obtain evidence which The People expect or expected to prove or tend to prove any part of any element of any charge against defendant in the above-entitled action; and a copy of any inventory of items seized pursuant to any such warrant.

DATED: . . . ., 197. .

. . . .
JUDGE OF THE SUPERIOR COURT

APPENDIX C

Notes and Sample Paragraphs for Second
(Third or Nth) Discovery Motion

The second discovery motion should be as broad as the first, containing the same categories, but with additional demands made more specific by reason of having learned more about the case. The really important differences occur in the supporting declaration (or affidavit).

For example, after a nominal change in the title (e.g., NOTICE OF SECOND MOTION FOR PRE-TRIAL DISCOVERY; SUPPORTING DECLARATION; POINTS AND AUTHORITIES; ORDER SHORTENING TIME) the paragraph requiring disclosure of arrest records of specific witnesses [see Appendix A, paragraph 11 of the sample motion] should be updated to include witnesses not known at the time of the first motion; and the paragraph concerning how much money has been paid to informers [see paragraph 12, of sample motion] should be amended slightly, so as to retain its general scope (all the informers may not be known even now), while adding a specific reference to informers who *are* known. This can be accomplished by adding a few words at the end of the paragraph, e.g.

"Without limiting the generality of the foregoing language, this paragraph is specifically addressed to information and records relating to the following named persons who are thought to be informers:

. . . .

. . . .

. . . .

. . . ."

The first important differences will occur in the supporting declaration [See Appendix A, paragraph 2 of the sample supporting declaration], which will now contain a longer list of items already supplied by the prosecution, noting the date each item was received. This is a convenient way to make a record of compliance and to preclude any later claim by the prosecution that they mistakenly thought something had been supplied at an early date, which had not been.

The declaration supporting a second discovery motion should be particular as to the reasons why the lawyer thinks the prosecution have evidence which they have not supplied to him, with special reference to evidence which they should have supplied under a previous order.

The following are illustrative of statements which might be included in an affidavit supporting a second discovery motion:

3. On about ...., the prosecution furnished me a copy of a three page Follow-Up Report dated ...., prepared and filed by Detective Smith. At about the middle of page 2, describing his observations and conversations at the scene of the alleged crime, Detective Smith states, 'Talked to Mr. Strobe, who arrived at 21:30.' Mr. Strobe is the chief photographer of the police crime laboratory.

4. On about ...., the prosecution furnished me a copy of an Evidence Booking Receipt signed by Sgt. Willhold dated .... This is a receipt for '50 black and white photographs.' I am familiar with the ordinary business practice of the .... police department; according to this practice, photographs taken at the scene of an alleged crime are usually taken by Mr. Strobe or someone else under his direction, and when developed and printed, they are normally booked into evidence and a receipt such as that mentioned above is given for them.

5. From these events it seems reasonable to infer that there are about 50 photographs now in The People's possession which are allegedly relevant to this case. As of the time of preparing this affidavit, none of these photographs has been made available to the defense.

Or to cite another example:

2. A Follow-Up Report written by Detective Smith dated ...., made available by the prosecution on ...., contains three references to the fact that fingerprints were taken at the scene of the alleged crime. In the normal course of business of the police crime laboratory it usually takes about ...... days to prepare fingerprint reports. On that schedule, it is reasonable to conclude that reports concerning the fingerprints lifted at the time of Detective Smith's

report may not have been available to the prosecution at the time of the first discovery order in this case, which was dated .... (and effective as of ....); but by now, those reports should have been completed and filed. No such reports have been available to us as of the time of preparing this declaration.

Or perhaps:

2. It is apparent from police reports previously made available by the prosecution (report of Detective Smith dated .... ; of Detective Jones dated .... ; and interview reports of Detective Brown dated ....); that a major prosecution witness is Richard Telltale. Mr. Telltale was subpoenaed by the defense and testified at the hearing of the first discovery motion. He stated that he was an informer, that he worked with the .... police department for a period of three months before the arrest in this case; that he never filed written reports; but that he was paid various sums of money as 'expenses' from time to time during this three month period. He testified that Detective Brown usually made these payments, and that no receipt was required.

3. The department routinely budgets and maintains funds and accounts for informer 'expense money.' In the usual course of business, records are kept of these outlays. Although The People were required to disclose to the defense the names and addresses of all persons having knowledge or records concerning such outlays [see Discovery Order in the above entitled action, dated ...., 197.., filed ...., 197.., page 3, lines 18–24], none of this information has so far been disclosed to us. I made additional, specific requests for compliance with this discovery order in telephone conversations with Mr. Waxear of the District Attorney's office. I telephoned him and specifically asked for this information on .... and again on .... He said he would look into it and get back to me, but he never called back. It appears that The People are holding back information which they are required to divulge by the discovery order, which they can easily get, and which is not otherwise available to the defense.

Another example would be:

3. It is apparent from the police reports previously sup-

plied to the defense, that the following persons have or claim to have material information concerning the alleged crime charged against defendant: ....

. . . .

All of these people were allegedly assulted by the defendant. It is imperative to the orderly preparation of the defense case that we be supplied with copies of records showing any convictions of any of these witnesses of any felonies, and moreover, of any records of arrest for any assaults allegedly committed by any of these persons against any other persons, since they are alleged victims, and since it is anticipated that self-defense will be an issue in this case. Further, we need to know whether any of them has been committed to any state mental institution for treatment of any mental condition which might be relevant to the question whether any of them was an aggressor rather than a victim in this case.

Sample Jury Instructions

[1] Curfew Instructions

[a] Sample Administrative Order Imposing Curfew

IN THE MATTER OF PRESCRIBING AND ISSUING RULES
AND REGULATIONS TO COPE WITH THE EXISTING
STATE OF EMERGENCY ADMINISTRATIVE ORDER NO. 70-14

Under the state of emergency now existing in State Barbara County and pursuant to the authority vested in me by Section 12-5 of the Santa Barbara County Code to make and issue rules and regulations reasonably related to the protection of life and property affected by such emergency, I hereby make and issue the following rules and regulations, subject to confirmation by the Board of Supervisors of Santa Barbara County at the earliest practicable time:

1. Except in cases of personal emergency, no person shall be outside, or remain outside, on any public place, including but not limited to any public street, public sidewalk, or public property within that area of the County of Santa Barbara described in the attached Exhibit "A" between the hours of 11:00 P.M. of one day and 6:00 A.M. of the following day.

2. Except in cases of personal emergency, no person shall be outside, or remain outside, on any public place, including but not limited to any public street, public sidewalk, or public property within that area of the County of Santa Barbara described in the attached Exhibit "B" and shown in the attached Exhibit "C" between the hours of 7:30 P.M. of one day and 6:00 A.M. of the following day.

3. No person shall conduct or participate in any meeting, assembly or parade, of more than 5 persons, or use voice or sound amplifying equipment, upon any public place, including but not limited to any public street, public sidewalk, or public property or in any meeting place open to the public, as defined herein, within the County of Santa Barbara in the area prescribed in the attached Exhibit "A".

4. As used in these regulations, "meeting place open to the public" means:

(a) The campus of the University of California at Santa Barbara, provided that scheduled classes shall not be affected and provided further that meetings and assemblies may be conducted on the campus of the University of California, Santa Barbara, at locations and in the manner designated for this purpose by the Chancellor.

(b) On improved real property owned by any public agency, including but not limited to the State of California, the County of Santa Barbara, or the City of Santa Barbara.

(c) Public parks, school playgrounds [provided that this provision shall not affect recreational activities of students of a public school district conducted on school property], municipal parking facilities, and property owned by the University of California.

5. No person, except a law enforcement officer or member of the National Guard, shall carry any firearm or other deadly weapon within the area prescribed in the attached Exhibit "A".

6. Regulations Nos. 1, 2, and 3 above shall not apply to policemen, peace officers, firemen, or other emergency personnel or civilians engaged in police or emergency work.

7. In determining whether an emergency exists for the purposes of interpreting or applying these regulations, the legal test as to whether a "personal emergency" exists shall be whether a reasonable person under the same or similar circumstances would believe that a personal emergency exists under such circumstances.

8. Regulations Nos. 1, 2, 3, 4, 5, 6, and 7 above shall become effective immediately and shall remain in effect until further notice. Any violation of these regulations is a misdemeanor as provided in Section 12-10 of the Santa Barbara County Code.

9. The sections, paragraphs, sentences, clauses, and phrases of these rules and regulations are severable, and if any phrase, clause, sentence, paragraph, or section of these rules and regulations shall be declared unconstitutional by the valid judgment or decree of a court of competent jurisdiction, such unconstitutionality shall not affect any of the remaining phrases, clauses, sentences, paragraphs and sections of these rules and regulations.

10. Administrative Order No. 70-13 and the regulations promulgated thereunder are hereby rescinded and superseded by these regulations; provided, however, that the rescission of said Administrative Order No. 70-13 and the rules and regulations adopted thereunder shall not affect the validity of any action heretofore taken

pursuant to said regulations, or any proceedings heretofore or hereafter commenced or prosecuted based on any violation of said rules and regulations prior to the effective date of their rescission.

In witness whereof, I have subscribed my signature this 11th day of June, 1970 at 6:00 P.M.

. . . .
RICHARD R. ROE,
Administrative Officer of the
County of Santa Barbara

[b] Sample Instruction: Knowledge of Curfew

DEFENDANT'S SPECIAL JURY INSTRUCTION NO. . . . . . .[1]

County Administrative Order No. . . . . . . requires the People to prove affirmatively knowledge, express or implied, of the curfew.

Knowledge may be proven by direct or circumstantial evidence.

If you find that the People fail to prove that the defendant had such knowledge, whether by direct or circumstantial evidence, then you must find the defendant not guilty.

GIVEN . . . .
MODIFIED . . . .
REFUSED . . . .
WITHDRAWN . . . .

. . . .
JUDGE OF THE SUPERIOR COURT

AUTHORITIES: *California Jury Instructions Criminal* (hereinafter cited as *CALJIC*) No. 1.21 (as adapted) (3d rev. ed. 1970).

[c] Sample Instruction: Defendant Authorized to Enter

DEFENDANT'S SPECIAL JURY INSTRUCTION NO. . . . . . .[2]

Nothing done under valid public authority is a crime if such authority is in no way exceeded or abused. If after considering the evidence in this case you find that an officer of the law authorized the defendant's entry into the curfew area and that such authorization was in no way exceeded or abused, then you must find the defendant not guilty.

GIVEN ....
MODIFIED ....
REFUSED ....
WITHDRAWN ....

....
JUDGE OF THE SUPERIOR COURT

AUTHORITIES: *People v. Ferguson*, 134 Cal. App. 41, 51–54, 24 P.2d 965, 967–971 (1933); R. Perkins, *Criminal Law*, 925, 977 (2d ed. 1969).

[d] Sample Instruction: Defendant Authorized to Enter

DEFENDANT'S SPECIAL JURY INSTRUCTION NO. ......[3]

If after weighing the evidence in this case you find that the police officers on duty at the entrance to the curfew area gave permission to the entry of defendant, you must find the defendant not guilty.

GIVEN ....
MODIFIED ....
REFUSED ....
WITHDRAWN ....

....
JUDGE OF THE SUPERIOR COURT

[e] Sample Instruction: Definition of "Loiter"

DEFENDANT'S SPECIAL JURY INSTRUCTION NO. ......[4]

As used in County Administrative Order No. ......, the term "loiter" is defined as follows:

To be slow in moving, to delay, to linger, to saunter, to lag behind, or to linger idly by the way.

However, you may not find the defendant guilty of the above stated ordinance, unless you find that the defendant "loitered" in such a nature that from the totality of his actions and in the light of the prevailing circumstances, you and each of you reasonably conclude that such "loitering" is being engaged in for the purpose of committing a crime as opportunity may be discovered.

GIVEN ....

MODIFIED ....

REFUSED ....

WITHDRAWN ....

....

JUDGE OF THE SUPERIOR COURT

AUTHORITIES: *In re Cregler*, 56 Cal. 2d 308, 311–312, 14 Cal. Rptr. 289, 291 (1961); *Mandell v. Municipal Court for Oakland-Piedmont Judicial District*, 276 Cal. App. 2d 649, 657, 81 Cal. Rptr. 173, 178–179 (1969).

[2] Jury Instructions Relating to Common Political Charges, as to Which Form Book Alternatives May Be Available

[a] Sample Statutes Relating to These Instructions (California Penal Code, Sections 148, 243 [in part] and 69)

California Penal Code, Section 148 provides:

"Every person who wilfully resists, delays, or obstructs any public officer, in the discharge or attempt to discharge any duty of his office, when no other punishment is prescribed, is punishable by a fine not exceeding one thousand dollars, or by imprisonment in a county jail not exceeding one year, or by both such fine and imprisonment."

California Penal Code, Section 243 provides in part:

"A battery is punishable by fine of not exceeding one thousand dollars ($1,000), or by imprisonment in the county jail not exceeding six months, or by both. When it is committed against the person of a peace officer or fireman, and the person committing the offense knows or reasonably should know that such victim is a peace officer or fireman engaged in the performance of his duties, and such peace officer or fireman is engaged in the performance of his duties, the offense shall be punished by imprisonment in the county jail not exceeding one year or by imprisonment in the state prison for not less than one nor more than 10 years."

California Penal Code, Section 69 provides:

"Every person who attempts, by means of any threat or violence, to deter or prevent an executive officer from performing any duty imposed upon such officer by law, or who knowingly resists, by the use of force or violence, such officer, in the performance of his duty, is punishable by a fine not exceeding five thousand dollars, or by imprisonment in the state prison not exceeding five years or in a county jail not exceeding one year, or by both such fine and imprisonment."

[b] Sample Instruction: Resisting Officer; Excessive Force

DEFENDANT'S SPECIAL JURY INSTRUCTION NO. ......

You are further instructed with respect to the charge of violating Section 148 of the Penal Code as follows:

It is a necessary element of this offense, which the People must prove beyond a reasonable doubt, that at the time defendant .... allegedly resisted, delayed and obstructed Sgt. ...., Sgt. .... was engaged in the performance of his duty as a police officer. It is not part of the duty of a police officer to use excessive force in detaining or arresting any person. Accordingly, even if you find that defendant knew or reasonably should have known that Sgt. .... was a police officer, if you also find that Sgt. .... or any of the other police officers involved in detaining defendant was himself guilty of exceeding the scope of his duty by using excessive force in detaining defendant, then defendant .... had a legal right to use reasonable force to defend himself against such excessive force on the part of such officer or officers. Provided defendant used only such reasonable force to defend himself, then defendant is entitled to a verdict of not guilty.

....
JUDGE OF THE MUNICIPAL COURT

DEFENDANT ....'s PROPOSED INSTRUCTION ...

GIVEN ....
MODIFIED ....
REFUSED ....
WITHDRAWN ....

AUTHORITIES: *People v. Curtis,* 70 Cal. 2d 347, 354–357, 450 P.2d 33, 36–39, 74 Cal. Rptr. 713, 717–719 (1969); *People v. Jones,* 8 Cal. App. 3d 710, 716–718, 87 Cal. Rptr. 625, 628–630 (1970); *People v. Muniz,* 4 Cal. App. 3d 562, 567, 84 Cal. Rptr. 501, 504 (1970); accord, *People v. Hood,* 1 Cal. 3d 444, 450–451, 82 Cal. Rptr. 618, 621, 462 P.2d 370, 373 (1969). Adaptation of *CALJIC* No. 5.65.

[c] Sample Instruction: Resisting Officer; Knowledge; Excessive Force

DEFENDANT'S SPECIAL JURY INSTRUCTION NO. ......

You are further instructed, with respect to Count .... of the Indictment, which charges a violation of Section 243 of the Penal Code, as follows:

It is a necessary element of this offense, which the People must prove beyond a reasonable doubt, that defendant .... knew or reasonably should have known at the time he allegedly used force and violence against Detective ...., first, that said .... was a police officer; and second, that he was then engaged in the performance of his duties. If such knowledge is not proved beyond a reasonable doubt, defendant is entitled to an acquittal on this count. In this connection, you are instructed that defendant was not required to guess either the officer's identity or his purpose.

If you find that defendant .... realized that Detective .... was a police officer, but also find either that said detective was himself guilty of exceeding the scope of his duties by using excessive force in detaining defendant, or that defendant .... reasonably thought that Detective .... was using excessive force, then defendant .... had a legal right to use reasonable force to defend himself against such excessive force on the part of Detective ...., and provided defendant used only such reasonable force to defend himself, then defendant is entitled to an acquittal on this count.

You are instructed that even if defendant .... knew or reasonably should have known that Detective .... was a police officer attempting to perform some legal duty, and even if defendant used force and violence against Detective .... which was not necessary or was more than necessary to defend himself, in order for defendant to be guilty of violating Section 243, it is also necessary that Detective .... shall have been engaged in making a lawful arrest or a lawful detention of defendant. If he was attempting to arrest defendant unlawfully, or to detain him without a proper legal cause, then defendant could not be guilty of violating Section 243, although such circumstances would not bar a conviction for the lesser included offense of battery, a misdemeanor. I shall presently define battery for you.

....
JUDGE OF THE SUPERIOR COURT

DEFENDANT'S PROPOSED SPECIAL INSTRUCTION NO. ....

GIVEN ....
MODIFIED ....
REFUSED ....
WITHDRAWN ....

AUTHORITIES: *People v. Curtis*, 70 Cal. 2d 347, 359, 450 P.2d 33, 74 Cal. Rptr. 713 (1969); accord: *People v. Hood*, 1 Cal. 3d 444, 450–451, 462 P.2d 370, 373, 82 Cal. Rptr. 618, 621 (1970).

[d] Sample Form Book Instruction: Resisting Arrest

If a person has knowledge, or by the exercise of reasonable care should have knowledge, that he is being arrested by a peace officer, it is the duty of such person to refrain from using force [or any weapon] to resist such arrest.

[However, if you find that the peace officer used excessive force in making the arrest, it is not the duty of such person to refrain from using force to resist such arrest.]

....
JUDGE OF THE SUPERIOR COURT

GIVEN ....
MODIFIED ....
REFUSED ....
WITHDRAWN ....

AUTHORITIES: Exact copy of *CALJIC* No. 5.65 (1972 rev.)

[e] Sample Instruction: Resisting Arrest; Unreasonable Force, Arising Out of Street Stop and Detention "For Purposes of Questioning"

DEFENDANT'S SPECIAL JURY INSTRUCTION NO. ......

You are further instructed, with reference to Counts ...., ... and .... of the information, each of which charges a violation of Section 69 of the Penal Code, a felony, as follows:

In order to establish a violation of this section, the People must prove beyond a reasonable doubt, first, that the deputies themselves were engaged in performing lawful duties when they stopped defendant on the street and used force to detain him for questioning; and second, he knew not only that the deputies were police officers, but that they were engaged in the performance of lawful duties. In this connection, you are further instructed that a police officer may not lawfully stop a citizen for questioning, or use any force whatsoever to detain him on the street, on the basis of a hunch or a suspicion, even though the officer may be acting in good faith, where the apparent facts are equally consistent with innocent activity on the part of the citizen as with any criminal activity. You are also instructed that the deputies were under a legal duty not only to identify themselves as police officers but also to state their purpose before initiating any form of violence or physical restraint against defendant ...., and that defendant was not required to guess the identity of any officer whom he could not see, nor was defendant required to guess the purpose of the officers whether or not he could see them.

If you find that the People have failed to prove beyond a reasonable doubt that the action of these officers in stopping defendant was in the lawful exercise of their duties, including their action in stopping defendant and using force to detain him, then defendant .... is entitled to an acquittal of all charges of violating Penal Code Section 69.

You are further instructed that even if you find that the People have proved beyond a reasonable doubt that the deputies were acting in the lawful exercise of their duties and that defendant knew this to be a fact, but also find either that one or more of the deputies was guilty of exceeding the scope of his duties by using excessive force in detaining defendant, or that defendant .... reasonably thought that he was using excessive force, then defendant .... had a legal right to use reasonable force himself against such excessive force on the part of the deputy; and provided defendant used only such reasonable force to defend himself, then defendant is entitled to an acquittal on these counts charging a violation of Penal Code Section 69.

. . . .
JUDGE OF THE SUPERIOR COURT

DEFENDANT'S PROPOSED SPECIAL INSTRUCTION NO. . . . .

GIVEN . . . .
MODIFIED . . . .
REFUSED . . . .
WITHDRAWN . . . .

AUTHORITIES: *Irwin v. Superior Court,* 1 Cal. 3d 423, 426–428, 462 P.2d 12, 14–15, 82 Cal. Rptr. 484, 485–487 (1969); *People v. Moore,* 69 Cal. 2d 674, 682–683, 446 P.2d 800, 805–806, 72 Cal. Rptr. 800, 805–806 (1968); *People v. One 1960 Cadillac Coupe,* 62 Cal. 2d 92, 96, 396 P.2d 706, 708–709, 41 Cal. Rptr. 290, 292–293 (1964); *People v. Lingo,* 3 Cal. App. 3d 661, 664–665, 83 Cal. Rptr. 755, 757 (1970); *People v. Escollias,* 264 Cal. App. 2d 16, 19–20, 70 Cal. Rptr. 65, 67 (1968); *People v. Henze,* 253 Cal. App. 2d 986, 988–990, 61 Cal. Rptr. 545, 547–548 (1967); *People v. Hunt,* 250 Cal. App. 2d 311, 314–315, 58 Cal. Rptr. 385, 387–388 (1967); accord: *Cunha v. Superior Court,* 2 Cal. 3d 352, 355–356, 466 P.2d 704, 85 Cal. Rptr. 160 (1970); *People v. Collins,* 1 Cal. 3d 658, 463 P.2d 403, 83 Cal. Rptr. 179 (1970); *Jackson v. Superior Court,* 274 Cal. App. 2d 656, 659, 79 Cal. Rptr. 502–504 (1969); *Terry v. Ohio,* 392 U.S. 1, 20 L. Ed. 2d 889, 88 S. Ct. 1868 (1968); *Sibron v. New York,* 392 U.S. 40, 20 L. Ed. 2d 917, 88 S. Ct. 1889 (1968); Fourth and Fourteenth Amendments to the Constitution of the United States; Article I, Sections 1, 2, 3, and 13 (Clause 6) of the California Constitution.

[f] Adaptation of Form Book Instruction: Resisting Arrest; Specific Intent; Knowledge

DEFENDANT'S SPECIAL JURY INSTRUCTION NO. . . . . . . [5]

In the crimes charged in each count of this information, there must exist a union or joint operation of act or conduct and a certain specific intent.

In the crime of violating Penal Code Section 69, there must exist in the mind of the perpetrator the specific intent to deter and prevent an executive officer from performing duties imposed upon such officer by law by means of threats and violence, and to knowingly resist an executive officer by means of force and violence in the performance of duties imposed upon such officer by law, and unless such intent so exists that crime is not committed.

In the crime of violating Penal Code Section 243, the perpetrator must have actual knowledge or reasonably should have actual knowledge that the peace officer is then and there engaged in the performance of his duties, and unless such knowledge exists that crime is not committed.

. . . .

JUDGE OF THE SUPERIOR COURT

GIVEN . . . .
MODIFIED . . . .
REFUSED . . . .
WITHDRAWN . . . .

AUTHORITIES: Adaptation of *CALJIC* No. 3.31.

[g] Sample Instruction: Resisting Arrest; Excessive Force (Example of Blockbuster Instruction)

[Author's Note: the following is an instruction which was given after the jury had been hung for more than a day, having received complicated instructions along the lines of several previously quoted in this appendix. This is cited as a prime example of the importance of any instruction given to the jury after it retires, and particularly after it requests further instructions. While minds may differ as to whether this instruction should have been included among those originally read to the jury (I think it should have been) it certainly broke things loose in favor of the defense.]

DEFENDANT'S SPECIAL JURY INSTRUCTION NO. . . . . . .

You are further instructed that if the deputies or any of them used excessive force in detaining defendant . . . ., and if any resistance offered by defendant . . . . was in response to such excessive force, then defendant may not be convicted of any crime but is entitled to an acquittal on all counts and to an acquittal on all lesser included offenses. This is true regardless whether the deputies were legally correct in stopping defendant.

. . . .
JUDGE OF THE SUPERIOR COURT

GIVEN . . . .
MODIFIED . . . .
REFUSED . . . .
WITHDRAWN . . . .

[h] Sample Instruction: Defendant Not to Be Convicted Because of Crimes of Other Persons

DEFENDANT'S SPECIAL JURY INSTRUCTION NO. . . . . . .

You are instructed that Defendant . . . . may not be convicted of any crime by reason of criminal actions, such as rock throwing, on the part of other persons. In these proceedings, he is responsible only for what he did alone, if anything.

. . . .
JUDGE OF THE SUPERIOR COURT

DEFENDANT'S PROPOSED SPECIAL INSTRUCTION NO. . . . .

GIVEN . . . .
MODIFIED . . . .
REFUSED . . . .
WITHDRAWN . . . .

[3] Where Government Interference Makes it Necessary to Stretch Jury Instructions Beyond Previous Limits

[a] Sample Form Book Instruction (Illustrating Conventional Instructions Regarding Entrapment) [6]

A person is not guilty of crime when he commits an act or engages in conduct, otherwise criminal, when the idea to commit the crime did not originate in the mind of the defendant but originated in the mind of another and was suggested to the defendant by a law enforcement officer or a person acting under the direction, suggestion or control of a law enforcement officer for the purpose of inducing defendant to commit the crime in order to entrap him and cause his arrest.

When law-enforcement officers are informed that a person intends to commit a crime, the law permits the officers to afford opportunity for the commission of the offense, and to lend the apparent cooperation of themselves or of a third person for the purpose of detecting the offender. When officers do this, if the suspect himself, originally and independently of the officers, intends to commit the acts constituting a crime, and if he does acts necessary to constitute the crime, he is guilty of the crime committed. He has no defense in the fact that an officer or other person engaged in detecting crime was present and provided the opportunity, or aided or encouraged the commission of the offense.

When a person acts as a detective for the purpose of apprehending another believed to be bent on crime, and to that end pretends to be an accomplice of the suspect, no act done by the detective may be imputed to or held against the suspect unless the latter, in exercise of his independent will, directs that the act be done.

. . . .

JUDGE OF THE SUPERIOR COURT

GIVEN . . . .
MODIFIED . . . .
REFUSED . . . .
WITHDRAWN . . . .

AUTHORITIES: Exact copy of *CALJIC* Nos. 4.60 (1970 revision), 4.61, 4.62 (3d rev. ed. 1970).

[b] Jury Instruction Given in *United States v. Anderson, et al.,* ("The Camden 28") [7]

Now, there is another defense available to the defendants but available only if you find the facts substantiate the principle of law which I am about to give you.

You have heard the terms "creative activity" and "overreaching governmental participation."

As you will recall the evidence regarding the Government's participation in this case focused to a great extent on the activities of Robert Hardy who has testified here. Before you consider this defense, you, as able judges of the facts, must determine what role Mr. Hardy played in this case.

The evidence varies at several points, and the inferences that you may or may not draw could vary on certain points, as to what actually happened. Only you as jurors can resolve the factual disputes as to what occurred in the spring and summer of 1971. Then you must determine whether these acts, as you find them, reach an intolerable degree of overreaching governmental participation.

These activities, you must find, must have been intolerable and have gone beyond the limits of permissible law enforcement techniques I have just discussed in giving you the charge of entrapment.

That is to say, if you find that the overreaching participation by Government agents or informers in the activities as you have heard them here was so fundamentally unfair [as] to be offensive to the basic standards of decency, and shocking to the universal sense of justice, then you may acquit any defendant to whom this defense applies.

Furthermore, under this particular defense, you need not consider the predisposition of any defendant; because if the governmental activities reached the point that I have just defined in your own minds, then the predisposition of any defendant would not matter.

[4] Jury Instructions for Use Where the Government Has Stretched Criminal Statutes in Order to Create Political Crimes (Selected Instructions Requested by Defense in *United States v. Russo and Ellsberg*) [8]

[a] Necessity of Making Information Public as Defense To All Counts; Reasonableness of Method [G-13]

I instruct you that even if you find that the government has proved beyond a reasonable doubt that the defendants committed the acts with which they are charged in any count of the indictment, you may nevertheless acquit them if you find that their acts were justified by the necessity of releasing Exhibits 1–20.

In order to find that the acts of the defendants were justified, you must find:

1) That the defendants were reasonable in their belief that the

continued suppression of the information in Exhibits 1-20 was a greater evil to the United States than any which might result from the reproduction and release of the exhibits.[1]

2) That the defendants were reasonable in their belief that the reproduction or release of the information was necessary to bring before Congress and the public the true facts concerning the war in Vietnam so as to permit the constitutional and democratic processes of the country to function.

With respect to the second of these two facts, the issue is not whether the reproduction or release of the information in these documents was the only possible means of bringing those facts to Congress or the public or that in fact it was successful to that end, but whether a reasonable man would have anticipated a direct causal relationship between the reproduction or release of the information and disclosure of the facts necessary to inform Congress and the public.[2]

If you find that the acts of Dr. Ellsberg and Mr. Russo were justified by the necessity of terminating a greater evil, they necessarily cannot have had the specific intent necessary for a finding of guilt, and they must therefore be acquitted.

[AUTHORITIES:] Generally: *United States v. Holmes*, 26 F. Cas. 360 (No. 15, 383), (E.D. Pa. 1842); *United States v. Ashton*, 24 F. Cas. 873 (No. 14, 470) (C.C.D. Mass. 1834); *United States v. Nye*, 27 F. Cas. 210 (No. 15, 906) (C.C.D. Mass. 1855); *Browning v. State*, 31 Ala. App. 137, 13 So. 2d 54 (1943); *Commonwealth v. Wheeler*, 53 N.E.2d 4 (Mass. 1944); *Rex v. Borne*, 1 K.B. 687, 3 All. E.R. 615 (1939); *United States v. Simpson*, 460 F.2d 515 (9th Cir. 1972); *United States v. Kroncke*, 459 F.2d 697 (8th Cir. 1972); A.L.I. *Model Penal Code*, §§ 3.01, 3.02 and *Comments* (Tent. Draft. No. 8, 1958); National Commission on Reform of Federal Criminal Laws, *Proposed Statutes*, §§ 608, 609 and *Working Papers*, pp. 261–272.

Defendants' Memorandum in Support of Offer of Proof for Paul McCloskey, filed 3/5/73, is hereby incorporated by reference.

---

[1] National Commission on Reform of Federal Criminal Laws, Proposed Statutes, 608, 609, and Working Papers, p. 263, para. 4.

[2] United States v. Simpson, 460 F.2d 515 (9th Cir. 1972); United States v. Kroncke, 459 F.2d 697 (8th Cir. 1972).

[b] 18 U.S.C. § 641; Language of Statute [T-2]

Count Two charges a violation of Section 641 of Title 18, United States Code, which provides, in the part pertinent to this count:

"Whoever embezzles, steals, . . . or knowingly converts to his use or the use of another . . . any . . . thing of value of the United States or of any department or agency thereof . . . shall be fined not more than $10,000 or imprisoned not more than ten years, or both, but if the value of such property does not exceed the sum of $100, he shall be find not more than $1,000 or imprisoned for not more than one year, or both."

AUTHORITY: 18 U.S.C. § 641.

[c] Elements of Offense (18 U.S.C. § 641); Prosecution Burden of Proof [T-3]

In order to find Dr. Ellsberg guilty of Count Two, you must find that the prosecution has proven beyond a reasonable doubt each and every one of the following elements of the offense:

First, that Dr. Ellsberg stole, embezzled or converted Exhibits 1, 3, 9-14 and 18-20 at the time and place charged. This means in turn that you must find that

> a. the exhibits listed in this count were properly classified;
> b. the provisions of the RAND manual applied to them;
> c. Dr. Ellsberg handled the exhibits in a manner that permanently or substantially deprived the United States of the use or benefit of the exhibits.

Second, that the exhibits listed in this count were the property of the United States at the time of the alleged offense.

Third, that Dr. Ellsberg had knowledge that the exhibits were the property of the United States.

Fourth, that Dr. Ellsberg specifically intended to permanently or substantially deprive the United States of its property.

Fifth, that the exhibits had a value in excess of $100.

Failure of the prosecution to prove beyond a reasonable doubt any one of these elements or sub-elements must result in a finding of not guilty of count two.

AUTHORITY: *Morissette v. United States,* 342 U.S. 246 (1952); *Ailsworth v. United States,* 448 F.2d 439, 442 (C.A. 9, 1971); *United States v. Collins,* 464 F.2d 1163 (C.A. 9, 1972); *United States v. Trinder,* 1 F. Supp. 659 (D. Mont. 1932) *Chappell v. United States,* 270 F.2d 274 (C.A. 9, 1959); *Government of the Virgin Islands v. Williams,* 424 F.2d 526 (C.A. 3, 1970); *United States v. Kemble,* 197 F.2d 316 (C.A. 3, 1952); *Kirby v. United States,* 174 U.S. 47 (1898); *Conerly v. United States,* 350 F.2d 679, 681 (C.A. 9, 1965); *United States v. Yokum,* 417 F.2d 253 (C.A. 4, 1962); *Findley v. United States,* 362 F.2d 921 (C.A. 10, 1965); *United States v. Johnston,* 268 U.S. 220, 226–227; *United States v. Alessio,* 439 F.2d 803 (C.A. 1, 1970); *United States v. Wilson,* 284 F.2d 407 (C.A. 4, 1960); *United States v. Payne,* 467 F.2d 828 (C.A. 5, 1972).

[d] Sub-Element: Exec. Order No. 10501; Propriety of Classification of Documents: Invalidity of Classification For Purpose of Avoiding Political Embarrassment; Necessity for Action by Person Solely Authorized [T-4]

The first element of Count Two involves three sub-elements as I have indicated, and I will deal with each separately.

The first sub-element requires that you find beyond a reasonable doubt that the exhibits listed in the count were properly classified.

There is only one basis for classifying information under the Government's classification system in Executive Order 10501. That is when a person with original classifying authority determines that the information is official information requiring protection in the interests of national defense.[1]

A document may be marked by an individual as being classified if it contains a reproduction or copy of information already properly classified at the time the new document is completed. This is called reproductive or derivative classification.[2]

I instruct you that Exhibits 1, 3, 9-14 and 18, all Pentagon Papers volumes, and Exhibit 20, the Gurtov memorandum, were not classified by the original classification method because the persons who classified them were not authorized to exercise original top secret classification. You may find therefore that these exhibits were properly classified only if you find that they were properly classified as an exercise of reproductive or derivative classification.

---

[1] Exec. Order 10501, §§ 1, 2, 3.

[2] Id. at § 5(g).

To find that an exhibit is properly classified by the reproductive or derivative classification method, you must first find that information in the exhibit was taken from the text of a source document bearing an outstanding, proper classification mark.[3] This means that the source document must have had a classification mark on it, and that the source document had not been declassified at the time that the exhibit was marked classified. [Amended] Indications in Exhibits 1, 3, 5, 9-14, and 18 and 20 themselves that information was taken from source documents marked classified are not to be considered at all by you in this regard.

For example, some footnotes in some of the exhibits have notations in parentheses that the source document was classified. These notations are what is called hearsay and are not proof of anything.

Second, you must find that information drawn from the source document was marked classified in that source document. You have heard testimony about markings by paragraphs. Even though a document as a whole may bear a classification marking, not all information within the document is necessarily classified. Any given paragraph may be marked "unclassified."[4] The prosecution must prove beyond a reasonable doubt that each of Exhibits 1-18 and Exhibit 20 contained information which was marked classified in the source document from which it was drawn.

Third, you must find that the person who classified the exhibit did so with reference to, and under the authority of applicable regulations within the Executive branch. You must find that the classifiers knew those regulations and made an effort to follow them in classifying the exhibit. If the exhibit was classified according to an office practice of marking "Top Secret" all documents relating to Vietnam to be sent to the Secretary of Defense, you must find that it was not properly classified. If you find that an exhibit was classified to avoid embarrassment or to cover up political mistakes, then you must find that the document was not properly classified.[5]

Fourth, you must find that the person who classified the exhibit either himself made an evaluation of the currency, accuracy and necessity of the classification of the source documents or referred them to the governmental agency which originally classified the source documents for such evaluation. If you find that no such evaluation was

---

[3] Dod Instr. 5210-47, § V, B.(1), (3).

[4] Id. at § VII, C.(3).

[5] Id. at § III, E.

made, then you must find that the document was not properly classified.[6]

Fifth, you must find that each of the paragraphs in each exhibit were given an individual classification marking or that a guide was attached to or included in each exhibit to indicate which information in the report was classified.[7]

You are instructed that there is no evidence in this case that Exhibit 19, the eight-page excerpt from the Wheeler Report, was classified as an exercise of reproductive or derivative classification. To convict, you must find beyond a reasonable doubt that the exhibit was properly classified as an exercise of original classification.

You must first find that Exhibit 19 was classified by a person authorized to exercise original top secret classification. There was testimony by General DePuy that General Wheeler made the ultimate decision on the full report's top secret classification. General Wheeler was a person authorized to exercise original top secret classification. However, you must find beyond a reasonable doubt that General Wheeler personally assigned the classification to Exhibit 19, because his classification authority could not be exercised for him or in his name by anyone else.[8] In making this determination, you may consider both General De Puy's testimony and the fact that the exhibit itself contains no indication that General Wheeler himself assigned the classification.

Second, with respect to Exhibit 19, you must find that each paragraph of the full Wheeler report was given an individual classification marking or that a guide was attached to or included in it to indicate the information in the report that was classified.[9]

[e] Sub-Element: Applicability of RAND Security Manual [T-5]

The second sub-element requires you to find beyond a reasonable doubt that the provisions of the RAND Manual applied to the documents listed in the count. This means that you must find beyond a reasonable doubt that the person under whose authority the docu-

---

[6] Id. at § V, B.(2), (3).

[7] Id. at § VIII, C.(3).

[8] Exec. Order 10501, § 2.

[9] Dod Instr. 5210.47, § VIII, C.(3).

632 / POLITICAL CRIMINAL TRIALS

ments were sent to RAND or stored at RAND intended that the RAND Security Manual apply to them.

In making this determination, you may consider:

Whether the Exhibits were sent to RAND under a specific work contract between RAND and a governmental agency;

Whether the Exhibits were sent to RAND under a specific agreement which differed from the terms of the RAND Security Manual;

Whether any RAND official gave instructions for the handling of the Exhibits which differed from the terms of the RAND Security Manual; and

Whether RAND officials treated the Exhibits in a manner different from the terms of the RAND Security Manual.

[f] Sub-Element: Handling Documents So As to Deprive Government of Use, Benefit and Value; Necessity for Direct Property Loss [T-6]

The third sub-element requires you to find beyond a reasonable doubt that Dr. Ellsberg handled the exhibits in a manner that permanently or substantially deprived the United States of their use and benefit.

In other words, you must find beyond a reasonable doubt that he used the Exhibits in a specifically unauthorized manner which completely or substantially deprived the owner of their use, benefit and value. Thus, as a result of Dr. Ellsberg's conduct, the government must have suffered an actual and direct property loss, either complete or substantial, of the use, benefit or value of the physical exhibits themselves. In making this determination, you are not to consider whether the government was deprived of its control of the information in the documents, or of any copies of the exhibits. There is no charge before you dealing with either the information in or copies of the exhibits.

Not every unauthorized use of the property of another is a stealing, embezzlement or conversion. The unauthorized use must result in a complete or substantial loss of the use, benefit and value of the physical property to its owner. Thus even if you find that the exhibits were properly classified and that the Rand Security Manual applied to them and that Dr. Ellsberg's conduct violated the provisions of the Rand Manual, you may not find him guilty of Count Two unless you also find beyond a reasonable doubt that his conduct completely or substantially deprived the government of the use, benefit or value of the physical exhibits.

In making a determination as to whether Dr. Ellsberg's conduct did so deprive the United States you may consider the following factors:

Whether anyone entitled to use the exhibits requested use of them or tried to use them and was deprived of using them as a result of Dr. Ellsberg's conduct;

Whether Dr. Ellsberg's conduct impaired the physical use, value or benefit of the exhibits in any way;

Whether the exhibits were returned to RAND;

Whether the exhibits' physical use, value or benefit was impaired when they were returned to RAND.

AUTHORITY: *United States v. Collins*, 464 F.2d 1163, 1165 (C.A. 9, 1972); *United States v. Johnston*, 268 U.S. 220, 226–227 (1925); *United States v. Alessio*, 439 F.2d 803 (C.A. 1, 1970).

[g] Sub-Element: Government Ownership of Documents; Classification Irrelevant to Ownership [T-7]

The second element of Count Two requires the prosecution to prove beyond a reasonable doubt that the exhibits were the property of the government at the time of the alleged offense. The mere fact that the government at the outset produced the exhibits does not determine ownership any more than the fact that a publishing company publishes a book forever determines its ownership. Nor does the fact that the exhibits bear the name of a government agency determine ownership any more than the fact that a book bears the publishing company's name forever determine its ownership.

In deciding who owned the exhibits you may consider the following factors:

Whether the Vietnam study exhibits were a complete set of study volumes and whether they were ever made a part of the formal files of the Department of Defense; and

Whether the study exhibits were transferred to RAND as privately owned, personal papers in accordance with the practice of senior officials leaving government. You may consider the manner in which the study exhibits were transferred to and stored at RAND. You may consider who controlled the use of the study exhibits while they were at RAND; and

Whether the study exhibits were treated as personal or private papers by RAND and government officials, and the manner in which the study exhibits were returned from RAND to the Department of Defense in 1971. You may consider whether other sets of the study were treated by the government as the private property of third persons; and

Whether other documents stored with the study exhibits were treated as the private property of third persons.

In considering whether the government owned the exhibits, you must not take into account at all the fact that they were classified. That fact is irrelevant to ownership. Classified documents may be owned by private persons.

AUTHORITY: *Morissette v. United States,* 342 U.S. 246 (1952); Defendants' Offer of Proof regarding Personal Papers.

[h] Sub-Element: Defendant's Knowledge That Documents Were Property of Government; Mistaken Belief to the Contrary as Defense [T-8]

The third element of Count Two requires the prosecution to prove beyond a reasonable doubt that Dr. Ellsberg knew that the documents were the property of the United States or any department or agency thereof at the time of the alleged taking. Thus, even if the government was the owner of the documents, if the defendant mistakenly believed in good faith that they belonged to someone other than the government, he cannot be convicted of Count Two.

AUTHORITY: *Kirby v. United States,* 174 U.S. 47, 53 (1898); *Conerly v. United States,* 350 U.S. 679, 681 (C.A. 9, 1965); *United States v. Yokum,* 417 F.2d 253 (C.A. 4, 1962); *Findley v. United States,* 362 F.2d 921 (C.A. 10, 1965).

[i] Sub-Element: Specific Intent to Deprive Government of Use of Property; Other Kinds of Wrongful Intent Not Sufficient; Factors to Consider [T-9]

The fourth element of Count Two requires the prosecution to prove beyond a reasonable doubt that Dr. Ellsberg specifically intended to permanently or substantially deprive the United States of its property. Specific intent may not be inferred from the fact of possession of the exhibits alone. It is a question of fact to be determined by you from a consideration of all the facts and circumstances in the case, including Dr. Ellsberg's conduct with respect to the documents, conversations he may have had regarding the documents and his own testimony.

An intent merely to use the exhibits in a wrongful manner temporarily and then to return them is not by itself enough for stealing, embezzlement or conversion. If Dr. Ellsberg merely intended to put them to a brief unauthorized use and then to return them, you may not find him guilty of Count Two. You must find that he intended that his conduct cause a complete or substantial loss of the use, benefit or value of the exhibits to the government or that he knew that his conduct was likely to result in such a loss.

In determining whether Dr. Ellsberg had such a specific intent, you may consider the following factors:

Whether he intended to return the exhibits to RAND;

Whether he intended to injure the exhibits in any way, and

Whether he intended to prevent any person entitled to use the exhibits from using them.

You may, of course, consider the length of time he took the exhibits away from the RAND building in Santa Monica.

Evidence that the classification markings were clipped from copies of the exhibits and that copying of the exhibits was done secretly is irrelevant to Dr. Ellsberg's intent under this count and is not to be considered at all in this regard. You must consider only Dr. Ellsberg's intent with respect to the exhibits. Anything he may have intended to do with copies of the exhibits or the information in the exhibits is irrelevant and is not to be considered at all in this regard.

AUTHORITY: *Morissette v. United States*, 342 U.S. 246, 266 (1952); *United States v. Trinder*, 1 F. Supp. 659 (D. Mont. (1932);

Ailsworth v. United States, 448 F.2d 439, 442 (C.A. 9, 1971); *United States v. Collins,* 464 F.2d 1163 (C.A. 9, 1972); *Government of Virgin Islands v. Williams,* 424 F.2d 526 (C.A. 3, 1970); Perkins, *Criminal Law* 266, 267 (2nd ed. 1969); Clark and Marshall, *Law of Crimes,* § 12.04 (6th ed. 1958); Holmes, *The Common Law* 71 (1881).

[j] Sub-Element: Value of Documents; Market Value, Not Cost of Research [T-10]

The fifth element of Count Two requires the prosecution to prove beyond a reasonable doubt that the value of the exhibits in this count exceeds $100.00.

The word "value" here means market value, the value at which property is sold in trade. You are not to consider here the cost of the whole study. The task force produced many studies other than those before you and there were numerous copies made of each study. You are to consider only the market value of the particular copies of the particular studies which are before you as Exhibits 1, 3, 9–14, 18 and 20. In determining the market value of the exhibits, you are not to consider the fact that the information in the exhibits was marked classified.

AUTHORITY: *United States v. Wilson,* 284 F.2d 407 (C.A. 4, 1960); *United States v. Payne,* 467 F.2d 828, 830 (C.A. 5, 1972); *United States v. Bottone,* 365 F.2d 389 (C.A. 2, 1966); 3 Wigmore, *Evidence* § 718(2) (Chiadbourn rev. ed.).

[k] Element (of Another Count): Concealment of Documents; From Whom Concealed; Factors to Consider [T-14]

The first element of Count Three requires that the prosecution prove beyond a reasonable doubt that Dr. Ellsberg concealed or retained the exhibits at the time and place charged with the intent to convert them to his own use or gain.

In order to find that Dr. Ellsberg concealed the exhibits, you must find beyond a reasonable doubt that he acted affirmatively to hide and prevent the discovery of the exhibits for the purpose of preventing the government from recovering them. You are to consider only whether Dr. Ellsberg concealed the exhibits from the authorities who transferred possession of them to him and not whether he may have concealed them from other persons. In making this determination, you may consider the following factors:

Whether the exhibits had been kept out of the RAND top secret control before Dr. Ellsberg obtained them;

Whether RAND officials knew Dr. Ellsberg had the exhibits and where he kept them;

Whether RAND records, including receipts signed by Ellsberg showed that Dr. Ellsberg had the exhibits;

Whether Dr. Ellsberg received special instructions from any RAND official regarding the manner in which he should keep the study exhibits.

In order to find that Dr. Ellsberg retained the exhibits, you must find beyond a reasonable doubt that he acted affirmatively to withhold them for a substantial period of time for the purpose of preventing the government from recovering them. Again, you are to consider only whether Dr. Ellsberg withheld the exhibits from the authorities who transferred them to him, and not whether he may have withheld them from other persons. In making this determination, you may consider the following factors:

Whether any authorized officials requested that Dr. Ellsberg return the exhibits;

Whether Dr. Ellsberg ever refused to return the exhibits;

Whether he ever did return the exhibits;

Whether he was ever specifically told that he could keep the exhibits only for a limited period of time, as with a library book.

In determining whether Dr. Ellsberg is guilty of Count Three, your consideration must be limited to the actual exhibits which are the subject of this count. No charge is made with respect to copies that Dr. Ellsberg may have made of the exhibits or which respect to the information in them. Dr. Ellsberg's conduct with regard to any such copies or such information is irrelevant and you must not consider it.

If you find that Dr. Ellsberg did conceal or retain the exhibits, you must also find beyond a reasonable doubt that he did so with the specific intent to convert the exhibits themselves to his own use or gain. This requires the prosecution to prove that he acted with the specific intent to deprive the government completely or substantially of the use, value, or benefit of the exhibits or that he actually knew that his conduct would create a substantial risk of such deprivation. I have already instructed you under Count Two as to the meaning of this intent and knowledge requirement.

AUTHORITY: Conceal: *Verdugo v. United States,* 402 F.2d 599, 604, 605 (C.A. 9, 1968); *United States v. Shapiro,* 113 F.2d 891, 893 (C.A. 2, 1940); *United States v. Mathies,* 203 F. Supp. 797, 800 (W.D. Pa. 1962); *Susnjar v. United States,* 27 F.2d 223, 224 (C.A. 6, 1928); *Feinstein v. United States,* 390 F.2d 50, 54 (C.A. 8, 1968), cert. denied 392 U.S. 943, Black's Law Dictionary (4th ed. 1968). Retain: *United States v. Mendoza,* 122 F. Supp. 367 (N.D. Cal. 1954); Burdick, Law of Crimes § 613; *People v. Williams,* 253 Cal. App. 2d 952, 957, 61 Cal. Rptr. 238, 242 (1967). See also DeVitt and Blackmar § 13.10.

[l] 18 U.S.C. § 793(c); Language of Statute [ND-2]

Count Nine charges violations of Section 793(c) of Title 18, United States Code, which provides in the parts pertinent to this count:

> "Whoever, for the purpose [of obtaining information respecting the national defense] receives or obtains . . . from any person, or from any source whatever, any documents . . . of anything connected with the national defense, knowing or having reason to believe, at the time he receives or obtains . . . it, that it . . . will be obtained . . . or disposed of by any person contrary to the provisions of this chapter . . . shall be fined not more than $10,000 or imprisoned not more than ten years, or both."

AUTHORITY: 18 U.S.C. § 793(c); Legislative History of 18 U.S.C. § 793, as described in Defendants' Memorandum in Support of Motion to Dismiss, pp. 31–41.

[m] Elements of Offense (18 U.S.C. § 793(c)) [ND-3]

In order to find Dr. Ellsberg guilty of Count Nine you must find that the Government has proven beyond a reasonable doubt each and every one of the following elements of this offense:

First, that he received and obtained Exhibit 19 (eight pages from the Wheeler Report) from the RAND Corporation (Santa Monica) on or about October 3, 1969;

Second, that Exhibit 19, the Wheeler Report, was, in fact, related to the national defense in October 1969 meaning that its release could have injured the national defense of the United States or given advantage to a foreign nation with respect to the national defense interests of the United States;

Third, that at the time he received or obtained Exhibit 19, Dr. Ellsberg knew or had reason to know that its contents could be used to injure the United States or give advantage to a foreign nation;

Fourth, that he received and obtained Exhibit 19, the Wheeler Report, for the purpose of obtaining information which could be used to injure the United States or to give advantage to a foreign nation.

Fifth, that at the time he received or obtained Exhibit 19, Dr. Ellsberg knew or had reason to know that the document had been properly classified;

Sixth, that at the time he received or obtained Exhibit 19, Dr. Ellsberg knew that he would communicate, deliver or transmit the document to a person who was not trustworthy or whose possession of the documents could cause injury to the national defense or advantage to a foreign nation;

Seventh, that at the time he received or obtained Exhibit 19, Dr. Ellsberg knew that communication of the document by him to such a person would be in violation of law.

Failure of the prosecution to prove beyond a reasonable doubt any one of these elements must result in a finding of not guilty of Count Nine.

AUTHORITY: 18 U.S.C. § 793(c), (d), and (e). Bill of Particulars. *Gorin v. United States*, 312 U.S. 19, 30–33 (1941).

[n] Element: Receiving Document [ND-4]

The first element of Count Nine requires the prosecution to prove beyond a reasonable doubt that Dr. Ellsberg received or obtained the Wheeler Report on or about October 3, 1969.

AUTHORITY: *Pearson v. United States*, 192 F.2d 681, 692 (6th Cir. 1951); DeVitt & Blackmar, I *Federal Jury Practice & Instructions*, § 13.10.

[o] Element: Document to Contain Information Related to National Defense [ND-5]

The second element of Count Nine requires that, to convict, you must find beyond a reasonable doubt that on or about October 3, 1969, the eight pages of the Wheeler Report which constitute Exhibit 19 contained information which related to national defense.

Relation to national defense is an element not only of this Count, but of others as well. From listening to the testimony for both sides in this case you know how much the parties to his case have concentrated upon it.

I will now define the concept of relation to national defense for you.

Information relates to national defense only if its release at the time of the alleged offense could have injured the national defense of the United States or given advantage to a foreign nation with respect to the national defense of the United States.

AUTHORITY: 18 U.S.C. § 793(c).

[p] Meaning of "Advantage to a Foreign Nation" [ND-6]

Information which could be of "advantage to a foreign nation" is information which could enable a foreign nation to take action which would significantly improve its military position in such a way as to impair the ability of the United States to defend itself militarily.

You cannot find an "advantage" if you conclude only that a piece of information could be "useful" or "interesting" to a foreign nation or to certain officials of that nation or to a hypothetical foreign analyst. There are, as you have heard testimony, vast amounts of information which may be of professional curiosity or interest to persons engaged in international, military, or intelligence activities. "Advantage" requires more than this; it must give an immediate or future tactical or strategic military advantage to a foreign nation over the United States with respect to its national defense.

AUTHORITY: *Gorin v. United States,* 312 U.S. 19; *United States v. Heine,* 151 F.2d 813, 815–817 (2d Cir., 1945); U.S. Constitution, Amend. 1, Amend. 5.

[q] Meaning of "Injury" to National Defense Interests [ND-7]

Turning to "injury" to the national defense interests of the United States, "injury" means harm or damage. To find such injury, you must find that disclosure of the information could harm or damage the defense activities of this country's military forces and the related activities of national preparedness. The injury must be immediate and direct and must produce harm or damage to the tactical or strategic military position of the United States in its own defense. Injury to the national defense of the United States includes only activities related to the military defense of the national borders of the continental United States and U.S. territories and possessions. Information that might cause harm to an ongoing military operation not directly related to the defense of the nation's borders and territories does not fall within the definition of national defense.

AUTHORITY: Same as Instruction ND-6.

[r] Meaning of "National Defense" [ND-8]

The term "national defense" refers solely to matters directly connected with the current defense activities of this country's military forces and the related current activities of national preparedness. It deals with current military secrets and must pertain to matters of current military significance.

Documents which were connected with the national defense when they were written may, through the passage of time, lose that connection. Information that has no current potential for injury to the national defense of the United States or advantage to a foreign nation does not relate to the national defense, even though it discusses military matters and even though it continues to carry classification markings. For example, information that a landing would take place at a certain location may relate to the national defense up to the time the landing occurs; but if the information were disclosed a year later, it would be outdated, and not related to the national defense. In deciding whether information has become outdated, you may consider any changes in military policies, deployments, or technology which occurred after the events described in the document.

AUTHORITY: *Gorin v. United States,* 312 U.S. 19, 30–33, aff'g 111 F.2d 712, 719 (9th Cir., 1940); *United States v. New York Times,* 328 F. Supp. 324 (S.D.N.Y. 1971).

[s] Meaning of "Injury or Advantage"; Defense Interests Distinguished from Diplomatic, Economic or Political Interests [ND-9]

Injury or advantage must be to the national defense of the United States and not to the United States' diplomatic, economic or political position. Information pertaining to diplomatic or political matters does not relate to the national defense unless its release could in a direct or reasonable way cause injury to the national defense of the United States or give advantage to a foreign power with respect to the national defense of the United States.

AUTHORITY: 18 U.S.C. § 793(e), *Gorin v. United States,* 312 U.S. 19, 30–31 (1941); *United States v. New York Times,* 328 F. Supp. 324 (S.D.N.Y. 1971).

[t] Injury to National Defense Distinguished From Diplomatic or Political Embarrassment [ND-10]

You must carefully distinguish between political or diplomatic embarrassment or discomfort on the one hand and on the other hand, injury to the national defense of the United States or advantage to a foreign nation with respect to the national defense of the United States.

It is true, of course, that disclosures of information may cause concern to the Government of the United States or to some of its officials or even to foreign governments who deal with this country or their officials. Government officials may be embarrassed by the revelation of their positions, attitudes and conduct. But the fact that disclosure of information would result in such concern or embarrassment is not enough to bring the information within the definition of relation to the national defense. The disclosure must do more than expose what the government or particular individuals have said or done; it must expose matters directly and reasonably connected with the military defense of our nation, in a manner which could injure the national defense of the United States or give advantage to a foreign nation with respect to the national defense of the United States.

AUTHORITY: Same as Instruction ND-9.

[u] Freedom of Discussion; Not to Convict For Isolated Facts if Outweighed By Need For Informed Citizenry and Congress [ND-11]

Freedom to discuss matters connected with the national defense is traditionally permitted in this country because it is protected by the constitutional guarantees of freedom of speech and freedom of the press.[1] Freedom of discussion is the essence of democratic self-government and its effectiveness depends on the free flow of information to the people concerning governmental matters.[2] The purpose of the statutes involving national defense is not to disrupt the free flow of information necessary for self-government but only to prevent disclosure of military secrets reasonably and directly related to the national defense of the United States with a current potential for injury or advantage as previously defined.

You may not convict even if you find that isolated or particular facts contained within an exhibit relate to the national defense of the United States in the manner required if on balance you conclude that the information in that exhibit in its totality was such that its disclosure was needed to keep the American people and the Congress adequately informed about the policies, decision-making processes and actions of their government, keeping in mind that a fully-informed citizenry and Congress is essential to the national defense.[3]

---

[1] Gorin v. United States, 312 U.S. 19, 23 (1941); United States v. Heine, 151 F.2d 813, 815 (2d Cir., 1945), cert. denied, 328 U.S. 833 (1946); United States v. New York Times Co., 328 F. Supp. 324, 331 (S.D.N.Y.), aff'd, 403 U.S. 713 (1971) (per curiam).

[2] Garrison v. Louisiana, 379 U.S. 64, 77 (1964); New York Times v. Sullivan, 376 U.S. 254 (1964); Stromberg v. California, 283 U.S. 359 (1931).

[3] Defendants' Motion to Dismiss.

[v] Necessity That National Defense Document Be Owned By Government [ND-12]

Documents relate to the national defense only if owned by the government. This does not mean that every document which is owned by the government relates to the national defense. In addition to government ownership of the documents, you must find that release of their contents could injure the national defense interests of the United States or give advantage to a foreign nation. But a document which is not the property of the United States cannot relate to national defense. Accordingly, to find a relation to national defense you must find that the government owned the actual exhibits listed in this count at the time of the alleged offense. I have instructed you previously under Count Two on what constitutes government ownership.

AUTHORITY: Exec. Order 10501, preamble. *United States v. Heine,* 151 F.2d 813 (2d Cir., 1945).

[w] Evidence of Particular Classification Irrelevant to Ownership [ND-13]

Exhibit 19 bears a classification marking. That is to be totally disregarded by you in determining whether the contents of the document could, if released at the time of the alleged offense, have caused injury to the national defense of the United States or given advantage to a foreign nation with respect to the national defense of the United States. So far as your deliberations on national defense issues are concerned, you must assume that the marking is just not there.

AUTHORITY: *Gorin v. United States,* 312 U.S. 19, 30–33 (1941); *United States v. Drummond,* 354 F.2d 132, 151–152 (2d Cir., 1965) (en banc).

[x] Release of Publicly Available Information No Crime; Examples [ND-14]

Information which was publicly available at the time of the alleged offense is not information which related to national defense as defined by the statute. This is because the release of information publicly available at the time of the alleged offense could not cause injury to the national defense of the United States or advantage to a foreign nation with respect to the national defense of the United States. This is true regardless of how the information has become publicly available, and regardless of the form in which the publicly available information is arranged. Information is accessible to the public if it is available to those who are willing to take the pains to find, sift and collate it. Information is publicly available if the substance and essence of it is available. The fact that some additional detail is contained in a document is not significant unless disclosure of the additional detail could itself injure the national defense of the United States or give advantage to a foreign nation with respect to the national defense of the United States. Examples of publicly available information include official announcements or reports, the Congressional Record, the State Department Bulletin, magazines, newspapers, public speeches, government press conferences, or other sources open to anyone industrious or interested enough to look for it.

Therefore, if you find that the information in Exhibit 19 was publicly available prior to October 3, 1969, then you must acquit Dr. Ellsberg of this count.

That completes my definition of relation to national defense for purposes of Exhibit 19 and Count Nine. I will have occasion again in further counts to say more about national defense.

If you do not find beyond a reasonable doubt that Exhibit 19 relates to national defense as I have defined that term, you must acquit Dr. Ellsberg of Count Nine.

AUTHORITY: *United States v. Heine*, 151 F.2d 813, 816 (2d Cir., 1945); *United States v. Soblen*, 301 F.2d 236, 239 (2d Cir., 1962); *Gorin v. United States*, 111 F.2d 712 (9th Cir. 1940) aff'd 312 U.S. 19 (1941).

[y] Element: Knowledge That Document Related to National Defense [ND-15]

The third element of Count Nine requires the prosecution to prove beyond a reasonable doubt that Dr. Ellsberg knew or had reason to know at the time he received Exhibit 19 that its contents related to national defense. This means that as of October 3, 1969, not only must the contents of Exhibit 19 have in fact related to national defense—on this I have just instructed you—but that in addition, Dr. Ellsberg must have known or had reason to know that they did.

You cannot surmise or speculate that Dr. Ellsberg knew or had reason to believe that the information related to the national defense. As with all other facts, the burden is upon the Government to present affirmative evidence to prove beyond a reasonable doubt the existence of the required unlawful knowledge.

You may consider Dr. Ellsberg's own testimony that he knew the exhibits did not relate to the national defense. If you believe Dr. Ellsberg on this point then you must acquit him of this count. Of course, you are not required to accept his testimony. However, in judging the credibility of his testimony you may consider the testimony of other reputable experts on the question of the relationship of the documents to national defense in 1969.

In addition to direct testimony, knowledge may be proved by inference, but unless such inferences exclude every possibility except that of guilty knowledge, such knowledge is not proved.

AUTHORITY: *Gorin v. United States*, 312 U.S. 19, 28, 30 (1941); *Ibid.* Supreme Court Record, pp. 426–29; *United States v. New York Times Co.*, 328 F. Supp. 324, 328 (S.D.N.Y., 1971).

[z] Element: Receiving for Purpose of Obtaining Information Respecting National Defense [ND-16]

The fourth element of Count Nine requires the prosecution to prove beyond a reasonable doubt that Dr. Ellsberg received or obtained the Wheeler Report for the purpose of obtaining information respecting the "national defense." That is, you must find that Dr. Ellsberg obtained the document for the purpose of obtaining information which could be used to injure the national defense of the United States or to give advantage to a foreign nation with respect to the national defense of the United States. If you find that it was not Dr. Ellsberg's purpose to obtain a document which could be so used, then you must acquit him of this count.

AUTHORITY: 18 U.S.C. § 793(c).

[aa] Element: Proper Classification of Document [ND-17]

The fifth element of Count Nine requires the prosecution to prove beyond a reasonable doubt that Exhibit 19 had been properly classified and that Dr. Ellsberg knew or had reason to know that it had been properly classified.

As I have previously instructed you, in order to find that Exhibit 19 was properly classified, you must first find that the exhibit was classified by a person authorized to exercise original top secret classification. There was testimony by General De Puy that General Wheeler made the ultimate decision on the full report's top secret classification. General Wheeler was a person authorized to exercise original top secret classification. However, you must find beyond a reasonable doubt that General Wheeler personally assigned the classification to Exhibit 19, because his classification authority could not be exercised for him or in his name by anyone else. In making this determination, you may consider both General De Puy's testimony and the fact that the exhibit itself contains no indication that General Wheeler himself assigned the classification.

Second you must find that each paragraph of the full Wheeler Report was given an individual classification marking or that a guide was attached to or included in it to indicate the information in the report that was classified.

However, as I have already stated, you shall not consider at all the markings on the document in determining whether it was properly classified.

[bb] Element: Intention to Communicate Document to One Who Would Use It to Injure National Defense [ND-18]

The sixth element of Count Nine requires the prosecution to prove beyond a reasonable doubt that when Dr. Ellsberg received or obtained the Wheeler Report he knew that he would communicate, deliver or transmit the document to a person who was not trustworthy or who could use the document to injure the national defense or give advantage to a foreign nation. Thus, to convict, you must find that on October 3, 1969, when Dr. Ellsberg allegedly received Exhibit 19, he knew he would give Anthony Russo management and control of the document or show its contents to him; and, that Anthony Russo was not trustworthy or that Anthony Russo could use the documents to injure the national defense or give advantage to a foreign nation.

AUTHORITY: 18 U.S.C. § 793(c). Defendants' Memorandum on "Not Entitled to Receive;" *Gorin v. United States,* Supreme Court Record, 418–419; Transcript Volume 71, pp. 12, 171.

[cc] Element: Knowledge That Showing Document to Co-Defendant Would Be Violation of Law [ND-19]

The seventh element of Count Nine requires the prosecution to prove beyond a reasonable doubt that Dr. Ellsberg had knowledge or reason to know that showing the contents of Exhibit 19 to Anthony Russo would be in violation of law. The laws in question here are 18 U.S.C. 793(d) and 18 U.S.C. 793(e). You must find, then, that on October 3, 1969, when Dr. Ellsberg is alleged to have received Exhibit 19, he was aware of the provisions of these two sections of law; that these provisions of law made his intended conduct illegal; and that he knew or had reason to know that fact.

In considering your finding you should consider the language of those sections, not for the purpose of interpreting them, for that is my task, but for the purpose of determining whether an intelligent man with the background and training of Dr. Ellsberg could have been expected to know their meaning.

AUTHORITY: 18 U.S.C. § 793(c).

Author's Footnotes

[1] This instruction is furnished by the Office of the Public Defender of Santa Barbara County.

[2] Id.

[3] Id.

[4] Id.

[5] This is an adaptation of an instruction on special intent. *California Jury Instructions Criminal* [CALJIC] No. 89 (3d rev. ed. 1970), usually cited as CALJIC No. 3.31.

[6] Id. at §§ 126–127; also 1972 Supplement 22.

[7] This instruction is furnished by Edward Carl Broege, Esq., who

advises that primary legal work concerning the instruction was done by David Kairys, Esq., and Mr. David Lavine, and that the language is that of the court, the Honorable Clarkson S. Fisher. For a short summary of evidence developed at the trial relating to government overreaching, see N.Y. Times, May 21, 1973, p. 1, col. 2.

[8] The following are selected by me from among a full set of the jury instructions requested by the defense in *United States v. Anthony Joseph Russo, Jr. and Daniel Ellsberg*, No. 9373–WMB–CD (C.D. Cal., dism'd May 11, 1973). These instructions, which as everyone knows turned out to be unnecessary, are made available through the courtesy of the defense lawyers in that case: Leonard B. Boudin, Esq., Charles R. Nesson, Esq., Charles E. Goodell, Esq., Dolores A. Donovan, Esq., Leonard I. Weinglass, Esq., and H. Peter Young, Esq.

The short descriptive titles preceding these instructions were added by me as a convenience in referring to them, and are not part of the instructions. The bracketed letter-numeral following each title, e.g. [ND-18], is the designation given that instruction by the lawyers who prepared it.

APPENDIX E

Sample Form of Agreement to Appear at Time Other Than Specified in Subpoena

JOHN J. DOE
111 Elm Street
Santa Barbara, California 93101
Telephone: (805) 444-4444

.... COURT OF CALIFORNIA,
COUNTY OF SANTA BARBARA

Plaintiff(s)	NO. ....
vs.	AGREEMENT TO APPEAR AT TIME OTHER THAN SPECIFIED IN SUBPOENA
Defendant(s)	(C.C.P. sec. 1985.1)

I, the person whose signature appears below, having been served with the attached subpoena, hereby agree with [Lawyer] to appear in the court from which that subpoena was issued, at a time other than the time specified in that subpoena, to wit: at any time on .... hour(s) notice to me by telephone, on any day during which the trial of the above-entitled action shall be in progress in said court.

I can be reached by telephone during the hours of 8 a.m. to 5 p.m. at telephone number ...., or in the evening at telephone number ....

I understand that only the court which issued this subpoena, or [Lawyer] can excuse my continued availability pursuant to said subpoena, during the trial of this action. I also understand that violation of this agreement would be violation of the attached subpoena and might be punished by the court as contempt.

Dated: ....

....
SIGNATURE

APPENDIX F

Sample Page From Combined Index
(For Use During Cross-Examination)

Officer Oldbadge (cont'd)
[Note: portions preceding this section have been omitted]

II. Observations Before Arrival at Scene

	Grand Jury Transcript	Discovery Motion Transcript
at about 7:30 p.m. was proceeding east on Green Street in the 100 block	3:9–12	9:5–7
saw defendant running along north side of street, going east, in that block; "he observed me and slowed down"	3:14–16	9:7–10
proceeded slowly past defendant, driving up to intersection of Green and Maple Streets, and defendant came abreast of this well-lit corner, and recognized defendant and observed he wore heavy shoes and light colored clothing; can't remember shirt	3:16 to 4:4	
defendant crossed Maple Street at 200 block of East Green Street, and "at about the vicinity of the hotel, I looked in my rear view mirror" and saw defendant talking to victim [marked on grand jury map]	4:8–10	
circled block, returning to make "routine check-out procedure" on parked vehicle; could not see defendant or victim at this time; resumed patrol	5:3–7	
got first radio call at about 8:30 p.m.	5:19–20	10:2–3

contra: crime was committed at 8:10 and reported at 8:20 p.m., see police report [evid. no. 1.01(c)] page 2

. . .

Main Objects in Cross-examining This Witness and Reasons:

1. Dislodge time schedule to show the first time he saw defendant was later and compress the time interval between then and when the victim was found. The reason is if defendant takes the stand, the interval of 30–40 minutes would kill him. That would conflict with leaving the store at 8:00 p.m., since the victim could not have been lying there very long. The approach should be: (1) ask him what he did after seeing defendant and before the radio message, minimizing time estimates; (2) shake him up with minor inconsistencies outlined above; (3) emphasize it was dark, that he needed a street light to recognize defendant, and back it up with evidence as to sunset time.
2. Pull the teeth out of that business of defendant running, by asking if there wasn't a traffic light, and if he didn't happen to see the defendant only because he had stopped for it. Obviously running to make the light, not for a guilty motive.
3. Ask him if it was routine to check out parked cars on every block in the city, or just around that park. He will probably say the car was suspicious because it was unfamiliar, but that it was not stolen. This should lead to why anybody would want to watch cars in a certain block so closely as to know when an unfamiliar car was parked there. The answer would be, this damn park is a hotbed of crime; it is the only area in town where two vehicle beats overlap, and that is a good argument point.

N.B. He is winsome with the jury and tends to overdo it with gratuitous explanations. Keep a tight rein, aim for these limited goals, get him off the stand fast, and *don't* get involved in lengthy cross-examination.

INDEX

[References are to sections]

A

B

C

[References are to sections]

[References are to sections]

[References are to sections]

F

[References are to sections]

G

Government
  Inferences which necessitate stretching jury
    instructions ....App. D[3]
  Stretching of criminal statutes by ....App. D[4]
Group trials 3.03

H

Handtooled jury instructions 8.05
Hearings
  Contested ....4.07[3]
  Preliminary 5.03
Hearsay evidence 13.06
Hostile judges 6.04

I

Immediate trial in multiple cases 6.04
Impeachment of prosecution witnesses ....14.02[6][a]
  Photographs for ....4.04[2]
    Nondisclosure of ....4.05[2]
Index for prosecution witnesses ....14.01[2][b], App. F
Inflammatory film footage 13.03
Inflammatory tapes of radio broadcasts 13.04
Informers
  Police protection of 14.04
  Unpaid 14.03
Intent, resisting arrest and ....App. D[2][f]
Instructions to jury
  Contents of 8.03
  Curfew ....App. D[1]
  Early preparation of 8.01
  Judge's ....16.01[3]
  Method of drafting 8.04
  On-going process of preparation of 8.02
  Presentation of hand-tooled 8.05

[References are to sections]

[References are to sections]

K

L

M

[References are to sections]

[References are to sections]

[References are to sections]

Q

R

S

[References are to sections]

T

U

[References are to sections]

V

W

[References are to sections]

Y

Younger clients